Small Ball in the Big Leagues

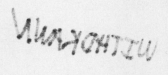

ALSO BY JAMES D. SZALONTAI
AND FROM MCFARLAND

_____

Teenager on First, Geezer at Bat, 4-F on Deck:
Major League Baseball in 1945 (2009)

Close Shave: The Life and Times
of Baseball's Sal Maglie (2002)

Small Ball in the Big Leagues

A History of Stealing, Bunting, Walking and Otherwise Scratching for Runs

JAMES D. SZALONTAI

McFarland & Company, Inc., Publishers

Jefferson, North Carolina, and London

LIBRARY OF CONGRESS CATALOGUING-IN-PUBLICATION DATA

Szalontai, James, 1974–
Small ball in the big leagues : a history of stealing, bunting,
walking and otherwise scratching for runs / James D. Szalontai.
    p.   cm.
Includes bibliographical references and index.

ISBN 978-0-7864-3793-1
softcover : 50# alkaline paper ∞

1. Baseball — United States — History.
2. Baseball — United States — Miscellanea.
I. Title.
GV863.A1S96   2010   796.3570973 — dc22   2010022570

British Library cataloguing data are available

On the cover: Portrait of Ty Cobb from the T227 Series of Champions cards,
American Tobacco Company, 1912 (Library of Congress)

Manufactured in the United States of America

McFarland & Company, Inc., Publishers
Box 611, Jefferson, North Carolina 28640
www.mcfarlandpub.com

Contents

Preface

When it comes to baseball strategy, the home run has garnered the bulk of the attention by historians, sportswriters, and fans alike. But to develop a complete understanding of the history of baseball, it is imperative to be knowledgeable about the history of small ball as well, which encompasses stolen bases, sacrifice bunts, the squeeze play, hit-and-run plays, productive outs, bunting for a hit, and making the opposition pay a price for walks and errors. Small ball strategies, small ball players, and managers who implement these strategies have been much maligned in the twenty-first century. But whether someone believes these strategies are effective or counterproductive, the history of small ball is an integral part of the game that cannot be dismissed.

The history of small ball has four primary phases. The nineteenth century was the first phase, when the rules were still developing. The 1887 St. Louis Browns of the American Association stole a major league record 581 bags by taking advantage of the generous stolen base rule of the era. The 1901 season was both the beginning of the Deadball Era (1901–1919) when small ball strategies were at their apex and also the beginning of the modern era (post–1900 baseball) as the game would be somewhat recognizable to the twenty-first century fan by this season. Naturally, with the low scoring games of the era, small ball strategies were ubiquitous throughout the major leagues as a quick, intelligent style of play was showcased upon the greensward. The third phase commenced in 1920, which is the year the so-called lively ball era began and was popularized by the majestic blasts by Babe Ruth. From 1920 to 1961 small ball strategies systematically declined. The number of stolen bases cratered, while the number of sacrifice bunts experienced a more modest decline. The nadir was perhaps in 1950 when the American League stole a major league low 278 bases, averaging a measly 34.8 steals per team. The final phase is the resurgence of small ball which began in 1962 when the Los Angeles Dodgers stole 198 bases and were led by Maury Wills who stole an exorbitant 104 bags. Small ball strategies experienced a renaissance during the late 1970s and 1980s. By the late twentieth century and early twenty-first century, small ball strategies were on the decline. But small ball enthusiasts still had plenty of hope as the game endured the Moneyball era in a way where stolen base totals still remain at healthy levels.

The most important small ball players, managers, teams, and games are examined in this book. It focuses not only on well-known small ball practitioners like Ty Cobb, Eddie Collins, Luis Aparicio, Bert Campaneris, and Kenny Lofton, but also on players who were not particularly gifted in bunting, place hitting, or stealing bases, but who had one or more memorable games. Al Lopez, for example, stole only 46 sacks during his Hall of Fame career, perhaps none bigger than his game-ending steal of home on July 2, 1933, which sent the Flatbush faithful into the streets, celebrating a doubleheader victory over the Cubs. People are well aware of the slugging feats of Babe Ruth. But he also participated in plenty of small ball activity, some of which are indelible moments of the autumn classic. In game five of the 1921 World Series he sparked the winning rally with a surprise bunt single. But during the following season's fall classic when the Yankees suffered an ignominious four-game sweep by John McGraw's Giants, a slumping Ruth laid down a sacrifice bunt in the opening frame of the final game. And then he committed perhaps the most unpardonable sin when the Yankees were trailing 3–2 with two outs in the last of the ninth in game seven of the 1926 classic, when he took off for second on the first pitch and was gunned down easily by Bob O'Farrell, which handed the St. Louis Cardinals the World Series title. This book examines the multitude of times small ball activities have secured victories through aggressive base-running, squeeze bunts, stolen bases, productive outs, and hit-and-run plays. But it also examines games where aggressive small ball activity led to a cataclysmic defeat.

One of the best ways to gain a better understanding of the history of baseball is through statistics. There are stolen base totals and sacrifice hit or bunt totals for a substantial portion of baseball's history. Unfortunately, this is not the case with the hit-and-run play and productive outs, making it harder to make objective judgments about these plays. Perhaps it will never be known, for example, if John McGraw's Giants of the Deadball Era or Whitey Herzog's Cardinals of the 1980s implemented the hit-and-run more often. But through the statistics that are available there is a great deal that can be learned.

A book such as this is possible because of the sportswriters, historians, and fans who have chronicled the game's history. Some of these scribes are well-known by twenty-first century fans, while others are more obscure but also tremendously talented. Among the many sportswriters I read included F.C. Lane, Frank Graham, I.E. Sanborn, Ring Lardner, William B. Hanna, Joe Vila, Frank H. Young, James C. Isaminger, William E. Brandt, Murray Tynan, James P. Dawson, Shirley Povich, Rud Rennie, Arthur Daley, Sid Gray, Howard M. Tuckner, Peter Gammons, Clif Keane, Fred Mitchell, and Ralph Wiley.

The sources are listed in the bibliography, but there were a few sources that were especially helpful. James Charlton edited *The Baseball Chronology: The Complete History of the Most Important Events in the Game of Baseball*, and was assisted by more than fifty people. After the baseball encyclopedia this was the source I consulted the most frequently and it helped me to identify the most important small ball events. Charlton's book was published in 1991, but a more detailed version of his chronology that includes games not listed in the book and also expands beyond the 1990 season can be found at the terrific website baseballlibrary.com. I relied on *The 2006 ESPN Baseball Encyclopedia* for most of the statistics in this book. This outstanding encyclopedia does not list sacrifice hit totals for position players, so I relied on the website, baseball-reference.com, for that information. For All-Star Game and postseason statistics I relied on retrosheet.org and if information wasn't listed there, then I consulted baseball-reference.com. I gained tremendous knowledge about the history of the game by reading many of the terrific publications by the Society for American Baseball Research, including *The Baseball Research Journal*, *The National Pastime: A Review of Baseball History*, *Deadball Stars of the National League*, *Deadball Stars of the American League*, and *The SABR Baseball List and Record Book: Baseball's Most Fascinating Records and Unusual Statistics*. Bill James's exhaustive tome *The New Bill James Historical Baseball Abstract* is an integral book to understand the history of the game. All of the sources I used helped me gain a better understanding of the history of baseball. These sources are far too many to list here but are acknowledged throughout the book and listed in the bibliography.

This book provides a much needed history of small ball. It is intended to educate, entertain, and persuade baseball enthusiasts to reassess their opinion of small ball activities.

1

The Nineteenth Century

The National Association of Professional Base Ball Players was formed on March 17, 1871, and became the first professional baseball league. Originally it consisted of the following organizations: the Boston Red Stockings, Chicago White Stockings, Cleveland Forest Citys, Fort Wayne Kekiongas, New York Mutuals, Philadelphia Athletics, Rockford Forest Citys, Troy Haymakers, and the Washington Olympics. However, during the league's five-year existence, teams were constantly joining the circuit and quitting the circuit. It was not unusual for teams to quit the circuit once the season began. And only three of the original nine members persevered through all five of the National Association campaigns: the Boston Red Stockings, New York Mutuals, and the Philadelphia Athletics. While the National Association is the first professional league, there has been significant disagreement as to whether it should be given "major league" status. The Special Baseball Records Committee decided to exclude the National Association from the major league category because of its "erratic schedule and procedures."[1] However, the editors of *The 2006 ESPN Baseball Encyclopedia* disagreed with this decision and included the National Association statistics in their encyclopedia, insisting that "it was indisputably the Major League Baseball of its day."[2]

One of the wonderful features of the National Association (1871–1875) is that stolen base totals are available for teams and players. Furthermore, they also kept track of the number of caught stealing. During the National League's first ten seasons (1876–1885) they did not officially record the number of stolen bases. And when the National League did employ the stolen base statistic beginning in 1886, runners were credited with a stolen base if they advanced two bases on a hit or moved up a base on a fly ball. A stolen base was credited to a player for every extra base he took on a hit. For example, if a runner advanced from first to third on a single he was credited with one steal. Stolen bases were also credited when basestealers overslid the bag and were tagged out. There cannot be a direct comparison between basestealers of the nineteenth century, playing before 1898, and those of the modern era because it cannot be determined how many of these steals were garnered against the pitcher and catcher, in a way that satisfied the modern era definition of a stolen base.

In 1892 the rules were modified insisting that a runner would not be charged with a steal unless there was a chance to throw him out or an effort was made to do so. If, for example, a runner tagged up at second and advanced to third on a deep fly ball to right field and there was no chance to throw him out at third, then a stolen base was not to be credited to the runner. However, not all of the official scorers applied the new rule. Furthermore, it didn't have much of an affect on the number of stolen bases. In 1891, the eight-team National League averaged 251.4 steals per team and then in 1892 the senior league expanded to twelve teams and averaged 266.8 steals per team. In 1892, the National League teams also played a longer schedule than they had in 1891. Because official scorers did not apply the rule under all circumstances, it was repealed before the 1897 season began.

The generous stolen base rule lasted through the 1897 season and it is primarily the reason why the 1887 St. Louis Browns of the American Association stole an all-time record 581 bases, while the 1896 Baltimore Orioles set the National League record with 441 thefts. Furthermore, Hugh Nicol of the 1887 Cincinnati Red Stockings of the American Association stole an all-time record 138 bags despite batting only .215 with a .341 on-base percentage in 125 games. Nicol's Red Stockings finished in second place (81–54) that season and surely a large percentage of his stolen bases resulted from advancing two bases on a hit or tagging up on a fly ball. Arlie Latham of the first-place St. Louis Browns (95–40) stole 129 bases that season and his 163 runs scored was ranked second behind his teammate Tip O'Neill (167). Charlie Comiskey of St. Louis (117) and Pete Browning of Louisville (103) also stole over 100 bases. In 1887, the National League had two players who surpassed the 100 steal plateau: John Ward of New York (111) and Jim Fogarty of Philadelphia (102). Ward's 111 steals would stand as the National League record until Lou Brock swiped 118 in 1974. Stolen bases plummeted when the modern stolen base rule was implemented in 1898. The Baltimore Orioles led the circuit with 441 and 401 steals in 1896 and 1897, respectively. However, in 1898 they led the NL with only 250 steals. The National League's stolen base totals from 1896 to 1898 were 3,059, 2,705, and 2,069.

The National Association's computation of the caught stealing totals was also very rare considering that the caught stealing statistic is only available for the NL in 1913, 1915, from 1920 to 1925, and for all the seasons from 1951 and beyond. The caught stealing statistic was compiled in the AL from 1914 to 1915 and for every season since 1920. To keep track of the number of stolen bases but not to keep track of the number of caught stealing is like compiling the number of hits but not the number of at-bats and therefore being unable to calculate a player's batting average. Just like there is a huge difference between a .250 hitter and a .300 hitter, there is also a huge difference between a player who steals 50 bags with a 60 percent basestealing average and one who steals 50 bags with an 80 percent basestealing average.

Baseball statistics are generally considered highly accurate. However, there have also been a myriad errors or discrepancies in the various baseball encyclopedias published throughout the years. Different sources, for example, have listed Cap Anson's hit total as 3,013, 3,509, 3,081, 3,423, 3,418, 2,995, and 3,022. While the errors in the Macmillan encyclopedias were plentiful, most of them were also very small in nature. Baseball encyclopedias remained largely inaccurate until the groundbreaking work *Total Baseball*, by John Thorn and Pete Palmer, which was first published in 1989 and corrected the old statistics. What made statistics especially inaccurate during the nineteenth century was that official scorers often used different standards when making decisions and sometimes their opinions were biased. Furthermore, it was believed that some corrupt official scorers had nefarious partnerships with players and deliberately augmented a player's batting average. Owners were also eager to manipulate the numbers, making their players more attractive to other teams who may want to acquire them. In 1879, Cap Anson of the National League's Chicago White Stockings was given a .407 batting average, which gave him the batting crown. Nick Young, the league secretary, was a Cap Anson partisan, and credited him with this gaudy number. However, Henry Chadwick insisted that the accurate number was tabulated by William Stevens of the *Boston Herald*, which gave him a .318 batting average. Because of such shenanigans by the league office, modern day encyclopedias are compelled to credit Anson with the batting crown. *The 2006 ESPN Baseball Encyclopedia* lists Anson at the top of the circuit with a .317 batting average, despite the fact that several players had higher batting averages, including Paul Hines of Providence who batted .357.[3]

While there are stolen base totals for the tenuous National Association, they are considered incomplete because they were compiled using box scores which did not always list them. The Boston Red Stockings dominated the league with a 205–50 record (.804) from 1872 to 1875, winning four consecutive pennants. The Red Stockings had a terrifying lineup which led the league in all of the following offensive categories from 1873 to 1875: batting average, on-base percentage, slugging percentage, runs scored, hits, doubles and home runs. Furthermore, they were known for their aggressive baserunning and stole 404 bases during the five National Association seasons. They led the league in thefts in 1871 (73), 1873 (145), and 1874 (45). The dynastic Red Stockings, who were led by player-manager Harry Wright, ran roughshod over the league with an exceptional 71–8 record in 1875 as they led the league in most of the offensive categories and finished third in steals with 93. The National Association disbanded after the 1875 campaign because of insolvent ballclubs; lack of competition; gambling; a lack of uniformity in the schedules; teams that were constantly quitting; and players who did not remain with one team for a long time.

In 1876 the National League began its inaugural season with rules that were significantly different than the ones that were used during the twentieth century. The pitcher delivered his offering underhanded and stood only 45 feet from home plate. The catcher stood a few feet behind the batter waiting for the offering and trying to corral it on one bounce. During the early days of the game the catcher did not wear a mask, but by 1877 masks were becoming commonplace in the professional ranks. The foul-bound catch was eliminated from the rule book in 1879, which had previously allowed catchers to record an out if they caught a foul tip on the first bounce. In 1879 catchers moved closer to the batter and needed extra protection. The ability to change speeds and put movement on the ball often determined whether pitchers were successful or not. The baseballs were not uniform and weighed between 5 and 5.5 ounces. The pitcher could not locate his pitches because batters had the right to instruct the hurler to throw the ball high or low. It took nine balls to walk a batter and the strike zone was not standardized. The first "good pitch" with two strikes which the batter did not swing at resulted in a warning. The second good pitch delivered after two strikes was called a strikeout. If a batter advanced to first base on a walk he was charged with an at-bat. And it wasn't until 1889 that a batter drew a walk after four balls. Before 1879 baserunners could deliberately run into the ball after being put in play by the batter and therefore prevent the infielder from making the play. Batting orders were not announced ahead of time and could be made up once the game started, allowing the manager to make decisions based on the circumstances. This lasted until 1879, which was the year that several new rules were implemented. Errors were plentiful because fielding gloves were not used until 1875, and even at that time not everybody embraced them. Furthermore, these were rudimentary gloves, with no padding, and therefore a player's hand would swell up even if he wore a glove. Baseball was a rough enterprise and players often performed even when they had serious injuries. During the 1870s gambling was rampant; drunkenness was a problem among the players; the rules were constantly changing; and scheduling was unpredictable.

If a batter hit a ball in fair territory and it rolled into foul territory it was ruled a fair ball. Ross Barnes perfected the fair-foul hit and used it to bat .429 for Chicago during the National League's inaugural season to win the batting crown. He usually took a full cut on his fair-foul hit, hitting the ball sharply on the ground, just inside the third base line. Others perfected the art of the fair-foul bunt, which involved bunting the ball with tremendous backspin so that after landing once in fair territory it would roll far off into foul territory. However, this rule was rescinded after the 1876 season. Dickey Pearce and Tom Barlow, who both played for the Brooklyn Atlantics, are credited with having developed the bunt. They played together on the 1873 Brooklyn Atlantics of the National Association while Dickey played for the original Brooklyn Atlantics in 1866. *The New Dickson Baseball Dictionary* insists that Pearce is credited with "introducing" the bunt as a member of the 1866 Brooklyn Atlantics.[4] Pearce is given credit for inventing the fair-foul hit, but according to historian Peter Morris there is considerable disagreement as to who invented the bunt. Herbert Worth, who played one major league game for the 1872 Brooklyn Atlantics, is one of several players who gave the credit to Barlow, saying, "Tommy Barlow was the inventor of the bunt hit, and was famous throughout the country for his skill. He had a short bat, not over two feet long, which when he hit the ball he imparted a wrist motion which gave the ball, when it came in contact with the bat, a sort of reversed twist and the ball after striking the ground would almost seem to remain where it struck and then dart off at an angle out of reach of the third baseman or the pitcher." However, many others insisted that Pearce was responsible for both the first bunt and the first fair-foul hit. The evidence suggests that Pearce invented the bunt but Barlow perfected it. Pearce's bunts are described in the *New York Clipper* on August 17, 1868, and September 10, 1868, which was before Barlow began his professional career. It also appears that the bunt developed as a variation of the fair-foul hit.[5]

Barlow's use of the bunt was considered bush league by some including an article in the *Boston Globe* on September 9, 1873, which referred to it as "the black game" and his attempted bunts were described as "a weak one for a professional club" and a "failure," when they were unsuccessful. They viewed Barlow's attempted bunts as a "weakness," and an indication that he couldn't succeed by taking a full swing at the ball. When Nick Young called Barlow's bunts "baby hits," a writer for the *Brooklyn Eagle* defended it, saying that it was the hitter's job to try to get on base and "the real baby hits are those which give easy chances for fly catches," which was a criticism of players who tried to drive the ball. It was "absurd" to ridicule Barlow because he tried to reach base via a bunt. Not many players adopted Barlow's bunting style, especially after the fair-foul hit was banned in 1877 and catchers stood closer to the plate, wearing masks.[6] Tim Murnane of the 1877 Boston Red Stockings was one player who did utilize the bunt using a flat-sided bat. The stolen base as it is defined in the modern era in which the runner took off with the pitch and raced safely to the next base, while the hitter did not put the ball in play, was also not very popular during the 1870s. Nor was the sacrifice bunt or the bunt in general. George Wright was one of the more respected players who used the bunt. Jim O'Rourke said that Pearce and Barlow were disadvantaged when their short bats were no longer allowed. They gave up bunting when they were forced to use the long bats and became "ordinary players."[7] Not only was the bunt used to get a hit but at a time when foul balls were not counted as strikes it was used to exhaust the pitcher. A foul ball was not counted as a strike until 1901 and it wasn't until 1909 that a batter was out if he bunted foul with two strikes.

By the late 1870s the delayed double steal was becoming popular. With runners on the corners, the runner on first took off and tried to get the catcher to throw to second so that the runner on third could steal home. The objective was not necessarily to steal two bags, but to allow the runner on first to get caught in a rundown and sacrifice himself, while the runner on third scampered home. If there were two outs the runner on third was expected to score before the out was recorded. The steal of home was rarely employed during the 1880s, but stolen bases in general were increasing in popularity. During the 1880s Mike "King" Kelly helped popularize basestealing by inventing the hook slide. The fans would reportedly chant, "Slide, Kelly, Slide," and in 1889 the chant became a famous song. During his sixteen-year major league career he batted .308 with a .438 slugging percentage and 368 steals. However, there are no stolen base totals for his first eight seasons. He was a terrific baserunner and exceptional defensive outfielder. Kelly received a large salary and was beloved by baseball fans. He invented his hook slide as a member of the Chicago White Stockings and it became known as the Chicago slide. There are some people who dispute whether Kelly invented sliding, but he certainly perfected it, made it popular and more ubiquitous by teaching it to his teammates. The 5'10", 170-pound right-handed player had terrific baseball intelligence. He was an extremely aggressive baserunner who would cut across the infield when running the bases if the umpire was not looking. He would pretend that he was injured, limp towards first base, and then steal second when the opposition relaxed. Kelly was versatile and played all nine positions in the field, including 583 games as a catcher. He was known to drop his catcher's mask in the baserunners' path so they would trip on it. Connie Mack compared Kelly to Ty Cobb.

The bunt would not become popular again until 1886 when players like Arlie Latham and John Ward began to use it. Latham was a member of player-manager Charlie Comiskey's 1886 pennant-winning St. Browns (93–46) of the American Association. In addition to bunting for hits they utilized the sacrifice bunt and helped it become popular among the fans and the players. Arlie was a member of the Browns from 1883 to 1889 and under the leadership of Comiskey they won the pennant four consecutive seasons from 1885 to 1888. St. Louis was the best small ball team in the circuit. They bunted frequently and ran the bases aggressively during their pennant-winning seasons. The American Association did not keep track of stolen bases until 1886 and from 1886 to 1888 the Browns stole 1,385 bags with totals of 336, 581, and 468. Latham stole 129 bags in 1887 but finished second in the circuit behind Hugh Nicol (138) and then he led the circuit with 109 thefts in 1888. Latham stole 742 bases during his career. His career appeared to be over after playing six games at the age of 39 for the 1899 Washington Senators of the National League. In 1907, John McGraw of the New York Giants signed him as a coach. He was the first official full-time coach and utilized the same tactics he had used as a player. Arlie was an irritant being loud, combative, vulgar, and pugilistic. In 1909 he appeared in four games for the Giants and stole the final base of his career, becoming the oldest man to steal a bag, doing so as a 49-year-old. Latham helped the Giants become better basestealers and in 1911 McGraw's club stole a modern era record of 347 bags.

The 1886 flag carriers, the St. Louis Browns of the American Association and the Chicago White Stockings of the National League, both won the pennant by using the bunt as a weapon. In addition to bunting for hits and sacrificing runners over, Latham used the bunt to draw the infielders in and then slapped the ball past them. However, some people were not amused with the reemergence of the bunt, including the *Detroit Free Press*, which wrote on May 9, 1886, that "Base Ball is essentially a manly spirit, and its patrons object to such infantile tricks." They took a cheap shot at Arthur Irwin, the weak-hitting shortstop for the Philadelphia Quakers of the National League, insisting that he must have been too feeble to swing the bat, and had to bunt to compensate for his weakness. The spectators let Irwin know that they disapproved of his performance.[8] By 1889 the hitter was rewarded

Arlie Latham was a jocular, intelligent, entertaining, controversial, and pugilistic ballplayer, who batted .269 lifetime in seventeen major league seasons. He was a renowned bunter and his St. Louis Browns of the 1880s were one of the earliest practitioners of the sacrifice bunt, helping to make it popular with fans and players alike. Latham was a great basestealer as well, taking advantage of the generous stolen base rule of the nineteenth century and stealing 742 hassocks during his career. He won his only stolen base crown in 1888 by pilfering 109 bags to beat out Hugh Nicol (103) for the American Association title. Latham made an impact as a highly effective bench jockey and his antics as a third base coach, running up and down the line while verbally harassing the pitcher as he was delivering the ball to the plate, led to the creation of the coach's box. (George Brace photograph).

with a sacrifice in the box score if he bunted a runner over. It was a statistic that made Henry Chadwick proud. While some people suggested that bunting allowed a club to coalesce as a unit with players sacrificing themselves for the good of the team, many players were reluctant to bunt because it hurt their batting average. However, in 1893 a new rule was adopted stipulating that batters who sacrificed were not to be charged with an at-bat, making it even more desirable. But this rule was not implemented until 1894 and was not used by all the official scorers until 1897. Flat bats were banned in 1893 and a foul bunt was called a strike during the following campaign. There were many people during the 1890s who wanted the bunt banned from the game. Cap Anson hated bunting and called it "baby hitting," and wanted it banned.[9] However, small ball tactics were becoming increasingly popular, evidenced by the fact that the stolen base statistic was officially compiled by the National League beginning in 1886 and sacrifice hits were compiled beginning in 1894. The bunt continued to have its critics into the twentieth century, including President William Howard Taft, who told reporters in 1909 that he preferred to see hitters try to slug the ball great distances.[10]

Variations of the bunt would develop over time: the bluff bunt, drag bunt, push bunt, surprise bunt, sacrifice bunt, squeeze bunt, safety squeeze, suicide squeeze, double squeeze, the bunt and run, and the swinging bunt. The double squeeze occurs with runners on second and third and fewer than two outs. When the pitcher delivers his offering to the catcher, the runners take off and the batter lays one down. The runner at third is acting in a suicidal manner and scores easily if the batter does his job. The runner at second, rounds third, and continues towards the plate as the out is being recorded at first base to score two runs on a bunt. The pennant-winning 1890 Boston Reds (81–48) of the Players League utilized the double squeeze play along with other small ball tactics and led the circuit with 412 steals, which was 136 more than the Chicago Pirates, who finished second in that category with 276. The Chicago Cubs pulled off a double squeeze on July 15, 1905, versus Brooklyn. Connie Mack, the Philadelphia Athletics manager, may have first observed the play in July 1905 when the Detroit Tigers plated two runs on Germany Schaefer's bunt, which first baseman Harry Davis quickly scooped up, and was dismayed to see the runner from second score after he threw to first for the out. When Davis became a coach for the Athletics in 1913, they began to practice this play during spring training, and then unleashed it as a potent weapon once the regular season began. The Philadelphia Athletics successfully executed the double squeeze at least eight times during the 1913 campaign. Jack Barry was at the dish each time and on three occasions he managed to leg out a hit while two runs scored. They clinched the pennant with a double squeeze on September 22, but their double squeeze attempt failed in the opening game of the World Series against the New York Giants. On April 29, 1914, Jack Barry popped up the double squeeze bunt attempt which led to a triple play, as the skipper, Connie Mack, was no longer a proponent of such trickery. However, he did use it successfully on August 16, 1927, against Cleveland.

The 1905 New York Highlanders helped make the squeeze bunt a respectable tactic. Jack Chesbro, a 5'9", 180-pound right-handed pitcher for the Highlanders, missed a sign while standing at third base in a 1904 contest. He broke for home with the pitch, believing he was ordered to steal, and Wee Willie Keeler bunted as Chesbro scored a run. Player-manager Clark Griffith knew that he had stumbled onto a new and effective strategy and had his men practice it during the 1905 spring training. Griffith didn't have a lot of power hitters on his team or players that could drive the ball. But they all knew how to bunt, so he recognized that the squeeze play would be an effective weapon, considering that most of his hitters weren't going to drive the ball into the outfield with a runner on third. The 1905 Highlanders were a formidable small ball outfit, leading the AL with 200 steals and finishing fifth in the circuit with 151 sacrifice hits. But their pitching staff compiled the worst ERA (2.93) in the AL and they finished the season in sixth place (71–78). While the Highlanders may have been the first team to use the squeeze play frequently, it had been employed by players during the nineteenth century. The two major leagues combined for 108 squeeze plays in 1908: 87 in the AL and 21 in the NL.

Interestingly, perhaps the greatest small ball tactician of the Deadball Era, manager John McGraw of the New York Giants, was not a fan of the sacrifice bunt or squeeze bunt. He was, however, fond of the stolen base, hit-and-run, and the steal and slam. Although he did acknowledge that the hit-and-run play was fundamentally flawed because a perceptive hurler could sense the runner in motion and pitch out. The steal and slam occurred when the runner on first took off for second as if he were going to pilfer the bag. If the batter liked the pitcher's offering he could take a cut at it, but if the hurler pitched out or delivered a difficult pitch to hit, then the batter would allow the baserunner to try to steal the bag without his interference. The evolution of the bunt and the stolen base is superbly detailed in Peter Morris's wonderful book *A Game of Inches: The Game on the Field: The Stories Behind the Innovations That Shaped Baseball.*

The game of baseball continued to evolve during the 1880s with rules that were constantly changing. Some of the notable changes included modifying the length of the pitcher's box to home plate; altering the definition of a legal delivery; changing the number of balls needed for a batter to draw a walk; going to a four-strike format for one season (1887); establishing a new strike zone; and disallowing batters from commanding the pitcher to throw a high pitch or a low pitch. Small ball strategies became increasingly popular during the 1880s. With two stable major leagues, the National League and the American Association, competition became fierce and the game became violent, dangerous, and rough. Player-manager Cap Anson's Chicago White Stockings were the best team in the National League during the 1880s, winning five pennants in 1880, 1881, 1882, 1885, and 1886. During three seasons they finished with over a .700 winning percentage. In 1880 they finished with a 67–17 record (.798); in 1885 they were 87–25 (.777); and in 1886 they concluded the season with a 90–34 mark (.726). Twenty-year-old Connie Mack observed Anson's White Stockings play an exhibition game in his hometown of East Brookfield, Massachusetts, in 1883, saying, "It was a bigger event to us than the inauguration of a president."[11] The White Stockings relied heavily on the inside game for success, which included teamwork between the infielders and outfielders and a baserunning approach that was scientific in nature. They had a powerful offense which was envied by the opposing teams.

The popular King Kelly played for Chicago from 1880 to 1886, while the fleet-footed Billy Sunday played for them from 1883 to 1887. Anson insisted that Sunday, who would become a famous evangelist, "ran like a deer" and was the fastest player in the game.[12] He later insisted that Sunday was a better player than Ty Cobb despite batting only .248 lifetime. In 1885 Sunday raced Arlie Latham of the St. Louis Browns to determine who was faster and Sunday pulled away for an easy victory in the foot race. Sunday's 71 steals for the 1888 Pittsburgh Alleghenys was third in the NL. He batted only .236 that year with a .256 on-base percentage. During his final major league season in 1890 with Pittsburgh (86 games) and Philadelphia (31 games) he stole a career high 84 bags to finish third in the National League. Cap Anson built a dynasty in Chicago during the 1880s, but his legacy is irreparably harmed by his disgraceful conduct in helping to implement baseball's color line.

Charlie Comiskey's St. Louis Browns were the best American Association team during the 1880s, winning four consecutive pennants from 1885 to 1888. They were a well-balanced team with terrific offensive players, pitchers, and fielders. Part of their winning formula was to verbally assault the umpires and their opponents. While coaching on the third-base line, Comiskey cursed the pitcher, incessantly challenged the umpire's judgment, and even stepped on the umpire's feet until blood came spilling out. He ran up and down the line, spewing his vulgar comments, and the rest of the team imitated the skipper. Players assumed the role as coaches and ran up and down the baselines yelling insults at the pitcher while they delivered the ball. Arlie Latham was especially talented when it came to antagonizing the opposition and he frequently started and participated in pugilistic activities. Because of Latham's disgraceful conduct, the coach's box was established in 1887. When pitchers were allowed to throw overhand, beanball wars developed, and headhunters were plentiful. Tony Mullane of the American Association's Cincinnati Red Stockings was a well-known beanball pitcher and the league adopted the hit-batsman rule because of these kinds of pitchers. At that time the National League was reluctant to adopt the rule believing that it "sissified" the game.[13] However, beanball pitchers threatened the health of players and therefore the amount of money the magnates could make, so the NL adopted the hit-by-pitch rule in 1887. The fans also became hostile, especially in the American Association where alcohol was sold and it became known as the "Beer Ball League." Pete Browning of Louisville was known to play drunk and once said, "I can't hit the ball until I hit the bottle."[14] Mickey Welch, a Hall of Fame pitcher who hurled for the Troy Trojans from 1880 to 1882 before playing for the New York Gothams/Giants for the rest of his career from 1883 to 1892, insisted that he was a successful pitcher because he drank beer.[15] There were a number of other players who were accused of drinking before and during games.

The National League had its inaugural season in 1876 and the competing American Association enjoyed their first campaign in 1882. Both leagues began compiling stolen bases in 1886 under the generous stolen base rule of the nineteenth century. The American Association teams swiped more hassocks during the late 1880s, pilfering 11,256 bases from 1886 to 1889, while the National League teams stole 8,408 bases during those four seasons. Both leagues had eight teams but the American Association played more games during that time period. Interestingly, both leagues' stolen base totals skyrocketed in 1887. In 1886 the American Association teams stole 1,904 bags and then they stole 3,664 bases in 1887. The National League teams pilfered 1,339 bases in 1886 and then swiped 2,681 bases in 1887. Harry Stovey of the Philadelphia Athletics stole 68 bags to lead the AA in 1886 and then in 1887 Hugh Nicol led the circuit with 138 steals. Similarly, in the NL, Ed Andrews of the Philadelphia Quakers led the circuit with 56 steals in 1886 and then John Ward swiped 111 cushions the following season. The St. Louis Browns of the American Association were the best bases-stealing team in the majors and stole an all-time record 581 bases in 1887. The next three teams on the all-time list also played in the American Association in 1887: Baltimore (545), Cincinnati (527), and Philadelphia (476). The seventh-place New York Metropolitans (44–89) finished last in the circuit with 305 steals. The National League's team stolen base leaders from 1886 to 1889 were the 1886 Philadelphia Quakers (226), the 1887 New York Giants (415), the 1888 Indianapolis Hoosiers (350), and the 1889 Boston Beaneaters (331). The 100-stolen-base level was crossed nine times by a player from 1886 to 1889. Hugh Nicol and Arlie Latham did it in back-to-back seasons during the 1887 and 1888 American Association campaigns while Charlie Comiskey, Pete Browning, and Billy Hamilton did it once. National Leaguers John Ward (111) and Jim Fogarty (102) each stole over 100 bags in 1887 and Fogarty just missed in 1889 with 99 thefts. The Union Association lasted for only one season in 1884, luring players away from the NL and AA and insisting that the reserve clause was illegitimate. There are no stolen base statistics available for the Union Association's only season.

Billy Hamilton stole 111 bags for the seventh-place Kansas City Cowboys (55–82), who led the American Association with 472 steals in 1889. He was known as "Sliding Billy" and finished his career with 914 steals, including four seasons with 100 or more. His three other

100-stolen-base seasons were accomplished as a member of Philadelphia's National League outfit in 1890 (102), 1891 (111), and 1894 (100). On August 31, 1894, he tied a major league record with seven stolen bases in a game. Hamilton scored at least 141 runs six times; he scored at least 103 runs during eleven of his fourteen major league seasons; he led the NL four times in that category, and set an all-time record of 198 runs scored in 1894, while batting .403 with a .522 on-base percentage. The Hall of Fame player batted .344 lifetime with a .455 on-base percentage. He was a terrific leadoff man with great patience and the ability to create chaos on the bases with his blazing speed. Hamilton led the NL in both walks and on-base percentage during five seasons. Sliding Billy was credited with the first head-first slide and popularized the drag bunt during the 1890s. He would frequently advance from first to third on a hit, an act which often earned him a stolen base under the rules until the 1898 season. Billy was a 5'6", 165-pound outfielder, who batted left-handed but threw right-handed. From 1891 to 1895 he joined Ed Delahanty and Sam Thompson in the outer garden for the Phillies to form perhaps the greatest outfield trio in major league history. All three of them earned induction into the Hall of Fame. From 1896 to 1901, Hamilton played for the Boston Beaneaters. The ninth edition of the Macmillan baseball encyclopedia credits Hamilton with 99 steals in 1894. But when the old statistics were corrected his total moved up to 100 making him the only player in major league history with four 100-steal seasons. Rickey Henderson and Vince Coleman each have three 100-steal seasons. Furthermore, his career stolen base total appears to have declined through the years. His Hall of Fame plaque credits him with 937 steals, while *The 2006 ESPN Baseball Encyclopedia* gives him 914.

Unlike speed merchants like Lou Brock or Rickey Henderson, Hamilton played in an era where stolen bases were at an all-time high and he benefited from the generous stolen base rule of that time period. During the three seasons when Hamilton stole 100 or more bases for the Phillies, the average number of steals for each team in the National League was as follows: In 1890 the NL averaged 282.4 steals per team, in 1891 the NL averaged 251.4 steals per team, and in 1894 the NL averaged 262.3 steals per team. Consult Appendix A to find out the average number of steals for each team, in each league, during each season.

The rules continued to be refined during the 1890s and by the end of the decade baseball was similar to the way it was played during the twentieth century. For most of the 1890s major league baseball consisted of only the National League as the American Association disbanded after the 1891 campaign, while the outlaw Players League lasted for one season in 1890. Baseball during the 1890s was played under a malleable set of rules. The game became even more violent as participation in the sport put a player at risk of bodily harm. This violent element became known as rowdyism or hoodlumism.

Players had to overcome several obstacles as they made their way around the bases. Only one umpire was used to officiate games and when he wasn't looking infielders tripped baserunners and held their belts or other pieces of their clothing. The infielders stood in the baserunners' way as they tried to advance to the next station and stepped on their feet while they were standing on the bag or sliding into it. While a stolen base attempt was being made, a hitter would slam the bat on the catcher's arm so he couldn't make the throw. Ed McKean, the Cleveland Spiders shortstop, was skilled at "giving the runner the hip." During one contest he put his hands around a player's neck and began to strangle him until he threw him to the ground and "his eyes stuck out of their sockets like doorknobs."[16] Patsy Tebeau, the player-manager of the Spiders, developed a play where the first baseman pushed the runner off the bag as the pitcher tried to pick him off. He was an aggressive baserunner who used his sharpened spikes as a weapon during an era when spike high slides were plentiful and the infielders would retaliate by spiking or stomping on the runner's feet so they couldn't run well.

The Baltimore Orioles brought out all their tricks when they played their hated rival, the Cleveland Spiders, like putting a mushy ball in play when the opposition was at the bat or blinding them by using a mirror to reflect the sunlight into their eyes. They were highly skilled at implementing these nefarious tricks and other teams emulated them. The Orioles used every artifice they could to gain an advantage and bend the rules: they tripped opposing players, filed their spikes to intimidate the opposition, and hid baseballs in the tall outfield grass that could be switched with the official ball when convenient. When there was only one umpire officiating the game they would take a shorter path around the bases, running through the infield, and refraining from touching each bag as they were required to do. The Oriole middle infielders would low bridge the runners as they made their throw to first on a double play ball. John McGraw, the Orioles third baseman, had his own tricks such as grabbing a runner's belt as he tagged up on a fly ball. The Orioles were not merely a bunch of thugs but they helped define baseball strategy and develop "inside baseball" and small ball tactics. They reportedly "invented" the hit-and-run, the sacrifice bunt, the squeeze play, the cutoff man, the double steal, and the "Baltimore chop."[17]

John Heydler was an umpire during the 1890s and insisted that the Orioles were "mean, vicious, ready at any time to maim a rival player or an umpire, if it helped their cause." He observed umpires with damaged feet, bruised and bloody, because John McGraw and some of the other players stomped on their feet with spikes that cut right through their shoes. Connie Mack was the skipper of the Pittsburgh Pirates from 1894 to 1896 and he froze baseballs and sent a spy to center field to steal signals. Despite showing a willingness to cheat and use rough tactics, Mack had no problem rendering judgment on the Orioles, insisting they were "not gentlemen," and "played the game like gladiators in ancient Roman arenas."[18] With owners reluctant to punish players and no unifying central authority in the game to punish unscrupulous players, the game was at the apogee of violent conduct and dishonest play.

Manager Ned Hanlon's Baltimore Orioles excelled at the inside game which was becoming increasingly popular during the 1890s. Thomas J. Murphy, their groundskeeper, would manipulate the foul lines so bunts had a better chance of staying fair. He was instructed to harden the ground in front of the plate so that they could execute the Baltimore Chop. Oriole hitters deliberately hit down on the ball so it struck the hardened area directly in front of home plate and bounced high in the air, giving the batter ample time to hustle down to first for an infield hit. Or perhaps the ball would bounce over the head of the first baseman or third baseman, especially if they were drawn in to guard against the bunt. Wee Willie Keeler perfected this play, while John McGraw and Wilbert Robinson were also very good at it.

The Orioles didn't invent the hit-and-run play, but they perfected it, and made it popular by using it ubiquitously. Some people have suggested that the 1876 Chicago White Stockings invented the play. Lave Cross insisted that Pete Browning accidentally discovered the hit-and-run. He was hard of hearing and misunderstood the instructions given to him by the coach and took off from first with the pitched ball and advanced to third as the batter hit a single. Hughie Jennings, the Orioles shortstop, heard of this serendipitous play, and told his teammates about it. There is ample evidence that shows that the hit-and-run play was used during the 1880s, not only by Chicago, but by other National League teams as well. It was John Ward's contention that the Boston Beaneaters had invented the play during the early 1890s and that Tommy McCarthy was their chief practitioner. Ward suggested that the hit-and run replaced the sacrifice bunt with a runner on first and no outs. The runner on first would take a few quick steps towards second as the pitcher delivered the ball and then retreat to the first base bag. They would observe whether the second baseman or shortstop went to cover the bag and then they would work the hit-and-run with the batter hitting the ball through the vacated hole. The hitter would know before the pitch was delivered whether to hit the ball through the vacated shortstop position or through the vacated second base position. Historian Bill James contends that because John McGraw was well-liked by the New York press he was allowed to claim credit for the hit-and-run play as the press passed the story on to gullible sportswriters. The Orioles began to use the hit-and-run play frequently beginning in 1894 when Willie Keeler joined the team. The 5'4", 140-pound left-handed fly chaser, was a superbly skilled place hitter and a terrific bad-ball hitter, which made him an ideal hit-and-run batter. Baltimore began the 1894 campaign against New York and utilized the hit-and-run play frequently during the series. They kept on using it throughout their three consecutive pennant-winning campaigns from 1894 to 1896.

Baltimore pitchers would cover first base on grounders to the right side and run behind the bag to back it up when a throw was coming into third. Thomas J. Murphy helped them out by raising the pitcher's box a foot above home plate during a time when the rules stipulated that it was supposed to be flat. Pieces of soap were spread around the mound and when the opposing pitchers tried to pick up dirt their hand would get slippery. The Oriole pitchers, meanwhile, kept the dry dirt in their back pockets. Ned Hanlon made sure that the Orioles were fundamentally sound in the inside baseball tactics. When the ball was hit deep into the outfield, an infielder went out and took the throw. If the opposing hitter made contact with the ball all of the Oriole fielders had a responsibility. On a line drive base hit to left field with a runner on first, the third baseman went out to take the relay throw, while the shortstop covered third, and the keystoner took care of second. The pitcher backed up third just in case a bad throw got away. Many of the opposing hitters were startled to be thrown out on what they thought was an easy double, as the Oriole outfielders substituted the original ball for one that was hidden in the outfield grass. Often they would simply remain at first as the Orioles quickly found a ball and threw it in. The outfield grass grew extremely high so that they could utilize this tactic but after considerable protest by their competition, the league ordered them to cut the grass regularly. The Oriole players loved the game and McGraw attributed their success to the fact that they "talked, lived and dreamed baseball."[19] They honed their skills in the early morning, 8 A.M. practices. Hanlon wanted all of his players to know how to bunt because when the pitcher's box was moved back in 1893 it made the bunt a more effective weapon. The innovative field general took control of the Orioles in 1892, managing for most of the season as they finished last in the National League with a 46–101 record and committed a league high 584 errors. In 1893 they committed 384 errors and then led the NL with only 293 errors in 1894. The Orioles were ruthless competitors who would outsmart the opposition to emerge victorious. Their style led to success on the field as they won the NL pennant for three straight seasons from 1894 to 1896 and finished second to Boston in 1897 and 1898.

When Baltimore defeated Brooklyn by a 5–2 score at Washington Park on September 8, 1898, the *New York Times* wrote that they "plainly demonstrated" why they were competing for the pennant down the stretch. "They played a fast and snappy game at every stage," and excelled at the "hit-and-run style of baseball," while also executing some "scientific bunt hitting." Brooklyn, meanwhile, was "painfully slow on the bases," and unable to hit in the clutch.[20] In 1898, Baltimore finished in second place with a 96–53 record and led the circuit with 250 steals during the first season in which the modern stolen base rule was implemented. Brooklyn was a tenth-place outfit (54–91) that pilfered 130 bags. From 1892 to 1899 the National League was a twelve-team circuit.

During McGraw's tenure with the Orioles he would generally lead off. He batted .334 lifetime with a .466 on-base percentage and led the NL in runs two times, walks twice, and on-base percentage three times. McGraw also had good wheels, stealing 436 bases during his career, including a career high of 78 in 1894 when he finished second in the NL. In 1899 he batted .391 for Baltimore during their final season in the NL and led the circuit with a .547 on-base percentage, 140 runs scored, and 124 walks. He also proved he could steal bases the conventional way, swiping 73 bags to finish second in the circuit behind his teammate Jimmy Sheckard (77) in 1899, one year after the modern stolen base rule was implemented. McGraw's .547 on-base percentage in 1899 stood as the major league record until Ted Williams surpassed him with a .553 on-base percentage in 1941. Before the 1901 campaign foul balls were not called strikes unless the umpire believed the hitter was doing so deliberately. Willie Keeler said, "There wasn't any of them that could foul 'em off harder than McGraw. He could slam 'em out on a line so fast that even the umpire couldn't tell he was doing it on purpose."[21] McGraw made a habit of spoiling pitches, frustrating and exhausting the pitcher in the process. Like many of the Orioles he was an aggressive baserunner who was also very intelligent. The 5'7", 155-pound McGraw, played mainly third base during his career and batted left-handed but threw right-handed. He choked up on the bat and swung down on the ball with a chopping motion. If the umpire threatened to call foul balls as strikes he would threaten them and intimidate them. When he reached first base he signaled Keeler, the two hole hitter, to execute the hit-and-run. Keeler, an exceptional place hitter, would hit the ball through the vacated hole and McGraw would scamper to third. The Oriole batters were excellent situational hitters who used their baseball savvy to win games. Johnny Evers described the Orioles as "a team of only fair players winning by dash, nerve, and courage."[22]

John McGraw would later take his strategies of scientific baseball to New York as the manager of the Giants. He was a big proponent of small ball, instructing his club the appropriate time to steal, bunt, or execute the hit-and-run. McGraw was known to use pinch-hitters, pinch-runners, and relief pitchers at a time when it wasn't done so often. He believed in developing ballplayers, showing faith in the youngsters and instructing them on the fundamentals of the game for several years before they became regulars. Mel Ott is one of several players who became great under McGraw's tutelage. McGraw's teams were generally overachievers who had good defense, excellent pitching, and ran the bases aggressively. During his tenure in New York from 1902 to 1932, McGraw led the Giants to ten pennants and three World Series titles. In addition to being a great leader and instructing his men concerning the tactical maneuvers of "inside baseball," he also excelled at the psychological part of the game. He was known to verbally and physically assault fans, players, and umpires. McGraw had intimate connections with gamblers and would incite the crowd until they were on the verge of rioting. When Babe Ruth arrived in New York in 1920, McGraw disdained the big ball game that Ruth played and disseminated around the country. He even persuaded Charles Stoneham, the Giants owner, to evict the Yankees from the Polo Grounds. McGraw simply detested the home runs and strikeouts piled up by Ruth.

There were two competing offensive styles during the 1890s, the "slugging" style and the "scientific" style.[23] The slugging style became a popular strategy beginning in 1893 as the moundsmen had difficulty adjusting to the longer pitching distance and hitters swung for the fences. In 1894 the NL teams hit a decade-high 629 homers, but by 1899 it declined to 352 and then to 254 in 1900 when the NL reduced to an eight-team circuit. In 1894 Boston led the circuit with 103 homers which was more than any team during the Deadball Era, which ranged from 1901 to 1919. The 1913 Philadelphia Phillies hit the most home runs during the Deadball Era with 73, while playing in their hitter's paradise, the Baker Bowl. Runs were plentiful for much of the 1890s and in 1894 the NL averaged 7.38 runs per game but this declined to 4.96 in 1898. In 1894 the third-place Boston Beaneaters (83–49) led the circuit with an exorbitant 1,220 runs. There were five teams that season that collected at least 1,024 runs. On June 29, 1897, Chicago took care of Louisville by a 36–7 score in which there were 12 doubles, 3 triples, 2 homers, 7 steals, and 2 sacrifice hits. Louisville used only two pitchers in the game. The first-place 1897 Boston Beaneaters (93–39) scored 1,025 runs becoming the last team to score over 1,000 runs until the 1930 St. Louis Cardinals (1,004) and the 1930 New York Yankees (1,062) did it. By the end of the decade scientific baseball or inside baseball was the prevailing strategy, which included small ball tactics such as aggressive baserunning, basestealing, bunting, and using the hit-and-run.

Baltimore and Boston dominated National League baseball during the 1890s, combining to win eight consecutive pennants from 1891 to 1898. Manager Frank Selee's Boston Beaneaters won the pennant in 1891, 1892, 1893, 1897, and 1898. Tommy McCarthy played for them from 1892 to 1895 and his outfield play led to a rule change. Because of McCarthy's shenanigans in the outer garden the rule was changed regarding when a player could leave a base on a fly ball and advance to the next station. At one point the rule stated that the baserunner couldn't leave the bag until the outfielder secured the ball so McCarthy would juggle the ball as he ran into the infield, circumventing the rule. When he came close enough to the infield where a runner could no longer advance he would take full possession of the spheroid. McCarthy joined Hugh Duffy in the Boston outfield and they became known as the "Heavenly Twins." Duffy was the more accomplished player, batting .326 lifetime with a .386 on-base percentage and a .451 slugging percentage during his Hall of Fame career. He scored at least 103 runs during nine seasons and drove in at least 100 runs during eight seasons. Duffy and McCarthy combined to steal 1,042 bases during their careers, with Duffy swiping 574 of them. Duffy was also a long ball threat, hitting more homers than any player during the 1890s and leading the NL in 1894 (18) and 1897 (11). While Baltimore and Boston dominated most of the decade, Brooklyn took the pennant in 1890 and then won again in 1899. Brooklyn also secured the flag in 1900 when the square, 12-inch home plate, was replaced with a five-sided, 17-inch wide version.

The American Association teams stole more bases than the National League teams during their final two seasons in 1890 and 1891. The fourth-place Toledo Maumees (68–64) led the circuit with 421 steals in 1890 and also paced the league with 108 triples. Tommy McCarthy of St. Louis batted .350 with a .430 on-base percentage, a .467 slugging percentage, and led the league with 83 steals. The 5'7", 170-pound right-handed fly chaser was good enough to be inducted into the Hall of Fame and batted .292 lifetime with a .364 on-base percentage, 1,066 runs scored, and 468 steals. For seven straight seasons from 1888 to 1894, while playing for St. Louis (AA) and Boston (NL), he scored at least 107 runs during each season, including a career high of 137 in 1890.

The Boston Red Stockings (93–42) captured the final AA pennant in 1891 and led the circuit with 447 steals. Boston's Tom Brown batted .321 with a .397 on-base percentage and led the circuit with 177 runs scored, 189 hits, 21 triples, and 106 steals. The speedy left-handed leadoff man batted .265 lifetime with a .336 on-base percentage, 1,523 runs scored, and 657 stolen bases. His teammate Hugh Duffy finished second in the circuit with a career high 85 steals, while Boston's Paul Radford finished fifth with 55 thefts. George Van Haltren of Baltimore finished third with 75 steals while Dummy Hoy, a deaf mute who played for St. Louis, finished fourth with 59 thefts. Van Haltren batted .316 lifetime with a .386 on-base percentage while stealing 583 bags, including his career high of 75 thefts in 1891. He shared the NL stolen base title with Patsy Donovan in 1900 with 45 thefts, while playing for New York. The speedy left-handed leadoff man scored at least 109 runs during eleven seasons. It was reported that during one game in 1897 when he was coaching third base and there was a runner on second, he stole a run when he ran down the third base line as if he were going to steal home. The catcher was already distracted, arguing with the umpire without calling time, and the pitcher, acting instinctively, fired the ball home. It got away from the catcher and the runner scored all the way from second base. Van Haltren wasn't the only player to use this trick. When Bill "Boileryard" Clarke of the Baltimore Orioles acted as the third base coach he would occasionally distract the pitcher with a runner on third by racing towards the plate while he was making his delivery. Hoy batted .288 during fourteen major league seasons. He had a .386 on-base percentage, scored 1,429 runs, including nine seasons with at least 104. Hoy had good wheels, swiping 596 bags during his career, and he led the NL in thefts during his rookie campaign with the 1888 Washington Senators by pilfering 82 sacks.

Hugh Duffy was a baseball lifer who played during the late nineteenth century when baseball men were trying to establish the best rules and tactics for the sport. By the turn of the century the scientific style with its prevailing small ball strategies had won out. Duffy, who pilfered 574 cushions during his career, watched the game change mightily as manager of the Boston Red Sox in 1921 and 1922, as Babe Ruth helped popularize the home run. While Ruth's Yankees led the major leagues with 134 homers in 1921, Duffy's Red Sox hit only 17, which was the worst in the big show. (George Brace photograph).

The Boston Reds won the Players League pennant during the circuit's only season in 1890 with an 81–48 record and they led the league with 412 steals, which was 136 more than the second team in that category. Boston's Harry Stovey (97) and Tom Brown (79) finished first and second in steals. Stovey was a 5'11", 175-pound right-handed player, who resided mainly in the outer garden (944 games), but also played 550 games at first base. He batted .289 lifetime with a .361 on-base percentage, 1,492 runs scored, and 509 steals. He led the AA in steals during the first season in which they were officially compiled, by swiping 68 in 1886. For nine consecutive seasons from 1883 to 1891 he scored at least 110 runs and led the AA four times, including with a career high of 152 in 1889 with Philadelphia. Stovey was also a good extra-base hitter, leading the AA or NL in doubles once, in triples four times, and homers five times. He led the AA with 119 RBIs in 1889, which was by far his best total.

From 1890 to 1899 the National League team stolen base leaders were as follows: 1890 Brooklyn (349), 1891 Brooklyn (337), 1892 Brooklyn (409), 1893 New York (299), 1894 Chicago (332), 1895 Cincinnati (326), 1896 Baltimore (441), 1897 Baltimore (401), 1898 Baltimore (250), and 1899 Baltimore (364). The individual stolen base titles went to Billy Hamilton of Philadelphia in 1890 (102); Billy Hamilton of Philadelphia in 1891 (111); John Ward of Brooklyn in 1892 (88); Tom Brown of Louisville in 1893 (66); Billy Hamilton of Philadelphia in 1894 (100); Billy Hamilton of Philadelphia in 1895 (97); Joe Kelley of Baltimore in 1896 (87); Bill Lange of Chicago in 1897 (73); Ed Delahanty of Philadelphia in 1898 (58); and Jimmy Sheckard of Baltimore in 1899 (77).

John Montgomery Ward compiled a 164–103 record during seven seasons as a big league pitcher before converting to an infielder. There are no stolen base totals for his first eight seasons, but he stole 540 bags during his final eight major league campaigns. Joe Kelley's 87 steals in 1896 were 33 more than his second best season in 1895 (54). This Hall of Fame player batted .317 lifetime with a .402 on-base percentage, a .451 slugging percentage, 1,421 runs scored, 1,194 RBIs, and 443 steals during a seventeen-year career. He was beloved by the female spectators and tried to make himself look good at all times, including when he played the field, carrying a mirror in his pocket which he used to fix himself up. Bill Lange stood 6'1" and weighed 190 pounds. Despite his powerful appearance he could race around the bases with great speed, stealing 400 bases during his seven-year major league career with Chicago (1893–1899) in which he played 813 games. The powerful Ed Delahanty had an excellent Hall of Fame career from 1888 to 1903 in which he batted .346 with a .411 on-base percentage, a .505 slugging percentage, 1,600 runs scored, 1,466 RBIs, and 455 stolen bases. Jimmy Sheckard's career began in 1897 and lasted well into the Deadball Era until 1913. He batted .274 lifetime with a .375 on-base percentage and 465 steals. Interestingly, Sheckard stole only eight bases in 1898 despite playing 105 games and having 408 at-bats. And then he stole 69 more the following season when he had a career high of 77 thefts.

In 1896 the NL averaged 254.9 steals per team before it declined to 225.4 in 1897. When the modern stolen base rule was implemented in 1898, the NL teams averaged 172.4 steals per team but this increased to 222.3 in 1899, an average that has not been surpassed in any subsequent senior circuit season and was only surpassed by the American League in 1912 when they averaged 227.9 steals per team. Although baserunners were no longer credited with a steal if they advanced on a fly ball or took two bases on a hit or infield out starting in 1898, they were awarded with a steal if they advanced a base on a double steal or triple steal attempt where one of the runners was thrown out. This lasted until 1909. Baserunners were also credited with a stolen base even if there was defensive indifference. Starting in 1920 if a runner advanced a base because of the defensive team's indifference, the official scorer gave the runner a fielder's choice, not a stolen base. Baltimore led the NL with 401 of the league's 2,705 steals in 1897 and then with the new rule in 1898, they led the circuit with only 250 of the league's 2,069 steals. However, in 1899 they increased their stolen base total to 364, which accounted for 13.6 percent of the league total of 2,668. Their 364 steals are the most thefts in a season under the modern stolen base rule. There were eighteen teams during the nineteenth century that stole at least 401 bases in the American Association, National League, or Players League. There were four stolen base duos that stole at least 200 bags: Billy Hamilton (111) and Herman Long (89) of the 1889 Kansas City Cowboys or Blues of the AA; Arlie Latham (109) and Tommy McCarthy (93) of the 1888 St. Louis Browns of the AA; Hugh Nicol (138) and Bid McPhee (95) of the 1887 Cincinnati Red Stockings of the AA; and Arlie Latham (129) and Charlie Comiskey (117) of the 1887 St. Louis Browns of the AA, who combined for an all-time record 246 steals. The best National League stolen base duo of the nineteenth century was Joe Kelley (87) and Jack Doyle (73) of the 1896 Baltimore Orioles. They rank as only the thirteenth best major league stolen base combination of the nineteenth century.

In 1893 a new rule was adopted stipulating that batters were not to be charged with an at-bat if they advanced a runner by laying down a bunt and the batter was put out at first base or he could have been put out. But the sacrifice bunt rule wasn't used until 1894 and it wasn't applied by all the official scorers until 1897. Starting in 1894 foul bunts were counted as strikes and it is the first season that the sacrifice bunt or hit totals are available for the National League. From 1894 to 1899 the NL sacrifice hit total was as follows: 1,156; 997; 1,163; 1,130; 1,346; and 1,323. In 1898 the NL averaged 112.2 sacrifices per team and they averaged 110.3 sacrifices per team in 1899. For a team to lay down over 100 sacrifices is a fairly high total, but for a league to average over 100 sacrifices per team is indicative of the ubiquitous nature of the sacrifice bunt. Sacrifice bunts would increase even more during the Deadball Era when the number of runs scored would decline sharply. From 1894 to 1899 there were 34 teams with 100 or more sacrifices, including eight in 1898 and seven in 1899. The sacrifice hit team leaders were as follows: 1894 Pittsburgh (163), 1895 Boston (127), 1896 Cincinnati (127), 1897 Cincinnati (135), 1898 Pittsburgh and Louisville (141), and 1899 Louisville (163). The individual sacrifice hit titles went to Patsy Donovan of Pittsburgh in 1894 (26); Hughie Jennings of Baltimore in 1895 (28); Dummy Hoy of Cincinnati in 1896 (33); Tom McCreery of Louisville and New York in 1897 (30); Claude Ritchey of Louisville in 1898 (31); and Bones Ely of Pittsburgh in 1899 (29). Chicago led the NL in sacrifices in 1900 with 130 and Jimmy Slagle of Philadelphia laid down the most sacrifices with 27.

The chaos of the nineteenth century would be replaced by stability in the twentieth century. The National League's major league monopoly was challenged by Ban Johnson's American League, which raided their players and went to war against them. Johnson declared in 1901 that the American League had major league status and in 1903 there would be a peace settlement between the two leagues, which allowed both of them to prosper.

2

The Deadball Era

Three miles north of Independence Hall in North Philadelphia stood the Huntingdon Street Grounds, surrounded by Huntingdon Street, Broad Street, Lehigh Avenue, and North 15th Street. The exterior looked like a medieval castle. When the ballpark opened in 1887 it was known as National League Park, but it also became known as the Philadelphia Baseball Grounds and in later vintage was known as the Baker Bowl. When the wooden structure burned to the ground in 1894, a more sturdy edifice was built out of steel, brick, and concrete in 1895. It was at Philadelphia's National League ballpark that what has become known as the Deadball Era unofficially began on April 18, 1901. National League games in New York, St. Louis, and Cincinnati were postponed that day because of the poor weather. But in Philadelphia, despite the overcast sky, the threat of rain which did not dissipate, and an atmosphere that was described as "raw and chilly," the Philadelphia Phillies played host to the Brooklyn Bridegrooms or Superbas, who were the defending National League champions.[1] The American League raids had impaired both teams: Philadelphia losing Nap Lajoie and Brooklyn losing Joe McGinnity and Lave Cross.

The 4,593 spectators who braved the elements were chagrined to watch their Phillies lose to Brooklyn by a 12–7 score, a final tally that was not befitting of the Deadball Era. This day belonged to Jimmy Sheckard, Brooklyn's third baseman, who collected three triples and scored four runs. Sheckard would play twelve games at third base during the campaign, replacing the departed Lave Cross at the hot corner. But he would eventually return to the more familiar and comfortable setting of the outer garden, playing 120 games in left field. On the following day when Brooklyn prevailed 10–2 and swiped four bases in the process, he was described as being "a little bit at sea" when a fly ball dropped behind third base.[2] Sheckard batted a robust .354 during the season, which tied for second in the National League with Philadelphia's Ed Delahanty. The 5'9", 175-pound, left-handed hitter had a .409 on-base percentage and led the league with a .534 slugging percentage. Sheckard scored 116 runs, hit 29 doubles, a league-leading 19 triples, 11 homers, had 104 RBIs and stole 35 bags. In 1899, the 20-year-old fly chaser led the National League in steals with 77, finishing four ahead of his Baltimore teammate, John McGraw. And in 1903 he would share the NL stolen base crown with Frank Chance as they both swiped 67. When Sheckard finished his career he had a .274 lifetime batting average and 465 stolen bases. He led the NL for at least one season in games, runs, triples, homers, walks, on-base and slugging percentage, and steals.

The April 18 contest between Philadelphia and Brooklyn was a true slugfest. There were thirty hits in the game, six doubles, and five triples. For the season, National League teams scored 4.63 runs per game, which was significantly below the American League's 5.35. The large discrepancy was largely due to the fact that the National League adopted the foul-strike rule in 1901, while the junior league would not adopt this rule until 1903. This rule stipulated that batters would be charged with a strike on a foul ball, except for the third strike, and unless it was caught before hitting the ground. However, batters could continue to bunt the ball into foul territory with two strikes without being penalized until 1909 when a foul bunt after the second strike became a strikeout. Prior to the adoption of the foul-strike rule, skilled batters would incessantly hit the ball foul or bunt the ball foul to wear out the pitcher and wait for the perfect pitch to hit hard. The foul-strike rule was one of several changes that led to decreased offensive productivity during the Deadball Era.

During the 1901 season Philadelphia swiped 199 bases which was third in the National League behind Pittsburgh (203) and Chicago (204). Swiping one bag for Philadelphia on Opening Day was Roy Thomas, a 5'11", 150-pound, left-handed hitter. Thomas was an excellent practitioner of small ball strategies and the inside game which was so prevalent during the early twentieth century. He was a pesky hitter, who was remarkably disciplined and possessed tremendous bat control, once fouling off a reported twenty-seven pitches in one at-bat. He was such an irritant to Brooklyn skipper Ned Hanlon with his ability to hit foul balls in 1900 that he helped persuade Hanlon, a member of the league's rules committee, to advocate for the adoption of the foul-strike rule in 1901. Thomas collected 115 walks during his rookie year in 1899 and accumulated the same number in 1900, which was the first of five consecutive seasons he would lead the National League in bases on balls. He led the league in walks during seven of the ten seasons in which he played at least 108 games. Thomas was recognized as the best bunter in the game. However, he generally bunted for a base hit and never accumulated more than the 23 sacrifices which he compiled during his rookie year. It is estimated that he attempted 200 bunts every season. But he was only credited with 166 sacrifice hits during his career, which is not an exceptionally large number for someone who bunted as frequently as he did. In fact there are 131 players in major league history with more sacrifice hits than Thomas.

Thomas was one of the best baserunners in the circuit and stole 244 bases during his thirteen-year career (1899–1911). He scored over 100 runs during four seasons: 1899 (137), 1900 (132), 1901 (102), and 1905 (118). His 132 runs scored in 1900 led the circuit. Historian Bill James asserts that he is the only everyday major leaguer to score three times as many runs as he drove in. In 1902 (.414) and 1903 (.453) he led the senior league in on-base percentage. He batted .290 lifetime and possessed a laudable .413 on-base percentage. Roy Allen Thomas, who was born in Norristown, Pennsylvania, on March 24, 1874, was ideally positioned as a player in the Deadball Era. In 5,296 at-bats he accumulated only 100 doubles, 53 triples, and 7 homers. He hit a single 89.6 percent of the time, which is the highest percentage in major league history. He scored 1,011 runs during his career, walked 1,042 times, but had only 299 RBIs. He was a complete player by Deadball Era standards, patrolling the center field position with great skill and his .972 fielding average was a record when his big league career ended. Thomas was a graduate of the University of Pennsylvania and coached its baseball team in 1903 and from 1909 to 1919.

On April 18 Brooklyn stole two bases, one apiece by Bill Dahlen and Joe Kelley. Shortstop Bill Dahlen would steal 23 bases on the season and an impressive 548 during his career. He was not exceptionally fast, but was an excellent baserunner, and knew how to slide while avoiding the tag with a well practiced hook slide. He stole at least twenty bags during fourteen seasons, including a career high of 60 with the 1892 Chicago Colts of the National League. Joe Kelley led the National League in steals with 87 in 1896 with Baltimore, but his stolen base totals would systematically decline during his final eleven major league seasons. On Opening Day 1901, the newly converted first baseman pilfered one of his eighteen bases during the season.

Brooklyn finished the 1901 season in third place (79–57), while Philadelphia finished second (83–57), seven and a half games behind Pittsburgh. The Superbas swiped 178 bags during the campaign, which was the fifth best in the National League. Their 80 sacrifice hits was only the sixth best in the league, finishing well behind league-leading Boston by 55, who were a fifth-place outfit (69–69). Bill Shettsline, the Phillies manager, led his club on a sustained small ball attack, finishing second in the National League with 126 sacrifice hits, including 29 by NL leader Bill Hallman, who batted .184 for Philadelphia in 445 at-bats. He began the 1901 campaign with the Cleveland Blues of the American League, playing five games at shortstop, before joining the Phillies where he compiled a career high .971 fielding average, while playing second base (90 games) and third base (33 games). The 5'8", 160-pound, right-handed infielder managed to play in 123 games for the Phils despite compiling a paltry .236 on-base percentage. Hallman wasn't much of a basestealer, swiping only 13 hassocks in 1901 and 201 during his fourteen-year career. William Wilson Hallman was an aging 34-year-old infielder who was not related to William Harry Hallman, a 25-year-old outfielder, who began his major league career for the 1901 Milwaukee Brewers of the American League.

The team that implemented small ball strategies the most often resided in the American League. Player-manager Clark Griffith finished third in the junior league in wins, compiling a 24–7 record on the bump and led the White Sox to a first-place conclusion with an 83–53 record. Frank Isbell, the team's first baseman, led the American League with 52 steals while Sam Mertes, their second baseman, finished second in the circuit with 46 and right fielder Fielder Jones tied for third with 38. Teams that accumulated large numbers of steals in the late twentieth century and early twenty-first century were often comprised of one or two players who garnered a large percentage of the team's thefts. This was not the case during the Deadball Era when a team's stolen base total was based on large contributions by many members. Isbell (253), Mertes (396), and Jones (359) would each finish their careers with large stolen base totals, but they paled in comparison to a deaf ballplayer named Dummy Hoy, who swiped 27 of his 596 career bases in 1901. In his second to last season he batted .294 with a .407 on-base percentage as Chicago's center fielder and led the league in walks (86) and hit by pitches (14). Herm McFarland swiped 33 bags and played left field; catcher Billy Sullivan stole 12 bases; third baseman Fred Hartman stole a career high 31; and shortstop Frank Shugart stole 12 bags in his final big league season. Everybody contributed to the prevailing small ball philosophy of the team and by executing the inside game better than their opponents, they prevailed and conquered the junior circuit in its inaugural season. Sam Mertes led the Sox with 20 sacrifice hits, while Fielder Jones was second with 18. The Pale Hose led the major leagues with 280 steals, which was 73 more than Baltimore, the team with the second most thefts. Furthermore, their 135 sacrifice hits were tied with the Detroit Tigers and Boston Beaneaters for the most in the majors. From 1901 to 1903, Chicago's American League outfit was most commonly known as the White Stockings, but an article in the *Washington Post* on April 26, 1901, referred to them as the Chicago American(s).

Fielder Jones, the Chicago Americans skilled offensive and defensive occupant of the outer garden, became the White Sox manager in 1904 and led the 1906 Sox, better known as the "Hitless Wonders," to a World Series victory over Chicago's National League representative who came into the series as heavy favorites. The *Chicago Tribune* wrote that "a White Sox rally at that time was described as a base on balls, a sacrifice, a stolen base, and a long fly."[3] Jones was an exceptional strategist of the inside game, a stern disciplinarian, who also conveyed a sympathetic side by helping former players who were in financial ruin and would advocate for players' rights. Like many of his contemporaries, he knew that the successful implementation of small ball strategies would bring success and strongly argued for effective teamwork. He railed against the implementation of the sacrifice fly rule in 1908. Under this rule if a batter produced a run scoring fly out, he was credited with an RBI and was not given an at-bat. Many, including Jones, believed this rule undermined team play and helped encourage players to become more attentive to individual statistics. Jones insisted that this was not what the game needed and added, "Team work is the goal of every club that wants to become a winner and individual records are a handicap."[4]

Fittingly, with three American League games postponed on Opening Day 1901, the inaugural junior league contest was played at Chicago's South Side Park on April 24. The championship flag was hoisted so the 8,000 spectators could acknowledge the team's accomplishment from the previous season and they were entertained with music. Chicago was buoyed by two first inning runs and five runs in the second frame as they defeated Cleveland, 8–2, on only seven hits. The box score did not credit either team with a sacrifice hit or a stolen base. With rookie Roy Patterson on the bump, a six-foot, 185-pounder nicknamed the "Boy Wonder," the Sox secured the victory, the first of twenty wins Patterson would be credited with during the campaign. Frank Shugart and Cleveland third baseman Bill Bradley fielded well and both outfields engaged in "sensational fielding." The game was a brisk one hour, thirty minute affair.[5]

Interestingly, Bradley who was a feared right-handed slugger who swung a heavy bat and was known for the large number of extra-base hits he accumulated, including home runs in four consecutive games in 1902 when he finished tied for second in the league with eleven long balls, was not an enthusiastic supporter of the inside game that was ubiquitous around the majors. In fact he hated it and wanted to slug. "Brilliant coaching makes me tired," he declared. "This idea … that coaches, teamwork, and the so-called inside ball … makes or unmakes a team, is foolishness."[6] However, despite his opposition and hostility towards the inside game he utilized small ball strategies throughout much of his career, particularly in his later years. In 1901, his third big league season, he stole 15 bases and 181 during his fourteen-year major league career. Remarkably, in 1908, when he managed to bat a paltry .243 for Cleveland in 548 at-bats, he was credited with 60 sacrifice hits, which is the second most in major league history as he did anything to help his team win. However, 1908 was the first of twenty-four major league seasons in which sacrifice flies were counted as sacrifice hits. Furthermore, the six-foot, 185-pounder is tied with Ed Konetchy for 38th all-time with 253 sacrifice hits. Fielder Jones ranks 37th with 254. Bradley, a .271 lifetime hitter with an unimpressive .317 on-base percentage, ran the bases aggressively and was a terrific fielder, leading the junior league's third baseman in fielding average during four seasons: 1901, 1904, 1905, and 1907. After batting .340, .313, and .300 from 1902 to 1904 his career began spiraling downhill in 1905 as a stomach ailment hindered his abilities and he batted just .268. For the next few seasons he battled various injuries as his productivity declined.

During the American League's second day as a major league circuit, on April 25, the game in Detroit at Bennett Park between the Tigers and the Milwaukee Brewers would not be easily forgotten by the spectators who witnessed the stunning developments upon the diamond. Hugh Duffy, the player-manager of the Milwaukee squad, was enjoying a 13–4 lead heading into the ninth inning. The last of the ninth took about thirty minutes to complete and when Pop Dillon hit his second double of the inning and fourth of the game to tie a major league record and drove in the go-ahead run to give Detroit a 14–13 win, a "great throng" ran onto the field and six men picked Dillon up, placed him upon their shoulders, and carried him around the field until Dillon persuaded the men to let him down.[7] In total, the Tigers collected nine doubles, including two by shortstop Kid Elberfeld, "The Tabasco Kid." This was a harbinger of things to come for Milwaukee as they finished the season in last place (48–89), while Detroit finished third (74–61). Manager George Stallings's Detroit squad compiled impressive small ball numbers in 1901, stealing 204 bases, which was third in the circuit and their 135 sacrifice hits was tied for first. In the lidlifter, third baseman Doc Casey swiped the first of his career high 34 bases in 1901 and Kid Gleason, their second baseman, stole one of his 32 bases on the season and 329 in his career.

The White Sox would also win on April 25 in Chicago by a 7–3 score despite a homer by Cleveland's Erve Beck that sailed over the right-field fence, served up by John Skopec. The White Sox were propelled to victory thanks to a terrific batting display and baserunning exhibition. They unleashed their small ball attack upon Cleveland, swiping five bags, three by Jones, and one apiece by Shugart and Isbell.

Standing upon the earth at the Polo Grounds on June 20 was a 5'11", 200-pound, right-handed player with a huge chest, powerful arms, and muscular shoulders. He was compact and awkward looking with bowed legs but ran extremely fast. His unique appearance belied his tremendous athletic ability. He was in his fifth major league campaign and had yet to settle in on a position, playing shortstop, the outfield, and third base during the 1901 season. In previous years he had played first and second base as well and had patrolled each of the three outfield stations. Teammate Tommy Leach insisted he was the greatest player in the league at all four infield positions and in the outfield as well. He was, of course, talking about his teammate Honus Wagner, a man who not only was amazingly talented in the field and at the bat, but also stole 723 bases to rank 10th all-time. Wagner also collected 221 sacrifice hits during his illustrious career, including a career high of 27 in 1909. And even before the 1908 rule change that counted sacrifice flies as sacrifice hits, he had his fair share of sacrifice hits, 81 in total during the eleven seasons from 1897 to 1907, including 14 in 1907. While many National League players succumbed to their desire to enrich themselves and eagerly jumped to the American League with its larger contracts, Wagner remained loyal to owner Barney Dreyfuss and rejected a $20,000 offer by Clark Griffith, the manager of Chicago's American League outfit.

Wagner led the National League in stolen bases in 1901 (49 steals), 1902 (42 steals), 1904 (53 steals), 1907 (61 steals), and 1908 (53 steals). During the Deadball Era stolen bases were more evenly distributed among many members of the team. In 1901 when Wagner led the NL with 49 steals, the average number of stolen bases in the National League for each team was 175.3. Wagner collected only 24.1 percent of Pittsburgh's 203 steals. In 1904 he led the NL with 53 steals and the average number of stolen bases for each National League team was 196.8. Compare this to 1982 when Rickey Henderson broke the modern-era stolen base record with 130 bags. The average number of steals that season for each American League team was 99.6. And Henderson stole 56 percent of the Athletics' 232 bags during a time period where the best basestealers would often steal 40 percent or more of their team's bases.

In 1901, Wagner batted .353 with a .417 on-base percentage. He led the league in RBIs with 126 and stolen bases with 49. Pittsburgh finished the season in first place (90–49). They ranked second in stolen bases (203) and fourth in sacrifice hits (117) among senior circuit teams. Wagner and his fellow fly chasers Ginger Beaumont (36), player-manager Fred Clarke (23), and Lefty Davis (22) collected 130 (64 percent) of the team's stolen bases.

Honus Wagner's notable achievement on June 20, 1901, was that he became the first of eleven major league players to steal home twice in a game. The New York Giants committed seven errors that day and had difficulty making contact against Jack Chesbro, who in his third big league season would compile a 21–10 record and a 2.38 ERA. New York collected three hits in total, while Pittsburgh had ten against Ed Doheny, who began the season with New York, compiling a 2–5 record and a 4.50 ERA, before being traded to Pittsburgh in June for Heinie Smith and going 6–2 with a 2.00 ERA for the Pirates. Pittsburgh pushed across five runs in the opening frame on one hit, a double, and cruised to a 7–0 victory. The Pirates had six steals in total, three by Wagner while Beaumont, Claude Ritchey and Bones Ely had one apiece. Amazingly, the nameless scribe who wrote a 105-word description of the game in the *New York Times* did not even bother to mention the fact that Wagner stole home twice and did not even mention a word about Pittsburgh's baserunning that day.[8] Yes, stolen bases were ubiquitous during this time period but even a neophyte would have recognized the significance of the moment.

Clarence Howeth Beaumont, who was better known as Ginger because of his red hair, was recognized as one of the game's best leadoff hitters during the early years of Deadball Era competition. In 1901 he batted .332, scored 120 runs, and stole a career high 36 bases which was the fifth best total in the National League. Beginning in 1905 he had problems with his knee, an injury that would persist through most of his final years, limiting his stolen base totals and having an adverse affect on his batting average because he relied on his foot speed to leg out a large number of infield hits and bunts. Beaumont's twelve-year major league career concluded after the 1910 season with a .311 batting average, 254 stolen bases, and 166 sacrifice hits. In 1900 (21) and 1904 (23) he finished third in the National League in sacrifice hits. He played his entire career in the senior circuit with Pittsburgh (1899–1906), Boston (1907–1909) and Chicago (1910). He contributed heavily to Pittsburgh's three consecutive National League pennant-winning ballclubs from 1901 to 1903. And when he hit a fly ball to center field on a delivery by Cy Young on October 1, 1903, at Boston's Huntington Avenue Grounds, he became the first batter in the first modern World Series. However, Boston prevailed five games to three as Beaumont batted .265 and had two of Pittsburgh's nine stolen bases in the series. He also led the Pirates with six runs scored.

Beaumont was fast, but he didn't look fast, and astonished the spectators who were seeing him play for the first time with his foot speed. He stood at 5'8", 190 pounds, batted left-handed but threw right-handed, and had what appeared to be a lazy, nonchalant disposition, literally dragging the bat to home plate and looking as if he just didn't care. But then Beaumont would step into the batter's box, put the ball in play, and take off like a rocket to first base, astonishing the neophytes and compelling one scribe to call him "one of the wonders of the century."[9] His foot speed was on full display before an August 4, 1901, game between Pittsburgh and Cincinnati. Before the contest players lined up at home plate and were timed as they ran to first base. Beaumont was the fastest, running the 90-foot sprint in three seconds flat.

Despite the decline in offensive productivity during the Deadball Era, the ball itself did not fundamentally change until 1911 when the new cork-centered ball replaced the ball whose core was filled with yarn. The American League scored 5,873 runs in 1901 and in 1903 when they also adopted the foul-strike rule the junior league teams collectively scored 4,543 runs. In 1911, the American League scored 5,658 runs, which was 1,081 more runs than the previous season. The National League increase was not as severe; a nearly ten percent augmentation in 1911 from the previous season's 5,007 to 5,506. However, it was the third season in a row that runs scored increased significantly; from 1908 to 1911 the senior league's runs scored totals were 4,136, 4,543, 5,007, and 5,506. The number of home runs hit in the NL increased from 214 in 1910 to 316 in 1911. The increased long ball hitting around the majors did not impact the running game as stolen bases increased in 1911 from the previous year, by 40 in the AL and 97 in the NL, but the number of sacrifice hits declined in both leagues. Offensive productivity actually decreased for the rest of the decade as did the running attack. In 1911 the NL teams averaged 211.4 stolen bases during the season and 177 sacrifice hits. In 1917 they averaged 143.1 stolen bases per team and 168.5 sacrifice hits. The number of stolen bases per team declined much more sharply in 1918, but they also played fewer games because of World War I and in 1919 both leagues played a 140-game schedule. In 1911 the American League stole an average of 213.9 bases per team and had 183.1 sacrifice hits. By 1917 the AL teams were averaging 158.5 stolen bases and they attained a major league record of 216.4 sacrifice hits per team. While stolen bases decreased during the Deadball Era's second decade, sacrifice hits increased or remained steady. But a direct comparison between sacrifice hits in the Deadball Era's first decade compared to the second decade is flawed because of the 1908 rule change.

The decline in offensive productivity during the Deadball Era had little to do with how the ball was constructed, but was largely influenced by how pitchers manipulated the ball. They threw the spitball, shine ball, emery ball, paraffin ball, licorice ball, mud ball, and a number of other pitches that involved doctoring the baseball, making part of the ball's surface, rough or smooth, which would alter the revolution and path of a delivery. It was not only the pitch itself that made it difficult for a batter to hit because of its erratic movement and dark color, but it was also employed as a psychological weapon. Pitchers would feign as if they were loading up the ball and then deliver another pitch from their repertoire. Ed Walsh provided his observations of Urban Shocker in the 1924 *Reach Guide*, insisting that Shocker was a great pitcher but not a great spitball pitcher. He added, "In nine innings today he threw exactly four spitballs. I was surprised. I expected a flock of them. But he came up with everything a good pitcher should have." There was great debate during the Deadball Era whether the spitball and other freak deliveries should be disallowed. F.C. Lane, the editor of *Baseball Magazine* and a strong advocate for power hitting, was against the wet pitch as was a commentary provided in *Spalding's Official Baseball Guide* of 1909. The *Reach Guide* vigorously debated the issue in 1909 and there was no consensus among the writers. W.A. Phelon of the *Chicago Journal* wrote, "While the spit ball is sloppy, dirty, and disgusting, it is, I fear, impossible to get rid of."[10] Although spitball pitchers and hurlers who mastered the other trick pitches may have had a considerable advantage against the hitter, they were easy targets for good basestealers who pilfered hassocks in large numbers, primarily because these pitches were difficult for the catcher to handle. By the 1920 season the spitball was outlawed along with other trick pitches such as the shine ball, mud ball, and emery ball as pitchers could no longer put a foreign substance on the ball, spit on it or deface it. However, the pitcher could still legally rub up the ball. Seventeen pitchers were allowed to throw the spitter until the end of their career, including future Hall of Famers Stan Coveleski, Urban (Red) Faber, and Burleigh Grimes.

Other factors leading to decreased offensive output during the Deadball Era included the pitchers' adjustment to the 60'6" pitching distance and improvements in fielding and fielding equipment. In 1901 there were 2,875 errors in the American League and by 1917 there were 1,871. The National League committed 2,456 errors in 1901, 2,590 in 1904, but by 1917 there were 1,875 miscues. Also consider that there were fewer games played in 1901

(140-game schedule) than in 1917 (154-game schedule). The configuration of the ballparks also affected run production. In the National League runs scored increased by 407 from 1908 to 1909. The Pirates opened Forbes Field on June 30, 1909, and although its dimensions of 360–462–376 were large, it was actually a significantly smaller distance down the lines and in the gaps than at their previous home at Exposition Park. Before the 1909 campaign the Giants significantly reduced their center field distance as well.

The foul-strike rule also contributed to the decreased offensive productivity. In 1901 the foul ball or foul-strike rule was implemented in the National League (1903 in the AL), which helped the pitcher and had the effect of decreasing batting averages and increasing strikeouts. The American League, for example, had a .275 batting average in 1902 with 2,744 strikeouts but in 1903 their collective batting average plummeted to .255 and their strikeouts soared to 4,199. After the rule there was a greater emphasis on manufacturing runs and "inside baseball."

Pittsburgh dominated National League competition in 1902, finishing 27 and a half games ahead of second-place Brooklyn with a 103–36 record. Wagner took the stolen base crown with 42, one ahead of Chicago's Jimmy Slagle, while Beaumont finished fourth with 33. Pittsburgh led the circuit in several offensive categories, including runs scored (775), hits (1,410), doubles (189), triples (95), batting average (.286), on-base percentage (.344), and slugging percentage (.374). For the second consecutive season the Cubs led the senior league in stolen bases, swiping 229 despite having only one player finish in the top five in that category. The only other National League team with over 200 steals was Pittsburgh with 222. The fifth-place Cubs (68–69) also led the circuit in sacrifice hits (156).

Other developments would prove meaningful in later years and help break Pittsburgh's dominant position in the senior circuit. The last-place Baltimore Orioles of the junior league were torn apart by John McGraw's feud with Ban Johnson. The quick-witted and volatile skipper, nicknamed "Little Napoleon," managed fifty-seven games for them (26–31) and then became the manager of the New York Giants (25–38) and would also manage New York's National League outfit for the next thirty seasons. McGraw was many things, including a leader and a strong advocate of the inside game. His wife Blanche said, "Life without baseball had little meaning for him … it was his meat, drink, dream, his blood and breath, his very reason for existence."[11] Another development occurred when Johnny Evers, a scrawny middle infielder, was called up to Chicago from Troy of the Class B New York State League. During his September call-up he batted .222 and stole the first of his 324 career bases. Evers was playing for Frank Selee's Chicago outfit for only a week before the big city papers lauded his fielding ability, writing he is "about the coolest man at handling a ball that has ever played on the Smoky City aggregation."[12] On September 15, 1902, the first Tinker to Evers to Chance double play was recorded. Shortstop Joe Tinker also played his first major league game in 1902, batting .263 in 501 at-bats and stealing 27 of his 336 career bases. Tinker is ranked 15th all-time in sacrifice hits (285) just behind Jimmy Sheckard's 286 and Evers is tied for 35th with 256. But neither Tinker nor Evers had more stolen bases than Frank Chance, who tied for the NL stolen base title with Jimmy Sheckard in 1903 with 67, and then won the crown outright in 1906 with 57. "The Peerless Leader" batted .296 lifetime with identical .394 on-base percentage and slugging percentages. He accumulated 403 stolen bases. He began his career with Chicago in 1898 but never played more than 76 games until 1903 when he played 125, the first of six seasons with at least 111 games played.

Alphonzo De Ford Davis, a promising 27-year-old fly chaser, who was better known as Lefty, suffered a gruesome injury at Exposition Park on July 11, 1902. He had debuted with Brooklyn in 1901, batting .209 with four steals before being traded to Pittsburgh in May and batting .313 with 22 steals in 87 games and 335 at-bats. He also compiled a gaudy .415 on-base percentage for Fred Clarke's club. In 1902 he was batting .280 with a .377 on-base percentage and had 19 stolen bases in 59 games when he broke his leg while trying to steal second base. It was reported that George Van Haltren, who had tied Patsy Donovan for the NL lead in steals in 1900 with 45 and would compile 583 bags during his distinguished career, suffered a similar fate two months prior to Davis at almost the same spot on the diamond. Davis, who appeared destined to be one of the circuit's best basestealers for years to come, was never the same after the injury. He played for the New York Highlanders in 1903, batting .237 with only 11 steals in 372 at-bats and then he didn't return to the big leagues until 1907 with Cincinnati, batting .229 with 9 steals during his final major league season. If it weren't for Davis's unfortunate predicament, the July 11 contest would have been a fine day for Pittsburgh as they won, 6–3, over New York. The only error of the game was committed by the Pirates second baseman, Claude Ritchey, and Deacon Phillippe outdueled Tully Sparks on the bump. Leadoff man Davis and Tommy Leach had one steal apiece, while Kitty Bransfield, who was in his second season as an everyday player, swiped two bags. The 5'11", 207-pound, right-handed first baseman stole 23 of his 175 career bases in 1902 and batted .305.

Pittsburgh won the next day as well, 4–0, as Jack Chesbro fanned eleven. Clarke had three hits and reached first each time he was up, Leach had a sacrifice, and Beaumont stole a base. Pittsburgh had five consecutive baserunners out on the basepaths because of poor judgment, a caught stealing, a pick off, or because they were trying to take an extra base. Again, the nameless scribe in the *New York Times* failed to mention a word about Pittsburgh's baserunning.[13] New York's leadoff man Steve Brodie also stole a bag, which was one of 11 on the season and 289 in his career. Brodie batted .281 in 1902 during his twelfth and final big league campaign. Wagner also stole a base, but it wasn't the J. Wagner who was listed in the box score and played right field for Pittsburgh. The J stood for John, but he was better known as Honus. The stolen base was credited to C. Wagner; Charles Wagner is better known as Heinie and in 1902 he played the first seventeen games of his big league career, batting .214 with three steals for the Giants. He would play twelve big league seasons, but after 1902 he wouldn't make an appearance in a major league game until 1906 with the Boston Americans.

Pittsburgh's potent offensive attack was on full display before nearly fifteen thousand Polo Grounds spectators on August 2. Player-manager Fred Clarke opened the proceedings with a single past New York's player-manager John McGraw, who was playing shortstop. Beaumont sacrificed Clarke to second and he scored on Leach's single. Leach advanced to third on left-fielder Jim Jones's wild throw and then scored on Wagner's "little hit." The second run was tallied despite the fact that Billy Lauder, the Giant's third baseman, unleashed an accurate throw to catcher Frank Bowerman, who muffed it and allowed Leach to cross the plate safely. When the ball got away, Wagner moved up to second and scored on Bransfield's hit to center. Ritchey then hit a double and manager McGraw had seen enough. The battery of Dummy Taylor and Bowerman was replaced with Jack Cronin and Roger Bresnahan. Pittsburgh won the game easily, 7–2, and right from the opening frame "their undoing was imminent and their defeat a certainty," according to a scribe in the *New York Times*, who insisted that New York was "overmatched."[14] Beaumont and Doheny had sacrifice hits while Clarke and Jones, the Giants leadoff man, stole one base apiece.

Cincinnati defeated Brooklyn, 2–1, on the day and scored their two markers in the first inning. Player-manager Joe Kelley of the Reds legged out a bunt down the third base line to open the game at Washington Park and then advanced to third on Jake Beckley's single. Sam Crawford bunted towards first and was safe as Tom McCreery failed to touch him. Kelley tallied the first run on the successful bunt. Then Cy Seymour sacrificed, and Heinie Peitz walked to load the bases. Beckley scored on a fly ball to center by Tommy Corcoran. Brooklyn scored their run in the seventh as a sacrifice by Tim Flood proved critical in the sequence that scored the run. The game was played in a fashion that was described as "fast and at times brilliant."[15] There was outstanding defense and good pitching. Brooklyn's backstop Duke Farrell was charged with the only error of the ballgame.

Under the leadership of John McGraw, New York's aggressive baserunning was on full display on August 1 when three runners were punched out at home in two innings during the opening game of a doubleheader versus St. Louis. Six runners were called out trying to steal or take an extra base. And Roger Bresnahan, who had come to New York from Baltimore with McGraw, scored from second base on a bunt. On October 2, the Giants stole one base and were caught stealing eight times. Additionally, they had three runners picked off and two thrown out at the plate. New York's small ball statistics would sky rocket in 1903 during McGraw's first full season with the team. From 1901 to 1905 the Giants stole 133, 187, 264, 283, and 291 bases. And from 1901 to 1903 their sacrifice hit totals were 73, 108, and then a whopping 185. During McGraw's thirty-one seasons managing the Giants from 1902 to 1932, which included a few years where he only managed for part of the season, the Giants led the league in stolen bases eleven times: 1904, 1905, 1906, 1911, 1912, 1913, 1914, 1916, 1917, 1921, and 1926. However, his Giants club only led the league in sacrifice hits during two seasons in 1903 and 1904.

The Philadelphia Athletics pulled away from St. Louis and Boston in September to win the American League flag in 1902 by five games with an 83–53 record. Chicago again led the league in stolen bases, swiping 265, while Philadelphia finished second with 201. The White Sox also led the circuit with 154 sacrifice hits. Topsy Hartsel of the Athletics led the league in stolen bases with 47. Sam Mertes of Chicago finished second with 46 and Dave Fultz of Connie Mack's Philadelphia outfit stole 44. During his final five seasons of his seven-year big league career with the Athletics and Highlanders from 1901 to 1905, Fultz stole 170 bases. In 1902 he led the majors in sacrifice hits with 35, which was six more than the National League leader, Fred Tenney, and eleven more than Doc Nance's junior league leading 24 sacrifices in 1901. Furthermore, he batted .302 and was tied with Hartsel for the American League lead in runs scored with 109. At 5'5" and 155 pounds, Hartsel was recognized as one of the finest leadoff men in the majors, while batting out of the left side of the batter's box. He batted .276 lifetime with a .384 on-base percentage and 247 steals. The diminutive fly chaser led the junior circuit in walks during five seasons and on-base percentage during two seasons.

Baseball's most famous stolen base in 1902 was accomplished not by a Punch-and-Judy hitter, but by one of the game's most powerful sluggers, who possessed great intelligence and tremendous insight about the game of baseball. Harry Davis, a right-handed slugger who guarded the gateway station for the Philadelphia Athletics, batted .307 in 1902 and stole 28 of his 285 career bases. He would lead the American League in homers for four consecutive seasons from 1904 to 1907. But on August 13, 1902, he was hugging first base while Dave Fultz was anchored at third. He conspired with Fultz to find a new residence and a double steal was attempted. Davis was caught in a rundown but advanced to second when Fultz dove back into third on a throw. Harry then ran back to first base, unsatisfied with the outcome because Fultz did not score. George Mullin, the Detroit Tigers' rookie pitcher, was on the bump and did not even deliver a pitch before Davis took off again for second. Mullin took the bait, threw to second but it was not in time and Fultz took off for home on the throw, scampering safely across home plate. Both Davis and Fultz were credited with a stolen base. Germany Schaefer became famous for stealing first base in 1911 with Washington and he may have pulled off this maneuver more than once. Fred Tenney stole first base as a member of the 1908 New York Giants on July 31.

The number of runs scored increased by a significant margin in the National League in 1903, from the previous year's 4,494 to 5,349. The increase in stolen bases was also noticeable; there were 200 more stolen bases in the senior circuit in 1903. Brooklyn (273), Chicago (259), and New York (264) were the only major league teams to steal over 200 bags in 1903. Stolen bases decreased in the AL by 142, while sacrifice hits increased by 158 over the 1902 total. Their 1,173 stolen bases were 396 less than the NL, which represented the widest differential between the two leagues during the Deadball Era. The Giants had the most sacrifice hits in the majors with 185 and their first baseman, Dan McGann, led the circuit with 30. Pittsburgh won the pennant with a 91–49 record, but their competition was gaining ground; New York finished 6.5 games off the pace with an 84–55 mark and Chicago was 8 games behind at 82–56. The collective small ball statistics skyrocketed in McGraw's first full year as the Giants manager. The team stolen base total increased by 77 over the previous season's total when he managed the club on a part-time basis and increased by 131 over 1901. Likewise, their sacrifice hit total increased by 77 when compared to 1902 and by 112 over the 1901 Giants outfit. Most importantly, McGraw increased the team's win total by 36 as the 1902 Giants finished in last place with a 48–88 mark. The stolen base crown was shared by Sheckard and Chance (67), while Wagner and Brooklyn's Sammy Strang finished tied for second with 46. Sam Mertes who had previously done his running on American League fields, played for a senior league outfit for the first time since 1900, putting on the uniform of the New York Giants in 1903 and swiping 45 bags which was only 17 percent of the club's stolen base total. In a ten-year career Mertes averaged 39.6 steals per season and 13.9 sacrifice hits during each campaign. He enjoyed his best season in 1903, batting .280 while scoring 100 runs, tying for the league lead in doubles (32), and leading the senior circuit with 104 RBIs.

Boston won the flag comfortably in the American League, by 14 and a half games over Philadelphia with a 91–47 record. Player-manager Jimmy Collins then led the Boston Americans to a victory in the first modern World Series over Pittsburgh, despite stealing four fewer bases than their opponent. After batting .296 with 23 steals during the regular season, the skipper stole three bags in the fall classic, while center-fielder Chick Stahl pilfered the other two cushions for Boston. When Collins began his big league career in 1895, it was customary for third baseman to play back, even when there was a skilled bunter at the dish. But Collins eschewed this flawed strategy and played in on the grass, using his blazing speed and lightning quick reflexes to scoop up bunts and then unleash an accurate sidearm or underhand throw. He played eleven games for the 1895 Boston Beaneaters and then finished the season by batting .279 with 12 steals for the Louisville Colonels, a team that would finish the campaign in last place with a 35–96 record, 52 and a half games behind the first-place Orioles. Baltimore was a skilled small ball aggregation with excellent bunters, and they forced the Louisville third baseman to make four miscues in one contest with their bunts. John McClosky, the Louisville skipper, had seen enough. McClosky has been credited by Hugh Fullerton as being the only manager who would signal his baserunners to slide feet first or headfirst as they were stealing second. Surely, this must have been a verbal signal. This innovative manager brought his 25-year-old rookie right fielder in to play third base against the feared Baltimore attack, replacing the despondent hot corner occupant who had just made four errors. The Orioles tried to bunt four consecutive times with the busher at third, including bunts by John McGraw and Willie Keeler. But four times they were out. A star had been born and his exploits became known around the country. The Boston bugs and newspapermen wanted him to return to the Beaneaters and he returned to Boston in 1896 and remained in the National League through the 1900 season, before joining Boston's American League aggregation in 1901. He completed his Hall of Fame career with a .294 lifetime batting average, 147 sacrifices, and 194 stolen bases.

In the 1903 World Series, Boston laid down six sacrifice bunts, while Pittsburgh had only three. Candy LaChance, the Boston first baseman, who was tied for ninth in the junior league with 22 sacrifices in 1903, laid down three in the series. During Boston's two-run sixth inning outburst in game seven, LaChance and Hobe Ferris had back-to-back sacrifices. LaChance reached first on an error by pitcher Deacon Phillippe during his sacrifice attempt. And then in the bottom of the sixth, the Pirates cleanup hitter, Honus Wagner, collected a sacrifice bunt. Wagner executed a squeeze play that sent Fred Clarke scampering safely across the plate, but the terrific moundsman, Cy Young, unleashed a throw to first that smacked into the glove of LaChance just before Wagner stepped on the first cushion.

The seventh-place White Sox (60–77) led the circuit in steals (180), while the fifth-place Tigers (65–71) had the most sacrifice hits (170). Detroit's Billy Lush led the major leagues in sacrifice hits with 34. Harry Bay won the stolen base crown with 45 bags for the third-place Cleveland Naps or Blues (77–63), who finished second in the league in stolen bases with 175. Bay was a 5'8", 138-pound, left-handed hitting and throwing center fielder. Many baseball experts believed he was the fastest man in the American League and the slightly built Bay delighted spectators with his great baserunning and outstanding catches. He played the game with reckless abandon, unconcerned about his own health, tossing his body around the field, and sliding headfirst into first base on bang-bang plays. At the plate he had a chop swing, hitting the ball on the ground, and utilizing his great speed. The pounding his legs took began to adversely affect his performance in 1904, but he still shared the AL stolen base crown with his teammate Elmer Flick as they both stole 38. Additional injuries impaired him in 1905, including an injury to his right knee when he was trying to catch fly balls in an aggressive manner on a muddy field. Bay played two games for Cleveland in 1908 and then his eight-year big league career was over with a .273 batting average and 169 steals. He had 107 sacrifice hits, finishing fourth in the AL in 1903 (25) and fifth in 1905 (30).

The New York Highlanders, who were destined to finish in fourth place (72–62) under their first-year skipper Clark Griffith, won 7–2, in their second game of the season against Washington at American League Park on April 23. The spectators were "blue" because of the weather that was reminiscent of winter and the fact that Washington committed five errors in defeat.[16] Washington, led by manager Tom Loftus, finished the season in last place (43–94) and had a major league low 81 sacrifice hits. Herman Long, New York's shortstop, who would steal fourteen bags in 1903 with the Highlanders and Tigers, made three errors. And this man who would steal 537 pillows during his career had to be replaced by Ernie Courtney because of his poor fielding. New York whose 129 sacrifice hits ranked fifth in the circuit had two in this game: John Ganzel and Jack O'Connor. Detroit defeated Cleveland on the day, 11–1, while the Athletics and White Sox also won in American League competition. In National League competition on April 22, New York defeated Brooklyn, 7–2, at Washington Park as the Giants stole four bases, including one by pitcher Joe McGinnity while Bill Dahlen had one for Brooklyn. Later in the month, on the 29th, the Washington Senators stole eight bags in a 9–5 win over Boston. On May 7, Dan McGann stole four of his 36 bases on the season in an 8–4 win over the Phillies. On July 9, the Chicago Cubs scored all six runs in the seventh inning on five one-base hits, an error, two steals, and a sacrifice to defeat Philadelphia, 6–1.

"Iron Man" Joe McGinnity toed the slab for the Giants on August 8. One week before this contest he had pitched both ends of a doubleheader against Boston and emerged victorious each time. On the 8th he did the same thing against Brooklyn, winning 6–1 and 4–3, in the second of three doubleheaders he would win that month. He singled off Henry Schmidt in the third inning of the second game, was sacrificed to second, and then he emerged safely at third on a bang-bang play. The Brooklyn players argued with the umpire, but they failed to call time, and McGinnity stole home to the disgust of Schmidt who threw the ball out of the ballpark. On August 15, Schmidt himself would steal home against St. Louis in the second game of a doubleheader. According to *The SABR Baseball List and Record Book*, there have been 46 steals of home by pitchers since 1900. The first pitcher was Win Mercer of Washington who stole home against Philadelphia on August 10, 1901. A huge 67.4 percent of these pitchers stole home during the Deadball Era from 1901 to 1919, 31 in total.

By 1904 John McGraw's Giants were a well-oiled small ball machine, stealing a major league leading 283 bags (12th best since 1900) and leading the National League with 166 sacrifice hits. The senior league implemented the 154-game schedule in 1904 and the Giants finished with a 106–47 mark, thirteen games ahead of second-place Chicago (93–60). Not surprisingly, Frank Selee's Chicago outfit was the second best small ball team in the circuit, finishing second in steals (227) and second in sacrifice hits (141). New York had three players finish in the top five in steals; Honus Wagner of Pittsburgh led the league with 53, followed by Sam Mertes and the newly acquired Bill Dahlen who both stole 47 for New York. Then Dan McGann and Chicago's Frank Chance were tied with 42. Kid Gleason of Philadelphia led the senior league in sacrifice hits (35) for the first of two consecutive seasons. The Giants were vilified by fans, writers, and players in opposing cities. The Pittsburgh newspapers, for example, began to call McGraw's Giants "rowdy" and "stuck-up."[17] McGraw himself was "loud-mouthed," and "the expressions he uses to occupants of the grandstand are not all within the bounds of propriety." It was "a shame" that the spectators had to hear such language. While the accusations against McGraw were largely true, they even made up stories about Christy Mathewson, New York's dignified college-educated pitcher, and accused him of using bad language.[18]

Boston won the junior circuit flag for the second consecutive season with a 95–59 record, finishing one and a half games ahead of second-place New York (92–59). Third-place Chicago (89–65) collected the most stolen bases (216) and sacrifice hits (197) in the league. George Davis, a 33-year-old shortstop who would swipe 619 career bases but never won a stolen base title, led the team in steals with 32 which was only 14.8 percent of the team's larcenous activity. Davis finished fourth in the circuit while teammates Elmer Flick and Harry Bay of Cleveland were tied for first with 38. Fielder Jones led the circuit in sacrifice hits with 36.

Elmer Flick stood at 5'9", 168 pounds, batted left-handed but threw right-handed, resided in the outer garden, and swung a thick-handled bat that helped him accumulate

268 doubles, 164 triples, and 48 homers during his thirteen-year career. He batted .313 lifetime with a .389 on-base percentage and a .445 slugging percentage. Flick, an extra-base machine, also stole 330 bags including thirty or more during seven seasons. It was not unusual during the Deadball Era for power hitters to run a lot. Cleveland thought so highly of Flick that they refused an offer from the Detroit Tigers to trade him for Ty Cobb in 1907. It was an offer they most likely regretted and not only because Cobb captured the first of nine consecutive batting titles in 1907. Flick batted .302 in 1907 and his 18 triples led the league for the third consecutive season. Additionally, he stole a career high 41 bases, which was tied for second in the league with Wid Conroy. But he developed a gastrointestinal ailment and played in only 99 more games during the next three seasons. He characterized his final three seasons as being "awful," regretted playing, and said, "there was a time in 1908 I was positive I wouldn't live another week."[19] But he did live until January 9, 1971, and in 1963 was voted into the Hall of Fame by the Veterans Committee.

On April 22 the New York Giants clobbered Philadelphia, 18–3, at the Polo Grounds. The game was knotted at three until the last of the fourth when Art Devlin hit a grand slam on a "tremendous" drive to center field. New York scored fifteen runs in their final five frames at the bat. Philadelphia, who would finish the campaign in last place (52–100) and were not proficient at the inside game, which included stealing bases (159, ranked 7th in NL) and garnering sacrifice hits (119, ranked 7th in NL), committed eight errors in this contest. New York stole eight bases, including two by Art Devlin and three by Bill Dahlen. But the Giants' terrific small ball stats on the day, including two sacrifice hits, were largely ignored by the scribe who wrote a long article in the *New York Times*. As in years past they appeared to salivate over every long drive and even mentioned that Dahlen hit a long foul ball to left field.[20]

In Boston, the Brooklyn Superbas won their game, 6–2. In the sixth inning consecutive successful bunt hits by John Dobbs and Charlie Babb loaded the bases but Jack Doyle hit into a double play, scoring one run. However, Brooklyn scored their second run in the inning when Mike McCormick, who was born in Scotland and batted .184 with 22 steals in his only major league season, collected a hit that scored Dobbs. At Washington's American League Park there were only two attempted steals with the New York Highlanders Dave Fultz the one who was successful. Fultz stole only 17 bags on the season, but then in his final big league campaign in 1905, he finished second in the junior league with 44 thefts. New York won the April 22 contest, 2–0, behind the fine pitching of Jack Chesbro. In Cleveland the Naps won, 10–2, before an overflowing crowd of 17,000 in their home opener as the spectators surrounded the diamond, forcing the umpires to implement a ground rule mandating that any ball hit into the crowd was a triple. Ground rules were also in place for Detroit's home opener as they fought to a 12 inning, 4–4, stalemate against St. Louis before the game was called on account of darkness. It was awkwardly reported that "The fielding was clever considering the cold weather." In Philadelphia, the Boston Americans won, 3–1, and the Athletics pitcher Weldon Henley's "three-base wild throw" proved critical.[21] At 6–1, Boston who was an average small ball team at best in 1904 (101 steals, last in the AL; 155 sacrifice hits, third in the AL), were off to a fast start.

Joe McGinnity stole home once again on April 29 versus Boston. And the Chicago White Sox pitcher Frank Owen stole home on August 2 against Washington. Owen, who would win twenty-one games in both 1904 and 1905 and then win twenty-two in 1906, also stole home against Washington on June 13, 1905. Interestingly, Bill Donovan of Detroit was the next pitcher to steal home, achieving the laudable feat against Cleveland on September

14, 1905. And then Donovan would steal second, third, and home against Cleveland in the fifth inning in the May 7, 1906, contest. Owen's third and final steal of home on April 27, 1908, was the tenth time a pitcher accomplished that feat in the twentieth century.

Dan McGann, a six-foot, 190-pound, switch hitting first baseman, who was quick tempered and eagerly threw punches when provoked, was John McGraw's type of player, keeping alive the rowdy spirit that was at the core of the old Baltimore Orioles. He would lead the National League in hit by pitches six times, and in 1904 stole a career high 42 bases. In 1903 he had stolen four bases in a game and then on May 27, 1904, he stole five bases in a single contest. This was a feat that would not be matched in National League competition until August 24, 1974, when Davey Lopes pulled it off. Lopes tried for a sixth steal but was thrown out.

The Giants were clearly the best team in baseball in 1904, winning eighteen in a row from June 16 to July 4. They won 53 of their first 71 games and coasted to the flag. They would get them on, get them over, and get them in, anyway they could and did not have one everyday player hit over .300. Despite the fact that McGann had the best batting average at .286 among the regulars, they still led the circuit in team batting average at .262. Early in the season they had plenty of competition, and on May 22 the Giants were in third place behind first-place Cincinnati and second-place Chicago. The crowd that assembled at Chicago's West Side Grounds on May 22 was the largest since 1899 as the Cubs and Giants battled each other. The Cubs scored their three runs in the fourth and behind Mordecai Brown, won 3–1. Johnny Evers's stolen base proved critical in scoring the final Cubs run. He singled, pilfered the second sack, moved to third on an out, and scored on an error by Dahlen at short. New York scored their lone marker in the fourth frame thanks to McGann's theft. He singled, stole second, and scored all the way from the keystone sack on catcher Johnny Kling's errant throw.

As for the 1904 World Series, well there wasn't one as McGraw and AL president Ban Johnson had come to loggerheads long ago and their irreconcilable differences prevented a series from happening. McGraw asked why he should play the Boston Americans because after all they played in a "minor league." He added, "The Giants would totally outclass them."[22]

The Giants took the National League flag again in 1905 (105–48), leading the major leagues in steals (291) and finishing fifth in sacrifice hits (138) in the senior circuit. Third-place Chicago (92–61) finished second in steals (267) and led the league in sacrifice hits (193). The Cubs won 17 of their final 20 games, serving as a harbinger of what would come in 1906. Billy Maloney, their right fielder, was tied with New York's third baseman Art Devlin with the most steals in the league with 59. Honus Wagner finished third with 57 during the only season between 1900 and 1912 in which he failed to lead the league in a major offensive category. The second-place Pirates finished nine games off the pace at 96–57 and were ranked third in the league in steals (202) and fourth in sacrifices (159).

Philadelphia was the most improved team in the league, concluding the campaign in fourth place (83–69) and winning 31 more games than the previous season. Hugh Duffy, their 38-year-old skipper, recognized that his playing career was almost complete, but inserted himself into fifteen games, batting .300. The Phillies finished with a .546 winning percentage despite failing to lead the league in one major offensive or defensive category. They stole 180 bags (6th, NL) and Kid Gleason's major league leading 43 sacrifices was 24.7 percent of the team's 174 total (tied 2nd, NL). Sherry Magee, the 21-year-old second-year outfielder manned the left field station in an excellent outfield that also included John Titus and Roy Thomas, and finished fifth in the senior league in steals (48). He began his big league career in 1904 at age nineteen, batting .277 in 364 at-bats and then rose to .299 in 603 at-bats in 1905. The powerful 5'11", 179-pound, right-handed hitter possessed a quick temper, a hunger to win, a pugilistic personality and was suspended many times during his career for arguing with umpires. Magee was a five-tool player who could run, field, throw, hit for average and power. He batted .291 lifetime with a .427 slugging percentage in a sixteen-year big league career with the Phillies, Braves, and Reds, finishing with over one thousand runs scored (1,112) and RBIs (1,176). He stole an impressive 441 bases during his excellent career and from 1905 to 1910 swiped 276 bags with totals of 48, 55, 46, 40, 38, and 49. In addition to his great offensive prowess, he also exhibited terrific glove work in the outer garden. He made crowd pleasing catches and had an accurate throwing arm.

Perhaps the most electrifying steal of 1905 occurred on September 12 when Harry Arndt's game-ending steal of home in the last of the ninth sent the Cardinals fans home gleeful because their club had just defeated Pittsburgh, 2–1. This was the first game-ending steal of home in the twentieth century. Arndt stole thirteen bags in 1905 and twenty-seven during his four-year big league career.

The Philadelphia Athletics won the American League flag in 1905 with a 92–56 mark, edging out Chicago by two games, and then lost the World Series to McGraw's Giants, four games to one. The New Yorkers swiped ten bases in the series, while Topsy Hartsel stole the only two bags for the White Elephants. Danny Hoffman, Philadelphia's center fielder, led the league in steals with 46 while their left fielder, Hartsel, finished fourth with 37. Connie Mack led a solid small ball attack, finishing third in the circuit in both steals (190) and sacrifice hits (165). The New York Highlanders, a sixth-place team (71–78), led the circuit in steals (200) while second-place Chicago (92–60) had 61 more sacrifice hits than any other league participant, collecting 241 in total.

Willie Keeler, the New York Highlanders 33-year-old right fielder, led the junior circuit with a career high 42 sacrifice bunts. Beginning in 1894, and not counting his first two seasons, Keeler compiled 366 sacrifice hits which ranks fourth all-time and he also stole 495 bags. He finished fifth or better in sacrifices in his league during nine seasons. The diminutive, five-foot-four-and-a-half-inch, 140-pound, left-handed slap hitter, was right at home in the Deadball Era when teams fought for every run and were aggressive on the basepaths, which included executing an abundance of delayed steals, straight steals, double steals, triple steals, and steals of home. Managers would try to outguess each other and would incessantly provide signals from the coach's box or the bench to inform their players that a specific play had been called, such as a pitch out or stolen base. They would sometimes signal the pitcher commanding him to throw a specific pitch and signal the batter to swing away or take a pitch. Bunting was also an integral part of the game: bunting for hits, the squeeze, and the sacrifice. Additionally, the hit-and-run and bunt-and-run were part of a manager's offensive arsenal.

Keeler, who used perhaps the lightest bat in major league history, choked up on it almost half way, and had perfected the hit-and-run with the 1890s Baltimore Orioles, astonishing opponents with his consistency in hitting the ball through the vacated hole at shortstop or second when the fielder went to cover the bag to take the throw from the catcher. Keeler rarely ever struck out and had great bat control. He was an amazingly gifted bunter and successfully did so even when the infield played in. If the corner infielders came in too far he would simply push the ball past the first or third baseman for a hit. If they played back he would bunt in a more traditional style. Keeler was fast and could leg out bunts or infield grounders. Honus Wagner said, "Keeler could bunt any time he chose," regardless of the positioning of the infielders.[23] His ability to hit the ball wherever he wanted, including fouling off pitches to wear out the pitcher, was partially why the foul-strike rule was implemented in the National League according to the *Chicago Daily Tribune*. From 1899 to 1902 he had played for Brooklyn's senior league outfit. His small stature earned him the nickname "Wee Willie" and he was well-liked, sociable, and always appeared to have a smile on his face. This was in stark contrast to many of his teammates with the old Baltimore Orioles. Jimmy Austin experienced his first big league campaign in 1909 with the New York Highlanders, while Keeler was playing his second to last season. He called Keeler a "wonderful fellow," and added, "He could loop'em over the infield better than anybody I ever saw."[24] It was a revealing statement considering that veterans often treated young ballplayers like dirt. The veteran informed the youngster that he would help him anyway he could. Keeler's small size caused confusion during one game when the umpire told his manager to get the batboy off the field. The manager retorted, "Heck no! He's no batboy! He's our best hitter."[25]

John McGraw had insisted that to win a pennant once did not make a team "outstanding." If a team won two in a row they were "good," but not until they won three in a row did they achieve true "greatness."[26] Little Napoleon was supremely confident in 1906 and made his team wear a menacing black uniform with the words "WORLD'S CHAMPIONS" inscribed across their chest, which surely made them a greater target in the senior league. They dressed in their hotel and went to the ballpark in carriages that were pulled by horses. The horses were decorated with yellow blankets that also had the words "world's champions" written across them.[27] McGraw did another fine job managing in 1906, but his team battled myriad injuries. Christy Mathewson left the team for a short time with diphtheria; Mike Donlin broke his leg sliding into the third sack in a game against the Reds; and Roger Bresnahan felt the effects of a serious beaning for a significant portion of the season as his productivity declined. The Giants were still what Noel Hynd called a "band of thieves," stealing 288 bases, which is tied for the ninth best in the modern era.[28] From 1903 to 1906, with McGraw steering the ship, the Giants stole an exorbitant 1,126 bases and led the major leagues during three seasons and finished second once. Despite finishing with an impressive 96–56 record, the Giants finished twenty games off the pace in McGraw's fourth full season as the Giants skipper.

The best small ball team in the National League, as well as the major leagues, resided on Chicago's West Side, and was led by player-manager Frank Chance who had replaced Frank Selee as the skipper during the previous season's campaign when he was diagnosed with tuberculosis. The Cubs compiled a major league best 116–36 record (.763 winning percentage), finishing 66 and a half games ahead of last-place Boston. They were ranked second in the major leagues in steals (283) and first in sacrifices (231). For the second time in his career, Chance was the king of thieves, winning the stolen base crown in the NL with 57. Sherry Magee finished second and stole 55 of fourth-place Philadelphia's 180 steals. Devlin (54), Wagner (53), and Evers (49) also stole a sizeable number of bases in senior league competition. On April 28, Chance had a game-ending steal of home against the Reds with 32-year-old southpaw hurler Jake Weimer on the mound, as Chicago won, 1–0. For the only time in major league history two managers stole home on the same day as Fred Clarke also accomplished this feat in Pittsburgh's 10–0 win over St. Louis.

Jimmy Sheckard joined the Cubs in 1906, batting .262 with 30 steals and leading the league in sacrifice hits (40). The acquisition of Sheckard and Harry Steinfeldt helped propel Chicago to a pennant in 1906. Sheckard was fundamentally sound and could bunt, hit-and-run, steal, and play excellent defense in the outfield. This was in addition to his solid extra-base hit power. Tom Jones of the St. Louis Browns won the American League sacrifice hit title with 40 as well. In an eight-year big league career spent entirely in the AL with Baltimore, St. Louis, and Detroit, Jones batted .251, stole 149 bags, and had an impressive 205 sacrifice hits. Jones was a 6'1", 195-pound, right-handed hitter who played first base.

Not surprisingly, the two worst small ball teams in the majors finished in last place in 1906 and coincidentally they both resided in the same city, Boston. Boston's National League outfit (49–102) had a major league low 93 steals and 119 sacrifice bunts. Meanwhile, the Boston Americans (49–105) ranked last in the junior circuit in both stolen bases (99) and sacrifice hits (138).

The best small ball team in the American League was the "Hitless Wonders," Chicago's South Side ballclub who finished third in the league in steals (216) and first in sacrifice hits (226). The White Sox were the junior league's best small ball team during the circuit's first six seasons at the major league level. From 1901 to 1906 they led the league in stolen bases four times and sacrifice hits during five campaigns. Charles Comiskey, their owner, believed in having a supremely fit team, excellent pitching, and the ability to score runs every way possible, including the utilization of small ball strategies. In 1906, the White Sox led by player-manager Fielder Jones finished last in the AL in batting average (.230) and home runs (7), but ranked third in runs scored (570). Frank Isbell led the Sox in steals with 37, which was only 17.1 percent of the team's stolen bases. Elmer Flick shared the stolen base crown with Washington's John Anderson who stole 39 of his career 338 bases. Isbell and Washington's rookie shortstop Dave Altizer finished second with 37 thefts while Chicago first baseman Jiggs Donahue finished fifth (36). The seventh-place Senators led the AL with 233 steals. In addition to Chicago and Washington, the American League had three other teams steal over 200 bags: St. Louis (221), Detroit (206), and Cleveland (203).

In 1903 Anderson attempted to steal second while a runner was anchored there and to pull off such a play became known as "pulling a John Anderson." However, evidence suggests that he may have simply been picked off first. The bases were loaded at the time as Anderson wandered off the bag with a large lead and then broke for second on a 3-and-2 pitch. When the batter struck out the catcher threw to first to double up Anderson.[29]

Heading into the World Series between Chicago's two big league clubs, who combined to steal 499 bases during the regular season, it would be reasonable to expect plenty of running and other small ball activities, including the hit-and-run and the sacrifice bunt during the game's autumn classic. The White Sox were not given much of a chance by the so-called experts and the gambling fraternity had the Cubs a three-to-one favorite heading into the series. The opening game at the Cubs' West Side Grounds was played in teeth-chattering weather, it was below freezing and a light snow fell intermittently throughout the contest. The White Sox prevailed, 2–1, thanks to Isbell's RBI single in the sixth. The Cubs clobbered the Sox in the second game, 7–1, and their successful execution of the inside game was partly why victory was achieved. They were able to send Doc White to the showers after only three frames, jumping ahead 4–0 as they executed a squeeze bunt by pitcher Ed Reulbach, a hit-and-run, a stolen base, aggressive baserunning, and when the infielders came in too far one batter bunted hard and the ball skipped past them. These were the elements that allowed the Cubs to win 116 games, a total that was not matched until the 2001 Seattle Mariners did it by playing ten more games than the 1906 Cubs. Chicago laid down three sacrifices and pilfered six cushions in game two, including two apiece by Chance and

Tinker. Tinker and Evers teamed up for a double steal in the sixth inning and Tinker scored after pilfering the third sack on the wild throw by catcher Billy Sullivan. To say that Sullivan had a tough series was an understatement, he went 0-for-21 at the plate and allowed nine stolen bases.

Ed Walsh, who threw a hard fastball, a sweeping curve, and the spitter, tossed a shutout for the Sox in game three as they scored all three runs in the sixth thanks to George Rohe's three-run triple. Game four, played at the Sox's South Side Grounds, was won by the Cubs, 1–0, behind Mordecai Brown's two-hitter. In the top of the seventh, Chance, the Cubs' cleanup hitter, dropped a single into right field. Harry Steinfeldt, the Cubs' exceptional third baseman who was playing his first year with Chicago after eight campaigns with Cincinnati, laid down a sacrifice bunt. During the regular season, Steinfeldt batted .327 with a career high 29 stolen bases. After Chance was sacrificed to second, Tinker amazingly sacrificed him to third. There could be arguments about the utility of the sacrifice bunt when sacrificing a runner to second with no outs. The positive arguments include staying out of a potential double play and advancing a runner into scoring position, while the main negative assessment bemoans that an out was literally sacrificed in obtaining this objective. And certainly sacrificing a runner to third with no outs could be beneficial because after the successful execution of such a play, the runner could score from third on a fly ball to the outfield or perhaps a dribbler in the infield. The runner could also score on an error, passed ball, or wild pitch. But two consecutive sacrifices are surely not beneficial to the offense as two outs are literally sacrificed for this questionable goal. Therefore, perhaps, it is safe to assume that Tinker was bunting for a hit and the sacrifice was an incidental development. Nonetheless, Evers followed with a single to left field, scoring Chance with the game's only run. Chicago had five sacrifices in the contest, three by Tinker and two by Steinfeldt.

Game five was played on the Cubs' home turf and despite committing six errors, the Sox prevailed, 8–6, as Isbell hit four doubles to pace a twelve-hit attack. With the hard-throwing southpaw Doc White on the hill, an eighteen-game winner in 1906 who battled through a tired arm and an illness down the stretch, the Sox wrapped up the series in game six with an 8–3 triumph. The White Sox stole six bases in the series, while the Cubs stole nine, including three by Tinker and two apiece by Evers and Chance. Chicago's National League outfit had twelve sacrifices, while the Pale Hose had six. Frank Chance said that the White Sox deserved credit for the win: "The Sox played grand, game baseball, and outclassed us in this series…. But there is one thing I never will believe, and that is that the White Sox are a better ball club than the Cubs. We did not play our game and that's all there is to it."[30]

On May 18, 1907, the Giants won their seventeenth in a row and despite having a 24–3 record the Cubs were only one game back. McGraw's club would soon begin a precipitous decline, finishing the campaign in fourth place (82–71) behind Philadelphia (83–64), Pittsburgh (91–63), and the pennant-winning Chicago Cubs (107–45). There were 198 fewer runs scored in 1907 during senior league games than the previous year as a new rule was implemented establishing the strike zone from the knee to the shoulder. Chicago's team ERA was an all-time record 1.73. There were slightly fewer stolen bases in 1907 than in 1906, a decline of 80 in the NL and 136 in the AL. Three National League teams stole over 200 bases: Pittsburgh (264), Chicago (235), and New York (205). Honus Wagner won his fourth stolen base crown with 61 and he was followed by Magee (46), Evers (46), Leach (43), and Devlin (38).

Tommy Leach was another diminutive player toiling in the big show during its formative years. He stood at five-foot-six-and-a-half-inches tall and weighed as little as 135 pounds by some accounts. Leach played slightly more games during his career in the outfield (1,079) than at third base (955). Despite his small stature he was considered a power hitter, finishing in the top ten in six different seasons in each of the following categories: triples, home runs, and total bases. In 1902 he led the senior circuit in home runs (6) and was tied for the NL lead in triples (22). He led the league in runs scored in 1909 (126) and shared the title with Max Carey in 1913 (99). Leach batted .269 lifetime with 1,355 runs scored, 266 doubles, 172 triples, and 63 home runs. As a sign of the times, 49 of his 63 homers were of the inside-the-park variety, tied for third all-time with Ty Cobb, and behind Sam Crawford (52) and Jesse Burkett (55). Leach insisted that the most exciting play in baseball was not the home run that sailed over the fence, but the inside-the-park variety, and the three-base hit. Leach was a solid small ball player; the 43 bases he stole in 1907 was a career high and he stole at least twenty bases during ten seasons. He pilfered 361 hassocks during his career and had 240 sacrifice hits. He entertained spectators during nineteen big league seasons and spent his entire career in the National League with Louisville (1898–1899), Pittsburgh (1900–1912 and 1918), Chicago (1912–1914), and Cincinnati (1915).

Manager Patsy Donovan's Brooklyn Superbas led the senior league in sacrifice hits with 197, while the Chicago White Sox led the American League with 181. Otto Knabe, a 23-year-old, 5'8", 175-pound second baseman, won his first of four sacrifice hit titles with Philadelphia's National League representative in 1907. Knabe led the league in 1907 (40), 1908 (42), 1910 (37), and 1913 (41). Otto was a weak-hitting .247 lifetime hitter with 265 sacrifices (28th all-time) and 143 stolen bases, who transformed baseball into a physical sport with his intimidating blows around the second base bag. Bill Bradley led the American League in sacrifices with 46, which was the first of two consecutive seasons he would do so. The number "46" is significant in major league history because it is the most sacrifices in the history of the game if you exclude the twenty-four seasons when the sacrifice hit statistic included sacrifice flies in its total, in addition to sacrifice bunts.

Perhaps St. Louis Cardinals rookie first baseman Ed Konetchy, who stood at six-foot-two-and-a-half-inches and weighed 195 pounds, was an unlikely candidate to make small ball history in 1907. During his fifteen-year career in which he batted .281 with a .403 slugging percentage and 255 stolen bases, Konetchy was known as Big Ed, the Candy Kid, the La Crosse Lulu, and the Big Bohemian. Despite never leading the league in triples, his 182 three-baggers ranks tied for 15th all-time. Jack Huston, an ivory hunter for the Cardinals, scouted Konetchy because he was being called "the next Hal Chase," and John McGraw once said that he "is worth the whole (St. Louis) team. With a little coaching on batting and base running, this player has the makings of the grandest man in the business at first sack."[31] Big Ed was an excellent defensive first baseman, skilled at digging balls out of the dirt, and led the NL in fielding average seven times with St. Louis, Pittsburgh, Boston, and Brooklyn. He had excellent range and a strong and accurate throwing arm. As a member of the Federal League's Pittsburgh Rebels in 1915, he also led the league's first baseman in fielding average and stole a career high 27 bases, a feat he also matched in two prior National League campaigns. Konetchy stood straight up in the batter's box, choked up slightly, batted cleanup throughout most of his career, and sent scorching line drives to the outfield with his potent bat. During his first season in 1907 he batted .251 with 13 stolen bases in 91 games and 331 at-bats. On September 30 against Boston he stole home twice in the Cardinals 5–1 triumph. St. Louis set a major league record with three steals of home in this game. The Cardinals finished the 1907 campaign in last place and stole only 125 bags (6th in the NL) which was a low number during the Deadball Era.

The Detroit Tigers won the American League flag (92–58) by one and a half games over Philadelphia with a potent, run producing juggernaut, scoring 693 runs in total, which was 88 more than the second-place occupant in that category. Their outfield from left to right consisting of Davy Jones, Sam Crawford, and Ty Cobb finished one-two-three in the league in runs scored: Crawford (102), Jones (101), and the twenty-year-old prodigy Ty Cobb (97). Cobb won the first of his six career stolen base titles with 53 thefts. As a team the Tigers stole 196 bags, which was third in the league behind last-place Washington (223) and fifth-place New York (206). Led by their skipper Hughie Jennings, Detroit won 21 more games in 1907 than the previous season. Hall of Famer Sam Crawford stole 367 bases during his career but the strong, left-handed hitting slugger was no fan of the inside game while at the dish, eschewing the bunt and place hitting in favor of a philosophy that attempted to hit the ball as hard as he could. Jones was an emotional, hot tempered, 5'10", 165-pound, left-handed hitter, who swiped 207 bags during his injury-plagued career with a career high of 30 steals in 1907. He was also an intelligent, college-educated man, who was predominantly a leadoff hitter and his excellent foot speed helped him win races to earn extra money.

Cobb, who was also a left-handed hitter, was the William Shakespeare of the inside game, swiping 897 career bases (fourth all-time) and compiling 291 sacrifices (twelfth all-time). Fifty-four times during his career he stole home, which is a major league record. This impetuous player was skilled at slugging but could also leg out bunts and grounders, steal bases, take the extra base, lay down a sacrifice or squeeze bunt, execute the hit-and-run or bunt-and-run, and excel at place hitting. He mastered the small ball game and had the brains to outwit and intimidate the opposition. In lopsided games he would run the bases recklessly, making the opposing fielders rush their throws and perhaps fumble the ball in the process. This would pay off in the close games. Cobb was hungry for success and wanted to win more than the opposition. He would often slide with his feet in the air and the spikes would tear through the skin of an opposing fielder who dared to get in his way. Donald Honig wrote that he had "a quick, hyperactive mind that seemed always thinking ahead, daring his body to keep pace; it was as though he were dichotomized — the evil-genius brain taunting, goading, and enraging the lightning-reflexed body toward ever more distant and daring goals."[32] Sam Crawford said that Cobb was "dynamite" when running the bases, adding, "It wasn't that he was so fast on his feet, although he was fast enough. There were others who were faster, though, like Clyde Milan, for instance. It was that Cobb was so fast in his *thinking*. He didn't outhit the opposition and he didn't outrun them. He outthought them!"[33]

He knew how to manufacture runs, using both his physical skills and psychological intimidation. Cobb would incessantly practice sliding and bunting. He was a great baserunner, had a terrific batting eye, and had excellent bat control, which allowed him to hit the ball precisely where he intended. At first base he would kick the bag a few inches towards second so he would be less vulnerable of being picked off. He had great sliding techniques and would watch the infielder's eyes so he could ascertain the direction of the ball and get hit by it as he slid into the bag. When he slid into the bag, he would sometimes pretend he was injured and when the pitcher and catcher relaxed, he would steal a base. Walter Johnson feared that his fastball might kill a man if it struck him in the head. Cobb crowded the plate against Johnson, taking advantage of the pitcher's fears, and forcing him to work the outside corner. Cobb would slide into the bag spikes high so he could kick the ball out of the infielder's glove, intimidate the infielder, and even deliberately injure the fielder. Cobb would say, "I have observed that baseball is not unlike a war."[34] He finished his career with a .366 batting average and a .433 on-base percentage. In F.C. Lane's book, *Batting: One Thousand Expert Opinions on Every Conceivable Angle of Batting Science*, Cobb states his preference for small ball over big ball: "My idea of a genuine hitter is a man who can bunt, who can place his hits and who, when the need comes, can slug. I believe that a batter should use his brains and his feet as well as his batting eye and his shoulders."[35] Cobb would continue to dislike the big ball style of play right up to the end of his life; in 1952 he wrote, "The hit and run, stolen base, bunt, and sacrifice are deteriorating from unuse and they only hit for their amusement and pleasure for the home run."[36]

The Chicago Cubs won the 1907 World Series in four straight games against Detroit as they ran wild around the bases. They stole fifteen bases, including five by

Tris Speaker (left) and Ty Cobb were the greatest center fielders of the Deadball Era and are among the best fly chasers in major league history. Speaker was the superior defensive outfielder and despite batting .345 lifetime, he was surpassed by Cobb as a hitter (.366). Cobb was also a better small ball player; Speaker (309) was credited with eighteen more sacrifice hits than Cobb (291), but Cobb pilfered more than twice as many sacks than Speaker, 897 to 436. (George Brace photograph).

Jimmy Slagle and three apiece by Chance and Evers. Detroit, in contrast, stole only six as Davy Jones led the way with three steals. Slagle in his second to last season batted .258 with 28 steals and then hit for a .273 clip in the series. He set the pace right away in game one, stealing two in three attempts. Chicago had seven steals in the opener, a hard fought contest where neither team emerged victorious because darkness fell upon Chicago's West Side Grounds with the score tied at three after twelve innings. The Cubs rallied for two runs in the last of the ninth to knot the game at three, as the tying run was plated because of a two-out, third-strike, passed ball by the backstop, Boss Schmidt. Del Howard stole second after the miscue and then Evers tried to garner a game-ending steal of home but was unsuccessful. Again in the tenth the Cubs tried to push the envelope as Slagle and Chance pulled off a double steal, but Jimmy got greedy and was called out for interference as he tried to manufacture the winning run. The steal of third was Slagle's second theft of the inning, as he also pilfered the second sack after a single to center. In the eleventh the Cubs mounted another rally that fell flat, as Evers and Frank Schulte legged out bunt singles to load the bases with one out, but the runners died on the sacks. Umpire Hank O'Day would not allow them to continue past the twelfth inning.

In the first inning of game two, Slagle was called out on the hidden ball trick, the only one in World Series history. The Cubs added four more stolen bases in the second contest off the catcher Fred Payne as they took a 1 to 0 lead in the series with a 3–1 triumph and then outscored the Tigers, 13 to 2, in the final three contests. Hughie Jennings had feared the worst coming into the series, saying, "I'd give a million dollars if I had a Kling behind the bat."[37] This was a reference to Johnny Kling, the Cubs' excellent defensive catcher, who is generally considered the best one during the Deadball Era. Detroit, in contrast, had Boss Schmidt as their regular catcher, a switch-hitting, 5'11", 200-pounder, who batted .244 with 8 steals during the regular season. An opposing team could run all day on Schmidt, who was not skilled at throwing runners out. Schmidt was backed up by Payne who batted .166 in 169 at-bats. The third catcher was Jimmy Archer who batted .119 in just 18 games and 42 at-bats. During the regular season the Cubs averaged 1.5 steals per game, but in the World Series they averaged three steals per contest. Furthermore, they had a 75 percent basestealing average in the big classic, which was considered excellent by Deadball Era standards. Kling held the Tigers to a 54.5 percent basestealing average, and threw out three runners in game two. Perhaps, his best accomplishment was that he did not surrender a steal to the American League basestealing champion, Ty Cobb, and threw him out twice.

For many years it was believed that the Cubs stole 18 bags in the 1907 World Series, which would have tied them with the 1909 Pittsburgh Pirates for the most steals in the autumn classic. The ninth edition of the Macmillan baseball encyclopedia credits them with eighteen steals as does a myriad other baseball books. But when the old statistics were corrected, the Cubs had three steals taken away. It was not unusual for World Series teams to lose one steal or gain one steal or for individual players to do the same, but a reduction of three steals in a single World Series was unusual. The fifteen steals is verified by examining the Retrosheet box scores of the 1907 series. This means that player-manager Fred Clarke's 1909 Pittsburgh Pirates should be recognized as the only team to steal eighteen bags in the fall classic, which stands as the record.

Manager Frank Chance's Cubs won the exhilarating 1908 pennant race, thanks partially to a 19-year-old busher named Fred Merkle, who was trying to make a name for himself in the big tent for John McGraw's Giants. On September 23, Merkle failed to touch second base on an apparent game-winning hit and the game was declared a tie. Chicago won the one-game playoff on October 8 to secure the flag. Merkle played sparingly in 1908, his second year, batting .268 in 41 at-bats and then with the infamous gaffe still fresh in people's minds, he batted just .191 in 236 at-bats with 8 steals during the 1909 campaign. In a sixteen-year big league career he batted .273 with 272 steals, including a career high of 49 in 1911. Chicago finished the campaign with a 99–55 record, finishing one game ahead of both Pittsburgh and New York. They were the majors best small ball team, leading the National League in stolen bases with 212 and both leagues with 270 sacrifice hits. Pittsburgh's 186 stolen bases ranked fourth in the league as Honus Wagner won his fifth and final stolen base crown with 53 thefts. In 1909 he stole 35 bases and then never stole more than 26 during his final eight seasons.

Following Wagner was Red Murray, who stole 48 of his 321 career bases for the last-place St. Louis Cardinals. During Murray's seven seasons as an everyday player from 1907 to 1913 with the Cardinals and Giants, he stole 297 bases, an average of 42.4 a season. He stole a career high 57 bags with the 1910 Giants and stole 48 in 1908, 1909, and 1911. There is a wonderful story about Murray told by Rube Marquard to Lawrence Ritter in his phenomenal book *The Glory of Their Times*. The score was tied against Pittsburgh one day with a runner on second and no outs in the ninth inning. Before stepping into the box, Murray asked McGraw what he should do and the skipper replied, "What are you doing in the National League? There's the winning run on second base and no one out." McGraw then asked Murray what he thought he should do if he were piloting the team and Red correctly replied that he should sacrifice the runner to second. When Murray stepped back into the batter's box, he looked perplexed, and looked at McGraw again. Murray got a high pitch just like he preferred in his wheelhouse and he hammered it for a home run over the left-field fence to end the game. Red was as happy as he had ever been while McGraw was apoplectic. McGraw confronted Murray in the clubhouse in front of the team and informed him that he was fined $100 in a way that made members of the team laugh uncontrollably.[38]

Finishing third with 47 steals was Cincinnati's Hans Lobert, followed by Sherry Magee who swiped 40 of fourth-place Philadelphia's 200 steals. Johnny Evers stole 36 to finish fifth in the circuit.

Hans Lobert, a 5'9", 170-pound, right-handed hitter, played his entire fourteen-year career in the National League with Pittsburgh (1903), Chicago (1905), Cincinnati (1906–1910), Philadelphia (1911–1914), and New York (1915–1917). Lobert manned the hot corner for most of his career and stole 316 bases, including 40 or more during four seasons: 1908 (47), 1910 (41), 1911 (40), and 1913 (41). He had 231 sacrifices and led the NL in 1911 (38). Lobert's foot speed was exhibited on October 12, 1910, when he rounded the bases in 13.8 seconds, which was hailed as a record-breaking achievement. He won many races including against Jim Thorpe, who had won an Olympic gold medal, against Vince Campbell, a track star on the collegiate level, and he also defeated a racehorse. He played in five games for the 1903 Pirates and his only hit in thirteen at-bats was a bunt single with two strikes. McGraw asked the youngster who taught him to bunt with two strikes. Lobert replied, "Nobody did," adding, "but I like to bunt and nobody was looking for a busher to do that."[39] McGraw encouraged him to keep it up and continue to outsmart the opposition. Lobert batted .274 during his career with a .337 on-base percentage and a .366 slugging percentage. On September 27, 1908, he stole second, third, and home against St. Louis in the third inning of game one. On that same day Ty Cobb swiped home for the third time during the campaign in the third inning of Detroit's 5–2 win over Philadelphia. His second theft of home was garnered in the opening game of that series, on the 24th, when the Tigers fought the Athletics to a 4–4 tie. All three of his steals of home came on the front end of a double steal.

The last-place New York Highlanders led the American League in steals with 231, but it was third-place Chicago who was the circuit's best small ball team (209 steals, 2nd AL; 236 sacrifices, 2nd AL). The American League pennant race was just as exciting as the National League as Detroit (90–63) won the flag by a half game over second-place Cleveland (90–64) and by one and a half games over Chicago. In many ways, Chicago was still the hitless wonders, finishing with a .224 batting average, which was only better than Philadelphia (.223) in the junior circuit who finished in sixth place. Cleveland's American League aggregation led by player-manager Nap Lajoie won 16 of 18 during the final month to take over first place before fading in the early autumn afternoons. Cleveland had the major leagues best ERA in 1908 (2.02) and they led the American League in sacrifice hits (243), thanks to Bill Bradley's astonishingly high 60 sacrifices. The White Sox were still living on the reputation of their 1906 world championship; therefore the Tigers respected and feared the Pale Hose more than the Naps. Ty Cobb didn't believe on waiting for someone to drive you in, but he literally tried to steal games from the enemy with his attack style of offense.

Cobb said, "I think the best way to beat the Sox is to play wild ball against them." He added, "Take any and every kind of chance. If you play stereo-typed baseball against them, you play right into their hands. Run wild and do everything least expected and least logical and you have a chance of beating them."[40] The Tigers were a slightly below average small ball team in 1908, finishing fifth in the junior league in steals (165) and fifth in sacrifices (191).

Patsy Dougherty, the White Sox's left fielder, led the circuit with a career high 47 stolen bases. He stole 261 lifetime and during his first three seasons with the Sox (1907–1909) his basestealing numbers increased significantly as he stole 33, 47, and 36. In 1907 Charlie Hemphill stole only 14 bases in 153 games and 603 at-bats for the St. Louis Browns. But after being traded to the New York Highlanders in 1908, he stole 42 bases for an outfit that had been running wild against American League teams for years. Detroit's Germany Schaefer finished third in the league with a career high 40 stolen bases. Schaefer was skilled at stealing signs and was an excellent bench jockey, which were both attributes that were coveted and used frequently during the Deadball Era. Cobb stole 39 bags to finish fourth and Josh Clarke of Cleveland stole 37 bases during his only season as an everyday player.

The Chicago Cubs won their second straight world championship in 1908, defeating Detroit four games to one. Just like in 1907, the Cubs stole significantly more bases than the Tigers. In the 1908 series they swiped 15 bases including five by Chance and two apiece by Tinker, Evers, Solly Hofman, and Frank "Wildfire" Schulte. Detroit stole only five bases, as Cobb led the way with two. The Cubs were credited with eight sacrifice bunts, including four in the opening game, while Detroit had four sacrifices. Chicago was charged with only two errors in the series as Evers and Chance had one apiece in the opener. Detroit's defense was not as good as they committed nine miscues.

In 1909 stolen bases increased by significant margins in both leagues; the National League increased from 1,372 in 1908 to 1,516 in 1909. The number of stolen bases per team increased from 171.5 to 189.5. The American League totals jumped from 1,350 to 1,539. In 1908 each junior league team stole an average of 168.8 bases, while in 1909 they stole 192.4 per team. Sacrifice hit totals which had jumped by 306 in the NL from 1907 to 1908, declined by 113 in 1909. The American League also saw a significant jump in sacrifices from 1907 to 1908, by 321. But in 1909 sacrifices remained steady as there were eight more than the previous year. The increase in sacrifices from 1907 to 1908 was due to the new rule mandating that sacrifice flies also count as sacrifice hits. The sacrifice fly rule was enacted in 1908, but instead of treating the sacrifice fly and the sacrifice bunt as two distinct plays, they were combined to form the sacrifice hit statistic, which had previously represented the number of sacrifice bunts that were accumulated. Under this new rule the number of sacrifice hits skyrocketed as it was to be expected. From 1904 to 1907, the four seasons before the new rule, there were 4,865 sacrifice hits in the senior circuit. But from 1908 to 1911, the first four seasons with the redefined sacrifice hit definition, there were 6,142. During these same time periods the American League sacrifice hit totals did not increase by as much, from 5,185 to 6,119.

For the first time since 1903, Pittsburgh captured the pennant in the senior circuit with a 110–42 record in 1909. Chicago finished second with a 104–49 record, which would have been good enough to win the flag during most seasons. In the American League the Detroit Tigers won their third consecutive pennant with a 98–54 mark, beating out Philadelphia (95–58) by three and a half games. Fourth-place Cincinnati led the senior league in steals with 280, followed by third-place New York who stole 240. Bob Bescher, the Reds left fielder, won the first of four consecutive NL stolen base crowns with 54 hassocks and was followed by New York's Red Murray (48). The Cubs stole 187 bags (3rd in NL) and led the circuit with 248 sacrifices, while their left fielder, Jimmy Sheckard, had the most in the circuit (46). In the American League, the four first division teams stole over 200 bases: Detroit (280), third-place Boston (215), fourth-place Chicago (211), and Philadelphia (201). The Athletics had the most sacrifices in the league with 247, beating out Chicago (243) and Detroit (232). Donie Bush, Detroit's second-year shortstop, led the circuit with 52 sacrifices. The AL stolen base crown was captured by Cobb (76), followed by Eddie Collins of Philadelphia (63) and Cobb's teammate, Bush (53). Each of these three players had young legs and were in the early stages of their career.

Despite stealing eighteen fewer bases in 1909 than the previous year, Honus Wagner had another spectacular season, capturing his fourth consecutive batting title (.339) and leading the league in doubles for the fourth consecutive season and RBIs for the fourth time during his career. On May 2 he stole second, third, and home in the first inning of the second game against the Chicago Cubs. Pittsburgh won the twin bill by scores of 5–2 and 6–0, stealing two in the opener and six in the first inning of the nightcap. Wagner garnered three steals in an inning for the third time in his career, which was an NL record.

In Chicago's South Side Park the White Sox stole twelve bases, including home three times as they defeated St. Louis by a 15–3 score on July 2. I.E. Sanborn of the *Chicago Daily Tribune* declared, "Comiskey's men made more runs than we thought there were in the whole world." Ed Walsh, who had won 40 games and pitched 464 innings during the 1908 campaign, would win 25 fewer games in 1909, and on July 2 he stole home for the second time in his career. He was hit "promiscuously," throughout the "sultry battle," but the "enemy's fire," was "kept down to the desultory class," except in the fifth frame. The White Sox, led by skipper Billy Sullivan, scored five markers in the first inning, which included a single by Freddy Parent who convinced the third baseman he was going to bunt and then hit the ball past him. Parent, a 33-year-old shortstop and outfielder, stole a career high 32 bases in 1909 and 184 during his career. Outfielder and first baseman, Dave Altizer, stole 27 bags in 1909 and beat out a bunt in the initial frame. Fred Payne had a "record breaking single," that scored three runs. He tripped while rounding the first base bag and was held to a one-base hit. Chicago scored five more in the fourth and stole a few more bases. Jake Atz and Billy Purtell pulled off a double steal in the inning. The White Sox pushed across two more in the fifth when Parent and Altizer pulled off a double steal. Lee Tannehill, a third baseman and shortstop, started the sixth with a line drive to left field that got past the outfielders but his attempt for an inside-the-park homer was cut short, one foot before home plate, after two good throws. Barney Reilly followed, was hit by a pitch, and "stole second professionally." Later in the inning, Ed Hahn and Walsh pulled off Chicago's third double steal of the game.[41]

The crowd at South Side Park, including the *Chicago Daily Tribune*'s, I.E. Sanborn, were enthused to see Yale graduate Barney Reilly make his big league debut. He replaced Atz at second base in the sixth inning with the game well in hand. Despite making the only White Sox error of the game, his debut was impressive and the "most decisive evidence of his having shaken the amateur hayseed out of his hair," was when he was hit by a pitched ball his first time up and stole second base. This impressed the crowd because the ball beat him to the bag. But Reilly, an unflappable busher, pulled off a beautiful hook slide, catching the base with his toe on his inner leg, and making it impossible for the fielder to tag any part of his body except his spikes. This "stamped him as having acquired more than the rudiments of baseball before taking his degree at Yale."[42] Reilly, however, would only play twelve major league games, each one with the 1909 White Sox. The 24-year-old second baseman batted .200 in 25 at-bats and stole two bags.

Interestingly, despite the fact that the traditional sacrifice bunt was now added with the sacrifice fly to form the sacrifice hit statistic, the box scores of major league games in 1909 and beyond listed the sacrifice flies and the sacrifice bunts separately. For example, the game in Brooklyn between the Giants and Superbas on July 2 had a total of three sacrifice flies and three sacrifice bunts. The box score in the *Chicago Daily Tribune* listed sacrifice bunts after the term "Sacrifice hits." The Giants won, 5–3, with Fred Tenney, an aging 37-year-old first baseman, leading off. Tenney was burdened with leg problems in 1909 and batted .235 in his next to last big league season, stealing 8 of his career 285 bases. He was a solid small ball player who stole fifteen or more bases during thirteen seasons and his 277 sacrifice hits is tied for 19th all-time.

On July 15, in the fourteenth inning of the second game between the Phillies and the Cardinals, Eddie Grant, Philadelphia's third baseman, had a game-ending steal of home with right hander Fred Beebe on the mound. Grant was on the front end of a double steal with Sherry Magee. The five-foot-eleven-and-a-half-inch, 168-pound, left-handed hitting but right-handed throwing hot corner occupant, was especially skilled with the glove at defending against the bunt. He would lose his life on October 5, 1918, during World War I in the Argonne Forest of France. From 1908 to 1911 he stole 27, 28, 25, and 28 bases, respectively. He stole 153 bases during his ten-year big league career and was skilled in moving the runner over with a sacrifice, compiling 129 during his career and finishing fourth in 1909 (31) and second in 1910 (34) in the senior league. There were six seasons in which Grant played in fewer than 97 games, including his first year with the 1905 Cleveland Naps when he played in two games.

In Detroit's 6–0 win over Boston at Bennett Park on July 22, Ty Cobb collected three hits and stole four bases. In the seventh inning he stole second, third, and home. Detroit's left fielder, Matty McIntyre, stole one of his thirteen bases on the season, while catcher Boss Schmidt and pitcher Ed Killian had two sacrifices apiece. Pitchers did not amass a large number of sacrifice hits during the Deadball Era, a custom that would prevail into future decades. Killian had three sacrifice hits and 62 at-bats in 1909. During his career, the southpaw hurler had 19 sacrifice hits and 609 at-bats. In Cleveland, Naps outfielder Bill Hinchman was out at the plate trying to stretch a triple into a homer as New York won a rain shortened game, 1–0. In National League play, Boston's two-hole hitter, Beals Becker, had three of the six sacrifices in the game but Pittsburgh won, 9–0. There were three stolen bases in the game: two by Boston third baseman, Bill Sweeney, who stole 172 during his career and one by Fred Clarke, the Pirates leadoff man.

At the Polo Grounds, the Cubs defeated the Giants, 3–1, as "a bit of comedy" played out in the "eighth round." Josh Devore, a 21-year-old backup, pinch-ran and was picked off first. The play happened so quickly that McGraw looked "dazed" in the third base coach's box. Chicago scored all their runs in the first. Evers walked to lead off the game, and then an effective, well executed bunt by Sheckard, sailed over the third baseman's head for a hit. It may have appeared to be an unintentional, fortuitous play, to the spectators in the crowd but the Cubs had actually practiced this style of attack. With runners on first and second with no outs, Frank Schulte came up to the box with orders to sacrifice the runners over. He finally was successful on his third attempt. When Chance grounded to pitcher Hooks Wiltse, R.W. Lardner of the *Chicago Daily Tribune* said Evers was at "death's door." But Evers danced along the third base line, eluding the attempted tags by Wiltse, and then

Wiltse threw it past his rookie catcher, Chief Meyers, as two runners scored and Chance moved up to third and scored on Steinfeldt's sacrifice fly. Lardner started his column by writing, "George Wiltse played the leading role today in a tragedy entitled, 'The Elusiveness of Evers.'"[43]

On August 8, New York Giants outfielder Bill O'Hara stole second, third, and home in the eighth inning as McGraw's club defeated St. Louis, 3–0. In his rookie season O'Hara batted .236 with 31 steals and then would play only nine more major league games with the 1910 St. Louis Cardinals. On August 23 with the ineffective southpaw Jim Pastorius on the hill, Brooklyn catcher Bill Bergen threw out six of eight Cardinals trying to steal, but St. Louis prevailed, 9–1, to split a twin bill. Bergen's achievement is tied for the most runners thrown out in a game during the modern era. Brooklyn swiped six in the 7–0 opening game victory. The Cubs also had their running shoes on as Johnny Evers and Del Howard stole home in the initial frame versus Boston, while Solly Hofman turned the trick in the second inning. All three steals of home were on the front end of a double steal and Chicago emerged victorious, 11–6.

The Detroit Tigers won the 1909 pennant with crucial wins down the stretch with the help of four new regular infielders: Tom Jones (first base), Jim Delahanty (second base), Donie Bush (shortstop), and George Moriarty (third base). There appeared to be further good news since they did not have to face the Cubs in the World Series, who had beaten them the previous two years. But just like the previous two seasons, the National League flag carrier, the Pittsburgh Pirates, ran wild on Detroit as the Tigers lost again, this time four games to three. The Pirates stole eighteen bases, including six by Wagner and three apiece by Clarke and rookie second baseman Dots Miller. Even George Gibson, a smart, highly skilled defensive backstop, stole two bases in the series. The slow-footed Gibson stole a career high of nine bases in 1909 and forty during his fourteen-year career. The eighteen steals surpassed the previous record of the 1907 and 1908 Cubs, who stole fifteen bags in the postseason during both years. Detroit stole only six bases and were led by Cobb who stole two. Pittsburgh had twelve errors in the series, while Detroit had seventeen. Babe Adams stole the show, winning three games for the Pirates, and compiling a 1.33 ERA in 27 innings pitched.

The highlights of the opening game included the first of two homers in the series by Clarke and a terrific running catch by Leach to rob Cobb in the seventh of a sure three-base hit with two ducks on the pond and two out. Leach "ran backward like a tiny land crab," according to the article in the *New York Times*.[44] Pittsburgh stole two bases, one by Miller and Owen "Chief" Wilson, while Cobb stole one for Detroit. Bush had a sacrifice bunt, while Leach had a sacrifice fly. Pittsburgh emerged victorious in the opener by a 4–1 score, which delighted the Forbes Field crowd. In the second game, Detroit won, 7–2, thanks in part to Cobb's steal of home in the third inning. Wagner led Pittsburgh to an 8–6 win in game three as he collected three singles, drove in two, and stole three bases on three different pitchers. In the fourth game, Wagner was "helpless" against George Mullin as Detroit knotted the series at two with a 5–0 win.[45] Bobby Byrne and Tommy Leach stole bases in the losing effort, while Detroit had no steals and two sacrifice bunts. Clarke's three-run homer proved critical in game five as Pittsburgh won, 8–4. Wagner stole a run in the four-run seventh inning, stealing second and third with two outs and then scampering home on a throwing error by the catcher Boss Schmidt. Tom Jones of the Tigers stole second with one out in the ninth, despite the fact his team was losing by four runs. Surely, this must have been because of defensive indifference, but stolen bases were credited under those circumstances during the time. Pittsburgh pilfered four hassocks in game five, while Detroit had two. The Pirates also laid down two sacrifice bunts. Detroit knotted the series in the next contest with a 5–4 win as the game ended on a strike'em-out-throw'em-out double play. Ed Abbaticchio pinch-hit for Deacon Phillippe with runners on first and second and one out. He struck out during his only at-bat of the series and Schmidt gunned down Wilson trying to pilfer the third sack. Adams was on the mound for Pittsburgh in the finale and he whitewashed the Tigers at Detroit's Bennett Park, leading them to an 8–0 victory. The Pirates decided to push the envelope in the finale, stealing four bases in five attempts.

Manager Hughie Jennings's Tigers lost the World Series for the third consecutive season and their inability to curtail the running game was a large reason why they fell flat. They allowed a whopping 48 stolen bases in sixteen games. To put that into perspective consider that if a team kept up that pace during the 154-game regular season, stealing three bases per game, they would steal 462 bases, which would shatter the modern major league record by 115 steals, which was later established by the 1911 New York Giants.

At the insistence of John McGraw the entire Giants team, including the veterans, spent part of their day practicing the proper sliding techniques during their spring training activities in 1910 at Marlin, Texas. With the masterful McGraw supervising, each player took their turn sliding into a ten-foot-long pit. He preferred the hook slide and the fadeaway, which gave the runner a better chance to avoid the tag and eschewed the headfirst slide because the runner went right into the tag and it was harder to contort one's body in a way which avoided the tag. The Giants in 1910 were rebuilding and except for Christy Mathewson and Art Devlin this was almost an entirely different squad than the outfit that had won the world championship in 1905. This club was replete with new players like Josh Devore, who made a name for himself in 1910, batting .304 with a .371 on-base percentage and 43 steals in his first season as an everyday player. The Giants finished the 1910 campaign in second place (91–63), while the Cubs took the flag for the fourth time in five seasons with a 104–50 mark. During most seasons, New York's 282 stolen bases were good enough to lead the league. However, in 1910 the Cincinnati Reds stole 310, the fifth most in the modern era and the sixth most since 1898 when a stolen base was no longer credited when a runner advanced on a fly ball or performed several other outcomes. Not surprisingly, Clark Griffith was the Cincinnati manager, a skipper whose Chicago and New York teams had previously run wild in the American League for years. The 1910 Cubs stole 173 bases (5th in NL) and had a major league leading 234 sacrifice hits.

Bob Bescher won his second consecutive NL stolen base crown in 1910 (70) and was followed by Red Murray (57), Cincinnati outfielder Dode Paskert (51), Magee (49), and Devore (43). Bescher was a 6'1", 200-pound, switch-hitting left fielder, whose 428 career stolen bases is an exorbitant number when you consider that during three of his eleven seasons (1908, 1917 and 1918) he played a combined 99 games. F.C. Lane declared Bescher the "King of Basestealers" in a 1912 article in *Baseball Magazine*.[46] He was an intelligent basestealer who studied the habits of the opposing pitchers. He played for John McGraw during one season with the 1914 Giants, batting .270 with 36 steals. It's unlikely that McGraw would have taken exception to Bescher's sliding technique because he always slid feet first and ubiquitously used the hook slide. He would quickly ascertain where the catcher's throw was going and then slide to the inner portion of the bag or the outer portion. The August 6, 1911, game against the Philadelphia Phillies is illustrative of his small ball style. Bescher advanced to the midway with aggressive baserunning, stretching what would have been a single for most players into a double and then he stole home on the front end of a double steal in the early innings. In the eighth frame he was anchored at the gateway station until a sacrifice was laid down and he came all the way around to score thanks to poor judgments on behalf of his opponent. Bescher was not a good average hitter, batting .258 lifetime, but he had a respectable .353 on-base percentage. He was not a well-rounded small ball player, collecting only 74 sacrifices, including a career high of 15 with the 1915 St. Louis Cardinals. This suggests that either he wasn't good at bunting or perhaps he didn't like it. His teammate Dode Paskert spent his entire fifteen-year career in the National League with the Reds, Phillies, and Cubs. The gifted defensive outfielder batted .268 lifetime with a .350 on-base percentage. He had 293 stolen bases and 224 sacrifice hits.

The American League flag was captured by Connie Mack's Philadelphia Athletics (102–48) as they finished third in the league in steals (207) and second in sacrifices (199). Second-place New York (88–63) swiped the most bases (288), followed by third-place Detroit (249). Manager Patsy Donovan's Boston Red Sox concluded the campaign in fourth place and led the league in sacrifice hits (227). Eddie Collins stole a career high 81 bases to win the first of four AL stolen base titles. He was followed by Cobb (65), Chicago's rookie infielder Rollie Zeider (49), Bush (49), and Clyde Milan of Washington (44). Harry Hooper, Boston's second-year outfielder, had the most sacrifice hits (34). In 1910 the Chicago White Sox were still hitless, but they were no longer wonderful. The sixth-place Sox had a major league low .211 batting average and finished seventh in the league in steals (183) and tied for fourth with 190 sacrifices. Future Hall of Famer, Ed Walsh, had a major league low 1.27 ERA but posted a losing record, 18–20. Walsh was a consultant to the architects who built Comiskey Park, where the White Sox began playing on July 1, 1910. The ballpark had spacious dimensions that made it salubrious for small ball play: 362 feet down the lines with a ten-foot fence and 420 feet to center with an eleven-foot fence.

On May 10, 1910, the Phillies executed a triple steal in the first inning versus Cincinnati but they lost, 8–6. Eddie Grant, Sherry Magee, and Kitty Bransfield were the three players involved in the triple steal. In Cincinnati's 6–5 win over Boston on May 23, Dode Paskert stole second, third, and home in the first inning. In the Chicago Cubs' 11–1 win against the Reds on June 28, Joe Tinker stole home twice. The Cubs took advantage of two pitchers who were each appearing in their first major league game: Rube Benton and Frederick "Mysterious" Walker.

Bobby Byrne, Pittsburgh's five-foot-seven-and-a-half-inch, 145-pound, right-handed third baseman, had his breakout season in 1910, batting .296 with a .366 on-base percentage and a career high 36 stolen bases. He was tied with his teammate Honus Wagner with the most hits in the circuit (178) and led the league in doubles (43). On August 25, against the Brooklyn Superbas at Forbes Field, he literally stole the game for the Pirates. The contest dragged on into the last of the twelfth, knotted at three. Byrne hit the ball sharply to left to open the Pirates half of the inning. However, he was not content with merely a single and aggressively made the turn towards second and ran like the wind until he was standing safely upon the second base bag. Leach tried to sacrifice him to third, but he failed and struck out. But when Leach was swinging futilely at the third strike, Byrne stole third. With George Bell, a right-handed pitcher who would go 10–27 with a 2.64 ERA during the season, standing on the bump, Brooklyn's hot-tempered skipper Bill Dahlen ordered Bell to walk Clarke and Wagner to load the bases, setting up a double play situation and a force at every base. Bell disagreed with Dahlen's strategy and told him so. But there would be no insubordination and he passed the two Pittsburgh hitters to load the sacks. Now the responsibility fell upon 26-year-old rookie John Flynn to drive in the winning run. With two strikes on Flynn, the diminutive runner at third "made a daring dash for home," and with the pitch delivered outside to the right-handed hitting Flynn, catcher Bill Bergen did not even have a chance to tag Byrne before he slid safely across the plate for a game-ending steal of home. Dahlen's strategy had backfired as he was outsmarted by the opposition and Bell appeared to be vindicated. Before the two men exited the field, "hot words" were exchanged.[47]

On September 3, the Philadelphia Athletics scored their only run in a 3–1 loss to Washington on a triple steal. Connie Mack's Athletics coasted to the title, but perhaps lost some concentration down the stretch. Joe Jackson of the *Washington Post* described the first game of a doubleheader between the Athletics and Senators on September 2 as "a dreary, long-drawn affair, entirely lacking in interest either as a batting or fielding demonstration."[48] However, Connie Mack had his boys ready once the calendar turned to October. Before the World Series between the Cubs and Athletics, a photo was taken of second baseman Johnny Evers and Eddie Collins. Unfortunately for Chicago, Evers was on crutches and had broken his leg late in the campaign. With an infield consisting of Collins, Harry Davis, Jack Barry, and Frank Baker and an outfield of Bris Lord, Amos Strunk, and Danny Murphy, the Athletics won the series, four games to one. Strunk had only played sixteen games during the regular season and filled in admirably in the series (.278), replacing the injured Rube Oldring. Ira Thomas was behind the dish catching the majors best pitching staff. Jack Coombs (31–9, 1.30 ERA) and Chief Bender (23–5, 1.58 ERA) led the mound corps as they compiled a major league low 1.79 ERA. Philadelphia stole seven bases during the World Series and were led by Collins who pilfered four. In contrast, the Cubs who had swiped thirty bags the last two times they played in the fall classic, stole only three bases.

The evolution and controversies of baseball statistics have been discussed in this book. Ty Cobb was at the center of one of those controversies in 1910. Nap Lajoie of the Cleveland Indians needed a perfect final day of the season to steal the batting title from Cobb, whose season had already concluded because of an injury. However, it has been suggested that Cobb was healthy and sat out because he wanted to reap the financial reward and not risk losing the batting crown. The St. Louis Browns, who were one of many teams who collectively hated Cobb, decided not to give their best effort when Lajoie came to the plate. Jack O'Connor, the Browns skipper, despised the fiery Cobb and instructed Red Corriden, the coffin corner occupant, to play on the grass. Not the infield grass, but the outfield grass. With St. Louis's third baseman playing too deep and intentionally out of position, Lajoie collected seven bunt hits in a doubleheader and also added a triple and a sacrifice. However, because of a mistake in adding up the numbers, it was Cobb, not Lajoie, who won the batting title. The corrected numbers for both players is Cobb with a .383 batting average and Lajoie with a .384 batting average. The Chalmers Company had promised to give a car to the player who had the highest batting average and in the end they decided to appropriately give each player a car. The mistake in Cobb's batting average wasn't corrected for seventy years and he is still considered the official 1910 batting champion despite having a lower average than Lajoie.

An article in the *Washington Post* dated September 4, 1910, examined the reasons why stolen bases had declined since the nineteenth century. It highlights what is obviously the most prominent reason, which is that up until 1898 stolen bases were credited when a baserunner advanced with the aid of a batted ball by moving up a base on a fly ball or advancing two bases on a hit or an infield out. There were additional circumstances that rewarded a stolen base to a runner as well, such as starting towards the next base while the ball was being delivered and safely advancing to the next station even if there was a clean hit. Teamwork is another reason for fewer steals as more hit-and-run plays were executed during the Deadball Era. Another reason why stolen bases decreased and the number of caught stealing increased was the introduction of the "big catcher's mitt." This larger mitt was first used in 1889, but was not used ubiquitously until much later. Arthur Irwin, a nineteenth century shortstop, originally used the padded fielder's glove, placing a piece of leather over the palm. This was perfected by Tom Daly and Pat Murphy, who developed a larger glove for catching. When catchers had used the small-fingered glove with less padding, their hands would give when catching the ball, and therefore it took them a little longer to unleash the throw. The thick-padded glove of the Deadball Era had practically no give, allowing the backstops to unleash the throw quicker. The *Washington Post* article written by a nameless scribe insisted that fewer stolen bases were not a "detriment" to the game. Baseball is more "scientific and interesting" when compared to the nineteenth century. Baserunners are also just as fast as in the old days and the only reason nineteenth century players accumulated more stolen bases was because of the rules and equipment.

As previously examined, stolen bases increased significantly from 1908 to 1909. This appears to have happened because of a modification of the rules. The 1907 guide provided the following rule for stolen bases: "A stolen base shall be credited to the base runner whenever he advances a base unaided by a base hit, a put-out, a fielding or a battery error." The rule was changed to allow a stolen base if there was a "battery" error as long as the runner started running towards the next base before that error.[49]

The exceptional book *Touching Second: The Science of Baseball*, written by John J. Evers, the second baseman of the Chicago Cubs, and Hugh S. Fullerton, a talented Chicago sportswriter, was published in 1910 and provides an assessment of scientific baseball, which was prevalent during the Deadball Era. Fullerton eschewed subjective observations, but instead relied on rigorous mathematical computations and statistical analysis to form objective conclusions. He lauded small ball strategies and was chagrined because baserunning "is fast becoming one of the lost arts of baseball."[50] As team work had become increasingly popular, aggressive baserunning had declined. Fullerton insisted that team work was "overdone," as players failed to take the initiative and waited for someone to flash them the steal sign, instead of running on their own.[51] They were no longer thinking for themselves and "there is less brain work exhibited on the bases than there was twenty years ago."[52] Stolen bases had decreased from the earlier days because of several factors, including the fact that pitchers did a better job of holding runners close and the popularity of the hit-and-run and bunt-and-run had reduced the number of opportunities to pilfer a sack. Fullerton wrote, "Baseball has been reduced to a science, and is in danger of becoming mechanical unless a few baserunners like Cobb, Collins, Evers and Clarke, exponents of the unexpected, convince managers that base-running pays, and that remaining anchored to bases is a poor policy."[53] Fullerton admired players who would incessantly try to steal, even if their judgment was occasionally lacking. He wrote the following about Ty Cobb:

> Cobb is one of the rare players who can play "inside ball" and individual ball at the same time. He is brilliant, thinks for himself and is not much hampered by bench orders. He runs mainly on his own judgment (or lack of judgment) but still he RUNS and he wins pennants for Detroit by running. The pitchers try harder to hold him to the bases than they do any other player in the league; the catchers give more pitch-out signs to catch him, but they do not stop him. He is a living proof of the fact that modern ball players could run bases with as much effect as the old-timers could — if it were not for their lack of individual thinking.[54]

The 1911 baseball season is largely remembered for the introduction of the new cork-centered ball, which was wound tighter than previous spheroids. There were 499 more runs scored in the NL and 1,081 more in the AL than in 1910. The speed game remained intact as stolen bases increased in both leagues. Cobb led the junior league in batting at .420, followed by Joe Jackson (.408), a left-handed pull hitter who took advantage of the short right field porch at Cleveland's League Park (290 feet with a 40-foot high wall) and stole a career high 41 bases in 1911. Philadelphia won the American League flag with a 101–50 record and led both leagues in sacrifice hits (231). The second-place Chicago Cubs (92–62) led the senior league in sacrifices with 202. Hans Lobert collected the most sacrifices (38) in the majors, playing for a sixth-place Cincinnati Reds team that stole 289 bases (2nd, NL) and collected 185 sacrifices (4th, NL). Bob Bescher's 81 stolen bases in 1911 would not be surpassed in the senior circuit until 1962 when Maury Wills stole 104. Despite the fact that official caught stealing statistics are unavailable for the 1911 season, it has been reported that Bescher was caught stealing only three times.

While three National League teams stole over 200 bases, the four first division teams in the AL stole over 200 as well: second-place Detroit (276), Philadelphia (226), third-place Cleveland (209), and fourth-place Chicago (201). Two second division junior league teams also surpassed the 200 steal barrier: sixth-place New York (269) and seventh-place Washington (215). Cobb led the circuit in steals with 83, followed by Washington's Clyde Milan (58). On April 18, Cobb stole home on the front end of a double steal in the first inning versus Cleveland. Detroit won, 5–1. Again, on May 1 he stole home against Cleveland as the Tigers won, 14–5. On July 12, with Philadelphia's southpaw Harry Krause on the bump, Cobb stole second, third, and home on consecutive pitches. This daring basestealer stole second and third despite a perfect throw by catcher Ira Thomas.

Both leagues were replete with terrific basestealing accomplishments in 1911. The most exceptional feat was perhaps accomplished by player-manager Hal Chase's New York Highlanders. However, contemporary accounts of the game were not impressed because it was garnered against the worst team in the American League, who played like bushers. On September 28 New York stole fifteen bases in an 18–12 win over St. Louis. Chase and Birdie Cree stole four bases apiece and the Highlanders stole seven cushions off catcher Jim Stephens in two innings before he was mercifully removed from the game. This contest featured an abundance of walks and errors and the *New York Times* criticized both teams for their incompetent play and declared in its unforgiving headline on the following day: "YANKS AND BROWNS IN BASEBALL FARCE: Hilltoppers Win Worst Game of Season with Few Persons Viewing the Travesty."[55] Prince Hal, the Highlanders skipper, was many things including a corrupt, devious human being, and perhaps the greatest glove man who ever guarded the gateway station. But Chase was also an excellent basestealer, pilfering 363 bags during his fifteen-year career, including 243 during his first eight seasons from 1905 to 1912.

Leading the AL in sacrifices was Jimmy Austin of St. Louis, a switch-hitting third baseman with excellent wheels, who could move a runner over with the best of them. He had 34 sacrifices during the campaign and 278 (18th all-time) during his career. Austin was enthusiastic about the game and would instill his team with energy when needed, helping him earn the nickname "Pepper" during his rookie year with the 1909 New York Highlanders. The five-foot-seven-and-a-half-inch, 155-pound, sparkplug batted .246 lifetime and stole 244 bases, including a total of 163 during his first six seasons as he stole 30, 22, 26, 28, 37, and 20. How fast was Jimmy Austin? To raise money for Doc Powers, a well-liked

Athletics catcher who died shortly after Opening Day 1909, a special day was put together on May 30 at Shibe Park where Athletic players competed against players from various clubs in special events with the proceeds going to Powers's family. Austin, a 29-year-old rookie in 1909, won the 100-yard-dash beating out several speedsters, including 21-year-old Harry Hooper who would steal 375 bases during his career.

The Chicago Cubs' Heinie Zimmerman and Al Kaiser both stole home in the seventh inning versus Brooklyn on June 7. During the 1911 campaign the Cubs stole home seventeen times, an achievement that was matched by the 1912 Giants and surpassed by the 1912 Yankees, who stole home eighteen times, establishing the all-time record.

On June 10, Bobby Byrne stole second, third, and home in a single inning versus Brooklyn. Byrne was hugging first base, but anxiously scheming to pilfer the second sack, and Clarke was edging off third. They conspired to engage in larceny at the same moment in time and the double steal was successful. While Brooklyn catcher Bill Bergen argued the safe call at home with the plate umpire, Byrne surreptitiously stole third, much to the consternation of Bergen who was already hot. Dots Miller walked to put runners on first and third. And then they pulled off the second double steal of the inning. The Pirates purloined six sacks in the five-run sixth inning on their way to a 9–0 rout.

On August 4, 1911, Germany Schaefer, baseball's playing comedian, stole first base while playing for the Washington Senators. Schaefer had already secured his place in baseball's history for calling his shot against Chicago's Doc White on June 24, 1906, to win the game for Detroit with a two-run, pinch-hit homer that cleared the left-field wall. He reportedly slid into every bag as he made his way around the diamond and informed the spectators that the performance for the day had concluded when he dusted himself off at home plate. What made Schaefer's called shot so impressive was that he was not a prodigious slugger like Babe Ruth. In fact he had only accumulated a handful of homers when he called his shot and hit nine during his career. He was built solidly at 5'9", 175 pounds, had strong shoulders and good wheels, stealing 201 bases during his career. When he stole first base there was no rule against such a play and it was intended to be strategic and not comedic, to push across a run and propel his team to victory. It was scorchingly hot that day at Comiskey Park and the contest was tied in the ninth inning. With Clyde Milan dancing off the midway, Schaefer laid down a bunt, intending to sacrifice, and when the White Sox unsuccessfully tried to catch Milan sliding into third, Schaefer was safe at first base with a knock. Kid Elberfeld, who was once described as "the dirtiest, scrappiest, most pestiferous, most rantankerous [sic], most rambunctious ball player that ever stood on spikes," stepped into the batter's box.[56] Schaefer stole second, hoping to draw a throw that would allow Milan to scamper home. However, Fred Payne, the White Sox's catcher, did not throw through and held the ball. Elberfeld popped out and Doc Gessler struck out, decreasing the chances of scoring a run. Now, Schaefer edged off second, but did so towards the first base bag on the right side of the second sack and then stole first base. The Sox manager, Hugh Duffy, had seen enough and vigorously argued with the umpire. While Duffy was arguing, Schaefer made his way for second and persuaded Payne to make the throw. Now the wily Schaefer was in a rundown and he believed that Milan, a man who possessed great wheels, would be able to cross the plate safely. A bang-bang play at the plate went against the Senators and the ploy backfired. Now it was the Senators turn to protest, arguing that there were ten men on the field for Chicago, counting Duffy. In the eleventh inning, Milan scored on a botched double play attempt to give Washington the victory. Officially, Schaefer's steal of first was not a stolen base. The umpire, Tommy Connolly, insisted that Germany had every right to go from second to first, but the official scorer only rewarded him one stolen base during that sequence when he pilfered the second base bag. Schaefer was always trying to get around the rules and once played the final few innings of a game in his raincoat, making the umpires red with anger.

The 1911 New York Giants literally began the season on fire. They opened the championship season with two losses to Philadelphia and after losing the second game, 6–1, on April 13, they were a homeless team by the following morning. That night at the Polo Grounds, the ballpark caught fire, perhaps because of a discarded cigarette left in the wooden stands. One of the most stunning fires in New York City history burned throughout the early hours of the next day, with flames as high as 100 feet in the air. The Giants played their home games at Hilltop Park until June 28, when the partially rebuilt Polo Grounds reopened. The story about how the 1911 Giants stole the pennant has been largely forgotten with the passage of time. When Frank Graham wrote his insightful 1952 book *The New York Giants: An Informal History of a Great Baseball Club*, he entitled the ninth chapter "A Pennant Is 'Stolen.'"[57] How actually did the Giants steal the flag? Did McGraw steal a sign at a crucial time or steal players? Not actually. This Giants outfit with young legs stole bases on straight steals, double steals, triple steals, steals of home and steals that made the opposing manager mad. They stole 347 bases, the most in the modern era. The infield had Fred Merkle (49 steals), Larry Doyle (38 steals), Art Fletcher (20 steals), and Buck Herzog (26 steals with Boston and 22 with New York). The outfield had fleet footed fly chasers Red Murray (48 steals), Fred Snodgrass (51 steals), and Josh Devore (61 steals). Coming off the bench they had the fast Beals Becker (19 steals).

The Deadball Era was a time when managers took control of the game, telling players when to hit, steal, bunt, take pitches or throw to first. But Fred Snodgrass insisted that McGraw allowed the players to run their own game most of the time, they had signals between themselves, and forged their own destiny, with McGraw's supervision and implementation of his small ball philosophy. The widely held belief that McGraw made every decision and called every play was "ridiculous," according to Snodgrass. Decisions about when to steal, hit-and-run, bunt-and-run, implement the double steal or triple steal, lay down a sacrifice bunt or squeeze bunt, were largely decided by the players. Lawrence Ritter interviewed Snodgrass, a nine-year big leaguer who stole 212 bases, for his magnificent book *The Glory of Their Times*. Snodgrass insisted that McGraw rarely used signs and when he did they were simple.[58] The Giants players were taught how to play baseball the right way, they didn't need to be told what to do once the battle began. Rogers Hornsby said, "When you train under most managers you merely get yourself in good physical condition. When you train under McGraw, you learn baseball."[59] Players were expected to know how to play the game the right way and how to execute the fundamentals, such as hitting the cutoff man, throwing to the right base, bunting, baserunning, and sliding. Snodgrass said that the two most important words for a ballplayer that encapsulated the way the game was played were "think" and "anticipate."[60] McGraw had players on his team who fit his small ball system. His failure to compile a great World Series record was partially due to the fact that the American League teams simply had better players. McGraw's men were mainly overachievers who got the most out of their ability.

The belief that McGraw allowed his players to run their own game was not universally held. Christy Mathewson insisted that McGraw gave orders for every aspect of a ballgame, that he made the players act like robots in a mechanical fashion, and they were forced to act like puppets, while the puppet master, McGraw, pulled the strings. It was Mathewson's opinion that players did not take matters into their own hands and improvise because they were not taught to.[61] Considering the Giants' aggressive nature, particularly on the bases, this view may have been misguided. However, McGraw himself admitted that in the early 1920s players were no longer taking the initiative and that ballplayers were told what to do by the skipper and were not good at thinking for themselves. McGraw began to take more control of a game with the passage of time. Perhaps Mathewson was frustrated because McGraw called the pitches and took the "initiative" and "improvisation" out of his own hands.

In F.C. Lane's terrific book *Batting: One Thousand Expert Opinions on Every Conceivable Angle of Batting Science*, McGraw provides many of his observations about the game. Concerning foot speed, McGraw said, "Fast base running and good sliding are great helps to hitting. This is the only way to make hits count for their full value."[62] As a member of the Baltimore Orioles, the large pitchers on the opposing teams would laugh at their small hitters, "But they presently began to laugh out of the other corner of their mouth, for we bunted the ball and they were so big and cumbrous they fell all over themselves. We got to first base time after time and then proceeded to make life miserable for them on the bases."[63] McGraw also said, "Most ball games are won in a single inning. Sooner or later by one move or another, you are able to launch an attack where it counts and by one vigorous assault win the game. A steady pounding away at the line and then an irresistible rush through the weakest place, that's the system."[64] McGraw held the similar view as Hugh Fullerton, who believed that ballplayers did not take the initiative and waited for the manager to direct them. Baseball had become a "machine proposition" and the managers did the thinking for the players. This was largely because ballplayers who did run the bases aggressively had low stolen base percentages, which convinced managers to play it safe and not to push the envelope.[65] Concerning the batting order, McGraw said, "A slow footed runner ... will often cripple an attack." He preferred leadoff hitters that had speed and patience; the two-hole hitter should also have good wheels and the ability to bunt and execute the hit-and-run; and then the next two hitters should possess power and the ability to drive in the table-setters.[66]

Decades later the Gas House Gang Cardinals would gain notoriety for their dirty uniforms. But in 1911 the Giants tore their uniforms to shreds with all the basestealing and sliding they did. McGraw recalled, "On one trip west we arrived in Chicago with a club in rags and tatters. Every player on the club had slid out of the seat of his pants. We had to telegraph (back to New York) for new uniforms." McGraw continued, saying that Josh Devore had ripped open his pants one day while sliding into second. So that it would not offend the spectators and cause embarrassment to Devore, the Giants players had to surround him as he exited the field.[67]

The Giants were in fine form on April 17, stealing four cushions in a 3–1 win over Brooklyn. "General McGraw" led his forces on a "successful invasion" of Washington Park on April 29 in a game that exhibited the exhilarating, daring, and perhaps reckless baserunning of the Deadball Era. Christy Mathewson was not at his best, allowing ten hits and three runs in the 7–3 New York triumph. But things could have been worse if not for Brooklyn's "foolish" baserunning.[68] The Giants' aggressive baserunning paid off in the opening chapter when they pushed across four runs, one of them being tallied when Larry Doyle scored from second on a Texas Leaguer to shallow center field. In the bottom of the first with one out, Brooklyn shortstop Bert Tooley hit a double to center field that sailed over Fred Snodgrass's head. Then Jake Daubert stepped into the box and hit a fly ball to left-fielder Josh Devore, who had been beaned in the top of the inning. Devore was most likely feeling the affects of the pitched ball that had hit him in the head, because he stumbled under the fly ball and then dropped it. Tooley had remained close to the bag, anticipating that the ball would be caught, and perhaps readying himself to tag up and advance to third. When he saw Devore's miscue and the ball lying on the ground, he advanced to third, but then was unsatisfied with that outcome and came running towards home plate where he was an easy out. On the scorecard the out was recorded 7–5–2.

In the top of the second, it was the Giants turn to run themselves out of an inning. Doyle was thrown out at third trying to steal. And then Brooklyn's catcher Bill Bergen threw out Murray "a moment later." In the last of the fourth, Daubert hit a bloop to left that fell safely on the grass and then was thrown out easily by right fielder, Murray, when he tried to advance to third on John Hummel's single.[69]

Cy Young of Boston and Mathewson of New York faced each other in the second game of a doubleheader at South End Grounds on September 12, as the Giants prevailed, 11–2. Young was 44 years old and pitching in his final major league season. He was hit early and often and when Mathewson and Devore pulled off a double steal in the second inning, the aging veteran was pulled from the game. Mathewson stole home on the play, the first of two in his career. New York stole six bases in the game, including two by Doyle. The Giants entered the ninth inning with a comfortable 9–2 lead as they prepared to take both ends of the doubleheader. But McGraw's men were not content as they continued to pulverize the bloody carcass that stood in their way. Buck Herzog opened the ninth with a double and advanced to third on pitcher Lefty Tyler's throwing error that allowed Art Fletcher to reach the gateway station. Herzog played for Boston in 1910 and for 79 games in 1911 before being traded to the Giants, where he had started his big league career in 1908 and 1909. He had an acrimonious relationship with McGraw, but perhaps he hated Boston's skipper Fred Tenney even more. The combative infielder was pacing the 1911 Rustlers with a .310 batting average before Tenney accused him and Doc Miller, their right fielder, of not putting forth their best effort. Herzog went on strike and was soon traded back to New York in a deal that brought Hank Gowdy and Al Bridwell to Boston. When Herzog was standing on the third base cushion he wanted to push the envelope regardless of the score, and he stole home as a bewildered and beaten Boston aggregation gazed upon him. Doc Crandall tallied the final run with a homer over the right field fence.

Also on September 12, Brooklyn destroyed Philadelphia, 11–6, at the Baker Bowl. The Superbas had two sacrifice bunts in the game and one sacrifice fly. Their three- and four-hole hitters, 23-year-old Zack Wheat and 21-year-old rookie third baseman Red Smith, laid down sacrifices in this contest. Hans Lobert, the speedy three-hole hitter for the Phillies, laid down one sacrifice. During the Deadball Era it was not unusual for power hitters or cleanup men to lay down sacrifice bunts. Furthermore, it was the position players, not the pitchers, who laid down the vast majority of sacrifice bunts. During the previous campaign on August 27, 1910, Red Killefer, a weak-hitting second baseman for Washington, established a major league record by collecting four sacrifices during the first of two contests versus Detroit.

In a poorly played game at the Palace of the Fans on the 12th, Chicago needed four double plays to defeat Cincinnati, 3–2. Bob Bescher stole two bags for the Reds, while Jimmy Sheckard also swiped two cushions for Chicago and Joe Tinker and Solly Hofman had one apiece. Tinker, the Cubs' three-hole hitter, had a sacrifice bunt, while Eddie Grant had one for the losing outfit. There were six errors in the contest, including three by Cincinnati's backstop, Larry McLean. On September 18, Larry Doyle stole home twice and Fred

Merkle purloined the pay station one time. McGraw's men swiped eight bags in total as they won, 7–2, against Pittsburgh.

In the 1910 World Series the Philadelphia Athletics with catcher Ira Thomas behind the dish were able to curtail the running game of the Chicago Cubs, a team that had run wild over Detroit during previous years. In 1911, Connie Mack's team won their second consecutive world championship and held the Giants to only three steals, two by Doyle and one by Herzog. Philadelphia had four steals, two apiece by Collins and Barry. Philadelphia's catcher Jack Lapp threw out four Giants runners trying to steal in game three. McGraw had intended to bunt all day and every day against Philadelphia's third baseman, Frank Baker, and then intimidate him with spike high slides. In many ways, McGraw was signaling a change in strategy with that statement because while he loved utilizing the hit-and-run and stolen base, he was not fond of the sacrifice bunt. In fact the Giants finished last in the National League in sacrifice hits from 1912 to 1915 and in 1911 they finished sixth. When Ty Cobb had famously spiked Baker in 1908, during Baker's introductory campaign in the big show, the *Detroit Free Press* called him a "soft-fleshed darling" for complaining. This reputation stuck with him during his first few seasons and McGraw was out for blood in the 1911 series. Snodgrass edged off second in the sixth inning of the opening game on October 14 and then took off for third when Merkle waved at a ball in the dirt to end his at-bat. The throw reached Baker at third ahead of the runner. Snodgrass slid, spikes high, tearing open Baker's left arm and knocking the ball out of his glove. New York won the opening game, 2–1, thanks to Devore's RBI-double in the seventh. A sacrifice bunt proved crucial in the only run scored by Philadelphia. The Athletics won the series, four games to two, and Baker batted .375 with two homers, which earned him his nickname, "Home Run." In game three, Snodgrass again spiked him, but this time he held onto the ball. Baker told a Philadelphia reporter that he was spiked "intentionally," and Snodgrass "acted like a swell-headed busher."[70] In addition to his ability to slug the ball a great distance, Baker was a solid small ball player. He stole 235 bases during his thirteen-year career, including a career high of 40 in 1912. He was also credited with 153 sacrifice hits and during three seasons from 1909 to 1911 he had 80.

New York committed sixteen errors in the series, while the Athletics had ten, including three apiece by Collins and Barry. Philadelphia's 1.29 ERA was superior to New York's 2.83. Neither team ran the bases effectively: Philadelphia had a 40 percent basestealing average, but that was considerably better than New York's abysmal 25 percent basestealing average as they went 3 for 12 in stolen base attempts. It was shocking for Gotham fans to witness their small ball juggernaut who stole 347 bases during the regular season be shut down in the autumn classic. The White Elephants had seven sacrifice bunts, while McGraw's Giants had only three. McGraw insisted that Philadelphia's middle infield combination of second baseman, Eddie Collins, and shortstop, Jack Barry, had exceptional teamwork and they were able to anticipate what the Giants would do, helping to curtail the running game. They were in McGraw's opinion, superior to Tinker and Evers, when it came to teamwork and executing the plays of the inside game.

Clyde Milan, Washington's speedy 5'9", 168-pound, left-handed hitting but right-handed throwing center fielder had struggled during his early seasons under the big tent. He batted .279 in 183 at-bats during his rookie campaign in 1907 and then in 1908 and 1909, playing 130 games during each season, he batted .239 and .200. What really frustrated Milan was when he was thrown out stealing and then a slower runner would steal a base off the same catcher. He stole only 8, 29, and 10 bases during his first three seasons, low numbers for a burner like Milan. Milan had a habit of running on the second pitch and he would slide right into the tag. When Jimmy McAleer became the skipper in 1910, Milan became schooled in the proper basestealing techniques, utilizing the hook slide, and breaking old habits such as stealing on the second pitch, which made him an easy target since a pitch out was often called. McAleer also helped put "The Big Train" back on the tracks in 1910; in his third big league season Walter Johnson went 13–25 with a 2.22 ERA in 1909. In 1910 he was allowed to pitch more innings, improving to 25–17 with a 1.36 ERA, the first of ten consecutive seasons he would win twenty or more games. Cliff Blankenship, a weak-hitting little-used backup catcher, who became injured in 1907, was dispatched out west to scout Milan and purchase his contract from Wichita of the Western Association. Afterwards, he traveled to Idaho and signed Johnson. This outstanding scouting trip yielded a sensational pitcher and a solid center fielder that combined to play thirty-seven seasons for Washington.

Milan batted .279 in 1910 and stole 44 bases, an increase of 34 over the previous season's total. By 1911 he was a .300 hitter, batting .315 with 58 steals. For three consecutive seasons from 1911 to 1913, he batted over .300 with averages of .315, .306, and .301, respectively. The speed game was clicking on all cylinders by 1912 as he won the AL stolen base title with 88 bags and then took the crown the subsequent year with 75. He batted a career high of .322 in 1920 and his sixteen-year major league career with Washington ended after the 1922 campaign with a .285 lifetime batting average, a .353 on-base percentage, 495 stolen bases, and 188 sacrifice hits. He scored over one hundred runs in both 1911 (109) and 1912 (105) and had a total of 1,004 during his career. Milan's foot speed was a strength in the field as well; playing what Clark Griffith believed was the shallowest center field in the majors.

If the 1911 Giants stole the flag, perhaps the same thing could be said about the 1912 outfit. McGraw's team finished with a 103–48 record with four more wins than the previous season. They stole 319 bases, which ranks third in the modern era, and also ubiquitously utilized the hit-and-run with effective precision throughout the campaign. Their sixteen-game winning streak ended on July 4, as their record stood at 54–12, far better than the nearest competitors. The Giants were truly a team, working together for a singular goal, executing the fundamentals and the various plays concocted and perfected by McGraw. There were no future Hall of Famers among the everyday players. Yet, they led the senior circuit in batting average (.286), on-base percentage (.360), runs scored (823), home runs (47), and hit-by-pitches (69). The 823 runs scored were the most in the National League since 1899 and the 69 hit batsman was 21 more than the team who ranked second in that category. Bescher won the NL stolen base crown (67) as the fourth-place Reds stole 248 bases during their first season at Redland Field. Max Carey of Pittsburgh finished second in steals (45), followed by Snodgrass (43) and Murray (38) of New York. Third-place Chicago had the most sacrifice hits in the National League with 182. Carey collected the most sacrifice hits in the majors (37), while Duffy Lewis of Boston led the junior circuit with 31.

The American League stole 247 more bases than the National League in 1912, 1,823 versus 1,576. With player-manager Jake Stahl leading the way, Boston took the flag with a 105–47 record as the Sox played their first season in Fenway Park. Tris Speaker, the Red Sox's left-handed-hitting center fielder, led the way, ranking third in the league in batting average (.383), first in on-base percentage (.464), third in slugging percentage (.567), second in runs scored (136), third in hits (222), first in doubles (53), and tied for first in homers (10). His 52 stolen bases ranked fourth in the league and was a career high. Speaker stole 436 bases during his twenty-two-year Hall of Fame career. Furthermore, he is ranked 10th all-time with 309 sacrifice hits. Tris garnered eleven or more sacrifices during eighteen seasons and had a career high of 28 in 1926 with Cleveland, which was tied for third in the junior league. He played a remarkably shallow center field, believing that more balls fell in front of the outfielders than sailed over their heads. In April of 1918 he executed two unassisted double plays at second base, catching a low liner in the shallow depth of the outer garden and then beating the runner to the second sack. It was reported that he was involved in a double play at the second sack as the pivot man at one time during his career.

Five American League teams stole over 200 bases in 1912: Detroit (277), Washington (273), Philadelphia (258), New York (247), and Chicago (213). Fourth-place Chicago led the majors with 211 sacrifice hits and they were followed by fifth-place Cleveland who had 208 and third-place Philadelphia who had 201. While Milan took the AL stolen base crown, Collins (63) and Cobb (61) finished second and third, respectively.

While Rickey Henderson is the undisputed king of thieves, Ty Cobb stole the most bases during the Deadball Era. But the greatest small ball player of all-time is most likely Eddie Collins. Collins ranks 8th all-time with 741 stolen bases and first all-time in sacrifices with 512. Eddie was a highly intelligent, supremely confident, fiercely competitive second baseman who had phenomenal defensive skills and offensive prowess as a left-handed place hitter. This exceptional fielder led American League second baseman in fielding average nine times. At the bat, he was a skilled place hitter, who possessed extra-base hit power. Collins was a cerebral player who used his Ivy League education to steal bases. He was not exceptionally fast like Clyde Milan, but he studied the pitchers incessantly. Collins analyzed how they held the ball when throwing different pitches. This way he knew when the pitcher was throwing a breaking ball, which is easier to steal on than a fastball because of its erratic movement which may be difficult for the catcher to handle and its slower speed. He studied what moves they used in different situations and while most basestealers focused on a pitcher's hands, Collins gazed intently at their feet and hips. It was the opinion of Rube Bressler that Collins was the smartest man to ever step between the white lines in a big league ballpark, while Cobb was a close second. Others have called Collins the greatest bunter to ever play the game; the greatest hit-and-run man; the best sign-stealer; the best player of the inside game; the best teammate; and the best defensive second baseman to ever step upon the field. John McGraw called him a "superb" all around player and wrote in his autobiography, "Rare are the occasions when Collins does not anticipate the play. To cross him is almost impossible. And he is just as forceful on the offensive as on the defensive."[71]

Eddie had fourteen seasons with twenty-one or more sacrifices. Despite his exorbitant number of sacrifice hits, he never led the AL in that category, and only finished second one time in 1923, when he accumulated 39 sacrifices as Roger Peckinpaugh garnered 40 to pace the circuit. Collins played for excellent teams for much of his career and also for teams that compiled large numbers of sacrifice hits. His first season where he saw significant playing time was in 1908, which was also the first season when sacrifice flies were counted as sacrifice hits. For twenty of his twenty-five seasons (80 percent) he played for a team that was ranked first, second, or third in sacrifices.

The 1,823 stolen bases accumulated by American League teams in 1912 was the highest number in either league during the Deadball Era. Stolen base totals would decline the following year in the American League and remain unchanged in the National League, and then drop precipitously by the end of the decade. Naturally, there was an abundance of eye-opening basestealing activity in 1912. Detroit defeated Chicago, 10–1, on April 16 as Sam Crawford garnered a theft of home on a double steal. On May 1, Ty Cobb stole home in the first inning, but the Tigers lost to the White Sox, 5–2. The Giants executed a successful triple steal (Buck Herzog, Tillie Shafer, and Chief Meyers) on May 3, but fell to Philadelphia, 8–6, in ten innings at the Polo Grounds. The *New York Times* teased its readers by insisting that something happened that probably will not occur again for "many moons." And then wrote: "If you insist on knowing, the Giants ripped off a triple steal. The triple steal business is about as scarce in the National pastime as whip sockets on automobiles."[72] George "Peaches" Graham, the Phillies catcher, was victimized for six steals, including three by Shafer and two by Meyers.

Graham was also behind the dish for the Phillies when New York stole nine bases on May 4 as McGraw's team won, 4–3. Their thievery helped propel them into the win column as they stole home twice, each time on a double steal. It was a horrendous day for the Phillies third baseman, Hans Lobert, who broke his kneecap chasing after a foul ball. On May 27, in a 6–2 win over Brooklyn, New York's pitcher Red Ames stole home on the front end of a double steal in the fifth inning. The *New York Times* declared that Ames's theft should be "perpetuated in bronze" and before this ball game "the best running Ames ever did was to catch a train."[73]

Clyde Milan stole five bags on June 14, including one of home. He accomplished his work in three innings as the surging Senators won their fifteenth straight game, with each victory coming away from Griffith Stadium. The Giants were in Boston on June 20, and emerged victorious in a wild 21–12 game. Both teams combined for 34 hits and New York stole eleven bases, four by Devore. Detroit celebrated the 4th of July with a 9–3 win over St. Louis in game one; Cobb stole

Eddie Collins (left) and Ty Cobb possessed a superb baseball intellect and used their brains to master the inside game with its prevailing small ball philosophy, which was ubiquitous during the Deadball Era. Cobb was a fearless basestealer, who terrorized the opposition by running the bases with reckless abandon, stealing sacks because of his great foot speed. Collins, meanwhile, did not have blazing speed but relied on his terrific ability to read pitchers. He outsmarted the opposition, instead of outrunning them. Collins ranks first all-time with 512 sacrifice hits and eighth with 741 steals. Cobb garnered the fourth most steals (897) and is ranked twelfth in sacrifices (291). While Collins is arguably the greatest small ball player of all-time — excelling as a baserunner, basestealer, bunter, hit-and-run man, and place hitter — it could also be argued that Cobb was the greatest small ball practitioner. (George Brace photograph).

second, third, and home in the fifth inning as he collected his fifth steal of home during the campaign. New York Highlanders pitcher Jack Warhop stole home on July 12. He was one of four pitchers to steal home during the season. Gavy Cravath's 11th inning steal of home on July 18 propelled the Phillies to a 9–8 win over the Cubs. The Phillies ended their five-game series in Chicago with a 14–2 rout on the 20th as Sherry Magee garnered two thefts of home. Also on July 20, the Highlanders pinch-runner Ray Caldwell stole home in the ninth to tie the game versus Cleveland. They won, 4–3, when pinch-runner Pat Maloney stole second and subsequently scored the winning run. Maloney stole only three bags during his 25-game major league career with the 1912 Highlanders. Caldwell, a pitcher who occasionally played the outfield, tossed a shutout in the second game that day to lead New York to the doubleheader victory. Joe Jackson led Cleveland to an 8–3 win over New York on August 11 as he stole home in the first inning and then stole second, third, and home in the seventh stanza. Guy Zinn of the Highlanders also stole home twice on August 15. New York's wild baserunning produced eight steals and led to a 5–4 triumph over Detroit. Larry Doyle stole home on the front end of a double steal, and Fred Merkle swiped second on the back end, as they pulled off this play in the first inning of a 7–4 Giant win over Chicago on August 16. The Giants collected seven thefts and stole home twice. Eddie Collins stole six bags on September 11 versus Detroit, three in the seventh inning. Then he stole six again on September 22 in the first of two versus St. Louis. The most stolen bases in a game during the modern era is six, an accomplishment achieved five times. And Collins did it twice within a span of eleven days.

The Giants batted .270 in the 1912 World Series compared to Boston's .220; New York's 1.59 ERA was significantly better than Boston's 2.92 ERA. McGraw's men had fourteen more hits in the series and six more stolen bases. The Giants collected eleven stolen bases and were led by Devore who had four. The Red Sox, in contrast, stole only five bags as Stahl had two to lead the team. New York's 50 percent basestealing average was unexceptional, but it was a significant improvement over their 25 percent basestealing average in the 1911 World Series. Despite New York's dominance in several offensive categories, Boston secured the world title with a 3–2 win in the final game on October 16. Fred Snodgrass had made what Hugh Fullerton called a "miracle catch" in New York's 5–2 win on October 14.[74] Harry Hooper made his own miracle grab in the fifth inning of the final game, a bare handed catch up against the right-field wall that Francis Richter described in the *Reach Guide* as "the most wonderful catch ever seen in a World's Series."[75] The 1912 World Series was sloppy but entertaining as both clubs combined for twenty-eight errors. Fittingly, perhaps, an error by Snodgrass on an easy fly opened the door for Boston to score the tying and winning runs in the last of the tenth inning in the final game. If a fan merely perused the box score it may appear that the Giants baserunning hurt them in the finale as they pilfered only one sack in four attempts and lost the contest by a 3–2 score. However, two of the runners who were caught stealing were safe because of errors by the infielders.

Those fans who picked up the *New York Times* on November 3, 1912, had the privilege to read an article by American League umpire Billy Evans under the headline, "LITTLE INSIDE BASEBALL SHOWN IN WORLD SERIES: Number of Games So Limited That Teams Do Not Dare to Play Anything but Straightaway Ball." It was Evans's opinion that the inside game was "bunk" in a short series and what he called the "baseball dope," which is essentially scouting reports, analysis, or evaluations based on statistics or observations, were worthless in a short series. What the prognosticators and so-called baseball experts predicted before a series rarely came true. Very few of the players were at their best. The fans generally expect the players to do something special in the series. And at the very least they expect them to play good fundamental baseball: field their positions well, throw to the right base, make the routine plays, and execute the plays of the inside game, including small ball strategies. They expect them to be "constantly pulling some trick from the book of inside baseball." Evans insisted that the World Series games are just like every other game, except sometimes worse. He stumbled upon a man from Vancouver who had come to see the series and was woefully disappointed. In game two, on October 9, the two teams fought to a 6–6 tie that was called on account of darkness after eleven innings. New York was charged with five errors that led to four unearned runs. It was this game that the man from Vancouver witnessed. It was a game in which the fans received their "thrills" not from good plays, but from bad ones. The stranger told Evans it would have been simply an "ordinary" game if not for the "rotten" play. It was a damning assessment by a visitor from a foreign land, and this stranger insisted he saw better games back home. What he saw in game two, he could have seen in the bushes, and he was expecting more of the inside game. Evans insisted that World Series games very rarely meet expectations. He surmised it was most unfortunate that Snodgrass would be remembered for his muff, because if not for his fine catch in game six, Boston would have won the game and the series right there. Evans concluded his article by writing that managers and players alike readily admit that there is less inside play in the series than in the regular season. In the series managers are fearful of using the aggressive and daring style they employ during the regular season. They are careful and conservative. They are content when one run is scored despite the fact that if they utilized the same strategies that were used in the championship season they would have scored more. Not until the Giants were down three games to one, on the brink of defeat, did McGraw allow his team to run wild on the bases and they almost came back to capture the title as a result. Evans's final argument was that players put too much pressure on themselves, trying to capture the larger monetary reward, the winner's share, and they couldn't play their best as a result.

John McGraw had once remarked that for a team to achieve greatness they must win three pennants in a row. By applying that definition the 1911–1913 Giants were truly great as they took their third consecutive flag in 1913 with a 101–51 record. New York's pitching led the way once again behind Mathewson, Rube Marquard, and Jeff Tesreau as the staff's 2.42 ERA was the best in the senior league, far better than Pittsburgh who finished second in that category (2.90 ERA). The regular position players boasted one player who batted over .300 (Meyers, .312), but collectively they led the circuit in batting average (.273) and on-base percentage (.338). They led the major leagues in stolen bases for the third consecutive year (296), but finished last in the National League in sacrifices (112). Their 60.2 percent basestealing average was the second best in the loop behind seventh-place Cincinnati (61.1 percent) who finished second with 226 thefts in the NL. McGraw continued to antagonize the opposition, placing targets on his batters, as they easily led the league in hit batsmen for the third straight campaign.

After losing their third consecutive World Series in 1913, McGraw and his old buddies from the Baltimore Orioles held a reunion at a New York saloon. Wilbert Robinson was McGraw's teammate with the Orioles and was a coach with the Giants from 1911 to 1913. McGraw got a few drinks in him and accused Robinson of making some poor decisions on the coaching line in the final game. Robinson insisted that McGraw made the most mistakes of any Giant during the series. Robby exited the premises but not before throwing beer on McGraw; by the following season he was managing in Brooklyn. In one incident during the series, Snodgrass was on first, and he should have been anchored there because he had a charley horse and couldn't run well. McGraw signaled the steal sign to Robinson along the coaching line and Robinson, obeying orders, signaled it to Snodgrass. As a result he was an easy out at second base. However, the Giants field general insisted that this story was apocryphal, that he didn't flash a steal sign and perhaps Robinson misconstrued a motion as a sign. McGraw and Robinson had been feuding all season and the incident at the saloon was the final dagger to their friendship as they reportedly didn't speak to each other for the next seventeen years. But Robinson was not the only one criticizing McGraw's managing decisions in the 1913 World Series and for their downfall in the previous two fall classics. They said he didn't rely on scouting reports and made quick, impulsive, emotional decisions that were subjective and lacking in scientific or objective reviews such as scouting reports. They said he didn't use the sacrifice bunt to move runners into scoring position. But instead he kept using the hit-and-run and the stolen base and ran the Giants out of potential rallies. In McGraw's defense it should be noted that his wild baserunning helped them win three consecutive flags and as Billy Evans had written at the end of the 1912 World Series, perhaps it was best that the managers employ the same strategy they used during the regular campaign.[76]

The second-place Phillies, who were led by Grover Alexander on the hill and Gavy Cravath at the bat, stole only 156 bags, which was tied for the fewest in the majors, but they led the senior circuit in sacrifices (183). Otto Knabe, Philadelphia's tough second baseman, led the league with 41 sacrifices. Red Dooin, the Phillies' fearless backup catcher, who stood at five-foot-nine-and-a-half-inches and 165 pounds (at least one source says he weighed no more than 145 pounds during his playing career) was also the manager of the ballclub and had his team residing at the top of the National League for most of the first half. McGraw believed that this reflected poorly upon the league, saying in June, "If a team like the Phillies can win a pennant in the National League, then the League is a joke."[77] New York took over first place on June 30 by defeating Philadelphia, 11–10, in an ugly game that included intense bench jockeying between the two teams. Ad Brennan, a member of the Phillies pitching staff, attacked McGraw after the game, and left him bruised and bloodied after landing with both fists and kicking him while on the ground.

On May 22, McGraw made a trade that perhaps he would later regret, sending Josh Devore, Red Ames, and Heinie Groh along with $20,000 to Cincinnati for Art Fromme and Eddie Grant. Devore was in McGraw's doghouse for dropping too many fly balls in left field. He was replaced in the Opening Day lineup by George Burns, a 5'7", 160-pound, 23-year-old speedster who McGraw had taken a liking to. By mid-season he was batting out of the leadoff hole, and by year's end he had compiled a .286 batting average and 40 steals. Burns was daring and aggressive on the bases, perhaps to a fault sometimes, and was caught stealing 35 times during the campaign. However, the large number of caught stealing was not unusual, considering there were 1,576 stolen bases in the NL in 1913 and 1,240 caught stealing. Burns's 53.3 percent basestealing average was only slightly worse than the 56 percent league average. The 40 steals were fourth in the league behind Hans Lobert (41), Hap Myers of Boston (57), and Max Carey who led the circuit with 61. George Joseph Burns shouldn't be confused with George Henry Burns who played in the American League from 1914 to 1929. George Joseph Burns played his entire career in the National League with New York (1911–1921), Cincinnati (1922–1924), and Philadelphia (1925). He led the league in steals in both 1914 (62) and 1919 (40) and had 383 during his career. The 112 sacrifice hits he accumulated is a low number by Deadball Era standards. Burns was a right-handed hitter who swung a mighty club, 42 inches and 52 ounces. He led the NL in runs scored five times: 1914 (100), 1916 (105), 1917 (103), 1919 (86), and 1920 (115). Burns also led the league in walks during five seasons, including a career high of 101 with the 1923 Cincinnati Reds. It is hard to find someone who has spoken badly about Burns, as he was well-liked, unassuming, and soft spoken.

Connie Mack's "$100,000 infield" of Stuffy McInnis, Eddie Collins, Jack Barry, and Frank Baker helped them win their third pennant in four seasons in 1913 as the took the flag with a 96–57 record. Mack was in many ways the antithesis of McGraw: mild-mannered, patient, temperate, and humble. He managed in civilian clothing, wearing a suit and starched white shirt. A straw hat or another piece of headgear that was the custom of the day was fixed upon his head. Mack rarely argued with umpires but when he did he didn't explode with hatred like McGraw but sent word to the arbiter that he should meet him in front of the dugout to discuss the relative merits of his decision. He didn't embarrass his players in public either, and took them behind closed doors for their scolding. The Tall Tactician rarely raised his voice or cursed. He was a deeply religious man and treated his players with compassion and as individuals. Mack told his players about the goals he had for the team and suggested ways in which they could achieve these goals. It was subsequently up to the players to carry out the plan of attack. The players were allowed to think on their own and decide when to steal, bunt, or hit-and-run. The signs they flashed were mainly between themselves. Mack's primary focus during a game was positioning his outfielders, depending on who was at the bat. In 1913, Philadelphia won their third World Series title in four seasons, defeating New York, four games to one. They led the way in most of the important categories and tied New York with five stolen bases. Collins had three steals to lead both teams.

During the junior league's regular season, second-place Washington led the American League with 287 steals, but they had the fewest sacrifices in the majors (111). The Cleveland Naps, who finished in third place, led the majors with 208 sacrifices and their shortstop Ray Chapman won the first of three sacrifice hit titles with 45. Milan stole the most bases in the circuit (75) and was followed by his teammate Danny Moeller (62). Moeller had a seven-year big league career and stole 171 lifetime, including 150 from 1912 to 1915. However, the 5'11", 165-pound, switch-hitting outfielder was not a very productive batter, hitting .243 lifetime. In addition to Philadelphia (221) and Washington (287), the three worst teams in the league also stole over 200 bases: sixth-place Detroit (218), seventh-place New York (203), and last-place St. Louis (209).

Wilbur Good was not a burner, but he did steal 31 bags in 1914 and 104 during his eleven-year career. Perhaps his most famous stolen base came on April 15, 1913, when he stole home in the tenth inning to give the Cubs a 5–4 win over Pittsburgh at Chicago's West Side Grounds. He pinch-ran in the tenth inning with right-hander Howie Camnitz on the bump. The most unusual small ball accomplishment in 1913 came on May 21, when the Pittsburgh Pirates had four sacrifice bunts in a single inning, the eighth, in their 5–2 win over Brooklyn, in the Dodgers new ballpark, Ebbets Field. The four sacrifices set a major league record. Jim Viox singled in the eighth, and Honus Wagner laid down a sacrifice bunt and was safe at first on a throwing error by pitcher Pat Ragan. Viox, who played only five big league seasons and had a career high of fourteen stolen bases in 1913, scored on the wild throw and Wagner pulled up to second. Dots Miller laid down another sacrifice and third baseman Red Smith came running in onto the infield grass, reached down to grab the ball, and flung it wildly to first. John Hummel was at the first sack, relieving Jake Daubert, who was kicked out of the game in the opening inning for arguing a third strike call with arbiter Bill Klem. Hummel couldn't gather in Smith's throw, allowing Wagner to score and Miller moved up to second. Owen Wilson sacrificed Miller to third, 5–3 on the scorecard. "Rice," who was most likely Tommy Rice, wrote in the *Brooklyn Daily Eagle*, "That should have been a plenty for any team with a heart, but the Pirates were not satisfied." Bobby Byrne stepped into the box and laid down a squeeze bunt that worked to perfection and Miller scampered across the plate. However, Byrne was out at first. Rice wrote, "One single, solitary single: four successive sacrifices, on two of which double-barreled errors were made, and three unclean runs. Good morning, Mr. Undertaker!" Earlier Rice wrote that these types of errors are occasionally committed by all teams, but those who think they bring "zest" to the game are wrong. However, he tried to cheer up Brooklyn's populace by writing, "but there was no occasion for looking through a glass bottom darkly and drowning vain regrets." In the headline he made the reference to "Four Saddening Sacrifices." In total, Pittsburgh had five sacrifices and two stolen bases. Brooklyn stole three bags, including two by their 22-year-old center fielder, Casey Stengel.[78]

On June 11, Ivy Olson of Cleveland stole home in the top of the 15th to break a 5–5 tie versus Boston. Another run was scored when Jack Graney also stole home. It was the only game in major league history that teammates stole home in extra innings. St. Louis Cardinals pitcher Slim Sallee stole home on July 22, as they defeated Brooklyn, 3–1. Ty Cobb stole home in the fifth inning to tie the game versus the Red Sox on August 25. Detroit won, 6–5. On September 6, Eddie Collins tied a major league record when he stole home twice in Philadelphia's 9–2 win against Boston. He was the eighth and final player during the Deadball Era to accomplish this feat. The Athletics pilfered seven cushions and Jack Barry plated two runs with a double squeeze bunt, inspiring Edgar Wolfe to write in the *Philadelphia Inquirer* that "the regularity with which the Mackmen get away with this play on opponents is getting positively monotonous. It takes all the novelty out of the thing."[79]

George Stallings was a highly intelligent baseball man, who managed in civilian clothing, and led his 1914 Boston Braves on a ferocious comeback to take the flag in a miraculous fashion. On July 15 they resided in last place, eleven and a half games behind first-place New York, but then they won 61 of their final 77 games. The Braves embraced only a portion of the small ball philosophy. Finishing last in the major leagues with 139 steals, they were first in the majors with 221 sacrifices. Boston's small stolen base total was partially due to the fact that they didn't have a lot of fast runners. However, basestealing is not solely about speed and judging from the Braves low stolen base totals during Stallings's tenure as their manager, Boston's lack of running may have been a strategic decision. The Philadelphia Athletics (99–53) were their opponent in the World Series, a team that had a much more balanced small ball attack: 231 steals (3rd, AL) and 217 sacrifice hits (1st, AL). The Braves miracle run continued in the series, sweeping the heavily favored Athletics in four games. Just like the regular season they got great pitching from Dick Rudolph and Bill James, who each won two games. They were also the more aggressive team on the bases, stealing nine, while their opponent stole two.

For the sixth consecutive season, the American League stole more bases than the National League. The junior circuit had 222 more stolen bases than the senior circuit in 1914 and they also had 20 more sacrifice hits. Five American League teams stole at least 211 bases, including the New York Yankees, who led both leagues with 251. The Yankees were managed by Frank Chance and Roger Peckinpaugh as they finished the campaign tied for sixth place. The National League had only three teams with 200 or more steals, including the second-place New York Giants who led the circuit with 239.

George Burns won the stolen base crown in the National League with 62 bags, while Fritz Maisel took the American League crown with 74. Maisel was nicknamed "Flash" and the five-foot-seven-and-a-half-inch, 170-pound, right-handed hitting third baseman could fly around the bases. He purloined hassocks for a very high percentage (81.3 percent), being caught only 17 times during the campaign. In 1914 there were 1,657 stolen bases in the junior league and 1,370 were caught stealing for a 54.7 percent basestealing average. The Detroit Tigers led the circuit with a 57.8 percent basestealing average, while the Yankees finished third (56.8 percent) despite the fact that Maisel stole 29.5 percent of their bases and had a phenomenal stolen base percentage. In 1915 he stole 51 bags and was caught stealing only twelve times for an 81 percent average. Maisel stole 194 bases during his six-year big league career, but batted only .242.

The National League sacrifice hit crown belonged to Lee Magee of St. Louis (35), while Chick Gandil of Washington and Terry Turner of Cleveland (38) tied for the junior league title. Turner was known as "Cotton Top," and by 1914 the 33-year-old infielder was playing in his twelfth big league campaign. He played predominantly shortstop (741 games) and third base (604 games) during his seventeen-year career with the Pittsburgh Pirates (1901), Cleveland Naps or Indians (1904–1918), and Philadelphia Athletics (1919). His contemporaries considered him one of the best defensive infielders in the game. Turner batted .253 lifetime, with 256 steals and 268 sacrifice hits (26th all-time). He strongly believed in the inside game, insisting that winning teams are not composed of players who are mainly concerned with individual achievements. Teams that work together as a cohesive unit are the ones that are successful. Eschewing the customary feet first slide of the Deadball Era, Turner preferred to slide headfirst. When he slid feet first, the spikes would occasionally get caught, and he would injure his ankle. He admitted that the headfirst slide could also be perilous and he had several scars on his hands when he was spiked by opposing infielders. Turner was often out of the lineup during his career because of injury or illness. His aggressiveness on the basepaths led to several injuries. In Lawrence Ritter's *The Glory of Their Times*, Bill Wambsganss tells the story of how Turner gave him some bad advice. Turner informed Wambsganss that Ty Cobb was a terrific bunter and he better be alert down the third-base line. He told him that Cobb would "grit his teeth" when he would bunt, giving the infielders the impression that he was going to murder the ball. Wambsganss observed this "teeth-gritting business," and crept in, down the line, to guard against the bunt. Cobb double crossed the youngster, sending a scorching liner right at him. Wambsganss reflexively moved the glove in front of his face, not in an effort to catch the ball but out of self defense. And by "sheer accident" the ball slammed into his mitt.[80]

Perhaps the 1914 Boston Braves were able to achieve greatness and win twenty-five more games than the previous season because of the lower talent level in both leagues. This was because the insurgent Federal League became a major league caliber circuit with its wealthy backers and attractive salaries that lured many National and American League players. The Indianapolis Hoosiers took the FL flag in 1914 with an 88–65 record and led the circuit in both stolen bases (273) and sacrifice hits (223). Benny Kauff, an excellent thief who stole 234 bases in eight major league seasons, led the circuit in batting average (.370), on-base percentage (.447), runs (120), hits (211), doubles (44), and stolen bases (75). His teammate Bill McKechnie finished second in the circuit with 47 steals. Kauff led the Federal League in steals in 1915 as well (55), this time playing for the Brooklyn Tip-Tops. Brooklyn was a seventh-place outfit that led the circuit with 249 steals. Frank Graham wrote that Kauff was a "husky coal miner" and "obscure minor-leaguer" before signing with Indianapolis in 1914. Kauff was the biggest gate attraction in the league; one writer observed he is "the Ty Cobb of the Federal League." Cobb was not amused by that title and strongly regretted it.[81] After the Federal League disbanded, Kauff played for the New York Giants from 1916 to 1920. He batted .264 in 1916 with 40 steals and then hit .308 with 30 steals the following season. At first McGraw took a liking to Kauff because he was always thinking about baseball, which reminded the skipper of the old Baltimore Orioles players. But over time McGraw soured on him and realized his initial observations were wrong. McGraw wrote in his autobiography, "It was almost impossible, though, to get his mind off himself and on the team as a whole." McGraw added that Kauff was eager to be a star, but a true star emerges when the team is successful and the player works for the team's goals.[82] Kauff enjoyed the night life, dressed in flashy clothing, and was not frugal when it came to spending money.

There were several notable basestealing accomplishments in the National and American Leagues in 1914. On April 14, the Yankees emerged victorious over the Athletics, 8–2, at the Polo Grounds. New York stole seven bags, including two apiece by Edward Francis Sweeney, who was better known as Jeff, and the speed merchant Fritz Maisel. On April 30, Cleveland executed a successful triple steal (Jack Graney, Ivy Olson, and Fred Carisch) in the ninth inning to tie the game at three with St. Louis. The game remained tied through twelve innings until they could no longer proceed because of darkness. The Boston Red Sox pulled off their own triple steal (Harry Hooper, Duffy Lewis, and Tris Speaker) in the third inning versus Cleveland on May 28, but lost 5–2. Lewis stole a career high twenty-two bases in 1914, but was caught stealing thirty-one times for a pitiful 41.5 percent basestealing average. In the second game between the Athletics and Browns on July 11, Philadelphia also pulled off a triple steal during the eighth inning when Amos Strunk, Jack Barry, and pitcher Chick Davies each walked and then stole bags during the same pitch. Davies was a 22-year-old southpaw who was making his major league debut.

The Boston Red Sox (101–50) secured the American League flag in 1915 by two and a half games over Detroit (100–54). Then the Sox defeated the Philadelphia Phillies (90–62) in the World Series, four games to one. Bill Carrigan, the Boston skipper, was nicknamed "Rough," and he was a tough, scrappy, pugilistic, 5'9", 175-pound backup catcher who led the Red Sox to World Series titles in both 1915 and 1916. During the 1915 regular season Boston stole a major league low 118 bases and were caught stealing 117 times. However, their 265 sacrifices ranked second in the majors behind the Chicago White Sox (270). Likewise, Philadelphia's National League aggregation led by skipper Pat Moran did not run a lot, stealing only 121 bags, which was tied with second-place Boston for the fewest in the senior circuit. Their 181 sacrifices ranked fourth in the NL behind fourth-place Chicago (182), seventh-place Cincinnati (192), and the Boston Braves who led the league with 194. It wasn't entirely surprising that both the Phillies and Red Sox combined for three stolen bases in the World Series. In the 1916 World Series between the Red Sox and Robins there would be only two steals.

In 1915 stolen bases took a sharp decline, but the American League once again led the National League in thievery, 1,443 versus 1,194. However, the dip in both leagues was noticeable; a decline of 214 steals in the AL from 1914 to 1915 while the NL total dropped by 241. For the first time in National League history the team that accumulated the most steals in the circuit finished with less than 200. Fifth-place Pittsburgh had 182 steals to lead the league. Max Carey (36) edged out Cincinnati's Buck Herzog (35) for the stolen base crown. The combative Herzog stole 320 bags during his thirteen-year career but Carey stole more than twice as much, 738 steals in twenty seasons.

Carey, a switch-hitting leadoff man, utilized his speed with great success, leading the National League in stolen bases for ten seasons: 1913, 1915, 1916, 1917, 1918, 1920, 1922, 1923, 1924, and 1925. During those ten seasons when he led the NL in steals, his stolen base totals ranged from a low of 36 in 1915 to a high of 63 in 1916. Carey's career total of 738 stolen bases was a modern era National League record until 1974 when Lou Brock surpassed him. He studied the pitchers carefully to determine when was the best time to attempt a stolen base. For example, many spitball pitchers who loaded up the ball would never throw to first base and therefore this was an ideal time to steal a bag. It was also a difficult pitch for the catcher to control and throw out the runner. During the era which Carey played in, it was commonplace for basestealers to be caught stealing nearly 50 percent of the time. Carey, however, compiled some outstanding success rates: In 1922 he stole 31 consecutive bases and finished the season with 51 bags in 53 attempts for a 96.2 percent basestealing average. The league average that season was only 54.4 percent. In 1923 he again stole 51 bases, but was caught stealing only 8 times for an 86.4 percent basestealing average, which was well ahead of the league average of 55.6 percent.

In the American League, Ty Cobb stole an eye-opening 96 bases, which was a career high and was accomplished while playing for a Tigers team that led the majors with 241 steals. Cobb's 96 thefts would stand as the major league record in the modern era until 1962 when Maury Wills stole 104 bases. In addition to Detroit, the third-place Chicago White Sox (233) and the sixth-place St. Louis Browns (202) also stole over 200 bases. The 1915 campaign is the only season during the Deadball Era in which caught stealing totals are available for both the American and National League. The junior circuit not only stole more bases, but they were more effective, swiping bags at a 57.9 percent clip, while the senior league pilfered hassocks at a 54.5 percent clip.

Bob Fisher of the Chicago Cubs played his fourth big league season in 1915 and second as an everyday player as the team's shortstop, batting .287 with 9 steals and 20 caught stealing for a deplorable 31 percent basestealing average. He did compile 42 sacrifice hits to lead the NL and tie Ossie Vitt of Detroit and Buck Weaver of the Chicago White Sox for the major league lead. Vitt was a weak-hitting 5'10", 150-pound, third baseman who batted .238 with a .322 on-base percentage and 114 steals during his ten-year big league career. Since he wasn't much of a hitter, he knew he had to contribute to the team in different ways and his 259 career sacrifice hits ranks 32nd all-time.

Buck Weaver was once described by Nelson Algren as a "territorial animal ... who guarded the spiked sand around third like his life."[83] Weaver was infamous for getting involved in the Black Sox scandal of 1919. He did not participate in the intentional bad play and batted .324 in the World Series, but he knew about his teammates intentions to throw games and apparently did nothing about it. He played mostly shortstop during his career, batting .272 lifetime with 173 steals and 242 sacrifice hits (43rd all-time). He also led the American League in sacrifices in 1916. In 1920, the ninth and final season of his career before being blacklisted, he batted .331 with a .365 on-base percentage and a .420 slugging percentage. He was only 30 years old at the time and could have been one of the best small ball players statistically to ever step on the field if it wasn't for his dishonorable conduct in 1919.

Just as in previous seasons there were many notable basestealing accomplishments in

1915. On April 15, the Chicago White Sox executed a triple steal in the first inning versus St. Louis with Eddie Collins swiping home. Chicago won the contest convincingly, 16–0. Collins batted .332 with a .460 on-base percentage in his first season with the Pale Hose in 1915. His 46 steals ranked third in the junior league. On April 28, Detroit pushed across ten runs in the eighth inning of their 12–3 win over St. Louis. The Tigers outfield of Cobb, Crawford, and Bobby Veach pulled off a triple steal in the third inning. Cobb swiped home on the play and would do so six times in 1915. Hippo Vaughn, a 6'4", 215-pound, south-paw hurler, who had his second consecutive twenty-win season in 1915 for the Chicago Cubs, stole second and third as a pinch-runner in the fourth inning before being called out try-ing to pilfer home in a wild game between the Cubs and Pirates on May 3. On June 4, Cobb stole home in the ninth inning of Detroit's 3–0 win over New York. In the Tigers 15–0 win against the Red Sox on June 9, Cobb stole home in the third frame with southpaw Ray Collins on the hilltop. In total, Detroit had six steals in the game, including one by Donie Bush, a 5'6", 140-pound, switch-hitting shortstop, who batted .250 lifetime with a .356 on-base percentage, 406 steals, and 337 sacrifice hits (5th all-time). While Detroit "rode roughshod" over Boston, Washington defeated St. Louis, 4–1, on the day.[84] St. Louis's left-handed-hitting leadoff man, Burt Shotton, stole two of his 43 bases on the season. Shot-ton was burdened with various injuries during his career: poor eyesight and problems with his legs and back. Despite these limitations he was able to put together a solid big league career, thanks to his ability to outsmart the opposition. The skilled place hitter batted .271 lifetime with a .365 on-base percentage and 293 steals. From 1913 to 1916 he stole 43, 40, 43, and 41 bases, respectively, for a St. Louis Browns team that was always fighting to stay out of the cellar. He was not a good outfielder and he was not a complete small ball player. His 62 career sacrifice hits is an extremely low number. Again, on June 18, Cobb stole three bases as he was involved in one triple steal and two double steals versus Washington in a 5–3 victory.

Heinie Zimmerman stole 175 bags during his thirteen-year career with the Chicago Cubs and New York Giants. His most exciting stolen base may have come on June 24, 1915, with right-hander Bill Doak on the hill for St. Louis, as his steal of home with two outs in the last of the ninth sent the Cubs fans home happy with a 14–13 victory. On July 9, Chicago's American League outfit executed a successful triple steal and two double steals in their 5–1 win over Washington. Sometimes stolen base achievements seem extraordinary and almost unbelievable until you are aware of the circumstances that surrounded such a feat. Chicago White Sox pitcher Red Faber became the second moundsman to steal home in 1915, when he stole three bases in the fourth inning versus Philadelphia on July 14. The Sox were ahead 4–2 in the bottom of the fourth, but storm clouds were threatening and such an event may force the arbiters to cease activity before the contest became official. Faber was hit by a pitch and then in an effort to move the game along, he tried to get thrown out on the bases but failed, as the Athletics refused to cut him down as part of their disgraceful stalling tactics. The Sox won the game, 6–4, as the inclement weather never came their way. Fourth-place Washington stole 186 bags during the 1915 campaign and also led both leagues in stolen base percentage (63.7 percent). Eight of those steals came in the first inning versus Cleveland on July 19. Danny Moeller had three of his thirty-two thefts on the season during the initial chapter in the 11–4 win.

In 1916, runs scored declined in the National League for the fourth consecutive sea-son and the junior circuit scored 309 more runs than the senior league. For the eighth con-secutive year the American League teams had more stolen bases than the National League:

1,425 versus 1,328. The AL would lead the NL in steals for one more season before the Nationals ended the streak in 1918, a season that ended on Labor Day because of World War I. The American League was also accumulating more sacrifice hits than the Nationals, a streak that extended to six straight seasons in 1916, 1,537 versus 1,293. This would not be a streak that ended anytime soon. In 1930, after nineteen consecutive seasons in which the American League had led their rivals in sacrifices, the National League finally broke through, finishing with 34 more sacrifice hits.

The Brooklyn Robins, led by manager Wilbert Robinson, won the NL pennant in 1916 with a 94–60 record, finishing second in the league in steals (187) and first in sacrifice hits (203). Despite Brooklyn's solid sacrifice hit total, it was reported in Frank Graham's wonderful book *The Brooklyn Dodgers: An Informal History* that Robinson was upset when they couldn't move runners over early in the season. "That's the trouble with this ball club. We get men on and can't move them around because nobody on the club knows how to bunt but Daubert," said Robinson. Robinson insisted that when he played with the old Baltimore Orioles, he could bunt just as well as anyone on the club despite carrying a few extra pounds. And likewise he expected everyone on his team to be able to move a runner along with a successful sacrifice bunt. He even demonstrated to his players that he could still lay one down at the age of fifty-two because once you learn to bunt you never forget how its done.[85] Fourth-place New York led the circuit with 206 steals and Max Carey took the individual crown with 63.

Only two seasons removed from a pennant-winning team and three seasons removed from a world championship club, the Philadelphia Athletics were 54 and a half games off the pace in 1916 with a 36–117 record in American League competition. They finished seventh in the league in both steals (151) and sacrifices hits (158). The first-place Boston Red Sox (91–63) were very similar to their 1915 aggregation, in that they finished at the bottom of the major leagues in steals (129) for the second consecutive season, and they moved up one spot in sacrifices to lead both leagues with 238. Four American League teams had over 200 sacrifices, including the top three teams: Boston, Chicago (221), and Detroit (202). Sixth-place Cleveland also crossed the 200 mark (234), while two NL teams did so as well, including the third-place Boston Braves (202). Cobb took the AL stolen base title (68), followed by Armando Marsans (46) and Burt Shotton (41) of the fifth-place St. Louis Browns, who compiled the most stolen bases in the majors with 234.

Buck Weaver led both leagues in sacrifice hits with 44, while Max Flack, a 5'7", 148-pound, left-handed-hitting right fielder, led the NL with 39. Flack was a solid small ball player who stole 200 bases during his twelve-year big league career with Chicago in the Federal League and National League and the St. Louis Cardinals. In both 1914 and 1915 he stole a career high 37 bags with the Chicago Whales of the FL. Flack batted .278 lifetime with a .342 on-base percentage and 147 sacrifice hits.

Hans Lobert, the skilled small ball practitioner, who had joined the New York Giants in 1915, his fifth major league team, and batted .251 with fourteen steals, would never be the same after an exhibition game in 1916. The 34-year-old Lobert injured his left knee while sliding into the bag as the Giants took on Yale University in New Haven, Connecticut, on April 11. He was never the same after the injury, playing briefly in 1916, batting .224 in 76 at-bats with two steals, and then he batted .192 in 50 games and 52 at-bats in 1917, his final big league season. He also stole the final two bases of his career in 1917. The Giants lost their first eight games of the 1916 campaign and never recovered, finishing the season situated on the final rung of the first division with an 86–66 record.

Ray Schalk, the Chicago White Sox's diminutive 5'9", 165-pound (some sources say he was 5'7", 155 pounds) catcher was a daring, intelligent, hard-working, and aggressive player. He played seventeen of his eighteen big league seasons with the Pale Hose, batting .253 lifetime with a .340 on-base percentage and 177 stolen bases. Schalk stole two of his career high 30 bases on April 15, 1916, as the Sox defeated Detroit, 9–4. His thirty steals was a record for catchers until 1982 when John Wathan of the Kansas City Royals stole thirty-six.

The New York Giants emerged victorious on May 26, 12–1, over Boston despite the fact that Benny Kauff was picked off first three times. On June 22, the Giants lost their eighth extra-inning game of the season, 3–1, in eleven innings to Boston at the Polo Grounds. The *New York Herald* declared that Johnny Evers and pitcher Art Nehf starred for Boston in the "Warlike Contest." This was a hotly contested affair with McGraw and Rube Benton of the Giants "chased to the shade of the bench," for arguing with the arbiters, while Boston's Hank Gowdy and Fred Snodgrass were not so lucky and were forced to the clubhouse. This game was described as an "exceptional exhibition," with great pitching, fielding, "rare plays," clutch hitting, aggressive baserunning, and the final outcome being influenced by great basestealing. All the small ball statistics belonged to Boston: six stolen bases, including two by Evers, who was playing with a right arm that was badly injured. Rabbit Maranville, the team's shortstop and leadoff man, stole a career high thirty-two bases during the season and had one steal and one sacrifice bunt in this game. Evers and Maranville teamed up for an excellent double play in the sixth inning, 4–6–3. When Evers stole home on a triple steal in the eleventh inning to score Boston's final run it was described as "an unusual play and one not seen at the Polo Ground(s) in several years." Nehf started the eleventh inning with a single to left field and was sacrificed to second by Maranville. Evers slugged the ball to deep center for a double, scoring Nehf. Zip Collins walked and Pete Compton singled to load the bases and set up the triple steal. Hank Gowdy's stolen base in the third inning set up Boston's first score. The fine double play combination of Evers and Maranville pulled off a double steal in the third frame, but they were left stranded on the bases. The fact that New York didn't steal was partially influenced by the fact that they had only five baserunners in the game. The nameless scribe who covered the game for the *New York Herald* was quite impressed by each team's effort, writing that there was more "fight and spirit" by both teams than in any other game that had been played during the season. It was reported that Boston got the "breaks," but they made their own good luck with Nehf's terrific pitching, a superb defensive contribution with no errors, and an exceptional small ball performance.[86]

On June 27, the Cubs defeated the Pirates, 1–0, in the first of two thanks to Vic Saier's home run. Manager Joe Tinker's Cubs won the second game, 10–4, partially thanks to a successful squeeze play and three sacrifice bunts. Lee Magee of the New York Yankees stole twenty-nine bags in 1916, but on June 29 in a 5–0 win over Philadelphia he was thrown out three times. Earlier in the season on April 26, Fritz Maisel of the Yankees was also thrown out three times. On August 13, the St. Louis Cardinals stole eleven bases in five innings in game two versus Pittsburgh, while the Pirates stole three. Several of the Cardinals' steals were because of defensive indifference, but there was no rule at the time which forbade crediting a stolen base under such circumstances. The thievery by manager Miller Huggins's team did not produce a victory as the Pirates prevailed, 9–5, to split the doubleheader. Ty Cobb batted .371 in 1916, but failed to win his tenth straight AL batting championship as Tris Speaker dethroned him with a .386 average. He did win his fifth stolen base crown in 1916 and on August 23 he proved why he was, perhaps, the smartest player in the game. In Detroit's 10–3 triumph over Philadelphia he advanced from first to third on a single and when he caught third baseman Charlie Pick napping with the spheroid in his hand, he stole home. Outfielder Jimmy Johnston of Brooklyn stole twenty-two bags in 1916 and on September 22 he stole second, third, and home in an 11–1 win over St. Louis. Tim Hendryx of the Yankees stole four bases in 1916 in fifteen games. However, three of those steals came on October 4 in the first game of two against Washington. In Hendryx's eight-year big league career in which he played 416 games, he stole only 26 bases.

The 1916 World Series between the Boston Red Sox and Brooklyn Robins may have appeared to have been played conservatively, considering that both teams combined for only two steals, but the Robins were caught stealing three times and the Red Sox were gunned down on six attempts for the second consecutive fall classic. While basestealing was curtailed, a sacrifice bunt was the most important small ball activity in the series. Game two, won by Boston, 2–1, was decided in the fourteenth frame when the Red Sox got a walk, sacrificed the runner to second, and pushed him home on pinch-hitter Del Gainer's single. Both teams combined for sixteen sacrifice bunts, ten by Boston and six by Brooklyn. Left-handed-hitting fly chaser Duffy Lewis, who ranks 29th all-time with 264 sacrifices despite playing only eleven major league seasons, collected four sacrifice bunts for the Sox in the 1916 autumn classic. The Red Sox won the series, four games to one.

In 1914 the emery ball had been outlawed by American League president Ban Johnson, who was also a member of the National Commission, a three member governing body that ruled baseball until November 1920. However, the ingenious pitchers came up with more mischievous ways to get batters out by coming up with new pitches. In 1917 the shine ball was the pitch that had batters protesting to Ban Johnson that should also be outlawed. The shine ball was made smooth or slick on one side by using licorice, tobacco, slippery elm, paraffin, or talcum powder, which is what Eddie Cicotte preferred. On May 28, 1917, Johnson ruled against the hitters, and declared that the shine ball was legal. The use of the shine ball and other trick pitches kept batting averages down in 1917. The American League's collective batting average in early June was .234 and at season's end it stood at .248, the same number it had been during the previous two seasons. The National League teams batted at a .249 clip during the season, but scored 132 fewer runs than the junior league. Stolen bases declined by 157 in the junior circuit compared to 1916 and they declined by 183 in the senior league. Sacrifice hits increased in both leagues, by 194 in the American League and by 55 in the National League.

The New York Giants won the National League flag (98–56), their first since 1913, as they were able to lead the league with only 162 steals and their 151 sacrifice hits ranked seventh in the circuit. Fifth-place Chicago was the only team in the National League with over 200 sacrifices as they finished with 202. Pittsburgh's Max Carey won his third consecutive stolen base crown with 46 thefts. Charlie Deal, the Cubs third baseman, led the senior league with 29 sacrifice hits. During spring training the *Chicago Tribune* declared, "Sox should win flag unless stars are hurt."[87] Their prediction was prescient as the White Sox won the pennant with a 100–54 record, finishing nine games ahead of second-place Boston (90–62). The White Sox led by manager Pants Rowland led the major leagues in stolen bases (219) and finished third with 232 sacrifices. Third-place Cleveland stole 210 bags and had 262 sacrifices, which were both ranked second in the majors. The most eye-opening small ball statistic in 1917 belonged to the Boston Red Sox, who were managed by Jack Barry. During the previous two seasons when the Red Sox won the World Series, they had a high number of sacrifice hits and a low number of steals. This trend continued in 1917 as they finished last in both leagues with 105 steals and first in sacrifices with 310. The 310 sacrifices are the most by any major league team in the history of baseball, including the nineteenth century. Remarkably, the man who led the American League in sacrifices did not even play for the Red Sox. Ray Chapman, Cleveland's well-liked, gregarious shortstop, collected 67 sacrifice hits in 1917, which is a major league record. It could be argued that if Chapman had not died in 1920 because of a Carl Mays fastball, he could have been the all-time leader in sacrifice hits. He ranks 6th all-time with 334 sacrifices. He averaged a sacrifice every 3.1 games. Eddie Collins ranks first all-time with 512 sacrifices and he averaged a sacrifice every 5.5 games. The 5'10", 170-pound Chapman could also steal bases, swiping a career high of 52 in 1917 and 238 during his career. The 52 steals ranked third in the league behind Eddie Collins (53) and Ty Cobb (55).

In 1917, the Boston Red Sox's player-manager Jack Barry was only thirty years old and this former member of the Athletics' $100,000 infield batted a paltry .214 on the season. However, he led the team with 54 sacrifice hits in just 116 games, while Everett Scott (41) and Larry Gardner (40) were among the Sox who collected large sacrifice hit totals. During Barry's eleven-year big league career he batted only .243 with 153 steals, but he did the little things to help his team win. He was an excellent practitioner of the inside game; a great clutch hitter; a solid defensive player during his career at shortstop (877 games) and second base (339 games); and an outstanding bunter, executing the sacrifice, squeeze, or that rare play, the double squeeze, where runners would score from second and third on a bunt. His 284 sacrifice hits ranks 16th all-time. As Edgar Wolfe wrote in the *Philadelphia Inquirer* in 1913, a critic must look beyond the statistics to value this player, "his hits are always timely and his sensational fielding is something that cannot be computed in cold, soulless figures."[88] Barry played in the World Series four times with the Philadelphia Athletics (1910, 1911, 1913, and 1914) and once with the Red Sox (1915). His only season as a big league skipper was in 1917. Not surprisingly, Barry was considered a player's manager and relied on the input of his men, especially captain Harry Hooper, before making judgments. Under Connie Mack he had learned the importance of defensive positioning and the necessity for the players to communicate with each other on the field. Boston hitters were instructed to never swing at the first pitch, which was a rule that was rarely violated. However, the players were largely allowed to make their own decisions as far as when to steal, hit-and-run, or bunt. An occasional steal sign was flashed from the coach's box, but most of the signs were transmitted between the players. Paul J. Zingg wrote in his biography of Harry Hooper that Barry did not embrace Connie Mack's "intrusive managerial style," and thus adopted "a more laissez-faire manner."[89]

On June 1, 1917, Guy Morton of Cleveland outdueled Babe Ruth of Boston, 3–0, as he tossed a one-hitter. Ray Chapman and Braggo Roth stole home in the fourth inning of this game. Robert Frank Roth was a five-foot-seven-and-a-half-inch, 170-pound right fielder, who was loquacious and eager to entertain people with stories about himself, which helped him earn the nickname "Braggo." He stole 51 bases in 1917, a career high, and 190 during his eight-year big league career. Roth's six steals of home in 1917 tied a major league record. Roth was coveted by many major league teams during his career, but once he arrived at a destination he never stayed long, whether in the bushes or under the big tent because of his temperamental and arrogant attitude. Once he arrived on a new team the skipper would often sour on him. He began his final big league season at the age of 28 with the 1921 New York Yankees, batting .283 in 152 at-bats. But despite hitting for a .291 clip with a .395 on-base percentage, a .432 slugging percentage, and 24 steals in 36 attempts in 1920 for Washington, his legs began to cause him problems during the following season and his mouth also got him into trouble with the Yankees skipper, Miller Huggins. In 1923 he was playing for the Kansas City Blues of the American Association and despite batting .339 on August 3, he was dismissed from the club because of his "indifferent play." Roth just didn't care anymore and didn't run out ground balls or hustle while in the field. The only time he would bust it down to first was when he had a chance for a knock.[90]

Catcher Mike Gonzalez stole only 52 bases in a seventeen-year career playing for five teams. Perhaps his greatest steal came on June 11 when he had a game-ending steal of home in the fifteenth inning to give the St. Louis Cardinals a 5–4 win over Philadelphia. Joe Oeschger, the Phillies right-hander who compiled a 15–14 record on the season, was on the bump when Gonzalez stole home. The Cardinals had to claw back from an early four-run deficit in the first, as the Phillies pushed across four runs thanks in part to a stolen base and a sacrifice. They also had two singles in the inning, two walks, a fielder's choice and they benefited from an error by the opposition. The third-place Cardinals stole 159 bases during the season (2nd, NL) and three of them came on a triple steal versus Brooklyn in the fifth inning on June 14. Dots Miller swiped home on the play, while Walton Cruise and Tom Long also stole bases. St. Louis prevailed in the contest, 5–4.

In 1917, Hy Myers of Brooklyn stole only five bases in 120 games. Myers ran awkwardly with his hands down on his sides and on August 25 in game one versus St. Louis, he was thrown out trying to steal three times. The next time a National League player was thrown out three times in a game was in 1979 when Rodney Scott was the unfortunate victim.

The worst nightmare of any player who steals home materialized for Tris Speaker of the Cleveland Indians on September 1. In a game versus Detroit, Speaker took off from third in the bottom of the first inning in an effort to steal home. Joe Evans, a .190 hitter during the campaign in 385 at-bats, was at the dish and perhaps he missed a sign that was flashed in his direction by Speaker or the third-base coach. When Speaker came running in, down the line towards the plate, Evans swung viciously at the ball and hit a scorching line drive at Speaker's direction and nailed him in the face. Detroit's skipper Hughie Jennings showed some compassion and allowed Speaker to return in the third inning after he was removed from the game in the second frame while Elmer Smith played center field. The Chicago White Sox had their running shoes on September 3, stealing eight bags in game one versus Detroit and five in game two. On September 24, the streaking Cleveland Indians won their tenth straight game, 5–4, against Connie Mack's Athletics. Ray Chapman stole third base and home in this game. It was his fourth steal of home during the month of September.

The Giants lost the World Series, four games to two, as the White Sox clinched the world championship on October 15. Many baseball fans blamed Heinie Zimmerman for losing the series in the fourth inning of the sixth game when he was unable to catch Eddie Collins in a botched rundown, as Collins scored. This was a breakdown of the inside game that relied on teamwork and as a result McGraw was incendiary. Zimmerman's primary sin was a lack of foot speed, and as McGraw pointed out, the man who was to blame was first baseman Walter Holke who failed to cover home plate and left it unguarded. Rube Benton was also to blame because instead of firing the ball to catcher Bill Rariden on the comebacker, he threw it to third base, where Zimmerman caught the spheroid. Benton also watched the rundown from the mound and did not cover the plate. The White Sox did slightly better than New York in most of the major statistical categories. The Sox stole six bags and were led by Eddie Collins who swiped three. New York stole four bags in the series as outfielder Dave Robertson led the way with two.

For Pants Rowland the 1917 world championship vindicated him as a manager even though the Sox finished in third place (1915) and second place (1916) during his first two seasons. Rowland never played in the big show and to many it was considered a big joke when Charles Comiskey had hired him. John McGraw, however, was perhaps at the low point of his managerial career and hadn't won a World Series title since 1905, losing his last four appearances in the fall classic (1911, 1912, 1913, and 1917). Rowland was triumphant but gracious after the final game despite the final two contests being played under intense conditions with hostile bench jockeying and with intentionally high slides with razor sharp spikes. He tried to shake McGraw's hand, saying in part, "I'm sorry you had to be the one to lose." McGraw replied, "Get away from me, you goddamned busher."[91] Chicago's American League outfit were the "Clean Sox" in 1917, but events were transpiring that would make many of their souls corrupt and willing to throw the fall classic in 1919. There had been a rumor that Charles Comiskey would give his players a bonus for winning the world championship in 1917, but instead the players received a case of champagne, which Ring Lardner of the *Chicago Tribune* said "tasted like stale piss."[92]

The major leagues were impacted by World War I in 1918 and were unable to complete their reduced 140-game schedule and ended the regular season on Labor Day. Baseball was considered a nonessential activity and their players, along with other Americans, were ordered to "work or fight."[93] Baseball officials were able to persuade the government not to take players from the pennant-winning Chicago Cubs (84–45) and Boston Red Sox (75–51) so that a competitive World Series could be played. In anticipation of the lower attendance, the owners reduced the salaries of the players. Major league attendance plummeted by 40 percent and the attendance was also low in the World Series. When it became apparent to the Cubs and Red Sox players that they would not receive the money that was promised to them as World Series participants, they very nearly decided not to take the field for game five, and they stepped between the white lines an hour after the scheduled start time. Boston won the series, four games to two, as both teams stole three bases apiece.

The fourth-place Pittsburgh Pirates stole 200 bases in 1918 to lead the majors. Max Carey won his fifth stolen base crown and his fourth consecutive with 58 bags. He was followed by George Burns (40); Charlie Hollocher, a rookie shortstop with the Chicago Cubs (26), who batted .316 during the campaign and led the NL with 161 hits; George Cutshaw of Pittsburgh who stole 25 of his career 271 bases; and third baseman Doug Baird of St. Louis who also stole 25. The Cubs led the NL with 190 sacrifice hits, while Edd Roush of Cincinnati paced the circuit with 33. Roush was 25 years old in 1918, and the Reds center fielder batted .333 during the season with a league leading .455 slugging percentage. The 5'11", 170-pound, left-handed hitting outer garden occupant, was a terrific hitter, batting .323 lifetime with two batting crowns (1917, .341 and 1919, .321). For eleven consecutive seasons from 1917 to 1927 he batted .304 or better while playing for the Reds and Giants. And during that time period the only season he batted below .323 was in 1927 (.304). He stepped into the batter's box with one of the heaviest bats in the game with a thick-handle. Roush said he took only a half swing at the ball, perhaps like a tennis player or the swing of Chase Utley, a modern day player. The quick footed fly chaser relied on his short, heavy bat, to drive the ball, not his compact swing. He was skilled at hitting them where they ain't and said that place hitting "is in a sense glorified bunting."[94] He would snap at the ball at the plate, playing on some fields that "weren't much better than a cow pasture."[95]

In addition to being an exceptional center fielder, Roush was also a solid small ball player, stealing 268 bases, including a career high of 36 in 1920. The Hall of Famer was also credited with 256 sacrifices, which is tied with Johnny Evers for 35th all-time.

Second-place Cleveland led the AL with 171 stolen bases, while the first-place Red Sox led the majors with 193 sacrifices. Despite having a new manager with Ed Barrow, the Red Sox again had a large number of sacrifices and a low number of stolen bases (110, 6th AL). George Sisler, the St. Louis Browns 25-year-old first baseman, won the first of four stolen base titles with 45 thefts. He was followed by Roth (36) and Chapman (35) of Cleveland; Cobb (34) of Detroit; and Speaker (27) of Cleveland. Dave Shean, the Boston Red Sox's second baseman, was 34 years old at the start of the season, and in his second to last major league campaign he batted .264 with 11 steals and led both leagues with 36 sacrifice hits.

In the New York Yankees 5–4 win over Boston on May 4, they were credited with eight sacrifice hits, although only six of them were sacrifice bunts. Merlin Kopp played only 187 games in his three-year big league career and the 5'8", 158-pound, switch-hitting outfielder stole 39 bases in total. His biggest steal most likely came on May 20, 1918, when his second theft of the game was a game-ending steal of home with two outs in the bottom of the fourteenth inning. Detroit's right-hander Hooks Dauss toed the slab when Kopp stole home to give the Athletics a 5–4 win. The ninth and final game-ending steal of home during the Deadball Era was garnered by Jim Thorpe of the New York Giants against Pittsburgh on June 5. Pirates hurler Wilbur Cooper delivered the pitch to the batter, Joe Wilhoit, while Jose Rodriguez who was the runner on first base took off for the midway, and Thorpe, who was on the third sack, took off late as the batter swung and missed the offering. Catcher Walter Schmidt rifled the spheroid to Cooper, who inexcusably threw the ball to third baseman Bill McKechnie. The throw home was off target, in the dirt, and McGraw's outfit emerged victorious.

Lee Fohl, the manager of the Cleveland Indians, was delighted to see his club steal seven bags in a 14–7 win against Boston on June 7. Braggo Roth was on the front end of a triple steal in the seventh inning. And then on June 11, the Indians beat the Yankees, 4–3, when Ray Chapman drew a walk in the home half of the twelfth inning, advanced two bases on Tris Speaker's sacrifice bunt, and scored on Bill Wambsganss's squeeze bunt. The Pittsburgh Pirates defeated the Boston Braves, 3–2, in sixteen frames that day, thanks to a squeeze play with three ducks on the pond. The Cincinnati Reds took two games from the Philadelphia Phillies on July 27, by scores of 14–5 and 3–0. They stole eight pillows in game one and the sacrifice bunt was featured prominently in the nightcap, as it helped them score each of their runs. Greasy Neale and Sherry Magee stole three bases apiece in the lidlifter, taking huge leads off right-hander Milt Watson.

On August 24, the Red Sox defeated the Browns, 3–1, as 23-year-old pitcher Babe Ruth stole home in the contest. It was the second time in 1918 that a pitcher had swiped home; Bob Steele of the New York Giants stole home against St. Louis on July 26. Ruth stole 123 bases during his career, including a career high of 17 in both 1921 and 1923. But Ruth's small ball statistic that is a true eye opener is his 113 career sacrifice hits, including a career high of 21 in 1930. However, this statistic is very misleading. For most players, especially during the Deadball Era, it can be assumed that most of their sacrifice hits were sacrifice bunts. This is based partly on the fact that during the 1908 season when sacrifice flies were first counted as sacrifice hits, there was an increase of 321 (25.6 percent) in the AL and 306 (22.7 percent) in the NL when compared to 1907. But for Ruth it is unlikely that he utilized the sacrifice bunt very often, if at all, and if he did so it was during his first few seasons in the majors. Consider that in 1930 he collected his career high of 21 sacrifice hits, but during his final five major league seasons when sacrifice flies were no longer counted as sacrifice hits, he never again was credited with a sacrifice hit. Furthermore, we know that sacrifice flies in general became a greater percentage of the sacrifice hit total in the 1920s, probably accounting for between 40 to 50 percent of the sacrifice hits by 1930.

While it is true that it was not at all unusual for cleanup hitters or sluggers to lay down a bunt to move a runner along during the Deadball Era, this certainly didn't apply to Ruth when he dominated the game in the 1920s. To be a home run hitter during the Deadball Era was very different than to be a slugger during the 1920s. During the Deadball Era it was not unusual for a player with less than ten homers to lead their league in long balls, in fact it happened thirteen times, including in 1902 when Tommy Leach led the NL with six homers. In 1918, Gavy Cravath of the Phillies led the NL with eight homers. Furthermore, many homers were of the inside-the-park variety during the Deadball Era. Ruth helped demolish the inside game with its small ball tactics that relied on brains, teamwork, and aggressive baserunning. However, his big bang style was what most fans preferred and brought them through the turnstiles. There were critics like Ty Cobb who said he ruined the scientific or inside game of the previous decade.

Allen Barra in his polemical book *Clearing the Bases: The Greatest Baseball Debates of the Last Century* is skeptical that Ruth saved the game after the Black Sox scandal and argues against it. He also contends that Ruth was not responsible for the lively ball era, writing, "evidence in this case simply doesn't support the legends that have grown up around Ruth." Babe Ruth, he asserts, "did not create the 'Lively Ball Era.'"[96] He is correct with this statement because the lively ball was created by the A.J. Reach Company, who in 1919 came up with a better yarn-winding machine that would make the yarn tighter around the ball and more lively. Furthermore, the ball was clean and easier to see and hit because the pitcher could no longer deface the ball. The shine ball, spitball, mud ball, emery ball, paraffin ball, and licorice ball were among the pitches that were outlawed beginning with the 1920 season. However, a few spitballers were able to load up until the end of their career. After the death of Ray Chapman in 1920, the umpires made an effort to keep clean baseballs in play at all times.

Donald Honig in *Baseball America: The Heroes of the Game and the Times of Their Glory* takes exception to Barra's conclusions, writing that the home run in New York became "the most exciting attraction in sports, with a veritable superman performing seemingly inexhaustible miracles," hitting home runs for great distances and with "wondrous frequency."[97] As Honig points out, Ruth doubled the attendance his first year in New York and Barra's argument, perhaps, would have been more convincing if he did not only rely on attendance figures for both the National and American Leagues, but instead examined the totals for individual Yankee games, which perhaps tells the true story. It was not fortuitous that the Yankees led the American League in attendance from 1920 to 1924 and from 1926 to 1933 as Ruth helped build the Yankee legacy. As Barra writes, "There was no drop in attendance following the Black Sox scandal or the death of Ray Chapman, so there was nothing for Ruth to save baseball from."[98] This argument has many holes. Attendance more than doubled in both leagues from 1918 to 1919 and rose sharply from 1919 to 1920 before decreasing slightly in 1921, by 463,972 in the AL and just 49,591 in the NL. However, the Black Sox scandal did not become public until late September 1920, so it had a minimal affect on that season's attendance totals. Furthermore, most of the players who threw the 1919 series were still playing in 1920. And as for the decline in 1921, the question to ask is if Ruth didn't keep people interested in the game with 54 homers in 1920 and 59 the subsequent season, then how many more people would have lost interest in the game? Or to say it differently, how high would the attendance figures have been if not for the Black Sox scandal? Ruth may have murdered small ball but he may have saved baseball in the process, which, of course, is the greater goal.

Through the 1920s into the 1930s, 1940s, and 1950s, inside baseball tactics became rare or less frequent as the caveman strategy of swinging the bat for the fences and trying to hit the ball great distances was embraced. Intelligence was no longer one of the most important qualities of a player as it was during the Deadball Era, but instead teams coveted power and the players who possessed this strength did not have to have the smarts to execute the plays of the inside game of a previous or ancient time, depending on one's outlook.

The 1919 Cincinnati Reds were led by several skilled practitioners of the inside game. Jake Daubert played first base and batted .276 with 11 steals. He was a five-foot-ten-and-a-half-inch, 160-pound, left-handed hitter, who would swing down on the ball and utilize his speed. Daubert accumulated 251 stolen bases during his fifteen-year career with Brooklyn and Cincinnati in the National League. During his first five seasons from 1910 to 1914, he stole at least 23 bases. Daubert's stolen base totals during those five years were 23, 32, 29, 25, and 25. However, his stolen base percentages left much to be desired as he compiled a basestealing average below 50 percent during five of the eight season's they are available during his career: 1915 (45.8 percent), 1920 (45.8 percent), 1922 (45.2 percent), 1923 (47.8 percent), and during his final big league campaign in 1924 (33.3 percent). In 1916 he swiped 21 bags with a 75 percent basestealing average, which is his highest percentage. At one point in his career it was believed that Daubert was faster than Eddie Collins.

His 392 sacrifice hits ranks second all-time, but his only sacrifice hit crown came in 1919 when he led the circuit with 39. Daubert has the most sacrifice hits in National League history. He would generally bunt the ball down the third base line and would occasionally surprise the defense and bunt with two strikes. If he couldn't beat out a bunt with his legs, he was content with taking the sacrifice and advancing the runner and playing scientific baseball. His ability to bunt was legendary and Milt Stock, the Philadelphia Phillies third baseman, said, "Jake Daubert was the greatest bunter I ever saw. In his prime he could bunt almost at will. I don't know exactly what he did to the ball, but he seemed to put reverse English on it some way so that it would stop just where he wanted it to stop."[99] Casey Stengel also lauded Daubert's skill, insisting he may have been the best bunter he ever saw, "He uster put a reverse twist on it like a pool ball. It would hit the ground and — oops— here it is coming back."[100] On August 15, 1914, he had four sacrifices in the second game of a doubleheader versus Philadelphia, tying the major league record. He had six sacrifices in the doubleheader on the day, which was also a record. Daubert generally batted second in the lineup, which was ideally suited for him because of his ability to bunt, his exceptional place hitting skills, and his fairly low strikeout totals. Jake's bunting ability allowed him to avoid long slumps and helped him win two batting championships, including in 1913 when he batted a career high .350. He insisted that his success in 1913 was due to the exorbitant number of infield hits that he legged out. Daubert collected thirty-one or more sacrifices during seven seasons. He led the National League with 39 sacrifices in 1919 and finished second in 1914 (33), 1915 (39), and 1916 (35).

The rest of Cincinnati's infield was filled out by second baseman Morrie Rath (.264, 17 steals), shortstop Larry Kopf (.270, 18 steals), and third baseman Heinie Groh (.310, 21 steals). Center fielder Edd Roush won the NL batting crown at .321 and stole twenty bags.

Greasy Neale (.242, 28 steals) along with the great small ball practitioner and slugger Sherry Magee also resided in the outer garden. In Magee's final season he batted .215 in 163 at-bats with 4 steals.

Cincinnati won the tainted World Series, five games to three. They stole seven bags, including two apiece by Rath and Roush, while Chicago swiped five. The Reds won eight more games than the White Sox during the regular campaign, finishing with a 96–44 mark. Skipper Pat Moran had his team leading the NL with 199 sacrifice hits with their 143 steals ranking sixth in the league. Fourth-place Pittsburgh led the circuit with 196 steals. New York's left fielder, George Burns, stole exactly forty bases for the third consecutive season and won his second stolen base crown. When Johnny Evers, the former senior league star, watched the Giants play against the Reds from his seat in the Polo Grounds bleachers on August 14, he was fascinated by the ability of Burns. "I had seen George Burns in many games, but this time I saw him from a new angle, and he struck me as better than ever before. Batting, fielding, base running, sliding — none do these various things better, and if he's called out he's up and away, with no words for the umpire," said Evers.[101] Pittsburgh's George Cutshaw (36) and Carson Bigbee (31) followed Burns in the stolen base category. Bigbee was a 5'9", 157-pound, left-handed-hitting but right-handed throwing outfielder. He batted .287 with 182 stolen bases during his eleven-year big league career with Pittsburgh from 1916 to 1926.

The Chicago White Sox won the American League flag with an 88–52 record and led the circuit with only 150 steals. A few years earlier 150 steals would have had a team ranked at or near the bottom of the league in thefts, but things had changed mightily by 1919 as there were only 916 stolen bases in the circuit, which was 249 fewer than the National League. Branch Rickey, the St. Louis Browns skipper, was a strict moralist and an innovative strategist who led his team to a 67–72 fifth-place conclusion as they finished last in the majors with a paltry 74 steals. The White Sox were a well-rounded small ball outfit, leading the majors with 223 sacrifices. Second-place Cleveland (221), fourth-place Detroit (209), and the St. Louis Browns (201) also compiled more than 200 sacrifices. Ray Chapman led the majors with 50 sacrifice hits, while Eddie Collins led the junior circuit with only 33 stolen bases and was followed by Sisler (28), Cobb (28), and Washington's 29-year-old fifth-year player Sam Rice, who played right field and batted .321 with a .411 slugging percentage and 26 stolen bases. In 1920 he would steal 63 bags to lead the circuit and he finished his Hall of Fame career in 1934 with 351 steals.

On June 14, the Giants defeated the Cubs, 1–0. George Burns took the initiative in the third inning, stealing home on the front end of a double steal for the only run. When McGraw's club had a 10–2 lead in the ninth inning in the first of two on July 7 versus Philadelphia, they ignored the Phillies baserunners and concentrated solely on the man standing in the batter's box. Fred Luderus, the Phillies' first baseman, who batted .293 during the campaign with only six steals, reached first. As did Ed Sicking (4 steals), Hick Cady (1 steal), and Gavy Cravath (8 steals). None of these players were burners, and none of them had even above average foot speed. But in that ninth inning they combined for eight steals to tie Washington's major league record that was set on July 19, 1915. The 1919 season was the final campaign in which stolen bases were rewarded when there was defensive indifference. Beginning in 1920, stolen bases were not credited to the runner if there was no effort by the defensive team to stop them. The play was scored as a fielder's choice.

The corrupt Hal Chase patrolled first base for the New York Giants in 1919, batting .284 with 16 steals before being banned for life because of his game-fixing activities. The

Reds would strengthen their hold on first place and move in front of the Giants by six and a half games by winning two doubleheaders from them in mid-August. In one of the doubleheaders, Chase was charged with four errors and cost them one game with a miscue in the fourteenth frame. New York dropped two games on August 15, as they played "grittily uphill" in the 4–3 opening game defeat before playing in a "dispirited fashion" in the 4–0 nightcap loss. It may have appeared to William B. Hanna of the *New York Herald* that Chase wasn't putting forth his best effort: "Chase was a dropping figure at bat all afternoon. He made a few miracle catches of bad throws, but he couldn't hit and seemed to know it."[102] Chase was removed from the game for a pinch-hitter in the ninth inning of game two and then missed most of the remaining games with a wrist injury, perhaps injured with one of his headfirst slides. But he hung around with the team, flashed signs along the baselines as a coach, and tried to manipulate the outcome of games.

Cincinnati scored a run in the top of the first inning of the lidlifter, thanks in part to a beautifully executed hit-and-run by Groh with Daubert on first. Moran's team had three sacrifice bunts in the opener, two by Roush and one by Magee, while Chase had one for New York. The Giants 20-year-old first-year player Frankie Frisch stole one base, as did Art Fletcher. Frisch batted .226 during the season with 15 stolen bases in 54 games. By the time his career ended with the 1937 St. Louis Cardinals, he stole 419 bases and secured three NL stolen base crowns. Frisch stole two more bags in the nightcap, while Burns collected one for New York. Cincinnati stole four, one by Magee and three by Neale in the ninth. Greasy Neale advanced to first on a walk with one away. After Kopf flied out, he stole second, and appeared to be injured. He limped around some, perhaps to lull the opposition to sleep, and then stole third. Magee advanced to the gateway with a walk to put runners on the corners. And they pulled off a double steal, as Neale slid across the plate. New York had lost four games to the Reds in three days, losing both ends of a doubleheader on August 13th and 15th, while winning the twin bill on the 14th, and by season's end they were situated in second place (87–53).

On August 23, the Detroit Tigers executed a triple steal with Cobb, Harry Heilmann, and Chick Shorten on the basepaths. Babe Ruth hit a grand slam for Boston but it wasn't enough as Detroit won, 8–4. Neither Heilmann nor Shorten distinguished themselves with their basestealing during their careers. In seventeen big league seasons, Heilmann stole only 113 bases, including a career high of thirteen in both 1918 and 1924. During his rookie season in 1914, he stole one base and was caught stealing eight times. Shorten was a six-foot, 175-pound, backup outfielder who participated in eight major league seasons, playing for four teams. He stole only twelve bags during his career.

A direct statistical comparison between the National and American Leagues cannot be made for many of the Deadball Era seasons because the rules varied in each league for some campaigns concerning the foul strike, infield fly, balk, the criteria for an earned run and a number of other scoring decisions. There was no established criteria for who would be declared the winning or losing pitcher of a game. Ban Johnson would sometimes intervene and change the official scorer's decision in this regard a few days or even a few weeks after a game. The height of the pitcher's mound could vary drastically from one ballpark to another. There were different judgments by the scorers in situations when a fielder unsuccessfully tried to throw out a baserunner. For example, if there was a runner situated at the second sack with one out and the batter grounded to the shortstop and then threw to third where the runner slid in safely, some official scorers credited the batter with a hit, while others gave him a fielder's choice, and some even gave him a sacrifice. The scribes were concerned about the lack of uniformity in scoring decisions. At the major league meetings in February 1913, several of the sportswriters (Jack Ryder, William Hanna, Fred Lieb, Tom Rice, and George McLinn) who also had the responsibility of scoring games could not come to a consensus regarding how this play should be scored. Ban Johnson provided the final verdict and for the sake of uniformity he declared that this play would be scored as a hit. Jack Ryder of the *Cincinnati Enquirer* was such a strong supporter for crediting the batter with a hit in these situations that it was called the "Cincinnati Base Hit." The hitters would benefit from this unofficial rule for only one season as it was later defined to be a fielder's choice. To make judgments about the statistics of the Deadball Era, it's important to have an understanding of the rules, which were constantly changing. The official scorers would often interpret the same play in significantly different ways and score it differently. This is true even today in the twenty-first century, but it was much more ubiquitous during the early twentieth century. John Heydler, the National League president, even suggested at one time that errors of judgment should be included in the box score, which would have made it even more subjective.[103]

The most important criteria for judging whether a team should be characterized as a "small ball team" is foot speed and the accumulation of large numbers of stolen bases. Teams that steal a large number of bases because of swift-footed players can utilize all the weapons of the small ball arsenal and they will be far more successful than slow-footed aggregations when doing so, assuming that they can execute the fundamentals, such as bunting, place hitting, and the ability to read the pitcher. They could use the hit-and-run if they chose and reduce the likelihood of a double play as a result. And although the hitter is the most important participant in this play, a fast runner is more likely to stay out of a double play if the batter hits the ball on the ground and during the Deadball Era with its expansive playing fields, they would have a greater possibility of scoring on such a play. Furthermore, if the batter fails to make contact with the ball, a speedy runner can outrun the mistake and pilfer a cushion. A speed merchant is more likely to score on a squeeze play, which is sometimes called the bunt and run. However, the bunt and run is an exhilarating play that can score a fast runner from second base and demoralize the opposition. For example, the runner at second base takes off for third as the pitcher delivers the ball to home plate. The batter lays down a bunt, down the third base line, and when the third baseman, catcher, or pitcher fields the ball and fires it to first to get the out, the baserunner does not break his stride and heads for home. If the first baseman is caught napping, the baserunner scores easily, and if not, he still has a good chance to score. However, let's imagine that the catcher fields the bunt and sees the baserunner round third out of the corner of his eye. If the catcher hesitates it may allow the batter to leg out a hit. The third baseman is out of position to take a throw at third because he came in to field the bunt. That makes it the responsibility of the shortstop or perhaps the left fielder if he is playing very shallow to cover third and take the throw. There are a number of positive outcomes that can benefit the offense in this situation, including the fact that the third baseman or pitcher may field the bunt and perhaps rush his throw to first if the batter also has good wheels. If the defense does not anticipate this play they could look very foolish once it happens.

A fast runner is more likely to take an extra base with aggressive baserunning and an outfielder may be in such a rush to gather the ball in and deliver it back to the infield that they may commit an error as a result. The defensive players' judgment and effectiveness may be adversely affected because of the intense psychological strain they feel with a fast runner on the bases or at the plate. If a batter with good wheels attempts to sacrifice a runner to second, they may beat the throw to first for a hit or perhaps the pitcher will make a bad throw to first as he rushes his throw. If the runner on first could also fly then it minimizes the chances of being forced at second on such a play. The suicide squeeze is more likely to work with some speed at third base. If a fast runner is situated at second base, the outfielders may play very shallow, so they could try to cut the runner down at the plate on a single. The batter would have a better opportunity of driving the ball over their heads in such a situation. Speed also has an adverse affect on the pitcher, who may lose his concentration with a fast runner on first and constantly try to pick him off, and then throw a fat pitch to the batter. With a burner on first, the pitcher will throw more fastballs because a curve or changeup is an easier pitch to run on. And naturally if the batter knows he's going to see more fastballs, it increases the likelihood of him getting a hit. The pitcher may also feel compelled to rush his delivery and go to a slide step, which could lower his velocity. With a fast runner at the bat, the infield may play in at the corners to guard against a bunt and therefore minimize the amount of space they could cover on a ground ball and increase the chances for the batter of getting a hit on such a play. Speed creates chaos and panic in the opposition, which helps the team at the bat. And, of course, with an exceptional swift-footed basestealer on the bases, the manager doesn't have to give up an out with a sacrifice bunt, but instead could simply have his runner swipe the bag.

If a manager has slow runners on his team then he is limited in the number of small ball strategies he could employ and if he uses these strategies anyhow, he may not be successful. Teams that steal a large number of bases, but have a modest or low number of sacrifice hits, are generally recognized as small ball teams. The 1911 New York Giants (347 steals), who were ranked sixth in the NL with 160 sacrifice hits, are considered a small ball team. So are the 1912 New York Giants, who stole 319 bags, but finished last in the senior circuit with 152 sacrifices. The same is true with the 1985 St. Louis Cardinals (314 steals), who finished seventh in the NL with 70 sacrifices. However, teams that have a high number of sacrifices and a low number of steals are generally not considered to be a small ball team. If you established a statistic measuring if a team should be considered a "small ball" outfit, then it would behoove you to count the stolen bases at least twice as much as the sacrifice hits. Teams that are capable of stealing large numbers of bases do not have to rely on the sacrifice bunt. The sacrifice bunt is a more effective strategy with slow or average baserunners.

The caught stealing totals are only available for two seasons in both the NL and AL during the Deadball Era. In the National League, in 1913, the stolen base percentages for individual teams ranged from 48.2 percent to 61.1 percent and in 1915 they ranged from 51 percent to 62.1 percent. The American League stolen base percentages ranged from 50.1 percent to 57.8 percent in 1914. And in 1915 they ranged from 50.2 percent to 63.7 percent. Many people in the twenty-first century may consider the baserunning of the Deadball Era to be reckless and foolish. However, imagine if you took Roger Clemens, perhaps the greatest pitcher of his generation, and allowed him to deface the ball and throw a spitter, shine ball, mud ball, or emery ball. Imagine if he played during a time when the ball would become darkened because of saliva, tobacco juice, licorice, and other substances that were placed upon it and the fact that it was rarely ever removed from a game. The ball would lose its elasticity or lively nature because it was constantly being battered. Imagine if Clemens played part of his career with a yarn-centered baseball, instead of a cork-centered ball. Furthermore, he would be playing in ballparks that are considered enormous by twenty-first century standards, so he wouldn't have to worry about too many balls sailing over the fence. Additionally, he would be allowed to throw as many beanballs as he liked with the knowledge that he wouldn't be suspended for doing so. And the hitters would step into the batter's box without a batting helmet. Under those circumstances, Clemens would be almost unhittable. When the conditions favor the pitchers by a wide margin, it is not so reckless to try to score a run anyone you can, whether by stealing large quantities of bases, bunting them over, utilizing the hit-and-run, taking an extra base with aggressive baserunning, or using the suicide squeeze. Those players who took the initiative may steal second, third, and home on their own. It is not surprising that the top nine players of all-time in career steals of home, played part or all of their career during the Deadball Era: Ty Cobb (54), Max Carey (33), George Burns (28), Honus Wagner (27), Sherry Magee (23), Frank Schulte (23), Johnny Evers (21), George Sisler (20), and Frankie Frisch (19). The players and managers of the Deadball Era were not a bunch of Neanderthals. In fact the players of these two decades probably had higher baseball intelligence than players from any other subsequent decade to follow. Once the home run became ubiquitous, brains were no longer a necessary or even coveted part of a ballplayer's makeup.

During the Deadball Era those teams that finished at or near the top of their league in winning percentage also accumulated significantly more stolen bases and sacrifice hits than teams in the second division. It is not surprising considering the conditions of this time period that the best teams were better small ball teams than the worst teams. This is not to suggest that small ball was the only reason why these teams were successful. A team's ability to pitch, field, and hit, are some of the other criteria that should be examined when discovering why a team is successful. But the results in Chart 1 and Chart 2, which shows that the best teams were collectively better in the two primary small ball statistics than the worst teams, is also not a coincidence.

Chart 1 below shows the number of stolen bases compiled in both the National and American Leagues by the nineteen teams who finished either first, second, third, etc., during the Deadball Era. It also provides the average number of stolen bases compiled by those nineteen teams, and how many of them ranked first or second in the league in stolen bases. The way to read this chart is as follows. Listed vertically on the far left-hand side are "1st Place," "2nd Place," etc. which represent the nineteen first-place, second-place, third-place, fourth-place, fifth-place, sixth-place, seventh-place, or eighth-place teams in each league. The second column is "NL-SBs (Avg)." For the nineteen first-place or pennant-winning teams in the NL, they collectively compiled 4,132 steals and averaged 217.5 steals per team. The next column is "Rank (1st-2nd)," which shows that seven of these pennant-winning teams led the National League in steals, while six finished second. The next column is "AL-SBs (Avg)," which shows that the nineteen first-place clubs in the junior league stole 3,566 bases and averaged 187.7 steals per team. In the last column, "Rank (1st-2nd)," we see that four of the pennant-winning teams finished first in their league in steals and two of them finished second. Chart 1 is as follows:

	NL-SBs (Avg)	Rank (1st, 2nd)	AL-SBs (Avg)	Rank (1st, 2nd)
1st Place	4,132 (217.5)	1st (7), 2nd (6)	3,566 (187.7)	1st (4), 2nd (2)
2nd Place	3,696 (194.5)	1st (3), 2nd (4)	3,647 (191.9)	1st (5), 2nd (3)
3rd Place	3,376 (177.7)	1st (0), 2nd (3)	3,656 (192.4)	1st (1), 2nd (6)
4th Place	3,561 (187.4)	1st (4), 2nd (3)	3,351 (176.4)	1st (1), 2nd (1)
5th Place	3,379 (177.8)	1st (4), 2nd (0)	3,343 (175.9)	1st (1), 2nd (5)
6th Place	3,189 (167.8)	1st (1), 2nd (1)	3,261 (171.6)	1st (3), 2nd (1)
7th Place	2,756 (145.1)	1st (0), 2nd (1)	3,078 (162)	1st (2), 2nd (1)
8th Place	2,891 (152.2)	1st (0), 2nd (1)	2,972 (156.4)	1st (2), 2nd (0)

Not only did the first-place teams in the NL steal significantly more bases (4,132 with a 217.5 average per team), but seven (36.8 percent) of these nineteen teams led their league in steals, while six (31.6 percent) of the nineteen teams finished second. Conversely, the last-place teams in the NL compiled only 2,891 steals for a 152.2 average per team. Furthermore, none of these teams finished first in steals and only one (5.3 percent) finished second. In the American League there was also a significant difference between the teams that finished first or second in winning percentage, compared to the teams that finished seventh or eighth. The nineteen pennant-winning junior league clubs compiled 3,566 stolen bases and averaged 187.7 per team. Four (21.1 percent) of these teams were ranked first in steals, while two (10.5 percent) were ranked second. Conversely, the last-place teams compiled only 2,972 stolen bases for a 156.4 average and had two (10.5 percent) first-place rankings in steals and no second-place rankings. The second-place American League teams had the most first and second-place rankings in steals, while the third-place teams stole slightly more bases than the second-place clubs.

Chart 2 shows a similar outcome for sacrifice hits:

	NL-SHs (Avg)	Rank (1st, 2nd)	AL-SHs (Avg)	Rank (1st, 2nd)
1st Place	3,358 (176.7)	1st (8), 2nd (1)	3,690 (194.2)	1st (7), 2nd (2)
2nd Place	3,199 (168.4)	1st (5), 2nd (4)	3,446 (181.4)	1st (4), 2nd (1)
3rd Place	3,162 (166.4)	1st (2), 2nd (6)	3,519 (185.2)	1st (5), 2nd (5)
4th Place	3,022 (159.1)	1st (0), 2nd (4)	3,391 (178.5)	1st (3), 2nd (4)
5th Place	3,232 (170.1)	1st (4), 2nd (3)	3,186 (167.7)	1st (1), 2nd (5)
6th Place	2,879 (151.5)	1st (0), 2nd (1)	3,001 (157.9)	1st (0), 2nd (1)
7th Place	2,644 (139.2)	1st (0), 2nd (2)	2,865 (150.8)	1st (0), 2nd (0)
8th Place	2,693 (141.7)	1st (0), 2nd (0)	2,689 (141.5)	1st (0), 2nd (1)

The nineteen pennant-winning NL teams compiled 3,358 sacrifices and averaged 176.7 sacrifice hits per team. Eight (42.1 percent) of these teams led the league in sacrifices, while one (4.8 percent) finished second. There were twenty-one NL teams that ranked second in sacrifice hits because there was a tie during two seasons. Conversely, the nineteen last-place teams in the NL compiled only 2,693 sacrifice hits and averaged 141.7 per team. Furthermore, none of these teams finished first or second in sacrifices. The difference in the American League was even more severe as the nineteen first-place teams compiled 3,690 sacrifice hits and averaged 194.2 per team. Seven (35 percent) out of the twenty teams (1 tie) that were ranked first in sacrifices were also a pennant-winning squad, while two (10.5 percent) of the nineteen teams that ranked second were pennant-winners. The last-place teams in the American League compiled only 2,689 sacrifice hits for a 141.5 average per team. There were no first-place rankings in sacrifices among these teams, while one (5.3 percent) was ranked second in that category.

The statistical evidence clearly shows that the teams with the most wins in each league were, in general, the best small ball teams during the Deadball Era.

3

The Decline of Small Ball: 1920–1961

The game of baseball as it was played during the Deadball Era was drastically different than the way it was played during the 1920s. Runs scored increased from 1919 to 1920 by 822 in the National League and by a whopping 1,283 in the American League as the game changed suddenly and spectacularly in one season. Babe Ruth slammed 54 long balls in 1920, which exceeded the home run total of fourteen teams. F.C. Lane, the editor of *Baseball Magazine*, insisted during the 1920–21 offseason that the Black Sox Scandal wasn't the biggest story in baseball, but rather it was "Can Babe Ruth Repeat?" Indeed, Ruth was up to the task, connecting for 59 home runs, which was more than eight major league teams. Lane pointed out that while there were only thousands of fans who could fit into the ballparks to witness Ruth's herculean achievements, there were millions of fans who read the newspapers and examined the box scores to see what Ruth had accomplished.[1]

Not everyone was pleased with the new long ball era in major league baseball. Ring Lardner insisted, "It ain't the old game which I have lost interest in, but it is a game which the magnates have fixed up to please the public with their usual good judgment."[2] At first John McGraw, the great small ball strategist, resisted the change and despised the increased home runs and strikeouts of the lively ball era. Before the 1919 season commenced he said that Ruth, who he described as a "bum," would ground into a hundred double plays during the season.[3] However, McGraw adapted over time and recognized that the small ball strategies of the Deadball Era, namely the sacrifice bunt, the hit-and-run, and the stolen base, were no longer as effective when hitters could slam the ball over the fence and the big inning was accomplished with the use of extra-base hits. Trying to steal large numbers of bases was no longer an effective strategy according to McGraw. To risk an out while trying to pilfer a bag didn't make a lot of sense when the batter had a realistic chance of going deep. McGraw said, "A manager would look foolish not to play the game as it is, meet the new situation with new tactics." But he still missed the way baseball was played during the Deadball Era when he saw "men shoot down the base paths, one after another, until they had stolen their way to a win. That was baseball — the kind of baseball that I learned to love when I got my first job."[4]

William Killefer, a Deadball Era catcher who began his nine-year managerial career with the 1921 Chicago Cubs, and Red Faber, who had a twenty-year Hall of Fame pitching career for the Chicago White Sox from 1914 to 1933, expressed their displeasure about the home run in F.C. Lane's *Batting*: Killefer said, "Of late years baseball has fallen into a rut. The game has become a slugging match. The fine points of pitching and aggressive base running have gone into the discard ... the lure of the home run has completely distorted batting values." Faber said, "The sluggers have wrecked baseball. They are a thorn in the side of every pitcher. You never know when you have the game won. A home run dumped into the stands may rob you of a victory any time until the last man is out."[5]

Joe Vila, in a 1921 edition of the *New York Sun*, wrote that the home run was no longer unique and had become "a daily incident and a joke." He advocated the elimination of the lively ball and wrote that the "large majority" of fans wanted to see some intelligent pitching exhibitions, terrific fielding, and a return to the inside game with its widespread use of small ball strategies.[6] In a 1925 interview for the *New York Sun*, Johnny Evers regretted the fact that ballplayers had "stopped thinking." Hitters held the bat at the bottom of the knob, instead of choking up, and swung for the fences. When Evers had played the game of baseball it was both a mental and physical contest as teams tried to outguess each other and players spent hours devising plays. The mental calculations and decisions needed to win a game were largely eliminated during the early 1920s. Many of the Deadball Era players refused to embrace baseball as a home run dominated enterprise. Mordecai Brown appeared to look down upon the modern ballplayer in a 1941 *Sporting News* interview. Ballplayers were intelligent in his day and batters would do anything to get on base, recognizing the value of on-base percentage long before that statistic existed. He would derive great enjoyment if he faced the modern-day hitters who are primarily concerned about hitting home runs. They would be an easy target for a crafty pitcher like himself.[7] Ed Walsh, who spent all but one season of his fourteen-year big league career toiling for Chicago's American League representative during the Deadball Era, advocated for the legalization of the spitball until his death on May 26, 1959. He insisted that the hitters had received all the advantages since the Deadball Era ended, including smaller ballparks and livelier baseballs. Walsh said, "They've practically got pitchers wearing straitjackets."[8] The durable pitcher threw one of the best spitballs in the majors during his playing career. In a 1957 *Sporting News* interview Walsh also insisted that the dead ball should return to the game. This way the game would be "decided inside the park, not outside it." The dead ball would result in more acrobatic catches and the aggressive baserunning with its surfeit number of bang-bang plays would make the game more exciting.[9]

In March 1952, Ty Cobb was the center of controversy as a result of his interview in *Life* magazine entitled "They Don't Play Baseball Any More." Cobb was on the offensive once again, this time verbally attacking the modern ballplayer, and blaming him for the national pastime's decline. The obsession with the home run had made baseball a boring game and it was the reason why people stayed away from the ballpark. Cobb believed that Stan Musial and Phil Rizzuto were the only ballplayers in the major leagues "who can be mentioned in the same breath with the oldtime greats." He also insisted that the ballplayer in the early 1950s was not schooled in the fundamentals and their only objective was to hit long balls. They were encouraged to do so because of the salubrious hitting conditions with shorter fences and a lively ball. The home run was "commonplace" and had "lost its thrill." The modern ballplayer was one-dimensional, and players like Ralph Kiner and Gus Zernial were neither good fielders nor in good playing condition. According to Cobb, "hitting a baseball 350 feet is mostly a feat of sheer momentary strength like carrying a piano up a stairway." There were only a few players in the 1950s who were good small ball practitioners—players that could execute the surprise bunt, squeeze bunt, or sacrifice bunt. Players who could hit behind the runner to advance him to third, or who could steal a base or execute the hit-and-run. In addition to having a great scarcity of good basestealers, there were also only a few catchers and pitchers who could stop such a player. Cobb criticized Ted Williams and called him lazy because he was uninterested in learning how to hit the ball the opposite way, which would render the "Williams shift" ineffective. Joe DiMaggio was also criticized for not hitting the ball to the opposite field and for not keeping himself in top physical condition. While most old-time ballplayers agreed with Cobb, some did not. Clark Griffith, who pitched in twenty major league seasons in the late nineteenth century and the early twentieth century, said that old players like Cobb should "keep their mouths shut." Bucky Harris, who played twelve big league seasons and was the manager of the Washington Senators in 1952, said "Ty Cobb is nuts." New York Giants manager Leo Durocher said that the old-time players "make me sick" when they talk about how great it was in the old days.[10]

During the four decades after the Deadball Era, small ball strategies declined sharply. As listed in Appendix A, during the 1920 season the eight NL teams stole 969 bases and averaged 121.1 steals per team. By 1930 the senior league teams stole only 481 bases and averaged 60.1 steals per team. During the 1938 campaign, the NL teams stole only 354 bags (44.3 per team), which was only seven more than the 1911 New York Giants. During the 1940s, the NL teams stole between 361 (1947) and 527 (1945) bases. The two seasons that were particularly noteworthy during the 1940s was the stolen base increase from 1944 (381) to 1945 (527). This happened despite the fact that the NL stolen base leader in 1944 (Johnny Barrett, 28) had two more steals than the stolen base leader in 1945 (Red Schoendienst, 26), indicating that the increase in steals was not because of one or two great basestealers joining the league, but instead the steals were widely distributed among many players. In 1953, there was an embarrassingly low 342 steals (42.8 per team) in the National League and steals even lower the following season (337, 42.1 per team) before a modest increase in 1955 (377, 47.1 per team). During the 1950s there were only two seasons (1951: 453 and 1959: 439) when the NL teams stole over 400 bags.

In 1920 there were 751 stolen bases (93.9 per team) in the American League, but there was a more modest decline by 1930 (598 steals, 74.8 per team) compared to the National League. Stolen bases declined during the 1930s in the AL: the junior circuit stolen base totals ranged from 452 (1933) to 624 (1931). There was only a small increase in stolen bases during the four World War II seasons (1942–1945: 2,156 steals) when compared to the four seasons before the war (1938–1941: 2,080 steals). However, there was a sharp decline during the first four seasons after the war (1946–1949: 1,534 steals). The highest stolen base total during the 1940s was in 1943, when the eight junior circuit teams stole 626 bags. Stolen bases declined to embarrassingly low levels during the 1950s and ranged from 278 (1950) to 414 (1959) in the junior league. In 1950 the eight AL teams stole a modern era, major league low 278 bags (34.8 per team), while second division clubs Washington and Philadelphia led the league with 42. Dom DiMaggio of Boston secured the AL stolen base crown with only fifteen steals, while Johnny Lipon of Detroit stole nine of his career twenty-eight bags, which was good enough for fifth best in the circuit. The Chicago White Sox stole only nineteen bags during the season, but that wasn't even close to the modern era major league record for the fewest steals by a team, which was later established by the 1957 Washington Senators who stole only thirteen bags. These were numbers that could make Deadball Era players physically ill to see how low their national game had fallen. Baseball had gone from one extreme to another, from the power outages of the Deadball Era to the stationary game of the 1950s.

During the 1920s the sacrifice hit became almost a worthless statistic. As home runs and runs scored increased significantly, it was no longer an effective strategy to use the sacrifice bunt in a ubiquitous fashion and give up an out. Furthermore, as sacrifice flies became a greater percentage of the sacrifice hit total, it could no longer be assumed that a team with a high level of sacrifice hits also amassed a large number of sacrifice bunts. The 1930 and 1939 seasons were the final two seasons when sacrifice flies were counted as sacrifice hits and as to be expected sacrifice hits plummeted during the 1931 and 1940 seasons. In 1930 there were a total of 2,600 sacrifice hits in the National and American Leagues. However, in 1931 both leagues combined for 1,439 sacrifice hits, a decline of 1,161 from the previous season. Likewise, in 1939, there were 2,193 sacrifice hits in the major leagues and in 1940 there were only 1,266. The sacrifice hit statistic in the 1920s would be similar to an extra-base hit statistic that did not distinguish between doubles, triples, and home runs.

Complicating the situation even more was the fact that the sacrifice fly rule was modified in 1926, crediting the batter with a sacrifice fly if his fly out or line drive out advanced any runner. Under the previous definition a batter was rewarded with a sacrifice fly only when his fly out with less than two outs scored a runner after he tagged up. Naturally, with the expanded definition of a sacrifice fly, sacrifice hits skyrocketed in 1926. The National League's total jumped from 1,079 in 1925 to 1,489 in 1926. The American League's total increased from 1,479 in 1925 to 1,709 in 1926. This version of the sacrifice fly rule lasted through the 1930 season. From 1931 to 1953, except for one season in 1939, the batter no longer had the benefit of the sacrifice fly rule, as he was charged with an official at-bat in those circumstances. When the sacrifice fly rule resurfaced in 1954, it was no longer part of the sacrifice hit statistic, as that statistic only represented the number of sacrifice bunts.

George Sisler of the St. Louis Browns played five seasons during the Deadball Era from 1915 to 1919 and then saw the game change drastically during the 1920s. Sisler defended the bunt in F.C. Lane's *Batting* and was chagrined to watch its decline as a strategic weapon:

> There is no reason why a Major League batter should not be able to bunt. But too many of them fail. This is largely because they dislike to bunt and won't take the trouble to learn. How any one can undervalue the bunt is beyond me. The bunt was the cornerstone of many of Ty Cobb's batting championships. It's an important play quite apart from its value in the sacrifice. It's the best possible weapon to break up speed pitching which you can't hit. It's always on ace in your sleeve at a critical time. I bunt perhaps fifty times a year. I have never kept accurate tally, but it is safe to say that five or six times a year I make a really bad attempt to bunt. But it is much easier to lay down a bunt than it is to make a safe hit. Dangerous as it seems, I favor bunting the third strike under certain circumstances.[11]

In 1931 there were 789 sacrifice hits or bunts (98.6 per team) in the senior circuit and sacrifice hit totals remained relatively steady until the late 1940s when they began to decline systematically. By 1957 there were only 510 sacrifice bunts (63.8 per team) in the National League. The senior league averaged at least 100 sacrifice hits per team during the four wartime seasons from 1942 to 1945, including a high of 878 in 1943 (109.8 per team). This was not all that surprising considering that the major leagues used a dead ball for part of World War II. Baseballs were considered nonessential items and with both crude and scrap rubber banned by the federal government, A.G. Spalding & Brothers had to devise a baseball made of unessential materials. The "balata ball" was used during the early part of the 1943 season and it was so dead that Spalding was soon forced to come up with a ball that traveled further. Frank McCormick said, "The ball wouldn't ride. If you hit it on the end of the bat, or even if you got good wood on it, it felt like you had a handful of bees. It stung. It was like hitting a piece of concrete. It reminded me of when I was a kid, I used to practice by swinging at stones."[12] In 1946 sacrifice hits remained high in the NL (901, 112.6 per team) before dropping significantly during the following season (687, 85.9 per team). Sacrifice bunts declined during the 1950s and after the 1946 campaign the NL teams would not accumulate over 900 sacrifices until 1971 (918). But the National League had four additional teams by then and averaged only 76.5 sacrifices per team.

The eight American League teams compiled 650 sacrifices (81.3 per team) in 1931, and they didn't drop below that total until 1940 (608, 76 per team). After the 1940 campaign it took eleven seasons before the AL teams averaged below 80 sacrifices per team: 1951 (619, 77.4 per team). Similar to the National League, the junior circuit's sacrifice hit totals increased during the war with three seasons (1943–1945) with at least 811 sacrifices and averaging over 101 sacrifices per team. Sacrifice hit totals declined during the 1950s, ranging from a decade high of 712 (89 per team) in 1952 to a decade low of 531 (66.4 per team) in 1958.

Neither the pennant-winning Brooklyn Robins (93–61) nor the Cleveland Indians (98–56) stole a lot of bases in 1920. Manager Wilbert Robinson's ballclub became known as the "Robins" when he took over as skipper in 1914 and it remained that way through the 1931 campaign, his last season as a big league manager. In 1932 with Max Carey as skipper they were called the Dodgers once again, reverting back to the nickname used from 1911 to 1913. Brooklyn stole only 70 bags in 1920, last in the NL, and they were caught stealing 80 times. Fourth-place Pittsburgh led the league with 181 steals and were led by the NL stolen base champion Max Carey (52). George Cutshaw, the Pirates second baseman, batted .252 with 17 steals and a league leading 37 sacrifices. Brooklyn finished fourth with 189 sacrifice hits, while Chicago led the circuit with 220.

In the American League, player-manager Tris Speaker rallied his club to a first-place finish despite the death of the beloved Ray Chapman during the season. Speaker liked to platoon players, i.e. have a right-handed hitter face a left-handed pitcher and vice versa. Furthermore, judging from the sacrifice hit totals during his tenure as manager from 1919 to 1926, he may have also been fond of the sacrifice bunt. Cleveland stole only 73 bags in 1920 (6th, AL), but led the majors with 256 sacrifices. Sixth-place Washington led the circuit with 160 steals as Sam Rice won his only stolen base crown with 63 thefts. Donie Bush of Detroit and Joe Gedeon of St. Louis led the majors with 48 sacrifices. In the World Series, Cleveland prevailed five games to two, as Bill Wambsganss's unassisted triple play in the fifth inning of game five was the most memorable moment of the series. Both teams combined for only three steals. Interestingly, brothers Doc Johnston of Cleveland and Jimmy Johnston of Brooklyn had one apiece. There were ten runners caught stealing; the Robins had four runners gunned down, while the Indians had six. The aggregate basestealing average in the series was an abysmal 23.1 percent. Brooklyn had five sacrifice bunts, while Cleveland had two.

The caught stealing statistic was compiled in 1920 and the percentages were significantly worse when compared to the few Deadball Era seasons in which they are available. The Pittsburgh Pirates (60.7 percent) and St. Louis Browns (60.5 percent) had almost a 61 percent basestealing average to lead the majors. There were seven teams with basestealing averages under 50 percent; the Robins (46.7 percent), Cubs (47.1 percent), Braves (47.3 percent), and Red Sox (46.9 percent) were around 47 percent. The Indians (44 percent) and Yankees (43.8 percent) were at 44 percent. Babe Ruth led the Yankees with fourteen steals, but he was caught stealing fourteen times as well. The last-place Philadelphia Athletics had a 42.7 percent stolen base average. The Athletics stole only fifty bags, which was the lowest total in the history of the National and American Leagues at this juncture of baseball history. Not surprisingly, the teams who stole the most bases had the better stolen base averages.

In Cleveland's 3–2 win over Chicago on May 5, Ray Chapman and Larry Gardner each stole a base. Gardner was a 34-year-old, exceptionally skilled defensive third baseman, who was known for his clutch hitting. He stole 165 bags during his seventeen-year career, which is at best a modest number. However, the fact that he kept getting caught stealing in 1920 did not dissuade him from trying as he stole only three bases in twenty-three attempts for a dreadful 13 percent basestealing average. By 1920, the 33-year-old Ty Cobb's best bases-tealing days were behind him as he stole only fifteen bags and was caught stealing ten times. But on May 18 in the eighth inning against the Athletics, he tripled and stole home. Detroit prevailed, 8–2, but by season's end the Tigers were situated in seventh place as their .396 winning percentage was a precipitous drop from the previous year's .571 percentage. Sam Rice, a 5'9", 150-pound, left-handed hitter but right-handed thrower, batted .338 during the campaign and on July 18 he collected three of Washington's seventeen hits in a 10–3 triumph over Detroit. He had two of the sixty-three steals he would garner during the season, but he would also lead the league with thirty times caught stealing.

The most memorable game of 1920 was a 26 inning, 1–1 tie, between Brooklyn and Boston at Braves Field on May 1. Leon Cadore of Brooklyn got batters out with his assortment of curveballs, while Joe Oeschger of Boston overpowered batters with his heater. These two contrasting pitchers threw the entire twenty-six innings for their club. Cadore estimated that he threw nearly 300 pitches, while Oeschger believed he had thrown about 250. Hy Myers, Brooklyn's terrific center fielder, who batted .304 during the campaign with a .462 slugging percentage and led the NL in triples (22) for the second season in a row, had one of the two stolen bases in this game. In 1919 he led the senior circuit with a .436 slugging percentage, but by 1920 his .462 slugging percentage ranked only as the sixth best in the league. Myers was a quick-witted player who would occasionally run in from center field to take the throw at second base from the catcher, and try to catch the baserunner at the midway napping. Despite possessing good wheels, he wasn't a good basestealer, swiping only 107 cushions in a fourteen-year career. In 1920 he stole nine, but was caught stealing thirteen times. Wally Hood, who played only nine games in 1920 (7 with Brooklyn) and sixty-seven during his three-year big league career, had the other stolen base for the Robins, one of only five during his career. Sacrifice bunts in this game were credited to Hood, which was the only one for the Robins, and to Oeschger, the Braves leadoff man Ray Powell, catcher Mickey O'Neil, first baseman Walter Holke, and right fielder Walton Cruise.

Brooklyn scored their run in the fifth frame, thanks to Oeschger's inability to start a double play on a comebacker. Then in the bottom of the sixth, Boston pushed across its lone run. Les Mann started the last of the eighth with a hit and Cruise sacrificed him to second, but Cadore handled Holke's liner up the middle, and then he subdued the opposition. In the last of the ninth it looked as if Boston would emerge victorious as pinch-hitter Lloyd Christenbury legged out a bunt to put runners at first and second with no outs. Oeschger laid down one of his five sacrifices on the season to put two runners into scoring position with one out. When Powell walked to load the bases, Brooklyn moved its infield in to increase their chances of preventing the winning run from scoring. Charlie Pick grounded sharply to Ivy Olson, who was generally a shortstop but was playing second base in this game. Olson was generally recognized as a poor fielder and was booed incessantly at Ebbets Field. As F.C. Lane wrote in *Baseball Magazine*, "Brooklyn fans, particularly on a week day, foregather at Ebbets Field with two fell purposes in view. One is to ride the ball players of the opposing team, which is more or less legitimate rooting. The other is to ring execration and vituperation on the hapless head of Ivan Olson."[13] However, Olson speared

Pick's sharp grounder and tried to tag Powell, who was called out for running out of the baseline, and threw to first for a double play.

In the fifteenth inning Boston again had two on with no outs. Tony Boeckel laid down a bunt with the intention of sacrificing the runners to second and third. However, Rowdy Elliott, the Brooklyn catcher, pounced on the ball as it died in the wet infield, and forced Cruise at third. Cadore again worked his way out of the inning. Zack Wheat started the seventeenth inning with a single and then was sacrificed to second by Hood. Ed Konetchy reached on an infield hit to put runners on the corners. Chuck Ward reached first to load the bases when shortstop Rabbit Maranville unsuccessfully tried to catch Wheat off third. Elliott hit a comebacker to Oeschger who threw home for one out, but the catcher's throw to first temporarily eluded Holke. Big Ed Konetchy rounded third and collided with the catcher Hank Gowdy at home plate, who held onto the throw from first to get the runner.

The game continued mercilessly and monotonously until the 26th inning. After Holke legged out a bunt in the last of the 26th with two outs and Boeckel flied out, the umpire called the game at 6:50. Ivy Olson pleaded with the umpire to continue the game, "One more. One more," as he pointed to the sky. His voice could be heard by the sportswriters in the press box. It was an epic battle and perhaps it was fitting that the score was tied in the end, because neither team deserved to lose. Some players got as many as eleven at-bats and Zack Wheat said, "I carried up enough lumber to the plate to build a house today."[14]

There was plenty of excitement later in the month on May 29 when the surging Cubs won their seventh straight with an 8–5 win over the Cardinals. Charlie Hollocher and Dode Paskert pulled off a double steal in the four-run third inning for Chicago. But the most eventful stolen base attempt occurred in the eighth inning when Chicago's right hander Claude Hendrix was driven off the slab. Doc Lavan, the St. Louis shortstop, had his career year in 1920, batting a career high .289. With Lavan at second and Jack Fournier at third and with the Cardinals trying to come back in the game, Lavan took off for third to the "amazement" of the crowd, and ended the inning with his baserunning mistake. I. E. Sanborn of the *Chicago Daily Tribune* wrote about Lavan's mistake and because "this one was not pulled in the limelight of a world's series it probably will not make as much noise in the corridors of the hall of fame," referring to Red Faber's similar goof in 1917.[15]

Frankie Frisch batted .341 with a .485 slugging percentage and won the first of three stolen base crowns in 1921 with 49 bags (13 caught stealing). McGraw's pennant-winning Giants (94–59) led the league in runs scored (840), walks (469), on-base percentage (.359), and stolen bases (137). Ruth's Yankees (98–55) outlasted Cleveland to take the flag as they stole 89 bags (5th, AL) and had 189 sacrifices (4th, AL) with most likely a large percentage of them as sacrifice flies since they led the majors with a .464 slugging percentage. Second-place Cleveland led the majors with 232 sacrifices, while fourth-place Washington was the only AL team with over 100 stolen bases (112). The Senators led the majors with a 62.9 percent basestealing average. George Sisler won his second stolen base crown (35 steals), while Bill Wambsganss won the first of two sacrifice hit titles with 43. In the senior league, Milt Stock, the St. Louis Cardinals third baseman, batted .307 and led the circuit with 36 sacrifice hits. The Chicago Cubs resided in the second division during the first three seasons of the lively ball era, and in 1921 this seventh-place occupant led the National League with 208 sacrifice hits and finished with the worst basestealing average in the majors (41.9 percent). With basestealing in decline there weren't too many spectacular moments in 1921. Brooklyn lost to New York, 3–2, on May 4 to end their eleven-game winning streak. However, Dutch Ruether, the Robins pitcher, stole home in the fifth inning. Ruether had also

Pictured from left to right is the starting infield of the 1921 Cleveland Indians: Bill Wambsganss (second base), Doc Johnston (first base), Larry Gardner (third base), Joe Sewell (shortstop), and backup first baseman George Burns. These five players combined for 1,280 sacrifice hits during their careers: Wambsganss (323), Gardner (311), Sewell (275), Burns (187), and Johnston (184). Wambsganss ranks seventh all-time in sacrifices; Gardner ranks ninth; and Sewell is tied for twenty-first. Ray Chapman, the most prolific sacrifice hitter in Cleveland Indians history, died tragically on August 17, 1920, after being beaned by a Carl Mays fastball on the previous day. He would have most likely accumulated the most sacrifices in major league history if not for his premature death. Chapman is credited with 334 sacrifices (sixth all-time) in nine seasons. (George Brace photograph).

stolen home as a member of the Cincinnati Reds on September 3, 1919. In the Chicago White Sox's 4–1 win against New York on July 8, the Pale Hose's pitcher Dickie Kerr stole home in the seventh on the front end of a double steal.

The only everyday player remaining from the Giants 1917 pennant-winning squad was the fleet footed leadoff hitter George Burns. Prior to the 1918 campaign, McGraw told a New York sportswriter that Burns was the second greatest player he ever managed after Christy Mathewson. "He is a marvel in every department of play, a superb fielder, a wonderful thrower, a grand batsman and with few peers in baseball history as a run scorer. Best of all. Burns, modest and retiring to an extreme, is the easiest player to handle that ever stepped upon a field," insisted the Giants' skipper.[16] The 31-year-old Burns batted .299 during the season with 19 steals before hitting .333 in the World Series. Babe Ruth received most of the attention heading into the series. During the regular campaign he continued to hit prolific blasts, including the first one to land in the center field bleachers at the Polo Grounds about 500 feet from home plate. However, while Ruth was pilfering third base in the second World Series contest, he injured his elbow, and it became infected as wild rumors of blood poisoning and amputation circulated about the populace when he was forced to sit out games six and seven. Ruth batted .313 in the series with only 16 at-bats. He hit his first World Series homer in the ninth inning of the fourth game. In game five a surprise bunt single by Ruth, while leading off the fourth inning, started what would be the winning rally. The Giants stole seven bags in the series, including three by Frisch. The Yankees stole six, as Ruth and Mike McNally had two apiece. McGraw found great satisfaction in his World Series triumph as the Giants prevailed in the nine-game series, five games to three.

In 1922, Max Carey batted .329 with a .408 on-base percentage; had a career high 140 runs scored and 207 hits; a league leading 80 walks and secured his seventh stolen base crown with 51 steals. It could be argued that Carey had the greatest basestealing season in major league history. At first glance this may appear to be an outrageous claim, but consider that Carey was caught stealing only two times during the entire season and had a 96.2 percent basestealing average. This is the highest success rate for a basestealing champion in major league history. Furthermore, he swiped thirty-one consecutive bags during the season, a record that wouldn't be broken until 1975 when Davey Lopes stole 38 straight. Thanks to Carey, Pittsburgh led the majors with 145 steals and had a major league high 71.1 percent basestealing average, which was an extremely high percentage during this time period. Carey stole 738 bags during his career, which ranks 9th all-time and won ten NL stolen base titles, including two periods with four consecutive stolen base crowns (1915 to 1918 and 1922 to 1925).

Carey's terrific skills were exhibited in an eighteen inning, 9–8, loss to the Giants at Forbes Field on July 7. George "Highpockets" Kelly, New York's 26-year-old slugging first baseman, hit a home run over the left-field fence in the ninth to put the Giants up by two before Pittsburgh tied the game at seven with two runs in the last of the ninth. Kelly was not swift of foot, stealing only 65 bases in a sixteen-year career, but when right-fielder Ray Rohwer misplayed his drive to the opposite field in the eighteenth inning, he scored on a two RBI inside-the-park homer and the Giants held on to win. Carey hit a double, triple, and homer on July 6 and then continued his hot hitting on the 7th when he collected six hits, walked three times, and stole three bags. Pittsburgh was held scoreless in the first two frames and then took a 3–2 lead in the third, thanks in part to Chief Yellowhorse's sacrifice bunt and a two RBI single by Carey, who stole second and home in the inning off New York's starter Jesse Barnes. Carey's baserunning exhibition in the fifth chapter was outstanding; he advanced to first on a base on balls and Pittsburgh attempted the hit-and-run play with Carson Bigbee at the dish. Bigbee grounded to shortstop, Dave Bancroft, who was a wide ranging, studious, highly skilled defensive shortstop, who was having his career year with the bat in 1922 (.321, .397 on-base percentage, 117 runs scored, 209 hits, 41 doubles, and 16 steals). While Bancroft threw to first to record the out, Carey rounded second and advanced to third. Kelly unsuccessfully tried to cut Pittsburgh's quick footed center fielder down at third, but the ball sailed over third baseman Frankie Frisch's head and Carey scampered across home plate. It is not often that a hit-and-run play can be deemed successful when the batter makes an out. New York's left fielder and cleanup man, Irish Meusel, had the only stolen base in the game for the Giants, one of 12 on the season and 113 in his career. Meusel had the only sacrifice for McGraw's club, while Pittsburgh had three: Yellowhorse, Clyde Barnhart, and Rohwer. Emil Frederick "Irish" Meusel should not be confused with Bob Meusel, his brother who played with the Yankees. One way to know the difference between the brothers is to remember that Irish had a weak throwing arm, while Bob's was terrific. Lee Allen insists that Irish and John McGraw were walking down the street one day when a drunken, one-armed man, stumbled into them and politely apologized and mentioned the fact he had the "misfortune" to lose his arm. McGraw growled, "Get on your way. Irish ain't got it."[17]

The Giants (93–61) and Yankees (94–60) would meet in the World Series once again. McGraw's club led the league in on-base percentage (.363), was second in slugging percentage (.428), and ranked third in steals (116). The Yankees didn't steal a lot of bases (62, 7th AL), but they didn't need too. Interestingly, the Yankees didn't lead the league in slugging percentage, finishing third in the circuit (.412), as Ruth slammed only 35 homers in 406 at-bats and his batting average plummeted from .378 in 1921 to .315. Ruth and Bob Meusel were suspended for the first month of the season as their barnstorming trip after the 1921 World Series was declared illegal by Commissioner Kenesaw Mountain Landis. Second-place St. Louis (93–61), managed by Lee Fohl, finished one game off the pace and led the junior league in batting average (.313), on-base percentage (.372), slugging percentage (.455), stolen bases (136), and stolen base percentage (64.2 percent). The Browns George Sisler won the AL stolen base crown with 51 thefts, while teammate Ken Williams finished second (37). Williams was a six-foot, 170-pound, left-handed hitting slugger, who had an exceptional season in 1922, batting .332 with a .413 on-base percentage, a .627 slugging percentage, 128 runs scored, and a league-leading 39 homers and 155 RBIs. He may have been the first player to use a corked bat and Sisler was once accused of driving nails into his bat.

The fifth-place Chicago Cubs led the NL with 205 sacrifices, while the top five teams in the AL had more than 200, including the third-place Detroit Tigers who led the majors with 244. Zeb Terry, the Cubs' 31-year-old second baseman, batted .286 during his final big league campaign, stole only two bases in thirteen attempts and led the NL with 39 sacrifice hits. Terry compiled 141 sacrifices during his seven-year career, an impressive number considering he played a total of thirty games in 1917 and 1918. Bill Wambsganss batted .262 for Cleveland, stole seventeen bags, and led the AL with 42 sacrifice hits. He ranks seventh all-time with 323 sacrifice hits. Wambsganss had twenty-six or more sacrifices during eight seasons. He garnered at least 40 sacrifices in 1920 (40), 1921 (43), and 1922 (42). Ray Chapman, who played with Wambsganss from 1914 until his death in 1920, ranks sixth all-time (334).

Perhaps John McGraw found greater satisfaction in his four-game sweep of the Yankees in the 1922 World Series than his previous season's world title. It wasn't that the Giants won, but it was how they won, as the Yankees made a fool of themselves, and conducted themselves in a manner that was befitting of the bush leagues. The Giants had a 1.76 ERA compared to the Yankees' 3.35 in the series. However, McGraw's club made six errors, while Miller Huggins's aggregation made only one. Frankie Frisch stole the only base for the National League representative, while Bob Meusel and Wally Pipp swiped one apiece for the Yankees. The second game of the series ended in a 3–3 tie after ten innings despite the fact that the fading sun was still shining. Commissioner Landis was pushed around by the angry crowd as he exited the ballpark. Landis was also furious with the arbiters for their decision and to quell the fears that the game had been called to give the owners an extra payday, Landis gave the entire receipts to New York charities. Babe Ruth batted only .118 in the fall classic as he couldn't handle the slow curves thrown at his direction. It was rumored that McGraw called every pitch his hurlers threw in the series.

The fourth game of the series when the Giants prevailed, 4–3, was when the Yankees embarrassed themselves. The inhabitants of New York who read the *New York Times* on

October 8 were confronted with the following headline that read in part, "BAD BASE RUN-NING BEAT THE YANKEES: Analysis Shows That Slow Thinking on Paths Cost Huggins's Team at Least 2 Runs." Bob Meusel and Wally Pipp were the worst culprits, while Wally Schang, manager Miller Huggins, and coach Charley O'Leary were also responsible. The mistakes that were made were not one of the intricate plays of the inside game. These were mistakes that a neophyte could pick up and they "were blunders that would have caused minor leaguers to blush." Meusel and Pipp's mistakes were "errors of omission rather than commission — lapses above the shoulder rather than physical."[18] Bob Meusel, a 6'3", 190-pound, right-handed hitter, stepped into the batter's box to lead off the seventh inning with the Yankees trailing, 4–2. Meusel grounded to Heinie Groh at third base and he didn't run hard and slowed up as he approached the bag, assuming that Groh would throw him out. He violated one of the unofficial rules of the game, demanding that a hitter should always run hard to first base. Meusel had no excuse, especially considering that the infield grass was wet. Groh's long throw across the diamond was off target, and it bounced in front of first baseman, George Kelly, who couldn't handle it. But Meusel had given up on the play and was not running to first, which allowed Kelly to retrieve the ball and beat Meusel to the bag. Two batters later, Aaron Ward hit a homer, and because of Meusel's indolence, the score stood at 4–3 instead of being tied.

Pipp's blunder came after he sent Hugh McQuillan's offering off the right-field wall for a double as the first batter in the last of the ninth. Meusel tried to sacrifice him to third on the first pitch, but the ball went foul. Pipp got a long lead off second and then Meusel swung away, hitting a grounder towards Groh at third. The play was in front of Pipp and he should have held up, but he ran towards the next base right into an out. He got into a rundown and was tagged out by shortstop Dave Bancroft. If he wanted to advance to third, he should have waited until Groh threw the ball to first, and then took off for the next station. Excuses were plentiful after the game, including the illogical one that insisted that Pipp was crossed up because he was expecting Meusel to bunt. There was more discontent in the ninth when Wally Schang followed with a single to center, sending Meusel to third. O'Leary was coaching at first base and he waved Schang to second. Schang, a switch-hitting catcher, was not a fast runner and with the difficult footing even a speed merchant would have had second thoughts about going to second. If there was ever a time for insubordination, this was it. The play was in front of Schang, it should have been his decision, not O'Leary's. Schang was an easy out at second base and then Ward flew out to Irish Meusel in left field and what could have been a great comeback became a demoralizing defeat.

Huggins's mistake came along the third base coaching lines when he held up Whitey Witt at third in the opening frame when he could have scored easily from second on Ruth's long drive to center field in the spacious Polo Grounds. Bill Cunningham, the Giants center fielder, almost ran out of room nearly 500 feet away from home plate but he caught the ball in front of the bleachers. Luckily for Huggins, the Yankees scored two runs in the inning as Witt and Joe Dugan made their way safely across home plate.

It was reported that the Giants got the breaks and luck allowed them to score their four runs. The Giants were unrestrained in their enthusiasm after the game. McGraw said that Bancroft, McQuillan, and Groh, were the most responsible for the win. The locker room was filled with shouting and laughter. They laughed at silly jokes that under normal conditions would not even crack a smile. Casey Stengel, who batted a career high .368 with a .436 on-base percentage and a .564 slugging percentage in 250 at-bats during the regular season, would stop and make an "exaggerated theatrical gesture" and recite "facetious quotations from the classics."[19] Heinie Groh sat in front of his locker, laughing uncontrollably, and shaking. Art Nehf was generally quiet and temperate, but he was among the Giants leading the joking. Coach Cozy Dolan had a grin on his face that didn't come off. The Giants needed one more win to secure the world championship, but the Yankees were done. In game five the Giants won, 5–3, as Babe Ruth went hitless for the third consecutive game. Amazingly, Ruth laid down a sacrifice bunt in the top of the first inning in that final contest. Joe Vila wrote the following at the conclusion of the series: "The exploded phenomenon didn't surprise the smart fans who long ago realized that he couldn't hit brainy pitching. Ruth, therefore, is no longer a wonder. The baseball public is onto his real worth as a batsman and in the future, let us hope, he will attract just ordinary attention."[20] For those who wanted a return to the way baseball was played during the Deadball Era, this was not reality but just a dream. It was a false hope that the great Ruth had fallen and would never get up.

The Giants (95–58) and the Yankees (98–54) would dominate major league baseball in 1923 once again and meet in the World Series for the third year in a row. Huggins's squad was playing their first season in Yankee Stadium and this team excelled at power hitting, leading the league in homers (105) and slugging percentage (.422), while performing poorly in the less meaningful small ball categories with 69 steals, which ranked seventh in the American League, and finishing last in the circuit with 145 sacrifices. The Babe was back, leading the majors in several categories, including runs scored (151), homers (41), RBIs (131), walks (170), on-base percentage (.545), and slugging percentage (.764). Cy Williams of the last-place Philadelphia Phillies also hit 41 homers as he prospered in the salubrious hitting grounds of the Baker Bowl. The Phillies led the majors with 112 homers. Despite the fact that some people thought that Williams was the fastest runner in the majors, he never stole more than 18 bags in a season and finished his nineteen-year career with 115 steals. After losing two consecutive World Series, the 1923 fall classic started poorly for the Yankees, as Casey Stengel of the Giants won the opener with a two-out inside-the-park homer in the top of the ninth. But the Yankees won the series, four games to two, as Ruth batted .368 with three homers. For the second year in a row there was little basestealing as Aaron Ward swiped the only base in the series for the Yankees, while Dave Bancroft had the only one for the Giants. Frankie Frisch was the only runner caught stealing, as Yankees catcher Wally Schang gunned him down trying to pilfer the second sack in the top of the first inning of the opening game. The Yankees had all four sacrifice bunts in the series, including three in their 8–4 game four triumph.

The fourth-place Chicago Cubs led the NL with 181 steals, while Chicago's American League outfit, a seventh-place team, led the AL with 191. With the help of Max Carey, who won another stolen base crown in an effective manner (51 steals, 8 caught stealing), the Pirates led the majors with a 67.2 percent stolen base average and finished second in the NL with 154 steals. The AL stolen base crown was secured by Eddie Collins (48) of the Pale Hose, while his teammate Johnny Mostil (41) finished second. Collins batted .360 during the campaign with a .455 on-base percentage and he stole bases at a 62.3 percent clip. Mostil patrolled the center field pasture for the Sox and batted .291 with a .376 on-base percentage and compiled an impressive 71.9 percent basestealing average. The junior league was in a long stretch of dominating the senior circuit in sacrifice hits, year after year, collecting 508 more in 1923. Second-place Cincinnati (91–63), led by skipper Pat Moran, led the NL with 185 sacrifices, while second-place Detroit (83–71) led the AL (256). Stuffy McInnis, the former member of the Philadelphia Athletics $100,000 infield, and a highly skilled defensive first baseman, who finished his career after playing one game in 1927 with a .307 lifetime batting average and 172 steals, led the NL in sacrifices in 1923 with 37, while playing for the Boston Braves. He ranks third all-time with 383 sacrifices and is the only right-handed batter in the top five in that category (three left-handed hitters and one switch hitter). McInnis had twelve seasons of twenty or more sacrifices and had a career high of 45 sacrifices in 1920 with the Boston Red Sox. Roger Peckinpaugh was also best known for his glove, but at the shortstop position. He was built solidly, a five-foot-ten-and-a-half-inch, 165-pound, right-handed pull hitter, who played for four AL teams during his seventeen-year career, batting .259 with 205 steals, including a high of 38 with the 1914 New York Yankees. Peckinpaugh's batting average was hurt by the fact he was a dead pull hitter and the defense playing him accordingly. However, he helped his teams in different ways and ranks 8th all-time with 314 sacrifice hits.

It is not surprising that the eleven major league players who collected 300 or more sacrifice hits during their careers either toiled predominantly during the Deadball Era when games were generally low scoring and there was more value placed on the sacrifice bunt in an attempt to push across that one run that can win you the ball game or they played most of their career at a time when sacrifice flies were counted as sacrifice hits. Willie Keeler is the only ballplayer on this list to play during the nineteenth century and the only one who did not play all or most of his career during the time when sacrifice flies were counted as sacrifice hits from 1908 to 1930 and in 1939. Keeler played big league ball from 1892 to 1910 and benefited from the sacrifice fly rule for only three seasons, from 1908 to 1910, when he played 209 games. The 300 sacrifice hit club is as follows:

Player	*Sacrifice Hits*
1. Eddie Collins	512
2. Jake Daubert	392
3. Stuffy McInnis	383
4. Willie Keeler	366
5. Donie Bush	337
6. Ray Chapman	334
7. Bill Wambsganss	323
8. Roger Peckinpaugh	314
9. Larry Gardner	311
10. Tris Speaker	309
11. Rabbit Maranville	300

Marty Callaghan, a 5'10", 157-pound, left-handed outfielder, who had a four-year big league career with the Chicago Cubs (1922–1923) and the Cincinnati Reds (1928 and 1930), had one of his ten career stolen bases on May 4, 1923. It was a steal of home in the tenth inning versus the Cardinals as Chicago prevailed, 2–1. The Cleveland Indians annihilated the Boston Red Sox, who were destined for a last-place finish in 1923, by a 27–3 score on July 7, and they also took the second game of the twin bill, 8–5. Lefty O'Doul, a 26-year-old relief pitcher for Boston, allowed thirteen unearned runs after two outs were recorded in the sixth frame of the opener. Manager Frank Chance was merciless and allowed his pitcher to take a beating because he was annoyed by his off-the-field activities. He walked eight batters, surrendered eleven hits, and yielded sixteen runs while working three innings, the fourth through sixth. The Indians ended the sixth inning massacre themselves by deliberately making an out on the bases: Joe Sewell stole a bag and then Riggs Stephenson was caught stealing. Lefty O'Doul's best days were ahead of him, as a hitter not as a pitcher.

The Pittsburgh Pirates' 18–5 triumph over Philadelphia may have looked like a big score on any other day.

When the Tribe defeated Washington, 22–2, on August 7, Frank H. Young of the *Washington Post* began his column as follows, "If the Indians who figured in Custer's last stand, famous in history, were any more blood-thirsty than Speaker's tribe was against the gentle Nats in yesterday's engagement, that early massacre must have been just as terrible as the press notices say it was." The "Redskins" were on the "war path," collecting twenty-six hits and running the bases like wild men. Washington skipper Donie Bush was criticized for sending three rookies to the slab: Monroe Mitchell, Skipper Friday, and Squire Potter. Interestingly, all three moundsmen pitched sparingly in 1923 and never pitched in the big leagues again. For Potter it was his only major league game, allowing nine runs on eleven hits and four walks in three innings. Young jokingly wrote that the fans were wondering if they were going to see the trainer, Mike Martin, or the bat boy pitch if Washington tied the game. With the game well in hand, Cleveland apparently tried to steal bases, getting caught stealing two times in the seventh and once apiece in the eighth and ninth. The way Frank Young described it, they were not running up the score but "allowed themselves to be put out" on the bases. One runner was out trying to stretch a double into a triple. Young reported that George Uhle, the Cleveland pitcher, was "lobbing 'em over" because Washington had lost their "ambition" in the later innings. The Indians first baseman, Frank Brower, stole the only base, while their leadoff man, Charlie Jamieson, who batted .345 during the season with a .422 on-base percentage and league leading 222 hits, had one sacrifice, while Sewell had the other.[21] Washington got their revenge over Cleveland with a 20–8 win on August 24 as they collected twenty-two hits and were the beneficiary of fourteen walks. The Senators cleanup hitter, Sam Rice, scored five runs, while Goose Goslin scored four. Washington stole four bags: Peckinpaugh, Bucky Harris (167 career steals), Joe Judge (213 career steals), and Rice. Stephenson (53 career steals) swiped the only bag for the Tribe. Peckinpaugh, Joe Evans, and Muddy Ruel had sacrifice hits for the Senators.

The Senators were at Comiskey Park in Chicago on August 15 and split a twin bill with the Sox. George Mogridge, a well-liked and respected southpaw moundsman, pitched Washington to a 5–1 twelve inning victory in the opener. Eddie Collins and Harry Hooper (.288, 18 steals) stole one base apiece for Chicago, while Judge (.314, 11 steals), Nemo Leibold (.294, 7 steals), and Mogridge (13–13) stole bases for Washington. Peckinpaugh had a sacrifice for the Senators, while Mostil and Collins had one apiece for the Sox. The White Sox started their ninth inning rally to tie the game when Hooper led off with a double, advanced to third on Mostil's bunt, and Collins drove him in with a sacrifice. But that was the only run allowed by Mogridge on the day. In the top of the twelfth when Washington pushed across four runs, Mogridge stole home on the front end of a double steal. He is reportedly the only pitcher to steal home in extra innings. Red Faber of the White Sox was the only other pitcher to steal home in 1923, when he accomplished this feat versus St. Louis on April 23, which was the second time he did so during his career. Mogridge was the last pitcher to steal home until September 23, 1943, when Johnny Vander Meer did it. Faber won the second game, 4–3, for Chicago. Hooper, Mostil, and Collins stole bases, while Peckinpaugh had a sacrifice hit and Chicago's first baseman and cleanup hitter, Earl Sheely, had two, while their left fielder, Bibb Falk, had one. Firpo Marberry, the Senators right-handed rookie pitcher, became unnerved in the eighth when Collins legged out a bunt after Mostil singled. The pair then pulled off a double steal as Collins stole his thirty-fifth. They scored on a fly ball by Sheely, one of his two sacrifices in the game, and a double by Falk. Interestingly, after the end of the Deadball Era most of the box scores no longer made a distinction between sacrifice flies and sacrifice bunts. When the White Sox whitewashed Philadelphia, 10–0, on August 23 they stole six bases: Collins, Hooper, rookie third baseman Willie Kamm (.292, 18 steals), and Mostil had one apiece, while Bill Barrett (.272, 12 steals in 44 games) had two.

During Hooper's five seasons with the White Sox from 1921 to 1925 they finished in the second division every year. He missed the scientific game which was prevalent during his seasons with the Red Sox and regretted the fact that players with excellent statistics on a club which could not bring home a pennant were lauded more extensively than players who made various contributions to team play such as Larry Gardner, Duffy Lewis, and Joe Wood. After three consecutive seasons of batting at least .304, he dipped to .288 in 1923 as the critics suggested that the end was near and his legs were giving out. Hooper bounced back in 1924, batting .328 with a .413 on-base percentage and sixteen steals before ending his Hall of Fame career after batting .265 with twelve steals in 1925.

In Pittsburgh's 5–2 win over Brooklyn on August 13 at Ebbets Field, the Pirates 29-year-old, right-handed pitcher Lee Meadows had his no-hit bid broken up in the seventh frame as Gene Bailey, a weak-hitting 29-year-old outfielder, laid down a bunt towards the first baseman and beat it out. In the first inning, Max Carey stole second and third and then swiped home on a delayed double steal. He "outguessed" Brooklyn during each of his steals and the throws were not even close to getting him. On the double steal, Johnny Rawlings enticed the catcher Hank DeBerry to throw to second and when he did, Carey broke for the plate.[22]

For Frank Chance, an excellent practitioner of the inside game, the national pastime had changed mightily since the end of the Deadball Era. He was a player-manager for ten seasons during the Deadball Era with the Chicago Cubs (1905–1912) and New York Yankees (1913–1914) and managed for one additional season in 1923, as his Boston Red Sox concluded the campaign in the cellar (61–91). Chance said, "I started out on the theory that it was wise to get a run, give my pitchers something to work on, but I early discovered that such a system wouldn't get you very far in the majors these days." Connie Mack summed up the new style of play in 1923, "Inside baseball is all right, but you gotta have the punch."[23] The new style of play impacted the batting orders, as managers no longer sought to put a great bunter in the two hole. Tris Speaker said, "I want a hitter up there." Managers relied on platooning more than ever, while Speaker used a different strategy of alternating left-handed and right-handed batters in the lineup.[24] Frank Chance was going to manage the Chicago White Sox in 1924, but he contracted bronchial asthma and his life ended far too soon on September 15, 1924, at the age of forty-seven.

In many ways the 1924 World Series was a battle between big ball and small ball. The Giants were the power hitting team in the series, as they led the National League with 95 homers and they were an unexceptional small ball aggregation. John McGraw led the Giants to his final pennant (93–60), edging out Brooklyn (92–62) by a game and a half. They led the National League with 857 runs scored, 1,634 hits, a .300 team batting average, a .358 on-base percentage, and a .432 slugging percentage. Their 82 stolen bases ranked fifth in the league, well behind third-place Pittsburgh who led the majors with 181 steals and a 66.3 percent basestealing average. New York's 127 sacrifices ranked seventh in the league, while fifth-place Chicago led the circuit with only 163. In the junior league, the Washington Senators won the pennant (92–62) despite finishing last in the majors with 22 homers, less than half the number accumulated by Babe Ruth (46). Despite leading the AL with 88 triples, they had a .387 slugging percentage, which was ranked sixth in the league. They ranked second in the AL in steals (116) behind last-place Chicago who accumulated 137. And they tied the White Sox with a major league leading 232 sacrifices. In the closely played World Series, the Senators won the decisive game seven contest, 4–3, in twelve innings to capture the title. Player-manager Bucky Harris captured the pennant during his first two seasons as skipper in 1924 and 1925. In the 1924 series, the Senators had a 2.42 ERA compared to New York's 3.11. They hit more homers than the Giants, 5 to 4, stole more bases, 5 to 3, and laid down more sacrifice bunts, 5 to 4.

Bucky Harris was only 27 years old in 1924 and was known as the "boy manager." He was a gentleman, who was well-liked by his players, and married the daughter of a U.S. Senator in 1926. In 1924 the second baseman batted .268 with 20 steals and 10 caught stealing. He led the majors with 46 sacrifice hits and would also lead the junior circuit in 1925 (41) and 1927 (30). His 249 career sacrifices (40th all-time) is an impressive number considering that during three of his twelve major league seasons, he played a total of nineteen games. The future Hall of Famer accomplished that feat by hitting out of the right hand side of the batter's box. Babe Pinelli, a right-handed hitting third baseman, batted .276 lifetime with 71 steals and 145 sacrifices in an eight-year career. He led the NL in sacrifices in 1924 (33) with Cincinnati and would do so again in 1925 (34). Max Carey won another stolen base crown in 1924 (49), while Eddie Collins won his second consecutive American League title with 42.

During Ty Cobb's first four seasons as the Detroit Tigers' player-manager from 1921 to 1924 they improved each season. In 1920 with Hughie Jennings as the skipper the Tigers finished in seventh place with a .396 winning percentage and during the next four seasons with Cobb steering the ship, the Tigers had winning percentages of .464, .513, .539, and .558. They had a terrific outfield consisting of Heinie Manush, Cobb, and Harry Heilmann. Third-place Detroit led the junior circuit in several categories in 1924, including runs scored (849), batting average (.298), and on-base percentage (.373). Their 100 stolen bases ranked third in the circuit, while their 225 sacrifices was second. Eddie Collins said that Cobb, "saw, decided, and acted all at once."[25] At 37 years old "The Georgia Peach" was slowing down, but for Cobb that meant batting .338 with a .418 on-base percentage, scoring 115 runs, collecting 211 hits, and stealing 23 bags. In Detroit's 8–4 victory over St. Louis on April 22, he stole home in the third inning. And then five days later he stole home again in a 4–3 triumph over Chicago. On August 10, while Detroit was in the process of defeating Boston, 13–7, he scored four runs, stole four bags, including third twice and home once.

Manager Johnny Evers's Chicago White Sox were in Cleveland on May 1 and defeated the Indians, 13–7. They scored four in the top of the first and never trailed in the game. The Sox stole six bags during the high scoring battle: one by Collins, two by Ray French, and three by Bill Barrett. Barrett was a 23-year-old, third-year player, who played shortstop (77 games), the outfield (28 games), and third base (8 games) during the campaign. He batted .271 with 15 steals. The May 1 game was most likely one of the highlights of his career as he scored three runs, collected three singles and a double, and stole home twice. His first steal of home came in the first inning against the battery of southpaw hurler Joe Shaute and catcher Glenn Myatt. Then in the ninth Barrett stole home on the front end of a double steal with French stealing a bag behind him. Both teams combined for four sacrifices, perhaps, the most important coming in the five-run ninth for Chicago when Collins led off the frame with a walk, was sacrificed to second by Earl Sheely, and he scored on Willie Kamm's single. Ray French had a three-year major league career with the Yankees (1920), Robins (1923), and White Sox (1924). He batted .193 lifetime in 187 at-bats and stole three bags, two of which came in this game.

In 1924 there were two game-ending steals of home. Pat McNulty, a 5'11", 160-pound, left-handed hitting outfielder, stole home against Boston's big, 6'2", 200-pound, right-hander George Murray in the eleventh inning on June 14 to give the Tribe a 3–2 win. Bill Hubbell, the Phillies' 27-year-old right-handed pitcher, was on the bump when Cliff Heathcote of the Chicago Cubs swiped home with two outs in the last of the ninth to send the Wrigley Field fans home happy with a 3–2 win on July 17. Heathcote was also an outer garden resident like McNulty, and finished tied for third in the NL in steals in 1923 (32) and also finished third in 1924 (26). In a fifteen-year National League career with the Cardinals (1918–1922), Cubs (1922–1930), Reds (1931–1932), and Phillies (1932), he batted .275 lifetime with 191 steals.

The game of baseball as it was played during the 1920s was very different than the way it is played in the twenty-first century. There were moves that were tolerated in the 1920s that are unacceptable by today's standards, such as stealing bases with a large lead. Consider the game between the St. Louis Cardinals and Brooklyn Robins at Ebbets Field on September 16, 1924. This was the game in which Jim Bottomley, the Cardinals 24-year-old first baseman, went 6 for 6 with 12 RBIs. St. Louis crushed Brooklyn, 17–3. Taylor Douthit, a 23-year-old backup outfielder for St. Louis, who was getting a rare start, pilfered second base in the sixth inning with the Cardinals comfortably ahead, 9–1. Jimmy Cooney, the Cardinals third baseman in this game, also stole second base in the sixth inning but the score was 13–1 at that juncture. With a 4–0 lead and runners on first and second with nobody out in the second frame, Douthit fouled out as he unsuccessfully tried to lay down a bunt. However, in the fourth inning with the score 5–1, he laid down a successful sacrifice bunt in a similar situation. Douthit again executed a sacrifice bunt in the seventh inning with the score, 13–1, but he advanced safely to first base on a fielder's choice as the pitcher unsuccessfully tried to cut down the runner at second. Amazingly, the next hitter, the great Rogers Hornsby, who stepped into the box with a .425 batting average and was on his way to leading the senior league in batting, on-base percentage, and slugging percentage for the fifth season in a row, also laid down a sacrifice bunt. At season's end he had a .424 batting average, a .507 on-base percentage, and a .696 slugging percentage. And yet he bunted with his team leading 13–1. Hornsby's sacrifice bunt was followed by a two-RBI single by Bottomley, which tied the single game RBI record and was later surpassed in the ninth inning with a run producing one-base hit. Ironically, the record was previously held by Brooklyn's manager, Wilbert Robinson, who drove in eleven runs for Baltimore on June 10, 1892. With runners on first and second and nobody out in the first inning, Hornsby also laid down a bunt, perhaps in an attempt to sacrifice the runners over, and legged it out for a hit.

Despite batting only .294 with little power in 1925, Roger Peckinpaugh was voted the AL MVP by the sportswriters, mainly because of his outstanding defensive play and leadership qualities. But in the World Series, things unraveled as he committed eight errors, including three at critical times that led to two Washington losses. Manager Bill McKechnie's Pittsburgh Pirates defeated the Senators, four games to three. The Pirates stole seven bags in the series, including three by Carey, while Washington stole two. The Senators laid down eight sacrifice bunts, while Pittsburgh had six. Kiki Cuyler, the Pirates three-hole hitter in the series, finished fourth in the NL with a .357 batting average during the regular season, and then hit .269 in the fall classic with three sacrifice bunts. Pittsburgh's potent offense led the majors in several categories, including runs scored (912), doubles (316), triples (105), slugging percentage (.449), stolen bases (159), and stolen base percentage (71.6 percent). They scored 188 more runs than the previous season, partially because the distance down the right-field line at Forbes Field was reduced from 376 to 300 feet. The National League had 400 fewer sacrifices than the American League and 44 fewer stolen bases. Third-place Cincinnati led the senior circuit with 173 sacrifices, while the fifth-place Chicago White Sox led the AL with 231. The White Sox, led by player-manager Eddie Collins, stole 131 bags, which was second in the league behind Washington (135). And just like during the previous few seasons, the Sox were a solid small ball outfit, but one that resided in the second division. Max Carey batted .343 with Pittsburgh and won his tenth and final stolen base crown with 46 thefts. Pirates outfielder Kiki Cuyler finished second with 41 steals (75.9 percent basestealing average) and led the majors in runs scored (144) and triples (26). Johnny Mostil of the White Sox won the first of two consecutive stolen base titles with 43 bags and he was followed by Goose Goslin (27) and Sam Rice (26) of Washington.

Lou Gehrig played a total of twenty-three games in 1923 and 1924. And then he batted .295 with a .365 on-base percentage and a .531 slugging percentage in 126 games in 1925. He stole six bases that season and 102 during his career (100 caught stealing). The first stolen base of his career was memorable as he stole home on the front end of a double steal in New York's 5–3 win against Washington on June 24, 1925. Wally Schang, a .284 lifetime hitter with 121 steals, stole second base while Gehrig was stealing home.

In an interview with Bill Van Fleet, Rogers Hornsby, who was the St. Louis Cardinals player-manager in 1926, said the following about that season's World Series: "We were brash Davids throwing rocks at the Yankee Goliaths and nobody can say we didn't give 'em a battle."[26] In fact the Cardinals gave them more than a battle and defeated the mighty Yankees aggregation, four games to three. Ruth batted .300 in the series with four homers, including three in game four. He had shown poor baserunning judgment in the past, but in this series it cost the Yankees dearly. The Yankees were trailing, 3–2, with two outs in the last of the ninth in game seven when Grover Alexander walked the Babe. To steal a bag in this situation would be fantastic, but you better be damn sure you're going to make it. If a young Ty Cobb was hugging first, or Max Carey, or Frankie Frisch, or George Sisler, or Eddie Collins, the risk may be justified. But if you're Babe Ruth you may want to stay anchored to the bag. Ruth took off for second on the first pitch, running on his own with no sign transmitted from the bench. Bob O'Farrell's throw reached the bag well in time for second baseman Hornsby to slap the tag on him. Lee Allen wrote that he was "out by a mile."[27] This was a slight exaggeration as Hornsby said Ruth was out by ten feet. There were only three steals in the 1926 World Series: one by Hornsby and Billy Southworth for St. Louis, while Ruth stole one for New York. This was the St. Louis Cardinals first world championship and the final out of the series was a gift.

The sacrifice bunt was the primary small ball weapon employed in the autumn classic as the Cardinals laid down nine sacrifices and the Yankees collected seven. And it wasn't just the pitchers and the Punch-and-Judy hitters who sacrificed runners over. Bob Meusel, the Yankees cleanup hitter, who led the junior circuit with 33 homers and 138 RBIs during the previous season and then hit 12 homers and drove in 81 in 1926, laid down two sacrifice bunts in the series. The Cardinals cleanup man, Jim Bottomley, who led the National League with 40 doubles, 305 total bases, and 120 RBIs, during the regular season, laid down one sacrifice in the fall classic. Hornsby and Gehrig also had sacrifice bunts.

In 1926 the National League teams stole only 608 bases, while the American League teams stole 667. There wasn't a single NL team that stole over 100 bases, which was the first time this occurred in the history of either league. The fifth-place New York Giants led the senior circuit with only 94 steals. Player-manager Eddie Collins's Chicago White Sox finished in fifth place and led the junior league with 123 steals. The second-place Cincinnati Reds of the NL and the third-place Philadelphia Athletics of the AL tied for the major league lead with 239 sacrifice hits. Taylor Douthit of St. Louis led the NL in sacrifices in 1926 with 37, while Freddy Spurgeon of Cleveland led the AL with 35. The stolen base crowns were secured by Kiki Cuyler of Pittsburgh in the NL (35) and Johnny Mostil of Chicago in the AL (35).

After four consecutive stolen base titles, 36-year-old Max Carey began showing his age in 1926. After batting .222 with 10 steals in 86 games, he was released by Pittsburgh when he got into a dispute with management over the presence of former manager Fred Clarke on the bench, who undermined and second guessed current skipper Bill McKechnie. With Brooklyn he batted .260 in 100 at-bats, but didn't steal a bag. However, he still possessed a strong and accurate throwing arm. He knew the tendencies of senior league batters and positioned himself superbly to catch enemy drives. Furthermore, Carey helped the young outfielders like Babe Herman and he would later manage the Dodgers in 1932 and 1933. Carey's basestealing average in 1926 is a mystery because the caught stealing statistic is not available for the 1926 National League season. From 1926 until 1950 the NL did not record caught stealing totals and they resumed doing so in 1951.

With two outs in the sixth inning at Sportsman's Park on May 3 in a contest between Cincinnati and St. Louis, the Reds executed a triple steal. Wally Pipp was at first base for the Reds when St. Louis pitcher Vic Keen walked the next three batters: Red Lucas, Val Picinich, and Walter "Cuckoo" Christensen. Perhaps the Cardinals should have known something was up when Sam Bohne ran for Lucas at third. The Reds pulled off the triple steal on the second pitch to Hughie Critz. Cincinnati won the game, 9–6. The Phillies were in Cincinnati on May 6 and lost 14–4 as the Reds were credited with eight sacrifices to tie a major league record. It was also a game with several attempted double steals, not all of which were successful. With Cincinnati up comfortably in the eighth inning they pushed across three more runs with the help of a sacrifice bunt and a stolen base. The headline in the *Philadelphia Inquirer* read, "REDLEGS SLAUGHTER QUAKERS IN FIRST FRAY." James C. Isaminger referred to the Reds as "blood-thirsty hostiles." The game was "a rout, a debacle," and manager Art Fletcher's Phillies played their worse game of the year up to this juncture.[28]

Ty Cobb stole home in the first inning on July 3 against Cleveland with George Uhle on the hill. However, the Indians prevailed, 7–5. Sluggers Lou Gehrig and Babe Ruth pulled off a double steal on April 13 and then did it again on July 24 in a 7–4 win against Chicago. On September 1, the Senators defeated the Red Sox, 14–12, in a game that Frank H. Young of the *Washington Post* insisted that almost all the pitchers were "mistreated" and the game "developed into a test as to which team's pitchers were the least ineffective, the Red Sox won the argument and the Nationals won the game."[29] This game is significant in the history of small ball because both teams combined for a major league record eleven sacrifices. Sam Rice and Joe Judge had two apiece for Washington. Buddy Myer, Bucky Harris, and Muddy Ruel had one apiece for the Senators. Topper Rigney, William "Baby Doll" Jacobson, Bill Regan, and Fred Haney had one apiece for Boston. Interestingly, there wasn't a single sacrifice credited to a pitcher. Several of the bunts helped produce runs, including Ruel's squeeze play in the third inning. Earl McNeely, the Washington leadoff man, who batted .303 with eighteen steals and only six caught stealing in 1926, swiped two bags in this game. Buddy Myer, their 22-year-old shortstop, who batted .304 during the season, stole one of his ten bases. And Simon Rosenthal, who was known as "Si" and was playing his second and last big league season for Boston, also stole a bag.

The 1927 New York Yankees ran roughshod over American League competition, compiling a 110–44 record, and then swept manager Donie Bush's Pittsburgh Pirates (94–60) in the World Series. Bob Meusel and Babe Ruth stole the only bases in the series. New York scored thirteen more runs than Pittsburgh (23 to 10) and their pitchers compiled a 2.00 ERA versus the Pirates, 5.19 ERA. During the regular season, Ruth hit sixty homers, which was more long balls than seven AL teams and five NL teams. The second-place St. Louis Cardinals led the senior circuit with 110 steals, while fifth-place Cincinnati compiled the most sacrifices with 219. In the American League, manager George Moriarty's fourth-place Detroit Tigers led the circuit with 139 steals, while fifth-place Chicago had the most sacrifices (234). Frankie Frisch won his second stolen base crown (48) during his first season as a member of the St. Louis Cardinals as he hit for a .337 clip. Max Carey batted .266 for Brooklyn and finished second in the circuit with 32 steals. The American League stolen base crown was secured by George Sisler (27) and he was followed by Bob Meusel (24), Johnny Neun (22), Tony Lazzeri (22), and Ty Cobb (22). The sacrifice hit titles belonged to Pie Traynor of Pittsburgh (35) and Bucky Harris of Washington (30).

After twenty-two seasons as a member of the Detroit Tigers, Ty Cobb wore the uniform of the Philadelphia Athletics in 1927 and batted .357 with a .440 on-base percentage. He scored 104 runs and stole 22 bags in his second to last season. In the Athletics 3–1 win over the Senators on April 19, he stole home on the front end of a triple steal. George Burns, the Cleveland first baseman, stole home for the second day in a row on May 27 as the Indians triumphed over the Browns, 7–3. He was on the front end of a double steal, while Joe Sewell swiped a bag on the back end. Sewell stole only three bases in nineteen attempts during the season and had a 15.8 percent basestealing average. This was not George Joseph Burns, who was best known for playing for John McGraw's Giants from 1911 to 1921. The Tribe's first sacker was George Henry Burns, also known as "Tioga George," who played for five American League teams from 1914 to 1929 and batted .307 lifetime with 154 steals. Also on May 27, Tris Speaker, who batted .327 with nine steals in his second to last big league season with the Washington Senators, stole home on a delayed double steal with Joe Judge in the first game of a doubleheader versus New York. The Senators won the opener, 7–2, but lost the nightcap, 5–0. Third-place Washington finished second in the junior league with 133 steals in 1927 and also led the circuit with a 71.9 percent basestealing average. The Browns fell to the Athletics, 11–9, at Shibe Park on June 7 as Cobb swiped one bag, while George Sisler stole three. In addition to winning his fourth and final stolen base crown in 1927, "Gorgeous George" Sisler had an impressive 79.4 percent basestealing average.

Johnny Neun, Detroit's switch-hitting first baseman, batted .324 with a .427 on-base percentage in 204 at-bats during the 1927 campaign. During his six-year big league career with the Tigers and Braves, he stole 41 bases, but 22 of them came in 1927 when he also compiled an impressive 75.9 percent stolen base average. There were at least two days when Neun had notable basestealing accomplishments, including the day he stole home in both ends of a doubleheader versus Washington. On July 9 in the second game of a bargain bill versus New York he went 5 for 5 and stole five bags, which was 22.7 percent of his 1927 total. The Tigers purloined eight sacks in the game, as Jack Warner, Harry Heilmann, and Johnny Bassler garnered one apiece. The Navin Field crowd enjoyed watching the home team win by a 14–4 score in the nightcap but it came after the Yankees clobbered the Tigers, 19–7, in the opener. Amazingly, Richards Vidmer's lengthy article in the *New York Times* did not even mention Johnny Neun's name, despite the fact that he became only the fourth player since 1900 to steal at least five bags in a game. He devoted nearly the entire article to Babe Ruth's two homers in the lidlifter, mesmerized by the accomplishment of the king of clout, and dismissive of small ball strategies which were in decline and part of the distant days of the Deadball Era.[30]

The Yankee pitchers, in general, did a poor job of holding the Detroit baserunners close to the bag in the series and starter Herb Pennock was perhaps the worst culprit on the following day. In the opening inning, Charlie Gehringer singled, stole second, and then got a huge lead off second base, which allowed him to score easily on Heinie Manush's single. Pennock, who was a six-foot, 160-pound, left-handed pitcher, finally began paying more attention to the baserunner and picked Manush off first. W.B. Hanna wrote in the *New York Herald Tribune*, "Our boys in their fourth showed their themselves a bit bereft of base running acumen." Lou Gehrig started the top of the fourth for New York with a double and then Meusel grounded to Jack Warner at third base. Warner fumbled the ball momentarily and then ran down Gehrig for the first out. Meanwhile, Meusel rounded first and headed for second where he was out by about ten feet. Detroit took a 6–1 lead when they pushed across four runs in the last of the fourth. The highlight of the inning was Jackie Tavener's three steals. His steal of home was part of a double steal. Larry Woodall, who stole nine bases in ten attempts in 1927, stole the bag on the back end. Hanna insisted, "The Tiger runners were making bushers out of the Yankees and particularly out of their pitcher." Tavener was a 5'5", 138-pound, left-handed hitting shortstop, who batted .274 during the season with nineteen steals and eight caught stealing. New York's only stolen base in the game was by second baseman Ray Morehart, who stole ten bags in a three-year major league career. Detroit won the game, 6–3. Hanna wrote that the Yankees have plenty of iron men on their pitching staff, but iron can sometimes be "malleable."[31]

Bill Barrett batted .286 with a career high twenty steals (13 caught stealing) in 1927 and his aggressive baserunning led to a 7–6 White Sox win over Boston at Comiskey Park on July 11. Barrett reached first on a single with two outs in the last of the ninth and then stole second. Catcher Fred Hofmann's throw was off target and the ball went into center field where Ira Flagstead misplayed it and Barrett scored with the winning run. Chicago tied a major league record with eight sacrifices and all of them were sacrifice bunts. Bibb Falk and Aaron Ward had two apiece. While Barrett, Roger Peckinpaugh, Willie Kamm, and Harry McCurdy had one apiece. Boston had one sacrifice, which was credited to Cleo Carlyle, who batted .234 in 278 at-bats with four steals in his only big league season. Peckinpaugh played his final campaign in 1927, batting .295 with two steals in 217 at-bats. His name appeared in the box score as "Peck," for this game.[32]

Also on July 11, the Senators emerged victorious in Cleveland by a 3–2 score. Bucky Harris singled in the top of the tenth with one out and Tris Speaker walked. The Senators player-manager advanced to third on Goose Goslin's fly ball to right field. Joe Judge stepped into the batter's box and Speaker began running towards the midway. George Grant, Cleveland's right-handed relief pitcher, threw to second and Harris stole home easily to put the Senators in the lead. On July 26, Max Carey and his Brooklyn Robins were in Pittsburgh but they lost, 6–5, despite the fact that he collected three hits, pilfered three sacks, and stole home in the sixth inning. For Carey it was his thirty-third and final steal of home during his illustrious career. He holds the NL record in that category, but he is well behind Ty

Cobb who stole home 54 times. Ultimately, it was a disappointing homecoming for Carey as Brooklyn lost three of the four games in the series. Doc Gautreau was a diminutive, 5' 4", 129-pound, second baseman, who batted .257 lifetime with 40 steals in 261 games. His Boston Braves stole seven bases in a 4–3 eleven inning victory over Brooklyn in the first of two on September 3. Gautreau stole home twice in the opening game, a feat that would not be duplicated until 1958 when Vic Power pulled it off.

The New York Yankees won their third consecutive pennant in 1928 with a 101–53 record by holding off an excellent Philadelphia Athletics team (98–55) by two and a half games. Again, the Yankees eschewed small ball strategies, finishing seventh in the junior circuit with 51 steals and last in the major leagues with 146 sacrifices. However, they led the majors in several pivotal categories, including runs scored (894), home runs (133), on-base percentage (.365), and slugging percentage (.450). The American League teams stole 132 more bases than the National League teams and had only six more sacrifice hits. The fifth-place Chicago White Sox led the majors with 144 steals and the third-place St. Louis Browns led both leagues with 214 sacrifices. Manager Bill McKechnie's St. Louis Cardinals won the NL pennant with a 95–59 mark, finishing two games ahead of John McGraw's Giants (93–61). And although the Cardinals finished second in the circuit with 82 steals behind Chicago and Cincinnati who had 83, this pennant-winning aggregation was far from being a small ballclub. The fifth-place Reds were managed by Jack Hendricks and led the circuit with 212 sacrifice hits. Miller Huggins was extremely concerned heading into the 1928 World Series because he was missing several players due to injury. But the Yankees swept the Cardinals in comfortable fashion and won each game by at least three runs. Tony Lazzeri, Bob Meusel, and the Cardinals Frankie Frisch had two steals apiece, while St. Louis's 36-year-old shortstop, Rabbit Maranville, had one. Ruth batted .625 in the series and hit three homers in game four. New York had a 2.00 ERA versus St. Louis's 6.09 ERA.

In Kiki Cuyler's first season with the Chicago Cubs he batted .285 and won his second stolen base title with 37 thefts. He was a five-foot-ten-and-a-half-inch, 180-pound, right-handed outfielder who batted .321 during his Hall of Fame career with 328 steals and 176 sacrifice hits. He had a solid .386 career on-base percentage and a .474 slugging percentage. He scored 1,305 runs, including a high of 155 in 1930. During five seasons he scored at least 110 runs and led the NL in both 1925 (144) and 1926 (113). Cuyler was not like the prototypical small ball practitioners who excelled at place hitting and could adroitly hit behind the runner to move him along. Kiki took big cuts at the ball and swung from his heels, which led to an above average number of strikeouts. He was a line drive hitter who led the NL in triples in 1925 (26) and tied for the lead in doubles in 1934 (42). He spent significant time at all three outfield positions during his career and covered a large area with his terrific foot speed. Cuyler possessed a great throwing arm and was an excellent baserunner. He led the senior league in stolen bases in 1926 (35), 1928 (37), 1929 (43), and 1930 (37). When he stole 32 bags in 1924 he had a 74.4 percent basestealing average and when he stole 41 the following year, he had a 75.9 percent basestealing average. From 1926 to 1950 the caught stealing statistic is not available in the National League according to The 2006 ESPN Baseball Encyclopedia. Despite the fact that stolen base percentages are needed to determine the true value of a basestealer, the caught stealing statistic was not recorded during this time period, at a time when many baseball men were unaware of the importance of statistics.

Fred Clarke was quoted in a 1925 issue of Baseball Magazine saying that Cuyler may become "a second Cobb." And he is as "fast as a flash."[33] Despite batting .321 in 1926, Kiki was relegated to manager Donie Bush's doghouse in 1927 and batted .309 with a .394 on-base percentage with 20 steals in only 85 games. Bush was infuriated when Cuyler failed to break up a double play with a take-out slide on August 6, earning him a permanent seat on the bench for the rest of the season. He hardly played during the second half of the season and the Pirates fans were outraged when their great fly chaser was benched in the 1927 World Series. Like Rogers Hornsby, Cuyler didn't smoke or drink and he copied Hornsby's batting style.

Pie Traynor was a six-foot, 170-pound, right-handed third baseman who won his second consecutive sacrifice hit title in 1928 with 42. He was inducted into the Hall of Fame in 1948, twenty years before his former teammate Kiki Cuyler went in. Traynor is considered one of the greatest third baseman in major league history. He possessed a terrific throwing arm and was highly skilled at handling bunts and slow dribblers down the third base line. He batted .320 lifetime with a .362 on-base percentage and a .435 slugging percentage. Traynor was a decent but unspectacular basestealer, swiping 158 bags, including a career high of 28 in 1923 when he was caught stealing 13 times. In 1922 he stole 17 bags, but was caught stealing only three times for an 85 percent basestealing average. Since many of the Pirates had great basestealing averages, perhaps they were influenced by the wisdom of Max Carey. From 1922 to 1925 he stole 84 bases, which was 53.2 percent of his career total. Traynor spent his entire seventeen-year career with the Pirates and had 231 sacrifice hits. The American League sacrifice hit title in 1928 was secured by the Boston Red Sox's slow-footed first baseman Phil Todt who had 31.

Harvey Hendrick batted .310 for Brooklyn with a career high 29 steals in 1927 and then batted .318 with a .397 on-base percentage, a .478 slugging percentage, and 16 steals in 1928. In Brooklyn's 13–1 victory against Chicago on June 12, he stole second, third, and home in the eighth inning. In 1927 Jackie Tavener stole three bases in an inning versus the Yankees and then pulled off the same feat in 1928. The last-place Tigers took a pair from New York on July 25 by 3–2 and 10–7 scores. Tavener stole second, third, and home in the fourth inning of game two. His steal of home was on the front end of a double steal, while Larry Woodall stole second on the back end. On September 28, the Cardinals scored seven runs in the fifteenth inning to defeat Boston, 10–3, at Braves Field. Frankie Frisch stole home in the inning and became the first player with two extra inning steals of home. He also pulled off this feat in the second game versus Brooklyn on July 20, 1927.

After seven consecutive last-place finishes from 1915 to 1921, Connie Mack began to slowly rebuild his team and for the first time since 1914 he found himself in the winner's circle once again by capturing the 1929 flag (104–46). Sluggers Al Simmons (.365, 34 homers, 157 RBIs) and Jimmie Foxx (.354, 33 homers, 118 RBIs) paced the offense, while Lefty Grove, George Earnshaw, and Rube Walberg led the best pitching staff in the majors. Despite having five players score 100 or more runs, they finished second in the circuit (901) behind sixth-place Detroit who scored 926 runs. The Athletics led both leagues in sacrifices (213), while the seventh-place Chicago White Sox led the circuit with 109 steals and a 62.6 percent basestealing average. Detroit's Charlie Gehringer needed only 27 steals to win the only stolen base crown of his career, while Joe Sewell of Cleveland won his only sacrifice hit title with 41. Sewell was a left-handed hitting but right-handed throwing shortstop and third baseman, who struck out only 114 times in 7,132 at-bats during his Hall of Fame career. After nine seasons in which he played almost all of his games at shortstop, he switched to third base in 1929 and batted .315 with six steals. He batted .312 lifetime with a .391 on-base percentage, 74 steals, and 275 sacrifice hits which is tied for 21st all-time.

Manager Joe McCarthy led the Chicago Cubs to their first pennant since 1918 as they compiled a 98–54 record. Chicago's right-handed hitting outfield trio put fear into opposing pitchers: Riggs Stephenson (.362, .445 on-base percentage, 17 homers, 110 RBIs), Hack Wilson (.345, 39 homers, 159 RBIs), and Kiki Cuyler (.360, 15 homers, 102 RBIs). Charlie Grimm (.298) patrolled first base; Rogers Hornsby (.380, 39 homers, 149 RBIs) was at second; Woody English (.276) at shortstop; and Norm McMillan (.271) at third base. Zack Taylor was acquired from the Boston Braves on July 6 and filled in for Gabby Hartnett behind the plate who missed most of the season because of a sore arm. The Athletics prevailed in the World Series, four games to one, as McMillan stole the only bag during the five games. Seventh-place Cincinnati led the senior circuit with 134 steals, while Chicago finished second with 103. The last-place Boston Braves had the most sacrifices in the league (197), while their second baseman Freddie Maguire led the league with 26. Kiki Cuyler won the stolen base crown (43), while Cincinnati's rookie outfielder Evar Swanson finished second (33).

Runs scored increased by 262 in the AL compared to 1928 and by 840 in the NL. National League teams scored 5.36 runs per game and the Philadelphia Phillies finished in fifth place despite a 6.13 team ERA. During the season a poll was published showing that most of the major and minor league managers wanted to return the dead ball into the game. Ten of the sixteen big league skippers were in favor of returning to the dead ball because they believed the lively ball had a deleterious affect on the game. John McGraw and Wilbert Robinson were the biggest proponents of bringing back the dead ball, while not surprisingly, Miller Huggins of the Yankees wanted to continue using the lively ball. Huggins died tragically and unexpectedly in late September because of blood poisoning.

John McGraw's third-place New York Giants stole only 85 bags in 1929, but they had several in their opening game of the campaign at the Baker Bowl on April 18. They had two double steals in their six-run ninth inning and defeated the Phillies, 11–9. Johnny Mostil of the White Sox won consecutive AL stolen base crowns in 1925 and 1926 before missing most of the 1927 season after he attempted to kill himself during spring training. He put together decent numbers in 1928, batting .270 with a .360 on-base percentage and 23 steals in 43 attempts. Disaster struck while playing his twelfth game of the 1929 campaign, on May 19, when Mostil stole home on the front end of a double steal in the fourth inning versus Detroit. He tripped over the plate, broke his right leg, and never appeared in a big league game again.

In Washington on June 4, the St. Louis Browns had a 7–2 lead as they entered the last of the ninth. However, the Senators rallied and scored six runs to win 8–7. The winning run scored when Ossie Bluege stole home against rookie right-hander Chad Kimsey. According to Frank H. Young of the *Washington Post*, Kimsey must have thought Bluege was "incapacitated" because of a knee injury and that he would remain anchored at third base. Bluege taught the busher a lesson when he went into a "lazy wind-up." Ossie broke for home, sliding over the plate before catcher Wally Schang could apply the tag. Stuffy Stewart, who would fail to get a hit in 22 at-bats during his final major league season, was at the dish with two strikes on him when Bluege took off from third. The pitch was called a low ball, but St. Louis coach Jimmy Austin disagreed and argued with the arbiter, Bill "Big Shot" McGowan.[34] Bluege was a 5'11", 162-pound, infielder who batted .297 with a career high 18 steals in 1928 before being limited to 64 games in 1929, batting .295 with six steals. When his eighteen-year career ended after 18 games with the 1939 Senators, he had a .272 lifetime batting average with 140 steals. Frank O'Rourke had two steals for the Browns on June

4. The five-foot-ten-and-a-half-inch, 165-pound, third baseman batted .251 during the season with 14 steals in 21 attempts.

Mule Haas is perhaps best remembered for the two home runs he hit in the 1929 World Series for the Athletics, including his homer in the bottom of the ninth in game five, which tied the game. The 6'1", 175-pound, left-handed hitting but right-handed throwing outfielder was also highly skilled at laying down sacrifice bunts. During his final three seasons with the Philadelphia Athletics, he led the AL in sacrifices: 1930 (33), 1931 (19), and 1932 (27). And he also led the circuit as a member of the Chicago White Sox in 1933 (30), 1934 (24), and 1936 (23). Haas batted .292 lifetime, but stole only twelve bases in 1,168 games. He had 227 sacrifice hits during his career. Adam Comorosky, a 5'10", 167-pound, right-handed outfielder led the majors with 23 triples in 1930 and secured the NL sacrifice hit title with 33. He batted .313 during the season, with a .371 on-base percentage, a .529 slugging percentage, 112 runs scored, 119 RBIs, 47 doubles, and 14 steals. Comorosky played predominantly left field for the Pirates. Kiki Cuyler batted .355, scored 155 runs, and won his third consecutive stolen base crown (37). Paul Waner of Pittsburgh and Babe Herman of Brooklyn finished a distant second with 18 steals. Marty McManus batted .320 for Detroit with a .396 on-base percentage and .475 slugging percentage. He also led the AL with a career high 23 steals and had a 74.2 percent basestealing average.

The 1930 baseball season was truly the year of the hitter as nine teams batted over .300 and the New York Giants led the majors with a .319 team batting average. The collective NL batting average was .303, while in the AL it was .288. Batting over .300 wasn't that big of a deal considering that seventy-one players did it in the NL who played at least ten games. Chuck Klein scored 158 runs to lead the NL, while Al Simmons scored 152 runs to lead the AL. Five players scored at least 150 runs: Klein, Simmons, Cuyler, Woody English (152) and Babe Ruth (150). Hack Wilson hit 56 homers and drove in 191. The offensive onslaught is correlated to the alteration of the baseball, which was wound tighter and the stitches were lower, making it more difficult for the pitcher to grip the spheroid. Naturally, in this hitting rich environment small ball activities tumbled even more: stolen bases fell to 481 in the NL, a whopping decline of 211 compared to 1929. There were 598 steals in the AL, a decline of 41 from 1929. Sacrifice hits declined by 106 in the AL and increased by 8 in the NL. The first-place Philadelphia Athletics (102–52) led the AL with 182 sacrifices, the second year in a row they led in that category. However, they stole only 48 bags, which was well behind second-place Washington (94–60), who stole 101 to lead the majors. The fifth-place Pittsburgh Pirates paced the senior circuit with only 76 steals and they also led the majors with 196 sacrifices. The pennant-winning St. Louis Cardinals (92–62) were one of two teams to score over 1,000 runs, while the third-place New York Yankees were the other. St. Louis plated 1,004 runs, while New York led both leagues with 1,062. As to be expected there wasn't much running in the 1930 fall classic as Frankie Frisch stole the only base and Philadelphia defeated St. Louis, four games to two.

Despite the decline in basestealing in 1930 there were several notable basestealing accomplishments. The Browns scratched out only five hits against Chicago's Red Faber on May 31 but won, 3–2. Oscar "Ski" Melillo won the game when he stole home with two outs in the last of the ninth. Melillo was a 5'8", 150-pound, right-handed second baseman who batted .256 during the campaign with a pitiful .287 on-base percentage and a career high 15 steals.

Ben Chapman made his major league debut for the 1930 New York Yankees and was considered by many to be the fastest player in the game. By the time he ended his career in baseball he would leave a negative mark on the game, which overshadowed his on-the-field achievements. He was a dirty player who got into several memorable fights during his career. Chapman was tough, aggressive, fiery, intemperate, volatile, racist, bigoted, and an immoral human being who's career is replete with dishonorable conduct. In 1930 he batted .316 with 14 steals. And then he would lead the AL in steals during the next three seasons, in 1931 (61), 1932 (38), and 1933 (27). He won his final AL stolen base crown in 1937 (35) and finished his career with a .302 batting average, a .383 on-base percentage, a .440 slugging percentage and 287 steals. He scored over 100 runs six times, including a career high of 120 in 1931. And he drove in over 100 twice: 1931 (122) and 1932 (107). After losing the opener in Cleveland on July 22, 1930, by a 6–5 score, Chapman slid "spectacularly" across the plate as he stole home to tie the game at eight in the nightcap.[35] Earl Averill hit a two-run homer in the last of the eighth to give the Indians a 10–8 lead, which they never relinquished. In the second game both teams combined for six steals: Johnny Hodapp and Dick Porter had one apiece for Cleveland, while Ed Morgan had two. Chapman and Bill Dickey had one apiece for New York.

On July 25 the Philadelphia Athletics won comfortably in Cleveland by a 14–1 score behind Lefty Grove. They had twelve hits, including three homers, walked ten times, and pulled off two triple steals. Al Simmons led the junior circuit with a .381 batting average in 1930 and he also picked up nine steals in eleven attempts. He stole home on the front end of a triple steal in the opening inning with Bing Miller and Dib Williams swiping bags on the back end. Then in the fourth inning, Mickey Cochrane was on the front end of a triple steal, while Simmons and Jimmie Foxx were on the back end. The Giants were at Wrigley Field on August 24 and were desperately trying to get back into the pennant race. The game was knotted at two in the last of the ninth, but the Cubs had the bases loaded with two outs. Then suddenly Danny Taylor shocked rookie right-hander, Joe Heving, when he broke for the plate with a 0 and 2 count on the batter and scored the winning run with a steal of home.

Much to the delight of John McGraw and other proponents of inside baseball, the ball was deader in 1931 as the horsehide covering the ball was thicker and the stitching was slightly higher, allowing the pitchers a better grip of the baseball. Furthermore, batting averages were going to be slightly impaired by the elimination of the sacrifice fly rule. The sacrifice hit statistic would now represent the number of sacrifice bunts a team or player accumulated because sacrifice flies were no longer counted in this statistic. Home runs and runs scored plummeted in 1931, as did batting averages with the NL having a .277 average and the AL a .278 average. The number of runs scored dropped by 1,488 in the NL and by 316 in the AL. Home runs declined in the NL from 892 in 1930 to 493 in 1931. The American League's decline was not as severe from 673 to 576. Because of the rule change, sacrifice hits plummeted by almost 50 percent in the majors, while surprisingly, stolen bases decreased in the NL by 19 and increased in the AL by only 26. The first-place St. Louis Cardinals (101–53) led the NL with 114 steals, while the second-place New York Yankees (94–59) led the AL with 138, thanks to Ben Chapman who led the majors with 61 thefts. Frankie Frisch paced the senior league with only 28 steals. The fifth-place Pittsburgh Pirates led the majors with 130 sacrifices, while last-place Chicago led the AL with 105. The AL team stolen base percentages ranged from 47.7 percent to 70.7 percent. Mule Haas of the Athletics (19) and Freddie Maguire of the Braves (31) both won their second sacrifice hit titles.

By spring training the players already knew the ball was deadened and John McGraw looked forward to implementing the strategies of the inside game and outsmarting his opponents. While the Giants trained in San Antonio, Texas, in 1931, McGraw was eager to return to the old days when one smart move, one well executed play, or a mental error could decide a ballgame. Anticipating that there would be lower scores in the game, McGraw diligently imparted his wisdom on basestealing to the Giants. A sliding pit was set up so that the Giant players could practice the proper techniques. The New York players also spent considerable time improving their bunting skills during spring training. However, despite the deadened baseball in 1931, and despite the fact that they practiced small ball plays during spring training, the second-place Giants would finish the season with only 83 steals (2nd, NL) and 59 sacrifices, which was last in the major leagues.

The St. Louis Cardinals had four of the senior league's top five best basestealers on their team in 1931: Frisch led the circuit with 28 steals and he was followed by Babe Herman of Brooklyn (17). The Cardinals Pepper Martin (16), Sparky Adams (16), and George Watkins (15), rounded out the top five. At a time when basestealing was in decline the St. Louis Cardinals of the 1930s brought some aggressive baserunning to the populace during depression-era baseball. Pepper Martin was a stocky, 5'8", 170-pound, thick-chested player with thinning hair and a disheveled appearance. He was a player who reacted on the field, instead of thinking through the situation, and ran the bases with reckless abandon, which often culminated with his trademark headfirst slide. Times were tough when he played and it was reported that he hitchhiked his way to spring training and rode the freight trains in a five day journey and arrived at his destination with a dirty appearance and in desperate need of a good meal. Leo Durocher mistakenly says that Martin "invented" the headfirst slide in his autobiography *Nice Guys Finish Last*. While Martin didn't invent the headfirst slide, a sliding technique that was used by several players during the Deadball Era, he may have popularized it. Martin and Frisch pulled off many double steals and together they were known as the "diving seals." Many of the Cardinal players imitated Martin and also slid headfirst. And the Gas House Gang Cardinals of the 1930s were not concerned about washing their uniform for the next day's game. Durocher wrote, "We looked horrible, we knew it and we gloried in it." According to Durocher, the Gas House Gang Cardinals were a rough and tumble unit, "generally unschooled, generally unspoiled, generally unsophisticated."[36]

Pepper Martin played the hot corner with fierce determination and his body was generally bruised, covered with black and blue spots because of all the line drives he knocked down with his anatomy. He chewed tobacco and when he should have been paying attention to the pitcher's delivery, he had his glove under his arm, putting tobacco into his mouth or shaking dirt from under his cleats. Leo Durocher, who joined the team in 1933 as their shortstop, yelled over to Martin to make sure he saw the pitcher's delivery and if the batter hit the ball. Naturally, with all the bruises on his body he hated to field bunts and for those courageous hitters who laid one down there was a price to be paid. Durocher describes a game where the Braves hitters were bunting on their pitcher, towards third base, and Martin was barely able to bend over because of his sore back. Martin had had enough. He went to the mound and called over first baseman, Ripper Collins, informing him that "The next guy that bunts on me, forget the bag and back up the runner. I'm going to bounce one off his noggin." According to Durocher he missed the first batter, but hit the second, and the Braves stopped bunting.[37] Similar stories have been told by other players like Lloyd Waner, who said, "When I bunted on Pepper, I always ran down the line with my hands covering my head."[38] In Martin's thirteen-year career he batted .298 with 146 steals. He won three NL stolen base titles, in 1933 (26), 1934 (23), and 1936 (23). Martin led the NL with 122 runs scored in 1933 and scored 121 in both 1935 and 1936.

Frankie Frisch began his major league career in 1919 as the Deadball Era was ending, batting .226 with 15 steals in 54 games for John McGraw's Giants. He remained with the Giants through the 1926 season before being sent to St. Louis in a deal that brought Rogers Hornsby to New York. Frisch played with the Redbirds from 1927 to 1937, including as a player-manager from 1933 to 1937. The 5'11", 165-pound, switch-hitting second baseman was a flashy and daring baserunner. He won three NL stolen base titles: 1921 (49), 1927 (48), and 1931 (28). Frisch batted .316 lifetime with 419 steals and 229 sacrifices. During his career small ball strategies became less fashionable as managers waited for the big inning, relying on long balls to score runs instead of manufacturing them. During his first season in 1919, the National League averaged 145.6 steals per team; in 1937 the senior circuit averaged only 57.4 steals per team. (George Brace photograph).

Pepper, known as "The Wild Horse of the Osage," was born as Johnny Leonard Roosevelt Martin in Temple, Oklahoma, on February 29, 1904. He got a cup of coffee with the Cardinals in 1928 and 1930, before playing in 123 games in 1931, batting .300. The 1931 World Series against the Philadelphia Athletics was his coming out party. He felt sorry for President Herbert Hoover, who was booed in the first game in Philadelphia (game three), while he was cheered. With Prohibition still the law of the land, Hoover heard chants of "We want beer!" when he arrived at Shibe Park.[39] Before the series commenced, manager Gabby Street told the Cardinals basestealers that they were going to run on catcher Mickey Cochrane and they were going to do so early in the count to surprise him. The theory was that they weren't going to get a lot of baserunners against Philadelphia's great pitching staff, therefore they would try to manufacture runs when they did. The stage was set for Pepper Martin to star in the fall classic. Lee Allen wrote that he was a "typical depression hero, and in his filthy uniform he looked like a man who might be drinking soup from a tin can at a Bowery mission, greasing a car in a filling station, standing in a breadline, or robbing a bank."[40]

Martin was engaged in thievery in the 1931 series and picked the Athletics clean. Philadelphia took the opener, 6–2, as Martin collected three hits, including a double and he stole one base. In the second inning of game two, Martin hit a ball in front of Al Simmons in left field and then tested his arm, sliding into second with a cloud of dust, as Simmons muttered, "Oh, a smart busher, huh."[41] Then Martin stole third and scored on Jimmie Wilson's fly ball to the outfield. In the seventh inning, he reached first on a one-base hit, then stole second on the first pitch to Wilson and went to third on a groundout. Then with Charlie Gelbert at the dish, the squeeze play was executed and Martin slid safely across the plate. Martin hit a single and double and scored two runs in the 2–0 win and when the Cardinals won game three, 5–2, he did the same thing. In a 3–0 loss in game four, he had the only two hits for St. Louis, including a double and he stole a base. Martin had three hits, including one homer and four RBIs in a 5–1 game five win. St. Louis won the series in seven games and despite the fact that Martin went hitless in the final two contests, he still batted .500 in the series with five runs scored, five RBIs, and five stolen bases. The Cardinals stole a total of eight bases, while the Athletics had none.

It was rumored that catcher Mickey Cochrane was not concentrating on the task at hand and defeating the Cardinals because he was still thinking about the considerable amount of money he lost in the stock market. His play seemed to support this theory, as he batted only .160 in the series and the stolen bases were predominantly his responsibility, not the pitchers, because his throws were so bad. Martin made his presence felt in the final game when he came to the plate in the opening inning with two runners in scoring position and then George Earnshaw was perhaps trying to be too perfect with his pitches and threw a wild pitch. Martin walked and then stole second. Cochrane was perhaps so unnerved by Martin's antics at second base that he allowed a third strike to get by him and the Cardinals scored their second run of the inning. Ernie Orsatti struck out on the play, but Cochrane couldn't squeeze the third strike, as the ball got away. The Philadelphia backstop threw to Jimmie Foxx at first to record the out, but Foxx's throw home was off target. George Watkins raced in from third to score the run and Martin moved up to third. Watkins hit a two-run circuit clout in the third inning, and the Cardinals had all the runs they needed to win the finale, as they prevailed, 4–2.

Connie Mack's Philadelphia Athletics won three consecutive AL pennants from 1929 to 1931 by winning a total of 313 games: 104, 102, and 107. They pilfered only 136 bases during that span and they did not steal a single base in eighteen World Series games. In 1929 (213) and 1930 (182) they led the junior circuit in sacrifice hits, but then they garnered only 79 sacrifices (5th, AL) in 1931. The decline had to do primarily with the elimination of the sacrifice fly rule in 1931 and sacrifice flies were no longer counted as sacrifice hits. In 1931 the Athletics were arguably the worst small ball team in the majors as they stole only 25 bags, which was last in the AL and only one better than the senior circuit's worst team, the Cincinnati Reds (58–96).

One of the notable small ball achievements in 1931 took place on May 13 when the Philadelphia Athletics defeated the Chicago White Sox, 7–5, in an eleven inning battle at Comiskey Park. Bing Miller hit a double down the third base line for his third extra-base hit on the day in the top of the eleventh to get things started. Jimmy Dykes was sent to the plate with orders to bunt, but instead of getting a sacrifice, he legged it out for a hit. James C. Isaminger of the *Philadelphia Inquirer* wrote that Joe Boley "fell over like a cedar tree in a Michigan forest," when he was hit by a pitched ball to load the bases. Philadelphia pitcher George Earnshaw then hit a fly ball that was deep enough to plate a run and Max Bishop reached on a fielder's choice. With Dykes hugging third and Bishop edging off first, the Athletics pulled off a double steal. Bishop took off when the pitcher made his offering and catcher Bennie Tate faked a throw to second and then threw a bullet to Willie Kamm at third. By this time Dykes was charging for the plate. Kamm handled the low throw in the dirt and threw back in the direction of Tate in hopes of cutting down Dykes. Dykes collided into the 5'8", 165-pound catcher and hit him like a "truckload of bricks." Isaminger wrote that "Tate went over in a heap as Dykes' spikes dented into his rubber goal." Tate was hit extremely hard and couldn't even put the tag on Dykes in the bang-bang play. The victory gave the Athletics their fifth straight triumph and Earnshaw won his third of the season. Both teams combined for five steals and three sacrifices. Luke Appling, Chicago's 24-year-old shortstop, had a sacrifice bunt in the sixth frame, as the runner then scored on Kamm's double.[42]

On June 25, Dazzy Vance of Brooklyn had a no-hitter through six innings, as he induced the first eighteen Cardinals to record an out before the hometown fans at Ebbets Field. He got two more outs in the seventh before George Watkins legged out a two-strike bunt and scampered to third on Jim Bottomley's one-base hit. When Vance threw to first for the second time, Watkins stole home. Bottomley advanced to second on the play and the official scorer credited the duo with a double steal despite the fact that he initially returned to first base on the softly thrown pickoff attempt. They took advantage of the right-handed Brooklyn pitcher because his system for holding runners was well-known: he would lob the ball over to first base a few times and then showcase his best move. Watkins was a six-foot, 175-pound, left-handed hitting but right-handed throwing outer garden resident, who batted .288 in seven big league seasons with 61 steals. His theft of home allowed the Cardinals to emerge triumphant, 1–0.

Manager Joe McCarthy's New York Yankees took both ends of a doubleheader from Detroit by scores of 2–1 and 4–3 on September 13. The opening game was decided in twelve innings when Tony Lazzeri stole second and home against southpaw Elon "Chief" Hogsett. William E. Brandt of the *New York Times* wrote that Lazzeri's basestealing exploits were "highly sensational." Lazzeri worked a walk with one out in the bottom of the twelfth inning. He swiped second on a delayed steal when catcher Muddy Ruel tried to pick him off first base. Brandt wrote that first baseman Dale Alexander "was trying to find him somewhere around first," when he caught the throw from Ruel. Lazzeri advanced to third when pitcher Lefty Gomez grounded out. On the first pitch to leadoff man, Earle Combs, Lazzeri broke for the plate and slid safely across it before Ruel could slap the tag on him.[43] Lazzeri was a quiet, intelligent player, who excelled in the big leagues despite having epilepsy. He played most of his career at second base, batting .292 during his fourteen-year career with a .380 on-base percentage and a .467 slugging percentage. He stole 148 bags, including a career high of 22 in 1927. During eight seasons he stole eleven or more bases.

John McGraw managed his final forty big league games in 1932, going 17–23, before being replaced with Bill Terry on June 3. McGraw's former teammate with the Baltimore Orioles, Wilbert Robinson, was no longer the Brooklyn skipper in 1932 and was replaced with Max Carey. Carey's last name was originally Carnarius and Tommy Holmes of the *Brooklyn Eagle* suggested that the team should be called the Brooklyn Canaries. Instead they became known as the Dodgers once again. Robinson had an easygoing personality and let his players do pretty much what they wanted. Carey was a strict disciplinarian and cracked the whip, getting his players in line, and demanding excellence. Carey wanted to bring the inside game back to Brooklyn with its intelligent plays and small ball strategies. Robinson and Carey were complete opposites on and off the field: Uncle Robbie liked to eat and drink prodigiously, while Carey was lean, drank only in moderation, and tried to eat healthy foods. Despite Carey's emphasis on the inside game, the third-place Dodgers stole only 61 bases (4th, NL) and had 99 sacrifice bunts (5th, NL). Carey himself had stolen 61 bases in 1913, but the game had deteriorated since then and was dominated with the long ball mentality.

Gabby Street's St. Louis Cardinals finished tied for sixth place with New York, leading the circuit with 92 steals. The fourth-place Philadelphia Phillies collected the most sacrifices (125) and led the league in several other categories, including runs scored (844), home runs (122), batting average (.292), on-base percentage (.348), and slugging percentage (.442). Left-handed hitting slugger Chuck Klein took advantage of the short right field porch at the Baker Bowl and batted .348 with 137 RBIs. He was tied with Mel Ott for the most homers (38) in the NL and led the circuit in slugging percentage (.646), runs scored (152), hits (226), and stolen bases (20). Ben Chapman won the AL stolen base crown (38) and was followed by Gee Walker of Detroit (30). Walker batted .323 during the season and had an 83.3 percent basestealing average. He stole home in the fourth inning of Detroit's 7–6 win over Washington on June 15. During his fifteen-year career, he stole 223 bases. In 1932 the AL teams stole 99 more bases than the NL and fifth-place Detroit led the majors with 103. Manager Roger Peckinpaugh's Cleveland Indians finished in fourth place and had the most sacrifices (110). The New York Yankees (107–47) swept the Chicago Cubs (90–64) in four games in the 1932 World Series. Chicago pilfered the only three cushions in the series: two by Billy Jurges and one by Kiki Cuyler. Both teams collected one sacrifice bunt: Jurges laid one down for the Cubs and the Yankees rookie infielder, Frankie Crosetti, also garnered one.

Dick Bartell batted .308 for the Philadelphia Phillies with a .379 on-base percentage, 118 runs scored, 48 doubles, and 8 steals. He won the first of two consecutive sacrifice hit titles with 35, which was eight ahead of Mule Haas who led the AL. Bartell was a fiery, 5'9", 160-pound, right-handed shortstop who never backed down from a fight and often sought to start one. He had a loud mouth and irritated plenty of enemy infielders when he spiked them with a slid. During his eighteen-year big league career with the Pirates, Phillies, Giants, Cubs, and Tigers, he batted .284 with 109 steals and 269 sacrifice hits (25th all-time). Not counting the one game he played for the 1927 Pittsburgh Pirates, Bartell played only four seasons when sacrifice flies were counted as sacrifice hits. "Rowdy Richard" played big league ball from 1927 to 1943 and in 1946.

For the fourth consecutive season, stolen bases declined in the senior league in 1933, as the eight NL teams stole only 408 bases. Player-manager Bill Terry's New York Giants won the pennant (91–61) and they stole a meager 31 bases in the process, which was ranked sixth in the circuit. They also finished last in the NL with 86 sacrifices. Pepper Martin won the NL stolen base crown with 26 thefts and the fifth-place Cardinals collected the most steals in the majors with 99. During the Deadball Era, George Gibson was a weak-hitting, rifle-armed catcher, who insisted that "*thinking* was my real specialty." In 1933 he was managing in his sixth big league season with the Pittsburgh Pirates and led them to a second-place finish as they led the league in several categories, including sacrifices (147), batting average (.285), on-base percentage (.333), and slugging percentage (.383). Gibson demanded perfection and discipline from his players, prompting one reporter to write, "The Pirates have more signals than the Notre Dame football team and Gibson insists that every order be carried out to the letter."[44]

In the American League, Ben Chapman won his third straight stolen base crown (27), beating out Gee Walker of Detroit by one steal. The second-place Yankees (91–59) led the circuit with 76 steals and first-place Washington (99–53) collected the most sacrifices (128). Manager Marty McManus's seventh-place Boston Red Sox led the circuit with a 61.1 percent basestealing average as they stole 58 cushions.

Before John McGraw died on February 25, 1934, he came back to manage one more game in 1933. He was the skipper for the National League in the first All-Star Game at Comiskey Park on July 6, 1933, as the junior circuit emerged victorious, 4–2. Charlie Gehringer had the only stolen base and Rick Ferrell the only sacrifice bunt. Babe Ruth was showing his age, gasping for air after running a short distance and grabbing a fly ball in pregame preparation. One reporter insisted that Ruth was such a liability in the outfield because of his slow speed that he would allow more runs because of poor defensive play than he would drive in. After Ruth singled with one out in the fifth inning, he pulled up at second on Al Simmons's one-base hit. A Chicago writer observed the following about the decaying ballplayer: "Ruth's wheels are gone. A fast runner could have made it to third on that hit."[45] The Babe was indeed at the end of the line and would only play until 1935. Robert Obojski wrote in his wonderful book *All-Star Baseball Since 1933* that Ruth had "single-handedly" sent inside baseball "the way of the extinct carrier pigeon."[46]

While the hourglass was almost on empty for the Babe, 24-year-old Al Lopez was playing his fifth big league season in 1933. The highly skilled and durable defensive catcher batted .301 during the season for Brooklyn and stole a career high ten bags. On July 2 the Dodgers defeated the Cubs, 7–3, in the first of two at Ebbets Field. Lopez went 3 for 4 in the opener with a home run. In the second game, Lopez had perhaps the biggest stolen base of his career. With two outs in the last of the ninth, he stole home against right hander, Charlie Root, to give the Dodgers a 4–3 victory. Murray Tynan of the *New York Herald Tribune* insisted that the Cubs thought the steal was a "mean trick," but Lopez "maintained it was just an old Spanish custom." Root was not expecting Lopez to sprint towards home and took a long windup. Lopez was safe by an "eyelash" and Root was "startled." Tynan insisted that "If Lopez had tossed a bushel of golden pesos into the stands he could not have received more applause."[47]

The Giants defeated the Senators, four games to one, in the 1933 World Series. Luke Sewell, Washington's catcher, stole the only base of the series. New York used small ball tactics to win the highly controversial fourth game by a 2–1 score in eleven frames. The controversial part developed in the sixth inning when Buddy Myer singled and was sacrificed to second. Heinie Manush, a left-handed hitting left fielder for Washington, stepped into the batter's box. During the regular season he batted .336 with six steals and led the junior circuit with 221 hits and 17 triples. Hughie Critz, the Giants second baseman, made an excellent play in fielding Manush's grounder and threw to pitcher Carl Hubbell covering the bag. Manush appeared to be safe but National League umpire, Charles Moran, called him out. Moran also appeared to call him out before the play was complete. What developed next was chaos. According to Rud Rennie of the *New York Herald Tribune*, Manush didn't bump the arbiter but he "slapped" him and was subsequently thrown out of the game. The slap occurred while he was running through the bag, past the umpire. There was considerable arguing after the play and then player-manager Joe Cronin struck out to end the inning. Manush tried to take the field for the next inning, apparently unaware he was kicked out, and he was told to exit the premises. The Senators once again argued with Moran. Skipper Joe Cronin grabbed hold of Manush, fearing that he might take a swing at the umpire. George Moriarty, who was one of the umpires in the game, led Manush off the field. Moriarty had been Manush's manager with the 1927 Detroit Tigers. When the Griffith Stadium fans realized what happened, they were incensed, and someone threw a pop bottle at Moran. The game culminated in the eleventh inning when Travis Jackson of New York bunted down the third base line for a hit. Gus Mancuso sacrificed him to second and Jackson came around to score on Blondy Ryan's single. Hubbell held the Senators scoreless in the last of the eleventh for his second win of the series. Rennie insisted, "Washington is bitter and angry in defeat."[48]

At the National League meetings during the 1934 off-season, Roscoe McGowen of the *New York Times* asked Giants skipper Bill Terry how Brooklyn would do in the upcoming season. Terry replied, "Is Brooklyn still in the league? I haven't heard from them."[49] This unintentional insult infuriated Dodger fans and their soon-to-be manager Casey Stengel. The Dodgers used this insult as motivation late in the season when they helped prevent the Giants from winning the pennant. For the fifth consecutive season, stolen bases declined in the NL, as the league amassed only 362 steals. The second-place Giants (93–60) stole a major league low 19 bags, which was fifty behind the first-place Cardinals (96–58), who led the circuit with only 69 steals. New York did, however, lead the league with 108 sacrifices. Pepper Martin secured his second consecutive stolen base crown with 23 thefts, while Kiki Cuyler of Chicago finished second with 15. Hughie Critz, New York's weak-hitting second baseman, batted .242 with a .269 on-base percentage and led the senior circuit with 22 sacrifices. During his twelve-year big league career, he stole 97 bags and had an impressive 187 sacrifices.

Bill Werber played four games for the 1930 New York Yankees and three games for them in 1933 before being traded to the Boston Red Sox along with George Pipgras for $100,000 on May 12, 1933. Werber batted .259 for Boston with fifteen steals in twenty attempts. Then he had his breakout year in 1934, batting .321 with a .397 on-base percentage, a .472 slugging percentage, 129 runs scored, 200 hits, 41 doubles, and a major league leading 40 steals in 55 attempts. In 1935 his batting average dipped considerably to .255, but he won his second stolen base crown with 29 bags. And then with the 1937 Philadelphia Athletics, he batted .292 and won his third and final stolen base title with 35 thefts. During his eleven-year career he batted .271 with 215 steals and 88 sacrifice hits. He scored at least 105 runs three times, including 115 with the 1939 Cincinnati Reds, which led the National League. Werber didn't run the bases wildly, but liked to take "calculated risks," similar to Buddy Lewis. In August of 1934 the first-place Detroit Tigers came into Fenway Park to battle the Red Sox. George Moriarty was one of the umpires and having a favorable opinion of the inside game and the excellent baserunners that are abundant with those strategies, he suggested to Werber that he may want to steal second on a walk. He gave Werber some advice on the subject, telling him how it is to be done. Werber recalled that he walked in the sixth or seventh inning and noticed that the middle infielders were turned towards the outfield, trying to take out the dirt from under their spikes. As he approached first base, about fifteen feet away, he started running full speed and rounded the bag. When catcher Ray Hayworth threw to second, nobody was covering the bag, allowing Werber to take third on the throw into center field.[50] Werber insisted that his low stolen base totals with the pennant-winning 1939 and 1940 Cincinnati Reds, when he stole 15 and 16 bases respectively, were due to the fact that manager Bill McKechnie discouraged him to run. Batting behind Werber were Frank McCormick, Ernie Lombardi, and Ival Goodman, who were all clutch hitters who could hit the long ball. Werber believed that basestealing had to do with "Good judgment, instinct, and a willingness to learn the pitcher's *normal* pitching patterns."[51]

The Detroit Tigers won the 1934 American League flag with a 101–53 record and led the majors with 125 steals. The fourth-place Red Sox compiled 116 steals and led the circuit with a 71.2 percent basestealing average. After their 1933 pennant-winning campaign, the Washington Senators fell to seventh place and lost 33 more games than the year before. They did, however, pace the majors with 131 sacrifices. Four junior league basestealers had more steals than the NL leader: Werber (40), Jo-Jo White of Detroit (28), Ben Chapman (26), and Pete Fox of Detroit (25). There were 547 stolen bases in the AL, which was 185 more than the NL. The American League won the All-Star game, 9–7, as their number one and two hitters, Charlie Gehringer and Heinie Manush, stole bases, while Pie Traynor and Mel Ott swiped bags for the NL.

St. Louis defeated Detroit, four games to three, in the World Series as Pepper Martin stole two bases for the Gas House Gang, while the Tigers collected five: Gehringer, Hank Greenberg, Marv Owen, Billy Rogell, and White. Player-manager Mickey Cochrane, a first-year skipper for Detroit, led his team on a sustained small ball attack in game four, as they prevailed 10–4. They had three stolen bases and four sacrifice bunts. Some of the heavy artillery, consisting of the number two, three, and four hitters Cochrane, Gehringer, and Goose Goslin, each laid down a sacrifice bunt. Dizzy Dean made the most unfortunate pinch-running appearance. Dean refused to slide with a force play at second base and short-stop, Billy Rogell, fired the ball into his head. There was great concern when he was removed from the field on a stretcher. The colorful pitcher later said, "They X-rayed my head and found nothing. I saw stars, moons, and all sorts of animals, but no Tigers."[52] Amazingly, he took his turn on the hill on the following day, pitched eight strong innings, but lost to Tommy Bridges, 3–1. In the top of the sixth inning in game seven at Briggs Stadium, Joe Medwick hit a triple and spiked Marv Owen at third base with his slide. The mob would not be appeased as they threw pop bottles, fruits, and vegetables at his direction when he tried to take his position in left field. Medwick was removed from the game for his protection, but the Cardinals were up comfortably by this juncture, 9–0.

The Brooklyn Dodgers were heading home on May 16 after a disappointing 5–14 road trip. Tommy Holmes of the *Brooklyn Daily Eagle* wrote that the Dodgers were "disillusioned" and were returning home after their "worst initial excursion through the provinces that a Brooklyn club has experienced in 15 years."[53] On May 15 they did manage to defeat St. Louis, 6–5, at Sportsman's Park. Lonny Frey, a 23-year-old second-year player, scored the go-ahead run when he stole home on the front end of a double steal in the eighth inning. Frey had three RBIs and two hits in the game. He batted .284 with eleven steals in 490 at-bats during the 1934 season. The 5'10", 160-pound, infielder batted .269 lifetime with 105 steals. The Boston Braves' 9–0 triumph over St. Louis at Sportsman's Park on June 13 was significant for two reasons, which involved the two shortstops: Leo Durocher of St. Louis was charged with four errors and Boston's Billy Urbanski came to the plate six times and had no at-bats because of four walks and two sacrifices.

Charlie Gehringer of the Detroit Tigers (93–58) and Stan Hack of the Chicago Cubs (100–54) stole the only bases in the 1935 World Series that was won by the Tigers in six games. Manager Charlie Grimm's Cubs won twenty-one straight games in September to secure the flag and they led the majors with 150 sacrifices. Billy Herman, who was born William Jennings Bryan Herman in New Albany, Indiana, on July 7, 1909, batted .341 with six steals in his fifth big league season. The talented second baseman led the majors with 227 hits, 57 doubles, and 24 sacrifices. He was an exceptional hit-and-run batter, perhaps the best in the history of the game according to historian Bill James. In a fifteen-year career he batted .304 with 67 steals and 171 sacrifice hits. Jack Burns, the St. Louis Browns' 28-year-old first baseman, batted .286 in 1935 with an AL leading 20 sacrifices. The sixth-place Cincinnati Reds led the NL with 72 steals. Augie Galan of the Chicago Cubs batted .314 with a .399 on-base percentage, a .467 slugging percentage, and a major league leading 133 runs scored. He led the NL with 22 steals, winning the first of two stolen base crowns during his career. Bill Werber won the AL stolen base crown with 29 bags, edging out Lyn Lary who stole 28 in 32 attempts for Washington and St. Louis. The fourth-place Boston Red Sox led the AL in both sacrifices (137) and stolen bases (91).

On May 15, Lou Gehrig stole home for the fifteenth and final time during his career as New York defeated Detroit, 4–0. Each of his thefts of home were on double steals. Tony Lazzeri secured his second extra inning steal of home during his career when he pulled it off in the eleventh inning of the second game of a doubleheader on July 6. New York defeated the Senators, 10–7, to split the twin bill. However, the most unlikely steal of home occurred on August 26 when Zeke Bonura, a lumbering, slow-footed, six-foot, 210-pound first baseman, stole home with two outs in the last of the fifteenth inning to give the Chicago White Sox a 9–8 win in the first game of a doubleheader versus New York. Bonura took several false starts against Yankees right-hander Jimmie DeShong and then he suddenly took off with a 3 and 2 count on Sox pitcher Whit Wyatt. He caught DeShong taking a long windup and stole home to win the game as umpire Bill Summers ruled that Bonura was safe. Bonura had whispered to third base coach Jimmy Austin that he was going to steal home and Austin pleaded with him not to, saying, "Don't you do it. It will cost me my job."[54] James P. Dawson of the *New York Times* wrote that Bonura "summoned an amazing burst of speed."[55] Both teams combined for five sacrifices in the opener and then the Yankees won the seven inning second game, 7–5, which ended early because of darkness. Zeke Bonura batted .307 lifetime with a .380 on-base percentage and a .487 slugging percentage in seven big league seasons. He managed to steal 19 bases in 26 attempts during his career. Despite leading American League first baseman in fielding percentage during three seasons, his manager Jimmy Dykes once insisted that he was the "worst first baseman who ever lived." As far as his impressive fielding percentage, Dykes said, "You can't miss what you can't get."[56] Bill Werber wrote that "He looked like a bouncing bear in his efforts to play first." Werber recalled that in the late inning of a tie game between the Red Sox and White Sox in 1935, he studied Bonura's habits from third base when the pitcher tried to pick off Dusty Cooke at first base. Bonura took his time returning the ball to the White Sox pitcher, Vern Kennedy, taking a hop, slapping his mitt, and then lobbing the ball to the pitcher. Kennedy threw to first once again and Bonura went through the same routine as Werber stole home in the enemy's ballpark to score what turned out to be the winning run.[57]

Babe Ruth played his final season for the Yankees in 1934, batting .288 with a .448 on-base percentage and a .537 slugging percentage. And then the man who had captured the public's imagination with his prodigious home run blasts and changed the way the game was played had a forgettable final season with the 1935 Boston Braves, batting .181 in 28 games. In 1936 the Yankees debuted a new star, Joe DiMaggio, who batted .323 in his rookie season with 132 runs scored, 125 RBIs, and was tied for the league lead with fifteen triples. While Ruth sought glory upon the bases and made some poor baserunning decisions during his career which hurt his team, the introverted DiMaggio was content to remain anchored to the bases and let his bat do his talking. He stole four bags in 1936 and only thirty during his career in thirty-nine attempts. DiMaggio could have stolen bases if he wanted to. He possessed good wheels when he first came to the big leagues and was a terrific baserunner, skilled at taking an extra base on a hit. American League players quickly learned that they shouldn't test DiMaggio's cannon arm in the outfield. The Yankee Clipper was a complete player, who excelled despite playing his career in Yankee Stadium, a ballpark that was not ideal for a right-handed pull hitter like himself.

A crowd of 69,812 packed into Lakefront Stadium in Cleveland to witness the American League win their third straight All-Star Game by a 4–1 score on July 8, 1935. The players were amazed that nearly 70,000 people would pay their way into a stadium to watch a baseball game as the country struggled to survive the Great Depression. Pepper Martin started the game with a Texas Leaguer off Lefty Gomez and then stole the only base of the contest after Arky Vaughan flied out.

Despite dominating the Giants in most of the important statistical categories in the 1936 World Series, the Yankees needed six games to secure the world championship. They scored twenty more runs than Bill Terry's team and had twenty-two more RBIs. The Yankees pitchers compiled a 3.50 ERA versus the Giants, 6.79. The volatile Jake Powell batted .455 in the series for McCarthy's Yankees and stole the only base. Powell spent the 1936 regular season playing for both Washington and New York, batting .299 with a career high 26 steals. The five-foot-eleven-and-a-half-inch, 180-pound, outfielder was extremely fast and a terrific bunter. However, he never fulfilled his potential because he was always getting into trouble, on and off the field.

Pepper Martin won his third and final NL stolen base crown with 23 steals and he was followed by his teammate Stu Martin (17), Stan Hack of Chicago (17), and Lou Chiozza of Philadelphia (17). Lyn Lary of the St. Louis Browns led the AL with 37 steals and had an 80.4 percent basestealing average. For the seventh consecutive season, the AL stole more bases than the NL, 562 to 401. However, the NL did compile more sacrifices than the AL, 761 to 654. The second-place St. Louis Cardinals led the NL with 69 steals, while the fourth-place Washington Senators paced the AL with 104. The Chicago Cubs were tied with the Cardinals in second place and led the majors with an impressive 137 sacrifices, while the sixth-place Boston Red Sox led the AL with 108. Mule Haas won his sixth and final sacrifice hit title in the AL with 23, while the Phillies middle infielder Leo Norris led the NL with 21.

The New York Yankees (102–52) defeated the New York Giants (95–57) for their second straight world championship in 1937, defeating the National League champions in five games. Burgess Whitehead, the Giants second baseman, stole the only base of the series. The Giants committed nine errors, including three by Dick Bartell, while the Yankees were charged with none. Furthermore, they were outscored by sixteen runs. Connie Mack and Earle Mack managed the seventh-place Philadelphia Athletics who led the majors with 95 stolen bases, while fourth-place St. Louis led the NL with 78. Augie Galan secured the NL stolen base crown with 23 thefts, while Ben Chapman and Bill Werber shared the title in the AL, as they both stole 35. The second-place Chicago Cubs accumulated the most sacrifices in the majors with 119, while Chicago's American League outfit led the AL with 111. Manager Charlie Grimm's Cubs led the majors in sacrifices for the third consecutive season. Jimmy Brown, the St. Louis Cardinals 27-year-old middle infielder, batted .276 in his rookie season with ten steals and a major league leading 26 sacrifices. Doc Cramer of Boston and Dixie Walker of Chicago led the AL with 17. Cramer patrolled center field during most of his career and was one of the game's best defensive outfielders. He covered a lot of ground and had a terrific throwing arm. During his twenty-year career in the American League with Philadelphia (1929–1935), Boston (1936–1940), Washington (1941), and Detroit (1942–1948), he batted .300 or better during eight seasons but didn't have a lot of power. The 6'2", 185-pound, left-handed hitting leadoff man batted .296 lifetime with 62 steals (45.9 percent stolen base average) and an impressive 180 sacrifice hits. He scored over 100 runs three times: 1933 (109), 1938 (116), and 1939 (110). Cramer finished his career with 2,705 hits. He was an excellent contact hitter, but didn't walk a lot, and had only a .340 on-base percentage.

When the Indians hosted the Senators on May 4, 1937, the game was knotted at five entering the eleventh inning. Washington scored seven runs in the eleventh and won the contest, 12–5. The Senators took the lead in the eleventh when Ben Chapman stole home on the front end of a triple steal. Whitlow Wyatt, the Indians 6'1", 185-pound, right-hander was "dazed" when he saw Chapman steal home just ahead of his delivery to the plate. Chapman began the top of the eleventh with a walk and moved up one base on Buddy Lewis's single. Joe Kuhel followed with a sacrifice bunt, moving both runners up one base to second and third. Then cleanup hitter, John Stone, struck out looking. At this juncture Indians skipper Steve O'Neill brought Wyatt in from the bullpen to face the right-handed hitting Al Simmons. Simmons walked to load the bases and set up the triple steal. Wyatt didn't get rattled when Chapman acted as if he were going to steal home several times during John Mihalic's at-bat. Shirley Povich of the *Washington Post* insisted that Chapman was "practically home" before Wyatt delivered the ball during his dash to the plate. Then it began to rain on the Indians in more ways than one: there was a "steady drizzle" and the Senators scored at will against the unnerved Wyatt and finished the game with twenty hits. Both teams combined for five stolen bases and three sacrifices. Washington scored two in the fifth when Buddy Lewis started the attack with a "clever bunt," towards John Kroner at third. The inning ended after Stone was cut down at the plate for the first out, while trying to score from second on a single as Roy Weatherly's throw beat him by a "dozen feet." And then Ossie Bluege hit into a double play. Washington catcher Johnny Riddle made a perfect throw to second in the fourth inning, catching Earl Averill trying to steal the second sack.[58]

The National League won the 1938 All-Star Game by a 4–1 score at Crosley Field as Ival Goodman of the Reds and Joe DiMaggio of the Yankees stole bases. The senior circuit had a 2–0 lead entering the last of the seventh and manager Bill Terry was looking for some insurance. Frank McCormick led off with a single off Lefty Grove and then Leo Durocher stepped into the box with orders to lay down a sacrifice bunt. Jimmie Foxx was playing out of position at third base so Lou Gehrig could patrol the gateway station. Durocher followed orders and laid a well placed bunt down the third base line. Foxx made a nice play on the ball, he charged in, fielded it cleanly, and threw accurately to first base. But Gehrig wasn't covering the bag because he had anticipated a bunt and moved in and therefore was in no position to take Foxx's throw. Therefore, it was second baseman Charlie Gehringer's responsibility to cover the bag and take the throw, but he failed in his obligation and the ball sailed into right field. Joe DiMaggio picked up the ball in right field, but his throw to the plate was over Bill Dickey's head as he tried to cut down McCormick and the ball went into the National League dugout. Casey Stengel, one of the NL coaches, reportedly picked up the ball and threw it in a bucket filled with ice water, saying, "This one is just too hot to handle." Durocher hit an unofficial bunt home run, but with all the errors in the play he wasn't even rewarded a single because Foxx was charged with an error on his throw.[59]

For the ninth straight season the AL stole more bases than the NL in 1938, 542 to 354. However, there was little difference in the number of sacrifice hits, as the AL had 681 versus the NL's 673. The New York Yankees won the pennant (99–53) and then won their third straight World Series, this time defeating the Chicago Cubs (89–63) in a four-game sweep. The Yankees stole all three bases in the series via thefts by Bill Dickey, Joe Gordon, and Red Rolfe. During the regular season these three players combined to steal twenty-seven bases and had an 87.1 percent basestealing average. McCarthy's club easily led the majors in both home runs (174) and stolen bases (91). They also led the AL with a 76.5 percent basestealing average. Burleigh Grimes's seventh-place Brooklyn Dodgers led the NL with 66 steals and the Cincinnati Reds had a major league low 19 steals. Only two players stole more than twenty bags and they both resided in the American League: Frankie Crosetti of New York (27) and Lyn Lary of Cleveland (23). Stan Hack led the NL with only sixteen steals and was followed by Cookie Lavagetto and Ernie Koy of Brooklyn, who each stole fifteen. "Smiling Stan" Hack was a consistent but unspectacular basestealer, swiping ten or more bags for eight straight seasons from 1934 to 1941. The .301 lifetime hitter stole 165 bags and won the NL stolen base crown in 1938 and shared the title in 1939.

There wasn't a large difference in the number of sacrifice bunts between the NL teams in 1938, ranging from 78 to 89. In the AL, the Yankees had the fewest sacrifices (61), while the second-place Boston Red Sox led the majors with 112. Del Young, a .229 hitter for the Philadelphia Phillies, led the circuit with 15 sacrifices, while Bobby Doerr of Boston led the AL with 22. The Hall of Fame second baseman ended his career with a .288 batting average, 223 home runs, 54 stolen bases (45.8 percent stolen base average), and 115 sacrifices.

On April 29, Bill Werber had a game-ending steal of home for the Philadelphia Athletics with little-used right hander Bill Phebus on the hill for Washington. The final score stood at 7–6. Werber began the last of the ninth with a walk and then was sacrificed to second by Mule Haas on a 2 and 0 count. Phebus was summoned from the bullpen to replace southpaw Joe Krakauskas after the first two balls to Haas. After the sacrifice, he walked two batters, one intentionally, to load the bases. Philadelphia second baseman Dario Lodigiani stepped into the batter's box. On the second pitch to Lodigiani, Werber "opened the speed throttle and bolted for the plate," while the pitcher was winding up. James C. Isaminger of the *Philadelphia Inquirer* insisted that the Washington battery of Rick Ferrell and Phebus acted as if the steal of home was a "complete surprise." Ferrell dropped the pitch but Werber would have stolen home even if he caught it.[60] Werber batted .259 during the season with a .377 on-base percentage, nineteen steals, and fifteen caught stealing.

In the top of the tenth inning of the fourth and final game of the 1939 World Series, the Yankees were content to get one run when Red Rolfe sacrificed Frankie Crosetti to second. But instead they pushed across three in the inning as it was highlighted by Joe DiMaggio's single to right field, which scored three runs. Shortstop Billy Myers booted Charlie Keller's grounder, putting two men on base. Crosetti scored on DiMaggio's one-base hit

George Case, the exciting speed merchant, played in the major leagues from 1937 to 1947, spending ten of his eleven seasons with the Washington Senators. The right-handed fly chaser batted .282 lifetime with 349 steals and 52 sacrifices. He won six American League stolen base crowns and he could have been one of the most prolific basestealers in big league history if he wasn't forced to retire because of a back injury at the age of thirty-one. Case averaged 31.7 steals per season, including his first and last big league season when he played a total of 58 games. (George Brace photograph).

and outfielder Ival Goodman allowed the spheroid to get by him. And then there was a bang-bang play at the plate as Charlie Keller collided with catcher Ernie Lombardi just as the throw arrived and knocked the backstop out cold. As Lombardi lay unconscious at home plate, DiMaggio went all the way around the bases and scored just before Lombardi began to awaken from his slumber. The Yankees dominated the series, scoring twenty runs, while Cincinnati scored only eight, despite the fact that New York's .206 batting average was only slightly better than Cincinnati's .203. Goodman had the only stolen base of the series. For the Yankees it was their fourth straight World Series triumph.

George Case brought exciting and daring baserunning to the game when it was largely absent in the late 1930s and 1940s, bringing excitement to the crowds who had been lulled asleep by the monotonous long ballgame. Case was a bonafide speed merchant and a terrific small ball practitioner, which included being a skilled bunter. The six-foot, 183-pound, right-handed fly chaser debuted in 1937 for Washington, playing just 22 games before hitting .305 with eleven steals in seventeen attempts the following year. In 1939 he batted .302 and scored over 100 runs (103) for the first of four seasons and led the AL with 51 steals. He led the AL in stolen bases from 1939 to 1943 with 51, 35, 33, 44, and 61. He stole 49 and 30 in 1944 and 1945 and then won his sixth and final stolen base crown with the 1946 Cleveland Indians (28). Case was a highly effective basestealer, compiling the following bases-tealing averages during his six seasons when he won the stolen base title: 75, 77.8, 78.6, 88, 81.3, and 71.8. He batted .282 during his career with 349 steals, despite battling several serious leg and shoulder injuries. He had a 76.2 percent career basestealing average. Not only did he use his speed to leg out a plethora of bunt hits and infield hits, but he was also one of the hardest players to double up in major league history. He used his blazing speed in the outfield and was able to catch balls in the outer garden that other players couldn't. And on the bases he terrorized the opposition, not only with stolen bases, but by taking an extra base when other players with average speed would have had no chance. He retired because of a back injury at the age of 31 after playing 36 games for the 1947 Washington Senators. If it wasn't for his injuries, he would have easily became a member of the 500 stolen base club.

For a promotional event at Griffith Stadium on September 14, 1943, the fans turned out to see if Case could circle the bases faster than Hans Lobert, who was credited with the record by many people. He circled the bases in 13.5 seconds, breaking Lobert's mark of 13.8. However, not only did Case have competent AAU officials timing him, but he started with one foot on home plate, while Lobert reportedly began with a running start. In a 1945 *Sporting News* article, Evar Swanson was credited with circling the bases in 13.4 seconds on September 15, 1929, as a member of the Cincinnati Reds and he was credited with running 13.3 seconds with the 1931 Columbus Red Birds.[61] Case participated in many promotional events, including the first one put on by Bill Veeck in the major leagues with the 1946 Cleveland Indians. He faced off against the famous Olympic sprinter Jesse Owens, but lost a close race. However, both participants were well past their prime. It was the only time Case lost a race with his baseball uniform on. He supplemented his big league salary by competing in 100-yard match races and won $1,000 in one race versus Gil Coan. In Rich Westcott's book *Diamond Greats: Profiles and Interviews with 65 of Baseball's History Makers*, Case is quoted as saying, "Running came naturally to me. I could run the 100 in 9.9 in full uniform. It was said that if I had trained, I would've been a world-class sprinter."[62] Clyde Milan, the crafty basestealer from the Deadball Era, was brought back to the Senators to instruct Case on the finer points of basestealing. Case's manager, Bucky Harris, even gave him the green light to steal whenever he wanted, which was rarely done during this time period. Harris said, "Get the jump whenever you can, but don't abuse it." Case felt he could steal off catcher Frankie Hayes of the Athletics all day, while Paul Richards of the Tigers was the most difficult to steal a base against. George was a cerebral basestealer, incessantly studying the habits of opposing catchers and pitchers. He believed that "60 percent of all stolen bases are gifts," usually because of a bad throw from the catcher or because the fielders are not in position to make a good tag. Not all bases are stolen on the pitcher, but a pitcher may reveal something with his move that makes it easier to steal a base. And even though the pitchout is the defense's biggest weapon against a basestealer, many catchers inadvertently reveal that a pitchout is coming with their positioning.[63]

The 1939 Chicago White Sox led the American League in both stolen bases (113) and sacrifices (154). In the senior league, first-place Cincinnati led the circuit with 193 sacrifices, while fourth-place Chicago paced the circuit with only 61 steals. The Reds more than doubled their sacrifice hit total from 1938, when they led the league with 89. This was predominantly because in 1939, the sacrifice fly was counted as a sacrifice hit for the final season in major league history and for the first time since 1930. While George Case easily won the AL stolen base crown with 51 thefts over second-place finishers Mike Kreevich and Pete Fox, who each had 23 bags, the NL title was shared by Lee Handley and Stan Hack who stole only 17. Yet again, the AL stole more bases than the NL, 589 to 368. Lonny Frey of Cincinnati and Pinky May of Philadelphia shared the NL sacrifice hit title with 25, while Mike Kreevich of the Chicago White Sox led the AL with 22. Kreevich, a five-foot-seven-and-a-half-inch, 168-pound, right-handed outfielder batted .323 during the season with a .390 on-base percentage. He was an excellent defensive outfielder with a terrific arm. He won the AL sacrifice hit title in 1939 and 1940 (21). Kreevich batted .283 lifetime with 115 steals and 119 sacrifices. Gene Moore of the Brooklyn Dodgers batted only .225 with four steals in 1939, but one of them was a game-ending steal of home versus Chicago on June 1, to give the Dodgers a 3–2 win in the last of the fourteenth. He stole home on a botched squeeze play, as Leo Durocher couldn't make contact with Charlie Root's delivery and catcher Bob Garbark allowed the ball to get away from him, allowing Moore enough time to cross the plate.

There were two sacrifices in the 1940 All-Star Game, won by the National League, 4–0. They were credited to senior league first baseman Frank McCormick and pitcher Larry French. The sacrifice bunt also proved to be an important weapon in the seventh game of the 1940 World Series as Bobo Newsom of Detroit and Paul Derringer of Cincinnati hooked up in a pitcher's duel. Billy Sullivan, the Tigers catcher, was sacrificed to second in the top of the third inning. And then Bill Werber, Cincinnati's third baseman, made a low throw to first on Charlie Gehringer's grounder, which allowed Sullivan to score. Detroit took a 1–0 lead into the last of the seventh, when the slow-footed Frank McCormick managed to score from second on Jimmy Ripple's double to tie the game. McCormick had hesitated along the basepaths to see if Bruce Campbell would catch the ball and when Dick Bartell took the relay throw there was a possibility they could cut McCormick down at the plate, but Bartell did not turn around in time. Jimmie Wilson sacrificed Ripple to third and he scored on Billy Myers fly ball to the outfield. The Reds won the final game, 2–1, and captured their first World Series since 1919.

Jimmie Wilson, Cincinnati's 40-year-old catcher, was the true hero of the series. His body was bruised and beaten after catching in the big leagues since 1923. In 1938 he played only three regular season games for the Phillies and then played four games the following season for Cincinnati before hitting .243 in 16 games for the 1940 Reds during his final major league season. Somehow, he willed himself to play in the 1940 World Series, overcoming the painful injuries that had taken its toll, and batted .353 in 17 at-bats and stole the only base of the series. Bill Werber wrote that it was "A truly heroic performance by a man with the heart of a lion."[64]

First-place Cincinnati (100–53) led the NL in sacrifices for the third consecutive season in 1940 with an impressive 125 total. The 1940 Reds were known for their pitching and defense and led the majors in both ERA (3.05) and fielding average (.981). Billy Southworth was one of three managers that were employed by the third-place St. Louis Cardinals in 1940 and they led the NL with 97 stolen bases. For the eleventh consecutive season the AL stole more bases than the NL, but this time the margin was only three, 478 to 475. In the junior circuit, Jimmy Dykes's Chicago White Sox finished tied for fourth place with Boston and led the league with 110 sacrifices, while seventh-place Washington collected the most stolen bases with 94. The Senators also had the best stolen base average in the AL by a wide margin with 70.1 percent. The stolen base champions were Lonny Frey of Cincinnati (22), who stole one more base than Stan Hack, while George Case took the American League crown (35). Mike McCormick, the Reds rookie outfielder, batted .300 with a paltry .326 on-base percentage. He stole eight of his career sixteen bases, and tied for the NL lead with 20 sacrifices. Ham Schulte, the Phillies second baseman, batted .236 in his only big league season and also collected twenty sacrifices. Meanwhile, in the American League, Mike Kreevich won his second consecutive sacrifice hit title with 21 and finished tied for fourth in the league with 15 steals.

At Shibe Park on August 20, the Athletics lost the opener, 6–1, to the White Sox and then took the nightcap by a 4–3 score in ten innings. Benny McCoy, a left-handed hitter, was at the bat with two outs in the last of the tenth, facing southpaw Thornton Lee, when Wally Moses suddenly took off for the plate and stole home with the winning run. Moses had started the inning with a single and moved to second on Sam Chapman's sacrifice. An intentional walk, a force out, and another intentional walk filled the bases and set up the exhilarating finale, which culminated with Moses's steal of home on the first pitch to McCoy. Wally Moses was a 5'10", 160-pound, left-handed fly chaser who batted .301 or better during his first seven major league seasons with the Athletics, including a career high of .345 in 1936. He was traded to the White Sox in December of 1941 and never batted over .300 again. Moses had plenty of speed, but apparently it wasn't utilized as often as it could have been. In 1942 he stole sixteen bags, which was his career high at that juncture of his career. And then in 1943 he turned on the jets and swiped 56 bases and had an 80 percent bases-stealing average. He also garnered his second game-ending steal of home that season on July 7 in the fourteenth inning versus the Boston Red Sox. He stole 21 and 11 during the following two seasons and then never stole more than five bags in a season the rest of his career. In 1937 he showed he could hit the long ball, connecting for 25 homers but he didn't hit more than nine in any other campaign. He finished his career with a .291 batting average and 174 steals with a 68.2 percent basestealing average. In 1937 he scored over 100 runs for the only time in his career, finishing with 113. He was tied for the AL lead in triples in 1943 with 12 and led the AL in doubles in 1945 with 35.

In 1941, Joe DiMaggio captured the attention of the nation with his 56-game hitting streak in the final season before the United States entered World War II. The Yankees won the pennant (101–53) and then defeated the Brooklyn Dodgers (100–54) in a closely fought World Series won by the Yankees in five games. Phil Rizzuto and Johnny Sturm of the Yankees stole the only bases of the series. McCarthy's Yankees were clinging to a 3–1 lead in the top of the seventh in game one. But Lew Riggs's pinch-hit single brought the visitors within one run and Brooklyn was threatening to add more with two runners on base and no outs. Leo Durocher, Brooklyn's skipper, sent Jimmy Wasdell up to pinch-hit for the pitcher and told him to "get in there and hit." Wasdell disregarded the bunt sign that was flashed to him after the first pitch and popped up near the third base dugout. Red Rolfe squeezed the ball for the out and threw to shortstop Phil Rizzuto who was covering third to catch Pee Wee Reese who tried to move up on the play. It was a disheartening double play and if Wasdell had simply followed orders and executed the sacrifice bunt, two runners would have been in scoring position with one out. Brooklyn lost the game, 3–2. Wasdell insisted, "I didn't see any bunt sign, but there must have been one because Durocher bawled hell out of me in the dugout. I can't blame him. It was my fault." After the game when the emotions that are exacerbated during battle subsided, Durocher took responsibility, trying to take the blame off his player. Although he still claimed that Wasdell missed the bunt sign. However, Washington skipper Bucky Harris, who had managed Wasdell during four seasons, challenged Durocher's statement, insisting that Wasdell was not a bright player but he had never missed a signal when he played for him.[65]

The American League won the 1941 All-Star Game at Briggs Stadium by a 7–5 score as Ted Williams hit a three-run homer in the last of the ninth. In the top of the sixth inning leadoff man, Stan Hack, sacrificed Bucky Walters to third and he scored on Terry Moore's fly ball. Al Lopez also had a sacrifice bunt for the National League.

The senior league had 136 more sacrifices than the junior league in 1941, but the AL led the NL in steals once again, 471 to 411. The third-place Cincinnati Reds led the NL with only 68 steals, while the second-place St. Louis Cardinals led the majors with an impressive 126 sacrifices. Second-place Boston had the most sacrifices in the AL (115), while third-place Chicago led both leagues with 91 steals. George Case led the majors in steals for the third straight season with 33, while Danny Murtaugh of the Philadelphia Phillies had 18 steals to lead the NL, one more than his teammate, Stan Benjamin. Murtaugh was a 23-year-old rookie second baseman in 1941 who secured the NL stolen base crown despite playing in only 85 games and batting .219 with a .275 on-base percentage. Marty Marion, the St. Louis Cardinals second-year highly skilled defensive shortstop, batted .252 with a major league leading 28 sacrifices. Marion stole only 35 bases during his career, but he had 151 sacrifices, which is a high total. The AL sacrifice hit title was shared by Lou Boudreau, Joe Cronin, and Bob Harris, who each had 14. Harris was a pitcher for the St. Louis Browns, which is significant because this was the first time in major league history that a full-time pitcher had led the league in sacrifices.

Johnny Rigney toed the slab for the Chicago White Sox on June 25 at Griffith Stadium and allowed six hits in a 2–0 thirteen inning triumph. Sid Hudson was the hard luck loser for Washington. He pitched a terrific game until the top of the thirteenth when he walked Luke Appling with the bases loaded to allow the first run and then the Sox pulled off a triple steal with Joe Kuhel leading the way. Kuhel finished second in the AL with 20 steals in 1941 with an 80 percent basestealing average. The six-foot, 180-pound, first baseman stole ten or more bases during nine seasons and 178 during his career. Mike Kreevich started the rally in the top of the thirteenth with a one-out single and moved to third on a hit-and-run play as the left-handed hitting Kuhel went the other way, down the third base line for a double. Taffy Wright was walked intentionally to load the bases. Entering the inning, Wright had collected the only three hits in the game for Chicago. Appling walked to force in the first run. According to Shirley Povich of the *Washington Post*, "Slyly flashing the signs among themselves," the runners then went into motion on Hudson's long windup. The 6′4″, 180-pound, right-hander was "startled," and "stood almost transfixed in the midst of his windup." In addition to the three stolen bases, the Sox also had two sacrifices by Kreevich and Bob Kennedy. George Case batted seventh for Washington and stole their only base.[66]

Don Kolloway played ten games for the 1940 Chicago White Sox and then started the 1941 campaign at the age of 22, and batted .271 with eleven steals in 280 at-bats. On June 28, the Sox were in Cleveland and Kolloway entered the game with a .168 batting average. He hit two homers, a single, and stole four bases in a 6–4 triumph. The 6′3″, 200-pounder, who played mainly second base, stole three bases in the ninth inning. Jeff Heath stole only 56 bases during his career, but there was probably none bigger than his game-ending steal of home with Jack Kramer on the hill to give the Indians a victory over the Browns in the first game of a doubleheader on July 4. In addition to his .340 batting average, .396 on-base percentage, and .586 slugging percentage, Heath led the major leagues with 20 triples and finished second with 123 RBIs in 1941. He finished third in the AL with a career high 18 steals.

Ernie Lombardi was so slow that the infielders would move back ten or fifteen feet when he came to the plate. And this is why he was able to beat out a few bunts during his career, because they played so far back that even Lombardi was able to leg out a bunt. The 6′3″, 230-pound Lombardi was a pull hitter and the infield would also shift to the left side. He was a good hitter and a skilled defensive catcher with a strong and accurate arm. Lombardi played seventeen big league seasons for the Dodgers, Reds, Braves, and Giants. He stole eight bases in 1,853 games. To Bill Werber this was a surprise, not because he stole so few but because he was able to steal so many. In Brooklyn's 4–2 victory over the Reds at Ebbets Field on August 27, Lombardi stole his first base since August 10, 1937, a drought that lasted nearly four years. In 1941 he played his final season for Cincinnati, batting .264, which was considerably less than his .319 average from the previous season.

The St. Louis Cardinals won 43 of their final 51 games to capture the first NL pennant during the war in 1942. Billy Southworth's club finished the season with a 106–48 record and led the majors with 130 sacrifices, while Leo Durocher's Dodgers finished two games out with a 104–50 record and led the NL with 81 stolen bases. Brooklyn finished second in the circuit with 119 sacrifices, while St. Louis was second in steals with 71. In the American League, second-place Boston finished nine games behind New York and led the league with 123 sacrifices. Jimmy Dykes's sixth-place Chicago White Sox led both leagues with 114 steals. The stolen base averages for AL teams ranged from 48.3 percent (Cleveland) to 77.2 percent (Washington). Once again, George Case led the majors in steals (44), which was more than double the NL leader's total by Pete Reiser, who stole 20 bags. Johnny Pesky was a 22-year-old rookie, who was an excellent contact hitter, using a heavy, long bat, which he choked up on. He was the Boston Red Sox's shortstop in 1942 and he led the AL in hits during his first three seasons with 205, 208, and 207 in 1942, 1946, and 1947. He batted .331 during his initial big league campaign and led the junior circuit with 22 sacrifices. Lennie Merullo batted .256 for the Chicago Cubs with a career high 14 steals and led the NL with 22 sacrifices. The 1942 World Series was captured by the Cardinals in five games. The Yankees stole three bases in the series as Phil Rizzuto had two and Roy Cullenbine had one. The Redbirds were unable to purloin a sack as Stan Musial was gunned down in their only attempt in game three. Southworth's club laid down seven of the eight sacrifice bunts, including three by Terry Moore.

On August 2, the Giants won the opening game over the Cardinals by a 7–1 score at the Polo Grounds as Mel Ott hit two homers, including a grand slam. The 34,505 spectators were dismayed to see their team lose the nightcap, 3–2. Hal Schumacher and Mort Cooper were hooked up in a 2–2 pitcher's duel entering the ninth inning. In the top of the ninth, Stan Musial led off by hitting Schumacher's offering towards shortstop, Dick Bartell, who made a poor throw to Babe Young at first base and Musial pulled up to the midway. Musial made it to third when Ray Sanders made an out. Catcher Ken O'Dea worked a walk and Johnny Hopp was sent in to pinch-run for him. Whitey Kurowski's squeeze bunt plated the go-ahead run. On August 5, Hal Newhouser of the Detroit Tigers and Thornton Lee of the Chicago White Sox hooked up in a pitcher's duel at Comiskey Park. The Sox were frustrated because they hit into four double plays. But Don Kolloway's steal of home in the last of the sixth produced the only run in the game and gave Chicago the victory. Kolloway stole a career high sixteen bases in thirty attempts during the season and led both leagues with 40 doubles.

For the fourteenth consecutive season the American League stole more bases than the National League in 1943, 626 to 384. However, the senior circuit amassed more sacrifices than the junior circuit for the fifth straight season, 878 to 811. With the infamous balata ball used for part of the 1943 season and with a less livelier ball than in years past, the 1943 campaign was in many ways a return to the Deadball Era. Steve O'Neill, who was the manager of the Detroit Tigers after being a big league catcher for seventeen seasons, said, "Any ball club would be lucky to get two runs in a game with this new ball. It's deader than the one in use when I was playing."[67] Not surprisingly, there were several impressive small ball achievements in 1943. For the first time since 1925 when the first-place Pittsburgh Pirates stole 159 bases, there was a major league team to steal over 150. The 1943 Chicago White Sox finished in fourth place and they stole 173 bases, while second-place Washington finished second in steals with 142. In the NL the fourth-place Pirates led the circuit with only 64 steals as Arky Vaughan of Brooklyn won the stolen base title with 20. It would take nineteen seasons before another big league team stole over 150 bases when the 1962 Los Angeles Dodgers did it, compiling 198 thefts. George Case's 61 stolen bases in 1943 was the highest total since Ben Chapman stole the same number in 1931. It would take nineteen seasons for a major league player to steal more than Case when Maury Wills swiped 104 for the 1962 Dodgers.

Excluding the Deadball Era when the sacrifice bunt was ubiquitously employed and excluding the twelve seasons after the Deadball Era when sacrifice flies were counted as sacrifice hits, then during the remaining major league seasons if a team accumulated over 100 sacrifices that would generally put them at or near the top of their league in that category. In 1943 there were eight major league teams with over 100 sacrifices, including the Detroit Tigers, who led the AL with 123. In the National League the first-place St. Louis Cardinals (105–49) amassed 172 sacrifices, which is the major league record if you exclude the thirty-one major league seasons mentioned above. Harry Walker of St. Louis led both leagues with 36 sacrifices, the highest total since Dick Bartell had 37 in 1933. Walker's total would not be surpassed until Bert Campaneris had 40 sacrifices for the 1977 Texas Rangers. And it wouldn't be surpassed by a National League player until 1990 when Jay Bell of Pittsburgh laid down 39 sacrifices. Joe Hoover of Detroit led the AL with 28 sacrifices in 1943.

The Cardinals, a highly efficient sacrifice bunting team, won their second consecutive pennant, but this time they lost the World Series to the Yankees in five games. They committed ten errors in the series, while New York had five and both teams combined for three stolen bases by Frankie Crosetti, Charlie Keller, and Marty Marion. Southworth's club laid down five sacrifice bunts, while the Yankees had four. The Cooper brothers, Walker and Mort, each laid down a sacrifice bunt in the 4–3 St. Louis victory in game two. Catcher Walker Cooper batted .318 during the regular season and batted fourth in game two. He garnered six sacrifices during the regular season, while his brother Mort, the team's ace pitcher (21–8, 2.30 ERA), had only five.

Wally Moses (56), Thurman Tucker (29), and Luke Appling (27) of the Chicago White Sox finished second, third, and fourth in the major leagues in steals. Appling was a .310 lifetime hitter with a .399 on-base percentage and he stole 179 career bases, five more than Moses's 174. But Moses had the most notable basestealing accomplishments in 1943. Chicago split a twin bill with Cleveland on May 5, winning the second game, 5–2, as Wally Moses had an extra inning steal of home for the second time in his career. And then on July 7 he had his third extra inning steal of home to set a major league record as he did it in the fourteenth inning at Comiskey Park with Boston's Mace Brown on the hill to give Chicago a 3–2 win. The bases were loaded when he took off on his successful journey to the plate. He began the last of the fourteenth with a single and was moved to second on a sacrifice bunt. Moses went to third on Guy Curtright's single and Appling walked to load the bases. Jimmy Grant struck out and he swiped home with Kolloway at the bat.

Huck Geary played only 55 major league games in two seasons with the Pittsburgh Pirates, batting .160 lifetime with three steals. However, one of his steals was a game winner. In the bottom of the fourteenth inning on June 1 against the Boston Braves with right hander Al Javery on the mound, he stole home to give the Pirates the victory. On September 23, in a 3–2 Reds victory over the Giants, pitcher Johnny Vander Meer of Cincinnati stole home. It was the only stolen base of his career and the first steal of home by a pitcher since August 15, 1923, when George Mogridge accomplished this feat. Vander Meer pilfered home in the fifth inning on a double steal with Max Marshall. Estel Crabtree struck out on the play and Vandy took off for home when catcher Gus Mancuso fired the pill to second. Shortstop Buddy Kerr, who had recently made his major league debut on September 8, tried to cut Vander Meer down at the plate, but his throw was off target, and Marshall alertly moved up to third. Bill McKechnie's Reds plated the winning run in the last of the ninth thanks to a surprise bunt by Lonny Frey, a sacrifice bunt by Marshall, and a pinch single by the little-used Chuck Aleno.

As the war progressed the quality of play declined as the number of players joining the military increased. Major league owners relied on teenagers, old-timers, and 4-F's to take the place of the departed players. Mexicans and Cubans were also employed because they were exempt from the military draft. Under this environment the St. Louis Browns, who were situated in the second division from 1930 to 1941, were able to break into the first division in 1942 and then capture the American League flag in 1944. The Yankees were good during the final two wartime seasons, but not great. By the final wartime campaign, Babe Ruth wasn't too impressed with the current Yankees aggregation, saying, "That sawed-off runt playing second base is the only ballplayer who could've gotten a uniform when the Yankees really had a ball club."[68] He was referring to George "Snuffy" Stirnweiss, who had a terrific season in both 1944 and 1945, and led the majors in stolen bases during both seasons with 55 and 33 respectively. His stolen base average was an impressive 83.3 percent in 1944 and 66 percent in 1945.

The Cardinals (105–49) defeated the Browns (89–65) in the 1944 World Series as neither team stole a base, which was the first time that had happened in the fall classic. There were only eight more sacrifice hits in the major leagues than in 1943, but six additional teams accumulated 100 or more sacrifices. There were fourteen teams in total with 100 or more sacrifices, seven from each league. The St. Louis Cardinals led the majors with 124 sacrifices, while the fifth-place Philadelphia Athletics finished second with 122. George Hausmann of the Giants paced the NL with 27 sacrifices, while Eddie Mayo of Detroit led both leagues with 28. For the fifteenth consecutive season, the AL stole more bases than the NL, 539 to 381. After leading the majors in stolen bases for five straight seasons, George Case was unseated from his throne, and finished second with 49 thefts, while his Washington teammate George Myatt finished third in the AL with 26. Johnny Barrett of Pittsburgh led the NL with 28 steals and led the majors with 19 triples. The New York Yankees finished in third place with an 83–71 record and led the AL with a 74.6 percent basestealing average, while last-place Washington paced both leagues with 127 steals (68.3 percent basestealing average). Manager Frankie Frisch's second-place Pittsburgh Pirates had the most stolen bases in the NL with 87, which was 34 more than the second-place finisher in that category.

On June 8, 1944, the Washington Senators defeated the Philadelphia Athletics by a 7–5 score in eleven innings at Shibe Park. John Sullivan began the winning rally in the top of the eleventh for manager Ossie Bluege's Senators by grounding to Irv Hall, the Athletics shortstop, and reached first when Hall committed an error on the play. Pitcher Milo Candini tried to sacrifice him to second, but his "line drive bunt" eluded the grasp of Athletics hurler, Joe Berry, and he legged it out for a hit. Sullivan moved up to third when he tagged up on leadoff man George Case's long fly ball to left field. And then left-handed hitting George Myatt hit a triple off the left-center-field wall plating two runs. Case had three of the five stolen bases by the Senators in the game. Ford Garrison, Philadelphia's leadoff man, stole the only base for the Athletics. Jake Powell of Washington had the only sacrifice bunt in the contest. Washington scored four runs in the fifth as Case and Myatt pulled off a double steal. They both scored on Powell's single to left field.[69]

Joe Hoover of the Detroit Tigers stole two bases in the fourth inning on August 25 versus St. Louis. One of his steals was a theft of home on a double steal. That was the only run of the contest as Detroit prevailed, 1–0. On September 17, the Browns and White Sox split two games. In the second contest won by Chicago, 8–2, the White Sox pulled off double steals in both the seventh and eighth inning. Chicago hurler Joe Haynes stole home in the eighth inning.

The 1945 Detroit Tigers (88–65) needed seven games to win the world championship over the Chicago Cubs (98–56). Doc Cramer, Roy Cullenbine, and Jimmy Outlaw stole bases for Detroit, while Don Johnson and Andy Pafko stole one apiece for Chicago. The Cubs were caught stealing three times, while the Tigers were gunned down only once. Chicago had ten sacrifices, while the Tigers collected only three. One of Detroit's sacrifice bunts was garnered by Hank Greenberg, who batted cleanup in game seven, and laid one down in the opening inning of that contest. For the first time since 1929, the National League teams stole more bases than the American League teams, 527 to 453. The senior league was working on their own streak in the sacrifice bunt department, leading the AL for the seventh straight season, 844 to 837. Nine major league teams had 100 or more sacrifices and the Chicago Cubs led both leagues with an impressive 150. The third-place St. Louis Browns led the AL with 124. Don Johnson, who played baseball on Chicago's North Side, led the NL with 22 sacrifices, while Southsider, Roy Schalk, led the AL with 24. Second-place Washington compiled the most stolen bases in the majors with 110 and led the AL with a 62.9 percent basestealing average. The last-place Philadelphia Athletics stole only 25 bags and had a pitiful 35.7 percent basestealing average. The sixth-place Boston Braves led the NL with 82 thefts. The stolen base titles were secured by Red Schoendienst of St. Louis (26) in the NL and by Snuffy Stirnweiss (33) in the AL.

On May 13 in Cleveland, the Yankees spilt a doubleheader with the Indians, winning the opener 1–0 in ten innings and losing the second contest by a 4–2 score. Atley Donald of New York and Red Embree of Cleveland hooked up in a pitcher's duel in the opener as the game remained scoreless after nine innings. Hersh Martin was on first base with no outs in the top of the tenth inning when Snuffy Stirnweiss, batting in the three hole, tried to move him over with a sacrifice bunt. But Embree slipped and fell to the ground and Stirnweiss was safe at first. Rud Rennie of the *New York Herald Tribune* insisted, "On a dry field it would have been a sacrifice." Cleanup man Johnny Lindell stepped into the batter's box and tried to move the runners along with another bunt. Again, Embree's footing gave out and he slipped. He was going to try to catch Martin at third, but now he unleashed a poor throw to first but catcher Jim Steiner retrieved the throw in time to catch Lindell at the gateway as two runners moved up. Nick Etten was walked intentionally to load the bases and then Martin scored the game's only run on Russ Derry's fly ball to center. Lindell had the only sacrifice on the day for New York, while Cleveland had three in the two games, including one by the powerful Pat Seerey in the second contest.[70]

Wally Moses's batting average increased each season from 1943 to 1945 from .245 to .280 to .295. Likewise his on-base percentages also increased from .310 to .345 to .373. However, his stolen base totals decreased during these three seasons from 56 to 21 to 11. His number of runs scored was constant with 82, 82, and 79. On July 7, 1945, Moses stole home in the bottom of the first inning versus the Philadelphia Athletics against right-hander Lou Knerr. That was the only run of the game as Bill Dietrich tossed a shutout for the Sox and then they swept the twin bill with a 12–4 win in the second contest. Chicago's number two hitter, Roy Schalk, had two sacrifices in the opening contest.

At Ebbets Field on August 28 a crowd of 20,530 fans, including about 11,000 "knothole kids" and 3,800 women, were happy to see their Dodgers jump to a 5–0 lead after the first four innings. Brooklyn pushed across a run in the last of the fifth to make the score 6–1 when Tommy Brown tripled off the center-field wall with two outs. Then while Rene Monteagudo of the Phillies was pitching to Brooklyn catcher John "Fats" Dantonio, Brown stole home just before Hal Spindel put the tag on him.[71] In 1945, Brown was experiencing his second big league season at the age of seventeen, batting .245 with three steals. He became the youngest big leaguer to steal home. Brooklyn won the game, 7–1.

George Case's daring baserunning helped the Senators secure a 3–2 victory over St. Louis on September 7 at Griffith Stadium. Because of injuries, Case stole only thirty bases during the season, which was tied for second in the major leagues with his teammate George Myatt. He had perhaps his best baserunning day on September 7 when he stole three bases. With right-hander Bob Muncrief on the hilltop for St. Louis, Case stole home with two outs in the bottom of the first. Case had reached first with a walk, stole second, and advanced to third on an infield out. He sparked a two-run rally in the third inning when he singled to left field, stole second, and scored when he advanced one base on two fly balls to center fielder Milt Byrnes. Neither fly ball was hit deep. Joe Kuhel produced the final run by hitting a home run to center field, which was the only one hit by the Senators in their spacious ballpark in 1945. They finished second to last in the major leagues with 27 homers and hit only one at home, while only the Chicago White Sox had fewer with 22.

With the quality of play perhaps at the lowest level in the history of the modern era during the 1945 season, the fans were eager for a return to normalcy in 1946 as the players in the military returned to pursue their passion by playing the national game. Attendance increased by 69 percent in the NL and 72 percent in the AL. The number of runs scored increased in the AL by 263 and decreased in the NL by 596 when compared to 1945. The senior league stole more bases than the junior league, 478 to 406, and they also had more sacrifices, 901 to 722. The Cardinals and Dodgers were deadlocked at season's end with a 96–58 record, but St. Louis prevailed in the three-game playoff to capture the flag. Leo Durocher's Dodgers led the major leagues in both sacrifices (141) and stolen bases (100). In the American League, the first-place Boston Red Sox (104–50) led the circuit with 106 sacrifices, while fifth-place Chicago had the most stolen bases (78). Eddie Stanky of Brooklyn compiled the most sacrifices in the majors with 20, while Lou Boudreau and George Kell tied for the AL lead with 15. The stolen base crowns belonged to Pete Reiser in the NL (34) and George Case in the AL (28).

Pete Reiser was Brooklyn's five-foot-ten-and-a-half-inch, 185-pound, fly chaser whose career was negatively impacted by the various injuries he suffered because of running into outfield walls and because of his aggressive baserunning. He had last played in 1942 when he batted .310 and led the circuit with twenty steals before joining the military and missing the next three seasons. In 1946, he batted .277 in 122 games. Leo Durocher insisted that Reiser was "the best I ever saw at stealing home."[72] That's quite a statement considering that he witnessed the daring baserunning of great basestealers like Jackie Robinson and Willie Mays during his managerial career. Reiser unnerved opposing pitchers when dancing off third, getting them to lose their concentration, throw a wild pitch or be charged with a balk. Durocher believed that Reiser "might" have been the best player he had the pleasure to see play. He might have been better than Willie Mays. Durocher insisted that Reiser had more power than Mays from both sides of the plate and threw just as good. He also wrote in his autobiography that Reiser was faster than any player he ever saw and he ran to first base "consistently" in 3.6 or 3.7 seconds. Durocher recalls that when Reiser slid at home plate he threw his body towards the left-hand side of the batter's box and this way the catcher could only tag the "tip of his hand."[73]

After splitting two games with Boston to begin the 1946 season, the Brooklyn Dodgers commenced their home schedule by defeating the Giants, 8–1, at Ebbets Field on April 18. They stole four bases in the fifth inning as Reiser stole second and home. On April 20, Rip Sewell of Pittsburgh and Bucky Walters of Cincinnati hooked up in a pitcher's duel at Forbes Field. Walters stole home in the sixth inning but the Pirates prevailed, 2–1. In 1946, Johnny Hopp batted .333 for the Boston Braves and finished third in the National League with 21 steals. On May 9 his steal of home broke a 2–2 tie in the twelfth inning against Chicago at Wrigley Field and Boston went on to win, 5–2. Jeff Cross began his big league career by playing one game for the 1942 St. Louis Cardinals and then he returned to the big leagues in 1946, batting .217 in 49 games and 69 at-bats with four steals. On May 16 he won a game for the Redbirds when he pinch-ran in the tenth inning at Boston and stole home to give St. Louis a 9–8 win. Pete Reiser tried to steal home on May 25 with Augie Galan at the plate, but Phillies catcher Andy Seminick interfered and his glove made contact with Galan's bat. Reiser was given a steal of home by the official scorer and Galan advanced to first base. Brooklyn won the contest, 7–1, at Shibe Park. Part of the headline on September 9 in the *New York Herald Tribune* was "Durocher Men Steal 8 Bases," in describing Brooklyn's thievery on the previous day. It was Eddie Stanky Day at Ebbets Field and the home fans were delighted to see the Dodgers win, 11–3, over the Giants. Reiser stole three bases, including home, Dixie Walker had two, while Galan, Stanky, and Carl Furillo each had one. Furillo also had a sacrifice. Pistol Pete's steal of home was his seventh on the season. Bob Cooke wrote, "Practically everything a Dodger did developed into prosperity, while the Giants, attired in the ragged clothes of realism, tumbled over themselves like men impacted with defeat."

There was plenty of small ball activity in the 1946 World Series between the St. Louis Cardinals and the Boston Red Sox. The Cardinals stole three bases in the series: Stan Musial, Red Schoendienst, and Enos Slaughter. Leon Culberson and Johnny Pesky stole bags for Boston. Marty Marion had three of St. Louis's eight sacrifices, while the Red Sox laid down three sacrifice bunts. Ted Williams had a frustrating series, batting just .200 in 25 at-bats, as the Cardinals moundsmen effectively pitched him inside. The Splendid Splinter was flummoxed, he was watching a lot of strikes sail past him, and he even tried to hit the ball the other way against the Williams shift. Then in the third game of the series, while the Sox were on their way to a 4–0 victory thanks to Rudy York's three-run blast in the first inning, Williams laid down a two-out bunt towards the vacated left side of the diamond in the third stanza. Williams insisted he did this to show the Cardinals that he was capable of doing so and furthermore the wind was blowing in. Whether Ted Williams should lay down a bunt towards the third base line and take an easy hit against the shift is debatable. But this was an astonishing act because he never did so. Williams's approach to the game was one of defiance, and refusal to swing at pitches outside the strike zone and refusal to let the Williams shift change his strategy. This was worthy of headlines, as one paper wrote, "WILLIAMS BUNTS."[74] Red Smith wrote the following: "The Kid's bunt was bigger than York's home run. Thirty-four thousand, five hundred witnesses gave off the same quaint animal cries that must have been heard at the bonfires of witches in Salem when Williams, whose mission in life is to hit baseballs across Suffolk county, pushed a small, safe roller past third base."[75]

In the top of the third inning of game four, Terry Moore of St. Louis tried to sacrifice Red Schoendienst to second. But Boston's hurler Tex Hughson bobbled the bunt and then threw wildly to first, over second baseman Bobby Doerr's head as he was covering the bag, and the two runners moved up to second and third. With first base open the Red Sox choose to pitch to Stan Musial and the strategy backfired as he drove them in with an extra-base hit. St. Louis won the contest, 12–3, and collected twenty hits and four sacrifices. In the bottom of the fifth inning of game seven, Marty Marion sacrificed Harry Walker to second and he scored on pitcher Murray Dickson's double. Generally, sacrificing a runner to second with the pitcher on deck is not a smart strategy. But Marion was struggling and Dickson had shown he could swing the bat during the regular season when he batted .277 in 65 at-bats. Dickson went 2 for 5 in the World Series with two doubles. In the last of the eighth, the Cardinals took a 4–3 lead on a hit-and-run play when Slaughter went in motion on Bob Klinger's pitch to Harry Walker. Walker hit a double and Slaughter scored when shortstop Johnny Pesky hesitated after receiving the relay throw. In the top of the ninth, Rudy York singled for Boston and Paul Campbell ran for him. Doerr hit a single to put runners on first and second. A successful sacrifice would put two runners in scoring position with one out and give the Sox a chance to win the game. As the series was coming down to the execution of the fundamentals, Pinky Higgins failed miserably. He bunted too hard and St. Louis's charging third baseman Whitey Kurowski was able to throw to second to catch Doerr; they almost turned a double play as the relay throw to first was very close.

Harry Brecheen got the final two outs and the world championship belonged to St. Louis.

By 1947 many of the good basestealers who had sustained the tradition of thievery in baseball during the decline of small ball were retired or on their way out. Bill Werber played his last game for the 1942 Yankees. Wally Moses was on the downside of his career and stole only eleven bags during his final five seasons from 1947 to 1951. Luke Appling, a consistent but unspectacular basestealer, was also playing his final few seasons. George Case was playing his final season in 1947 for Washington, batting .150 in 36 games and 80 at-bats and stealing five bases in six attempts. Snuffy Stirnweiss stole 18 bags in 1946 and then never stole more than five during his final six big league seasons. Injuries would begin to take there toll on Pete Reiser, and after batting .309 with 14 steals in 110 games in 1947, his career took a sharp decline. And finally there was that disgraceful and vile human being, Ben Chapman, who ended his playing career with one game for the 1946 Phillies. Chapman and his 1947 Philadelphia Phillies replete with white Southerners were trying to end the career of Jackie Robinson with racial taunts and insults, beanballs, spikings, and cheap shots. The Phillies weren't the only team trying to destroy the hopes and dreams of millions of Americans, but their members were perhaps the worst of a sick and twisted bunch of conspirators. The St. Louis Cardinals had a number of players who spiked Robinson and they even planned to strike and refuse to take the field in protest of his presence in the lineup. Robinson endured the toughest major league season of any player to walk between the white lines and received a plethora of death threats. In response the Phillies players lined up in the dugout, pointed their bats at Jackie Robinson as if they were guns, and made machine gun noises. Roger Kahn wrote that the success of Jackie Robinson and of integration "was seriously in doubt" during the early part of 1947. He added, "(So, indeed, was Robinson's mental health.)"[76]

It was perhaps miraculous that Jack Roosevelt Robinson did not get seriously injured in 1947. In fact he played 151 games, a testament to his mental toughness, and ability to endure the substantial abuse that came in his direction. He was a phenomenal small ball practitioner, who stole 29 bases to lead the NL during his rookie campaign. The 5'11", 204-pound, right-handed first baseman bunted successfully 42 times and fourteen of them were hits. The other 28 were sacrifices. He won *The Sporting News* Rookie of the Year Award by batting .297 with a .383 on-base percentage and a .427 slugging percentage. He scored 125 runs and drove in 48. September 23, 1947, was Jackie Robinson Day at Ebbets Field and Bill "Bojangles" Robinson said, "I'm sixty-nine years old but never thought I'd live to see the day when I'd stand face-to-face with Ty Cobb in Technicolor."[77] Before the 1947 season concluded, Jackie was being called the "Ebony Ty Cobb."[78] Not since Ty Cobb had a player terrorized opponents on the basepaths like Jackie Robinson did. Both Robinson and Cobb were filled with anger: Jackie because of the injustices and racist behavior he encountered and Cobb because of the contrived injustices that filled his psychotic brain. Some historians suggest that Robinson brought back the art of basestealing. This perhaps is an overstatement, but he may have popularized it.

When Robinson came to the big leagues he was instructed not to fight back against the racists that were determined to end his career. Jackie was not a docile man, content with the status quo, and content that the big leagues were letting a single black man to perform in a hostile condition that threatened his physical and mental health. The eloquent Donald Honig wrote, "This was a black American releasing torrents of pent-up rage and resentment against a lifetime portion of bigotry, ignorance, and neglect; this was a messenger from the brooding, restless ghettos."[79] If Robinson couldn't walk over to the other side of the field, like any white man was allowed to do, and put his fist through Ben Chapman's skull, then how could he fight back against the racists? This was done by using his small ball skills, especially his baserunning. Robinson would infuriate the opposition with his aggressive baserunning. He took extra bases, going from first to third or second to home or scoring from the gateway station on a double when it didn't seem possible. Jackie challenged the outfielders when he collected a hit, turning singles into doubles and doubles into triples. He danced off the bases, distracting the pitchers who threw beanballs at his skull and infuriated them when he stole a bag. He made rundown plays difficult. Jackie took long leads off the bases and was constantly performing fake breaks. The pitcher would lose his concentration; he would throw a wild pitch, balk, or serve up a fat pitch to the batter. When pitchers tried to rush the ball to the plate, the batter had a distinct advantage because their velocity declined as a result. When the batter flew out to the outfield, Jackie was always tagging up ready to take that extra base. He took the initiative, he was perhaps the most daring and aggressive baserunner since Cobb. And he loved to steal home. When beanball pitchers threw at his head, he would bunt down the first base line hoping to run over the pitcher as they tried to cover first or tried to pick up the ball.

Robinson's aggressive baserunning was how he released his anger and fought back against the racists that were out to maim him. Russ "The Mad Monk" Meyer was interviewed for the book *The Whiz Kids and the 1950 Pennant,* by Robin Roberts and C. Paul Rogers III. Meyer recalled one game at Ebbets Field when he yelled over to Robinson at third base, "Go ahead you nigger, try to steal." Robinson did just that and infuriated Meyer when he was safe on a bang-bang play at home plate. Meyer got into the face of umpire Frank Dascoli because it appeared that Robinson was out; according to Meyer this was confirmed with pictures in the next day's paper. Robinson, meanwhile, was laughing at Meyer in the dugout. The Mad Monk exploded even more and confronted Jackie, telling him that they should meet down the runways, which were underneath the stands to settle the score. Thankfully, that confrontation never came to fruition.[80]

If Jackie Robinson played for one of these organizations or managers who wanted their players to remain anchored to the bases, his fate may have been very different. Not only did his small ball skills help the Dodgers win games, but they were a retaliatory act and a way to release his anger and fight back. Not with his fists, but with his legs. Branch Rickey told Robinson during the spring of 1947 as he prepared to play against the Dodgers in an exhibition game, "I want you to concentrate, to hit that ball, to get on base *by any means necessary.* I want you to run wild, to steal the pants off them, to be the most conspicuous player on the field — but conspicuous only because of the kind of baseball you're playing."[81] There are some modern day critics of small ball strategies who insist that a Jackie Robinson or a Rickey Henderson would have been better off not stealing bases. They are mistaken in this regard. In the case of Jackie Robinson that mentality could have had disastrous results. There is a subjective side to small ball that can't be quantified entirely with statistics. It has to do predominantly with the psychological impact it has on the pitcher and the rest of the defense. It also affects the positioning. If somebody like Jackie Robinson steps into the batter's box, the corner infielders are going to have to play in or otherwise Robinson could get an easy bunt single. And if the third baseman, for example, plays in, there is a bigger hole on the left side for Jackie to hit the ball through. If Robinson is standing at third base with less than two outs in a tie game in the last of the ninth, the outfielders are going to have to play extremely shallow to have a chance to throw out Robinson at the plate on a fly ball. Again, the batter benefits from this because what ordinarily could be a routine fly ball might fall gently upon the earth. As highlighted in Chapter Two, a team benefits greatly if they have fast runners who can execute small ball strategies. In Peter Golenbock's book *Bums: An Oral History of the Brooklyn Dodgers*, Ed Charles recalls watching Robinson play in a spring training game: "He got a couple of hits, he ran and was aggressive on the base paths. He danced and excited the crowds and excited the players, and he excited everybody."[82] It would most likely be difficult to find one person who saw Robinson run the bases aggressively who would think that he would have been better off if he had remained anchored to the bags.

Jackie broke into the white majors at the age of 28. His career statistics are remarkable, considering the abuse that he had to take. Robinson had a .311 lifetime batting average and led the NL in 1949 (.342). He had a .409 career on-base percentage and led both leagues in 1952 with .440. His career slugging percentage stood at .474 with a career high of .528 in 1949 when he collected 38 doubles, 12 triples, and 16 homers and had a career high 124 RBIs. During his ten-year career he scored 947 runs and scored at least 104 runs during six seasons. He stole 197 bases during his career and won the NL stolen base crown in 1947 (29) and led both leagues in 1949 (37). The caught stealing statistic did not resume being compiled in the NL until 1951, but Robinson had excellent basestealing averages during those seasons when they were compiled. In 1951 he stole 25 bags and had a 75.8 percent basestealing average. The following year he stole 24 and had a 77.4 percent basestealing average and then in 1953 he stole 17 and had an 81 percent basestealing average. From 1951 to 1953, Robinson's basestealing average easily surpassed the aggregate National League average of 60.7, 56.1, and 61.1 percent, respectively. Robinson laid down 104 sacrifice bunts during his career. He led both leagues in 1947 (28) and tied for the NL lead in 1949 with Marty Marion (17).

In 1947 stolen bases plummeted in the junior circuit when compared to wartime levels and declined slightly in the senior circuit. There were only 399 stolen bases in the AL and 361 in the NL. For the first time since 1938, the junior league teams amassed more sacrifices than the senior league teams, 719 to 687. Sacrifices plummeted in the NL when compared to 1946, a decline of 214. There were only three major league teams with over 100 sacrifices: the Philadelphia Athletics (144), the Boston Braves (129), and the Brooklyn Dodgers (115). While Jackie Robinson laid down the most sacrifice bunts with 28, Eddie Joost of the Athletics led the AL with 24. Joost, the Athletics everyday shortstop in 1947, batted a paltry .206 but he walked 114 times and had a .348 on-base percentage. None of the major league teams stole over 100 bases in 1947. The pennant-winning Brooklyn Dodgers (94–60) led the NL with 88 thefts, while the sixth-place Chicago White Sox led the AL with 91. The American League stolen base averages ranged from 46.4 percent (Detroit) to 61.5 percent (Chicago). Jackie Robinson led the NL with 29 steals, while Bob Dillinger of St. Louis won the first of three consecutive AL stolen base crowns with 34. Dillinger was a 28-year-old third baseman, playing his second big league season. He batted .294 and had a 72.3 percent basestealing average.

The Brooklyn Dodgers got off to a good start to begin the 1947 campaign. They won their fourth in a row on April 26 versus the Giants by a 7–3 score and were situated in first place, a half game ahead of Pittsburgh. Gene Hermanski hit a two-run homer in the sixth inning to give them the lead which they would never relinquish before 33,565 approving fans at Ebbets Field. The five-foot-eleven-and-a-half-inch, 185-pound, left fielder threw out Bobby Thomson trying to stretch a single into a double in the top of the fifth. In the last of the eighth the Dodgers pushed across their final marker. Eddie Stanky walked and was sacrificed to second by Jackie Robinson. After a walk to Pete Reiser, Stanky scored on Dixie Walker's fourth consecutive hit. With the bases loaded and two outs, Reiser attempted his first steal of home during the campaign but was called out by the arbiter, George Magerkurth. The Dodgers emerged victorious on the following day against their hated rivals when Stanky executed a squeeze bunt in the ninth inning to give them a 9–8 win. On May 30, the Boston Braves won two games from the Dodgers, 6–3 and 3–0, and executed a run producing double steal in each game. Fritz Ostermueller, a 39-year-old southpaw, was on the bump for the Pittsburgh Pirates on June 24 versus Brooklyn at Forbes Field. The game was tied at two in the top of the fifth and Jackie Robinson was dancing off third base taking fake breaks and a long, audacious lead. Bob Cooke of the *New York Herald Tribune* wrote, "Robinson turned on an added burst of speed and contrived as pretty a steal of home as one would care to see." In the opening paragraph, Cooke wrote that Ostermueller's windup "resembles a counter-rotating propeller," and he became "ensnared" in his pitching motion when Robinson pilfered home. For Robinson it was the first of nineteen steals of home during his career. Jackie is tied for 9th all-time in that category and out of the top thirteen players he is the only one not to have played during the Deadball Era. His steal of home plated the winning run as the Dodgers emerged triumphant, 4–2. Carl Furillo, a 25-year-old second-year player, also stole a bag for Brooklyn, as did backup Al Gionfriddo who was getting a rare start. As for Pete Reiser he was on his way to Johns Hopkins Hospital to be examined for "dizzy spells."[83] In a game against the Cubs in June, Jackie Robinson scored from first base on a sacrifice.

The 1947 All-Star Game at Wrigley Field on July 8 was a pitcher's duel and conducive to small ball activity. The American League prevailed, 2–1. In the top of the seventh, Bobby Doerr, the American League second baseman who had replaced starter Joe Gordon at the position, singled off Johnny Sain with one out. Doerr got a huge jump off Sain and took off for second. Instead of coming home with the ball, Sain turned towards second, and unleashed a late throw that hit Doerr in the back. The ball went onto the outfield grass and Doerr advanced to third. The Americans took a 2–1 lead when Stan Spence hit a single into center field to score Doerr. On August 29, Detroit defeated St. Louis, 5–4, at Sportsman's Park. Fred Hutchinson, the Tigers 6'2", 200-pound, left-handed hitting but right-handed throwing pitcher, tripled off Ellis Kinder in the third inning and then stole home. It was the first time a pitcher had tripled and then swiped home.

Burt Shotton was the Brooklyn Dodgers skipper in 1947, except for two games that were managed by Clyde Sukeforth. Leo Durocher was suspended for the entire season for an "accumulation of unpleasant incidents detrimental to baseball," by commissioner Happy Chandler.[84] Bucky Harris led the Yankees to a pennant during his first season as their skipper and led them into battle against the Dodgers in the 1947 World Series. The Yankees won two of the first three games and then Brooklyn took the fourth contest, 3–2, in a terrific battle that is considered one of the greatest World Series games ever. The Yankees took a 2–0 lead into the last of the fifth. Bill Bevens, the Yankees six-foot-three-and-a-half-inch, 210-pound, right-handed pitcher, was having control problems but had not allowed a hit. Brooklyn scored their first run on two walks, a sacrifice, and an infield out. Bevens was still working on a no-hitter heading into the last of the ninth with a 2–1 lead, but he had walked eight. After Bruce Edwards flied out to left field, Carl Furillo got on base via a walk, which was Brooklyn's ninth free pass of the game. Spider Jorgensen popped out to the first baseman and then Al Gionfriddo pinch-ran for Furillo. Despite stealing only two bags during the campaign, the little-used backup outfielder said he was most likely the fastest man on the club. This, of course, was probably a dubious assertion considering the presence of Jackie Robinson and Pete Reiser. Furthermore, Gionfriddo insisted that Furillo had a habit of missing bases, for example, when he went from first to third he would occasionally step over second base and was called out. Reiser was called on to pinch-hit for reliever Hugh Casey. But Pistol Pete had injured his ankle the previous day in a slide and was not in top shape. Gionfriddo stole second on a 2–1 count. "I sort of slipped a little bit when I took off for second. I slid in head-first under the throw. It was a little close," insisted the diminutive 5'6", 165-pound, baserunner.[85] Now with the tying run in scoring position and first base open, Bucky Harris shocked many people when he walked Reiser to put the winning run on base. Eddie Miksis ran for him. The wheels were in motion and Shotton sent up a pinch-hitter for Eddie Stanky, right-handed hitting Cookie Lavagetto. He hit a double scoring two runs to end the game with Brooklyn's first hit. The Yankees would regroup and win the series in seven games. Phil Rizzuto stole the only two bases in the series for the Yankees. Brooklyn, meanwhile, stole seven, including three by Pee Wee Reese and two by Jackie Robinson. Robinson batted .259 in the series and had one of Brooklyn's three sacrifices. Harris's team also laid down three sacrifice bunts. The final game started ominously for Brooklyn when Stanky and Reese were caught stealing in the first inning. They lost the finale by a 5–2 score.

The Cleveland Indians and the Boston Red Sox finished the 1948 campaign with an identical 96–58 record atop the American League standings. Player-manager Lou Boudreau's Indians won the one-game playoff by an 8–3 score to secure their first pennant since 1920. The Indians went on to win the World Series over the Boston Braves (91–62) in six games. Both teams scored seventeen runs in the series and Boston collected more hits than the Indians, 43 to 38. Billy Southworth's Braves collected at least one sacrifice bunt in each game, and had seven in total, while the Indians had three. Joe Gordon and Jim Hegan swiped bags for the Tribe, while Earl Torgeson stole the only base for Boston. During the regular season, the NL stole more bases than the AL, 449 to 363, but the junior league had more sacrifices, 749 to 668. There were five teams with at least 100 sacrifices, including the Braves, who led the majors with 140 and the fifth-place Detroit Tigers who led the AL with 130. Johnny Sain of the Boston Braves led the majors with twenty-four wins and also led the NL with sixteen sacrifices. Bob Harris tied for the AL lead in 1941, but Sain became the first pitcher to win a sacrifice hit title outright. Barney McCosky of the Athletics led the AL with 22.

Leo Durocher managed the Dodgers for only part of the season before becoming the skipper of the New York Giants on July 16 in a move that shocked the baseball community, especially Giant fans who hated Durocher. The third-place Dodgers led the majors with 114 steals as Pee Wee Reese led the team with 25 thefts, finishing second behind Richie Ashburn of Philadelphia (32) in the NL. Ashburn was a 21-year-old fly chaser, who batted .333 with a .410 on-base percentage with little power during his rookie campaign. He had a 23-game hitting streak in 1948, but he only played 117 games because his season ended in late August when he fractured a finger sliding into second base. When his Hall of Fame career ended with the 1962 New York Mets, Ashburn had accumulated 234 stolen bases, including ten or more during twelve seasons. The 5'10", 170-pound, left-handed hitter also laid down 112 sacrifice bunts, including five seasons with eleven or more. He was an excellent leadoff man, who was difficult to strike out, and walked a lot. Ashburn led the senior league in hits three times, triples two times, walks four times, batting average twice, and on-base percentage four times. Additionally, he was one of the best defensive center fielders to play the game. Stan Rojek of Pittsburgh stole 24 of his career 32 bags to finish third in steals and Jackie Robinson finished fourth with 22 steals. The seventh-place Washington Senators paced the AL with 76 thefts and Bob Dillinger of St. Louis led the circuit with 28 steals. Washington's Gil Coan (23) and Mickey Vernon (15) finished second and third in the circuit. Vernon stole 137 bases during his twenty-year career, including a career high of 25 in 1942 with an 80.6 percent basestealing average.

In his first season as an everyday player in the big show during 1948, Alvin Dark of the Boston Braves batted .322 with four steals. On July 9 he tripled and stole home in the fourth inning, as the Braves defeated the Phillies, 13–2, at Braves Field. The American League won their third consecutive All-Star Game on July 13 at Sportsman's Park by a 5–2 score. Richie Ashburn, the National League leadoff man, went 2 for 4 with a run scored and a stolen base. Mickey Vernon, Pat Mullin, and George McQuinn stole bases for the American League. Vernon and Mullin pulled off a double steal in the third inning. Philadelphia Athletics pitcher, Joe Coleman, laid down the only sacrifice bunt.

On August 22, the Dodgers stole eight bases before a paid crowd of 33,151 at Ebbets Field but managed to lose to Boston, 4–3, because of a lack of clutch hitting. The Dodgers ran on Bill Salkeld, the starting catcher for Boston, "until his arm was ready to fall off." Shotton's team scored their first marker in the second frame when Pee Wee Reese singled, advanced to third on two throwing errors by right-handed pitcher Bill Voiselle, and scored on Gil Hodges's single. Brooklyn scored two runs in the fifth inning and stole five bases. With Jackie Robinson on third, Gene Hermanski on second, and Pee Wee Reese on first, the Dodgers pulled off a triple steal with Bill Voiselle on the mound and Billy Cox at the bat. It was Robinson's fourth steal of home during the season. Hermanski stole three bases in the game, Reese stole two, while Marv Rackley, Robinson, and Pete Reiser stole one apiece. Roy Campanella, the Dodgers 26-year-old rookie catcher, laid down the only sacrifice bunt in the game. The official caught stealing statistics were not compiled in the National League since 1925 and would not be resumed until 1951. But according to the *New York Herald Tribune*, Brooklyn was successful in thirty-one of their last thirty-two stolen base attempts.[86]

The Dodgers were in St. Louis on August 29 and defeated the Cardinals in two games, 12–7 and 6–4. Robinson hit for the cycle in the opener and stole the only base of the game. Carl Furillo had two sacrifices and Gil Hodges had one. In the tenth inning of the second contest, Robinson sacrificed Reiser to second. Reese struck out and George Shuba was walked intentionally. Reiser scored the go-ahead run on pinch-hitter Arky Vaughan's single and Shuba scored when catcher Del Wilber couldn't handle the throw. Pittsburgh won two games from Boston on the day at Forbes Field by scores of 6–1 and 5–2. Both teams combined for four sacrifices in the second game. On September 12, the Braves lost the opener to the Phillies, 6–4, and won the nightcap, 2–1, in thirteen innings. They plated the winning run when Alvin Dark singled to lead off the top of the thirteenth, advanced two bases on Earl Torgeson's sacrifice bunt, and later scored on Bill Salkeld's bases-loaded fly ball.

On October 12, the day after the 1948 World Series, Casey Stengel was named the new manager of the New York Yankees. Many critics thought this announcement was some sort of joke because Stengel was not perceived as a serious person. They thought he was a clown, who was always joking and not taking the game seriously. Furthermore, during his nine big league managerial seasons with the Brooklyn Dodgers and Boston Braves, he never finished higher than fifth place. Those people associated with the Boston Red Sox couldn't have been any happier. Dave Egan of the *Boston Daily Record* wrote, "The Yankees have now been mathematically eliminated from the 1949 pennant race."[87] However, beneath the jocular exterior was a knowledgeable baseball man, a strategic genius who often went against the book, and an excellent teacher who had several decades worth of baseball experience to pass down to the younger players. The reason why he was not successful managing the Dodgers and Braves was because he didn't have good players, but in 1949 that was going to change. When Stengel played in the big leagues during the Deadball Era and the early 1920s, managers were already platooning players and engaging in various other specializations. John McGraw, his manager with the New York Giants, was known for using full-time pinch-runners. Historian Bill James notes that from 1915 to 1925, which also corresponded with Stengel's final eleven seasons in the big leagues, was the "heyday of platooning." Then from 1926 to 1940, platooning declined sharply in the big leagues. In 1949 Stengel ubiquitously platooned players and revitalized the practice.[88]

At the 1949 Yankees spring training at St. Petersburg, Florida, Stengel worked his players extremely hard with two workouts per day. He trained his players for hours on the fundamentals, making sure they knew how to bunt, hit behind the runner, and steal bases. Some of the stars on the team were allowed to train at their own pace. Stengel told his players he didn't know anything about the American League and he was going to simply observe and allow the players to do what they wanted. He wasn't even going to give them signs, allowing the players to make their own decisions like it was done during the Deadball Era.[89]

Stengel would prove that the critics were wrong as the Yankees captured the flag with a 97–57 record and then defeated manager Burt Shotton's Brooklyn Dodgers (97–57) in five games to capture the World Series title. Billy Johnson and Phil Rizzuto stole the only bases for New York, while Pee Wee Reese stole a bag for Brooklyn. Jackie Robinson and the power-hitting Gil Hodges laid down sacrifice bunts for the Dodgers, while Cliff Mapes had one for the Yankees and Rizzuto led both teams with two sacrifices. There were 82 fewer steals in the major leagues than the previous season as the AL teams stole 366 bags and the NL teams stole 364. The Brooklyn Dodgers led the majors with 117 steals, which was 32.1 percent of the stolen bases in the senior league. On September 8, Red Schoendienst stole the seventeenth and final base of the season for the St. Louis Cardinals. At that juncture of major league history it was the lowest total ever and it is currently tied for the third lowest. In the American League, the sixth-place Chicago White Sox led the circuit with a measly 62 steals. Jackie Robinson led the majors with 37 steals and was followed by his teammate Pee Wee Reese (26). Bob Dillinger led the AL with only 20 thefts and Phil Rizzuto finished second with 18. Rizzuto was a terrific small ball player who swiped 149 bases during his career with a 72 percent basestealing average. He stole eleven or more bases during eight seasons. In 1949 he captured the first of four consecutive AL sacrifice hit titles with 25. The Scooter was an excellent bunter, who laid down 193 sacrifices, which ranks 90th all-time. Almost all of the players that are ranked ahead of him played all or part of their career when sacrifice flies were counted as sacrifice hits. Marty Marion and Jackie Robinson shared the NL sacrifice bunt title in 1949 with seventeen. The Brooklyn Dodgers led the NL with 102 sacrifices, while the fifth-place Philadelphia Athletics led the AL with 117.

On September 20, Jackie Robinson stole home for the fifth time in 1949 in a 5–0 win over Chicago. It was his thirteenth steal of home in three seasons. The Yankees defeated the Athletics on September 28, 7–5, as they scored the go-ahead run in the bottom of the seventh on Phil Rizzuto's squeeze bunt.

The Baseball Writers Association of America gave the 1950 NL Rookie of the Year Award to Sam Jethroe of the Boston Braves. Jethroe was among hundreds of black players who had been relegated to the Negro Leagues until Jackie Robinson integrated the sport and even then only a few players got a fair opportunity to make a major league team. The Boston Red Sox pretended as if they were giving Jackie Robinson, Marvin Williams, and Jethroe a legitimate tryout in April 1945 at Fenway Park but they were only doing so to appease the black press, a few members of the Boston city council, and a vocal sportswriter named Dave Egan, who was critical of the all-white Red Sox. Even as they went through their fundamentals in the deserted ballpark with two coaches, they were still harassed with hate speech as a voice yelled from the grandstand, "Get those niggers off the field!"[90] Jethroe spent eleven seasons in the Negro Leagues from 1938 to 1948 and spent two seasons playing for Montreal of the International League, which was a Brooklyn Dodger farm team. He reportedly stole 89 bags for Montreal in 1949. By the time he got his opportunity in the major leagues, he was 32 years old. However, the 6'1", 178-pound, switch-hitter had a terrific big league debut, batting .273 with a .338 on-base percentage, a .442 slugging percentage, 100 runs scored, and a major league leading 35 stolen bases. During the following season he improved to .280 with a .356 on-base percentage, a .460 slugging percentage, 101 runs scored, a major league leading 35 stolen bases with an excellent 87.5 percent stolen base average. In 1952 Jethroe played his final season as an everyday player, hitting .232 with 28 steals and ended his big league career with two games for the 1954 Pittsburgh Pirates. He was nicknamed "Jet," but he was more than a burner and connected for eighteen homers in both 1950 and 1951. He patrolled center field during most of his career but according to Johnny Antonelli he wasn't a good outfielder, which was probably because of his poor eyesight. Jethroe was a well-liked member of the Braves and although he was past his prime when he finally got to play in the big leagues, he performed extremely well.

The 1950 Philadelphia Phillies, known as the Whiz Kids, won the NL flag (91–63) but then dropped the World Series in four straight games to the New York Yankees (98–56) as they managed to score only five runs. Phil Rizzuto stole the only base for Stengel's team, while Granny Hamner pilfered the only bag for Eddie Sawyer's Phillies. In 1950 the junior circuit stole an embarrassing 278 bases, which was 34.8 per team, which is the lowest total amassed by either league in the history of major league baseball. The fifth-place Washington Senators and the last-place Philadelphia Athletics shared the AL stolen base title with 42 bags, which is the lowest total for a league leader in the history of the big leagues. Dom DiMaggio of the Boston Red Sox batted .328 with a .414 on-base percentage and a major league leading 131 runs scored. He tied for the AL lead with eleven triples and his fifteen stolen bases led the AL. DiMaggio had an impressive 78.9 percent stolen base average. The senior circuit teams stole 94 more bases than the junior league teams, 372 in total. Second-place Brooklyn paced the circuit in both stolen bases (77) and sacrifices (88). There were two teams with over 100 sacrifices in the AL: the second-place Detroit Tigers, who amassed 110 and the sixth-place Chicago White Sox, who had 106. Red Schoendienst captured the NL sacrifice hit title with 16, while Phil Rizzuto led the AL with 19.

On June 2, the St. Louis Browns swept a twin bill from the Washington Senators, 10–5 and 9–3. In the second game they pulled off a double steal with pitcher Harry Dorish stealing home and outfielder Ray Coleman swiping a bag on the back end. Dorish is the last AL pitcher to steal home. Leo Durocher's Giants finished the season in third place with an 86–68 record and stole only 42 bases (5th, NL). The Giants stole four bases against Johnny Sain on September 23 as they won 4–3 at Braves Field. Durocher insisted that Sain was easy to steal on. And then they won their next game, 12–4, over Boston as they stole four more, including one by pitcher Jim Hearn. The Giants swiped 19 percent of their stolen bases in two consecutive games.

The New York Giants rallied from a thirteen and a half game deficit on August 12 to tie the Brooklyn Dodgers with a 96–58 record at the end of the 1951 season. This exhilarating pennant race continued into a three-game playoff, which was won by the Giants in the third game on Bobby Thomson's three-run homer in the last of the ninth. Durocher's Giants committed ten errors in the World Series against the Yankees and lost it in six games. Monte Irvin, the Giants outfielder, batted .458 in the series and pilfered the only two bases. He collected four hits in the opening game and stole home. Southpaw Dave Koslo pitched a complete game in the opener and led the Giants to a 5–1 victory. He also laid down the only two sacrifice bunts of the series during that game.

Stolen bases rose significantly in both leagues in 1951, an increase of 81 in the NL and 135 in the AL. The senior circuit teams collected two more sacrifices than the junior league, 621 to 619. The Philadelphia Phillies and the Chicago White Sox led the majors with 103 sacrifices. The fourth-place White Sox also led the majors with 99 stolen bases, while second-place Brooklyn led the NL with 89. For the first time since 1925 the caught stealing statistic was once again compiled in the NL. The fourth-place Boston Braves stole 80 bags to finish second in the circuit and led both leagues with a 70.2 percent basestealing average. Sam Jethroe led the majors with 35 steals, while Minnie Minoso led the AL with 31. Jim Busby, Minoso's White Sox teammate, finished second in the junior league with 26 steals. Willie Jones of the Phillies paced the NL with 19 sacrifices, while Phil Rizzuto led the majors with 26.

Minnie Minoso was born in Havana, Cuba, on November 29, 1922, and played four seasons in the Negro Leagues from 1945 to 1948 before making his big league debut for the 1949 Cleveland Indians. He played nine games for them and eight more to start the 1951 campaign before being traded to the White Sox. The 5'10", 175-pound, right-handed outfielder blossomed with the Sox, batting .324 with a .419 on-base percentage and a .498 slugging percentage. He scored 109 runs for Chicago and 112 during the season. Additionally, he led the majors with 14 triples and stole 31 bases in 41 attempts. Minoso was once described by a scout as the "fastest thing on legs," and he played the game in a daring, aggressive fashion by stealing bases, taking the extra base, and running into the outfield walls to catch the ball.[91] The Sox fans encouraged him to steal bags with the chant of "Go! Go!" And that's precisely what he did in 1951, winning the first of three consecutive AL stolen base titles and reviving the tradition of the running game, which was once so ubiquitous within the White Sox organization. In 1950 the Sox stole only 19 bases as a team and that increased to 99 in 1951. Minoso thrived in the big leagues despite having to overcome various hardships, a language barrier, and a racist society. There were a plethora of beanball pitchers and bigots throwing at him and he led the American League in hit by pitches a remarkable ten times. The "Cuban Comet" was fearless and he even came back to the game after Bob Grim fractured his skull in 1955. Despite all the abuse that he had to endure, Minoso was not a bitter man, and was well-liked with an affable personality. He had an unending amount of enthusiasm and was determined to succeed and fulfill his big league obligations despite the harsh conditions. During Minoso's seventeen-year major league career, he batted .298 with a .389 on-base percentage and a .459 slugging percentage. He scored at least 104 runs during four seasons and amassed 1,136 runs scored during his career. Minoso tied for the AL lead in doubles in 1957 with 36 and led the junior league in triples three times, including a career high of eighteen in 1954. From 1951 to 1953 he stole 78 bases. He stole 205 bases during his career and pilfered twelve or more cushions during nine seasons. Minoso had a terrific major league career, one that is worthy of serious Hall of Fame consideration.

On May 6, 1951, the Cincinnati Reds won the opening game against New York, 4–3, in ten innings at the Polo Grounds. The Giants failed to win in the last of the ninth despite the fact that Eddie Stanky started the inning with a double. Spider Jorgensen failed in his attempt to sacrifice him to third and then Artie Wilson, who was running for Stanky, didn't tag up on a long fly ball. After Virgil Stallcup hit a homer in the tenth inning to give manager Luke Sewell's team the lead, the Giants were threatening once again when Whitey Lockman led off with a single in the bottom half. Alvin Dark sacrificed Lockman to second and Connie Ryan persuaded him to get off the bag and tagged him out on the hidden-ball trick. Lockman apparently thought that time had been called. Both teams combined for four sacrifices in the opener, including two by Dark. New York won the nightcap, 8–5, as Bobby Thomson stole a base and Jorgensen had a sacrifice. The Red Sox won two games from the Yankees on May 30, 11–10 in fifteen innings and 9–4. Ted Williams was edging off second in the opener and then he scored on a sacrifice. Frank Hiller tossed a one-hitter for the Cubs on June 28 as they defeated St. Louis, 8–0. In the four-run ninth inning, Chicago pulled off a double steal with Jack Cusick stealing home and Hiller swiping third. The Giants defeated the Braves, 4–1, at Braves Field on July 1. In the top of the fourth, Monte Irvin was at third base and Warren Spahn was working on Bill Rigney and paying no attention to Irvin. With a 2 and 1 count, Irvin stole home easily. The Dodgers won two games from the Giants, 6–5 and 4–2, before 34,620 fans at Ebbets Field on the 4th of July. Brooklyn won the opener in eleven innings on Preacher Roe's squeeze bunt, which scored Jackie Robinson. Robinson had moved up to third on the previous pitch when catcher Ray Noble tried to pick him off second.

Richie Ashburn had an outstanding performance in the 1951 All-Star Game, going 2 for 4 at the bat and playing sensational defense as the National League prevailed by an 8–3 score on July 10 at Briggs Stadium. Jackie Robinson legged out a squeeze bunt in the seventh that scored Ashburn. George Kell laid down a sacrifice bunt for the AL, while Cardinals star Stan Musial was caught stealing twice. The small ball activities were overshadowed by the six home runs that were launched in the game.

The Giants were at Crosley Field on July 29 and won two games, 3–1 and 6–4. Willie Mays stole the first base of his career in the opener and then was promptly picked off by hurler Willie Ramsdell. New York pulled off a double steal in the fourth inning of the nightcap, as Irvin stole home and Mays stole third. Irvin went 2 for 2 with two steals in the contest. The Dodgers swept a doubleheader from the Giants on August 8 by scores of 7–2 and 7–6 to extend their lead to eleven and a half games. Pee Wee Reese stole two bases in the opener and Robinson had one. In the nightcap, Robinson stole two, while Duke Snider and Billy Cox had one. On September 17, the Yankees emerged victorious over Cleveland, 2–1, thanks to Phil Rizzuto's squeeze bunt in the last of the ninth with the bases loaded. The Cardinals defeated the Dodgers on the following day, 7–1, as Stan Musial and Enos Slaughter pulled off a double steal with Musial swiping home on the play.

Ty Cobb's attack on the modern day player in *Life* magazine caused quite a controversy in the spring of 1952. The Brooklyn Dodgers finished the job in 1952 and didn't wilt down the stretch, finishing the season with a 96–57 record, four and a half games ahead of second-place New York. They led the majors in stolen bases with 90 and in stolen base average (64.7 percent). Their 104 sacrifices were ranked second in the NL behind fourth-place Philadelphia, who amassed 107. Stolen bases declined in both leagues in 1952 and third-place Chicago led the AL with only 61 stolen bases. Manager Paul Richards White Sox led the majors with 121 sacrifices. Pee Wee Reese led the senior circuit in steals (30) and had an 85.7 percent stolen base average, while Sam Jethroe finished a close second with 28 bags. Reese stole a praiseworthy 232 bases during his career, including five seasons with twenty or more. Minnie Minoso accumulated the most steals in the AL with 22 and Jim Rivera, who played for both the Browns and White Sox during the season, finished second with 21. The Phillies shortstop, Granny Hamner, led the NL with 17 sacrifices, while Phil Rizzuto won once again in the AL with 23. The Yankees needed seven games to defeat the Dodgers in the World Series as Gil McDougald stole the only base for the winners. Brooklyn stole five bases, including two by Jackie Robinson. The Dodgers had a 55.6 percent basestealing average, while the Yankees were caught stealing three times and pilfered bags at a 25 percent clip. Brooklyn laid down six sacrifice bunts, including three in game five, while the Yankees had two.

Giants pitcher Sal Maglie tossed a three-hitter on April 29 before 19,531 Crosley Field fans and drove in the winning run in the ninth inning with a single to give Leo Durocher's aggregation a 2–1 win. He had two sacrifices in the game. During the season he batted only .072 but contributed twelve sacrifices. New York scored the first run in the third inning when Wes Westrum hit a double to lead off and was sacrificed to third by Maglie. The squeeze play was executed perfectly when Davey Williams bunted down the third base line and Westrum scored. The Dodgers prevailed over the Cubs, 3–1, on May 2. Chicago's only run was scored when Bob Addis and Frank Baumholtz executed a double steal in the initial frame. In a six-year major league career, Luke Easter stole only one base in nine attempts. On July 15, the big six-foot-four-and-a-half-inch, 240-pound, left-handed hitter was standing at the gateway station in the first inning versus the Yankees. The sacks were full as Larry Doby was on second and Al Rosen was on third base. The Indians pulled off a triple steal and went on to win, 7–3. The Boston Red Sox finished second in the AL with 59 stolen bases. On September 19 they lost to Washington, 5–3, but stole six bases. Faye Throneberry, the Red Sox's 21-year-old rookie outfielder and brother of future major leaguer Marv, stole two of his sixteen bases on the season. Al Zarilla, Dick Gernert, Del Wilber, and Gene Stephens stole one apiece.

The first-place Brooklyn Dodgers (105–49) and New York Yankees (99–52) led their league in batting average, on-base percentage, and slugging percentage in 1953. Casey Stengel's Yankees won their fifth consecutive World Series championship, defeating the Dodgers in six games. Both teams stole two bases in the series: Billy Martin and Phil Rizzuto for New York and Gil Hodges and Jackie Robinson for Chuck Dressen's Dodgers. Once again, the Yankees had a low basestealing average (33.3 percent), while the Dodgers had only one runner caught stealing. The Yankees had four of the six sacrifices. Brooklyn was charged with seven errors, while the Yankees had only one.

The National League scored 756 more runs than in 1952, while the American League's total increased by 321. On August 30 there were fifteen major league games played with 171 runs scored, 298 hits, and 31 homers. The Milwaukee Braves connected for twelve homers in their twin bill and two of the scores on the day were 20–4 and 19–4. Arthur Daley was compelled to write an article in the *New York Times* titled "Too Much Jackrabbit?" He facetiously suggested that Ty Cobb had probably "blown a gasket by now," and then made the somewhat dubious claim that the dead ball was the reason he was able to amass a .367

career batting average (the current baseball encyclopedia gives Cobb a .366 average). Daley insisted that some recent World Series games that ended, 1–0, were "a bit on the dull side," but agreed with Cobb that the high scoring games were "damaging the sport." And he understood why a fan might think that the baseball was manipulated to make it livelier despite the denials by the owners.[92]

With a significant increase in home runs in 1953, stolen bases declined as there were only 342 in the NL and an even more pathetic 326 in the AL. The last-place St. Louis Browns stole only seventeen bases, which is tied for the third lowest in major league baseball's modern era. The Brooklyn Dodgers led the majors with 90 thefts, while the third-place Chicago White Sox paced the AL with 73. The stolen base crowns were won by Milwaukee Braves rookie center fielder Bill Bruton in the NL, who stole 26, and Minnie Minoso in the AL with 25. For the second season in a row Jim Rivera finished second in the junior league in thefts, this time with 22. Bruton was a left-handed hitting, six-foot-and-a-half-inch, 169-pound speed merchant, who led the NL in steals during his first three seasons with 26, 34, and 25. He stole 207 bases during his career and had a 69.9 percent basestealing average. His career batting average stands at .273 and he scored at least 106 runs during two seasons, including in 1960 when he led the NL with 112. He led the major leagues in triples two times, including a career high of fifteen in 1956. Bruton did not walk a lot and had a .328 career on-base percentage. He struck out 100 times during his rookie season, but made better contact in subsequent campaigns. Bruton played eight seasons for the Milwaukee Braves from 1953 to 1960 and four campaigns for the Detroit Tigers from 1961 to 1964. Some people thought that he should have bunted more often and utilized his speed in trying to get on base. Bob Buhl described Bruton as a "very fine gentleman, speedy center fielder, stolen base champion, and good team player."[93]

Sacrifices declined in both leagues in 1953 as the AL compiled 671 and the NL teams had 574. The Chicago White Sox amassed 120 sacrifices and were the only team with over 100. Last-place Pittsburgh led the NL with only 89. Pee Wee Reese was a complete small ball player and in addition to his laudable basestealing accomplishments, he was also a good bunter. He had 157 career sacrifices, including ten or more during seven seasons. He won his only sacrifice hit crown in 1953, leading the NL with fifteen. Jim Piersall batted .272 in his first season as an everyday player for the Boston Red Sox. The six-foot, 175-pound, right-handed outfielder stole eleven bases in twenty-one attempts and led the AL with nineteen sacrifices.

The Braves organization had resided in Boston since 1876, which was the National League's first season. The attendance declined systematically after their 1948 pennant-winning campaign and it became clear to owner Lou Perini that the town could no longer support two major league teams. In 1953, the Braves relocated to Milwaukee in the first franchise shift since the American League's Baltimore franchise moved to New York in 1903. On April 13, 1953, in the Milwaukee Braves' opening game in Cincinnati, Bruton stole a base and scored the first run as they prevailed, 2–0. On the following day, Bruton hit the first home run at Milwaukee County Stadium and then wouldn't hit another long ball for a year and a half. He became a better power-hitter later in his career and from 1960 to 1962 he hit 12, 17, and 16 homers, respectively.

Bob Lemon tossed a one-hitter for Cleveland on April 14 as they defeated Chicago, 6–0. Jim Rivera of the White Sox stole second base in the second inning and was called out trying to steal home. Before 29,406 spectators at the Polo Grounds on April 17, Jim Hearn of the Giants pitched four scoreless innings against Brooklyn before collapsing in the fifth inning when he surrendered six markers. It was a cold evening with a light rain falling and Hearn became unnerved in the fifth, unleashing two of his three wild pitches as Brooklyn's baserunners ran wild. In the four-run sixth inning the Dodgers had two sacrifices and executed a perfect hit-and-run play with Jackie Robinson at the bat, who slapped Ruben Gomez's offering through the vacated second base hole and sent Duke Snider to third. Jackie took second base when Gomez lost his concentration while holding the ball in the middle of the diamond. The Dodgers stole four bases in the game: two by Duke Snider and one apiece by Robinson and Roy Campanella. The Giants had won earlier in the day by a 6–3 score but lost the night game, 12–4.

The National League won the All-Star Game on July 14 at Crosley Field by a 5–1 score as Enos Slaughter went 2 for 3 with two runs scored, an RBI, and a stolen base. Brooklyn destroyed Chicago, 15–4, on July 21. In the third inning, Robinson stole second and third base. Duke Snider also had a stolen base. Snider batted .336 during the season with a .419 on-base percentage, a .627 slugging percentage, 132 runs scored, 126 RBIs, and a career high 16 steals. The Cubs won two games from the Reds on September 6 by scores of 7–6 and 7–2. Dee Fondy was standing on third base with two outs and two strikes on the batter in the last of the ninth in the opener. He stole home with Bob Kelly on the mound to give the Cubs the win. Fondy stole a respectable 84 bases during his eight-year big league career, including a career high of twenty in 1954 when he had an 80 percent basestealing average.

The 1954 Cleveland Indians compiled a 111–43 regular season record and then got swept in the World Series by the New York Giants (97–57). It was the first time since the 1922 Giants swept the Yankees that a National League team had swept the series. Davey Williams, the Giants second baseman, went 0 for 11, but his two sacrifices led both teams. Leo Durocher's outfit laid down six sacrifice bunts, while Al Lopez's Indians had three. Willie Mays stole the only base of the series and New York's pitchers had a 1.46 ERA versus Cleveland's 4.84. Mays's catch off the bat of Vic Wertz in the eighth inning of the opening game is considered one of the greatest in major league history.

Willie Howard Mays was arguably the greatest player in big league history. He combined the potent combination of speed and power in a way that had not been seen before, hitting 660 career home runs and stealing 338 bases. Mays could do it all: hit for average and power, field his position and unleash terrific throws, and run the bases superbly. He won four consecutive NL stolen base titles from 1956 to 1959 with 40, 38, 31, and 27 steals. Willie also stole bases at an effective clip, having a career 76.6 percent basestealing average. It took him a while to get accustomed to stealing bases in the big leagues as he stole a combined nineteen bases during his first three seasons. But then in 1955 he swiped 24 bags and had an 85.7 percent basestealing average. During his four seasons as the NL stolen base champion his stolen base percentages were 80, 66.7, 83.8, and 87.1. Mays stole at least eighteen bases during ten seasons. In 1962 when he purloined 18 sacks, he had a 90 percent basestealing average and when he stole 23 in 1971 at the age of forty, he compiled an 88.5 percent basestealing average. In Arnold Hano's biography of Willie Mays, he recalls that Mays tried to bunt with runners on first and second and no outs early in the 1954 season. Mays was unsuccessful in his sacrifice attempt as he bunted to the pitcher who forced the runner at third. Somebody said, "Ah! They have at last found Willie Mays's weakness. He can't bunt."[94] But Mays was the best or one of the best in the game at doing everything else. His job wasn't to sacrifice runners over, but he is credited with thirteen sacrifices during his career.

Entering the 1954 season, Mays had only played 155 major league games and was not yet the star he was about to become. Al Lopez, the manager of the Cleveland Indians, noticed that the infielders played him far back and to the left in the spring of 1954 and said, "Mays is a .270 hitter who might hit .300 if they teach him to bunt down the third-base line."[95] But Mays didn't need to bunt to be successful and led both leagues in batting average (.345) and slugging percentage (.667) in 1954. He also scored 119 runs, which was the first of twelve consecutive seasons with at least 101 runs scored. Mays led the NL with 13 triples in 1954, the first of three seasons he would do so and he drove in 110 runs. He would accumulate 103 or more RBIs during ten seasons. Leo Durocher insisted in his autobiography that nobody will ever play the game of baseball better than Willie Mays. He added, "And he had the other magic ingredient that turns a superstar into a super Superstar. Charisma. He lit the room up when he came in. He was a joy to be around."[96]

The sacrifice fly rule returned to the game in 1954, but this time sacrifice flies were counted as their own statistic apart from sacrifice hits or bunts. Only three teams compiled over 100 sacrifice hits in 1954: the Milwaukee Braves (110), Cleveland Indians (107), and the Cincinnati Reds (101). Roy McMillan, the Reds 24-year-old shortstop, batted only .250 during the season but contributed to the team effort with a major-league-leading 31 sacrifices. He batted .243 in a sixteen-year big league career with 41 stolen bases and 140 sacrifice bunts. Bobby Avila, the Indians second baseman, was from Mexico and became the first player from Latin America to win a batting title (.341) in 1954. This was a controversial title because Ted Williams batted .345, but at the time he needed 400 at-bats to be eligible for the crown and he fell fourteen short. The reason why he didn't have over 400 at-bats was because he walked 136 times. The rule would later be changed and the new criteria was based on the number of plate appearances, not at-bats. Avila's accomplishment was truly remarkable considering he played half the season with a broken thumb. The 5'10", 175-pounder was a very capable small ball player who ran the bases aggressively, who could execute the hit-and-run, and the various bunt plays. He won the AL sacrifice hit title in 1954 (19) and 1955 (18). During his eleven-year major league career he swiped 78 bags, including a career high of 17 in 1956 when he had an 81 percent basestealing average. His career stolen base average was less impressive at 60 percent. He was credited with 134 sacrifices.

Stolen bases remained extremely low in 1954 as the AL stole only 358 bags and the NL compiled 337. The third-place Chicago White Sox led the AL with 98 steals, while sixth-place St. Louis led the NL with only 63. The stolen base crowns were secured by Bill Bruton in the senior league (34) and Jackie Jensen of Boston in the junior circuit (22). Jensen stole 143 bases during his eleven-year career and had a 72.2 percent basestealing average. For the third consecutive season Jim Rivera finished second in the AL in steals. In 1954 he pilfered 18 bags, which was tied with Minnie Minoso.

There were two rookies who stole four bases in a game in 1954. Wally Moon of the St. Louis Cardinals batted .304 during the season with 106 runs scored and 18 stolen bases. He was the NL Rookie of the Year selection by both the BBWAA and *The Sporting News*. The six-foot, 175-pound, left-handed hitting but right-handed throwing fly chaser stole four bases on May 25 while the Cardinals were defeating the Cubs, 9–4. Spook Jacobs, the Philadelphia Athletics rookie second baseman, batted .258 during the season with seventeen steals in twenty attempts. He stole four bases on August 22 as the Athletics defeated the Senators, 3–2, in twelve innings in the lidlifter at Shibe Park. The second game was called after nine innings with a 4–4 tie because under Pennsylvania law an inning could not start after 6:40 P.M. on a Sunday. Philadelphia almost won the second game in the last of the ninth when Bill Wilson singled and was sacrificed to second. After a strikeout and a walk, Spec Shea, "The Naugatuck Nugget," unleashed a wild pitch and Wilson tried to score all the way from second, but was thrown out.

In 1954, Dee Fondy batted .285 for the Cubs as their first baseman with a career high twenty steals and an 80 percent basestealing average. On Opening Day against the Cardinals at Busch Stadium the Cubs emerged victorious, 13–4, as Fondy went 4 for 4 with two runs scored, one RBI, and two stolen bases. Brooklyn needed thirteen innings to defeat Pittsburgh on April 23 by a 6–5 score. Jackie Robinson stole three bags, including home in the sixth inning when he was on the front end of a triple steal. Gil Hodges and Sandy Amoros stole bases behind him. For Amoros it was his only steal of the season in five attempts. On May 25, the White Sox defeated the Indians, 4–2, as Sox catcher Sherm Lollar allowed his final stolen base of the campaign when Al Smith pilfered a bag. He threw out the next eighteen runners trying to steal. The American League won the All-Star Game, 11–9, on July 13 at Municipal Stadium. In the eighth inning with southpaw Dean Stone on the hill, Red Schoendienst unsuccessfully tried to steal home. National League coaches Leo Durocher and Charlie Grimm argued vigorously, insisting that Stone had balked as he rushed his delivery to the plate.

Pitcher Gene Conley of the Milwaukee Braves misplayed Sal Maglie's sacrifice bunt attempt in the top of the third inning on August 27. It took him too long to unleash the throw to second to try to catch Wes Westrum and the throw was high, which allowed the runner to slide in safely at the midway station. Whitey Lockman sacrificed the runners to second and third and they both scored in the inning on a groundout and a double. Conley threw a wild pitch in the sixth stanza when the Giants scored their final run. Durocher's team prevailed, 3–1, before a disappointed record breaking Milwaukee County Stadium crowd of 46,944. On that same day at Wrigley Field, the Cubs won, 4–3, in twelve innings over Philadelphia. Hal Jeffcoat scored the winning run on Gene Baker's squeeze bunt. With the Giants and Cubs tied at six at the Polo Grounds with two outs and the bases loaded on September 9, Hank Thompson laid down a squeeze bunt that scored Don Mueller with the winning run in the last of the ninth. Chicago prevailed in the nightcap, 3–0, as Ernie Banks stole a base for the Cubs, while Willie Mays and Monte Irvin pilfered a bag for the Giants. When the Giants secured the flag with a 7–1 triumph over Brooklyn on September 20, they had four sacrifices, including two by Sal Maglie.

The Brooklyn Dodgers won their first ten games of the 1955 campaign and never looked back, winning the pennant by thirteen and a half games over second-place Milwaukee (85–69). The Dodgers were 22–2 on May 10 and finished the season with a 98–55 record. Since the modern World Series began in 1903, they had participated seven times and seven times they went home in defeat. However, in 1955 they wrote a new ending, defeating the Yankees (96–58) in seven games. The Yankees won the opening game, 6–5, as Billy Martin was called out trying to steal home in the sixth inning and Jackie Robinson successfully stole home with Whitey Ford on the mound in the eighth inning. Phil Rizzuto stole two bases in the series, while Joe Collins also had one for the Yankees. They won the first two games of the autumn classic, despite having two caught stealing in each game. In the last of the sixth inning in game seven with the Dodgers leading, 2–0, Gil McDougald laid down a beautifully executed bunt and legged it out to put runners on first and second. Then Yogi Berra lifted a fly ball towards left field and Sandy Amoros made a sensational catch in front of the stands down the left field line. McDougald had already rounded the second base bag when the catch was made and was doubled up. Brooklyn won the game, 2–0, thanks in part to the shutout pitching by southpaw Johnny Podres and next year had finally arrived. Jim Gilliam and Jackie Robinson stole one base apiece in the series for Brooklyn. The Dodgers had six of the seven sacrifice bunts, including back-to-back sacrifices by their three and four hole hitters, Duke Snider and Roy Campanella, in the sixth inning of the seventh game. However, Snider reached first on an error during his sacrifice. Gil Hodges laid down a sacrifice bunt in the fifth game. This is not surprising, considering that Hodges collected 56 sacrifices during his career, including a career high of 11 in 1950 (tied 3rd, NL) when he launched 32 homers. Snider was also known to sacrifice, laying down 52 during his career.

The versatile Jim Gilliam batted .265 lifetime with 203 stolen bases and a 64.6 percent stolen base average. He stole a career high 26 bases in 1957 and twenty-one or more during four seasons. Additionally, he pilfered twelve or more bases during nine seasons. The five-foot-ten-and-a-half-inch, 175-pounder played several positions, but spent most of his career at second base. He secured the NL Rookie of the Year Award in 1953 with a .278 batting average, a .383 on-base percentage, 125 runs scored, and a major league leading 17 triples. He also stole 21 bases in 35 attempts. He scored at least 102 runs during his first four seasons. Gilliam was able to draw a fairly large number of walks, including a career high of 100 during his rookie season. He possessed the attributes of a good leadoff man: the ability to draw walks, put the ball in play, steal bases, and score runs. He also could bunt, laying down 98 sacrifices, including eleven or more during four seasons. Despite his .265 career batting average, he had a .360 on-base percentage.

In 1955 there were 377 stolen bases in the NL and 317 in the AL. Sacrifices declined in both leagues compared to 1954 as there were 624 in the AL and 563 in the NL. The Dodgers led the NL with 79 steals, while the third-place Chicago White Sox led the AL in both steals (69) and sacrifices (111). Manager Fred Haney's last-place Pittsburgh Pirates accumulated the most sacrifice bunts in the NL with 93. The Boston Red Sox, who finished in fourth place, stole 43 bags and led the majors with a 71.7 percent basestealing average. Bill Bruton collected one more steal than Willie Mays to secure the senior circuit stolen base crown with 25 thefts. After three consecutive second-place finishes, Jim Rivera led the AL with 25. Gene Baker of the Cubs and Bobby Avila of the Indians led the majors with 18 sacrifices. Avila and Billy Pierce laid down sacrifice bunts in the All-Star Game, won by the senior league, 6–5, in twelve innings.

On April 22, Walter Alston, the manager of the Brooklyn Dodgers, was ejected for arguing with the umpire after Don Zimmer was called out at home on Jackie Robinson's squeeze bunt. The Dodgers defeated Pittsburgh, 6–2, on May 26 as pitcher Don Newcombe hit a triple in the ninth inning and then stole home. Newcombe was a good hitting pitcher, batting .271 lifetime with fifteen homers. Earl Torgeson, the Detroit Tigers first baseman, had a game-ending steal of home in the tenth inning on July 17 with right hander Bob Turley on the mound for the Yankees. Casey Stengel's Yankees defeated the Red Sox, 4–1, on September 17. Phil Rizzuto and Bob Cerv executed a double steal in the first inning.

Luis Aparicio Sr. was one of the greatest shortstops in Venezuela and his son became a Hall of Fame shortstop in the majors. In 1956, Aparicio replaced fellow Venezuelan Chico Carrasquel as the shortstop of the Chicago White Sox. He won the AL Rookie of the Year Award that season at the age of 22 and began one of the greatest small ball careers in big league history. The 5'9", 160-pound, right-handed player stole 21 bases in 25 attempts during his rookie season. During his first nine seasons from 1956 to 1964, he led the junior league in steals with 21, 28, 29, 56, 51, 53, 31, 40, and 57. He stole 21 or more bases during twelve seasons. His final total stood at 506 and he had an impressive 78.8 percent basestealing average. Peter C. Bjarkman wrote in his terrific book *Baseball with a Latin Beat* that "unlike Cobb, Brock, or Henderson, Aparicio was a magician on the base paths in an era altogether undistinguished for base-running wizardry." Aparicio was playing his career towards the end of the dark age of small ball when teams rarely manufactured runs with aggressive baserunning and instead waited for the long ball. Bjarkman added that unlike Maury Wills, Lou Brock, and Rickey Henderson, who pilfered bags in an era when stolen bases were plentiful, Aparicio "ran not only against enemy pitchers and catchers but also smack against the grain of the game itself."[97] When he was at first base he would watch the pitcher's eyes to determine whether he was going to steal. He got a huge lead on the bases and a great jump when he took off. Aparicio was a good contact hitter, putting the ball in play and utilizing his speed but he had one deficiency. He didn't walk a lot and had only a .311 career on-base percentage. Aparicio was also a good bunter, sharing the AL sacrifice hit title in 1956 with George Kell and winning it outright in 1960. He is credited with an impressive 161 sacrifices. Defensively, Aparicio was brilliant and led American League shortstops in fielding percentage from 1959 to 1966. He played for the Chicago White Sox from 1956 to 1962 and again from 1968 to 1970. He was in Baltimore from 1963 to 1967 and he ended his career with the Boston Red Sox from 1971 to 1973.

Aparicio's double play partner with the White Sox, Nellie Fox, helped form a potent small ball duo. Fox was a hard-working second baseman, who overachieved because of his drive for success, and also had a Hall of Fame career. He batted .288 lifetime with 76 steals. Fox was a phenomenal contact hitter, who struck out only 216 times during his nineteen-year career, and used an old style bottle bat with a large handle. He would drive pitchers crazy by fouling off pitches. And when Aparicio stole a bag with no outs, he would hit behind the runner to move him along with a productive out if he didn't get a hit. These productive outs contributed to the team effort, but hurt his batting average. He was the perfect two hole hitter behind Aparicio and his great ability to make contact made him a terrific hit-and-run man. If Fox was in the hole it didn't bother him and he was a good two strike hitter, which allowed Aparicio to see more pitches and gauge the pitcher's delivery as he prepared to steal a bag. He laid down a whopping 208 sacrifices during his career, which ranks 79th all-time. He had twenty sacrifices in both 1951 and 1964 and ten or more during fourteen seasons. With the 1961 Chicago White Sox, he tied for the AL lead with 15 sacrifices and won the NL title outright with the 1964 Houston Colt .45s when he accumulated 20. Fox, who was a left-handed batter, liked to utilize the drag bunt to leg out a hit. At the bat he was known for being an excellent clutch hitter and in the field he was a very good defensive second baseman, who led the American League in fielding percentage six times. He had an abundance of energy and was always in motion. Nellie was beloved by the Sox fans and he was the team leader because of his willingness to give advice, his great work ethic, his willingness to sacrifice his body and to help the team even if it hurt his statistics. Al Lopez said, "Fox hustled his way to stardom."[98] Tom Withers of the Associated Press wrote on the day of his election to the Hall of Fame in 1997, "Pitchers couldn't strike out Fox, and neither could the Hall of Fame."[99] Fox and Aparicio helped the "Go-Go" Sox win the 1959 pennant despite finishing last in the majors in homers.

However, in 1956 the White Sox were a third-place outfit, finishing with an 85–69 record. The Dodgers (93–61) met the Yankees (97–57) for the second consecutive season in the World Series and again it took seven games to crown the champion. This time it was New York who prevailed as Hank Bauer and Mickey Mantle stole bases for the world champions, while Jim Gilliam swiped the only bag for Brooklyn. During the regular season the

White Sox led the majors with 70 steals, which was three more than the sixth-place New York Giants who paced the National League. The Sox also led the AL in sacrifices with 86, but this was far behind the second-place Milwaukee Braves who paced the NL with an exorbitant 142 sacrifices. Willie Mays won his first stolen base crown with 40 bags, while Aparicio won in the AL (21). Jim Rivera again finished second as he pilfered 20 hassocks. Johnny Logan, the Milwaukee Braves shortstop, batted .281 and led the NL with 31 sacrifices, which were more than twice as many as the AL leader. Logan stole only 19 bases during his thirteen-year career, but laid down 125 sacrifice bunts. In the junior circuit, Aparicio and George Kell shared the title with 14 sacrifices. Kell had 149 sacrifices during his career and also shared the title in 1946. During the two seasons in which Kell was tied for the AL sacrifice hit title, he played for two teams during each season.

Luis Aparicio was taught the game by his father, a terrific shortstop in Venezuela, and he passed down the knowledge to his son. He was a brilliant defensive shortstop and outstanding small ball player, who led the AL in stolen bases during his first nine seasons from 1956 to 1964, and he won the AL sacrifice hit title in 1956 and 1960. Luis batted .262 lifetime with 161 sacrifices and 506 steals with an impressive 78.8 percent basestealing average. Because of his glove and terrific small ball abilities, he was inducted into the Hall of Fame in 1984 and is rightfully recognized as one of the greatest shortstops in major league history. He is shown here with his son Nelson. (George Brace photograph).

After batting .319 with a major league leading 51 homers in 1955, Willie Mays's numbers declined sharply in 1956 to .296 and 36 long balls. He drove in only 84 runs, which was a decline of 43 compared to the previous year, but he pilfered 16 more bases. Mays stole 59.7 percent of the Giants bases during the season. He became the first National League player to hit thirty homers and steal thirty bases in 1956. Ken Williams of the 1922 St. Louis Browns was the first 30–30 man, when he led the AL with 39 homers and finished second with 37 steals. Perhaps Mays's declining numbers in 1956 had to do with the managerial change as Bill Rigney replaced Leo Durocher. Arnold Hano wrote, "Manager Rigney did not have the natural ebullience of Durocher; he was a silent man, tortured by what was happening, his gray hair turning white — a wrinkled cadaver of a man who was not yet forty years old but sometimes looked nearer sixty."[100] New York started the season in a promising manner on April 17 with a 4–3 triumph over Pittsburgh. Mays showed his terrific speed in the eighth inning when he scored from second on a groundout to the second baseman. He stole four bases on May 6 when the Giants defeated the Cardinals, 5–4.

The Cincinnati Reds defeated the Brooklyn Dodgers on July 19 at Crosley Field by a 7–2 score before 20,958 fans. Wally Post and Rocky Bridges stole bases for manager Birdie Tebbetts's Reds, while Sandy Amoros swiped a bag for Brooklyn. Amoros walked in the fourth inning, stole second, went to third on a wild pitch and scored on Chico Fernandez's single. Also, on July 19, Bill Rigney returned a $25 fine to Willie Mays, which was levied when he didn't run out a pop fly in the July 13 game against St. Louis. Mays was the final out in the contest. Rigney said he was returning the money because Mays was hustling in recent games. The 1956 All-Star Game was won by the National League, 7–3, at Griffith Stadium on July 10. Johnny Temple, the senior league's leadoff man, stole a base and pitcher Bob Friend had a sacrifice bunt. Temple was a 5'11", 175-pound, right-handed second baseman, who batted .284 lifetime with 140 steals and a 74.5 percent basestealing average. The Dodgers won two games from the Giants on September 1 at the Polo Grounds by 5–3 and 5–0 scores. Jackie Robinson stole second and third in the ninth inning of the nightcap and had five thefts in the series. On September 11 against Milwaukee at Ebbets Field, Jackie Robinson was dancing off second base when Ernie Johnson tried to pick him off and threw the ball into center field. Robinson scored all the way from second on the play.

To the disappointment of many fans, teams were being uprooted and moved to different cities in the 1950s. First there was the Boston Braves moving to Milwaukee in 1953. St. Louis's American League franchise moved to Baltimore in 1954 when Bill Veeck was forced to sell the club. Arnold Johnson purchased the Philadelphia Athletics and moved them to Kansas City in 1955. For more than a half century if an eastern team went on a western swing it meant traveling to Cincinnati, Chicago, Cleveland, Detroit or St. Louis. Pittsburgh was even characterized as being a western city. But in 1957, much to the consternation of the fans of the Brooklyn Dodgers and New York Giants, the ballclub owners decided to move to Los Angeles and San Francisco, respectively, for the 1958 season. After the Giants were the first team to announce that they were officially moving, Roger Angell expressed the following sentiment in *Holiday* magazine, "The end of the World came on Monday, August 19, 1957…. It was a funny way for the world to end: no trumpets, no clap of thunder, no fireball — just a brief announcement of the vote by a plump, pin-striped businessman named Horace C. Stoneham."[101]

Many things were different for the Brooklyn Dodgers in 1957, including the absence of Jackie Robinson who retired after the 1956 season. Stolen bases increased modestly in each league as there were 399 in the NL and 368 in the AL. The sixth-place Giants led the NL with a measly 64 steals, which was four more than third-place Brooklyn. Willie Mays led the majors with 38 steals and Jim Gilliam finished second in the circuit with 26. They were followed by Don Blasingame of St. Louis (21), Johnny Temple of Cincinnati (19), and Chico Fernandez of Philadelphia (18). It had been eleven years since Jackie Robinson broke the color line, but yet it shamefully took the Phillies until April 16, 1957, to allow an outwardly dark-skinned man to wear their uniform and officially integrate the team. John Kennedy was expected to play a major role in integrating their club, but this former Kansas City Monarch and the last player to jump to the majors from the Negro leagues injured his shoulder after his second big league at-bat and never played again. Fernandez, an excellent defensive shortstop, who stole 68 bases during his eight-year career, earned an every-day position in the lineup and broke the Phillies color line. According to historian Peter C. Bjarkman, Kennedy was wrongfully acknowledged as being the first black Phillie by many people, despite the fact that Fernandez was in the lineup for the opening game.[102] Disgracefully, the Detroit Tigers and Boston Red Sox remained as the final two teams not to have had a black man wear their uniform. Jackie Robinson had broken the color line, but the pace of integration was painfully slow.

Luis Aparicio (28), Jim Rivera (18), and Minnie Minoso (18), who each played for the White Sox, finished at the top of the AL in thefts. Mickey Mantle finished the season with a .365 batting average, a .512 on-base percentage, a .665 slugging percentage and was ranked fourth in the AL with 16 steals (84.2 percent stolen base average). The second-place White Sox led the AL with 109 steals, while the last-place Washington Senators stole an all-time low thirteen bases.

Sacrifice hits declined by 142 in the NL and increased by four in the AL. The Pittsburgh Pirates were tied with the Chicago Cubs as the worst team in the senior circuit with a 62–92 record and they led the league with 97 sacrifices. The Giants laid down only 32 sacrifice bunts, which was the lowest total in major league history until the 1973 New York Yankees had only 27. But the 1973 Yankees played in a league with the designated hitter. They were a fourth-place outfit in the AL East and eschewed both the sacrifice bunt and the stolen base (47). The fifth-place Baltimore Orioles led the majors with 110 sacrifices in 1957. In addition to stealing a sizeable number of bases, Johnny Temple also laid down 122 sacrifices during his career, including ten or more during eight seasons. He led the senior league with 16 in 1957 and tied for the lead in 1958 with Jim Davenport (17). Gil McDougald collected the most sacrifices in the majors during 1957 with 19.

For the third season in a row the New York Yankees (98–56) participated in the World Series and needed seven games to decide the winner. However, they lost for the second time in three years as Milwaukee (95–59) prevailed and secured the world championship. Wes Covington stole the only base for the Braves, while Gil McDougald had one for New York. Milwaukee had one runner caught stealing, while the Yankees had four, as they stole bags at an abysmal 20 percent clip. Manager Fred Haney's Braves laid down six of the nine sacrifices in the fall classic, and one of them was by slugger Eddie Mathews.

Despite the fact that stolen bases were still at historically low levels in 1957, the *New York Times* found reason to be optimistic with the headline "Stolen Base Is Returned to Baseball by Willie the Wonder" on May 24. John Drebinger began his article by discussing how the art of basestealing had declined after the Deadball Era. Before the introduction of the lively ball in 1920, even players with average speed knew how to slide several different ways. But the modern-day player doesn't know the proper technique and many of them risks injury when they do slide. Drebinger insisted that "Willie almost single-handedly has added luster and liveliness to a second-division ball club, something his home run hitting alone could never accomplish." When Mays advanced to first base, the pitcher became tense, and "the crowd vibrates with anticipation." In a recent interview, Ty Cobb saw signs that the stolen base was returning to the game and the primary reason for this return was Willie Mays. Drebinger more than implied that Mays was a better basestealer than Cobb because he had a better basestealing average. Of course, there are no caught stealing statistics available for half of Cobb's career so an exact comparison could not be made. Drebinger makes the dubious claim that Cobb's basestealing average in 1915, when he stole 96 bags and was caught stealing 38 times for a 71.6 percent basestealing average, would not be tolerated by the modern-day manager who plays for the "big inning." The Chicago White Sox led the major leagues with a 68 percent basestealing average in 1956 and the Philadelphia Phillies led both leagues with a 68.7 percent basestealing average in 1957. The major league average in 1956 and 1957 were only 59.2 percent and 57.9 percent, respectively. So it is not Cobb's basestealing average that would have prevented him from stealing a large number of bases, but he would be hindered only because some big league managers object to aggressive baserunning.

Mays was such a great baserunner not only because of his thievery, but because he took a plethora of extra bases. He would stretch singles into doubles, doubles into triples, and triples into home runs. Mays would go from first to third or second to home with the best of them and tag up and advance a base on shallow fly balls. He would sometimes advance two bases on a groundout to the infield. Regrettably, there is no statistic that measures the number of extra bases that a player takes and if there were it would provide us with a better understanding of a great baserunner's value to the team. Mays won games single-handedly with his speed. Like the time he defeated the Phillies with Robin Roberts on the hill. He legged out an infield hit by sliding head first into the gateway station in the ninth inning and then took second as the shortstop's throw got away from the first baseman by only a few feet. He promptly stole third and scored on a "short pop-fly single" behind first base. In May of 1957, he almost won a game by collecting a single and then advancing to third on a routine groundout to the first baseman. He scored when he teamed up with Ray Katt on a double steal: the catcher threw to second trying to get Katt and Mays scored the tying run from third. In his next plate appearance, Mays gave the Giants the lead with a homer, but two errors in the ninth allowed the opponent to win. Willie was a strong advocate of stealing third base because many players got "mighty careless" with a runner on second. It was Drebinger's contention that despite the fact the Giants were a second division outfit, they were an exciting team to watch because of Mays, regardless of whether they won or lost.[103]

There were a number of brawls in 1957. The Milwaukee Braves defeated the Brooklyn Dodgers by an 8 to 5 score on June 13 as there was "a wild brawl and equally wild ball game," before 14,778 spectators at Ebbets Field, including about 6,000 knothole kids. Johnny Logan, Milwaukee's two-hole hitter behind Bill Bruton, went 1 for 1 with a stolen base. Don Drysdale tried to pick him off first in the opening inning and hit him with the throw, allowing Logan to advance to second. The Braves were up 4–0 with two outs in the next inning when Drysdale drilled him in the back with his first pitch. Naturally, Logan took exception to this action and words were exchanged as he went to first base. And then Drysdale invited him to come to the mound to settle the issue and Logan accepted the invitation. Drysdale landed with a right hook but the on-deck hitter, Eddie Mathews, jumped on Drysdale and pummeled him with both fists. A bench-clearing brawl ensued.[104] The Dodgers defeated the Cardinals, 2–1, in ten innings on the following day. Lindy McDaniel was on the bump when Jim Gilliam stole home with the winning run in the tenth inning. Rip Repulski of the Phillies helped spark a three-run rally in game two versus Brooklyn on July 7 with a "scratch single" and a stolen base. Philadelphia won twice, 2–1 and 5–3. Chuck Harmon, a former Negro league player, stole one of his twenty-five career bases in the opener for the Phillies.[105]

The Dodgers were involved in another brawl on July 11 versus Cincinnati at Ebbets Field. Charlie Neal's vicious blow against Don Hoak, the former Dodger and current Cincinnati third baseman, was the highlight of the brawl. The pugilistic engagement happened in the seventh inning when Reds reliever, Raul Sanchez, delivered a "duster" at Jim Gilliam with the visitors winning 4–3. Gilliam had to hit the dirt to avoid being nailed. Then with the count 2 and 0, Gilliam employed an innovative trick that was used during the 1950s to retaliate against beanball pitchers. He bunted down the first base line hoping that Sanchez would field the ball or cover first and he could physically confront the pitcher. However, Gilliam popped it up in foul territory and there was no chance to make the play. But Sanchez had moved towards the ball and met Gilliam halfway down the line when they "both hit the ground with fists flying." Hoak was stunned by Neal's vicious punch in the bench-clearing brawl that followed. He was knocked to the ground but he didn't stay down and got back on his feet seeking retaliation. Gil Hodges, the Dodgers first baseman, got a hold of Hoak and made sure there would be no retribution. Hoak, Neal, Gilliam, and Sanchez, were all thrown out of the game. Sid Gray of the *New York Herald Tribune* wrote, "In getting rid of Sanchez by foul means—foul bunt means, that is—the Dodgers apparently retained enough fight to win the ball game." Brooklyn won the game, 5–4, as Hodges connected for two homers that were both two-run shots.[106] Hoak batted .293 during the season with a .381 on-base percentage and led both leagues with 39 doubles. He stole eight bases, but had an extremely poor 34.8 percent basestealing average.

Also on July 11, the Phillies defeated the Cubs in two games at Connie Mack Stadium by 1–0 and 3–1 scores. Chico Fernandez stole three bags in the opener and Harvey Haddix and Willie Jones had sacrifices for the Phillies. For part of the season, manager Al Lopez of the White Sox used three terrific small ball practitioners at the top of his lineup: Luis Aparicio leading off, Nellie Fox batting second, and Minnie Minoso batting third. On August 8, Minoso batted cleanup in a 7–4 win over Kansas City. Aparicio stole two bags in this game, while three-hole hitter, Earl Torgeson, had one.

The Yankees (92–62) won their fourth consecutive pennant in 1958 and for the fourth straight season they went the distance in the World Series. They got their revenge over Milwaukee (92–62), who beat them the year before, and they became the first team since 1925 to rally from a three games to one deficit to become world champions. There were six sacrifice bunts in the autumn classic, four by Milwaukee and two by New York, and only one of them was by a pitcher. Elston Howard stole a bag for the Yankees, while Eddie Mathews swiped one for Fred Haney's Braves. Stolen bases declined slightly in each league in 1958 as the second-place Chicago White Sox led the majors with 101 steals and had an impressive 75.4 percent basestealing average, which was only surpassed by the Milwaukee Braves, who swiped only 26 bags (76.5 percent). The Los Angeles Dodgers finished the season in seventh place and led the circuit with 73 steals. Milwaukee led both leagues with only 79 sacrifices, while fifth-place Detroit paced the AL with 75. Willie Mays led the NL with 31 steals, which surpassed Richie Ashburn's total by one theft. When Mays swiped his thirtieth bag in a 5–1 win over St. Louis on September 20, he became the first National League player to swipe thirty or more bases in three consecutive seasons since Kiki Cuyler in 1930. For the second consecutive season three members of the Chicago White Sox finished first, second, and third in steals and were followed by Mickey Mantle: Aparicio (29), Jim Rivera (21), Jim Landis (19), and Mantle (18). Rivera finished second in the AL in steals during six of the last seven seasons and the only season he didn't finished second was in 1955 when he led the league. Johnny Temple and Jim Davenport accumulated the most sacrifices in the NL with 17, while Billy Martin led the AL with 13.

Billy Martin, the Tigers 30-year-old infielder, was on the front end of a triple steal with Red Wilson and Frank Bolling in the second inning versus Kansas City on June 30.

None of these players were known for their basestealing ability. Wilson, however, was perfect in 1958, stealing ten bases in ten attempts. Detroit prevailed in the contest, 7–6. Another player who was not known for his basestealing ability was Vic Power, who stole 45 bags during his career, including three in 1958: one with Kansas City and two with Cleveland. Power played several positions during his career, but he was predominantly a first baseman with excellent defensive skills. He was an individualistic, flashy, unconventional, misunderstood player, who didn't quite fit in with the homogenous, conservative, and bigoted 1950s. The bigots were angered that he dated white women and drove flashy automobiles. And then they didn't like his one-handed fielding style and the way he held his bat in the batter's box. Power was interviewed by Danny Peary for his outstanding book *We Played the Game: 65 Players Remember Baseball's Greatest Era, 1947–1964*. One of the subjects he discusses is the game in which he stole home twice versus Detroit in the eighth and tenth innings on August 14, 1958. In 1958 there was still a large number of racists throwing beanballs at black and brown players and trying to injure them with spike high slides. Victor Pellot from Puerto Rico was one of their biggest targets. Vic Pellot became known as Vic Power when baseball men and writers mispronounced his last name while playing in Canada in 1949. Power says that he stole home against the Tigers two times on August 14 because their pitchers were always throwing at him and this was his way of retaliating. Power stole both bases easily and said that if either play was close, he would have been out. "Black players didn't get many close calls. I know I didn't," said Power. His second steal of home in the contest was a game winner in the last of the tenth with two outs and Frank Lary on the mound to give the Indians a 10–9 win. He became the first AL player since 1927 with two steals of home in a game. He insisted that he was a good basestealer, saying, "I could have stolen more bases if that was the style then."[107]

St. Louis defeated Los Angeles, 4–2, in the first game of a twin bill on July 3 at the Memorial Coliseum. Both teams combined for seven steals, including two by Ken Boyer, the Cardinals third baseman. Willie Mays manufactured a run in the 1958 All-Star Game at Memorial Stadium on July 8, which was won by the American League, 4–3. He stole second in the second inning and advanced to third on Gus Triandos's errant throw. He scored on Bob Skinner's single. Billy O'Dell, a southpaw pitcher with the Baltimore Orioles, laid down the only sacrifice bunt in the game for the AL.

The Chicago White Sox of 1959 were not lacking in offensive productivity and power in a way that compared to the hitless wonders of 1906. While the "Go-Go" Sox's small ball activity is somewhat overstated, the 1959 aggregation did win the pennant with great pitching, excellent defense, and the ability to manufacture runs. They led the majors with a 3.29 ERA and paced the AL with a .979 fielding average. Manager Al Lopez's Sox were the only major league team not to hit over 100 homers (97). Their .250 batting average ranked sixth in the league, their .327 on-base percentage was third, and their .364 slugging percentage was seventh. Chicago's small ball statistics were good but not great, as they led the majors with 113 steals and finished second in the junior league with 84 sacrifices. They had a plethora of good contact hitters on their club and accumulated the fewest strikeouts in the majors with 634. Bill Veeck, the owner of the team, said in September, "We connive, scrounge and hustle to get just one measly run. We can't afford to give any away, so we don't."[108] The 1959 White Sox showed baseball men that they could win with pitching, defense, and small ball. This was a team that thrived in the clutch, winning 35 of 50 one-run games. Additionally, they had excellent records against second-place Cleveland (15–7) and third-place New York (13–9). Their 94–60 record was the best in the game.

The Los Angeles Dodgers won the NL pennant with an 88–68 mark. Walter Alston's club led the NL in both stolen bases (84) and sacrifices (100). After four consecutive pennants the Yankees found themselves situated in the basement of the American League in late May. And according to historian David Quentin Voigt, "In a desperate move to rally his forces, Stengel shifted to a conservative 'hit, bunt, and run' style."[109] If the Yankees were playing small ball they probably weren't doing it that successfully or they were relying heavily on the hit-and-run. The third-place Yankees finished the season with a measly 45 steals, which was actually good enough for fourth best in the circuit, while they did compile a more respectable 76 sacrifices (3rd, AL). Only a few people believed that the Dodgers would compete for the pennant coming off a seventh-place finish in 1958. And they were similar to the White Sox with good pitching, excellent fielding, and the ability to manufacture runs, although they had more power. They won the World Series in six games and stole five bases in the process, including two by Jim Gilliam. Luis Aparicio and Jim Landis pilfered bags for the losers. Johnny Roseboro, the Dodgers catcher, had two of the team's four sacrifices, while Sox pitcher Bob Shaw had two of the three sacrifice bunts for Chicago. The Dodgers prevailed in the third game by a 3–1 score as the Pale Hose hurt themselves with three caught stealing and three double plays.

Both sacrifice bunts and stolen bases rose in each league in 1959. Luis Aparicio secured his fourth consecutive AL stolen base crown as he led the majors with 56 bags. Mickey Mantle finished second with 21 steals. Willie Mays batted .313 with a .381 on-base percentage and a .583 slugging percentage. He compiled an impressive 125 runs scored and 104 RBIs. He also won his fourth consecutive stolen base title with 27 sacks. Tony Taylor of Chicago, Jim Gilliam of Los Angeles, and Orlando Cepeda of San Francisco, finished tied for second with 23 thefts. Taylor played in the big leagues for nineteen seasons from 1958 to 1976 with the Cubs, Phillies, and Tigers. He played second base during most of his career and batted .261 lifetime with a .321 on-base percentage, 1,005 runs scored, 2,007 hits, and 234 steals with a 67.8 percent stolen base average. He stole at least twenty bases during six seasons, but never won a stolen base title. Cepeda swiped 142 bases during his Hall of Fame career and his 23 steals in 1959 was a career high. Charlie Neal of Los Angeles batted .287 during the season with 103 runs scored and tied for the major league lead with eleven triples. He stole a career high 17 bases and led the majors with 21 sacrifices. Tony Kubek, Jim Landis, and Al Pilarcik were tied in the AL with 13.

In 1959, 26-year-old Maurice Morning Wills, who was known as Maury, proved that persistence pays off as he got the call to the big show on June 6 after more than eight years in the bushes. He was cocky and loquacious, playing shortstop and possessing excellent speed, but was not yet known for being a prolific basestealer. He batted .260 during his rookie campaign with only seven extra-base hits (five doubles, two triples) and stole seven bases in ten attempts. He led the NL in steals during the next six seasons with 50, 35, 104, 40, 53, and 94. Wills did not just steal bases, but did so efficiently with stolen base percentages of 80.6, 70, 88.9, 67.8, 75.7, and 75.2, respectively, during his reign as the National League's top thief. He helped change the way the game of baseball was played with his 104 steals in 1962 with an outstanding 88.9 percent basestealing average. Wills was well deserving of his MVP award that season with a .299 batting average, 130 runs scored, 208 hits, 10 triples, which was tied for the NL lead, and his remarkable 104 steals. Just like Babe Ruth changed the game with his home run hitting at the end of the Deadball Era, Wills had a similar affect with the stolen base, showing baseball men that they didn't have to sit back waiting patiently for the home run to produce runs, but they could manufacture runs with their speed. However, it would take a while for major league teams to adopt this strategy because after Wills's terrific accomplishment in 1962, stolen bases did not increase in the NL for the rest of the decade, but the AL did see a significant increase during the middle of the decade that accelerated towards the end of the 1960s. By the mid–1970s stolen bases were once again fashionable and major league teams were accumulating a large number of steals. Wills became the first player in the twentieth century to steal over 100 bags in a season, an accomplishment that wasn't even achieved during the Deadball Era. This was a revolutionary achievement. Consider, for example, that during the 1950s, from 1950 to 1959 there were only two major league teams to steal over 104 bags: the 1957 Chicago White Sox (109) and the 1959 White Sox (113).

Wills wasn't the fastest basestealer in the game, but he was probably the smartest. He knew precisely when to run and would alter his slide depending on the situation. He would often slide very hard and at the last possible moment. On close plays he often tried to kick the ball out of the fielder's glove. Sometimes he surmised that it would be best to try to avoid the tag and he slid to the outside and grabbed the corner of the bag with his hand. Ed Roebuck said, "Wills was a good shortstop and terrific leadoff hitter and definitely the igniter for our offense. He changed the game of baseball, and I think that made him deserving of the Hall of Fame." In the minor leagues, Wills became a switch-hitter so he could utilize his speed out of the left-hand side of the batter's box against right-handers. Roebuck said, "His steals were very important to our success. But I'd have to say his running was a bit of a distraction." By distraction he meant that the two-hole hitter, Jim Gilliam, was often hitting behind in the count because he took pitches and his concentration was broken when the pitcher constantly threw over to first base or quick-pitched him.[110] Not all hitters could bat behind a great basestealer and are comfortable hitting behind in the count. But there are plenty of hitters capable of handling this responsibility. Furthermore, a fast runner like Wills will give the hitter the advantage of seeing more fastballs.

What about Maury Wills as a Hall of Famer? He finished his career with a .281 batting average, a low .330 on-base percentage, 1,067 runs scored, 2,134 hits, and 586 steals with a 73.8 percent basestealing average. Wills helped transform the game with his 1962 season and for that alone he should merit consideration. But in an age where small ball players are misunderstood and constantly being denigrated, it is unlikely that Wills will ever be enshrined in the hallowed hall. He only collected 268 extra-base hits: 177 doubles, 71 triples, and 20 homers. However, he stole 586 bags, which means that 586 times he essentially turned a walk into a double or triple, a single into a double, a single into a triple, a double into a triple, stole home or stole a bag after a fielder's choice. This doesn't even take into account the number of extra bases he took or the psychological affect he had on the defense. How many times did Wills take two bases on a stolen base because the catcher threw the ball into center field or left field or it wasn't handled properly by the infielder? How many times did the infielders rush their throw to first when Wills hit a slow grounder and threw it away? Or the outfielders rushed their throw into the infield and it was off target, allowing Wills to take an extra base. How many times did he help manufacture a run when the rest of his team was slumping and ignited the offense? Wills was a complete small ball player, who also laid down 119 sacrifices, including ten or more during seven seasons.

There were two All-Star Games in 1959. The first one was won by the National League, 5–4, at Forbes Field on July 7. Dick Groat had a sacrifice bunt for the winning team. On August 3 at the Memorial Coliseum, the AL won 5–3 as Aparicio stole a bag.

Bill Mazeroski's homer in the last of the ninth in game seven of the 1960 World Series gave the Pittsburgh Pirates their first world championship since 1925. Danny Murtaugh's Pirates (95–59) won the world championship over Casey Stengel's Yankees (97–57) despite the fact that their pitchers compiled a 7.11 ERA in the series versus New York's 3.54. Bob Skinner and Bill Virdon of Pittsburgh stole the only bases of the series. The Pirates collected three of the five sacrifice bunts, including one by Skinner in the five-run eighth inning in game seven. During the regular season, stolen bases increased for the second consecutive season in each league, a total of 501 in the NL and 422 in the AL. The last time that either league stole over 500 bags was in 1945 when the senior circuit teams compiled 527 steals. Maury Wills won the NL stolen base crown with 50 thefts, while Vada Pinson of Cincinnati finished second with 32.

Pinson was a laid back, relaxed, quiet, and pleasant personality, who played in the big leagues from 1958 to 1975 with the Cincinnati Reds (1958–1968), St. Louis Cardinals (1969), Cleveland Indians (1970–1971), California Angels (1972–1973), and Kansas City Royals (1974–1975). The 5'11", 181-pound, left-handed fly chaser possessed both power and speed. As a youngster he was timed at 3.3 seconds running from home plate to first base. Pinson utilized his blazing speed on the bases, swiping 305 bags during his career with a 71.4 percent basestealing average. He stole 21 or more during nine seasons, but never won a stolen base title. Pinson was known as a terrific drag bunter, but was often criticized for not bunting enough and trying to hit home runs. From 1959 to 1962 he scored at least 101 runs, including 131 in 1959 when he led the majors. He led the senior league in hits, doubles, and triples during two seasons each. During seven seasons he hit twenty or more homers and during five seasons he hit at least twenty homers and stole twenty or more bags. His lifetime batting average stands at .286 with a .327 on-base percentage and a .442 slugging percentage. Pinson accumulated only 52 sacrifice bunts during his career. Jim O'Toole, who was Pinson's teammate with the Reds, said he was a "great, great ballplayer," and some people were insisting that he would have a Hall of Fame career. However, Pinson was "too laidback," and lacked the intensity and "heart" to become one of the best players in the game.[111] Despite the fact that he didn't meet the expectations of some people, Pinson had a terrific career, one that is worthy of Hall of Fame consideration. He finished with 2,757 hits and if he would have gotten 243 more hits to get him to 3,000 he probably would have been inducted into the hallowed hall.

Luis Aparicio won his fifth consecutive stolen base crown in the AL with 51 bags and was followed by his teammate Jim Landis (23). The third-place Chicago White Sox led the majors with 122 steals and a 71.8 percent basestealing average. They also finished second in the league in sacrifice bunts (95) behind fourth-place Cleveland who compiled 97. The fourth-place Los Angeles Dodgers paced the NL with 95 steals and 102 sacrifices. Julian Javier of St. Louis led the NL with 15 sacrifices, while Aparicio took the crown in the AL with 20.

On June 4, the Tigers prevailed over the Indians, 7–4. Chico Fernandez scored Detroit's final run in the tenth inning when he tripled and stole home. The National League won both All-Star Games in 1960. In the first contest on July 11 in scorching 101-degree heat in Kansas City, Bob Skinner stole a base, while Willie Mays stole one bag and was caught once in the second game on July 13. National League pitcher Bill Henry was credited with the only sacrifice bunt in either game during the second contest at Yankee Stadium. Willie Mays had a terrific game in a 5–3 win over Cincinnati on June 24 as he hit two homers, had three RBIs, three runs scored, and stole home. Ted Williams stole only 24 bags during his Hall of Fame career. He batted .316 with a .451 on-base percentage and a .645 slugging percentage during his final season in 1960. When he stole his final base of his career on July 22 in a 6–4 win over Cleveland, he became the first major leaguer to steal a base during four consecutive decades. Rickey Henderson would also accomplish this feat in 2000. And Tim Raines pulled it off in 2001.

The American League expanded to ten teams in 1961 with new franchises in Los Angeles and Washington, after the original Washington franchise had moved to Minnesota. They also adopted a 162-game schedule. The National League would lengthen its schedule to 162 games in 1962 and expand to ten teams as well with new franchises in New York and Houston. The New York Yankees slugged their way to their second consecutive pennant in 1961, finishing with a 109–53 record, which was eight games ahead of second-place Detroit (101–61). Roger Maris broke Babe Ruth's sacrosanct home run record by slugging 61, while Mickey Mantle finished second in the majors with 54 homers. Ralph Houk replaced Casey Stengel as the Yankees manager in 1961 and brought stability to the ballclub. Stengel was incessantly juggling his lineup through the years and platooning players, while Houk believed in having a set lineup, which was appreciated by the Yankee players. Fred Hutchinson's Cincinnati Reds won the NL flag with a 93–61 mark as the strength of their offense was an outfield consisting of Frank Robinson, Vada Pinson, and Wally Post. Robinson batted .323 with a .404 on-base percentage and led the NL in slugging percentage (.611), while stealing 22 bases with an 88 percent stolen base average. He also scored 117 runs and compiled 124 RBIs. He stole 204 bases during his Hall of Fame career and had a 72.6 percent basestealing average. Pinson batted a career high .343 during the campaign and stole 23 bases in 33 attempts. Post batted .294 with 20 homers in 282 at-bats, but did not steal a base. Despite this talented group of fly chasers the Reds were overmatched in the World Series and lost to New York in five games. Bobby Richardson of the Yankees stole the only base of the series. It wasn't surprising that there were only three sacrifice bunts in the fall classic, considering that both Cincinnati (50) and New York (57) finished last in their respective leagues in sacrifices. The Yankees laid down all three sacrifices in the fifth game, by Ralph Terry, Hector Lopez, and Bud Daley.

The fourth-place Chicago White Sox led the majors with 100 steals, while second-place Los Angeles paced the NL with 86. The two last-place teams led their leagues in sacrifices: the Philadelphia Phillies accumulated 108 sacrifice bunts, while the Kansas City Athletics, had 89 sacrifices. Maury Wills led the NL with 35 steals, while Luis Aparicio led both leagues with 53. Dick Howser, Kansas City's 25-year-old rookie shortstop, batted .280 with a .377 on-base percentage, 108 runs scored, and stole 37 bases to finish second in that category. Maury Wills led the NL with 13 sacrifices, while American Leaguers Nellie Fox and Danny O'Connell led both leagues with 15.

Frank Robinson stole a base in the season's first All-Star Game on July 11 at Candlestick Park as the National League won, 5–4, in ten innings. The second game ended in a 1–1 tie on July 31 at Fenway Park as heavy rain forced the end of the game after nine innings. Al Kaline stole the only base in this contest. Kaline stole fourteen bases in 1961 and was caught stealing only one time for a 93.3 percent basestealing average. Ty Cobb, the great small ball practitioner of the Deadball Era, died on July 17. Hank Aaron of Milwaukee led the way in a sixth inning triple steal against the Reds on July 18 with Joe Adcock and Joe Torre stealing bags on the back end. On July 27, Vada Pinson tried to steal home in the top of the ninth inning and produced an unearned run when he jarred the ball loose from the catcher Sammy White. The Reds held on to defeat the Braves, 2–1. Roger Maris hit his 55th homer on September 7 as the Yankees defeated the Indians, 7–3, before 18,549 Yankee Stadium fans. In the opening inning, Maris proved he was a true team player and did something that not many power hitters would have done if they were chasing the great Babe Ruth's home run record. The Yankees jumped out to a 1–0 lead in the first when Tony Kubek tripled and scored on Maris's bunt single.

In the September 8 issue of the *New York Times*, Arthur Daley's interview with Jimmy Dykes was presented. Dykes was the manager of the Cleveland Indians in 1961 and was managing his twenty-first and final major league season. Daley interviewed Dykes concerning his recollections of Babe Ruth. Dykes recalled one game as a member of the Philadelphia Athletics when they were tied with the Yankees in extra innings. The Yankees had a runner at third base with two outs and Babe Ruth at the plate. Naturally, the Athletics were expecting the Babe to try to slug the ball a great distance, but Dykes recalls he "bunted down the third-base line and went laughingly — and I mean laughingly — to first. It was a perfect bunt, of course — I told you he could do everything — and I just looked at it. The game was over."

As noted in Chapter Two, teams that have the ability to steal a large number of bases should be considered small ball teams. These teams can utilize their terrific speed while bunting, running the bases, stealing bases, executing the hit-and-run, or in the field. Most importantly, managers that have fast players on their team don't have to give up outs by sacrificing runners over. The sacrifice is often a secondary outcome with a fast runner at the plate. For example, if there is a runner on first with no outs and a hitter at the plate with excellent wheels and the ability to lay down a bunt, it may be an excellent situation to do so because if the hitter fails to leg out a bunt hit, he could still have a productive at-bat and be credited with a sacrifice. An authentic small ball team is able to utilize all the small ball strategies effectively, and in large quantities, and teams that fit this criterion are ones that have the ability to steal large numbers of bases.

So how many steals must a team compile to be considered an authentic small ball team? Teams that steal 150 or more bases should surely be considered authentic small ball teams but this, of course, is a highly subjective number. During the forty-two seasons from 1920 to 1961 there were only nine teams that stole 150 or more bases: the 1920 Washington Senators, 1920 Cincinnati Reds, 1920 Pittsburgh Pirates, 1923 Chicago White Sox, 1923 Pittsburgh Pirates, 1923 Chicago Cubs, 1924 Pittsburgh Pirates, 1925 Pittsburgh Pirates, and the 1943 Chicago White Sox. These teams collectively performed well and were ten games over .500 with an 81.7–71.8 record. From 1920 to 1961 there were twenty-five teams who stole 130 or more bases: 1920 Washington Senators, 1920 New York Giants, 1920 Cincinnati Reds, 1920 Pittsburgh Pirates, 1921 New York Giants, 1921 Pittsburgh Pirates, 1922 St. Louis Browns, 1922 Cincinnati Reds, 1922 Pittsburgh Pirates, 1923 Chicago White Sox, 1923 Pittsburgh Pirates, 1923 Chicago Cubs, 1924 Chicago White Sox, 1924 Pittsburgh Pirates, 1924 Chicago Cubs, 1925 Washington Senators, 1925 Chicago White Sox, 1925 Pittsburgh Pirates, 1927 Washington Senators, 1927 Detroit Tigers, 1928 Chicago White Sox, 1929 Cincinnati Reds, 1931 New York Yankees, 1943 Washington Senators, and the 1943 Chicago White Sox. These teams performed slightly better with an 83–70.4 average record, which was nearly thirteen games over .500.

Charts 3 and 4 are designed to find out if the teams that finished at or near the top of their league in winning percentage had more or less stolen bases and sacrifice hits than teams who finished at or near the bottom of their league in winning percentage. The methodology is the same as charts 1 and 2 in Chapter Two. To ensure that there could be a direct comparison in the number of steals and sacrifices in the top eight places, the following methodology is used: If two teams are tied in winning percentage than the team that is listed first in *The 2006 ESPN Baseball Encyclopedia* is represented in the first spot, while the team that is listed second is represented in the second spot. For example, the St. Louis Cardinals and Chicago Cubs were tied for fifth place in the National League in 1920 with 75–79 records. Since the Cardinals are listed first, their totals are counted with the fifth-place teams; the Cubs totals are added to the sixth-place teams. This ensures that the first-place through eighth-place spots each have forty-two teams and a direct comparison can be made in the number of steals and sacrifices.

When examining chart 3, the steep decline in stolen bases during the four decades after the Deadball Era is noticeable and striking. During the Deadball Era the nineteen first-place teams compiled 4,132 stolen bases. The forty-two pennant-winning senior league teams from 1920 to 1961 compiled only 2,896 steals. The difference in the American League was also similar with 3,566 steals for pennant-winning teams during the Deadball Era and only 2,673 for first-place teams during the next forty-two seasons.

From 1920 to 1961 the first-division teams in the NL stole significantly more bases than the second-division teams, 11,148 versus 9,385. National League teams that finished in first place during this time period stole 2,896 bases versus only 2,022 for the eight-place or last-place teams. Furthermore, the first-place teams led their league in steals ten (23.3 percent) out of the forty-three times (1 tie) during this time period. They ranked second in steals six (13.3 percent) out of the forty-five times (3 ties). Conversely, the last-place teams did not rank first in steals during a single season and only had three second-place finishes (6.7 percent). Thirty of the first-division teams led their league in steals, which represents 69.8 percent of the league leaders in that category. Thirty-two of the first-division teams were ranked second in steals, which represents 71.1 percent of the teams that finished second in steals. The first-division teams in the junior league also stole more bases than the second-division teams, but the difference wasn't as great as the senior league, 11,347 versus 10,473. However, the junior circuit had two extra second-division teams with the ten-team league in 1961. The fourth-place junior league teams stole the most bases with 3,065, averaging 73 thefts per team. There is a significant drop off with the eighth-place teams, who stole only 2,173 bases for a 51.7 average. The eighth-place team in the American League represents the last-place team in 41 of the 42 seasons. Chart 3 is as follows:

	NL-SBs (Avg)	Rank (1st, 2nd)	AL-SBs (Avg)	Rank (1st, 2nd)
1st Place	2,896 (69)	1st (10), 2nd (6)	2,673 (63.6)	1st (4), 2nd (9)
2nd Place	2,687 (64)	1st (8), 2nd (6)	2,903 (69.1)	1st (7), 2nd (4)
3rd Place	2,826 (67.3)	1st (5), 2nd (13)	2,706 (64.4)	1st (7), 2nd (3)
4th Place	2,739 (65.2)	1st (7), 2nd (7)	3,065 (73)	1st (8), 2nd (6)
5th Place	2,536 (60.4)	1st (4), 2nd (3)	2,764 (65.8)	1st (5), 2nd (6)
6th Place	2,543 (60.5)	1st (6), 2nd (5)	2,734 (65.1)	1st (4), 2nd (9)
7th Place	2,284 (54.4)	1st (3), 2nd (2)	2,663 (63.4)	1st (5), 2nd (3)
8th Place	2,022 (48.1)	1st (0), 2nd (3)	2,173 (51.7)	1st (3), 2nd (2)
9th Place	x	x	81 (81)	1st (0), 2nd (0)
10th Place	x	x	58 (58)	1st (0), 2nd (0)

Stolen bases fell to all-time lows during the 1950s. However, this cannot be said of sacrifice bunts, which also declined sharply from the 1930s and 1940s, but were not abnormally low during the 1950s when compared to the subsequent decades. From 1920 to 1961 the first-division teams in both leagues accumulated more sacrifices than the second-division teams. The pennant-winning teams in the National League compiled 5,059 sacrifices for a 120.5 average. Furthermore, they had 11 of the 42 teams (26.2 percent) that led their league in sacrifices and 10 of the 43 teams (1 tie) that finished second, which was 23.3 percent of the teams. The eighth-place teams had only 4,311 sacrifices for a 102.6 average and four of these teams led their league in sacrifices (9.5 percent) and they had only one team that finished second (2.3 percent). The first-division teams in the NL had 28 out of the 42 teams (66.7 percent) that led their league in sacrifices. Furthermore, they had a whopping 36 out of the 43 teams (83.7 percent), who ranked second in sacrifices. The first-division teams in the AL didn't dominate by as much. There was a significant drop off in the number of sacrifices for AL teams that finished in sixth, seventh, or eighth places. Chart 4 is as follows:

	NL-SHs (Avg)	Rank (1st, 2nd)	AL-SHs (Avg)	Rank (1st, 2nd)
1st Place	5,059 (120.5)	1st (11), 2nd (10)	4,860 (115.7)	1st (7), 2nd (2)
2nd Place	4,785 (113.9)	1st (9), 2nd (9)	4,945 (117.7)	1st (6), 2nd (5)
3rd Place	4,725 (112.5)	1st (4), 2nd (10)	5,031 (119.8)	1st (9), 2nd (9)
4th Place	4,574 (108.9)	1st (4), 2nd (7)	5,071 (120.7)	1st (6), 2nd (6)
5th Place	4,441 (105.7)	1st (7), 2nd (3)	5,130 (122.1)	1st (9), 2nd (7)
6th Place	4,308 (102.6)	1st (1), 2nd (0)	4,592 (109.3)	1st (2), 2nd (5)
7th Place	4,384 (104.4)	1st (2), 2nd (3)	4,641 (110.5)	1st (1), 2nd (6)
8th Place	4,311 (102.6)	1st (4), 2nd (1)	4,409 (105)	1st (2), 2nd (4)
9th Place	x	x	73 (73)	1st (0), 2nd (0)
10th Place	x	x	89 (89)	1st (1), 2nd (0)

With terrific small ball players during the late 1950s—in particular terrific basestealers like Luis Aparicio, Willie Mays, and Maury Wills—the dark age of small ball was close to coming to an end. Wills's extraordinary basestealing accomplishment in 1962 may not have been the end of the dark age, but it certainly was the beginning of the end at the very least.

4

The Resurgence of Small Ball:
1962–2009

Stolen bases increased in both leagues during the 1960s. The National League teams averaged a decade low of 58.5 steals per team in 1961 but then jumped considerably by over twenty steals per team to a decade high of 78.8 in 1962. The 78.8 steals per team was the highest average in the senior circuit since 1929 (86.5). In the American League the lowest number of steals per team during the decade was 52.8 in 1960 and the circuit's high for the decade occurred in 1969 with 86.1 steals per team. Again, stolen bases increased in both leagues during the 1970s. In 1971, the National League teams had a decade low of 75 steals per team and in 1977 they established the high of the decade with 129.6 thefts per team. The decade low in the junior circuit was 71.1 thefts per team in 1972 and in 1976 each team averaged 140.8 steals, which was the highest average during the decade. The senior circuit had a significant increase in steals during the 1980s, while the AL totals remained relatively steady when compared to the 1970s and increased slightly. Both leagues accumulated their highest number of steals per team in 1987: 154.3 in the NL and 123.9 in the AL. Not counting the strike-shortened season of 1981, the lowest average in the NL was attained in 1989 with 127.4, while the AL's lowest average was 93.1 in 1984. After the halcyon decade of the 1980s, when thieves ran wild on National League basepaths, stolen bases declined in the senior circuit during the 1990s, while the American League experienced a small uptick in larceny. Not counting the strike-shortened 1994 season, the lowest steals per team in the NL was 100.6 in 1998. In 1990, the senior league teams stole a decade high of 148.9 bases per team. The American League had a decade low of 95.1 steals per team in 1995 when the season started late and each team played about 144 games. In 1992 the AL teams averaged a decade high of 121.7 steals per team. From 2000 to 2009 stolen bases were not near historically high levels, but they were also not at historically low levels either. However, the average number of steals per team declined from the 1990s level, which is the second consecutive decade that stolen bases have declined in the major leagues. The highest NL average from 2000 to 2009 was 101.7 steals per team in 2000. The AL's highest average was 117.6 in 2001.

In the National League during the 1960s the number of sacrifice bunts per team ranged from a low of 65.6 in 1962 to a high of 79.4 in 1968. The American League's lowest average was in 1969 as each team laid down 64.8 sacrifices. In 1960, the AL teams had a decade high of 82.6 sacrifice bunts per team. The senior circuit had a range of 68.3 (1970) to 90.2 (1975) during the 1970s. The American League's highest average was in 1972 with 74.4 sacrifices per team and the following season they experienced their lowest average with 49.3 sacrifices per team. Of course, the decline in sacrifices from 1972 to 1973 in the AL was correlated to the use of the designated hitter in 1973, the first season that rule was in use. Surprisingly, sacrifice bunts rebounded in 1974 and remained steady for the rest of the decade. From 1974 to 1979 the average number of sacrifices for AL teams was 62.6, 65.9, 68.2, 65.5, 72.6, and 67.6. Excluding the strike-shortened season of 1981, the senior league had a decade low of 67.4 sacrifices per team in 1984. In 1982, the NL teams averaged a decade high of 81.5 sacrifices per team, as they amassed 978 sacrifice bunts. During the 1980s sacrifice bunts declined by a significant number in the AL. The low of the decade was established in 1984 with 44.7 sacrifices per team and the highest average was in 1980 with 65.4. Excluding the strike-shortened 1994 season, the lowest average during the 1990s in the NL was 67.6 sacrifices per team in 1995. The highest average was 81.9 in 1992. After the first four seasons of the 1990s from 1990 to 1993, there was a sharp decline in the AL for the rest of the decade. The highest number of sacrifices per team was established in 1991 with 52.4 and the lowest average, excluding the 1994 season, was in 1999 with 36.2. From 2000 to 2009, the American League has seen further declines in sacrifice bunts, while the National League has remained relatively steady.

In 1962 Maury Wills helped propel the Dodgers within reach of the pennant, stealing an unheard of 104 bases. Not only did the Los Angeles Dodgers lead the majors with 198 steals, but they became the first major league team with a basestealing average over 80 percent. Of course, this is only counting the seasons when caught stealing totals were compiled, so it is possible that a team stole bases at an 80 percent clip or better and it wasn't recorded. The 1962 Dodgers were caught stealing only 43 times and had an 82.2 percent basestealing average. They were also tied with seventh-place Philadelphia with the most sacrifices in the majors with 83. Los Angeles could also hit the long ball, hitting a modest 140 home runs, which was the fifth best in the National League. Tommy Davis provided the muscle, leading the majors in batting (.346), hits (230), and RBIs (153). He also scored 120 runs and hit 27 homers. Willie Davis batted .285, scored 103 runs, and finished second in the major leagues with 32 steals in 39 attempts. Tommy, Willie, and Maury could all fly around the bases. Tommy stole 68 bases during a single season while playing in the bush leagues. As a young player, Tommy was timed at 3.4 seconds running to first base. He broke his ankle on May 1, 1965, and wasn't a fast runner after the injury. According to Stan Williams, Tommy Davis was only a step slower than Wills in the 60-yard dash. Willie Davis was the fastest runner: Wills would take a huge lead in the first ten yards and then Davis would catch up and win easily. Wills accelerated faster out of the batter's box but once Willie Davis got going, he was flying, and third base coaches couldn't stop him when he was running at top speed.[1]

The boastful Leo Durocher insists in his autobiography *Nice Guys Finish Last* that he was the brains behind the 1962 Dodgers. Walter Alston, the Dodgers manager, would flash the signals to Durocher in the third base coach's box and Durocher ignored them and implemented his own strategies. Durocher accused Alston of being too conservative and when the manager gave him the take sign, he would flash the hit sign. When Alston wanted to bunt, Leo would signal the batter and baserunner that the hit-and-run was on. He told Maury Wills to swing at the first pitch and not to take a strike. The pitchers had been throwing a first pitch strike to Wills because he was often looking to walk or was content with a walk. Wills's hitting improved as he got more aggressive, he stole more bases and his fielding also got better. Wills had been unaccustomed in hitting ahead of the count with 2–0 counts and 3–1 counts, as he was often ordered to take a pitch, but with Durocher's encouragement he began to hit away as Leo gave him the green light. Durocher would give all the speedsters the green light and would never flash the take sign. Leo also let his speed merchants pilfer sacks at their discretion. He wrote, "*Forget the signs*. Speed overcomes everything. *Let them run*." But then according to Durocher everything changed one day when Alston held a meeting: "As of tonight, starting with this ball game, I will take complete charge of this ball club. And Leo, that means you. If I give you the bunt sign, that's what I want. The bunt. And if I give you the take sign, I want that hitter to take." Alston said that if Leo missed a sign he would be charged with a $200 fine and worst of all he would be directly responsible for the $200 fine levied on the player who received the sign and followed Durocher's insubordinate signal. From that point forward Leo just flashed the signs to the players and became the puppet instead of the puppet master. Worst of all, Alston would hold a meeting every day to discuss the opposition. Durocher believed this was the worst thing that a manager could do when things were going extremely good or extremely bad.[2]

Maury Wills had a multitude of incandescent memories in 1962. President John F. Kennedy and Vice President Lyndon B. Johnson were among the spectators at District of Columbia Stadium to watch the National League defeat the American League, 3–1, on July 10 in the season's first All-Star Game. Stan Musial hit a pinch-hit single in the sixth frame and was replaced with pinch-runner Maury Wills. Wills got a huge jump on pitcher Camilo Pascual and stole second base easily. Catcher Earl Battey didn't even attempt a throw. Then Dick Groat hit a single, scoring Wills. Wills collected a single to lead off the top of the eighth. Jim Davenport followed with a single to shallow left field and Wills stopped when he rounded the midway, but when the throw went into second, he took off for third and made it with a terrific slide. Wills scored on a sacrifice fly. Having grown up in Washington, D.C., he was given a huge ovation by the 45,480 fans in attendance.

On August 10 and 11, the Giants won their first two games of their series against the Dodgers at Candlestick Park. Members of the Dodgers organization were extremely perturbed because the basepaths between first and second were saturated with water in an obvious attempt to slow down the Dodgers baserunning attack. Umpire Bill Jackowski forced the grounds crew to place sand over the area that was covered in water before the final game on August 12, but the Giants won anyway, 5–1. The Dodgers were at the Polo Grounds on August 26 and defeated the Mets, 16–5, partially thanks to three steals by Wills and twelve "gift" runs because of five errors by the opposition. Howard M. Tuckner of the *New York Times* wrote, "Maury Wills was busy turning the Polo Grounds into a freeway — or maybe a Maury-go-round."[3] Wills went 2 for 3 with a double, three runs scored, and one RBI. His three steals increased his season total to seventy-two. The two records he was chasing were Bob Bescher's modern National League record of 81 steals in 1911 and Ty Cobb's modern major league record of 96 steals in 1915.

Bill Mazeroski belted a grand slam homer and drove in six runs as the Pirates defeated the Dodgers, 10–1, in Los Angeles on September 7. The Dodgers committed five errors and were charged with twelve in their last three games. They had lost four out of their last five contests. Despite the poor team performance on September 7, Maury Wills stole four bases and broke Bescher's modern National League record with his final steal of the game, his 82nd of the season. An article in the *New York Times* credited Billy Hamilton with having established the all-time NL stolen base record with 115 bags in 1891. However, most modern baseball encyclopedias like *The 2006 ESPN Baseball Encyclopedia* credit Hamilton with 111 steals in 1891, while John Ward who played for New York's National League aggregation in 1887 also stole 111. The *New York Times* credited Bescher with only 80 steals in 1911, instead of 81. And the paper insisted that Harry Stovey set the all-time record by pilfering

156 hassocks for Philadelphia's 1888 American Association outfit, but he is only credited with 87 bags by modern encyclopedias. Wills went 2 for 3 in the game. He singled in the first inning and stole second and third. In the third frame, he walked and stole second as the *New York Times* credited Wills with the record.[4] But the real record-breaker came in the sixth inning when he singled and stole his fourth bag of the game.

In his 156th game of the season, Maury Wills stole his 96th and 97th base to break Cobb's modern major league record. However, the Cardinals emerged triumphant with a 12–2 win at Busch Stadium on September 23. Wills stole second base in the third stanza to tie the record as shortstop Dal Maxvill couldn't handle Carl Sawatski's throw. The crowd gave Wills a terrific ovation. Then he singled in the seventh and stole second to break the record. When Wills stepped into the batter's box in the ninth inning the game was stopped. He was given a base in the in-game ceremony as the public address announcer said, "And you won't have to steal this one." The actual base he stole to break the record was given to him after the contest. Despite Wills's great accomplishment, the Dodgers had lost five of their last seven games and were desperately trying to hold on to win the pennant.[5]

At season's end, Alvin Dark's San Francisco Giants caught the Dodgers as they had identical 101–61 records. The Giants won the first playoff game, 8–0, but the Dodgers won the must-win second game, 8–7, partially thanks to Maury Wills's baserunning. Wills stole his 103rd and 104th bases in the seventh inning of the final game on October 3. He stole three bases in that final contest and when he pilfered the third sack in the seventh, he scampered safely across the plate on catcher Ed Bailey's throwing error. October 3 is a date that the Dodger fan would like to forget because it was on that day in 1951 that Bobby Thomson hit a three-run homer off Ralph Branca in the last of the ninth to give the Giants an improbable pennant victory. But on October 3, 1962, disaster struck again. The Dodgers gave the home crowd plenty to cheer about as they took a 4–2 lead into the ninth. Four Giant runs crossed the plate on a single to right field, an infield single, a sacrifice fly, four walks (one intentional), one wild pitch, and a Dodger error.

Just like in 1951, the Giants lost the World Series to the Yankees after their three-game playoff win against the Dodgers. In the bottom of the second inning of the opening game, Jose Pagan's squeeze bunt plated a run for the Giants but the Yankees won the contest, 6–2. Matty Alou legged out a bunt to lead off the last of the ninth inning in the seventh and deciding game but he couldn't score as the Yankees won, 1–0, behind Ralph Terry's shutout pitching. Mickey Mantle and Tom Tresh stole two bags apiece for manager Ralph Houk's Yankees, while Willie Mays stole the only base for San Francisco. The Giants laid down four of the five sacrifices in the series.

Maury Wills did not have the intensity of Ty Cobb. He wasn't dirty, violent, and dangerous, and did not utilize spike high slides with razor sharp spikes. Wills was capable of sliding hard into the bag or sliding beautifully around the base to avoid the tag. He took huge leads but was rarely picked off. Wills was relatively mild-mannered, but when the Giants watered down the infield with excessive water and hindered his running game, it infuriated Wills and he was thrown out of a contest. Wills wasn't the fastest player in the game, but he got an excellent jump and could be up to full speed in two strides. He was the seventh of thirteen children in his family and was taught the Ten Commandments by his mother, but as one scribe put it, "Obviously, he took the Eighth lightly." At Cardozo High School in Washington, D.C., he was known more for his talents on the gridiron as a talented quarterback. He was offered scholarships to play football at nine universities, but decided to play professional baseball instead. Wills signed with the Dodgers in 1951 for only $500. He spent over eight seasons in the bushes and the Detroit Tigers almost purchased his contract in 1959, but they thought the $35,000 asking price was too much. One scribe described him as follows: "A wide-eyed young man who looks like a church deacon and runs as if the hounds of Hades were eternally snapping at his heels."[6]

When records are broken there are always critics who cling to the status quo, failing to recognize the achievements of the record-breakers, and finding ways to undermine them. Roger Maris felt this in 1961 when the expanded 162-game schedule allowed him to break Babe Ruth's sacrosanct home run record of sixty long balls. Commissioner Ford Frick placed an asterisk next to Maris's achievement, signifying that Ruth was the true record-holder. And despite the fact that Maury Wills broke Cobb's record in 156 games, which was the same number of games that Cobb played in during 1915, there were still critics trying to undermine his achievement by using the 162-game schedule as their primary argument.

Ed Charles of Kansas City had a game-ending steal of home versus Minnesota with 36-year-old right hander Ray Moore on the mound on August 8, 1962. On August 26, the Cubs emerged victorious over the Braves, 4–1, at Wrigley Field. They had four consecutive bunts in the sixth inning and three straight sacrifices. Dick Ellsworth, the Cubs pitcher, had a bunt single followed by a sacrifice by leadoff hitter Ken Hubbs, who was safe on a fielder's choice. And then the next two hitters, Ron Santo and Don Landrum, also laid down sacrifice bunts.

The New York Yankees won their fourth

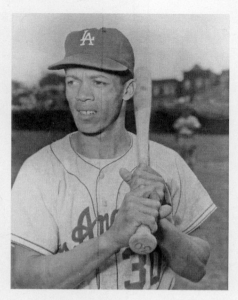

Maury Wills's record-breaking 104 steals in 1962 surely must have been more shocking than Roger Maris's 61 homers in 1961 that surpassed Babe Ruth. During the 1950s there were only two teams to steal over 104 bags and eleven of the twenty stolen base crowns during the decade were awarded to players who pilfered fewer than thirty bags. Wills stole more bases than every major league team in 1962. Furthermore, he had a phenomenal 88.9 percent basestealing average. While Maris's accomplishment is celebrated in the early twenty-first century, Wills's achievement has been largely ignored, overlooked, and worst of all, denigrated with the passage of time. But his contemporaries recognized the achievement by awarding him the 1962 NL MVP Award. He won six straight NL stolen base crowns from 1960 to 1965 and led the NL in sacrifices in 1961. (George Brace photograph).

straight pennant in 1963 with a 104–57 record. There was no meltdown in Los Angeles as Walter Alston led the Dodgers to their fourth pennant in ten seasons under his leadership with a 99–63 record. The Dodgers were not the same small ball juggernaut as they were in 1962 and despite leading the majors with 124 steals in 1963, they stole 74 fewer cushions than the previous season and they were far less successful when engaging in thievery. Their basestealing average plummeted from 82.2 percent in 1962 to 63.9 percent in 1963. The Dodgers' stolen base decline was almost entirely attributed to Wills, who stole 64 fewer bags than the previous season as he played 31 fewer games. After compiling a phenomenal 88.9 percent basestealing average in 1962, it plummeted to 67.8 percent in 1963.

The Dodgers relied on their great pitching, led by Sandy Koufax and Don Drysdale to sweep the World Series in four games. They allowed only four runs in the series as Koufax won two games, while Drysdale and Johnny Podres won one apiece. Koufax struck out fifteen in the 5–2 opening game triumph, while Drysdale pitched a three-hit shutout in game three. Los Angeles batted only .214 in the series, but they hit three homers and drove in twelve runs. Tommy Davis and Maury Wills stole the only bases of the series. Lee Allen described Wills's stolen base in game two as follows: "Wills singled to open the game; Downing then threw over to first and discovered that Maury had gone to second."[7] In game four, the Dodgers took a 2–1 lead in the bottom of the seventh inning. Jim Gilliam led off with a grounder to Clete Boyer at third, who threw it past first baseman Joe Pepitone, which allowed Gilliam to advance to third. Pepitone lost the ball in the shirts of the crowd and was charged with the Yankees only error of the series. But it proved costly when Willie Davis drove Gilliam in with a sacrifice fly and the Dodgers held on for the championship clinching victory. Interestingly, Willie Davis, the Dodgers three-hole hitter, laid down the only two sacrifice bunts in the series for Los Angeles. Davis was a good bunter and laid down 83 sacrifices during his career in regular season competition. Bobby Richardson collected the only sacrifice for New York. Mickey Mantle, the Yankees cleanup hitter, had only two hits in the series, a bunt single to lead off the top of the second inning in game three and a solo homer in game four.

On September 1, Cardinals pitcher Curt Simmons hit an RBI-triple in the second inning and then stole home on a botched squeeze play. St. Louis prevailed, 7–3, over Philadelphia. For Simmons it was the second and last stolen base of his career. The first one was pilfered in 1953. It would take twenty-one seasons before another pitcher stole home when Pascual Perez did it on September 7, 1984.

Perhaps it was not surprising that stolen bases began to increase once again during the 1960s as offensive productivity decreased because of several factors, including the expansion of the strike zone in 1963. Bill James attributes the decline in offense to several other factors, including increased night games; advertisements in center field that impaired the hitter's vision and were allowed until 1969; better equipment such as larger fielding gloves; pitching mounds which were not checked regularly until 1969 and therefore some teams were alleged to have pitching mounds that were higher than the maximum height allowed by the rules; and finally several teams relocated into new ballparks with more foul territory, which resulted in fewer hits.[8]

Louis Clark Brock, a five-foot-eleven-and-a-half-inch, 170-pound, left-handed fly chaser, began his career in 1961 with the Chicago Cubs, appearing in four games. He stole a total of forty bags during the next two seasons and then was traded to the St. Louis Cardinals on June 15, 1964, in one of the most lopsided trades in major league history. Brock batted .251 with ten steals for the Cubs in 1964 before being traded to St. Louis where he batted .348 with 33 steals. He never thought of himself as a basestealer until Cardinals manager Johnny Keane and his coaching staff convinced Brock that he would be a much better player if he utilized his speed. Bob Gibson wrote in his autobiography *Stranger to the Game* that Brock's speed and baserunning ability were "mind-boggling." The first baseman was forced to hold Brock close to the bag and Gibson points out that Curt Flood and Dick Groat benefited greatly by this. Brock distracted the pitcher while on base and this also helped the hitters. Despite Brock's presence on the team in 1964, Gibson insists that there were two things preventing the Cardinals from achieving their goals: The Phillies were playing great and Johnny Keane and Dick Groat came to loggerheads over the use of the hit-and-run play. When the season commenced, Groat was allowed to use the hit-and-run whenever he wanted. However, in a game against Los Angeles the hit-and-run failed to work three times. Keane took away Groat's green light to use the hit-and-run and they stopped talking to each other, which brought tension to the clubhouse and divided the team.[9]

Lou Brock, a former math teacher, achieved his success on the basepaths through intensive study and hard work. With a plethora of great basestealers in the game since the late 1950s, catchers were slowly getting better at throwing out burglars with fast, low throws. Brock became a master of reading the pitchers' movements by watching film. He also watched films about great basestealers and studied their habits. During the later years of his career he used statistics, charts, and computers to help him gain the edge. The cerebral basestealer knew precisely how long it was needed for a pitcher to deliver the ball and allow enough time for his catcher to throw him out. If the pitcher took more than a second and a half to deliver the ball, he knew that he had the base stolen. He timed himself going from one base to another. He timed the pitchers and the catchers and calculated precisely what was needed to steal a bag. Brock studied the movements of pitchers and looked for keys, such as focusing on the heel of a right-handed pitcher. If the pitcher shifted his weight forward towards his right knee, he was going home with the ball. In his interview with Rich Westcott, Brock said that a basestealer has to "understand the movable parts of the body. If, for instance, a righthanded pitcher is going to throw to first, do you know the first thing that moves when he goes from his stretch to the throw? It's his butt. So, if you watch that, you'll be able to tell if he's going home with the pitch or to first."[10] Where a pitcher distributes his weight on his feet tells the basestealer what he is going to do next and how he is going to do it. Brock believed that it was the pitcher's responsibility to stop a basestealer. If the pitcher did not hold him close to the bag then not even a rifle-armed catcher like Johnny Bench is capable of throwing him out. When he first came to the Cardinals he was desperate for knowledge about basestealing, but there were very few people who could speak knowledgably about the subject. He spoke to Cool Papa Bell, who lived in St. Louis. The former Negro League star and great basestealer gave Brock information that could not be learned in any book. For example, he told him how to read a pitcher in a way that would put the hitter in an advantageous position. Brock described basestealing as follows: "You've got to have a passion for the art. It's a love affair. When you're in love with something, you have no fear. You combine that with arrogance, and you have a person who can beat a pitcher every time." To become knowledgeable about basestealing you must study and only after you became knowledgeable can you become arrogant or confident. Each time he faced off against a pitcher on the bases, it was like a "duel." Brock also said that you can't be intimidated by the pitcher, even if they threw at you after you stole a base when one of the unwritten rules said you shouldn't.[11] Brock broke down basestealing in a scientific manner and believed that basestealing was a "concept" and it should be taught as such.[12]

By the time Brock's Hall of Fame career ended in 1979, he was the all-time stolen base leader with 938 and he broke Maury Wills's single season record in 1974 with 118 bags. Rickey Henderson would later break both records during his career. Brock had a respectable 75.3 percent basestealing average during his wondrous journey through major league ballparks. After being traded to the Cardinals, he spent the rest of his career with that team. In a nineteen-year career he batted .293 with 1,610 runs scored, and 3,023 hits. Brock possessed plenty of power and had 486 doubles, 141 triples, and 149 homers. But he also struck out too much, didn't draw a lot of walks as a leadoff hitter, and had only 47 career sacrifice bunts. But he used his speed to ground into a low number of double plays. He won eight NL stolen base crowns: 1966 (74), 1967 (52), 1968 (62), 1969 (53), 1971 (64), 1972 (63), 1973

(70), and in 1974 (118). Brock stole over fifty bases during twelve seasons. He was well-liked and a terrific competitor, who ignited the offense out of the leadoff spot.

With a great basestealer like Brock batting first in the lineup, it is important to find the right hitter to handle the responsibility of batting second. Two-hole hitters are going to be hitting behind in the count and must be patient in taking pitches, which allows the basestealer to pilfer a bag and they must keep their concentration while the pitcher works slowly and constantly throws over to first base. However, there are plenty of benefits as well, such as seeing more fastballs, large holes in the infield because of shifting defenses, and the pitcher may go to a slide step to quicken his delivery to the plate, which may lower his velocity. Curt Flood, a selfless man, who would later challenge baseball's reserve clause by refusing a trade to the Phillies after the 1969 season, batted second during much of his career with the Cardinals. He was a true team player who sacrificed himself in that role by taking pitches so Brock could steal a base and by making productive outs by hitting behind the runner. Flood batted .293 lifetime with 88 steals and 72 sacrifices. Furthermore, he was one of the greatest defensive center fielders in major league history. There is nothing spectacular about Flood's small ball statistics. But small ball is more than the mere accumulation of stolen bases and sacrifices. Small ball entails a willingness to contribute to the team effort where everyone contributes through bunts, productive outs, stolen bases, and the hit-and-run play. It is unlike the home run, which is largely an individual accomplishment, which does not engender teamwork.

It was still dark outside when the Philadelphia Phillies arrived at Philadelphia International Airport on the morning of September 21, 1964. Mayor James Tate showed up with about two thousand loyal fans to greet the conquering heroes. The pennant appeared to be secured with a six and a half game lead with twelve games to go. World Series tickets had already been printed. They were going to wrap up the pennant on their seven-game home stand, but shockingly they lost all seven. Allen Lewis wrote in the *Philadelphia Inquirer* that it was "the blackest seven days in Philadelphia baseball history."[13] In the first game of the homestand on September 21, the Reds' Chico Ruiz stole home in the sixth inning and scored the only run in the game. Art Mahaffey, the Phillies right-handed pitcher, was concentrating solely on cleanup man Frank Robinson and was shocked to see Ruiz sprinting home out of the corner of his eye as he delivered the 1 and 0 pitch. Mahaffey used a slow windup to deliver the first pitch and Ruiz saw an opportunity to pilfer home on the next offering. Clay Dalrymple, the Phillies catcher, was unable to catch Mahaffey's wild delivery and Ruiz stole home without having to slide. Both Dick Sisler, the interim manager of the Reds who was replacing Fred Hutchinson, who was dying of cancer, and Robinson, were also stunned. Robinson couldn't recall anybody stealing home with him at the plate. He also thought that if Mahaffey threw a strike then Ruiz would have been out. Gene Mauch, the Phillies skipper, said, "If you're thrown out on that play, you're on your way back to the minors."[14]

Both the Cincinnati Reds and St. Louis Cardinals put together long winning streaks, while Gene Mauch's Phillies lost ten straight. The Phillies finished second in the NL with 97 sacrifices, but they stole only 30 bases and had a 46.2 percent basestealing average. The Cardinals and Reds had more speed, stealing 73 and 90 bases, respectively. The Reds tried to use small ball strategies to defeat the Pirates on September 30, but Pittsburgh's small ball execution is what won them the game. Both teams combined for thirty-six strikeouts in a pitching duel between Jim Maloney, the Reds hard-throwing right hander, and Bob Veale, the Bucs flame-throwing southpaw, at Crosley Field. Cincinnati's Frank Robinson stole two bags in the thirteenth inning and Tommy Harper stole second to put two runners in scoring position. After a walk to Steve Boros to load the bases, the next two batters popped up to end the inning. Donn Clendenon doubled for the Pirates in the top of the sixteenth inning. Bill Mazeroski sacrificed him to third and then Jerry May, a 20-year-old first-year catcher who played just eleven games during the season, caught third baseman Chico Ruiz sleeping with the suicide squeeze. Clendenon took off for the plate with the pitch and May executed the bunt to score what would prove to be the winning run. Jerry May played 556 major league games and stole only one base during his career. At season's end it was the Cardinals who won the pennant with a 93–69 record.

Stolen bases declined slightly in both leagues in 1964, by 48 in the NL and 12 in the AL. Sacrifice bunts increased by 57 in the NL and declined by 43 in the AL. The Los Angeles Dodgers were tied for sixth place with Pittsburgh and led the majors with an impressive 141 steals. They also led both leagues with 120 sacrifices. However, they produced little power, hitting just 79 homers, which was second to last in the majors.

On May 24, Lou Brock of the Cubs stole home for the first time in his career on the front end of a double steal with Billy Williams on the back end. The theft took place in the first inning of game one versus Cincinnati. The Reds swept the twin bill, 6–5 and 12–4. On September 19, the Phillies' Johnny Callison was caught stealing home in the fourteenth inning on a botched squeeze attempt. Bobby Wine failed to lay down a bunt and Callison who took off from third was an easy out. With two outs in the last of the sixteenth, the Dodgers Willie Davis singled, stole second, and advanced to third on a wild pitch. Morrie Steevens's major league experience consisted of twelve games he pitched in for the 1962 Cubs. The 6'2", 175-pound, southpaw was called up from Philadelphia's bush league team in Little Rock, Arkansas, and was pitching in his first game as a Phillie. The first batter he faced was Ron Fairly with Davis at third. Leo Durocher, the Dodgers third base coach, encouraged Davis to steal home and that's precisely what Davis did with two strikes on the batter. Davis said, "There's a kid out there. You always try to do something to shake up a kid."[15]

Yogi Berra led the Yankees to their fifth straight pennant during his first season as their manager. They won thirty of their last forty games and finished with a 99–63 record. The Yankees hit more homers than the Cardinals in the 1964 World Series, 10 to 5, and scored more runs, 33 to 32, but lost the series in seven games. In the final game at Busch Stadium, won by the Cardinals, 7–5, behind Bob Gibson's route-going performance, Tim McCarver and Mike Shannon, two players who did not run well and combined for eighty career stolen bases, pulled off an unlikely double steal in the fourth inning. McCarver was at third base and Shannon at first base when manager Johnny Keane decided to try the double steal. When Shannon took off for second nobody covered the bag and catcher Elston Howard had to double pump before unleashing a throw that was off target. Bobby Richardson threw home and tried to catch McCarver at the plate, but the ball skipped past Howard. Then Dal Maxvill singled to center and Shannon challenged Mickey Mantle's arm and was safe. Bill White also stole a base in the series for St. Louis, while Clete Boyer and Bobby Richardson had one apiece for New York. It was not surprising that Johnny Keane's Cardinals had the most sacrifice bunts in the autumn classic considering that they laid down 26 more sacrifices than New York during the regular season, 94 to 68. Gibson, Curt Simmons, Shannon, and Maxvill garnered sacrifices for St. Louis, while Richardson laid down the only sacrifice for New York.

Stolen bases increased in both leagues in 1965, by 109 in the NL and by about 30 percent in the AL, an increase of 164. Sacrifice bunts decreased by 80 in the NL and increased by 106 in the AL when compared to 1964. The Los Angeles Dodgers were a powerful small ball aggregation, who won the pennant and then the World Series because of their ability to manufacture runs, good defense, and great pitching. Walter Alston's club led the major leagues in both stolen bases (172) and sacrifices (103). Their .245 batting average ranked only seventh in the circuit; their .312 on-base percentage ranked sixth; and their .335 slugging percentage ranked ninth. The Dodgers slugged only 78 homers, which was last in the majors. The pitching staff was led by Sandy Koufax (26–8) and Don Drysdale (23–12) as the Dodgers compiled the best ERA in the majors (2.81). They faced off against Sam Mele's Minnesota Twins (102–60) in the World Series and created havoc on the bases just like the regular season, as they won the title in seven games. Willie Davis stole three bases in game five. In total, the Dodgers stole nine in the series: three apiece by Davis and Maury Wills, while Wes Parker stole two and Johnny Roseboro pilfered one. The Twins stole only two bags: one piece by Bob Allison and Zoilo Versalles. Los Angeles had six of the eight sacrifice bunts, including two apiece by Davis and Parker. Walter Alston won his fourth world championship as manager of the Dodgers, which was the most by any National League manager.

Bert Campaneris of the Kansas City Athletics was able to unseat Luis Aparicio by winning the AL stolen base crown with 51 thefts in his second major league season. Campaneris would often steal two bases in a game and it was not unusual for him to take two bases on a sacrifice bunt. He batted .259 lifetime with a .311 on-base percentage and stole 649 bases with a 76.5 percent basestealing average. He led the AL in stolen bases during six seasons: 1965 (51), 1966 (52), 1967 (55), 1968 (62), 1970 (42), and 1972 (52). He stole 62 bases in both 1968 and 1969 with stolen base averages of 73.8 percent and 88.6 percent, respectively. He stole at least 51 bases during seven seasons. Campy was a complete small ball player, who laid down 199 sacrifice bunts during his career, which ranks 83rd all-time. During eight seasons he had ten or more sacrifices and led the AL in 1972 (20), 1977 (40), and 1978 (25). His forty sacrifices in 1977 is tied for 36th most all-time during a single season and every player who accumulated more sacrifices in a season either played during the Deadball Era or during a season when sacrifice flies were counted as sacrifice hits.

Maury Wills led the NL in thefts for the sixth straight season with a whopping 94 steals and was followed by Lou Brock (63), Jimmy Wynn of Houston (43), Tommy Harper of Cincinnati (35), and Willie Davis (25). Wynn had an outstanding 91.5 percent basestealing average in 1965. He stole 225 career bases and had a 69 percent basestealing average, while playing for five major league teams. Wynn laid down only 32 sacrifice bunts in a fifteen-year big league career. Tommy Harper was an excellent baserunner, who stole 408 bases during his career, and had a 77.9 percent basestealing average. He possessed both blazing speed and occasional power, hitting 146 career homers, including 31 for the 1970 Milwaukee Brewers when he also stole 38 bags. He stole at least 23 bases during eleven seasons and led the AL in steals with the 1969 Seattle Pilots (73) and the 1973 Boston Red Sox (54). His 73 steals in 1969 was the largest total in the AL since Ty Cobb pilfered 96 bags in 1915. He laid down 76 sacrifice bunts during his career. When he was a member of the Red Sox from 1972 to 1974 some people thought he was the team's best baserunner since Tris Speaker. During his three seasons with the Red Sox he stole 107 bases and excited the Fenway faithful with aggressive baserunning plays, like running from first to third on a sacrifice bunt.

The New York Mets committed three errors at Shea Stadium on April 14 and allowed the Houston Astros to escape with a 7–6, eleven-inning victory, in a game that had a significant small ball achievement. Warren Spahn, who was pitching in his final season, took the pill for New York and lasted eight innings, surrendering three runs. Roy McMillan, the Mets shortstop, couldn't handle a double play grounder in the seventh and Ron Brand followed with a two-run single. In the top of the eleventh the Astros scored four runs on a bunt single, four walks, two errors, two wild pitches, and Al Spangler's steal of home. The final run of the inning was tallied on Spangler's theft of home, which came on a double steal as Brand stole third. Spangler was a 31-year-old left fielder, who stood at six-feet tall, weighed 175 pounds, and threw and batted left-handed. During his thirteen-year career, he batted .262 with only 37 steals.

Frank Robinson won the 1961 NL MVP with Cincinnati and then in 1966 he won the AL MVP by leading the Baltimore Orioles (97–63) to a pennant victory and World Series championship. Manager Hank Bauer's Orioles swept the Dodgers in the World Series as they allowed only two runs in the opener and then Jim Palmer, Wally Bunker, and Dave McNally pitched shutouts in the final three games. Maury Wills stole 38 sacks for the Dodgers during the regular season with a mediocre 61.3 percent basestealing average and then pilfered the only base in the fall classic. Baltimore collected two of the three sacrifices, including one by big Boog Powell. Powell was a powerful slugger who stood at 6' 4" and about 240 pounds. His 34 homers in 1966 ranked third in the American League. He was not the ideal man to lay down a sacrifice bunt, but he did have more sacrifices (27) during his career than stolen bases (20). With Baltimore leading 4–0 in the top of the eighth inning of game two, Powell laid down a sacrifice that moved Frank Robinson to third and Brooks Robinson to second. Everything worked out fine when Davey Johnson had an infield single that scored both runs, thanks to Ron Perranoski's throwing error.

Bert Campaneris stole one more base in 1966 than in 1965. His stolen base average was an impressive 83.9 percent. That 52nd stolen base earned him his second straight AL stolen base crown as Don Buford of the Chicago White Sox finished second with 51 sacks. Buford's teammate, Tommie Agee, pilfered 44 bags to finish third. The switch-hitting, 5' 8", 165-pound, Buford was a terrific leadoff man but a questionable fielder, playing mainly second base and third base early in his career with the White Sox and switching to the outfield when he became a member of the Baltimore Orioles. He batted .264 lifetime with a .362 on-base percentage and a .379 slugging percentage. He scored 99 runs during each season from 1969 to 1971. From 1966 to 1968 he stole 51, 34, and 27 cushions, respectively, with stolen base averages of 69.9, 61.8, and 69.2. After stealing 51 bags in 1966 his stolen base totals declined each season for the rest of his career with 34, 27, 19, 16, 15, and 8. He played with the White Sox from 1963 to 1967 and for the Orioles from 1968 to 1972. With Baltimore he didn't run as much because he had home run hitters behind him and he played for a manager, Earl Weaver, who preferred power hitting and generally eschewed small ball strategies. Buford led the AL with 17 sacrifices in 1966 and compiled 47 during his career. He grounded into only 34 double plays in 4,553 at-bats. Buford enjoyed playing chess and reading in his spare time. Tommie Agee's best seasons of thievery came in 1966 (44) and 1967 (28) with the White Sox. And in 1970 (31) and 1971 (28) with the Mets. His career stolen base average stood at 67.3 percent, as he purloined 167 cushions.

The Pale Hose nickel-and-dimed their way to a fourth-place conclusion in 1966. The White Sox had a tradition of putting together excellent small ball teams and the 1966 outfit was another small ball juggernaut. They led the majors in both steals (153) and sacrifices (109). Their .231 batting average was ranked last in the majors and their 87 home runs were second to last. Eddie Stanky's team had the junior league's best ERA (2.68) and relied on small ball and great pitching to win games. Chicago's .976 fielding average was ninth in the AL.

In the National League, Lou Brock won his first stolen base crown with 74 thefts and was followed by Sonny Jackson (49) and Maury Wills (38). Brock stole bases at an impressive 80.4 percent rate. Jackson batted .292 as Houston's shortstop and led the majors with 27 sacrifices in his first season as an everyday player. Interestingly, he never had more than eight sacrifices in any other big league season and had only 57 during his career.

The Impossible Dream came true in 1967 as the Boston Red Sox transformed themselves from a ninth-place team in 1966 to a pennant-winning outfit in 1967. The country club atmosphere that permeated the Boston clubhouse was gone with a no-nonsense, competitive skipper, leading the way. Dick Williams, the Sox rookie manager, implemented strict rules that helped discipline the players and brought the team within one game of a world championship. They were tied for second in the league with 85 sacrifices and they stole 68 bags, which was good enough for the third best in the AL. Boston bludgeoned the opposition, leading the junior league in batting average (.255), slugging percentage (.395), runs scored (722), hits (1,394), doubles (216), and home runs (158).

The Red Sox won the pennant on the season's final day, October 1, with a 5–3 win over Minnesota. The victory only secured a tie, but when Detroit lost the second game of their doubleheader to California, 8–5, the pennant was Boston's. Both Minnesota and Detroit finished the season in second place. That final game for Boston turned on a bunt single by pitcher Jim Lonborg. The Sox were losing 2–0 in the last of the sixth when Lonborg led off. Lonborg worked hard to improve his bunting skills during batting practice because manager Dick Williams insisted that he do so. Not only did the Red Sox win twenty more games in 1967, but they had twenty more sacrifice bunts as well. Cesar Tovar, the Minnesota third baseman, was playing on the dirt against Lonborg. The Red Sox pitcher took advantage of the situation and laid down a bunt on a fastball by Dean Chance and legged it out for a single as Tovar rushed in onto the grass and bobbled the ball. This brought the crowd to a frenzy as a rally appeared imminent. By the end of the inning the Red Sox had pushed across five runs. After the game, Minnesota's skipper Cal Ermer said, "The game turned on Lonborg's bunt and it wasn't that good a bunt." He also criticized Tovar for not anticipating the bunt.[16]

Standing in Boston's way for the world championship was Red Schoendienst's St. Louis Cardinals (101–60), an outfit with good speed (102 steals, 1st NL) and power (115 homers, 4th NL). Lou Brock was simply sensational in the 1967 World Series. St. Louis won the opening game, 2–1, at Fenway Park on October 4 as Bob Gibson went the distance. Brock had four singles, two steals, and scored both runs for the Red Birds. In the seventh inning, he collected his fourth single, stole second, and advanced to third on Curt Flood's productive groundout. Then Roger Maris, a left-handed hitter, deliberately tried to pull the ball, and hit a grounder to second that scored Brock. In the 5–2 Cardinals victory in game three at Busch Memorial Stadium, Brock collected a triple and single. Gibson pitched a five-hit shutout in game four as St. Louis won, 6–0. Brock had a single, double, and stolen base. Boston won game five, 3–1, and game six, 8–4, to force a game seven. In the sixth game, Brock hit a single, homer, and pilfered a bag. In the fifth inning of game seven at Fenway Park, Brock singled and then stole second and third. Maris hit a sacrifice fly to plate the second run of the frame. St. Louis won the finale, 7–2, as Gibson went the distance and the World Series was theirs. Brock led both teams with a .414 batting average, 12 hits, and 8 runs. He collected two doubles, one triple, and one homer. He also stole seven bags, which was a World Series record and swiped three of them in the final game. The only other stolen base of the series belonged to Boston's Jerry Adair. Gibson went 3–0 and had a 1.00 ERA with 26 strikeouts in 27 innings. He won the series MVP award, but believed it should have been given to Brock.

In 1967, Lou Brock put together another terrific season, batting .299 with 206 hits and 76 RBIs. He led the NL with 52 steals and was tied with Hank Aaron for the most runs scored in the senior circuit (113). Brock had 65 extra-base hits: 32 doubles, 12 triples, and 21 homers. While he continued to excel at the bat and on the bases, Brock was not a very good defensive left fielder and led NL outfielders in errors for the fourth consecutive season. In Glenn Dickey's informative book *The History of the World Series Since 1903*, he makes some trenchant observations about Brock. Brock was no Punch-and-Judy hitter, who didn't hit a lot of extra-base hits. According to Dickey, most of the best basestealers were singles hitters, but this wasn't true of Brock. And if a player singles it puts him in the best position to steal a base because second base is the "easiest" base to pilfer. Furthermore, it is the "most logical" because a steal of second puts a runner in scoring position. This last point by Dickey is somewhat debatable because if a baserunner pilfers third with less than two outs it puts them in position to score on a sacrifice fly, infield grounder, a wild pitch or passed ball. Dickey points out that because players steal second far more often than they steal third or home that Brock's 65 extra-base hits "basically removed any chance he would steal," and therefore his basestealing achievement was "more impressive."[17] Bert Campaneris, the American League's basestealing champion in 1967 (55), had only 38 extra-base hits. And only three of them were home runs.

St. Louis's excellent leadoff man was able to irritate and anger the opposition with his baserunning exploits. The pitcher and the rest of the defense were distracted with Brock on the bases and this diverted their attention from their primary goal which was to get the batter out. During the Deadball Era and for many seasons after, if a baserunner stole a bag with their team leading by several runs it was not considered showing up the opposition. But somewhere along the way as small ball activities declined it became an unwritten rule that you don't steal bases with your team in front by several runs. Lou Brock, being independent minded and a competitive player, disregarded this rule and many people hated him for it. If, for example, a team is leading by seven runs, they are not going to stop trying to get base hits and batters may still swing for the fences without causing retribution. But if a basestealer pilfers a bag, it is for some reason frowned upon and regarded as showing up the opposing team. Just like Hank Aaron or any power-hitter was paid to hit homers and would continue to try to hit homers with his team leading by a few runs, Lou Brock was paid to steal bases and believed he should continue to do so irrespective of the score. Bob Gibson insists that even a few of Brock's teammates disapproved of his approach and preferred that he remain anchored to the bag when they had a big lead. They thought he was doing this simply to pad his statistics, but if a power-hitter padded their home run statistics with a long ball, that would not have been frowned upon. This was just another example of the bias and double standard that great basestealers had to deal with during their career. Bob Gibson wrote, "Brock was a winner because he was a competitor, and a competitor doesn't stop competing just because his team has pulled reasonably ahead."[18]

Brock would often have to dodge beanballs, brushback and knockdown pitches, because of his inclination to steal bags regardless of the score. Bob Gibson, the Cardinals outstanding pitcher, was not afraid in defending Brock. "The worst baseball fight" Gibson ever saw took place on July 3, 1967, in a game versus Cincinnati at Busch Memorial Stadium. Gibson was in a foul mood, coming off the worst start of his career by yielding eleven runs to San Francisco and failing to make it past the first inning. The Cardinals had no problem hitting Milt Pappas, the Reds 28-year-old right-handed pitcher. The score was already 7–0 when Brock stepped into the batter's box for the second time in the first inning. He got on base, tried to steal second, and was thrown out. While a seven-run lead is a large margin, this was only the first inning and the Reds had plenty of time to come back, especially with Gibson coming off such a bad outing. The Reds, however, considered Brock's stolen base attempt as a way to show them up. Relief pitcher Don Nottebart took over the mound duties and sent Julian Javier sprawling into the dirt with a knockdown pitch. In the fourth frame, Nottebart nailed Brock with his delivery. Gibson knew right away that he needed to respond and he threw a pitch past Tony Perez's ear as he was leading off the top of the fifth inning. Gibson wasn't trying to hit Perez, but simply send a message with a brushback pitch. Perez flied out to left field and the two players exchanged words as Perez was making his way back to the dugout. When Orlando Cepeda, the Cardinals first baseman, got between the two players, the benches emptied as the players from each dugout rushed onto the field. Cepeda nailed Reds reliever, Bob Lee, with a vicious punch. Then an ugly brawl ensued between the two clubs as nineteen police officers went on the field and tried to break it up. The players were spread out all over the field and in the dugouts.[19]

The 1968 season is known as the "Year of the Pitcher." Stolen bases remained steady in the NL, an increase of 10, but shot up by 132 in the AL. Sacrifice bunts increased by 65 in the NL and decreased by 38 in the AL. For the first time since 1944 the Pittsburgh Pirates led the NL in steals (130). The sixth-place Oakland Athletics led the majors with 147 steals. The Athletics, Pirates, Indians (115 steals), and Cardinals (110 steals) were the only teams to steal over 100 bags. The Cardinals, Orioles, and Athletics each stole bases at about a 71 percent clip to lead the majors. Phil Niekro, the Atlanta Braves pitcher, led the majors with 18 sacrifices while Denny McLain, the Detroit Tigers pitcher, led the AL with 16. This was the first time in major league history that a pitcher from each league led their circuit in sacrifices during the same season. Furthermore, it was the first time since Johnny Sain led the NL in sacrifices in 1948 that a pitcher led either league in that category. Niekro laid down 129 sacrifices during his career, while McLain had 64. Lou Brock won his third straight NL stolen base crown with 62 steals and compiled an impressive 83.8 percent basestealing average. He had 66 extra-base hits and led the majors in both doubles (46) and triples (14). Bert Campaneris won his fourth straight title in the AL and each season he improved his total with 51, 52, 55, and 62 steals.

At Atlanta-Fulton County Stadium on September 24, the Mets lost, 7–4. The Aaron brothers, Tommie and Hank, pulled off a double steal in the seventh as Hank stole home on the play. The batter missed the squeeze sign and the Mets catcher, J. C. Martin, threw the ball into center field. Hank was about ten feet or less from the plate when Martin "foolishly" threw the ball into center field.[20] Also on September 24, the Giants prevailed over Houston, 5–4. The final two Giant runs scored in the eighth inning when Willie Mays laid down a bunt with runners on second and third and both runners scored.

The St. Louis Cardinals won the pennant once again in 1968, relying on great pitching as they led the majors with a 2.49 ERA. They hit only 73 homers (8th, NL), stole 110 bases (2nd, NL), and laid down 67 sacrifices (8th, NL). The Cardinals team batting average was only .249 (4th, NL) and their .298 on-base percentage was tied for fifth in the NL. Mayo Smith's Detroit Tigers (103–59) became the fifth team in five years to win the AL pennant. This was a powerful aggregation that led the majors with 185 homers, which was 52 more than the second-place Baltimore Orioles, who were ranked second in the majors with 133 homers. Denny McLain led the staff with a 31–6 record and a 1.96 ERA and Detroit was ranked third in the junior circuit with a 2.71 staff ERA. They had the fewest stolen bases in the major leagues (26), the worst basestealing average (44.8 percent), and accumulated a modest 73 sacrifice bunts (6th, AL).

Bob Gibson outdueled McLain in game one of the World Series as the Cardinals pitcher fanned a record seventeen batters in the 4–0 victory. Lou Brock hit a homer and stole a bag. The teams split the next two games and Lou Brock stole three bags in a 7–3 game three triumph. St. Louis won game four, 10–1, behind Gibson as they took a three games to one lead in the series. Brock hit another homer, collected three hits, scored two runs, drove in four runs, and stole his final base in World Series competition. The final steal was his seventh of the series, which matched his total from the year before. His fourteen steals in World Series competition tied Eddie Collins's record. It looked as if the Cardinals would win their second straight world championship when Brock doubled in the opening inning of game five and scored on Flood's single. And then Cepeda hit a two-run homer after Flood pilfered the second sack. In the top of the fifth inning, Brock doubled once again and he tried to score on Julian Javier's single to left field. He decided not to slide on a bang-bang play at the plate and Willie Horton's throw to Bill Freehan arrived just in time as umpire Doug Harvey signaled that the runner was out. As a result, Brock was widely criticized for his decision not to slide. Mickey Lolich settled down after his shaky first inning and he didn't give up a run the rest of the way as Detroit won, 5–3. McLain went the distance in a game six, 13–1 win, to force a game seven. Brock singled in the bottom of the sixth inning of the final game and took a huge lead off first. Neither team had pushed across a run at this juncture of the contest. When he took off for second, Lolich threw to Norm Cash at first and Cash's throw arrived in time to catch Brock at second. Javier lined out and then Curt Flood followed with a single and was picked off first by the southpaw hurler. To have two runners picked off in a single inning during the sixth stanza of the deciding game of the autumn classic in a scoreless contest was devastating and the Tigers carried the momentum into the following inning. In the top of the seventh inning, the Tigers got a break when Flood misplayed Jim Northrup's fly ball and two runs scored as a result. Northrup pulled into third with a triple and scored on Freehan's double. Detroit won the finale, 4–1, to take the world championship. They won the World Series despite committing eleven errors, while St. Louis only had two. Brock had another sensational series, batting .464 with 13 hits, 3 doubles, 1 triple, 2 homers, six runs, 5 RBIs, and 7 steals. Not surprisingly, Detroit did not steal a bag in the series, while the Cardinals had eleven: seven by Brock, three by Flood, and one by Javier. Gibson laid down the only sacrifice bunt for the Red Birds, while McLain and the weak-hitting shortstop, Ray Oyler, who batted .135 in 215 at-bats during the regular season, had one apiece for Detroit.

Earl Weaver had begun his big league managerial career in 1968, managing the second half of the season with a 48–34 record. In his first full season in 1969, he led the Orioles to first place in the AL East with the majors best record, 109–53. Weaver was fiery, combative, strong-minded, decisive and knowledgeable. He never played in the big leagues and developed his knowledge of the game by spending considerable time playing and managing in the bushes. Baltimore was a decent small ball outfit, swiping 82 bags (7th, AL) and laying down 74 sacrifices, which was tied for second in the junior league. In the ALCS they met the Minnesota Twins (97–85), who won the AL West under first-year skipper Billy Martin. The Twins stole 115 bags (4th, AL) and laid down 65 sacrifices (7th, AL).

In the first game of the ALCS at Memorial Stadium in Baltimore, the game was tied at three in the last of the twelfth. There were two outs in the inning and two strikes on outfielder Paul Blair with Mark Belanger on third. Belanger took off with the next pitch and Blair laid down a successful suicide squeeze bunt as Baltimore won the game, 4–3. Belanger scored standing up as pitcher Ron Perranoski fielded the bunt, but the Twins catcher vacated home plate and went out to field the ball and therefore Perranoski was forced to try to tag Belanger unassisted. Baltimore swept the series in three games. Tony Oliva and Cesar Tovar stole the only bases in the series. Weaver's outfit had two caught stealing in game one and game two. Brooks Robinson stole a measly 28 bases in 23 major league seasons and was caught stealing twice in the opening game. The most notable attempt came in the last of the ninth with two outs and pinch-hitter Merv Rettenmund at the dish, when Robinson was thrown out trying to steal home. Baltimore had the only two sacrifice bunts in the series: Andy Etchebarren and Brooks Robinson. Robinson's sacrifice proved critical, as he moved Boog Powell into scoring position in the bottom of the eleventh frame in game two and he scored on Curt Motton's pinch hit single with two outs.

In the NL, the Amazin' Mets, winners of the NL East (100–62) took on the Atlanta Braves, who won the NL West (93–69). New York won in three straight high scoring games as they plated twelve more runs than the Braves, 27 to 15. Orlando Cepeda stole the only base for manager Lum Harris's Braves. Gil Hodges's Mets pilfered five bags: two apiece by Tommie Agee and Cleon Jones, while rookie Wayne Garrett stole one. Bud Harrelson's sacrifice bunt in game three was the only one of the series. The Orioles batted only .146 in the World Series and lost it in five games as New York's pitching was superior. Agee stole a bag for the world champions, while Paul Blair swiped one for Baltimore. Garrett and J.C. Martin had the only sacrifice bunts.

Lou Brock led the NL with 53 steals and was followed by Joe Morgan (49), Bobby Bonds (45), and Maury Wills (40). Little Joe Morgan was small in size, standing at 5'7" and weighing between 148 and 165 pounds, but his game was large and he put together one of the finest careers in big league history. Joe was a selfless player and a good teammate, who laid down 51 sacrifice bunts during his career. He was aggressive on the bases, but also efficient, with an 81 percent basestealing average, while pilfering a whopping 689 bags. Maury Wills persuaded Morgan to steal bags in any situation, even swiping third with two outs, which Wills argued, it benefited the team. However, both players agreed that to steal third is a gamble and it should only be done if they are certain that they could make it. These two great basestealers believed that with a runner at third base, the batter will get a better pitch to hit. With a man at third, pitchers are cautious, and they do not want to unleash a wild pitch so they may not throw their slider or a pitch low in the strike zone. Morgan, unlike Lou Brock, was not a proponent of stealing a bag while your team is leading by several runs.[21]

After four consecutive AL stolen base crowns, Bert Campaneris was unseated for the title in 1969 as Tommy Harper led the AL with 73 steals. Campaneris finished second with 62 thefts and had an excellent 88.6 percent basestealing average. Jim Merritt, a pitcher for the Cincinnati Reds, led the majors with 15 sacrifice bunts in 1969, while Paul Blair of Baltimore and Denny McLain of Detroit, led the AL with 13.

Rod Carew had a nineteen-year Hall of Fame career with the Minnesota Twins (1967–1978) and the California Angels (1979–1985). He batted .328 lifetime and led the AL in batting seven times, including a career high of .388 in 1977. When he won his second batting championship in 1972 (.318), he was the first player to do so without hitting a homer and he had 15 bunt singles among his 170 hits. This talented offensive player had terrific bat control and could bunt well, laying down 128 sacrifices, including a career high of 16 in 1982. Carew was a disciplined hitter, who knew the strike zone, and used the entire field. Because of his exceptional bunting skills, the third baseman was forced to play in, which opened up the hole on the left side. He batted left-handed and became known as one of the best drag bunters in the game.

Carew was a threat to steal while on base, pilfering 353 bags with a not so impressive 65.4 percent basestealing average. From 1973 to 1976 he stole 163 bags, including a career high of 49 in 1976. He also stole over 40 in 1973 (41). During seven seasons he stole 23 or more cushions. Despite his high number of steals, he never won a stolen base title. It took him a while to start pilfering large numbers of bases, as he stole only 58 during his first six seasons. Carew won his first batting crown in 1969 (.332) and stole 19 bags. There is nothing special about nineteen bags unless you consider that seven of them were steals of home (36.8 percent). Indeed, he stole home seven times to tie what was considered Pete Reiser's 1946 record, although in later years researchers found out that Ty Cobb stole home eight times in 1912. Carew is tied with Eddie Collins and Larry Doyle for 14th all-time with seventeen steals of home during his career. Many great basestealers are reluctant to steal home. Maury

Joe Morgan is the greatest second baseman in major league history and was accustomed to bringing home the hardware, winning back-to-back NL MVP Awards in 1975 and 1976, and winning five straight Gold Gloves from 1973 to 1977. This high percentage player batted .271 lifetime with a .392 on-base percentage and a .427 slugging percentage. He is ranked eleventh all-time with 689 steals, pilfering sacks at an outstanding 81 percent rate. (George Brace photograph).

Wills only tried it once. Lou Brock and Joe Morgan were not advocates of trying it. Davey Lopes, a prodigious basestealer with 557 steals, who began his career with the 1972 Los Angeles Dodgers, said in 1977, "That's for amateurs. I've never tried to steal home. Your only chance is if the pitcher's mind is in the next county."[22] Billy Martin, who managed the Twins for one season in 1969, is the person who persuaded Carew to begin stealing home. He did it twice in spring training and when Minnesota was having difficultly scoring runs during the 1969 regular season, he began to steal home. Carew was successful in his first six attempts to steal home. He would study the movements of the pitcher: how they held the ball while in the glove or in their hand and how they wound up. Whether he broke for home depended on how much of a walking lead he would get. Nolan Ryan found it humiliating to lose a game when a player stole home against him. He said, "I felt like a nickel" when Amos Otis slid safely across the plate with a theft of home after he delivered a 2 and 2 pitch. The Angels lost that game, 1–0. With Carew on third, Ryan would work from the stretch, which benefited the hitter because the third baseman was forced to hold the runner close, which opened up a big hole on the left side. Furthermore, the pitcher is often less effective pitching in the stretch than in the windup.[23] Carew garnered his first sixteen steals of home in only nineteen attempts for an 84.2 percent basestealing average. Melvin Durslag wrote the following in *Baseball Digest* in 1977 regarding his sixteen steals at that juncture of his career: "You may try to minimize this accomplishment, but to those artists especially gifted at stealing bases, the theft of home 16 times is the Pulitzer Prize, the Nobel Prize, the Congressional Medal and the Triple Crown, all in one."[24]

Rod Carew's first steal of home during his career came in the fifth inning on April 9, 1969, with Kansas City right-hander Roger Nelson standing on the slab. The theft of home gave the Twins a 3–2 lead but they lost, 4–3, in seventeen frames. The streaking Twins faced the Angels at Metropolitan Stadium in Bloomington, Minnesota, on April 19. Ted Uhlaender was the Twins leadoff man in 1969 as Carew batted out of the two hole. Uhlaender played predominantly center field and batted .273 with a .328 on-base percentage, 93 runs scored, and 15 steals. He went 3 for 4 on April 19 with two runs scored, while Carew was 1 for 5. Carew's only run of the contest was a steal of home. There was one out in the last of the seventh inning when he got a walking lead off reliever Hoyt Wilhelm and got about a third of the way to the plate before he broke for home. The steal of home tied the game at five. In the ninth inning, Uhlaender worked a base on balls and pilfered second. Carew made an out. And then Tony Oliva was passed intentionally to bring up Harmon Killebrew. Killebrew was a right-handed pull hitter who batted .276 in 1969, and led the junior league in homers (49), RBIs (140), walks (145), and on-base percentage (.427). The Angels went into the "Killebrew shift" and shifted their defense to the left side, but Killebrew crossed them up and went the other way, hitting the ball through the vacated right side to give Minnesota a 6–5 triumph. It was their fifth straight win.[25]

The Twins defeated the Seattle Pilots at Metropolitan Stadium on April 30 by a 6–4 score, winning their fifth straight game. Carew went 2 for 5, scored two runs and drove in two. The Twins scored four runs in the fifth stanza. With runners on first and second, the southpaw pitcher Tom Hall tried to lay down a sacrifice bunt. He did move the runners over, but also got himself a bunt single. Uhlaender followed with a two-run single and Carew reached on a fielder's choice as Hall scored on the play. Tony Oliva and Harmon Killebrew walked and then the Twins pulled off a triple steal as Carew stole home for the third time in April. Minnesota pulled off three triple steals in 1969. Oliva batted .309 during the season and led the AL in hits (197) and doubles (39). He also stole ten bags with an unimpressive 43.5 percent basestealing average. It was the sixth year in a row he stole ten or more. He collected 86 steals during his career with a 61 percent basestealing average. Killebrew stole only 19 bases during his Hall of Fame career with a 51.4 percent basestealing average. However, eight of his steals came in 1969 as he was caught stealing only two times. Minnesota swiped four bags on the 30th as Cesar Tovar (45 steals) also pilfered one. Tommy Davis and Jose Vidal stole bags for Seattle. Davis stole twenty bases in 1969, nineteen with Seattle, while Vidal pilfered one of his four sacks during his four-year career.

On May 18, Tovar stole third and home against Detroit's Mickey Lolich in the third inning. Then later in the inning, Carew stole second, third, and home. The two steals of home in a single inning tied a big league record. However, there was a price to be paid for their basestealing. Lolich beaned Tovar in his next at-bat with a pitch that nailed him in the head. The two steals of home accounted for the only two runs for Minnesota as Detroit won, 8–2. On June 4 in Bloomington, Minnesota, the Twins defeated the Yankees, 4–2. Carew went 3 for 4 with a double and two runs scored. He improved his batting average to .399. Graig Nettles drove him home with a sacrifice fly in the sixth inning for what proved to be the deciding run. In the eighth inning, Carew singled, advanced to second on a walk, took third on a fly out, and then stole home with Lindy McDaniel on the slab. He was on the front end of a triple steal. The Twins stole four bases in the game: two by Killebrew and one apiece by Carew and Johnny Roseboro (5 steals in 1969).

Also on June 4, the Cincinnati Reds rallied for three runs in the ninth to defeat Pittsburgh, 5–3, at Forbes Field. Cincinnati pushed across the go-ahead run when Woody Woodward scored from second on an infield single by Jimmy Stewart. The first run in the ninth was tallied when Johnny Bench singled, was sacrificed to second, and scored on pinch-hitter Fred Whitfield's single. Then Woodward pinch-ran for Whitfield and was sacrificed to second. Stewart then hit the ball up the middle over the second base bag and shortstop Freddie Patek ranged far to his left, gloved the ball, and tried to get Stewart at first. Meanwhile, Woodward rounded third and raced home. Stewart was able to beat the throw and collect an infield single and then he stole second. Catcher Manny Sanguillen overthrew the bag and Stewart went to third and scored on Bobby Tolan's double. It was simply a beautiful exhibition of small ball activity in the ninth inning by Dave Bristol's Reds. For Cincinnati it was their tenth victory in their last eleven games.

Tom Murphy, a 23-year-old right hander, was on the mound for the California Angels on June 16 when Carew and Oliva pulled off a double steal in the first inning for the Twins with Carew stealing third and Oliva taking second. The two baserunners didn't waste any time taking off again as they pulled off another double steal on the next pitch. For Carew it was his sixth steal of home during the season and at that time it was believed to have tied the AL record. The Twins won the game, 8–2.

The Twins were involved in a controversial play against the Royals on July 9. Johnny Roseboro, the Twins catcher, pushed Ellie Rodriguez's bat out of the way and threw out Bob Oliver trying to steal second. It took the umpires eight minutes to render a judgment at which time they declared that Rodriguez was out for interference and Oliver was sent back to first base. However, the out should have nullified the interference. The Royals won, 4–3. The Twins won both games of a doubleheader at Metropolitan Stadium on July 16, defeating the White Sox, 9–8 and 6–3. Minnesota stole five bags in the opener: two by Carew and one apiece by Tovar, Killebrew, and Charlie Manuel. For Manuel it was the only steal in a six-year big league career. Carew stole home in the game and it was reported that he broke the AL record and tied Pete Reiser for the major league record for seven steals of home in a season. Minnesota had two more steals in game two: one apiece by Killebrew and Frank Quilici, who had two of his three career steals in 1969. Walt Williams, the White Sox leadoff man, laid down a sacrifice bunt in game one, while Twins catcher George Mitterwald had one in game two.

The Cincinnati Reds defeated the San Francisco Giants, 6–4, on September 13. Bobby Bonds hit his thirtieth homer to become the fourth member of the 30–30 club. On August 13 he broke Willie Mays's San Francisco record with his 32nd steal. Mays stole 31 bases in 1958, which was the team's first season in San Francisco. Bobby Bonds had a terrific career and like his son, Barry, he possessed both speed (461 steals) and power (332 homers). Bobby joined the 30–30 club during five seasons: in 1969 and 1973 with San Francisco; in 1975 with the New York Yankees; in 1977 with the California Angels; and in 1978 with the Chicago White Sox and Texas Rangers. When he reached the 30–30 mark in 1978, it was only the tenth time in which that feat was accomplished. Bonds had a 73.2 percent basestealing average during his career. He stole over 40 bags during seven seasons, but never won a stolen base crown: 1969 (45), 1970 (48), 1972 (44), 1973 (43), 1974 (41), 1977 (41), and 1978 (43). Bonds had an impressive 91.8 percent basestealing average in 1969 and 88 percent in 1972. During his final few seasons, his stolen base average declined significantly, like in 1979 when he stole 34 bags for the Cleveland Indians at the age of 33 and had a 59.6 percent bases-stealing average. He laid down only sixteen sacrifice bunts during his career. In his first major league game on June 25, 1968, he hit a grand slam.

In 1970 stolen bases increased by 228 in the NL, which represented about a 28 percent increase. The senior league averaged 87.1 steals per team, which was the highest level since 1924 (94.3). The AL teams stole fewer bases than in 1969, a decline of 170, which was slightly less than twenty percent. Both leagues laid down nearly the same number of sacrifices: the NL had 819, while the AL had 811. The second-place Los Angeles Dodgers (87–74, NL West) led the NL with 138 steals, while the second-place Oakland Athletics (89–73, AL West) led the AL with 131. The Milwaukee Brewers finished tied for fourth in the AL West and led the majors with 115 sacrifices. Gene Mauch's Montreal Expos finished in last place in the NL East and led the senior circuit with 107 sacrifices. The Expos had 21 more wins in 1970 and a whopping 50 more sacrifices. Eddie Kasko's Boston Red Sox had by far the fewest sacrifice bunts in the majors with 34.

Bobby Tolan, the Reds 24-year-old left-handed center fielder, batted .316 with a solid .384 on-base percentage and led both leagues with 57 steals. Lou Brock finished second in the NL with 51 sacks and was followed by Bobby Bonds (48), Joe Morgan (42), and Willie Davis (38). Bert Campaneris won his fifth stolen base crown in the AL with 42 bags and was followed by Tommy Harper of Milwaukee (38) and Sandy Alomar of California (35). Pat Kelly (34) and Amos Otis (33) of the Kansas City Royals finished fourth and fifth. Pat Dobson, a pitcher with the San Diego Padres, led the NL with 19 sacrifices, while Cleveland middle infielder Eddie Leon led both leagues with 23.

Tolan batted .417 in the NLCS and stole a bag as the Reds (102–60) swept the Pirates (89–73) in three games. Dock Ellis, Pittsburgh's right-handed pitcher, laid down only four sacrifices during the regular season and then he had two sacrifices in game one of the NLCS. He pitched nine scoreless innings before the Reds tallied three runs in the tenth stanza. Baltimore (108–54) destroyed Minnesota (98–64) in three straight contests to win the ALCS, scoring seventeen more runs, 27 to 10. There were no stolen base attempts in the three games. Leo Cardenas of Minnesota and Paul Blair of Baltimore laid down the only two sacrifice bunts. Most of the experts picked Cincinnati to win the 1970 World Series, but Baltimore slugged ten homers to win four games to one. Brooks Robinson batted .429 and made sensational fielding plays at the hot corner. Bobby Tolan cooled off, batting only .211 in the series and stealing the only base. Both teams had two sacrifices: Blair and twenty-four-game winner Mike Cuellar laid one down for the world champions, while the Reds' eighteen-game winner Gary Nolan and backup outfielder Angel Bravo had one for the vanquished.

On July 14, the National League needed twelve innings to defeat the American League, 5–4, in the All-Star Game at Cincinnati's new Riverfront Stadium. Pete Rose exhibited his aggressive baserunning when he scored the winning run from second on Jim Hickman's single to center in the last of the twelfth and ran over catcher Ray Fosse. Amos Otis made a strong throw on the play. Rose felt that he had no choice but to run Fosse over because he was blocking the plate. Tommy Harper was caught stealing in this game. Sam McDowell, the Cleveland Indians left-handed pitcher, who would win twenty games in 1970, laid down the only sacrifice bunt.

On July 24, the New York Mets had the bases loaded in the last of the tenth before 53,657 fans at Shea Stadium when Tommie Agee stole home to give them a 2–1 win over the Dodgers. Relief pitcher Tug McGraw led off the tenth inning with a single. Agee tried to sacrifice McGraw to second, but reached on a fielder's choice when the Dodgers shortstop Billy Grabarkewitz dropped the throw to second and was charged with an error. Al Weis replaced McGraw at second as a pinch-runner and was picked off. Then Agee stole second and advanced to third on a wild pitch. Ken Singleton and Donn Clendenon walked with two outs. Jim Brewer, a 32-year-old southpaw reliever, had a 1 and 1 count on Cleon Jones when Agee took off from third on Brewer's next delivery and "blasted" into the catcher, Tom Haller, and the plate umpire, Shag Crawford. Gerald Eskenazi provided his observations in the *New York Times* and noted that all three of the men wound up in one pile and wrote, "The winning run came around in typical Met fashion — that is, the hard way." It was Agee's second steal of home. It was also his 23rd theft of the campaign, which tied him with Cleon Jones for the team record. Jones pilfered 23 bags in 1968. Agee batted .286 in 1970 with 24 homers, 107 runs scored, 75 RBIs, and 31 steals. The Dodgers pulled off a double steal in the eighth inning with Willie Davis leading the way. All four umpires made controversial calls during the game, including when the Mets thought they threw Davis out at third in the eighth. Frank Dezelan, the third base umpire, called him safe and manager Gil Hodges came out to argue.[26]

Lou Brock only stole home twice during his career. The second time was on August 6, 1970, when he stole home on the front end of a double steal in the first inning, while Joe Hague took a bag on the back end. The Cardinals shut out the Mets in that game, 3–0, behind the strong pitching of Nelson Briles.

Brock batted .313 in 1971 with a .385 on-base percentage and led the majors in both runs (126) and stolen bases (64). He had a 77.1 percent stolen base average and collected 200 hits, which was the fourth time during his career with 200 or more. In the American League, Amos Otis led the way with 52 steals and he was followed by Freddie Patek (49), Sandy Alomar (39), and Bert Campaneris (34). Otis and Patek stole 101 of the Royals' major-league-leading 130 steals, which was 77.7 percent of the team's stolen bases. Otis was a terrific hitter, fielder, and baserunner, who batted .277 lifetime with 54 sacrifices, 341 steals, and a 78.6 percent basestealing average. He scored 1,092 runs, drove in 1,007, and garnered 2,020 hits. In the field, he flashed the leather, and won three Gold Gloves as a center fielder. This 5'11", 166-pound, fly chaser was arguably the best center fielder during the 1970s, fielding his position with grace, magnificence, and by making many difficult plays look easy. In 1971 he won his only basestealing title and stole thirty or more cushions during five seasons. For twelve consecutive seasons from 1970 to 1981, he stole at least thirteen bags during each season. He had some impressive basestealing averages, like in 1970 when he stole 33 bags and was caught stealing only 2 times for a 94.3 percent average. The only times he was caught stealing that season was when he was picked off first base and when he was out trying to steal home on the front end of a double steal. When he won his stolen base title in 1971, he had an 86.7 percent basestealing average. He stole seven bases during the course of two consecutive games on April 30 and May 1, 1975, to tie the AL record. Bill James called him "the best percentage player on that team," and noted that Otis would read pitchers extremely well and occasionally notice a flaw in the pitcher's move, which enabled him to break for second base about a second before the moundsman released the ball. As a result Otis stole about fifteen bags each season while standing up.[27] When the Royals moved into Royals Stadium in 1973 they played on an artificial turf surface, which made the game faster and benefited teams that had an abundance of speed. Otis spent fourteen of his seventeen big league seasons with the Royals from 1970 to 1983 and played in the postseason five times. Amos Otis was known as A.O. and the Royals Stadium fans would chant "A-O, A-O!"[28]

Freddie Patek was a diminutive 5'5", 148-pound, shortstop who was far ranging with a strong throwing arm and highly skilled at turning the double play. Patek had excellent wheels and was aggressive while running the bases. His lifetime batting average stands at .242 and he compiled a .309 on-base percentage. Patek made his biggest impact on the bases, stealing 385 bags with a 74.6 percent basestealing average. He laid down 119 sacrifice bunts, including five seasons with ten or more. Patek stole 325 bases during eight seasons from 1971 to 1978 with totals of 49, 33, 36, 33, 32, 51, 53, and 38. In 1977 he stole a career high 53 bags and won his only stolen base title. His stolen base average that season was 80.3 percent.

In 1971 stolen bases declined in the NL by 145 and increased in the AL by 2 steals. Sacrifice bunts increased in both leagues, by 99 in the NL and by 73 in the AL. For the second season in a row, Gene Mauch's Montreal Expos led the NL in sacrifices (102), while Dave Bristol's Milwaukee Brewers led the majors for the second straight season, collecting 107. Earl Weaver's Baltimore Orioles (101–57) became the first team since the 1942 to 1944 St. Louis Cardinals to win over 100 games in three straight seasons. The Orioles finished tied for eighth in the junior circuit with 66 steals, but their 85 sacrifices were ranked second. Dick Williams's Oakland Athletics (101–60) won the AL West and accumulated 80 steals (4th, AL) and 80 sacrifices (5th, AL). However, they were no match for the Orioles in the ALCS as Weaver's club won in three straight games behind a pitching staff that compiled a league best 2.99 ERA during the regular season and a 2.33 ERA in the ALCS. It was the third consecutive season that the Orioles won the ALCS in three straight games. Neither Baltimore nor Oakland pilfered a bag. In the top of the second inning in game one, Dick Green, the Athletics weak-hitting second baseman, sacrificed catcher Dave Duncan to third and then Duncan, a man who stole only five bases in eighteen attempts during an eleven-year career, was caught stealing home with pitcher Vida Blue standing at the dish. Duncan took off for home on the suicide squeeze, but southpaw Dave McNally anticipated the play and delivered a pitch that Blue could not reach. Oakland's cleanup man, Tommy Davis, laid down a sacrifice bunt in game two.

In the NLCS, the Pittsburgh Pirates (97–65) defeated the San Francisco Giants (90–72), three games to one. Dave Cash and Manny Sanguillen stole bases for Danny Murtaugh's Pirates, while Ken Henderson and Willie Mays pilfered bags for Charlie Fox's Giants. Pittsburgh won the World Series in seven games as they stole five bags in the process, including two by Sanguillen. Mark Belanger stole the only base for Baltimore. Sanguillen stole only six bags during the regular season and then pilfered three in the playoffs. Pittsburgh collected four sacrifice bunts, two by Nelson Briles and one apiece by Jackie Hernandez and Bob Moose. Jim Palmer and Tom Shopay garnered sacrifices for the losing team. Hernandez's sacrifice came in Pittsburgh's three-run second inning at Memorial Stadium in game one. It was a successful squeeze bunt that sent Sanguillen across the plate and Hernandez moved to second on an error by catcher Elrod Hendricks, which was Baltimore's second miscue of the frame. The error proved costly as Hernandez scored on Dave Cash's single. However, Baltimore emerged victorious in the contest, 5–3, winning the battle before eventually losing the war.

On May 7, 1971, Joe Morgan had a great game with four hits, three runs scored, two RBIs, and two steals. The Astros won 8–1 at Philadelphia's new ballpark, Veterans Stadium, with its Astroturf surface. This fast surface helped Astros pitcher Don Wilson have a bunt double. Larry Bowa, the Phillies shortstop, ran towards third to cover the bag and the ball scooted past his vacated shortstop position. Detroit defeated Kansas City by a 3–1 score at

Tiger Stadium as they prevailed thanks to a four-base throwing error that scored two runs. Mickey Lolich laid down a bunt in the seventh inning and the Royals right-handed pitcher, Mike Hedlund, had difficulty fielding it. He tried to cut down Ed Brinkman at third base, but his throw was off target and went into the outfield. Brinkman scored easily and Lolich hurriedly ran around the bases and also scored on the play.

The Los Angeles Dodgers had their first Old-Timers Game on June 6 before a contest with the Mets. Dodger players from the 1950s took on the Dodger players from the 1960s. Despite being an active player with the Dodgers, Maury Wills played in the Old-Timers Game and stole a few bags with the encouragement of the fans. There were many famous Brooklyn Dodger players who participated, including Duke Snider, Pee Wee Reese, Gil Hodges, and 80-year-old Casey Stengel, who had a bird fly out of his hat when he raised it to the crowd after being introduced. The Dodgers won the regular game, 4–3, before 48,227 fans as the Mets ninth-inning rally ended with a line drive double play by Jerry Grote with the bases loaded to conclude the game. New York scored two in the fourth, but they also hurt themselves when catcher Duffy Dyer grounded into a double play. Wills batted in the leadoff spot and went 1 for 4. In his second to last season, the 38-year-old Wills batted .281 and stole 15 bags.

On September 6, the Cardinals emerged triumphant over the Phillies, 6–3, in the first game of a twin bill before dropping the nightcap, 2–1. Lou Brock stole four bags in game one for the second of three times during his career. The running Redbirds purloined six sacks in the opening game as Matty Alou and Jose Cruz also had one. And then Amos Otis stole five bags on the following day in a 4–3 win over Milwaukee. Otis batted third in the lineup and hit four singles. In the seventh frame, he collected a one-base hit with two outs, stole second and third, and scored the winning run after 19-year-old catcher Darrell Porter made a poor throw trying to throw him out at third base.

The 1972 season was the final American League campaign without the designated hitter, allowing pitchers the opportunity to hit. It can be assumed that a team's sacrifice hit or bunt total has a fairly large number of sacrifice bunts laid down by the pitcher. The fifth-place Montreal Expos led the senior circuit in sacrifices for the third straight season in 1972 with 108. Twenty-eight of those sacrifice bunts were laid down by pitchers or 25.9 percent of the team's total. The Oakland Athletics won the AL West title in 1972 (93–62) and paced the junior circuit with 100 sacrifices as 32 of them were laid down by pitchers. During the Deadball Era a very low percentage of the sacrifice hits were credited to pitchers. Bunting was a specialty of position players. When the 1917 Boston Red Sox compiled an all-time record 310 sacrifices, only 21 of them were credited to the team's pitchers, which was 6.8 percent of the team's total. During that same season the Cincinnati Reds had the fewest sacrifices in the majors and 16 of their 131 sacrifices (12.2 percent) were credited to the pitchers. However, when the Deadball Era ended, pitchers began to lay down more sacrifices and position players laid down less. In 1931, which was the first season since 1907 that sacrifice flies were not counted as sacrifice hits, the Pittsburgh Pirates led the majors with 130 sacrifices and 27 of them came from the team's pitchers, which was 20.8 percent. In 1943 when the St. Louis Cardinals had a whopping 172 sacrifices only 36 of them (20.9 percent) were laid down by the pitchers. The 1943 Chicago White Sox had the fewest sacrifices in the majors that season and 25 of their 72 (34.7 percent) sacrifices were credited to the pitchers. When the 1950 Brooklyn Dodgers led the NL with 88 sacrifices, 27 of them (30.7 percent) were credited to the team's pitchers. The Detroit Tigers led the AL with 110 sacrifices in 1950 and 32 of them were by pitchers (29.1 percent). The 1960 Cleveland Indians led the

AL with 97 sacrifices and 33 of them were by pitchers (34 percent). The 1971 Milwaukee Brewers had 42 of their major-league-leading 107 sacrifices (39.3 percent) credited to the pitchers. In 1969 the Montreal Expos laid down only 57 sacrifices and improved to 107 the following season. The 1969 Expos had 19 sacrifice bunts by pitchers (33.3 percent), while the 1970 version had 31 by pitchers (29 percent). Teams with more sacrifice bunts do not always have a lower percentage of them credited to pitchers when compared to teams with a low number of sacrifice bunts, however, this is often the case. The 1961 Cincinnati Reds were a first-place outfit, but they had the fewest sacrifice bunts in the majors (50). Nineteen of them were credited to pitchers (38 percent). The 1970 Boston Red Sox had only 34 sacrifice bunts and 19 of them (55.9 percent) were credited to pitchers. And the 1971 Kansas City Royals had the fewest sacrifice bunts in the majors (45) and 26 of them were credited to pitchers (57.8 percent).

During the first season of the designated hitter, sacrifice bunts declined sharply and then rebounded to levels that were modestly below the 1972 level. It wasn't until the 1980s that sacrifice bunts tanked in the AL. In the National League the percentage of sacrifice bunts attributed to pitchers increased towards the end of the decade and into the twenty-first century. The 1982 Los Angeles Dodgers led the NL with 106 sacrifices and 51 of them were laid down by pitchers (48.1 percent). For a team to compile 106 sacrifices is impressive, but what is really impressive is that the California Angels had more sacrifice bunts (114) than the Dodgers in 1982. Since the implementation of the designated hitter in the AL, there have been four AL teams to lead the majors in sacrifice bunts: the 1977 Texas Rangers (116), 1979 Minnesota Twins (142), 1980 Seattle Mariners (106), and the 1982 California Angels (114).

The 1988 San Diego Padres had the most sacrifices in the NL with 106 and 44 of them were credited to pitchers (41.5 percent). The 1998 Colorado Rockies had 45 of their 98 sacrifices (45.9 percent) credited to the team's pitchers. The 2004 Montreal Expos had 52 of their 100 major league leading sacrifices credited to pitchers. In 2007 the Colorado Rockies had the most sacrifices with 83 and 46 of them were by pitchers (55.4 percent). Meanwhile, the 2007 Chicago Cubs had the fewest sacrifices in the senior league with 48 and 20 of them were by pitchers (41.7 percent).

Lou Brock led the NL with 63 steals in 1972 and compiled a 77.8 percent basestealing average. He was followed by Joe Morgan (58), Cesar Cedeno (55), Bobby Bonds (44), and Bobby Tolan (42). Cedeno stood at 6′2″ and weighed between 175 and 200 pounds during his seventeen-year career. He was a talented right-handed center fielder with a good arm and the ability to field his position. Cedeno was also a good hitter with decent power (199 homers) and blazing speed (550 steals). He burst onto the big league scene in 1970 at the age of nineteen, batting .310 with 17 steals in 90 games and 355 at-bats for the Houston Astros. Leo Durocher managed him for part of the 1972 season and in 1973 and compared him to Willie Mays. However, the comparison ended with natural talent because while Mays had an ebullient personality, Cedeno was sullen and withdrawn. Durocher insisted he was often complaining about the umpires or because he didn't feel well. He also did not follow instructions from the manager. According to Durocher, Cedeno would often throw his bat and helmet after being punched out on a borderline pitch and continue to complain in the dugout. As a result he more than implied that the umpires had it in for him. Durocher wrote in his autobiography *Nice Guys Finish Last* that "I can tell you that just as sure as 2 plus 2 equal 4, I saw Cedeno steal second base so cleanly that he was sliding and on the way up. Out! One series, he was called out three straight times on bases he had stolen so cleanly that you could have umpired from the bench."[29] Cedeno could fly around the bases, stealing 550 lifetime with a 75.4 percent basestealing average. He stole 337 bags in six seasons from 1972 to 1977 with 55, 56, 57, 50, 58, and 61 swipes. He laid down only 32 sacrifice bunts during his career.

In 1972, Bert Campaneris won his sixth and final stolen base crown by pilfering 52 bags with a 78.8 percent basestealing average. Perhaps his final stolen base title was the most impressive if you consider that he batted just .240 with a paltry .278 on-base percentage. In addition to winning another stolen base crown in 1972, Campaneris also led the majors with twenty sacrifices. Larry Bowa of the Phillies paced the NL with eighteen. Bowa was a terrific defensive shortstop: wide ranging with quick hands and a strong throwing arm. He was skilled in the fundamentals of the game and was a complete small ball player with 318 steals and 151 sacrifices. He stole thirty or more cushions during three seasons, including a career high of 39 in 1974 and he stole twenty or more during nine seasons. As a 24-year-old rookie in 1970, he batted .250 and pilfered 24 bags. Bowa laid down eleven or more sacrifices during seven seasons.

Early in the 1972 season, the New York Yankees had a three-base wild pitch, but it didn't cost them a ballgame. On May 27 they had a two-base wild pitch and it did as they lost to the Tigers, 2–1, at Yankee Stadium. Cesar Tovar of Minnesota had taken advantage of the three-base wild pitch from Jack Aker on a ball-four delivery and raced from home plate to third base. Thurman Munson, the Yankees catcher, was largely to blame because he walked after the ball because he thought it was ball three. In the fifth inning on the 27th, Mel Stottlemyre bounced a pitch in the dirt that Munson couldn't handle as Mickey Stanley, who advanced to the gateway station on a walk, raced from first base to third base. The ball bounced about fifteen feet in the air and went towards the backstop. Billy Martin, the Tigers skipper, being the riverboat gambler that he was, decided it was time to shake things up. Ed Brinkman, a weak-hitting shortstop who batted .203 during the season and .224 lifetime, was ordered to bunt on the next pitch. It was not just any bunt, it was the suicide squeeze, as the third base coach whispered into Stanley's ear that it was time to take off. Brinkman bunted down the right side between the first base line and the pitcher's mound and Stanley raced across the plate. Ron Blomberg, the Yankees first baseman, came in on the grass and fielded the ball, but he didn't have a play at home and quickly realized that he wasn't going to get Brinkman at first. Joe Coleman, the Tigers pitcher, followed Brinkman to the plate and laid down a sacrifice bunt and Ed scored on Dick McAuliffe's single.

New York plated their only run in the seventh inning when Jerry Kenney singled and scored from first on a one-base hit by Horace Clarke. There were two factors that allowed Kenney to score from first base on a single: Clarke got his one-base hit on a two-out, 3 and 2 pitch, as Kenney was off and running with the delivery by Coleman. Secondly, Al Kaline was forced from the game in the second inning because of a strained muscle in his right calf. And therefore first-year player Paul Jata replaced him in right field and when Clarke hit the single, he threw to second instead of coming home with the ball. Dick Howser, the Yankees third base coach, was alert and noticed Jata's throw to second and waved Kenney home. After his run producing single, Clarke was thrown out trying to steal second with southpaw reliever Fred Scherman on the mound, who had just replaced Coleman after Clarke's hit. Clarke stole 18 bags in 24 attempts in 1972 and 151 during his ten-year career. It was the second time in Kenney's career that he scored from first on a single. New York had an opportunity to score in the second inning when Stottlemyre sacrificed runners to second and third, but Clarke flied out. The game ended on a double play grounder by Rusty Torres. Roy White stole one of his 23 bases of the season for the Yankees. White was a complete ball player except for a weak throwing arm and this skilled outfielder batted .271 lifetime with a .360 on-base percentage and a .404 slugging percentage. He stole 233 bases, but his stolen base average was on the low side (66.6 percent). White stole twenty or more bags during four seasons, including a career high of 31 in 1976. He also laid down 53 sacrifices.

Billy Martin's 1972 Detroit Tigers stole only 17 bags, which is tied with the 1949 St. Louis Cardinals and the 1953 St. Louis Browns for the third fewest steals in major league baseball's modern era. On June 7, 1972, the Pirates took two games from the Padres, 12–5 and 1–0 in eighteen innings. The Pirates pulled off a double steal in the eighteenth inning of the nightcap as Al Oliver and Willie Stargell purloined sacks. What made this accomplishment so unique is that Oliver and Stargell were the most unlikely of thieves that you will ever find pull off a dual theft: Oliver stole two bags in 1972 in six attempts, while Stargell's steal was his only attempt during the season. They won the game when Gene Alley worked a bases loaded walk. The National League needed ten innings to defeat the American League, 4–3, at Atlanta-Fulton County Stadium on July 23. The winning run scored when Nate Colbert worked a walk in the last of the tenth, was sacrificed to second by Chris Speier, and he scored on Joe Morgan's single. Morgan was awarded the Arch Ward MVP Trophy. Little Joe played excellent defense and also stole a base in the game. American League pitcher Jim Palmer had a sacrifice bunt. In the fourth inning in a contest between Kansas City and California on July 31, Amos Otis walked and then reached third on an errant pickoff throw by Nolan Ryan, which was one of three throwing errors he committed during the parsimonious affair. The next two hitters failed to drive Otis in and then he stole home with John Mayberry at the bat for the only run of the game. Rod Carew had a game-ending steal of home versus Cleveland with right hander Ed Farmer on the mound with two outs in the tenth inning on September 1. The Twins won, 5–4.

Johnny Bench stole only six bags during the 1972 regular season, but he stole two of Cincinnati's four bases in the NLCS as the Reds (95–59) defeated the Pirates (96–59) in five games. Al Oliver of Pittsburgh averaged less than one sacrifice bunt a season in regular season competition during his eighteen-year career, so he was not the most likely player to lay one down, but he did so in game five. The Oakland Athletics (93–62) also went the distance in their series with Detroit (86–70), winning three games to two. They stole seven bases, including two apiece by Campaneris and Reggie Jackson. In addition to being a terrific home run hitter (563), Jackson also stole 228 bases with a 66.5 percent basestealing average. He stole twenty-two or more during four seasons, including a career high of 28 for the 1976 Baltimore Orioles. Detroit failed to pilfer a sack: Jim Northrup was gunned down in game two and middle infielder, Dick McAuliffe, was caught stealing home in the eighth inning of game four. The Athletics won the finale, 2–1, at Tiger Stadium because they manufactured two runs and got strong pitching by Blue Moon Odom (five innings) and Vida Blue (four innings). Sal Bando had two of their three sacrifices in game five, one of which led to a run. But it was Reggie Jackson who stole the show, swiping two bags in the second inning, including a steal of home on the front end of a double steal. Oakland defeated Cincinnati in seven games to capture the franchise's first World Series title since 1930. They did so despite the fact that the Reds ran wild against the Athletics, stealing twelve bags, while Oakland swiped only one. Bobby Tolan led the way with five steals, while Bench and Morgan had two apiece. Cincinnati won the third game, 1–0, because of small ball. Tony Perez advanced to first on a one-base hit in the seventh inning. He went to second on a sacrifice bunt by Denis Menke and scored on a single by Cesar Geronimo. Statistically, the Reds dominated the series with a better ERA, 2.17 versus 3.05; more runs scored, 21 to 16; and fewer errors, five for the Reds and nine for the Athletics. Manager Dick Williams's Athletics won because they secured four one run victories. Oakland laid down six sacrifice bunts in the autumn classic, while Cincinnati had five. Campaneris and Menke had two apiece to lead their teams.

Stolen bases increased in both leagues in 1973, by 22 in the NL and by 205 in the AL. Naturally, sacrifice bunts plummeted in the AL in the first season with the designated hitter rule. There were 301 fewer sacrifice bunts in the junior circuit in 1973 and this represented a decrease of almost 34 percent. However, sacrifice bunts would increase sharply in 1974. The National League had 93 more sacrifice bunts in 1973 than in 1972, 958 to 865. The Cincinnati Reds led the majors with 148 steals, while the Montreal Expos had the most sacrifices (115), leading the NL for the fourth straight season. The Oakland Athletics led the AL with 67 sacrifices, while Earl Weaver's Baltimore Orioles led the AL with 146 steals. Weaver is often believed to have eschewed small ball strategies, so it may be surprising to some people that his team led the league despite not having one player finish in the top five in steals. Tommy Harper won his second stolen base crown in the AL with 54 bags. He was the first Boston Red Sox player to lead the league in steals since Jackie Jensen pilfered 22 sacks for the 1954 Sox. Billy North of Oakland finished second in the league with 53 steals. Lou Brock led the majors with 70 steals and was followed in the NL by Joe Morgan (67) and Cesar Cedeno (56). Ted Sizemore of the St. Louis Cardinals led the majors with 25 sacrifice bunts and he had 110 during a twelve-year career. While Mark Belanger was an outstanding defensive shortstop for the Baltimore Orioles, he wasn't much of a hitter, batting .226 in 1973 and .228 lifetime. He led the AL in sacrifices in both 1973 (15) and 1975 (23). The 6'1", 170-pound, right-handed player was a good small ball practitioner with 167 steals and 155 sacrifices.

Billy North was a terrific, wide ranging defensive center fielder, who batted .261 lifetime with a .365 on-base percentage. Bill James wrote that he was "underrated" in *The New Bill James Historical Baseball Abstract*, adding, "He couldn't throw the ball across a minivan, and he took a lot of grief for that, plus he played in conditions which depressed batting averages so much that he couldn't hit .300."[30] His weak throwing arm was his only liability in the field. North was a true speed merchant, who stole 395 bases and had a 70.9 percent basestealing average. He swiped 53 or more in 1973 (53), 1974 (54), 1976 (75), and in 1979 (58). The 5'11", 185-pound, switch-hitter won the AL stolen base crown in 1974 and 1976. He probably would have won the title in 1973, but he badly sprained his right ankle tripping over the first base bag on September 20 in a game versus Minnesota and lost a great chance to win the AL stolen base crown and an opportunity to play in the postseason. However, he played in the postseason with the 1974 and 1975 Athletics and the 1978 Dodgers. North had very little power and hit just twenty home runs during his eleven-year career and had a .323 slugging percentage. He batted .259 for the 1979 San Francisco Giants with a .386 on-base percentage, 87 runs, and a San Francisco record 58 steals, which was four short of the modern era Giants record. He missed twenty games that season because of an injury. George Burns stole 62 bags in 1914 for the modern era Giants record, while John Ward stole 111 in 1887 for the all-time record. North laid down 55 sacrifices during his career.

Peter Gammons of the *Boston Globe* wrote that the Detroit Tigers "finished their vacation prom with their fourth straight butchery" over the Boston Red Sox by an 11–7 score on April 19. Gammons also wrote, "And the local entry really looked bad. Woof-Woof bad." In the four-game set, Detroit scored 37 runs and had 56 hits, in their own version of the

Boston Massacre. Eddie Kasko's Sox were particularly bad in the pitching and fielding departments. Gammons described the double steal by 38-year-old Al Kaline (4 steals in 1973) and 30-year-old Willie Horton (1 steal in 1973) as "the insult of insults." The sequence that took place was as follows: 37-year-old southpaw hurler, Bob Veale, threw to Carl Yastrzemski at first when Horton broke for second. Yastrzemski chased after Horton while also keeping an eye on Kaline at third base. He threw over second baseman Doug Griffin's head to Luis Aparicio, the team's shortstop, who was backing up second. Kaline stole home and Horton found himself safe at the midway. Also of interest in this game, Yastrzemski slammed into second baseman Tony Taylor in the third inning. Reggie Smith hit a double play grounder to Ed Brinkman at shortstop. He flipped to Taylor, who jumped in the air to throw to first when Yastrzemski "hit him like Ty Cobb." Taylor's errant throw rolled towards the Red Sox dugout. Ike Brown, the Tigers first baseman, ran after the ball and dove a few yards from the dugout. This was not a good decision: he gathered the ball in, but skidded over the dugout steps and landed on his chin. The Red Sox, of course, watched patiently as the situation transpired and offered no assistance to Brown. Rick Miller, an outfielder with the Red Sox, called it "suicide," but also "a great play" and something that "you really have to admire." Detroit stole three bags in the game: one apiece by Taylor, Kaline, and Horton. Tommy Harper went 2 for 5 as the Red Sox leadoff man with a run scored and a stolen base. Brinkman laid down the only sacrifice bunt.[31]

At the age of 39, Luis Aparicio played his final big league season in 1973, batting .271 with a .324 on-base percentage and 13 steals in 14 attempts for the Boston Red Sox. On July 1, the Red Sox split a twin bill with Milwaukee at Fenway Park by losing the opener, 9–5, and taking the nightcap, 4–2. After scoring two in the first inning of the lidlifter, manager Del Crandall's Brewers tallied another run in the second on a double, a sacrifice bunt, an infield out and a single. Johnny Briggs had doubled, moved to third on Bob Coluccio's sacrifice, but was thrown out at the plate on Bob Heise's infield out, but Heise scored on a single by Pedro Garcia. Milwaukee scored two more in the third stanza and pulled off a double steal. But the primary story in this contest was the base that was pilfered by Aparicio, the 500th of his career.

Since the 1950s there had been a gradual decline in the amount of space allocated to small ball achievements in the articles produced by the sportswriters. For example, there are myriad games when a team executed a triple steal or a double steal and it was not mentioned in the story. Clif Keane of the *Boston Globe* wrote a column examining the intricate details of the doubleheader on July 1. There was no mention of Aparicio's major small ball achievement. He did, however, write a small 47-word piece about Aparicio's accomplishment on another page under the headline, "Luis hits 500."[32] Keane's approach was not unusual but emblematic of how some sportswriters felt towards small ball achievements. Aparicio's accomplishment took place in the sixth inning. It was the highest number of steals by an American League player since Eddie Collins retired in 1930. He was also the first player in the AL to reach the 500-steal plateau since Collins. There were no stolen bases in the second game of the doubleheader that day, but Tommy Harper, who batted sixth and went hitless in three at-bats, laid down a sacrifice. Aparicio batted seventh and also went hitless in three at-bats. These two players combined to steal 914 bags during their career and they were buried towards the bottom of the order.

The Oakland Athletics were able to repeat in 1973. They won the AL West with a 94–68 record and then defeated Baltimore (97–65) in five games to capture the ALCS. And then the Athletics defeated the New York Mets (82–79) in seven games to win the World Series.

Campaneris batted .290 with one homer and three steals. New York's inability to execute the fundamentals cost them dearly in game one as they lost 2–1. Wayne Garrett, the Mets leadoff man, popped up a bunt with Jon Matlack standing off first base in the fifth inning and it turned into a 1–3 double play right before Felix Millan hit a triple. Gene Tenace, the Athletics catcher, was caught stealing home in the third inning of the second game, a 10–7 Mets win in twelve innings. The Mets had four of the six sacrifice bunts in the series. Their inability to lay down a bunt had cost them a chance to win game one of the fall classic. But in the NLCS it was Sparky Anderson's Reds who failed to execute in the clutch. The score was knotted at two in game five when Garrett led off with a double in the bottom of the fifth inning. Millan stepped into the batter's box, willing to give himself up with a bunt, and move the potential go-ahead run to third base. The Reds botched the play and both runners were safe as the Mets went on to score four runs in the inning and break the game wide open.

In 1974 records that were once considered unbreakable were shattered. Hammerin' Hank Aaron became the all-time home run king when he connected for his 715th home run off Al Downing of the Dodgers at 9:07 P.M. EST on April 8. Lou Brock became the most prodigious thief in the history of the modern era for a single season when he stole 118 bags to break Maury Wills's 1962 record (104). While a direct comparison cannot be made between nineteenth-century thieves and the modern-era thieves, Brock was ranked third all-time in steals behind Hugh Nicol (138) and Arlie Latham (129). Both of the latter players achieved their feats in the American Association in 1887. However, when Rickey Henderson stole 130 bags in 1982, Brock dropped to fourth all-time and second in the modern era. In 1974, Brock batted .306 with a .368 on-base percentage, 105 runs scored, 35 extra-base hits, and 61 walks. His stolen base average was 78.1 percent, which is a good number for anyone, especially for someone who swiped 118 bags. Brock was an authentic speed merchant, but it wasn't only his foot speed that allowed him to break the stolen base record. In fact he turned 35 years old on June 18 and had slowed down considerably and was not as fast as he once was. Bake McBride, a 6'2", 187-pound, center fielder who batted left-handed but threw right-handed, patrolled center field and was considered the fastest player on the 1974 Cardinals. "Shake and Bake" McBride batted .309 in his first season as an every-day player and stole 30 of his career 183 bases. Brock achieved his accomplishment not by sheer foot speed but by intelligence, cunning, daring, and guile. He had been studying pitchers for years and could read them better than anybody else.

Manager Red Schoendienst's Cardinals finished second in the NL East (86–75), one and a half games behind Pittsburgh, and led the majors with 172 steals. Brock stole 68.6 percent of the team's bags and had more thefts than sixteen major league teams. Perhaps, not surprisingly, with so much speed the Cardinals didn't have to rely on the sacrifice bunt and had only 68, which was tied for tenth in the league, well behind the Atlanta Braves (109), who led the majors. In the American League the first-place Oakland Athletics (90–72, AL West) led the circuit with an impressive 164 steals, while last-place California accumulated 82 sacrifices, which was better than five National League teams. The Cincinnati Reds finished second in the NL West and were also third in the NL with 146 steals. Sparky Anderson's club led the majors with a 74.9 percent basestealing average. Stolen bases increased significantly in both leagues in 1974. In 1973 the NL teams stole 976 bags and averaged 81.3 steals per team, while in 1974 they stole 1,254 bases and averaged 104.5 per team. Likewise, the American League also saw a considerable increase from 1,058 in 1973 with an 88.2 per team average to 1,234 in 1974 with a 102.8 per team average. Sacrifice bunts increased in both leagues in 1974, by 25 in the NL and 159 in the AL.

Davey Lopes finished second in the NL with 59 steals, while Joe Morgan (58), Cesar Cedeno (57), and Larry Lintz (50), also finished in the top five. Lopes batted .263 during his sixteen-year career with a .349 on-base percentage, a .388 slugging percentage, and 557 steals. He stood at 5'9", weighed 170 pounds, batted and threw right-handed, played mainly second base, and participated in the postseason six times. Lopes hit 155 homers during his career, including ten or more during eight seasons and a career high of 28 in 1979. Not only did he steal bases, but did so efficiently with a terrific 83 percent basestealing average. During a seven season period from 1973 to 1979, he stole 371 bases with totals of 36, 59, 77, 63, 47, 45, and 44. His stolen base averages during those seasons were 69.2, 76.6, 86.5, 86.3, 79.7, 91.8, and 91.7. He led the NL in steals in 1975 (77) and 1976 (63). Lopes established a new major league record in 1975 by stealing 38 consecutive bags without being thrown out. In 1985 he batted .284 for the Chicago Cubs with a .383 on-base percentage, 47 steals, and a fabulous 92.2 percent basestealing average. That would have been impressive for any player, but especially for a 40-year-old man. And also consider he only played 99 games that season and had 275 at-bats. Bill James wrote regarding his 1985 accomplishment, "If you watched him play in those days he looked like he had arthritis, but he would steal second base standing up."[33] Lopes swiped twenty or more bases during thirteen seasons and laid down 74 sacrifice bunts. He was just as prolific stealing bases in the postseason, swiping nine in the NLCS to establish a record and ten in the World Series. Lopes stole five bags in the 1981 NLCS and four in the 1981 World Series.

Billy North led the AL with 54 steals and he was followed by Rod Carew (38), John Lowenstein (36), Bert Campaneris (34), and Freddie Patek (33). Felix Millan of the New York Mets led the majors with 24 sacrifice bunts, while Bucky Dent of the Chicago White Sox led the AL with 23. Interestingly, both Millan and Dent finished their careers with 121 sacrifice bunts. Millan had six seasons with eleven or more, while Dent had five seasons with thirteen or more. Neither one of them was a basestealing threat with Millan pilfering 67 bags and Dent only 17 in a twelve-year career.

Don Baylor stood at 6'1" and weighed between 190 and 210 pounds during his career. Baylor had power (338 homers), but he could also steal a bag (285 steals, 70.4 percent basestealing average). For eight consecutive seasons from 1972 to 1979, he stole twenty-two or more bases. During his rookie campaign in 1972 for the Baltimore Orioles he swiped 24 in 26 attempts and in 1976 for the Oakland Athletics, he finished fourth in the AL with a career high 52 steals and had an impressive 81.3 percent basestealing average. On June 15, 1974, the Orioles defeated the White Sox, 4–3, in eleven innings. Baylor pinch-ran in the ninth inning and had the most unusual of baserunning accomplishments: one steal and two caught stealing in a single inning. He tried to pilfer second and catcher Ed Herrmann's throw to second baseman, Ron Santo, was on the money. However, Santo dropped the ball and was charged with an error. Baylor later stole third and was caught stealing home because Andy Etchebarren couldn't lay down a squeeze bunt. Between 1987 and 1992 his unique baserunning accomplishment was matched in the NL four times.

On August 24, the Dodgers shut out the Cardinals, 3–0. Davey Lopes stole five bags and was caught stealing trying to pilfer his sixth base. He became the first National League player to steal five bags in a game since Dan McGann of the New York Giants turned the trick on May 27, 1904. Since McGann's five steals there had been five AL players who had stolen at least five in a game: Eddie Collins did it twice (6 steals each time), while Clyde Milan, Johnny Neun, and Amos Otis did it once. On August 30, the Cleveland Indians defeated the Texas Rangers, 7–3, at Arlington Stadium. Dave Nelson stole second, third, and home in the first inning, and it was only the third time this had been done in the big leagues since 1928. Nelson batted .236 during the season and stole 25 bags.

Despite losing to Philadelphia, 8–2, on September 10, Lou Brock stole his 104th and 105th bases to surpass Maury Wills for the most steals in a season. He stole his bases in the first and seventh innings after hitting a single. Both times there was a 0 and 1 count on batter Ron Hunt when catcher Bob Boone was unable to throw Brock out. Brock actually surpassed two records in this game as he also broke Max Carey's National League record of 738 career steals. His stolen base in the first inning was his 739th. Each time he was given the second base bag as a gift and after he broke Wills's record in the seventh, the game was halted for eleven minutes as the Cardinals dugout and bullpen emptied, as his teammates congratulated him at second base. Then they moved in front of the Cardinals dugout and James "Cool Papa" Bell participated in the ceremonies, congratulating the king of thieves. It was far from being a capacity crowd at Busch Memorial Stadium as the crowd numbered 30,812 for the Tuesday night game. But they were enthusiastic and vocal after he broke Wills's record, and they even threw firecrackers from the stands in a celebratory mood. Brock graciously thanked others for their help, including Ted Sizemore, who usually batted in the two hole, and therefore was his "partner in crime." He also thanked his fellow fly chasers Bake McBride and Reggie Smith, as well as Trainer Gene Gieselmann. As Brock approached the record the question that he was asked the most often was why at the age of thirty-five was he able to accomplish this terrific feat. He answered, "I can't explain it. All I can say is it's been a combination of a lot of things over the years. Speed has little to do with it." Despite the lopsided score the crowd refused to leave early. Jim Toomey, the Cardinals Assistant General Manager, said, "I've heard of them sticking around to see a guy hit a home run. But I've never seen 'em stick around to see a guy steal a base before."[34] In the ninth inning Brock advanced to first thanks to an error, tried to pilfer second, but he was cut down by Boone. "Lectrifyin'" Lou Brock was a great competitor, a gentleman, and the best stolen base artist since Ty Cobb had sharpened his spikes and terrorized the opposition.

The Cardinals won, 7–3, at Wrigley Field on September 29 as Chicago played poor defense. Don Kessinger, the Cubs shortstop, dropped a pop-up in the four-run sixth inning for the second Chicago error in the frame. "I just dropped it. No excuses," said Kessinger after someone asked him if the sun got into his eyes. The Cubs hit into four double plays in the game. Jim Marshall, the Cubs skipper, described the first St. Louis run as a gift, "we ran the base runner the wrong way." Lou Brock led off the game with a double to left field. When Sizemore hit the ball to pitcher Steve Stone, Brock was caught off second base but avoided the tag long enough to allow Sizemore to reach second. Brock was tagged out and later Ted Simmons, the fifth batter in the lineup, singled to right field for the first run. Brock went 2 for 5 in the game, including an RBI single. Stone made an errant throw on a sacrifice attempt by the pitcher John Curtis in the sixth inning, and then later Sizemore hit a pop-up behind the mound and Kessinger dropped it. Then Jose Cruz hit a three-run homer. Cruz would steal 317 bags during his career, including a career high of 44 in 1977 with Houston. The victory allowed the Cardinals to be tied with Pittsburgh atop the NL East (85–74) with three games left to play for each team.[35]

The Dodgers (102–60) needed four games to defeat the Pirates (88–74) in the 1974 NLCS. Walter Alston's team stole the only two bags in the series and they were both pilfered by Lopes. The Dodgers were a terrific small ball team with 149 steals (2nd, NL) and 86 sacrifices (4th, NL), while Danny Murtaugh's Pirates were not, with only 55 steals (11th, NL) and 54 sacrifices (12th or last, NL). Both teams laid down two sacrifice bunts in the NLCS. In the

ALCS, Baltimore won the opener, 6–3, but Oakland won the final three games to take the series as catcher Gene Tenace stole the only base of the series after swiping two cushions during the regular season in eleven attempts for a horrible 18.2 percent basestealing average. Both teams were excellent small ball outfits, with Oakland stealing more bases during the regular season, 164 to 145, but the Orioles laid down more sacrifices, 72 to 60. They laid down two sacrifices apiece in the ALCS: Mark Belanger had both of them for the Orioles, while Dick Green and Ray Fosse garnered them for the Athletics. The aggregate basestealing average in the series was a dreadful 14.3 percent, as each team was caught stealing three times. Baltimore's Paul Blair and Oakland's Herb Washington were each gunned down twice. Oakland went on to win their third straight World Series title, defeating the Dodgers in five games.

The opening game of the 1974 World Series took place at Dodger Stadium on October 12. Ken Holtzman, the Athletics starting pitcher, hit a double in the fifth inning and later scored on a squeeze bunt by Campaneris. Holtzman didn't last through the fifth inning but Oakland won, 3–2, as Rollie Fingers earned the win in relief. Herb Washington, a swift-footed pinch-running specialist, was picked off first base in the ninth inning of game two by Mike Marshall to kill a rally and Oakland fell short, 3–2. Washington had a unique two-year big league career. In 1974 he appeared in 92 games, scored 29 runs, and stole 29 bases with a not so impressive 64.4 percent basestealing average. Then in 1975 he played in 13 games, scored four runs, and stole two bases in three attempts. What makes Washington's career so amazing is that he never had a major league at-bat. All of his appearances were as a pinch-runner and a new baseball term was created when people began referring to him as a "designated runner."[36] Washington was a world-class sprinter, but he had no baseball experience. This experiment was widely criticized, but the Kansas City Royals Baseball Academy of the 1970s proved that you could turn athletes into good ballplayers with limited success. Oakland won the final three games to secure the world championship. They stole three bags in the series: Campaneris, Jackson, and North, while Los Angeles also stole three, two by Lopes and one by Joe Ferguson. The Athletics laid down seven sacrifices, including four in the opening game, while the Dodgers had three.

When the old baseball statistics were corrected by the amazing efforts by men like Gary Gillette, Pete Palmer, and John Thorn, they were not only correcting statistics during baseball's early years, but also statistics of a more recent vintage as well. The ninth edition of the Macmillan baseball encyclopedia has, for example, the stolen base totals listed incorrectly for five postseason series during the 1970s: the 1970 ALCS, 1972 ALCS, 1973 ALCS, 1974 NLCS, and the 1974 ALCS. Macmillan credits the Dodgers with five steals in the 1974 NLCS when they had two and they give Pittsburgh one steal when they should have none. Baseball-Reference.com lists the accurate totals and this is verified by reviewing the Retrosheet box scores.

In 1975 for the second season in a row a slow-footed Pittsburgh Pirates team (92–69) lost to a small ball juggernaut that accumulated large numbers of stolen bases. The Cincinnati Reds (108–54) could hit the long ball (124, 3rd NL), but they also led the NL with an impressive 168 stolen bases. They needed only three games to defeat the Pirates in the 1975 NLCS and scored twelve more runs than their opponents (19 to 7) and stole all eleven bases in the series. Joe Morgan led the running Reds with four sacks. The Reds ran wild in the 6–1 game two victory, pilfering seven hassocks. Most impressively, they had a perfect 100 percent basestealing average in the series as the Pirates catcher Manny Sanguillen couldn't throw out any of the burglars. This was not an aberration because they led the majors with an exceptional 82.4 percent basestealing average during the regular season.

The Oakland Athletics (98–64) were a battle tested aggregation having won three consecutive World Series titles and naturally were expected to defeat Darrell Johnson's Red Sox (96–65) in the ALCS. The Red Sox led the AL in batting average (.275), on-base percentage (.344), and slugging percentage (.417). But Oakland led Boston in the home run category (151, 2nd AL) and finished second in the AL with a whopping 183 steals, while Boston stole a measly 66 bags. However, Boston's pitching dominated the series (1.67 ERA) as they won in three straight and Oakland's basestealers failed to pilfer a bag, while Boston stole three: two by Juan Beniquez and one by Carlton Fisk. The Athletics did not even have a stolen base attempt.

One of the interesting things about the 1975 Athletics is that their stolen bases were distributed more evenly than many other teams with large numbers of steals. In the preceding seasons, if a team had a large number of steals they usually had one or two players with a large percentage of their thefts. This wasn't true during the Deadball Era, but became more commonplace after the first two decades of the twentieth century. For example, in 1973, Lou Brock stole 70 of the Cardinals 100 bases. However, with stolen bases once again becoming fashionable in the 1970s they began being compiled by more members of the team. In 1975, Claudell Washington led the Athletics with 40 steals, which was only 21.9 percent of their total. The California Angels, a last-place outfit, stole an exorbitant 220 bags and became the first major league team to steal 200 or more bases since the 1918 Pittsburgh Pirates (200). Manager Dick Williams's Angels also accumulated the highest total since the 1916 St. Louis Browns (234). Mickey Rivers led the team and the AL with 70 steals, 31.8 percent of the team's total. The 1975 Kansas City Royals were one of four major league teams and three AL West teams to steal over 150 bases (155). Amos Otis led the team with 39 steals, which was only 25.2 percent of the team's total. Davey Lopes led the NL with 77 steals, which was 55.8 percent of the Dodgers total (138). Meanwhile, Joe Morgan finished second in the NL with 67 steals, which was 39.9 percent of the Reds total. Some of the other prolific basestealers in 1975 included Lou Brock (56) and Cesar Cedeno (50) in the NL and Rod Carew (35) and Jerry Remy (34) in the AL.

The Cincinnati Reds won the closely fought 1975 World Series in seven games. This was an exhilarating series with tightly fought games like game six, which ended in the twelfth inning when Carlton Fisk homered off the foul pole to give Boston a 7–6 win at Fenway Park. The Reds won the third game, 6–5, in ten innings as each team hit three homers. Ed Armbrister of Cincinnati laid down a sacrifice bunt in the last of the tenth and hesitated out of the box. Fisk made a throwing error and the Sox's argument insisting there was interference was fruitless. Armbrister advanced to second base on the play, while Cesar Geronimo pulled into third and later scored the winning run on Joe Morgan's single. Once again the Reds dominated in the stolen base department, swiping nine bags, while Boston had none. Dave Concepcion stole three bases, Ken Griffey and Morgan stole two apiece, while George Foster and Tony Perez stole one. Boston accumulated more sacrifices, 4 to 2, but Cincinnati's second sacrifice led them to the promised land. In the top of the ninth inning in the seventh game with the score tied at three, Geronimo laid down a sacrifice bunt that moved Griffey to second. Griffey scored the final run of the series on Morgan's two-out single.

Sacrifice bunts increased in both leagues in 1975, by 99 in the NL and by 40 in the AL. The National League's 90.2 per team average was the highest level in the senior league since 1946 (112.6). Four National League teams had at least 104 sacrifices, including the fourth-place San Diego Padres who led the majors with 133. In the American League, the California Angels led the circuit with 97 sacrifice bunts. The Angels were a potent small ball team, but they needed to manufacture runs considering they hit only 55 homers, which was last in the majors. Enzo Hernandez of the Padres led the majors with 24 sacrifices, while Mark Belanger of the Orioles led the AL with 23.

On April 29, the Houston Astros exploded for an eight-run seventh inning, using the sacrifice bunt as an effective small ball weapon, as they prevailed over San Diego, 8–2. Roger Metzger, the weak-hitting Astros shortstop who batted eighth, tried to lay down a sacrifice bunt with runners on first and second and no outs in the seventh frame. Dave Freisleben, the Padres right-handed pitcher, tried unsuccessfully to cut down the runner at third, and Houston's starter J.R. Richard followed with a two-run single. This sequence was unusual because the eighth hitter rarely attempts to sacrifice with the pitcher on deck. It was even more perplexing because Richard was not an accomplished hitter, batting .203 in 1975 and .168 lifetime. The Astros stole three bags in the game and were credited with two sacrifice bunts.

In Houston's 6–2 win over Atlanta on July 6 they had four sacrifices, including three in the ninth inning. The number one and two hitters, Wilbur Howard and Greg Gross laid one down. As did rookie second baseman Rob Andrews and relief pitcher Mike Cosgrove. Perhaps Greg Gross found out he wasn't a basestealer during the previous season in 1974 when he stole twelve bags, but was thrown out twenty times for a pathetic 37.5 percent basestealing average. In a seventeen-year career, he batted .287 with 39 steals in 83 attempts for a 47 percent basestealing average.

On July 15, the National League won the All-Star Game, 6–3, at Milwaukee County Stadium as Lou Brock stole a base for the NL and Claudell Washington, George Hendrick, and Graig Nettles stole bags for the AL. There were six attempts as Dave Concepcion and Washington were thrown out. The four steals matched an All-Star Game record that was established in 1934 and also accomplished in 1948.

The headline in the *Los Angeles Times* on August 25 said it all, "Dr. Buckner Called for Surgery on Bat: Umpire Disallows Game-Winning Hit and Dodgers Are Beaten in 14th, 5–3." Ross Newhan began his article as follows: "Bill Buckner will soon undergo an operation on his ankle. Sunday, at Dodger Stadium, he was cited with malpractice for having performed illegal surgery on his bat." Buckner used a grooved bat in the sixth frame as a pinch-hitter and what would have been a game-winning hit was disallowed. Despite all the controversy surrounding this game it had significant small ball value. Davey Lopes, the Dodgers leadoff hitter, went 4 for 6 with one double, one run scored, one RBI, and three stolen bases. The three thefts brought his major league record of consecutive steals to 38. He hadn't been thrown out since June 4, but then in the twelfth inning Gary Carter threw him out trying to pilfer second base. Carter was also the catcher who threw him out in that June 4th game. There were four sacrifice bunts in this game, including two by Montreal's two-hole hitter, Jim Dwyer. Also on August 24, Lou Brock stole his 800th bag in a 6–2 Cardinals win over Atlanta. The only players with more steals in major league history were Ty Cobb (897) and Billy Hamilton (914).

In 1976 as the United States celebrated its bicentennial the National League celebrated its centennial season. If anybody had any lingering doubts that the stolen base had returned to its glorious heights than these doubts were assuaged in 1976. Chuck Tanner's Oakland Athletics did not steal the pennant like the 1911 New York Giants, but they had one helluva team, running wild on the bases, driving opposing pitchers to distraction, and stealing an American League record 341 bases. The only team in the modern era with more steals is the 1911 New York Giants, who swiped 347 bags. Three of the Athletics players had at least 52 steals: Billy North led the majors with 75, Bert Campaneris finished third in the junior circuit (54) and Don Baylor was fourth (52). Ron LeFlore of Detroit was second in the AL with 58 steals, while Freddie Patek of Kansas City was fifth with 51 thefts. Davey Lopes led the NL with 63 steals and was followed by Joe Morgan (60), Frank Taveras (58), Cesar Cedeno (58), and Lou Brock (56). Stolen bases increased by significant margins in 1976: In 1975 the NL teams stole 1,176 bases and had 98 steals per team. The NL increased to 1,364 steals in 1976, an average of 113.7 steals per team, which was the highest average in the senior circuit since 1920 (121.1). In 1975, the AL teams stole 1,348 bases and averaged 112.3 per team. During the 1976 campaign they increased their total by 342 to 1,690 steals. Their 140.8 steals per team average was the highest in the AL since 1917 when each junior circuit team averaged 158.5 thefts per team.

In 1976 there were six big league teams with at least 150 steals and all but one of them finished significantly over .500. The Athletics with their prodigious 341 thefts finished second in the AL West with an 87–74 record. They were beaten out by Whitey Herzog's Kansas City Royals (90–72), who finished second in the majors with 218 steals. After two seasons of playing at Shea Stadium, the Yankees moved into the newly renovated Yankee Stadium in 1976 and with Billy Martin as the skipper they won the AL East with a 97–62 record and stole 163 bases. Earl Weaver's Baltimore Orioles finished second with an 88–74 record and stole 150 bags. In the National League, the Big Red Machine was clicking on all cylinders and led the senior league in batting average (.280), on-base percentage (.357), slugging percentage (.424), runs (857), hits (1,599), doubles (271), triples (63), homers (141), walks (681), and stolen bases (210). They won the NL West by ten games, finishing with a 102–60 record, which was the best in the senior circuit. Bill Virdon's Houston Astros finished third in the NL West and stole 150 bags. There were eight teams with at least 144 steals and the two additional teams to meet this criteria, the Los Angeles Dodgers (92–70, 144 steals) and the Minnesota Twins (85–77, 146 steals), also had good records.

There were 107 fewer sacrifice bunts in the NL in 1976, when compared to 1975, which was a decline of a little more than 10 percent. The junior circuit had a modest 27 sacrifice bunt increase in 1976. For the second consecutive season, John McNamara's San Diego Padres led the majors in sacrifices, laying down 125. Gene Mauch was a strong advocate of small ball strategies and during his first season as the manager of the Minnesota Twins they led the AL with 93 sacrifices. Rod Gilbreath batted .251 for the Atlanta Braves in 116 games and led the NL with 20 sacrifices. Roy Smalley split the season between Texas and Minnesota and led the majors with 25 sacrifices. He batted .257 lifetime in thirteen seasons with 27 steals and 98 sacrifices.

Arguably the fastest runner in the major leagues in 1976 resided in center field at Tiger Stadium. As a young man Ron LeFlore got into trouble with the law and he said he used his terrific speed to run away from cops after throwing rocks at their cars. In January of 1970 he was arrested for armed robbery and sent away to Jackson State Prison, which was considered the toughest prison in Michigan. He joined the prison baseball team and became friends with Jimmy Karalla. LeFlore wrote the Tigers asking for a tryout upon his release, but they said no. However, when Billy Martin became the team's skipper things began to change. Karalla knew someone who knew Martin and he tried to get his friend to persuade Billy to sign LeFlore. The Tigers visited the prison in May of 1973 as part of a public service appearance and Martin decided to take a look at LeFlore's skills. By 1974, Ron LeFlore was in the big leagues, batting .260 with 23 steals in only 59 games. During his initial cam-

Ron LeFlore (left), a gifted basestealer, is honored by Lou Brock, who had accumulated the most steals in major league history by the time he retired. Brock stole 483 more bases than LeFlore, 938 to 455, but LeFlore's 50.6 steals per season average was slightly better than Brock's 49.4 steals per season. The two speed merchants also had similar basestealing averages: 75.3 percent for Brock and 76.2 percent for LeFlore. Brock won eight NL stolen base crowns and his 118 bags in 1974 broke Maury Wills's modern-era major league record of 104 steals in 1962. LeFlore stole a career high 97 bags in 1980 with Montreal and sported an impressive 83.6 percent basestealing average. (George Brace photograph).

paign his basestealing average was 71.9 percent. He batted .258 with 28 steals, but had a poor 58.3 percent basestealing average in 1975. And then he came into his own in 1976, batting .316 with a .376 on-base percentage, a .410 slugging percentage, 58 steals, and a much improved 74.4 percent basestealing average. These were all significant improvements: his on-base percentage during his first two seasons was only .301 and .302, while his 93 runs scored in 1976 was 27 more than the year before. He could have made a run for the stolen base crown in 1976, but a leg injury forced him to shut it down early and he only played 135 games. LeFlore found refuge between the white lines in 1976, dealing with the death of his younger brother Gerald, who was shot and killed in April.

When LeFlore began his major league career he was simply a raw, but talented young man, with little baseball experience since he didn't play the game as a boy. Unlike other players who were fundamentally sound after years in the bushes, LeFlore was learning the game at the big league level. From 1978 to 1980 he stole 68, 78, and 97 bases respectively with impressive stolen base averages of 81, 84.8, and 83.6. He led each league in steals: in 1978 with Detroit (68) and in 1980 with Montreal (97). After two seasons with the Chicago White Sox in 1981 and 1982, LeFlore completed his nine-year career with a .288 batting average, a .342 on-base percentage, a .392 slugging percentage, 455 steals, and a respectable 76.2 percent basestealing average. LeFlore averaged 50.6 steals per season, which compares favorably to the great basestealers. Lou Brock, for example, averaged 49.4 steals per season, while Davey Lopes averaged 34.8 and Maury Wills averaged 41.9. He laid down only fourteen sacrifice bunts during his career.

When LeFlore joined the Tigers in 1974, he had to deal with inhospitable fans, who verbally attacked him because of his race and criminal record. He also faced discrimination from the press box. Some writers appeared to find pleasure in the fact that an ex-convict was wearing Tiger "stripes" and leading the team "in what else?–stolen bases!"[37]

Frank Taveras, the 26-year-old shortstop for the Pittsburgh Pirates, finished tied for third in the National League with 58 steals in 1976 and had an 84.1 percent basestealing average. He was an inconsistent defensive shortstop, who batted only .255 lifetime with a .301 on-base percentage, a .313 slugging percentage, 300 steals, and a 73.9 percent basestealing average. From 1976 to 1979 he stole 218 bases with totals of 58, 70, 46, and 44. In 1977, he had a major league leading 70 steals and had a 79.5 percent basestealing average. The seventy steals shattered Max Carey's Pirate record of 63 steals in 1916. Carey passed away on May 30, 1976. Taveras laid down 67 sacrifice bunts during his eleven-year career with the Pirates, Mets, and Expos.

At the age of 34, Bert Campaneris batted .256 for the Athletics, stealing 54 bags with a good 81.8 percent basestealing average. On April 24 he became the seventh player in the modern era to pilfer five or more cushions in a game. He stole five bags as the Athletics defeated the Indians, 8–7. President Gerald Ford was among the 63,974 fans who packed into Veterans Stadium on July 13 to watch the National League win their fifth straight All-Star Game, by a 7–1 score. Despite excellent basestealers like Ron LeFlore, Freddie Patek, Mickey Rivers, Joe Morgan, and Cesar Cedeno in the game, there was only one stolen base, pilfered by Rod Carew. Dave LaRoche was on the hill for Cleveland on August 17 when George Brett stole home in the last of the tenth to give the Royals a 4–3 triumph.

Sparky Anderson's Cincinnati Reds (102–60) stole five bases in the 1976 NLCS as they swept the Phillies (101–61) in three games. Ken Griffey and Joe Morgan stole two bases apiece, while Johnny Bench also pilfered a bag. In game three, the Reds scored three in the last of the ninth for a come from behind 7–6 triumph. The winning run was able to score because Ed Armbrister sacrificed two runners into scoring position. And two batters later Dave Concepcion raced home from third on Griffey's infield single. Billy Martin's Yankees (97–62) needed five games to defeat the Royals (90–72) in the ALCS. Both teams ran the bases aggressively during the regular season and this continued into the playoffs as they combined to steal nine bags. However, neither team pilfered sacks at a good rate: Kansas City had a 50 percent basestealing average, while the Yankees were slightly better at 57.1 percent. Freddie Patek batted .389 in the series, but was caught stealing three times. The Big Red Machine swept the Yankees in the World Series as they stole seven bags, while Mickey Rivers stole the only base for New York.

After the exhilarating 1976 small ball campaign, stolen bases rose once again in the National League from 1,364 (113.7 per team) in 1976 to 1,555 (129.6 per team) in 1977. Despite the fact that the American League added two additional teams in 1977 (Seattle and Toronto), stolen bases declined from the previous year. In 1976 there were 1,690 steals (140.8 per team), but in 1977 the AL teams stole only 1,462 bases (104.4 per team), which represented a significant drop from the year before. Sacrifice bunts declined by 128 in the NL, which was a little more than thirteen percent and they increased by 99 in the AL, which represented a little more than a twelve percent increase. Interestingly, the 1977 and 1978 campaigns are the only seasons in which the AL had more sacrifice bunts than the NL since the designated hitter was adopted in the junior circuit. Of course, the junior league did benefit from having two extra teams, but the senior league's average sacrifice bunts per team (70.6) in 1977 was only slightly better than the junior league's average of 65.5 sacrifices per team. Thanks to expansion runs per team increased by 13 percent in the AL and home runs skyrocketed. In 1976 there were 1,122 long balls in the AL, which was 93.5 per team. However, in 1977, the junior league teams slugged 2,013 homers, which was 143.8 per team. Home runs also increased in the National League by 518, as did runs scored, an increase of 817.

In 1977 there were six AL teams with at least 105 steals and they all resided in the AL West. The last-place Oakland Athletics led the AL with 176 steals. Mitchell Page led the team with 42 thefts, which represented only 23.9 percent of the team's total. The Royals finished first in the AL West with a 102–60 record and stole 170 bags, which was second in the junior circuit. Both Oakland and Kansas City, the two most prolific stolen base clubs in the AL, also had the best stolen base averages. The Athletics had a 66.4 percent stolen base average, while Kansas City stole bases at a 66.1 percent clip. Despite having four managers during the season, the Texas Rangers finished in second place and had 154 steals, while fifth-place California had two skippers and stole 159 bags. In 1976 Chuck Tanner's Oakland Athletics stole bases at dizzying heights and in 1977 he moved on to Pittsburgh and just like the year before his rampaging runners finished in second place. The Pirates stole an exorbitant 260 bases, which was the highest total in the National League since John McGraw's Giants swiped 296 in 1913. The Houston Astros finished third in the NL West and stole 187 bags (2nd, NL), while second-place Cincinnati stole 170 bags (3rd, NL) and led the majors with a 72.6 percent basestealing average. Sparky Anderson's Reds not only stole large numbers of bases, but they were efficient. In 1977 they led the majors in stolen base percentage for the fifth straight season.

Whitey Herzog, a small ball advocate, managed the Kansas City Royals for part of the 1975 campaign and for four complete seasons from 1976 to 1979 before moving on to the St. Louis Cardinals. He compiled a 410–304 record (.574) as the manager of the Royals and then this master tactician was fired after the 1979 campaign by an ungrateful owner. Herzog then went to St. Louis and put together an 822–728 record (.530) in eleven seasons with the Cardinals. During his four complete seasons in Kansas City from 1976 to 1979, the Royals finished first in the AL West three times (1976–1978) and second once (1979). Herzog's Royals stole 811 bases from 1976 to 1979 and averaged an exorbitant 202.8 steals per season. They led the majors in 1978 (216) and in 1979 (207). Not only were they running the bases aggressively on the carpet at Royals Stadium, but most importantly they were winning. Despite being competitive with the Yankees in the postseason, they lost three straight ALCS's to them from 1976 to 1978 and this led to Herzog's downfall in Kansas City. Additionally, he didn't get along with the owner.

Freddie Patek led the AL with 53 steals and he was followed by Mitchell Page of Oakland (42), Jerry Remy of California (41), Bobby Bonds of California (41), and Ron LeFlore (39). In the NL, Frank Taveras led the circuit with 70 steals and was followed by Cesar Cedeno (61), Gene Richards of San Diego (56), Omar Moreno of Pittsburgh (53), and Joe Morgan (49). Both Mitchell Page and Gene Richards put together terrific rookie campaigns in 1977, batting .307 and .290 respectively. Page stole 42 bags at a superb 89.4 percent clip, while Richards garnered 56 cushions at an 82.4 percent rate.

John McNamara managed the San Diego Padres for only 48 games in 1977, and perhaps as a result the Padres sacrifice bunt total plummeted by 35 as they finished with 90. McNamara's Padres led the majors in sacrifice bunts during the 1975 (133) and 1976 (125) seasons. Despite the decline in 1977 their 90 sacrifices was good enough to lead the National League, but it wasn't good enough to lead the majors as the Texas Rangers laid down 116 sacrifices. The fifth-place Cleveland Indians also laid down more sacrifices than the Padres with 94. Three American League teams had 81 sacrifices: Minnesota along with the two expansion teams, Seattle and Toronto. Bill Almon, the Padres shortstop, batted .261 with 20 steals and an NL leading 20 sacrifice bunts. In Bert Campaneris's first season with Texas, he batted .254 with 27 steals, while his stolen base average declined from 81.8 percent in 1976 to only 57.4 percent in 1977. He led the majors with a whopping forty sacrifices.

Skip Jutze was a 5'11", 190-pound, catcher who batted .220 for Seattle in 1977 and failed to steal a base in four attempts. During his six-year big league career, he batted .215 with one steal in seven attempts. He tried to steal home two times on May 22 in a 6–2 triumph over Oakland and each time he was thrown out. Vida Blue was on the bump and Earl Williams behind the plate for Oakland and they combined to catch three runners stealing home, including two in the fourth frame.

The 2006 ESPN Baseball Encyclopedia and other up-to-date baseball encyclopedias of the twenty-first century credit Ty Cobb with 897 steals. However, when Lou Brock stole his 892nd and 893rd career bases on August 29 in a 4–3 Cardinals loss at San Diego Stadium, the newspapers around the country lauded Brock for breaking Cobb's modern-era record of what was believed to be 892 steals. He stole second base in the first and seventh innings. Brock pilfered both bags against the battery of pitcher Dave Freisleben and catcher Dave Roberts. The game was stopped after the record-tying and record-breaking steals and Brock was presented the base. After the record-breaking top of the seventh when he apparently became the most prolific thief in baseball's modern era, Brock went out to left field and was surrounded by members of the San Diego Padres bullpen who wanted his autograph. Manager Vern Rapp decided to pull Brock from the game and give him some rest despite the fact that St. Louis was clinging to a 3–2 lead. Mike Ivie connected for a two-run jack in the eighth inning and gave the Padres a 4–3 lead, which they never relinquished. It was reported that Brock needed only 2,376 games to steal number 892, while Cobb did it in 3,033 games. However, those numbers are probably slightly off because of the discrepancy in Cobb's career total. Brock turned 38 on June 18th and batted .272 during the season with 35 steals and a poor 59.3 percent stolen base average.

The Braves defeated the Padres on September 11 by a 7–3 score. Atlanta pulled off a triple steal with Gary Matthews (22 steals), Biff Pocoroba (3 steals), and Pat Rockett (1 steal) involved in the thievery. Pocoroba and Rockett combined to steal only eight bases during their big league careers, while Matthews stole 183 bags during a sixteen-year career and had a 71.2 percent basestealing average. When the Pirates defeated the Expos, 6–3, on September 17 there was a legitimate record-breaking performance. Frank Taveras stole his 64th bag to break Max Carey's Pirate record.

For the second consecutive season the Yankees (100–62) needed five games to defeat Kansas City (102–60) in the ALCS. Whitey Herzog's club lost despite having a better ERA during the series, 3.27 to 4.50; scoring more runs, 22 to 21; hitting more homers, 3 to 2; hitting more triples, 3 to 0; stealing more bases, 5 to 2; and laying down more sacrifices, 2 to 1. The Dodgers (98–64) had the best ERA (3.22) in the majors during the regular season and their mound corps led them to a four-game NLCS victory over the Phillies (101–61).

Ron Cey, Steve Garvey, and Reggie Smith stole bags for Los Angeles, while Greg Luzinski pilfered the only bag for the Phillies. Los Angeles won the fourth and final game by a 4–1 score. They tallied two markers in the second and fifth innings. They silenced the hostile Veterans Stadium crowd with two runs in the top of the fifth as one run scored on a wild pitch and the second run scored because of Bill Russell's squeeze bunt, which turned into an RBI single. After being embarrassed in a four-game sweep by the Cincinnati Reds in the 1976 World Series, the Yankees bounced back and defeated the Dodgers in six games to win the 1977 world title. Mickey Rivers stole a bag for the champions, while Davey Lopes swiped two for Tom Lasorda's Dodgers. Billy Martin's team did not have a runner caught stealing, while the vanquished had four caught stealing for a poor 33.3 percent basestealing average. Rick Monday was caught stealing home in the top of the fourth inning of game two with pitcher Burt Hooton at the plate. It was recorded as a 2–5–2 on the scorecard and it did not prove costly as Los Angeles won the game comfortably by a 6–1 score. The Yankees collected all four sacrifice bunts in the series, including two by southpaw hurler, Don Gullett, in game one.

After capturing their first world championship since 1962, the Yankees looked as if they would fail to repeat and appeared buried by July 1978. Billy Martin disciplined Reggie Jackson and levied a fine and suspension, but George Steinbrenner backed his egotistical slugger and threw his skipper under the bus. Martin told a reporter, "The two of them deserve each other. One's a born liar, the other's convicted."[38] With the Boston Red Sox surging in the AL East with a fourteen and a half game lead, Bob Lemon replaced Martin as the Yankees skipper. The Yankees began to win under the leadership of Lemon, thanks partially to the new manager's calm disposition and the fact that several injured players had returned. They went into Fenway Park in early September and humiliated the Red Sox in a four-game sweep by scores of 15–3, 13–2, 7–0, and 7–4. This demoralizing defeat became known as the "Boston Massacre."[39] By season's end the Yankees and Red Sox were tied with identical 99–63 records. When Lemon's crew prevailed in the one-game playoff thanks to Bucky Dent's three-run homer in the seventh inning, Boston's collapse was complete.

For the third consecutive season the Yankees (100–63) defeated the Royals (92–70) in the ALCS, this time in four games. New York did not pilfer a bag, while the Royals stole six: four by Amos Otis, and one apiece by Pete LaCock and Hal McRae. Otis had a terrific regular season, batting .298 with a .380 on-base percentage, 22 homers, 96 RBIs, and 32 steals with an 80 percent basestealing average. Then he continued his hot hitting in the ALCS, batting .429 with a record four steals in a five-game playoff. For the second consecutive season the Dodgers (95–67) defeated the Phillies (90–72) in four games in the NLCS as Davey Lopes and Steve Yeager stole bags for the senior league champions. And for the second consecutive season the Dodgers lost the World Series to the Yankees in six games. New York pilfered five bags, including two by Roy White and one by speedster Mickey Rivers, while the Dodgers also stole five, including two by Lopes and one by the terrific basestealer Billy North. Both teams laid down one sacrifice bunt: Roy White for New York and Vic Davalillo for Los Angeles.

Stolen bases remained steady in 1978, while sacrifice bunts increased by 123 in the NL and by 99 in the AL. There were two teams that stole over 200 bases and they were both very good. Chuck Tanner's Pirates once again led the NL in steals (213) and finished second in the NL East (88–73) behind Philadelphia for the third consecutive season. Meanwhile, Whitey Herzog's running Royals won the AL West for the third straight season and led the majors with 216 steals. There were five teams with at least 108 sacrifices: San Francisco Giants (127), San Diego Padres (114), Los Angeles Dodgers (111), Minnesota Twins (109), and the Oakland Athletics (108). Ron LeFlore led the AL with 68 steals and he was followed by Julio Cruz of Seattle (59), Bump Wills of Texas (52), Miguel Dilone of Oakland (50), and Willie Wilson of Kansas City (46). In the National League, Omar Moreno led the circuit with 71 steals and he was followed by fellow Pirate, Frank Taveras (46), Davey Lopes of Los Angeles (45), Ivan DeJesus of Chicago (41), and Ozzie Smith of San Diego (40).

Ozzie Smith was a 23-year-old rookie shortstop for the San Diego Padres, who batted .258 with 40 steals in 52 attempts and led the majors with 28 sacrifices, which was three ahead of the AL leader, Bert Campaneris. "The Wizard of Oz" was one of the greatest defensive players in big league history, who led NL shortstops in fielding average eight times. He was also a capable hitter, who was one of the most talented all-around small ball players to ever walk between the white lines. Smith spent four seasons in San Diego and fifteen in St. Louis before completing his Hall of Fame career in 1996 with a .262 lifetime batting average, a .337 on-base percentage, 580 steals, a 79.7 percent basestealing average, and a whopping 214 sacrifice bunts. For sixteen consecutive seasons from 1978 to 1993, he stole at least 21 bases. He swiped a career high 57 bags in 1980 with San Diego and he matched that total in 1988 with St. Louis. During his first three seasons from 1978 to 1980, he laid down 73 sacrifices with totals of 28, 22, and 23. He captured the NL sacrifice bunt title in both 1978 (28) and in 1980 (23). Smith was an excellent contact hitter, which made him skilled at executing the hit-and-run.

Ivan DeJesus could also play the shortstop position extremely well. He batted .254 lifetime with 87 sacrifices, 194 steals, and a 68.8 percent basestealing average. DeJesus was involved in arguably the worst trade in the history of the Philadelphia Phillies when they sent Ryne Sandberg and Larry Bowa to the Chicago Cubs in exchange for DeJesus on January 27, 1982.

Omar Moreno was a gifted defensive center fielder, who was the leadoff man for the 1979 world champion Pittsburgh Pirates. He stole 297 cushions from 1977 to 1980 with totals of 53, 71, 77, and 96. The 6'2", 180-pound, left-handed fly chaser was caught stealing 92 times during those four seasons and had an aggregate 76.3 percent basestealing average. He captured the National League stolen base crown in 1978 and 1979, but when he purloined a career high 96 stations in 1980, Ron LeFlore stole one more base than he did to secure the crown. In 1982, which was his final season in Pittsburgh, he stole 60 bases to finish third in the senior circuit. Despite his sizeable stolen base totals he only scored over 100 runs one time, in 1979 (110), as he was hindered by a pitiful .306 career on-base percentage. He had his best season in 1979 when he batted .282 as Harry Walker, the hitting instructor for the Pirates, got him to discard his deleterious habit of trying to hit the long ball and persuaded him to chop down on the ball and use his speed. At the conclusion of his career, he had five seasons with at least 53 steals and had 487 in total with a 72.8 percent basestealing average. He laid down 52 sacrifice bunts, including a career high of 17 in 1978.

Julio Cruz was a weak-hitting shortstop, who batted .237 lifetime with a .321 on-base percentage in ten big league seasons with the Seattle Mariners (1977–1983) and Chicago White Sox (1983–1986). The 5'9", 165-pound, switch-hitter laid down 56 sacrifices and stole 343 bases with a good 81.5 percent basestealing average. From 1978 to 1982 he stole 242 bags with totals of 59, 49, 45, 43, and 46. His stolen base averages during those five seasons were 85.5, 84.5, 86.5, 84.3, and 78. Cruz split the 1983 campaign between the

Mariners and White Sox and stole a total of 57 bags with an 82.6 percent basestealing average. Maury Wills's son, Bump, garnered 196 steals during his career and a 75.1 percent basestealing average. He stole at least 28 hassocks during five of his six seasons, including 35 during his final big league campaign with the 1982 Chicago Cubs. Wills laid down 53 sacrifices, including 14 in 1979 and 15 in 1980. Miguel Dilone became a member of the Oakland Athletics in 1978 and stole 50 bags in 73 attempts despite batting only .229 with a .294 on-base percentage, collecting a paltry nine extra-base hits, and compiling only 258 at-bats in 135 games. He had only 59 hits and 23 walks which meant that he was probably trying to steal a bag almost every time he got on base. Dilone batted .341 for the 1980 Cleveland Indians and stole a career high 61 cushions, which was 22.8 percent of his career total of 267.

Willie Wilson was a 6'3", switch-hitting outfielder who weighed between 187 and 200 pounds during his career. Many people considered him the fastest player in the game. This speed merchant forced the infielders to move in while he was at the bat and put themselves at a disadvantageous position. Not only did the corner infielders have to play at a shallow depth, but the shortstop also had to move in, to give himself a chance to throw Wilson out on a grounder. Likewise, the outfielders had to play extremely shallow when he was on second base if they wanted any chance of throwing him out at the plate. He rarely ever hit into a double play unless he drilled the ball at someone or stumbled out of the batter's box. He turned singles into doubles; doubles into triples; triples into homers; stole bases efficiently and ran wild on the artificial turf at Royals Stadium, which was a perfect surface for a speed merchant like Wilson. Defensively, he had a weak throwing arm but he ran down everything west of the Mississippi River. Bill James wrote, "What I remember most is the routine plays ... the way he would materialize in front of a ball ripped down the left field line, cutting off doubles so quickly that hitters felt lucky to have a single. He ran effortlessly, fluidly, accelerated instantly, and ran without strides, all in one continuous, easy motion."[40]

Wilson had a cup of coffee with the Royals in 1976 and 1977. In 1978 he batted only .217 with a .280 on-base percentage, ten extra-base hits (8 doubles, 2 triples), and still managed to steal 46 bags with a 79.3 percent basestealing average despite collecting only 43 hits and 16 walks. Under the guidance of Whitey Herzog he worked hard to improve his swing and developed a batting style where he simply dropped the head of the bat on the ball. The hard work paid off in 1979 when he improved to a .315 batting average with a .351 on-base percentage and 37 extra-base hits. He also won his only stolen base crown that season, swiping a major league best 83 bags with a terrific 87.4 percent basestealing average. He batted .326 in 1980 with 79 steals in only 89 attempts and led the majors in runs (133), hits (230), and he finished in a tie with 15 triples. After concluding his nineteen-year career with the 1994 Chicago Cubs, he finished with a .285 lifetime batting average, a .326 on-base percentage, 1,169 runs scored, 2,207 hits, and 147 triples. Thirteen of his forty-one homers were of the inside-the-park variety. He laid down 64 sacrifices, including a career high of 13 in 1979. But most impressively, he stole 668 bags with a fabulous 83.3 percent basestealing average. From 1978 to 1992 he stole at least twenty bags each season and his basestealing averages were terrific. For example, in 1983, he stole 59 bags and had an 88.1 percent basestealing average and then he swiped 47 in 1984 with a 90.4 percent basestealing average.

Willie Wilson and Hal McRae singled on April 18 to begin a game against Toronto and then they pulled off a double steal. A batter was passed intentionally with two outs and then Amos Otis connected for a grand slam to propel the Royals to their eighth straight victory with a 5–0 triumph. On July 11, the National League won their seventh straight All-Star Game with a 7–3 victory over the junior circuit at San Diego Stadium. Larry Bowa and George Brett stole bases, while Richie Zisk, Rod Carew, and Davey Lopes were thrown out trying to steal a bag. Pete Rose of Cincinnati put together a 44-game hitting streak in 1978 and on July 19 he needed a bunt single in the ninth inning in a 7–2 win over Philadelphia to extend the streak. The Tigers were at Metropolitan Stadium in Bloomington, Minnesota, on August 22 and Ron LeFlore set a junior circuit record with his 27th consecutive successful steal. LeFlore broke Mitchell Page's AL record of 26 straight steals that was established in 1977 and he was chasing Davey Lopes, who stole 38 straight bags in 1975 for the major league record. Detroit won the game, 7–3, as LeFlore went 2 for 5 out of the leadoff spot with one run and one RBI.

Willie "Pops" Stargell had an embarrassing moment in the Pirates 12–11 win against the Cubs on September 19, sliding about ten feet short of the second sack on a stolen base attempt. Pittsburgh purloined six bags in the eleven inning affair and Chuck Tanner ordered his men to keep running despite a 10–2 lead in the sixth, sagely insisting that anything could happen in the salubrious hitting environment of Wrigley Field. Two days later the Pirates prevailed over the Cubs, 3–2, in fourteen frames. Matt Alexander pinch-ran in the fourteenth inning, stole second, went to third on catcher Dave Rader's throw into center field, and he scored after the center fielder, Bobby Murcer, hit him in the shoulder while trying to cut him down at third base. Alexander had terrific wheels and stole 103 bags in nine big league seasons with the Cubs, Athletics, and Pirates. He batted .214 lifetime in only 168 at-bats and 374 games and had a 71 percent basestealing average.

After finishing in second place in the NL East for three consecutive seasons, the Pittsburgh Pirates finally broke through in 1979 and won the division with a 98–64 record, edging out Dick Williams's resurgent Montreal Expos team (95–65) that won nineteen more games than the previous season. Chuck Tanner's Pirates embraced the song "We Are Family," an anthem that reflected the divergent and colorful cast of characters that came together as a cohesive unit. They could beat their opponents with power (148 homers, 2nd NL) and by manufacturing runs as their 98 sacrifices ranked third in the NL and their 180 steals were second in the circuit. The Pirates led the league in slugging percentage (.416), runs scored (775), and stolen base percentage (73.2 percent).

Bill Virdon's Houston Astros gave an aging Cincinnati Reds outfit (90–71) all they could handle in the NL West, finishing second with a 89–73 record and relying heavily on small ball activities, stealing 190 bags (1st, NL) and laying down 109 sacrifices (2nd, NL). Houston hit only 49 homers during the season, which was the lowest total in the NL since the 1946 Boston Braves slugged only 44 homers. And only fifteen of their forty-nine homers (30.6 percent) came in the spacious Astrodome. John McNamara was the new Reds skipper in 1979 and their 99 steals and 67.8 percent basestealing average were their lowest totals since 1971.

The Pirates swept the Reds in three games in the NLCS as both teams stole four bags and the Pirates pitchers' compiled a 1.50 ERA. Chuck Tanner's well-balanced offensive attack scored the winning run in game two in the top of the tenth inning as Omar Moreno led off with a single, was sacrificed to second by Tim Foli, and scored on Dave Parker's one-base hit. The Pirates won, 3–2, as they rallied late for the second straight game after winning the opening contest, 5–2, on Willie Stargell's three-run bomb in the eleventh inning. The Baltimore Orioles (102–57) needed four games to defeat the California Angels (88–74) in the ALCS as Earl Weaver's Orioles pilfered five bags, including two apiece by Al Bumbry and Pat Kelly, while Jim Fregosi's Angels stole two (Rod Carew and Carney Lansford). The Pirates lost three of the first four games in the 1979 World Series against Baltimore and then came storming back to take the final three games to win the world championship. Tanner's club failed to pilfer a sack, going 0 for 4 in stolen base attempts. The Orioles swiped two bags: Doug DeCinces and Eddie Murray. Pittsburgh laid down three of the four sacrifice bunts, including one by cleanup hitter, Bill Robinson, in game five.

The American League stole only eleven more bases than the National League in 1979, 1,497 to 1,486. Whitey Herzog's second-place Kansas City Royals (85–77, AL West) led the majors with 207 steals and had the junior circuit's best stolen base average (73.1 percent). Willie Wilson was the most prolific burglar in the big leagues with 83 steals and was followed in the AL by Ron LeFlore, who swiped 78, Julio Cruz (49), Al Bumbry (37), and Bump Wills (35). Omar Moreno paced the NL with 77 steals and was followed by Billy North of San Francisco (58); Frank Taveras (44), who played for both the Pirates (11 games) and the Mets (153 games); Davey Lopes of Los Angeles (44), and Rodney Scott of Montreal (39).

Gene Mauch loved the sacrifice bunt and therefore it was not surprising that his Minnesota Twins led the AL in sacrifices during three of his first four seasons managing the club from 1976 to 1979. However, it must have been a surprise to some observers to watch his fourth-place Twins lay down a major league leading 142 sacrifice bunts in 1979, which was 29 more than the San Diego Padres, who led the NL with 113 sacrifices and had its total augmented by the fact that the senior league did not use the designated hitter. Minnesota had 63 more sacrifices than California, who finished second in the AL with 79. Craig Reynolds, a good defensive shortstop with the Houston Astros, batted .265 in 1979 with a low .292 on-base percentage and he compiled career highs in steals (12) and sacrifices (34). He stole only 58 bases during a fifteen-year career, but laid down 124 sacrifices and led the NL in 1979 (34), 1981 (18), and 1984 (16). His 34 sacrifices in 1979 was the highest total in the NL since Harry Walker laid down 36 for the 1943 St. Louis Cardinals, which was a team that garnered an exorbitant 172 sacrifice bunts. In 1979, Rob Wilfong of Minnesota led the AL with 25 sacrifices, which was 29.1 percent of his career total (86). Wilfong was an excellent defensive second baseman, who batted only .248 lifetime with 54 steals, but in 1979 he had career highs in several categories, including batting average (.313), on-base percentage (.352), slugging percentage (.458), runs scored (71), RBIs (59), and stolen bases (11).

On May 2, Bobby Bonds of the Cleveland Indians connected for his 300th homer to go along with his 413 steals to become the second player after Willie Mays with 300 homers and 300 steals. Bonds homered off right hander, Moose Haas, as the Indians lost to the Brewers, 6–1. The San Diego Padres had existed as a big league outfit since 1969, but it wasn't until May 13, 1979, that one of their pitchers stole a bag. The Padres defeated the Mets, 5–4, and Randy Jones swiped second base.

Eddie Murray stole only 110 bases during a 21-year Hall of Fame career and ten of them were purloined in 1979. His most memorable theft most likely came on August 15, 1979, when he stole home in the last of the twelfth inning to give the Orioles a 2–1 win over the White Sox. Guy Hoffman, a 23-year-old rookie southpaw, was on the hill for first-year manager Tony LaRussa's White Sox when the game-ending steal occurred. Murray was hugging third, while Doug DeCinces was standing on first and the weak-hitting Benny Ayala was at the dish with two outs. Earl Weaver surmised that it was time for young Mr. Hoffman to commence his education. With the count 1 and 2 on the batter, DeCinces stumbled off the gateway station with a fake break, as if he were taking off for second in an attempt to divert the pitcher's attention. Hoffman stepped off the pitching rubber and faked two throws towards first base and when he turned around Murray was well on his way home with the winning run. Weaver admitted that he was reluctant to use this play because "it's something you want to keep up your sleeve." Furthermore, this deceptive maneuver did not always work. LaRussa, the Sox's young 34-year-old field general, insisted he wasn't fooled and outmaneuvered by the Orioles skipper, but conceded that Weaver found "the perfect time to use it." Hoffman admitted that the responsibility belonged to him and that he couldn't hear catcher Bill Nahorodny screaming at him when Murray broke for home. He admitted that he forgot about the runner at third once he got ahead of the count and focused only on the batter: "I ruled out anything else. My looking at first base cost us the game. If I'd looked at third, like I've been taught all my life, I'd have gotten him." Weaver refused to provide too many details of how the play works. He said that Hoffman was "in pretty good company," and he had used that play to defeat Oakland when Vida Blue first came to the big leagues. DeCinces said that the Orioles third base coach, Cal Ripken, worked with the players in perfecting the play and he signals the runner at first when it should be used. Once he stumbles at first base as if he were getting picked off, the runner at third has to be going at full speed towards home plate. Murray, who had reached first base on a single, advanced to second on a sacrifice bunt, and then went to third on a fly ball to center after tagging up, had stolen only two bases up to this juncture of the campaign. This contest was a well-rounded small ball affair, especially for the American League with two stolen bases and four sacrifice bunts.[41]

Lou Brock turned forty years old on June 18 and batted .304 during his final big league season with 21 steals in 120 games. The final stolen base of his career, number 938, came on September 23 in a 7–4 win over the Mets at Shea Stadium. Again, there was a reference to a statistical record which since has been changed. It was believed that Brock's 938th steal made him the all-time leader, surpassing Billy Hamilton's 937 steals. However, *The 2006 ESPN Baseball Encyclopedia* credits Hamilton with only 914 steals. The Red Sox and Tigers split two games on September 23 at Fenway Park as Ron LeFlore, the Tigers leadoff man, went 4 for 9 with six steals in the doubleheader. He stole four in the nightcap, including one in the top of the tenth inning and scored the winning run on Champ Summers's single to give the Tigers a 3–2 win.

Stolen bases skyrocketed in the NL in 1980, increasing their total by almost 24 percent from the previous season, 1,486 to 1,839. The NL teams stole 384 more bases than the AL teams in 1980 and their 153.3 per team average was the highest in the NL since 1916 (166). Three senior league teams stole at least 209 bases: the San Diego Padres (239), Montreal Expos (237), and the Pittsburgh Pirates (209). Ron LeFlore of Montreal (97) stole one more base than Omar Moreno of Pittsburgh (96) to win the NL stolen base crown. Dave Collins of Cincinnati (79), Rodney Scott of Montreal (63), and Gene Richards of San Diego (61), also had large totals. Collins batted .272 lifetime in sixteen seasons for eight major league teams and stole 395 bases with a 74 percent basestealing average. He stole 24 or more cushions during nine seasons.

In 1980 stolen base prodigy Rickey Henderson batted .303 with an outstanding .420 on-base percentage at the age of twenty-one. He also swiped 100 bases to lead the majors with a 79.4 percent basestealing average. The 5'10", 195-pound, fly chaser had debuted in 1979, batting .274 with 33 steals in 89 games. And by 1980 he was already showing the skills that would make him the greatest leadoff man in major league history, by collecting 111 runs, 117 walks, and 100 steals. With the precocious Henderson now running wild across American League infields, Willie Wilson's 79 steals was only good enough for second in the circuit. Miguel Dilone of Cleveland (61), Julio Cruz of Seattle (45), and Al Bumbry of Baltimore (44) also stole their share of bases. The Cincinnati Reds stole 156 bags and led the NL with a 78.4 percent basestealing average. However, they were surpassed by the Kansas City Royals, who had an 81.1 percent basestealing average. Perhaps it wasn't surprising that the Toronto Blue Jays, who finished last in the AL with 67 thefts, would also have the worst stolen base average (48.2 percent) in the majors. Similarly, the Atlanta Braves who swiped the fewest bags in the NL (73) also had the circuit's worst stolen base average (58.4 percent).

After collecting fewer sacrifices than the junior league in both 1977 and 1978, the National League led the rival circuit by only two in 1979 and by fifty-one in 1980. The fifth-place San Francisco Giants led the NL with 100 sacrifices, but they were surpassed by the last-place Seattle Mariners who had 106 sacrifice bunts. Ozzie Smith of San Diego stole 57 bags and led the majors with 23 sacrifices. Dwayne Murphy of Oakland stole 26 bases, which is tied for his career high and was also accomplished in 1982. And he led the AL with a career high 22 sacrifices. Murphy batted .246 lifetime with a .356 on-base percentage, 100 steals in 161 attempts, and 84 sacrifices.

The fiery Billy Martin became the manager of the Oakland Athletics in 1980 and his aggressive, daring style of play was a big hit with the fans. Billy was a volatile, capricious, and unpredictable personality and he embraced a style of play called "Billy Ball" that mirrored his personality. "Billy Ball" was a combination of aggressive baserunning, daring plays, small ball activities, the execution of the fundamentals and the willingness and ability to intimidate the opposition. Paul Dickson in the *The New Dickson Baseball Dictionary* quotes Red Smith as writing: "In Billy Ball, the players run. Rickey Henderson stole 100 bases last year, breaking Ty Cobb's American League record. They work the double steal, they squeeze and they steal home. They sacrifice and they hit behind the runner. They worry runs out of the opposition, while their pitchers hold the varmints off at the pass."[42] The term "Billy Ball" also became associated with Martin's violent outbursts and controversial behavior. It was not merely a reference to the manager's strategic philosophy, but a state of mind. Martin embraced the totality of small ball, not only with steals and sacrifices but with hit-and runs, squeeze plays, and the ability to move up a runner with a productive out. Oakland finished second in the AL West in 1980 with an 83–79 record. Their 175 steals was second in the circuit behind Kansas City, only ten off the pace, but their 68.1 percent basestealing average was far worse than the 81.1 percent rate of the running Royals. The Athletics laid down 99 sacrifices, which was also second in the AL. Martin was resorting back to old style baseball in more ways than one. He allowed his starting pitchers to finish 94 games, the most in the AL since 1946. Their 94 complete games was 46 more than Milwaukee (48), who finished second in the AL. Furthermore, they had 81 more complete games than the Cubs, who finished last in the majors with 13. This strategy certainly did not hinder their hurlers performance, as the mound corps put together a 3.46 ERA, which was the best in the AL. Oakland's attendance increased by nearly 175 percent in 1980, from 306,763 to 842,259.

Rickey Henderson stole home on April 20 as Oakland prevailed over California, 8–2, to secure a doubleheader sweep. Billy Martin's aggressive and fun style of play was slowly winning over the fans in Oakland. The small ball activities consisting of bunting, stealing, and using the hit-and-run were once again fashionable. The 7,062 partisans who showed up at the Oakland-Alameda County Coliseum on Saturday, May 3, were delighted to see two Athletic players steal home in a 5–3 victory over Detroit. Wayne Gross stole home in the second inning, which was one of only five steals he would have during the season. Then in the third inning, Dwayne Murphy stole home on the front end of a triple steal. It was reported that Jack Morris, a 24-year-old right-handed pitcher, became "so unnerved" by the daring baserunning that he had to leave the game after only three innings.[43] Oakland was off to a fast start and they were situated in first place. In 1979 they were 8–14 after 22 games, but in 1980 they reversed that and were 14–8. The Athletics stole four bases in the contest: two by Gross and one apiece by Murphy and Mitchell Page (14 steals). Kirk Gibson, a 22-year-old center fielder, stole one of his four bases on the season for Detroit and Alan Trammell (12 steals), who went 3 for 5 batting second behind Lou Whitaker, also stole a bag. Catcher Jeff Newman laid down a sacrifice bunt for the Athletics. The hard-working Kirk Gibson stole 284 bags during his career with a good 78.5 percent basestealing average.

Despite his aggressive baserunning, Pete Rose averaged only 8.3 steals a season and in 1980 he batted .282 with 12 steals for the Phillies. Interestingly, Rose had 44 extra-base hits during the season, but 42 of them were doubles as he led the NL in that category. On May 11 in a 7–3 Philadelphia win over Cincinnati, the 39-year-old Rose stole second, third, and home in a single inning to become the first NL player to do so since Jackie Robinson did it in 1954.

On Wednesday afternoon, May 28, the Athletics aggressive baserunning landed them into the record books before 4,094 fans in Oakland. The Royals were probably not anticipating an aggressive running display with two slow runners on the corners in the first inning. Kansas City's huge 6'7", 225-pound, right-handed pitcher Rich Gale was already unnerved when Dwayne Murphy and Mitchell Page had pulled off a double steal to score Oakland's first run. But surely, Gale must have thought, the slow-footed catcher Jeff Newman (3 steals in 1980), who was standing on first base and Wayne Gross (5 steals), who was standing on third, were not going to pull off any mischievous activities. But Newman took off for second with the pitch and after a few steps, fell flat on his face. John Wathan, the Royals catcher, fell for the trap, and fired the ball to Willie Aikens at first base. Aikens saw Gross sprinting for the plate and came home with the ball. Gross was safe and so was Newman who moved up to second on the successful double steal. Gale lasted only two-thirds of an inning, yielding four runs, and the Royals were done as they fell, 6–3. Two steals of home in an inning by teammates was certainly a rare trick. Minnesota had last pulled it off in the AL on May 18, 1969, and the St. Louis Cardinals last did it in the NL on September 19, 1925. Oakland stole seven bags in the game, while Kansas City pilfered one. Mickey Klutts, the Athletics shortstop, went 2 for 4 with an RBI and stole the only base of his 199-game, eight-year big league career. Billy Martin said that they worked on the trick play in spring training and that Gross's timing while breaking for home was "sensational." The Royals were psychologically damaged by the play. In the second frame, Tony Armas took off for second base with runners on the corners and Wathan just held the ball, not daring to try to get the runner at second and risk a steal of home. "They were paranoid by then," insisted Gross. Wathan gave credit to Martin and said he had heard of the trick play that was utilized in the opening frame, but never saw it. Newman said, "That play is designed for guys like me and Wayne who aren't considered fast runners. They're not expecting us to steal, so when I fell down they thought they'd caught me napping." Martin insisted that none of the teams in the Western Division scared him. Kansas City, he surmised, was not the same team away from the artificial turf at Royals Stadium. He added, "I still think we belong in the race. Besides, we haven't even used all our tricks." The Athletics were not hitting any more homers than the year before, but they were averaging an extra run per game.[44]

Ray Knight, the Cincinnati Reds 27-year-old third baseman, batted .264 in 1980 with one steal in three attempts. He stole only fourteen bags during a thirteen-year career and generated a pitiful 35.9 percent basestealing average. However, Knight was one of three players, including Phil Garner and Rod Carew, who stole a base in the 1980 All-Star Game on July 8 at Dodger Stadium, which was won by the National League, 4–2.

Rudy Law got a cup of coffee with the 1978 Los Angeles Dodgers (11 games) and returned to the big leagues in 1980, batting .260 with 40 steals and a 75.5 percent basestealing average. The 6'1" left-handed outfielder weighed between 165 and 176 pounds during his seven-year career and batted .271 with a .325 on-base percentage, 22 sacrifices, 228 steals, and a 77.8 percent basestealing average. Not counting his brief 1978 campaign, Law averaged 37.5 steals per season and stole 77 cushions with the 1983 Chicago White Sox, while compiling an excellent 86.5 percent basestealing average. He ignited the Sox offense out of the leadoff spot and helped lead them to an AL Western Division title. Furthermore, his 77 steals crushed the former White Sox record of 56 by Luis Aparicio in 1959. On July 27, 1980, his Dodgers defeated the Cubs, 3–2, in twelve frames. Law singled in the twelfth, stole second, and advanced to third on a poor throw by the catcher. He scored the winning run on a sacrifice fly. Jerry Coleman, the San Diego Padres skipper, facetiously insisted that the only way to stop Rudy Law from stealing was "to shoot him."[45]

When Ron LeFlore stole his 62nd bag in the seventh inning of a 5–4 Expos win against the Reds on July 28, he was then tagged out while reading the scoreboard. In 1980 LeFlore (97 steals) and Rodney Scott (63 steals) accounted for 67.5 percent of the Expos stolen bases (237). Furthermore, they became the greatest basestealing duo in the history of the modern era. Their 160 steals was later surpassed by Vince Coleman (110 steals) and Willie McGee (56 steals), who combined for 166 thefts with the 1985 St. Louis Cardinals. Omar Moreno joined the record books on August 20 when he stole his 70th bag in a 5–1 Pirates loss to the Astros. He had stolen seventy or more bags for three consecutive seasons, becoming the first player to do so in the twentieth century. The record breaking game for the two Montreal Expos speedsters came on September 11 in a 6–5 win over Chicago: Scott entered the contest with 58 thefts and LeFlore pilfered his 91st sack in the fourth inning to break the record for steals by two teammates, which was previously held by Lou Brock (118 steals) and Bake McBride (30 steals) with the 1974 St. Louis Cardinals. While Ron LeFlore was breaking a record in September of 1980, he also had to see one fall. On September 18, Willie Wilson stole second and third in the second inning in a 5–2 Royals triumph over California. The second steal was his 28th consecutive theft to break LeFlore's AL record. Jerry Mumphrey of San Diego stole his 50th bag on September 25 as the Reds defeated the Padres, 5–3. Gene Richards (61 steals), Ozzie Smith (57 steals), and Mumphrey (52 steals) helped the Padres become the first modern-era major league team with three players who stole 50 or more bags in a season. Not only did this trio steal 170 bags, but they were caught stealing only 36 times for a terrific 82.5 percent basestealing average. On September 30, the Athletics defeated the White Sox, 5–1, as Rickey Henderson stole his 97th bag to break Ty Cobb's single season AL record that was established in 1915. The 1980 campaign was truly a historic season for the great basestealers of the game.

The Phillies needed five games to win the exciting, tightly played NLCS, with the final four games going into extra innings. It was the Phillies first pennant since the Whiz Kids captured the flag in 1950. Philadelphia stole seven bags in the series, while Houston had four. Garry Maddox and Bake McBride had two apiece for the fighten Phils, while Terry Puhl also had two for Houston. Philadelphia had five sacrifice bunts in the NLCS, while Houston had seven, including three by Enos Cabell.

Jim Frey was managing his first big league season in 1980 with Kansas City and he benefited from the great team that was left behind by Whitey Herzog. They won the West with a 97–65 record, leading the junior circuit in steals (185) but also finishing last in sacrifice bunts (34). They went on to sweep Dick Howser's Yankees (103–59) in the ALCS. Amos Otis stole two bags and Frank White swiped one for the only thefts of the series. During the regular season, Hal McRae pilfered ten sacks and was gunned down only two times. But in the ALCS he was caught stealing three times and was largely responsible for Kansas City's poor 37.5 percent basestealing average. The only sacrifice bunt of the series was laid down by New York's shortstop, Bucky Dent, in the top of the first inning in game one. The Phillies needed six games to capture the world title as Larry Bowa stole three bags for the champions and Kansas City swiped six, including two by Willie Wilson. Interestingly, two of Kansas City's steals were by Clint Hurdle and Dave Chalk. Hurdle's only stolen base during his ten-year big league career (515 games) in regular season competition came in 1978 and Chalk stole 36 bags in 74 attempts during a nine-year career and had only one in 1980. Both of the World Series participants laid down two sacrifices: U.L. Washington and White for the Royals, while Greg Gross and Keith Moreland moved runners over for the Phillies.

During the truncated 1981 season when 713 games were canceled because of the players' strike, the Houston Astros led the majors with 79 sacrifices and the Montreal Expos stole 138 bags, which were nineteen more than the Cleveland Indians (119), who led the AL. Craig Reynolds of Houston (18) and Alan Trammell of Detroit (16) led their respective leagues in sacrifices. The stolen base crowns were secured by Tim Raines (71) and Rickey Henderson (56). Raines had a sensational season, playing in 88 of Montreal's 108 games, but was beaten out for the NL Rookie of the Year Award by Fernando Valenzuela. He batted .304 with a .391 on-base percentage and stole a major league rookie record 71 bags with a terrific 86.6 percent basestealing average despite playing in a little more than half the games of a normal season. From 1981 to 1984 he led the NL in steals and from 1981 to 1986 he stole an exorbitant 454 bags with totals of 71, 78, 90, 75, 70, and 70. His stolen base averages were equally impressive at 86.6, 83, 86.5, 88.2, 88.6, and 88.6. When his 23-year career ended after the 2002 season he was one of only five players with 800 steals in major league history and his stolen base average was most likely superior to the four players ranked ahead of him. There are no caught stealing statistics for Billy Hamilton's career and the statistics are incomplete for Ty Cobb's career. Lou Brock had a 75.3 percent basestealing average and Rickey Henderson had an impressive 80.8 percent basestealing average. Raines, meanwhile, stole 808 career bases and had a whopping 84.7 percent basestealing average.

Dave McKay's only theft in 1980 was a steal of home and he would have another steal of home in May of 1981. Billy North played for Dick Williams during the Oakland Athletics' 1973 world championship campaign. Williams was a huge fan of North, but was dismayed to see him perform well as a member of the San Francisco Giants against his Montreal Expos in early May. On Friday, May 8, North stole three bags, scored a run, and drove in one in a San Francisco victory. And then on May 9 he had perhaps the greatest game of his career when he hit a grand slam for his only homer of the season and hit a two-run double in an 8–2 triumph over Montreal at Olympic Stadium. After the May 8 game, Dick

Williams said, "I love Bill North. He played his butt off for me when we were together in Oakland and he's a hard-nosed player."[46] North played his final big league season in 1981, batting only .221 but with a respectable .354 on-base percentage and swiping 26 bases in only 46 games. Julio Cruz pilfered 43 sacks to finish second in the American League and he tied Willie Wilson's junior circuit record with 32 consecutive successful steals. The streak ended on August 10 when California's Ed Ott was able to throw him out on a pitchout.

Jerry White stole three bags for Montreal in the NL Eastern Division Playoff, while Andre Dawson stole two and Terry Francona pilfered one as they downed Philadelphia in five games. The Expos were caught stealing six times, while the Phillies were 0 for 4 in stolen base attempts. Perhaps the most questionable stolen base attempt was by Expos pitcher Steve Rogers, who was gunned down trying to steal third base in the eighth inning of game one. Montreal earned the right to play the Dodgers, who defeated the Astros in five games in the NL Western Division Playoff as both teams combined to steal six bags. Davey Lopes stole five bags in the NLCS for Los Angeles as they defeated the Expos, three games to two, to earn a trip to the World Series. Rickey Henderson stole four bases in the postseason, but after Oakland defeated the Royals in three straight games they were swept by New York in the ALCS. The Yankees defeated Milwaukee in the AL Eastern Division Playoff in five games as Jerry Mumphrey swiped a bag for them and Robin Yount stole one for the Brewers. Tom Lasorda's Dodgers won the 1981 World Series in six games against the Yankees. They swiped six cushions, including four by Lopes, who pilfered ten bags in the postseason. The Yankees stole four bases in the fall classic and had five of the nine sacrifice bunts.

In 1982 the National League stole more bases than the American League for the third straight season despite having two fewer teams. The senior circuit stole 1,782 bases versus 1,394 for the junior league. The most important weapon in the small ball arsenal, the stolen base, was ubiquitously utilized by all twelve NL teams. There were six NL teams with at least 151 steals and no team had below 128. The AL was a different story altogether, as Billy Gardner's last-place Minnesota Twins stole only 38 bags, while Billy Martin's Oakland Athletics disappointed with a fifth-place finish but led the majors with 232 steals and finished second in the AL with a 72.7 percent basestealing average, which was only fractionally worse than Kansas City (73.5 percent). Jim Fanning's third-place Montreal Expos stole 156 bags and led the majors with a 73.6 percent basestealing average. Rickey Henderson broke Lou Brock's single-season, modern-era stolen base record with 130 steals. Henderson had a good 75.6 percent basestealing average and broke Ty Cobb's 1915 record of 38 caught stealing as he was gunned down 42 times. But most importantly, Henderson pilfered sacks at a better rate than Cobb, who had a 71.6 percent basestealing average in 1915. However, Cobb's average was considered exceptional during that time period. Damaso Garcia of Toronto finished second in the AL with 54 steals and was followed by Julio Cruz (46), Paul Molitor (41), and Willie Wilson (37). Tim Raines won the stolen base crown in the NL with 78 thefts and was followed by Lonnie Smith (68), Omar Moreno (60), Mookie Wilson (58), and Steve Sax (49).

While Rickey Henderson should have been lauded for breaking the single-season stolen base record in 1982, instead he was ridiculed and denigrated by a small but vocal segment of the baseball population. Bill James had spearheaded a revolutionary movement called sabermetrics that sought to find objective knowledge through statistics. Their discoveries were often ground-breaking and they were well on their way to educating baseball people about the importance of statistics. For far too long managers had misvalued players and made decisions based on gut feelings instead of objective knowledge. While the sabermetric revolution certainly changed the game for the better, it also led to extremes on the opposite spectrum where some people want to evaluate players solely on statistics, excluding the human element.

In the *1983 Baseball Abstract*, James mounted a one-sided savage attack against Henderson in which he called him "selfish" for having the audacity to try and break the stolen base record. He said that his stolen base attempts hurt the team, insisted that the thievery only produced four and a half runs for the Athletics, and scoffed at the idea that he should be considered for the MVP Award.[47] Henderson batted .267 in 1982, but with a .398 on-base percentage and a .382 slugging percentage. For the second time in his career he amassed over 100 runs (119), over 100 walks (116), and at least 100 stolen bases (130). James was on the mark in saying that Henderson had no right winning the AL MVP, as that honor went to Robin Yount. Henderson had much better seasons during his other two 100-steal campaigns in 1980 and 1983. As for Henderson being selfish, well all players are selfish. Players are selfish when they refuse to hit the ball the other way to move the runner over and make a productive out, instead of pulling the ball and hitting a lazy fly to left field. During the nineteenth century, players were selfish when they refused to sacrifice bunt, making the team goals subordinate to their personal goals, because they would be charged with an at-bat and this would hurt their batting average and their salary. Players are selfish when they're trying to win the doubles title and instead of moving on to third with a ball in the gap, they jog into the middle bag. If a batter has a chance to hit for the cycle and he needs a single to accomplish this feat, he may stop at first base even though they could easily make it to second. Or if the batter needs a triple for the cycle, he may run recklessly to third despite knowing he has a small chance to make it and that he is most likely an easy out. With a deficit of two or more runs in the ninth inning and the bases empty, a batter may try to take low percentage home run swings instead of simply trying to get on base. Players are selfish who want to win batting titles, home run titles, doubles titles, or triples titles. If a pitcher has a clause in his contract saying he would get a bonus if he works 200 innings or wins 15 games, he may push himself when he is injured, knowing full well it is going to hurt the team. There are players who get upset and sulk because they're riding the pine and want to play every day. When a player is in the final year of his contract he often gives an extra effort that perhaps was lacking in previous seasons just so he could get a large multi-year contract when he becomes a free agent. Selfishness is inherent in all players. Rickey Henderson was selfish, but so were most of the other players in the game.

James wrote about how Dwayne Murphy, a left-handed batter who hit in the two hole, was always behind in the count, taking pitches for Henderson to steal second. This is a valid point. Ideally, you want somebody batting second who takes a lot of pitches regardless of where they are batting in the order. Murphy appeared to fit this role well because he drew a lot of walks, including a career high of 102 in 1980. But there are also a number of benefits to batting second behind a great basestealer. That batter will see more fastballs because the pitcher doesn't want to bounce a breaking ball and wants to give his catcher the best chance to throw the runner out; he may go to a slide step, which may lower the velocity on his fastball or lead to a hanging breaking ball; and he may become distracted and lose focus on the hitter. Juan Pierre and Luis Castillo batted one and two for the 2003 world champion Florida Marlins. When Pierre reached first base in the late innings of a close game against a right-handed pitcher, the opposing manager would often bring in a left-handed hurler with the sole purpose of dissuading Pierre from stealing a bag. The beneficiary of this approach was Castillo, a switch-hitter, who batted much better and with more power from the right side. From the left side Castillo is a slap hitter with virtually no power, but he has a different batting stance from the right side of the plate and could turn on a ball. Furthermore, with a fast runner on the bases, the defense may put itself in a disadvantageous position and Castillo would see more fastballs. Perhaps with a speed merchant like Rickey Henderson at third the infield could move in knowing that it is the only way to cut him down at the plate. Obviously, the batter has a huge advantage in this situation because the fielders could only cover a limited amount of ground.

Dwayne Murphy's batting average and on-base percentage declined every year from 1980 to 1983. In 1980 he also batted second when Henderson stole 100 bags and he had a respectable .274 batting average and a .384 on-base percentage. He proved that he was capable of doing well as the two-hole hitter. But then the number of times he reached base systematically declined the next three seasons as it appeared that he began swinging for the fences more often and by 1983 he concluded the campaign with a paltry .227 batting average and .314 on-base percentage.

James's other point of contention was the fact that when Henderson tried to steal 172 times in 1982, he closed up the hole on the right side. Murphy was a left-handed hitter and with Henderson on the gateway station, the first baseman is forced to hold the runner on, which opens up a huge hole on the right side. This is obviously a legitimate point by James, but is it better to have Henderson in scoring position or is it better to have him anchored at first base just so Murphy could have a big hole to hit through? While this is a debatable situation, most people would probably want Henderson in scoring position. If Henderson pilfers the second sack with no outs in the inning and then Murphy pulls the ball on the ground, Henderson moves up to third where he could score on an infield out, a fly ball, wild pitch or passed ball. Furthermore, when Henderson steals second base that takes away the most likely double play combinations. There is certainly a situation when it would be advisable for a basestealer to remain anchored at first base. If, for example, there was a feared slugger at the plate who was hitting homers at a prodigious rate, then it may be counterproductive to swipe a bag because the hitter is likely to be passed intentionally and therefore the stolen base resulted in taking the bat out of the slugger's hands. This is especially true if the next batter is unexceptional with the lumber. However, Dwayne Murphy was not that kind of hitter.

Ralph Wiley wrote the following criticism about sabermetrics in his article "Squeeze play: Baseball's troubling issue":

It is usually the American-born blacks' records and place that are resented instead of celebrated. For example, it's the stolen base that is denigrated as a weapon by baseball sabermaticians like Bill James, at precisely the time when a Rickey Henderson steals 130 bases in a season. There are sour grapes when a baseball man uses stats to tell you a stolen base isn't important. Any time a baseball manager will give up an out for a base, as with a sac bunt or groundball to the right side, any time a base is so precious, then it goes without saying that the stolen base must be important. Not the CS, the caught stealing, or stats of success rates, but the stolen base itself.

So Rickey Henderson becomes, in the media and our oral history of the day, a bad guy, "this guy," who did something meaningless, and refers to himself in the third person and, oh yeah (with a decidedly sour look), maybe the best leadoff hitter ever, whatever that means. Barry Bonds becomes somebody who is excoriated for the limitations of his personality, even though we do not know him as a late-night talk-show host, but as a big-league baseball player. That skill set is all that should matter. But anything to keep from judging him on those merits. Look at the personalities of most timeless baseball stars; Ty Cobb, Ted Williams, Joe DiMaggio— none of them was a day at the beach.

When Rickey Henderson stole two bags on June 1, 1982, in Oakland's 3–2 win over Boston, he had 51 steals in 51 games. Furthermore, his 51 steals were accomplished in fewer games than any player in big league history. He also hit a two-run homer in the game, his fifth of the season.

After two cups of coffee for ten games apiece in 1980 and 1981, Bob Dernier batted .249 with a .315 on-base percentage, sixteen extra-base hits, and 42 steals in 54 attempts during his rookie season in 1982. The six-foot, 165-pound, right-handed fly chaser stole 218 bags with a 77.6 percent basestealing average during a ten-year career with the Phillies and Cubs. In 1982, Gary Carter said, "It's nice to see a guy who doesn't have white man's disease."[48] This was a reference to the fact that blacks had dominated the stolen base category ever since Jackie Robinson integrated the game in 1947. And for Dernier, a white man, to be stealing a large number of bases was an anomaly in Carter's opinion. Carter may have been joking when he said that, but there were some people who held to these insidious stereotypes. Then why did the African American and Latin American players dominate the stolen base leaderboard after Robinson integrated the game? This obviously had to do with the fact that African Americans had a long history of using small ball strategies, especially aggressive baserunning. So if you're an African American youngster in 1947 and Jackie Robinson is your hero and you're watching him steal bases, run the bases aggressively and lay down bunts, then you're probably going to want to emulate him and do the same thing. This is also true of Luis Aparicio and the Latin American kids. If a young black boy is a fan of Willie Mays and Mays is stealing bases, then he is going to want to steal bases himself. Ever since Babe Ruth changed the game with his home run hitting, whites have gravitated more towards home run hitters as their heroes.

Marshall Edwards had one of his ten stolen bases of the season for Milwaukee on June 10 and Paul Molitor laid down a sacrifice bunt. Milwaukee's 9–7 win over Baltimore was thoroughly examined in Daniel Okrent's wonderful book *Nine Innings: The Anatomy of a Baseball Game.* He wrote the following:

> Some teams, though — Milwaukee and Baltimore among them — saw that a stolen-base-dominated offense was an illusion: the number of runs scored simply did not increase in proportion to the risk that constant running entailed. Earl Weaver viewed the steal much as he did the bunt: the risk of losing an out was costlier than the potential advantage of picking up an extra base. In his younger years, Al Bumbry stole bases with relative frequency, but the Orioles by and large eschewed hyperaggressive basepath tactics.[49]

Despite all the talk of how Weaver eschewed small ball strategies and built his philosophy around the concept that if you play for one run, you get one run, his Orioles compiled very respectable small ball statistics. During Weaver's seventeen season managerial career with Baltimore, which included managing for only part of the 1968 and 1985 seasons, the Orioles averaged 90.1 steals per season, which is counting the strike-shortened 1981 campaign. If you exclude the 1981 strike-shortened season, then his teams stole a respectable 93.1 bases per season. The Orioles stole at least 104 bags during five seasons with Weaver as their skipper: 1973 (146) when they led the AL in steals; 1974 (145) when they were ranked third in the junior circuit; 1975 when their 104 steals was good enough for fifth in the circuit; 1976 when they stole 150 bags, the fourth most in the circuit and the highest total accumulated with Weaver steering the ship; and finally 1980 when they were ranked sixth in the circuit with 111 steals. Furthermore, it wasn't just Al Bumbry who was stealing bases. Don Baylor led the 1973 Orioles with 32 thefts and there were eight players with eleven or more steals. Baylor also led the 1974 Orioles with 29 steals and there were three players with 26 or more. The 1976 Orioles were led by Al Bumbry (42 steals) and there were five players with 14 or more.

Weaver's Orioles also laid down a very respectable number of sacrifice bunts, averaging 55.8 during his seventeen seasons and 57.6 if you exclude the strike-shortened 1981 campaign. They were ranked second in the league three times: In 1968 (80); tied for second in 1969 (74); and in 1971 (85). In 1974 they finished third in the junior league with 72 sacrifices. However, his teams didn't do much stealing and sacrificing during his final two seasons in 1985 and 1986 when they stole 69 and 64 and had 31 and 33 sacrifices, respectively. The Orioles' respectable stolen base and sacrifice bunt totals do not indicate that Weaver hated small ball strategies as some suggest. Let's examine the number of sacrifices of a team that truly hated the sacrifice bunt. During J.P. Ricciardi's first season as the general manager of the Toronto Blue Jays in 2003, he let it be known that he was going to follow strict sabermetric orthodoxy and eschew small ball strategies. He truly hated the sacrifice bunt. That is not a pejorative, but something he was proud of, and he even boasted in August of 2003 that the team's goal was to finish with less than ten sacrifices.[50] From 2003 to 2007 the Blue Jays' sacrifice bunt totals were 11, 20, 21, 16, and 33, for an average of only 20.2 a season. Because of Weaver's limited small ball activities during his final three seasons, it may indicate that he developed a disdain for small ball strategies with the passage of time. But the totality of his career suggests that here was a man who was more than willing to play small ball. The Orioles' sacrifice bunt totals with Weaver as the skipper were augmented during his first five seasons because there was no designated hitter rule in the American League. However, they were ranked second in the junior circuit in sacrifices during three of those five seasons. During Weaver's seventeen seasons the Orioles were ranked last in sacrifices only twice: in 1979 when they were tied with Boston with 42 sacrifices and during the strike-shortened 1981 campaign when they laid down 26 sacrifice bunts. Furthermore, they were never ranked last in the AL in steals during Weaver's tenure.

One manager who truly disdained small ball strategies was Billy Gardner, the manager of the Minnesota Twins from 1981 to 1985 and the Kansas City Royals in 1987. During his three full seasons as a big league skipper from 1982 to 1984, his Twins finished last in the AL in sacrifices during each season with totals of 22, 29, and 26. Furthermore, they finished last in the majors in stolen bases in 1982 (38); 12th in the junior circuit in 1983 (44); and 13th in the junior circuit in 1984 (39).

The 1982 All-Star Game was played at Stade Olympique, which was better known as Olympic Stadium in the United States. On July 13 the National League downed the American League, 4–1, continuing their dominance over the junior league with their eleventh straight victory. Rickey Henderson went 3 for 4 with a run scored and a stolen base. The NL attempted five thefts, but were only successful two times. Tony Pena and Tim Raines were successful, while Steve Sax, Ozzie Smith, and Al Oliver were thrown out. On July 27, Henderson stole his 95th bag but was also caught stealing three times in an 8–7 thirteen inning loss to California. It was reported that Henderson was the first AL player with three caught stealing in a game since 1916. He stole his 100th cushion in a 6–5 win over Seattle on August 2 and scored the winning run on Dan Meyer's squeeze bunt. Glenn Brummer was a third-string catcher for the St. Louis Cardinals in 1982. He batted .234 in 35 games with two steals and he would steal four bases in twelve attempts during his 178-game, five-year major league career. When he had a game-ending steal of home on August 22 to give the Cardinals a 5–4 win over the Giants, he was perhaps the most unlikely player to ever accomplish this feat. He pinch-ran in the eighth frame and remained in the game to catch.

He fanned in the tenth and then singled in the twelfth, his first safety since July 16. Brummer made his way to third on a single and an infield hit and then with David Green at the dish with two outs and a 1 and 2 count, he stole home. Gary Lavelle, a 6'1", 200-pound, southpaw pitcher, was ignoring him and he took the initiative and slid under the tag of catcher Milt May. Dave Pallone, the home plate umpire, did not appear to give a signal on the pitch. The Giants insisted that the pitch was a strike and that the inning should have concluded, but Pallone was adamant that he ruled that the delivery was a ball.

Catcher John Wathan of Kansas City entered the record books on August 24 when he stole his 31st bag in a 5–3 win over the Texas Rangers to break Ray Schalk's 1916 record for steals by a catcher. Wathan stole a career high 36 bags in 1982 with an 80 percent bases-tealing average. On August 27, Henderson stole his 119th bag on a pitchout in the third inning to break Lou Brock's single-season modern-era record of 118 steals in 1974. He would steal four in the contest to push his total to 122, but his Athletics fell to Milwaukee, 5–4. The record-breaking theft was accomplished against the battery of pitcher Doc Medich and catcher Ted Simmons. On September 4, Jack Clark hit a two-out, three-run jack in the ninth inning at Candlestick Park to give the Giants a 5–4 triumph over the Cardinals. Lonnie Smith of St. Louis went 3 for 3 with three runs scored and five stolen bases. He became the eighth player in the modern era with at least five steals in a game and it was the ninth time it was accomplished since 1900.

Whitey Herzog's running Redbirds won the 1982 World Series by defeating Harvey Kuenn's Brewers in seven games. These two teams had contrasting styles that represented the philosophies of their managers. The Cardinals (92–70) manufactured runs, finishing first in the NL with 200 steals and fourth in the circuit with 87 sacrifices. Their 67 homers were the fewest in the major leagues, but they managed to finish fifth in the senior circuit with 685 runs scored as they led the league in on-base percentage (.334) and tied for the lead in triples (52). Harvey Kuenn, meanwhile, had begun his fifteen-year big league career with the 1952 Detroit Tigers when small ball was in the midst of the dark age and 61 steals by the Chicago White Sox was good enough to lead the junior circuit. He devised a philosophy that was cautious running the bases and his 1982 Brewers stole a modest 84 bags (8th, AL) and laid down 56 sacrifices (5th, AL). Harvey's Wallbangers pounded opposing pitchers into submission, connecting for a major league leading 216 homers, which was 149 more long balls than the crafty Cardinals. St. Louis did have a better pitching staff (3.37 ERA) than Milwaukee (3.98 ERA), but they also played in a league that averaged fewer runs per game. Buck Rodgers (23–24) began the season as the Brewers skipper and was replaced by Kuenn (72–43) after forty-seven games. Kuenn insisted that the players have fun and rescinded the rule which prohibited the players from drinking in the hotel bar on the road. With their new skipper leading the way, the Brewers began to take off in June and by mid–July they resided in first place in the AL East.

The Cardinals had no problem defeating Joe Torre's Atlanta Braves (89–73) in the NLCS, sweeping them in three games, as Ozzie Smith of St. Louis and Dale Murphy of Atlanta stole the only bases of the series. St. Louis collected five of the seven sacrifice bunts, including three in the third game. Tom Herr's sacrifice bunt proved critical in a 4–3 game two triumph. David Green singled to left field to lead off the bottom of the ninth, advanced to second on Herr's sacrifice, and scored the winning run on Ken Oberkfell's single. Meanwhile, the Brewers (95–67) needed five games to defeat Gene Mauch's California Angels (93–69) in the ALCS as both teams combined for three steals. Rod Carew stole the only base for California, while Marshall Edwards and Paul Molitor pilfered bags for Milwaukee.

It wasn't surprising that Gene Mauch's 1982 club would lead the majors in sacrifices (114), collecting eight more than the second-place Los Angeles Dodgers who led the senior league. In fact, the Angels led the AL in sacrifices during Mauch's five seasons managing the club in 1981, 1982, 1985, 1986, and 1987. California laid down five of the seven sacrifices in the ALCS, including three in game five, when they came up short by a 4–3 score. The most noteworthy sacrifice bunt was garnered by catcher Bob Boone. He had a bases-loaded sacrifice bunt in the second inning of game two that plated one run and advanced two runners into scoring position. The Angels prevailed in that contest by a 4–2 score at Anaheim Stadium.

In the World Series the Cardinals stole seven bags, while Milwaukee pilfered one. Willie McGee, Ken Oberkfell, and Lonnie Smith stole two apiece for the world champions. Lonnie played a major role in St. Louis's aggressive baserunning exhibition in game six of the fall classic. Smith reached on an error in the bottom of the third inning, stole second, advanced to third on a groundout to the second baseman with one away, and was caught stealing home. In the fourth inning, the running Redbirds plated a run with a well-timed squeeze play. Dane Iorg was standing on third base, a man who stole only five bases in twelve attempts during a ten-year big league career. He raced home on Tom Herr's squeeze bunt and the Cardinals were well on their way to a 13–1 blowout victory. Herr was credited with a sacrifice on the play as he was thrown out at first base. That was the only sacrifice of the series for St. Louis, while Jim Gantner laid down the only sacrifice bunt for Milwaukee in game one. The Cardinals wrapped up the series with a 6–3 game seven win as small ball prevailed over wall ball.

For the fourth straight season the National League stole more bases than the American League in 1983, 1,786 to 1,539. The senior league pilfered only four more bases than they did in 1982, but the AL increased its total by 145, which was more than ten percent. Eleven of the twelve NL teams had at least 124 steals as the fourth-place St. Louis Cardinals led the senior circuit with 207 thefts. There were three AL teams with at least 165 steals and they all resided in the Western Division: Oakland (235), Kansas City (182), and Chicago (165). The National League stolen base averages ranged from a low of 61.7 percent (Pittsburgh) to 75.8 percent (Montreal). The American League stolen base averages ranged from a low of 51.3 percent (California) to 79.5 percent (Kansas City). For the first time since 1968, excluding the 1981 campaign, neither league had a team with at least 100 sacrifice bunts. The San Diego Padres paced the majors with 89 sacrifices, while the Angels led the AL with 68 sacrifices. With John McNamara replacing Gene Mauch as the Angels skipper in 1983, the team laid down 46 fewer sacrifices than the previous season and they won 23 fewer games. Steve Rogers, a right-handed pitcher with Montreal, led the majors by collecting 20 of his 101 career sacrifices. He became the first pitcher to lead the senior or junior league in sacrifices since San Diego's Pat Dobson laid down 19 in 1970. Alan Trammell paced the AL in 1983 with 15 sacrifice bunts. Rudy Law (77), Willie Wilson (59), Julio Cruz (57), and Bill Sample (44) had high stolen base totals in the AL, as did Alan Wiggins (66), Steve Sax (56), Mookie Wilson (54), and Lonnie Smith (43) in the NL. Rickey Henderson and Tim Raines were the top burglars in each league as they both ran away with the stolen base title.

Rickey Henderson collected at least 100 runs (105), walks (103), and stolen bases (108) for the third straight complete season. He stole at least 100 bases for the third time in his career, an achievement that would later be matched by Vince Coleman. During the nineteenth century, Billy Hamilton had four seasons with at least 100 steals, three in the National

League and one in the American Association. In addition to having another terrific season stealing bases, Henderson also improved his stolen base average from 75.6 percent in 1982 to an outstanding 85 percent in 1983. However, he was surpassed by Tim Raines who won his third straight NL stolen base crown with 90 thefts and had an 86.5 percent stolen base average, which was a record for players who tried to steal 100 or more bags in a season. While Montreal languished with an 82–80 record, Raines thrived, stealing 65.2 percent of Montreal's 138 thefts and leading the majors with 133 runs scored. Furthermore, he batted .298 with a .393 on-base percentage, 32 doubles, 8 triples, 11 homers, 71 RBIs, and 97 walks. He had a banner day on September 27 in a 10–4 win over St. Louis at Busch Memorial Stadium, which included a three-run homer. He went 3 for 4 with a triple, a homer, two runs scored, four RBIs, and his 86th stolen base. Raines collected his 70th RBI in the game and became the first modern-era NL player with 70 steals and 70 RBIs in a season. Ty Cobb did it three times in the AL, in 1909, 1911, and 1915. He was the last player to do so before Raines turned the trick.

Dale Murphy, a powerful slugger for the Atlanta Braves, won his second consecutive NL MVP Award in 1983. When he stole his 30th bag in a 3–2 win over Los Angeles on September 24 at Atlanta-Fulton County Stadium, he became the sixth member of the 30 homer, 30 steal club. The game was knotted at two in the eighth inning when Bill Russell walked and Dusty Baker singled to put runners on the corners. Pedro Guerrero, who was described by Mark Heisler of the *Los Angeles Times* as "the boss Dodger, strong enough to bunt one into Noc-a-Homa's newly-reinstalled teepee," swung meekly at a Pascual Perez breaking pitch with the infield drawn in. Rafael Ramirez, the Braves shortstop, fielded it, took a look at Russell at third to freeze the runner and flipped the ball to Glenn Hubbard covering second for the force out. Russell, who had decent speed and stole 167 bags during his eighteen-year big league career, took off for the plate when Ramirez flipped the ball to second. Baker was "on top" of Hubbard at second, making it difficult for him to unleash a good throw to the plate. Hubbard's throw was described as "quick, weak" and "accurate" and it was good enough to get Russell with a bang-bang play and catcher Bruce Benedict applied the tag.[51]

Murphy drew a one-out walk in the ninth inning off right-hander Tom Niedenfuer. After an unsuccessful pickoff attempt, Murphy pilfered second base and just beat Jack Fimple's strong throw. Heisler made note that Murphy "is also the first Caucasian to reach 30–30 since Jackie Robinson broke the color line." This was Murphy's final stolen base attempt of the season and he finished with a terrific 88.2 percent basestealing average. With first base open, Chris Chambliss, a slow-footed runner, was passed intentionally to set up a potential double play. And then after falling behind 0 and 2, Ramirez worked the count even and then frustrated Niedenfuer by fouling off several pitches. Manager Joe Torre called his at-bat "just tremendous." In Tuesday's game he put the squeeze play on with Ramirez at bat with no outs and runners on the corners in a tie game. He bunted into a double play and Atlanta fans lambasted Torre as a result, wondering why a man who was batting .336 with runners in scoring position was told to bunt. But now he let Ramirez hit away and he muscled the ball into left field, just beyond the reach of the shortstop, and Murphy raced home with the winning run as Atlanta pulled within four and a half games of Los Angeles to remain alive in the pennant race. Dusty Baker, the Dodgers three-hole hitter, went 4 for 4 and stole his sixth bag of the season, while Ken Landreaux, their fifth hitter, went 0 for 4 and stole his thirtieth. Heisler began his column by writing, "Hope still rustled among the ashes of the Braves' dynasty. Late Saturday afternoon, a tough little Dominican named

Rafael Ramirez lined a Tom Niedenfuer pitch through the falling shadows and just over shortstop, a single in the gloaming that broke up the game."[52] At season's end the Braves would fall short, finishing in second place in the NL West, three games behind Los Angeles with an 88–74 record.

In 1950 the "Whiz Kids" won the National League pennant, but in 1983 that achievement was secured by Philadelphia's senior league aggregation known as the "Wheeze Kids." Despite being the oldest team in the majors, Paul Owens's Phillies (90–72) stole an impressive 143 bags (7th, NL) and laid down 80 sacrifices (5th, NL). The Phillies needed four games to secure the NLCS title over Tom Lasorda's Dodgers (91–71), as they compiled a 1.03 ERA and stole two of the five bases in the series. Philadelphia had only one runner caught stealing, while Los Angeles had three, including two by Mike Marshall, an undistinguished burglar who stole only 26 bases during an eleven-year career with an unacceptable 44.1 percent basestealing average. While the Dodgers were on their way to a 4–1 win in game two, Marshall was caught stealing home in the bottom of the fourth inning, 2–4–2–5 on the scorecard.

In 1983, Joe Altobelli replaced Earl Weaver as the Baltimore Orioles skipper and led them to a world championship with a team that relied on homers (168, 1st AL) and eschewed small ball strategies with 61 steals (11th, AL) and 46 sacrifices (8th, AL). Tony LaRussa's small ball proficient Chicago White Sox managed only three runs in the ALCS and were shut out twice while losing the series, three games to one. Eddie Murray and John Shelby stole bags for the AL champions, while Julio Cruz and Rudy Law stole two apiece for Chicago. Cruz and Law were the two best hitters for the Sox in the series, batting .333 and .389 respectively for a team that had a power outage and failed to hit a homer. Baltimore's great pitching stymied an offensive attack that displayed the potent combination of power (157 homers, 3rd AL) and speed (165 steals, 3rd AL) during the regular season. Tito Landrum of Baltimore and Joe Morgan of Philadelphia stole the only two bases of the World Series as Baltimore prevailed in five games. Morgan was the only player caught stealing as he was gunned down on two occasions. Neither team laid down a sacrifice bunt in the fall classic.

Despite having two fewer teams the National League (1,728) once again stole more bases than the American League (1,304) by a total of 424 in 1984. The NL teams stole a modest 58 fewer bases than in 1983, but the AL total dropped by 235, which was over 15 percent. The AL teams averaged 93.1 steals per team in 1984, which was the lowest level in the junior circuit since 1973 (excluding 1981) when the AL averaged 88.2 steals per team. The last-place Pittsburgh Pirates in the NL East were the only senior league team with fewer than 100 steals (96), while seven AL teams failed to cross the 100 steal plateau. The St. Louis Cardinals led the majors with 220 steals, while the Montreal Expos stole 131 bags and led both leagues with a 77.5 percent basestealing average. The Chicago Cubs' 154 steals (4th, NL) was noteworthy because it was the organization's highest total since 1923 when they led the NL with 181 steals. Bobby Cox's Toronto Blue Jays finished in second place in the AL East with an 89–73 record, which was the identical number of wins and losses they had in 1983 when they concluded the season in fourth place. They paced the American League with 193 steals and a 74.2 percent basestealing average. The 1984 stolen base champions were Tim Raines (75) and Rickey Henderson (66). Juan Samuel, a 23-year-old second baseman with the Philadelphia Phillies, set a rookie record with 72 steals.

The NL (809) had 183 more sacrifice bunts than the AL (626) in 1984. The fourth-place Los Angeles Dodgers in the NL West led the NL with 92 sacrifices, while the Seattle Mariners, an outfit that was tied for fifth place in the AL West, led the AL with 66 sacrifice bunts. The Houston Astros finished second in the circuit with 87 sacrifices and were led by Craig Reynolds (16), who won his third and final NL sacrifice hit title. The New York Yankees finished third in the AL with 64 sacrifices and were led by the league leader, Bob Meacham, who had 14.

Brett Butler was a gifted small ball practitioner who would have felt comfortable playing during the Deadball Era. In 1984 he stole 52 bags for Cleveland, which was the third best in the American League. The diminutive left-handed center fielder stood at 5'10", weighed 160 pounds, and excelled at place hitting, bunting, stealing, the hit-and-run, and outsmarting the opposition. The slap-hitting lead-off man didn't hit a lot of homers (54), but he drew a good number of walks (1,129) and never struck out more than 79 times in a season. He scored at least 100 runs during six campaigns. His 41 bunt hits in 1992 with the Dodgers was a major league record. Butler insisted that he wouldn't have had a seventeen-year big league career if he couldn't bunt. It made him a complete player. Hitting out of the left-hand side of the batter's box, he was especially skilled at the drag bunt, but he also excelled at the push bunt, sacrifice, squeeze and any other bunting play. The corner infielders would have to respect his bunting skills and they would play in and then

Brett Butler did not have great physical tools but he willed himself into a great player through hard work, perseverance, and intelligence. He was a superb small ball player and leadoff man, who batted .290 lifetime with a .377 on-base percentage, 147 sacrifices, and 558 steals. Despite stealing 38 bags or more during eight seasons, including over 50 twice, he never led either league in stolen bases. The left-handed slap hitter was an exceptional bunter, collecting a record 41 bunt hits in 1992 and leading the NL with 24 sacrifices that season. (George Brace photograph).

Butler would skillfully guide the ball through one of the enlarged holes in the defense. He laid down 147 sacrifice bunts during his career and led the majors in 1992 (24) with the Dodgers. On April 12, 1990, he exhibited his patience at the plate by walking five times to tie a major league record. Once he got on base he was a threat to run and he stole 558 bases during his career with a 68.5 percent basestealing average. From 1983 to 1993 he stole no fewer than 31 bags in each season and stole at least 41 in 1984 (52) and 1985 (47) with the Cleveland Indians; in 1988 (43) and 1990 (51) with the San Francisco Giants; and in 1992 with the Los Angeles Dodgers (41). However, despite his prodigious stolen base totals he often had poor or unexceptional basestealing averages, like in 1983 (62.9 percent), 1988 (68.3 percent), 1991 (57.6 percent) and in his final season in 1997 (60 percent). Ironically, some of his best stolen base averages came very late in his career: From 1994 to 1996 he stole 67 bags and had a 77.9 percent basestealing average, which was well above his career rate. This pesky singles hitter batted .290 lifetime with a .377 on-base percentage and amassed 1,359 runs and 2,375 hits.

Butler had good speed, but he wasn't a burner like Willie Wilson or Rickey Henderson. His high baseball intelligence was exhibited in the various kinds of stolen bases he employed. He was skilled at the delayed steal, which according to *The New Dickson Baseball Dictionary* occurs "after the ball has been returned to the pitcher or after the defensive team has started another play."[53] The delayed steal, a maneuver that is intended to catch the defense while they are asleep, also occurs once the catcher secures the ball from the pitcher and his inclination may be to lower his head and relax, while reflexively tossing the ball back to the pitcher. The runner can also take off while the ball is being returned to the pitcher. The New York Mets had a catcher named Mackey Sasser, who played for them from 1988 to 1992. He was a poor defensive backstop, who had great difficulty throwing the ball back to the pitcher and therefore had to lob the ball back. When Sasser would throw his parachutes back to the pitcher, Butler would pick his pocket all day, stealing second and then third. It was the most unfortunate thing to watch, a big league catcher who couldn't throw the ball back to the pitcher with any velocity unless he risked making an errant throw.

Ryne Sandberg won the NL MVP Award in 1984 by batting .314 and leading the senior circuit in runs scored (114) and tying Juan Samuel for the major league lead in triples (19). He also collected 200 hits, had 36 doubles, 19 homers, drove in 84 runs, and stole 32 bags. He helped secure a Cubs win over San Diego on April 8 with a tenth inning RBI triple and a steal of home. Alan Wiggins stole five bags in San Diego's 5–4 win over Montreal on May 17.

The headline in the *Chicago Tribune* on June 11 read, "Men of steal: Cubs' triple theft finishes off Cards." Fred Mitchell wrote that stealing home is something the Cubs were becoming accustomed to and therefore it was "no big deal," although a triple steal required "remarkable feet." The Cubs were clinging to a 1–0 lead in the top of the ninth at Busch Stadium and were looking for some insurance. The bases were juiced with two outs. Starter Joaquin Andujar was still toeing the slab for St. Louis and Cubs pitcher Lee Smith was at the dish. There wasn't a lot of speed on the bases with Leon Durham on third (16 steals in 1984), Jody Davis on second (5 steals), and Larry Bowa on first (10 steals). However, their right-handed closer was at the dish. Smith worked a scoreless eighth inning and was staying in the game to try and secure a two-inning save. He rarely hit and when he did the results were not encouraging. Therefore it was a good time to roll the dice. Durham stole home on a high fastball and Davis and Bowa moved up behind him. He credited third base coach Don Zimmer for putting the idea in his head and he said, "If Smitty had swung I would have been dead. I just slid in and grabbed the bottom of his pants. I don't remember hearing anything except 'safe.'"

The game started auspiciously for Chicago when leadoff man Bob Dernier hit a double to start the game but then he was promptly picked off second. He went 2 for 4 in the contest and made a terrific catch in center field in the bottom of the fourth inning. The speedy fly chaser, who stole 45 bags during the season, took exception when the fans in center field began to harass him and Dernier exchanged words with them and later said, "I just let them know that they'd better watch it in case a ball came flying up there or something." Andujar had one sacrifice bunt in the game, but helped kill a potential rally with a failed sacrifice attempt in the fifth as he popped up. There was more small ball ineptitude in the last of the fifth. With runners on the corners and a 1 and 2 count on Andy Van Slyke, Tom Herr (13 steals) tried the delayed double steal. The delayed double steal usually works better with one out because you could sacrifice an out for a run, but Herr tried it with two away. It is a maneuver where the runner on first takes off for second as if he is trying to steal the bag. Then the runner stops before the catcher unleashes his throw to give the appearance as if he has second thoughts about the stolen base attempt and is about to return to first base. If the catcher hesitates, the runner on first continues to second at full speed and when he belatedly throws to second, the runner on third takes off for home. On June 10 it appeared that Herr was trying to get in a rundown long enough for Ozzie Smith to steal home. Jody Davis threw to second when Herr took off and then he went back towards first, apparently trying to get in a rundown. Smith took off for the plate but got "hung up" when Bowa threw the ball to Ron Cey at third. Cey unleashed a strong throw to Davis to catch Smith before he crossed home plate. With the 2–0 victory on June 10, the Cubs had a one game lead over Philadelphia in the NL East.[54]

Johnnie B. Baker batted .292 for the 1984 San Francisco Giants and stole four bases in five attempts. Dusty wasn't known for his wheels, but he did steal 137 bases during his career with a 65.2 percent basestealing average. He had eight seasons with ten or more steals and a career high of 24 with the 1973 Atlanta Braves when he also compiled a terrific 88.9 percent basestealing average. What made Baker's four steals in 1984 unique, was that three of them came in the same inning. On June 27 he stole second, third, and home in the third inning versus Cincinnati. Interestingly, the last player to accomplish this feat, Pete Rose, on May 11, 1980, was also not a great basestealing threat. San Francisco won the game, 14–9, thanks to Chili Davis's pinch-hit grand slam. On July 10, the National League prevailed in the All-Star Game, 3–1, at Candlestick Park as Ryne Sandberg, Tony Gwynn, Ozzie Smith, and Darryl Strawberry each stole second base for the senior league. Chet Lemon of the American League team was picked off first by right-hander Charlie Lea.

Pitcher Pascual Perez's only stolen base during his career was memorable. On September 7, in a 5–4 Atlanta loss to San Francisco, he stole home on the front end of a double steal with Milt Thompson on the back end. Thompson stole 214 bags during his thirteen-year career and had a career high of 46 thefts with the 1987 Philadelphia Phillies. His career stolen base average was a respectable 76.4 percent and he laid down only 20 sacrifices. Tim Raines stole four bags on September 18 in a 7–4 win over St. Louis and became the first big leaguer to steal 70 or more in four consecutive seasons. He would extend his streak to six straight seasons as he stole 70 bags in both 1985 and 1986.

Sparky Anderson's Detroit Tigers won the AL East in 1984 with a 104–58 record and the Tigers returned to the postseason for the first time since 1972 when Billy Martin was the skipper. And then they won seven of their eight postseason games to capture the World Series title, their first since 1968. Detroit stole an impressive eleven bases in the postseason: four in their three-game sweep of Dick Howser's Kansas City Royals (84–78) in the ALCS and seven in their four games to one victory over San Diego (92–70) in the World Series. Kirk Gibson stole four bases in the postseason, including three in the World Series and Chet Lemon stole two bags in the fall classic. Lemon batted .273 lifetime in regular season competition with a .355 on-base percentage, a .442 slugging percentage, 58 steals and an abysmal 43.3 percent stolen base average. He had good wheels but couldn't take advantage of his speed by stealing large numbers of bases. Tony Gwynn and Alan Wiggins stole the only bases for San Diego in the World Series. Gwynn was a prolific basestealer early in his career and stole 206 bases during a six-year stretch from 1984 to 1989 with totals of 33, 14, 37, 56, 26, and 40. He would finish his brilliant Hall of Fame career with 319 steals and a 71.8 percent basestealing average. Wiggins pilfered 242 cushions during his seven-year career, including 66 in 1983 and 70 in 1984. Dick Williams's San Diego Padres needed five games to defeat Jim Frey's Chicago Cubs (96–65) in the NLCS as they stole two bags and the Cubs pilfered six. Ryne Sandberg batted .368 in the series and pilfered three bags for Chicago, while Bob Dernier stole two.

The Padres lost the first two games of the NLCS before storming back to win the final three contests to break the hearts of Cub fans around the nation. Two errors by Leon Durham opened the door for a four-run seventh inning in the finale and the Padres won 6–3 at Jack Murphy Stadium. Chicago was 2 for 4 in stolen base attempts and Luis Salazar of San Diego had perhaps the most aggressive baserunning play of the series. He led off the eighth inning with a triple and was caught stealing home. San Diego stole 152 bags (5th, NL) during the regular season and had a 69.1 percent basestealing average (7th, NL). However, they hurt themselves with a poor 28.6 percent basestealing average in the World Series, while Detroit pilfered sacks at a decent 63.6 percent clip. Steve Garvey laid down the only sacrifice bunt in the series for the vanquished, while the world champions had two. In the bottom of the eighth inning in game five, which turned out to be the final contest of the series, Lou Whitaker and Alan Trammell had back-to-back sacrifice bunts right before Kirk Gibson broke open the game with a three-run homer. Whitaker reached on a fielder's choice during his sacrifice. The 8–4 victory gave Sparky Anderson the honor of being the first skipper to manage a world champion in both leagues.

In 1985 Whitey Herzog's running Redbirds (101–61) won the NL pennant and they did it the hard way by manufacturing runs. They stole an exorbitant 314 bases to become only the fifth team in the modern era with over 300 steals. The other four teams were the 1911 New York Giants (347), 1976 Oakland Athletics (341), 1912 New York Giants (319), and the 1910 Cincinnati Reds (310). Furthermore, the Cardinals' 76.6 percent stolen base average was the second best in the majors behind the Chicago Cubs, who were ranked second in the majors with 182 steals and pilfered sacks at a 78.8 percent clip. The Cardinals led the NL in batting average (.264), on-base percentage (.335), triples (59), and walks (586). This small ball juggernaut was also able to lead the NL with 747 runs scored despite hitting only 87 homers, which was the second fewest in the majors. With a lineup dominated by slap-hitters and line-drive hitters who could run well, they took advantage of the spacious dimensions of Busch Stadium and despite their anemic home run power, they finished sixth in the circuit in slugging percentage (.379) because they hit so many doubles (245, 4th NL) and triples. Their 70 sacrifice bunts ranked only seventh in the senior circuit, but with their speed they didn't need to give up outs by sacrificing runners over. Instead they could simply steal a bag or execute the hit-and-run. And even if a player like Willie McGee did lay down a bunt, intending to move the runner over, he may have been able to leg it out for a single. Also consider that only 37 of their 70 sacrifices (52.9 percent) were by position players. There were ten AL teams with more than 37 sacrifices in 1985, including California (99), Oakland (63), Chicago (59), Milwaukee (54), and Boston (50), who each had at least 50.

The championship series expanded to a seven-game format in 1985 and the Cardinals needed six games to dispose of the Dodgers (95–67) and secure the NL pennant. After losing the first two games at Dodger Stadium they returned to the artificial turf at Busch Stadium and used their speed to secure a 4–2 victory in game three. Their first three runs were tallied thanks to two stolen bases and two errors on pickoff attempts. Vince Coleman was the burglar who benefited from the errant pickoff throws, advancing two bases on both occasions, and infuriated the Dodgers as he advanced safely to the next station when he should have been thrown out. The two errors led to three runs. In the first inning, Bob Welch became obsessed with trying to pick off Coleman after he had singled to left field.

Then with a 1 and 1 count on Willie McGee, the Dodgers guessed right, as Welch fired a pitchout, but Coleman slid into second base safely. McGee walked and with a 3 and 2 count on Tom Herr, Welch threw to second base on a pickoff attempt, but neither of the middle infielders ran to the bag to take the throw, and Coleman raced home with the first run. Welch threw the ball at the first person he saw, the umpire, as his throw just missed hitting the arbiter and the ball went into right-center field. With McGee at third base, Herr drew a walk and then stole second on Welch's fourth pitch to Jack Clark. The Cardinals cleanup man struck out, but Andy Van Slyke was passed intentionally to fill the sacks, and McGee scored on Terry Pendleton's groundout. Coleman was hung out to dry on a pitchout in the second inning, but catcher Mike Scioscia hesitated and then threw the ball waywardly into right field as Coleman raced from first to third and scored on McGee's single. The frustrated Dodger starter failed to make it out of the third inning and was visibly shaken by the Cardinals running attack.

The Cardinals stormed back to win games three through six to secure the pennant. They pilfered six bags in the series: two by McGee (56 steals) and one apiece by Coleman (110 steals), Tom Herr (31 steals), Tito Landrum (1 steal), and Ozzie Smith (31 steals). Herr encapsulated the way the 1985 Cardinals played the game, hitting only 8 homers with a whopping 110 RBIs (3rd, NL) during the regular season and then batting .333 in the NLCS and leading the team with six RBIs. Smith batted .435 in the series and he hit a game-winning, one-out homer, off Tom Niedenfuer in the last of the ninth in game five to give St. Louis a 3–2 win. He had hit only thirteen homers in regular season competition during his eight-year career, all from the right side of the batter's box, and his circuit shot off Niedenfuer was especially surprising because it came while he was batting left-handed. Tom Lasorda's Dodgers stole four bags in the NLCS: two by Pedro Guerrero (12 steals) and one apiece by Mariano Duncan (38 steals) and Bill Madlock (10 steals). There were only three sacrifices in this fight for National League supremacy and two of the most notable bunts came in game one. Candy Maldonado, a 25-year-old outfielder for Los Angeles, had an RBI bunt single for his only hit of the series (1 for 7) that also advanced a runner to second base. But a successful squeeze play wasn't as surprising as the bunt single that was secured by St. Louis slugger Jack Clark.

The Cardinals faced the Kansas City Royals (91–71) in the World Series. Dick Howser's club needed seven games to defeat Toronto (99–62) in the ALCS as both teams combined for only four steals. The Cardinals took a three games to one lead in the I-70 World Series and they won game four, 3–0, as one of their runs scored on a surprise two strike squeeze bunt by Tom Nieto. However, the Royals stormed back to win the final three games to take the title. The Royals stole seven bases, including three by Willie Wilson and two by former Cardinal Lonnie Smith. Smith stole 12 bases in 28 games for the 1985 Cardinals before being traded to Kansas City on May 17 for John Morris. This allowed Vince Coleman to play every day in left field. The Cardinals were limited to only two steals in the fall classic, garnered by Willie McGee and Ozzie Smith. Whitey Herzog's track team that stole 314 bags during the regular season attempted only five steals in the autumn classic and had a 40 percent basestealing average. The Royals purloined 128 cushions (5th, AL) during the preliminary games and had eleven attempts in the World Series, pilfering sacks at a 63.6 percent rate. The Cardinals' catalyst, Vince Coleman, was missing from the fall classic because he injured his leg on October 13 in a freak accident at Busch Stadium when the automatic tarp was unrolling across the infield and he got his leg caught underneath for about thirty seconds. Both teams laid down three sacrifices and Nieto's squeeze bunt was the most noteworthy as he was credited with a sacrifice on the play. However, he advanced safely to second base on an error by pitcher Bud Black.

Vince Coleman and Willie McGee accounted for 166 of the Cardinals 314 steals. Coleman was a 23-year-old, switch-hitting, right-handed throwing left fielder, who won the NL Rookie of the Year Award by batting .267, but with a low .320 on-base percentage, 107 runs scored, and an eye-opening 110 stolen bases. He shattered Juan Samuel's rookie record of 72 thefts, which lasted only one season. Coleman had foreshadowed his great basestealing achievement by leading the league in steals during all of his minor league seasons. While playing in the South Atlantic League in 1983, he stole a record 145 bags despite missing a month with a broken hand. He led the National League in thefts during his first six seasons from 1985 to 1990 with totals of 110, 107, 109, 81, 65, and 77. Equally impressive was his stolen base averages during these seasons, which were 81.5, 88.4, 83.2, 75, 86.7, and 81.9. He became the first modern-era player with three consecutive seasons of 100 or more steals and the second player in the modern era along with Rickey Henderson with three 100 steal seasons. In 1989 the Cardinals speedster stole 50 consecutive bags to break Davey Lopes's 1975 record of 38 straight steals. Coleman surmised that it was easier to steal third than second and in 1987 he pilfered second and third thirteen times in the same inning. While Coleman's best attribute was his wheels, he didn't help himself by having low on-base percentages and high strikeout totals. Clearly, with his speed he could have been a great player if he drew more walks and put the ball in play more often, preferably on the ground. His 107 steals in 1986 was achieved despite having a .232 batting average, a .301 on-base percentage, only 139 hits and 60 walks. In 1987 he improved to .289 with a .363 on-base percentage and as a result scored 121 runs, an increase of 27 from the previous season. He struck out 450 times during his first four seasons with totals of 115, 98, 126, and 111.

When Coleman signed with the Mets as a free agent on December 5, 1990, things fell apart as he was saddled with injuries, off-the-field problems, and disagreements with management. He played for six teams during his thirteen-year career, finishing with a .264 batting average and an unspectacular .324 on-base percentage. He stole 752 bags with a terrific 80.9 percent basestealing average and laid down 48 sacrifices. With his speed he would often leg out a hit, while laying down a bunt, intending to advance one or more runners with a sacrifice. He averaged 57.8 steals per season and this is counting his final season in 1997 when he failed to steal a bag in six games for the Detroit Tigers.

Coleman is ranked sixth all-time in steals and is the worst player among those in the top ten. Out of the top ten all-time best basestealers, there are seven Hall of Famers (Rickey Henderson, Lou Brock, Billy Hamilton, Ty Cobb, Eddie Collins, Max Carey, and Honus Wagner) and one player, Tim Raines, who perhaps should be in the Hall of Fame.

Willie McGee was a 6'1", switch-hitting slap hitter, with a short swing and a quick bat, who was skilled at hitting pitches out of the strike zone. He weighed between 160 and 195 pounds during his eighteen-year big league career with the Cardinals (1982–1990 and 1996–1999), Athletics (1990), Giants (1991–1994), and Red Sox (1995). He batted .295 lifetime with 30 sacrifices, 352 stolen bases, and a 74.4 percent basestealing average. In 1985 he led the National League in batting average (.353), hits (216), and triples (18), while also scoring 114 runs and knocking in 82. From 1983 to 1985, McGee stole 138 bags with totals of 39, 43, and 56. His stolen base averages during these three campaigns were 83 percent, 81.1 percent, and 77.8 percent. Then in 1986 while playing in only 124 games and having his batting average plummet to .256, he stole 19 bags with a poor 54.3 percent basestealing average. He swiped 16 in 20 attempts in 1987 and then had his third season with over

40 thefts in 1988, when he swiped 41 with a terrific 87.2 percent basestealing average. He stole 274 of his 352 bases during his first nine seasons with the Cardinals. And then when he was traded to Oakland in 1990 through his final season in 1999, he stole only 78 bases.

In 1985, manager Whitey Herzog expressed his frustration because the hard-working McGee wasn't getting the credit he deserved. He made the All-Star team that season for the second of four times during his career, but Darryl Strawberry was selected in the popular vote despite having a batting average hovering around .220 and missing most of the first half because of an injury. McGee was a humble, deeply religious man, who did not seek the adulations and was well respected by the fans in St. Louis. Despite walking only 34 times in 1985, McGee insisted that hitting second behind Coleman made him a more patient hitter because he would have to take a pitch or two to allow Coleman a chance to steal a bag. Joaquin Andujar, a right-handed pitcher, who was his teammate in 1985, said, "If I was pitching against this team, I wouldn't want him on base. I'd rather face a power hitter because you can strike him out. But guys like McGee, you make a good pitch and they hit it no matter how hard you throw it. They get a single and then they're on second."[55]

Many of the Cardinals had terrific basestealing averages in 1985 and this included Tom Herr, who stole a career high 31 bags with a 91.2 percent basestealing average. However, the best stolen base percentage in the major leagues for a player with at least 20 steals in 1985 was attained by Jack Perconte of the Seattle Mariners, who stole a career high 31 bags and was caught stealing only two times for a stratospheric 93.9 percent basestealing average.

The National League teams stole 175 more bases than the American League aggregations in 1985 and they had 253 more sacrifices. There were five teams in the two leagues who had at least 155 steals: the St. Louis Cardinals (314), Chicago Cubs (182), Montreal Expos (169), Cincinnati Reds (159), and the New York Yankees (155). The second-place Yankees (97–64, AL East), who were managed by first Yogi Berra (6–10) and then Billy Martin (91–54), not only led the junior league in steals (155), but also had the circuit's best stolen base average (74.5 percent). Gene Mauch's California Angels (90–72) finished one game behind Kansas City in the AL West. They stole a respectable 106 bags (8th, AL) and laid down 99 sacrifices, which was the second best in the major leagues behind the Los Angeles Dodgers, who accumulated 104 sacrifices. Bobby Cox's Toronto Blue Jays laid down the fewest sacrifices in the majors with 21, but they finished second in the junior league with 144 steals. Wally Backman and Nolan Ryan shared the NL sacrifice bunt title with 14, while Bob Meacham took the crown in the AL for the second straight season with 23.

Rickey Henderson's first season in the Big Apple with the Yankees was a resounding success as he won his sixth straight AL stolen base title with 80 thefts. Furthermore, he was caught stealing only 10 times for an outstanding 88.9 percent basestealing average. He batted .314 with a .419 on-base percentage, a .516 slugging percentage, and a major league leading 146 runs scored, which was 28 more than Dale Murphy of the Atlanta Braves, who finished second in the majors with 118. Henderson hit 28 doubles, 5 triples, 24 homers, drove in 72, and walked 99 times. He became the first AL player with at least 20 homers and 50 steals in a season and he would accomplish that feat once again in 1986 with 28 homers and 87 steals and also in 1990 and 1993. Despite his gaudy numbers, the 1985 AL MVP Award went to teammate Don Mattingly who batted .324 out of the three hole and led the majors in doubles (48) and RBIs (145). He obviously benefited greatly by having Henderson as the leadoff hitter, giving him plenty of RBI opportunities.

Gary Pettis finished second in the AL in steals with 56 and he was followed by Brett

Butler (47) and Kansas City teammates Willie Wilson (43) and Lonnie Smith (40). Wilson and Smith accounted for 64.8 percent of Kansas City's 128 steals. Smith pilfered a total of 52 bags in 1985, counting his 12 thefts with the Cardinals. In the NL, Tim Raines (70) finished second behind Vince Coleman and he was followed by Willie McGee (56), Ryne Sandberg (54), and Juan Samuel (53). In the All-Star Game on July 16 at the Hubert H. Humphrey Metrodome, the two leagues combined for five steals in five attempts as the NL won, 6–1. Darryl Strawberry and Jose Cruz stole bases for the NL, while Dave Winfield, Rickey Henderson, and Damaso Garcia swiped bags for the AL.

On August 1, the Cubs and Cardinals were deadlocked at eight in the last of the fourteenth with the bases loaded and one out when the Cubs decided to use the element of surprise to end the marathon affair. Larry Bowa, Chicago's 39-year-old shortstop, was sent to the dish with orders to lay down a squeeze bunt, which would allow Keith Moreland to scamper home with the winning run if executed successfully. Moreland didn't have great wheels, but he did steal twelve bases in fifteen attempts in 1985, which was 42.9 percent of his career total of 28 steals. Bowa failed on the first pitch, bunting it foul, and then the Cardinals 26-year-old southpaw Ken Dayley worked the count to 1 and 2. Don Zimmer, the Cubs' third base coach, heard Hal Lanier, the Cardinals third base coach, whistle from the dugout. Zimmer surmised that the enemy had picked up their signal for the squeeze bunt, so he called Bowa over and informed him that they would use a new signal for the squeeze bunt. Zimmer didn't flash the sign for the squeeze before the next offering, anticipating that the enemy would be looking for it. Dayley and the Cards were indeed anticipating the squeeze play and pitched out hoping to catch the runner at third off the bag. However, Moreland was able to stay within the safe vicinity of the pillow. Then with the count 2 and 2, Zimmer flashed the new squeeze sign and Bowa laid one down in front of the plate on a fastball. Dayley's toss to catcher Darrell Porter was not handled and the five hour and two minute contest finally concluded before 36,164 Wrigley Field fans. Bowa, who also had a bases-loaded triple in the third inning, said, "It took a lot of guts on Jim Frey's part. With two strikes on me, that thing could backfire. I could miss the bunt for strike three and Zonk (Moreland) would be hung out to dry." He insisted that the signs were changed "about five times."[56]

Vince Coleman went 4 for 7 in the game with two triples, three runs scored, and his 73rd and 74th steals of the season. McGee also had two steals in the game and he teamed with Coleman for a double steal in the first inning. The effective St. Louis table-setters led off the game with a single and a walk off right-hander Scott Sanderson and then pulled off their double steal. Coleman overslid the third base bag, was hung up, and decided to keep on going towards home plate. Ron Cey, the Cubs third baseman, couldn't tag him and Coleman got himself into a rundown and eventually scored when no one was covering home, as McGee moved up to third base. Jim Frey, the Cubs skipper, argued unsuccessfully with the umpire, insisting that Coleman had run out of the basepath and should be called out. Amazingly, Coleman and McGee were both credited with two stolen bases each on that play. Randy Minkoff, the official scorer, initially ruled the play a double steal with each player receiving one stolen base. Then he called Seymour Siwoff, the NL chief statistician, who insisted that the rule book did not indicate how this play should be scored. And therefore both players were credited with two steals on the play. Whitey Herzog, the Cardinals skipper, scoffed and actually argued against his players receiving two stolen bases apiece, "It can't be four steals. It's a fielder's choice. I don't care who he called, he still can't give four steals on that play." With McGee on third, the Cubs brought their infield in with slugger

Jack Clark at the dish. It backfired and Clark singled past the drawn-in infield for the second run of the inning. Coleman's first steal of the game broke Juan Samuel's rookie record.[57]

Davey Lopes, the Cubs leadoff man, also stole two bases in the contest and laid down a sacrifice bunt. He walked and stole second in the bottom of the first inning and when Ryne Sandberg walked, they tried the double steal. Lopes was thrown out at third, as he was gunned down at the far corner for the first time in eleven attempts. Sandberg scored on Leon Durham's single and Chicago scored two more runs in the last of the second to take a 3–2 lead. Jody Davis and Ron Cey singled to start the inning, Bowa sacrificed them to second and third, and starter Scott Sanderson laid down a squeeze bunt for a hit as Davis scored. Cey scored after second baseman, Tom Herr, dropped the ball as he was trying to turn a 5–4–3 double play. The Cubs blew an 8–2 lead after four innings and the Cardinals eventually tied the game with three in the ninth. Before Bowa batted in the fourteenth, Bob Dernier checked his swing on two pitches and each time the first base umpire, Billy Williams, insisted he did not swing. Dernier drew a walk to load the bases. Herzog believed he was out both times and said that "We play all day and let those suckers (the umpires) take it away from us." Asked if he was surprised to see Bowa lay down a squeeze bunt on a 2 and 2 pitch, he said, "Sure, we thought he might still squeeze. What the heck, he can't hit." He also said it was hard for a manager to pitch out on a 2 and 2 count. Bowa's squeeze play was the most precarious of maneuvers, a suicide, with Moreland breaking for the plate with the pitch. However, in this situation the suicide squeeze was the only way to play it because the sacks were full and there were two balls on the batter. Dayley was most likely going to give Bowa a pitch he could lay down because he didn't want to go to a full count where another wayward delivery would force in the winning run.[58]

Thanks to the heads-up play by 21-year-old rookie shortstop Ozzie Guillen, the White Sox defeated the Yankees by a 6–5 score before 27,118 fans at Yankee Stadium on August 2. He singled off Rich Bordi, a 6'7", 220-pound right hander, with two outs in the eleventh inning and then stole second. Luis Salazar followed with a slow roller down the first base line. Bordi lazily went after the ball and his flip to Don Mattingly at first base was not in time. Guillen was not content at stopping at the coffin corner and made the turn at third and scored without a throw as the Yankees stunned first baseman held the ball. Guillen said, "I was coming all the way. You have to be aggressive."[59] This was an unusual game with the Sox's Carlton Fisk tagging out two runners back-to-back at the plate. Dale Berra was on first and Bob Meacham on second when Rickey Henderson connected for a deep drive to center field. Berra had judged that Luis Salazar would not catch the ball and started running, while Meacham played it cautious, and remained close to the second base bag. When Meacham began running, he slipped, and by the time he was running at full speed, Berra was on his heels. Salazar made an impressive throw to Guillen and the Sox shortstop hit Fisk with a one-hopper. Fisk was waiting for the two runners while standing up and he endured a good blow by Meacham but held onto the ball, staggered a bit, and then slapped the tag on Berra. Salazar, the Chicago leadoff man, had a sacrifice bunt in the contest and the Sox stole six bases: two by Reid Nichols (6 steals in 1985) and one apiece by Greg Walker (5 steals), Salazar (14 steals), Carlton Fisk (17 steals), and Guillen (7 steals). Tony LaRussa's White Sox finished the season in third place in the AL West with an 85–77 record. They stole 108 bases (7th, AL) and laid down 59 sacrifices (3rd, AL).

Dave Winfield stole home on September 7 with the eventual winning run in a 3–2 Yankees victory over the Athletics. It wasn't the most aesthetically pleasing steal of home as he got hung up after a pitchout in the sixth inning and found a way to score on the botched rundown. Vince Coleman stole his 100th bag on September 19, but the running Redbirds came up short by a 6–3 score to Philadelphia. Rickey Henderson broke another stolen base record on September 25 when he stole his 75th bag in a 10–2 win over Detroit to break the Yankees single-season record, which was held by Fritz Maisel who stole 74 in 1914. Also on the 25th, Davey Lopes broke a 4–4 tie against a division rival, the Mets, in the last of the ninth when he walked, stole second and third, and scored the winning run on a single. The aging speed merchant pilfered his final three sacks of the season, including one in the seventh inning when he entered the game as a pinch-runner. After his two-out walk in the ninth, Lopes was picked off, but first baseman Keith Hernandez couldn't get the ball out of his glove in time to cut down Lopes at second. In 1985, the 40-year-old Lopes batted .284 for the Cubs with 11 homers in 99 games and stole 47 bases with an outstanding 92.2 percent basestealing average. He turned 40 on May 3 and set a record for the most steals in a season by a player over 40.

The National League averaged a whopping 153.5 steals per team in 1986, while the American League averaged 105 steals per team. Eight NL teams stole at least 148 bags: St. Louis (262), Montreal (193), Cincinnati (177), Houston (163), Los Angeles (155), Philadelphia (153), Pittsburgh (152), and San Francisco (148). The Cardinals hit a measly 58 homers, which was 52 fewer than Montreal (110), who had the second fewest homers in the majors. Herzog's third-place team (79–82, NL East) led the majors in steals (262), sacrifices (108), and stolen base average (77.1 percent). However, after leading the National League in batting average and on-base percentage in 1985, they finished last in the majors in both categories in 1986 and they also had the worst slugging percentage. As a result they scored the fewest runs in the majors. The running Redbirds had great speed, but it's wasted if you can't get on base.

In the AL, Pat Corrales's fifth-place Cleveland Indians led the loop with 141 steals, while rookie manager Lou Piniella's second-place Yankees finished tied for second in the circuit with 139 steals and had the junior league's best stolen base average (74.3 percent). Not surprisingly, Gene Mauch's Angels led the AL with 91 sacrifices. Rookie second baseman Robby Thompson of the Giants shared the major league sacrifice bunt title with second baseman Marty Barrett of Boston as they both had 18.

Rickey Henderson led the majors in runs scored (130) for the second consecutive season and he won his seventh straight AL stolen base title with 87 thefts, while compiling an impressive 82.9 percent basestealing average. California's fast moving fly chaser, Gary Pettis, swiped 50 bags to finish second in the junior league for the second straight season and he was tied with John Cangelosi of the White Sox. Willie Wilson and Kirk Gibson each had 34 thefts, which was good enough to rank in the top five. In the NL, Coleman's 107 steals led the circuit, while Eric Davis (80), Tim Raines (70), and Mariano Duncan (48), also had large totals.

Eric Davis made headlines in 1986, batting .277 in 132 games with a .378 on-base percentage, a .523 slugging percentage, 97 runs scored, 71 RBIs, and 80 steals with a terrific 87.9 percent basestealing average. He smashed 27 homers and became only the second player behind Henderson to have a 20 homer, 80 steal season, despite not cracking the Reds starting lineup until June 15. The supremely talented, 6'3", 185-pound, fly chaser had a myriad of injuries during his career, which curtailed his performance. In the outer garden he tracked down numerous balls that many outfielders would not get to because of his great foot speed and then robbed many batters of homers with his exceptional leaping ability. He batted .269 lifetime with a .359 on-base percentage, a .482 slugging percentage, 282 homers, and 349 steals with an outstanding 84.1 percent basestealing average. Despite the fact that his stolen base totals declined or remained the same each year for five straight seasons after he pilfered an exorbitant 80 bags in 1986 (50, 35, 21, 21, and 14), his stolen base averages remained extremely high for all but one season at 89.3, 92.1, 75, 87.5, and 87.5. Davis had a quick, violent swing, but wasn't much of a bunter, laying down only three sacrifices during his career. If he wasn't burdened with performance depleting injuries and illnesses, he would have been a sure Hall of Famer. Despite his unfulfilled potential, Bill James thought enough about him to rank him as the 33rd best center fielder in *The New Bill James Historical Baseball Abstract*.

The Giants squeezed their way to a 3–1 win over the Reds on June 8 in the second game of a doubleheader to emerge with a split. Mike Woodard and Robby Thompson had back-to-back squeeze bunts in the eighth inning that plated two runs and gave San Francisco a 3–1 lead. Jeffrey Leonard laid down a sacrifice bunt in the inning, his second in four years. On June 10, Los Angeles defeated Cincinnati, 1–0, as Mariano Duncan scored from second on a grounder to third by Bill Madlock. The Reds tried to turn a 5–4–3 double play, but Madlock beat the relay throw to first and Duncan raced safely across the plate. Robby Thompson stole ten or more bases during seven seasons and 103 during his career with a poor 62.4 percent basestealing average. On June 27 in the Giants, 7–6, twelve inning triumph over Cincinnati, he was caught stealing four times to establish a new major league record. Catcher Bo Diaz gunned him down in the 4th, 6th, 9th, and 11th. Kirby Puckett stole third base for the AL and Lloyd Moseby stole second in the junior circuit's 3–2 win over the NL on July 15 in the All-Star Game at the Astrodome. Steve Sax stole the only base for the National League. When Vince Coleman decided to steal bases with a 10–2 lead on July 22 against the Giants, Roger Craig's team decided that he had broken one of baseball's unwritten rules and they would retaliate. They nailed him later in the contest, which led to a bench-clearing brawl. Mike Krukow, the Giants All-Star pitcher, injured his ribcage trying to take Coleman down and as a result he would have to miss three starts, which broke San Francisco's momentum. Houston defeated San Diego, 10–6, on September 20, but Tony Gwynn pilfered five bags and became the tenth player in the modern era to steal at least five in a game.

Out of the four playoff teams in 1986, Hal Lanier's Houston Astros had the most steals with 163, followed by Davey Johnson's Mets (118), Gene Mauch's Angels (109), and John McNamara's Red Sox (41). It was a thrilling postseason as the ALCS and the World Series went the distance, while the NLCS went six games before the Mets clinched the flag with a 7–6, sixteen inning affair, in game six. Houston pilfered eight bags in the fight for National League supremacy: three by Billy Hatcher (38 steals), two apiece by Kevin Bass (22 steals) and Bill Doran (42 steals), and one by Terry Puhl (3 steals). The Mets stole four in the series, one apiece by Wally Backman (13 steals), Lenny Dykstra (31 steals), Darryl Strawberry (28 steals), and Mookie Wilson (25 steals). Strawberry stole 221 bases during his seventeen-year career with a 69.1 percent basestealing average. He stole 146 bags during five seasons from 1984 to 1988 with totals of 27, 26, 28, 36, and 29. Wilson and Dykstra were also basestealing threats, stealing 327 and 285 respectively during their careers. There were only three sacrifice bunts during the NLCS: two by Hatcher and one by the Mets southpaw reliever, Jesse Orosco.

The Red Sox were down three games to one in the ALCS and 5–2 in the top of the ninth inning of game five before they rallied for a 7–6 eleven inning victory and then took the final two games of the series comfortably by 10–4 and 8–1 scores to secure the flag.

Spike Owen of Boston (4 steals) and Dick Schofield of California (23 steals) pilfered the only bags of the series. Wade Boggs had perhaps the most interesting sacrifice bunt of the series when he moved Owen to second base with his team leading 6–2 in the last of the eighth in game two. Instead of going for the jugular, they appeared to be trying to tack-on one more run by having the batting champion (.357) and the on-base percentage leader (.453) lay down a bunt. However, everything worked out fine as Owen moved to third on a single and scored on a sacrifice fly and Boston scored three runs in the frame to break open the game.

In the World Series it was the Mets who came back from the dead in game six and then secured the title with an 8–5 win on October 27. They stole all the bases in the series, seven in total: Strawberry and Wilson stole three apiece, while Backman pilfered one. The miraculous Mets garnered six of the ten sacrifices, including two apiece by Lenny Dykstra and Rafael Santana. Left-handed pitcher Bruce Hurst led the Sox with two sacrifice bunts, which was a good accomplishment for a player who was unaccustomed to handling the bat because he played in the junior circuit which used the DH.

Despite the fact that home runs and runs scored skyrocketed in both leagues in 1987, stolen bases also increased by only 9 in the NL and 264 in the AL, which was 18 percent. The NL averaged 154.3 steals per team, which was the highest level since 1916 (166). Meanwhile, the AL's 123.9 steals per team was the highest level in the junior league since 1976 (140.8). The average number of steals per team in each league in 1987 would not be surpassed in any subsequent season entering the 2010 campaign. Sacrifice bunts declined by 46 in the NL and by 14 in the AL when compared to 1986. Atlanta pitcher Zane Smith led the NL with 14 sacrifices, while Marty Barrett led the majors with 22. With Rickey Henderson saddled with injuries in 1987 and limited to 95 games, it allowed Harold Reynolds to win the AL stolen base title with 60 thefts. He was followed by Willie Wilson (59), Gary Redus (52), Paul Molitor (45), and Henderson (41).

The versatile Paul Molitor laid down 75 sacrifices, stole 504 bases, and had a 79.4 percent basestealing average during his Hall of Fame career. His 45 steals in 1987 represented a career high and his second highest total was 41 achieved in 1982, 1983, and 1988. Molitor was a high percentage player and this was exemplified in 1994 and 1995. With the 1994 Toronto Blue Jays, he played in all of their 115 games during the strike-shortened season, primarily as a designated hitter (110 games), and batted .341 with a .410 on-base percentage, a .518 slugging percentage, and 20 steals in 20 attempts. This 100 percent basestealing average was a record for a player with at least 20 steals since 1951 and is matched only by Kevin McReynolds, who stole 21 bags in 21 attempts for the 1988 New York Mets. Molitor's batting average (.270), on-base percentage (.350), and slugging percentage (.423), all declined in 1995, but he stole 12 bases in 12 attempts, going two consecutive seasons without being caught stealing. When Molitor came up to the big show in 1978, he walked only 19 times in 521 at-bats, but he developed into a patient hitter over time, understanding his responsibility as a leadoff hitter. Molitor, a right-handed hitter, was timed running to first base in about four seconds and had been taught the intricacies of stealing home by his coach at the University of Minnesota. He amassed modest strikeout totals during his career and his ability to hit the ball to all fields made him a good hit-and-run man. Daniel Okrent described him in *Nine Innings: The Anatomy of a Baseball Game* as "a handsome, charming, intelligent, and unfailingly polite young man, and he could play ball immaculately. He was somehow different from his teammates, a generally quiet man, out of place in the roisterous life of a clubhouse whose other occupants nonetheless treasured his skills."[60]

In the National League, Vince Coleman cruised to his third straight stolen base crown, collecting 53 more bags than Tony Gwynn (56), who finished second in the circuit. Billy Hatcher finished third with 53 thefts and was followed by Tim Raines and Eric Davis, who each had fifty.

Against the Mets on April 18 at Busch Stadium, the Cardinals tied the game at seven in the ninth frame when Ozzie Smith stole third and scored on catcher Gary Carter's errant throw. Tom Herr connected for a grand slam in the tenth as the Cardinals prevailed, 12–8. On April 18, Reggie Jackson was one month shy of his 41st birthday and proved that his tires were not completely flat by stealing home on the front end of a double steal with Jose Canseco on the back end as Oakland emerged triumphant over Seattle, 7–5. Jackson played his final season in 1987, batting .220 with 15 home runs and two steals in three attempts. Cardinal table-setters, one and two hitters, Coleman and Smith, went a combined 0 for 7 against Pittsburgh in a 3–1 loss at Busch Stadium on June 15. But Coleman managed to collect his 42nd steal and five-hole hitter, McGee, had one of the two sacrifice bunts in the game. Jim Morrison, the Pirates third baseman, was caught stealing home two times in the eighth inning. There was an error on his first caught stealing, which allowed him to return to third and then he tried once again unsuccessfully.

Andy Van Slyke went 3 for 3 with a homer, a run scored, and three RBIs during a 5–2 win over Chicago at Three Rivers Stadium on June 26. After catching a fly ball in center field in the fourth inning with the base loaded, he threw out Chicago leadoff man, Dave Martinez, trying to score from third. Andre Dawson's throwing error opened the door for Pittsburgh to score three markers in the seventh frame, prompting Fred Mitchell to write in the *Chicago Tribune*, "Oops! The cannon misfired Friday night."[61] This game was also significant for the inept baserunning of Cubs second baseman Paul Noce, whose major league career consisted of 70 games with the 1987 Cubs and one game with the 1990 Reds. He became the third player in big league history to be caught stealing twice in an inning. He was caught stealing second base in the third inning, but remained on the bag when shortstop Al Pedrique dropped the ball for an error. Noce then took off for third base but catcher Mike LaValliere's throw was on target and he was out. Amazingly, this unique accomplishment had only been attained once before on June 15, 1974, when Don Baylor had done it and then it happened twice in the span of twelve days in 1987.

The National League won the All-Star Game in Oakland on July 14, 2–0, in thirteen innings. Tim Raines went 3 for 3 with a triple, two runs driven in, and a stolen base. Mike Schmidt was caught stealing for the NL. The junior league had all three of the sacrifice bunts in the game: Matt Nokes, Tony Fernandez, and Harold Reynolds. Paul Molitor served as the catalyst in the Brewers 7–4 win over the Athletics on July 26 when he stole second, third, and home in the first inning. The resurgent Brew Crew (91–71, 3rd AL East) led the American League in larceny, garnering 176 bags, as they pilfered 76 more cushions than 1986 and won 14 more games. Eric Davis hit his 30th homer on August 2 in a 5–4 win against the Giants to become the seventh player in the 30 homer, 30 steal club. Molitor needed a bunt single in the third inning to extend his hitting streak to 32 games in a 5–3 win over Cleveland on August 17. He had a remarkable season in 1987, batting .353 with a .438 on-base percentage, a .566 slugging percentage, putting together a 39-game hitting streak and leading the AL in runs (114) and doubles (41). The Cardinals defeated the Mets, 6–4, in ten innings on September 11, but Howard Johnson stole his 30th bag to become the eighth player to hit 30 homers and steal 30 bags in a season. By 1987 major league baseball was changing mightily and this was exemplified by the fact that before the season began there were only six members of the 30–30 club, who accomplished the feat eleven times. The number of home runs skyrocketed in 1987 and naturally, the 30–30 club expanded, adding four new members: Davis, Johnson, Joe Carter, and Darryl Strawberry. From 1987 to 2009, the 30–30 mark was achieved forty-three times by twenty-eight players.

The Cardinals began to hit again in 1987 and as a result they won the NL East with a 95–67 record and then defeated San Francisco (90–72) in seven games in the NLCS to win the pennant. They batted .263 (6th, NL) and led the senior circuit in walks (644) and on-base percentage (.340), as they tallied the second most runs in the loop (798). The running Redbirds led the majors with 248 thefts and ranked third in the NL with an impressive 77.5 percent basestealing average. Their 84 sacrifices ranked second in the NL behind Atlanta (86) and was 14 more than Gene Mauch's California Angels, who led the AL with 70. The Cardinals stole four bags in the NLCS: one apiece by Vince Coleman (109 steals), Tom Herr (19 steals), fleet footed first-year player Lance Johnson (6 steals), and Tony Pena (6 steals). By the time Johnson's career ended with the 2000 New York Yankees, he would compile a .291 batting average, 327 steals, and a 75.7 percent basestealing average.

Roger Craig's Giants stole five bags in the 1987 NLCS: two by Robby Thompson and one apiece by Will Clark, Kevin Mitchell, and Jose Uribe. They won game two, 5–0, but also had an ignominious accomplishment as two of their runners were caught stealing home: Uribe and Clark. While Clark's 22.7 percent basestealing average in 1987 was truly abysmal, he joined a long list of players with horrible stolen base percentages. According to the *The SABR Baseball List and Record Book: Baseball's Most Fascinating Records and Unusual Statistics*, Clark's disgraceful achievement is the thirteenth worst stolen base percentage for players with at least 10 caught stealing since 1951 and through the 2006 season. Pete Runnels of Washington ranks first as he failed to steal a bag in ten attempts with the 1952 Washington Senators. Eddie Yost (1957) and Jose Vizcaino (1994) each stole one base in twelve attempts for an 8.3 percent stolen base average. Jerry Morales (1974) and Curt Flood (1958) were both 2 for 14 (14.3 percent). Elliott Maddox of the 1978 Mets was 2 for 13 (15.4 percent). Luis Gomez (1978), Johnny Groth (1952), Charlie Moore (1982), and Todd Cruz (1982) were all 2 for 12 (16.7 percent). Rick Miller (1978) and Tony Johnson (1982) were also ranked ahead of Clark as they stole 3 bags in 16 attempts (18.8 percent).

Tom Kelly's Minnesota Twins were dominant at home in the Hubert H. Humphrey Metrodome, compiling a 56–25 home record, but they fell flat on the road with a 29–52 mark. The Twins took on Sparky Anderson's Tigers in the ALCS and neither team had a huge advantage in the small ball department: Detroit stole 106 bags and laid down 39 sacrifices, while Minnesota had 113 steals and 47 sacrifices. Despite winning thirteen fewer games than Detroit in the regular season, the Twins prevailed in the ALCS, four games to one, in a high scoring series. The Twins stole four bags, including three by Randy Bush, who stole a career high of 10 bases during the regular season. Detroit pilfered five in the series, including three by Kirk Gibson (26 steals). With their upset victory over Detroit, the Twins kept on rolling in the World Series, winning their four home games and losing the three on the road to take the world title. The two teams combined for a whopping eighteen steals with St. Louis swiping twelve and Minnesota six. Gary Gaetti and Dan Gladden led the Twins with two thefts apiece. Coleman led the Cardinals in steals in the fall classic, pilfering six, despite batting only .143 in the series. Terry Pendleton and Ozzie Smith had two apiece, while Lance Johnson and Tony Pena each stole one. Both teams compiled outstanding stolen base percentages in the series: St. Louis pilfered bags at an 80 percent clip, while the Twins had an 85.7 percent basestealing average. In the bottom of the fifth inning in game five, the Twins pulled off a rare strike 'em out-throw 'em out double play. Jose Oquendo was caught stealing home, 2–5 on the scorecard, after pitcher Danny Cox struck out. There were only three sacrifice bunts in the autumn classic, garnered by Pendleton and Cox for the Cardinals and Bert Blyleven for the Twins.

After the robust offensive campaign in 1987, runs scored and home runs plummeted in both leagues in 1988. Stolen bases declined in the NL by 62 and in the AL by 222. The St. Louis Cardinals led the NL in steals for the seventh straight season and also led the majors for the fifth consecutive season. Whitey Herzog's running Redbirds pilfered 234 bags and their 78.5 percent stolen base average was the third best in the majors, only fractionally lower than the Cincinnati Reds (78.7 percent) and New York Yankees (78.9 percent). As is often the case, the teams with the most steals have the best stolen base averages and vice versa. This trend continued in 1988, as the Reds (207) and Yankees (146) finished second in thefts in their respective leagues. Houston (198) and Montreal (189) also compiled large stolen base totals in the National League. Tom Trebelhorn's Milwaukee Brewers, an outfit that was tied for third place in the AL East with an 87–75 record, led the AL in steals (159) for the second season in a row and finished third in the circuit with a 74.3 percent basestealing average. Rickey Henderson of the Yankees returned to form in 1988, winning his eighth AL stolen base crown with 93 thefts and compiling an outstanding 87.7 percent stolen base average. Nobody gave him any real competition for the crown as Gary Pettis of Detroit finished second with 44 steals, followed by Paul Molitor (41) and Jose Canseco (40). Vince Coleman led the NL with 81 steals and was followed by Gerald Young of Houston (65), Ozzie Smith (57), Chris Sabo of Cincinnati (46), and Otis Nixon of Montreal (46). The Cardinals, a fifth-place aggregation in the NL East, laid down 105 sacrifice bunts, which was second in the majors behind San Diego (106). The Chicago White Sox led the junior league with 67 sacrifices. Pitchers Orel Hershiser of Los Angeles and Rick Reuschel of San Francisco led the NL with 19 sacrifice bunts, while Marty Barrett led the AL with 20. Both Hershiser (101) and Reuschel (135) would help themselves at the plate and lay down over 100 sacrifices during their careers.

While neither Canseco, Young, nor Sabo could sustain their high basestealing totals during subsequent campaigns, Otis Nixon could. Nixon had blazing speed and was a prototypical leadoff man who could bunt, steal bases, negatively impact the psychological well being of a pitcher, and alter the positioning of the defense. He started his big league career with the 1983 New York Yankees (13 games) before spending four seasons in Cleveland, stealing a total of 57 bags with limited playing time. With the 1988 Montreal Expos, he batted .244 with a .312 on-base percentage, 46 steals, and a 78 percent basestealing average. He stole 498 bases from 1988 to 1997, playing for the Expos, Braves, Red Sox, Rangers, Blue Jays, and Dodgers, with totals of 46, 37, 50, 72, 41, 47, 42, 50, 54, and 59. Then at the age of 39, he batted .297 for the 1998 Minnesota Twins with 37 steals and an 84.1 percent stolen base average. He finished his career with the 1999 Atlanta Braves, batting .205 and stealing 26 bags despite collecting only 31 hits and 23 walks. He stole more bases than any player during the 1990s (478). Nixon batted .270 lifetime with a .343 on-base percentage, 67 sacrifices, 620 steals, and a 76.9 percent stolen base average. He garnered only 142 doubles, 27 triples, and 11 homers as 86.9 percent of his hits were singles. Nixon never led his league in steals, but finished second two times and third three times. This was because he played more than 133 games during only three seasons. In 1991, for example, his 72 bags was second in the NL behind Marquis Grissom (76). But Grissom played in 24 more games and had 157 more at-bats. Nixon's six steals on June 16, 1991, established a new modern-era National League record.

The Cubs defeated the Padres by a 1–0 score on May 11 thanks to Vance Law's squeeze bunt in the tenth inning. The Yankees blew a 6–4 lead in the fourteenth inning on June 4 at Memorial Stadium as they made two errors in the frame and lost to Baltimore, 7–6. Rickey Henderson singled in the first inning and stole his 248th bag as a Yankee, tying Hal Chase for the team record. Mike Boddicker tried to pick him off second, but his poor throw allowed Henderson to advance to third and then he scored on Claudell Washington's bunt single. Henderson, who had stolen three bags in the previous game, had two on the 4th to break Chase's team record.

When Oakland pitcher Gene Nelson stole a bag while pinch-running for Don Baylor on July 3, he became the first AL pitcher since Blue Moon Odom (1973) to pilfer a bag. Oakland prevailed in the contest, 9–8, in sixteen frames against Toronto. Baylor stole 285 bags during his career and was a formidable basestealing threat during his early years. But during his final five seasons from 1984 to 1988, he stole only 14 bags in 31 attempts (45.2 percent). Pitcher Rick Sutcliffe of the Chicago Cubs had his own basestealing accomplishment in Chicago's 8–3 win over Philadelphia at Veterans Stadium on July 29. A botched pickoff attempt allowed Sutcliffe to steal home and Mitch Webster to swipe a bag on the back end of a double steal. Sutcliffe became the first Cubs pitcher to steal home since Hippo Vaughn did it on August 9, 1919. The 1988 All-Star Game was played at Riverfront Stadium on July 12 as the American League prevailed, 2–1. Vince Coleman and Chris Sabo each stole a bag for the NL. Felix Jose made his major league debut in 1988 with Oakland and batted .333 with one steal in eight games and six at-bats. On September 23, Oakland manufactured a run in the fourteenth inning to defeat Milwaukee, 9–8. Jose singled, was sacrificed to second, stole third, and scored on a sacrifice fly. This game was also significant because Jose Canseco stole two bags to become the first 40–40 man.

Tony LaRussa's Oakland Athletics (104–58) truly sparkled in the AL as the "Bash Brothers" of Jose Canseco (42) and Mark McGwire (32) hit 74 of the team's 156 homers (2nd, AL). Their 129 steals (5th, AL) was a respectable number as were their 54 sacrifices, which ranked sixth in the circuit. Jose Canseco was the primary stolen base threat with 40 thefts as he became the first member of the 40 homer, 40 steal club, and won the AL MVP Award. In addition to scoring the second most runs in the majors (800), LaRussa's club could also pitch and had the best ERA in the AL (3.44). Oakland bashed seven homers in the ALCS and outscored Boston, 20 to 11, in the four-game sweep as Canseco stole the only bag of the series. Joe Morgan's Red Sox laid down the only two sacrifices by Jody Reed and Marty Barrett.

Oakland faced Tom Lasorda's weak-hitting Los Angeles Dodgers (94–67) in the World Series. The Dodgers stole 131 bags (6th, NL) during the campaign and finished third in the circuit with 95 sacrifices. The strength of their team was the pitching staff, which compiled a 2.96 ERA (2nd, NL). They needed seven games to defeat the New York Mets (100–60) in the NLCS as they stole nine sacks, while the Mets pilfered six bags. Steve Sax stole five bags for Los Angeles, while Kirk Gibson and John Shelby each had two. Davey Johnson's Mets were led by Kevin McReynolds, who had two. The National League Eastern Division champions had a good 75 percent basestealing average during the series, while Los Angeles pilfered bags at an outstanding 90 percent clip.

A hobbled Kirk Gibson hit a pinch-hit, two-out, two-run homer, in the last of the ninth off Dennis Eckersley to win the opening game of the fall classic for Los Angeles in a dramatic 5–4 triumph. The Dodgers went on to win the series, four games to one, as pitching prevailed over power. The world champions stole four bags: two by Mike Davis and one apiece by Sax and Shelby. Oakland stole three: one apiece by Canseco, Glenn Hubbard, and AL Rookie of the Year Walt Weiss. Los Angeles won game four, 4–3, thanks to several inopportune defensive miscues by their opponent. They escaped with a win despite going 1 for 4 in stolen base attempts. The two shortstops laid down the only two sacrifice bunts in the series: Weiss and Alfredo Griffin, who batted only .199 for the Dodgers during the regular season.

Rickey Henderson was batting .247 with a .392 on-base percentage and 25 steals in 65 games for the Yankees in 1989, when he was traded back to Oakland on June 21. Henderson was going to be a free agent after the 1989 season and negotiations had not gone well between the club and the player. Despite making the All-Star team during his four complete seasons in New York, from 1985 to 1988, Henderson had ruffled some feathers. He was often described as selfish, lazy, arrogant, and individualistic. Dallas Green was the Yankees manager for the first 121 games in 1989 and said, "I'm not saying Rickey didn't bust his tail every day, but I just didn't see the juice and enthusiasm people said Rickey had when he's on a hot streak." Reliever Dave Righetti, however, expressed the sentiment of many of his teammates, saying he "wasn't thrilled" about the trade, especially since they had trouble scoring runs. He added that the Yankees became a "damn good team" when Henderson arrived in 1985. "He had that try-to-get-me-out arrogance. Our whole lineup was like that last year," Righetti insisted. However, by 1989 people were questioning his motivation, physical skills, and consistency. Rumors about the trade had been circulating and the Oakland players had actually held a private meeting discussing whether they wanted Henderson on their team. They emerged with a message for the front office, saying that they approved of the deal and that it should be made. Tony LaRussa, the Athletics skipper, insisted that if Henderson did not go along with what they're trying to achieve then he would hear about it. Dave Stewart was happy to have him aboard, "It's a run whenever he gets on base. It's automatic offense. You'll see the difference immediately." Dave Parker insisted, "In New York, Rickey was the whole show. He felt he had to do it all. Here, he just has to do his job. *Now* he'll put on the show."[62]

Henderson did put on a show the rest of the way, batting .294 for Oakland in 85 games with a .425 on-base percentage, 72 runs scored, 52 steals, and a terrific 89.7 percent basestealing average. But he saved his best for the bright lights of the postseason as Oakland (99–63) defeated Toronto (89–73), four games to one, in the ALCS. After taking the opener, 7–3, at the Oakland–Alameda County Coliseum, partially thanks to a takeout slide by Henderson, which led to a crucial throwing error, the Athletics also won game two, 6–3. Henderson's four steals in game two was a postseason record for a single game. He walked in the fourth inning, stole second and third, and then scored on Carney Lansford's single. After losing game three, 7–3, Oakland won game four, 6–5, as Henderson hit two, two-run homers, and Jose Canseco launched one into the upper deck of the SkyDome. Oakland wrapped it up on October 8 with a 4–3 triumph. Henderson was the series MVP, batting .400 with a .609 on-base percentage, eight runs scored, one double, one triple, two homers, five RBIs, seven walks, and eight steals. In total, Oakland stole thirteen bags: eight by Henderson, two apiece by Carney Lansford and Tony Phillips, and one by Walt Weiss. Ordinarily, Toronto's eleven steals would have easily led a series, but not this time. Cito Gaston's Blue Jays were led by Tony Fernandez, who batted .350 and swiped five bags, while Nelson Liriano stole three and Kelly Gruber, Lloyd Moseby, and Mookie Wilson had one apiece. Toronto had a perfect 100 percent basestealing average, while Canseco was caught stealing twice for Oakland as they pilfered bags at an exceptional 86.7 rate. There were a total of five steals in the NLCS as the Giants (92–70) defeated the Cubs (93–69), four games to one. Not even an earthquake before game three of the World Series and a ten-day postponement could slow down the Athletics, as they outscored the Giants, 32 to 14, in the four-game sweep. Henderson batted .474 in the series and stole three of the four cushions for Oakland. Brett Butler stole the only two bases for San Francisco.

For nine straight seasons from 1980 to 1988 the National League stole more bases than the American League despite having two fewer teams. The streak came to an end in 1989, as the AL teams pilfered 1,587 bags while the NL teams stole 1,529 bags. For the first time since 1974, excluding the strike-shortened 1981 season, no major league team stole over 200 bases. Buck Rodgers's fourth-place Montreal Expos (81–81, NL East) led the NL with 160 steals, while another fourth-place outfit, the Brewers of the AL East, had an identical 81–81 record and led the AL with 165 steals. Tom Trebelhorn's Milwaukee Brewers led the junior league in steals for the third straight season. Davey Johnson's Mets led the NL with a 74.9 percent stolen base average, while John Wathan's Royals led the AL with a 75.1 percent average. New York's National League ballclub purloined 158 sacks (2nd, NL), while Kansas City pilfered 154 bags (3rd, AL).

The senior circuit only had 172 more sacrifices than the junior circuit. This was not unusual because ever since the AL adopted the designated hitter rule in 1973, the AL position players were consistently laying down more sacrifice bunts than the NL position players. Jack McKeon's second-place San Diego Padres led the NL with 95 sacrifice bunts, while Jeff Torborg's last-place Chicago White Sox finished second in the majors with 85 sacrifices. Roberto Alomar of San Diego led the NL with 17 sacrifices, while Cleveland Indians weak-hitting shortstop Felix Fermin led the majors with 32 sacrifices. It was the highest total in the AL since Bert Campaneris laid down 40 in 1977. Fermin batted .259 lifetime in ten seasons with 96 sacrifices and 27 steals in 48 attempts (56.3 percent).

In addition to leading the AL in runs (113) and walks (126), Henderson also stole 77 bags to win his ninth AL stolen base crown and had a sensational 84.6 percent basestealing average. Cecil Espy of Texas finished second with 45 thefts; Devon White of California had 44; Steve Sax of New York and Gary Pettis of Detroit were ranked fourth with 43 steals. Vince Coleman won his fifth straight NL stolen base title with 65 bags while also compiling an outstanding 86.7 percent basestealing average. Juan Samuel stole 42 bags, while playing for both Philadelphia and New York, and shared second place with 21-year-old second-year player Roberto Alomar. Tim Raines and Howard Johnson each stole 41. Espy had two good basestealing seasons in 1988 (33) and 1989 (45). White was an accomplished small ball player with 61 sacrifices, 346 steals, and a 77.9 percent basestealing average during his seventeen-year career. He stole at least 32 bases during five seasons: 1987 (32), 1989 (44), 1991 (33), 1992 (37), and 1993 (34). Roberto Alomar garnered 474 steals and an 80.6 percent stolen base average. In 1991 he stole four bases in a game to tie a Blue Jays record and in 1993 he stole a career high 55 bags and had a stretch of 18 consecutive steals without being caught. He was also a terrific bunter, whether it was trying to beat out a hit or sacrifice a runner over. Alomar had a whopping 148 sacrifices, including six seasons of eleven or more and a career high of 17 in 1989 when he led the NL.

In *The New Bill James Historical Baseball Abstract*, James credits Alfredo Griffin as being the most aggressive baserunner of the 1980s, writing, "I personally saw him score from second on a ground ball to second ... I have heard about Alfredo doing things like going first-to-third on infield outs, moving second-to-third on a pop up to short, scoring on a pop out to the catcher, and taking second after grounding into a forceout." He also wrote that any base that was unguarded was his for the taking.[63] Griffin had some terrific baserunning accomplishments, but he certainly wasn't the only one taking chances on the basepaths and making things happen. And surely, there is much more to aggressive running than compiling stolen bases. But the most prolific thieves are usually the most aggressive baserunners in the majors, because they often times possess lightning-quick speed that can be used to push the envelope. Was Griffin really more aggressive than a Rickey Henderson or Vince Coleman considering he stole only 192 bases in 326 attempts (58.9 percent) during his eighteen-year career? The stolen base by nature is an aggressive baserunning action. In 1980, Griffin batted .254 with a low .283 on-base percentage, and scored only 63 runs, despite playing in 155 games and compiling 653 at-bats. He was tied with Willie Wilson for the AL lead in triples (15), and he stole 18 bases in 41 attempts for a pitiful 43.9 percent basestealing average. Considering his dreadful stolen base percentages during the 1980s, he may have been the most reckless baserunner during that decade.

Rickey Henderson entered the 1989 season with 794 steals, which was accomplished in only ten seasons. On April 9, the Yankees fell to Cleveland, 4–3, and Henderson stole his 800th bag.

The first two hitters in the St. Louis Cardinals lineup, Vince Coleman and Milt Thompson, stole two bases apiece in a 5–2 loss to Pittsburgh on June 24 at Three Rivers Stadium. Coleman swiped second base in the third inning for his 39th consecutive steal, which broke Davey Lopes's record of 38 in 1975. He reached first on an infield single and then with the count 3 and 1 on Thompson, he pilfered the record-breaking bag. Then Thompson walked and he teamed with Coleman for a double steal. Coleman was becoming accustomed to stealing second and third in the same inning and had already done so seven times that season. Bob Walk, the Pirates 32-year-old right-handed pitcher, tried his best to stop Coleman from breaking the record and tried eight pickoff throws before the fleet-footed runner picked his pocket. Walk desperately tried to stop Coleman from breaking the record and insisted that "Pride comes into it" and it was like facing Mike Schmidt when he had 499 homers. The Cardinals speedster had actually started the streak during the previous season and finished the 1988 campaign with six straight successful steals. The last time he was gunned down was on September 15, 1988, in Philadelphia. Coleman said, "Any time you establish a record it's great, but when you don't win it's not as much fun. There's not much to celebrate."[64] He extended his streak to 50 before Montreal catcher Nelson Santovenia threw him out trying to steal second base in the fourth inning on July 28 at Olympic Stadium. He did steal his 45th bag of the season in the ninth inning and at this juncture of the campaign with only one caught stealing, he was sporting an incredible 97.8 percent basestealing average. Coleman had singled in the ninth, was sacrificed to second, stole third, and then came across to score. The Cardinals prevailed, 2–0.

The American League won the All-Star Game, 5–3, at Anaheim Stadium on July 11 as leadoff man Bo Jackson lit the fuse by going 2 for 4 with one homer, one run scored, two RBIs, and one stolen base. Tony Gwynn, Eric Davis, and Howard Johnson each stole bases for the NL, while Ozzie Smith was caught stealing. Rickey Henderson had a banner day on July 29 when he scored four runs, walked four times, and stole five bags despite not having an official at-bat in a 14–6 loss to Seattle. The five steals matched an Oakland record, which was set by Bert Campaneris on April 24, 1976. However, Eddie Collins stole six bags during two different games in September of 1912 for the Philadelphia Athletics. Oakland stole eight bases in the game: five by Henderson, two by Carney Lansford (37 steals in 1989) and one by Stan Javier (12 steals). Javier batted .269 lifetime with a .345 on-base percentage, 67 sacrifices, 246 steals, and a magnificent 82.8 percent stolen base average. This was a sloppy game by Seattle as they committed three errors and had their starter, Randy Johnson, walk seven in six innings of work. However, Oakland tied a team record by walking thirteen in the game and allowed Seattle to win before a crowd of 40,734 at the Oakland–Alameda County Coliseum. The Angels defeated Boston, 8–5, on September 9 as Devon White stole four bags, including second, third, and home in the same inning.

Despite the fact that the owners locked out the players during the 1990 spring training, all teams played a 162-game schedule even though the season started late and the players had only two and a half weeks to prepare for the lidlifter. Oakland had acquired Rickey Henderson in a midseason deal in 1989 to put them over the top and on August 29, 1990, they acquired Harold Baines and Willie McGee to strengthen their team. Tony LaRussa's potent offensive team was well-balanced, hitting 164 homers (3rd, AL) and also manufacturing runs with 60 sacrifices (3rd, AL) and 141 steals (2nd, AL). While many people held to the misguided belief that the Athletics relied on the three-run homer to win games, LaRussa insisted that most games are won "with singles and baserunning and clutch hitting."[65]

Oakland (103–59) crushed Boston (88–74) in the ALCS as they outscored them 20 to 4 in the four-game sweep. The Athletics didn't bludgeon them with power as they failed to hit a homer in the series and all four of their extra-base hits were doubles. But instead they compiled an exceptional .299 batting average, .399 on-base percentage, and stole nine bags, including two apiece by Jose Canseco, Rickey Henderson, and Willie McGee. They stole four bases in the first two games after the seventh inning and each time the baserunner came around to score. After fourteen straight steals in the postseason, Henderson was gunned down by Tony Pena trying to steal third base in the seventh inning of game three. His 33 thefts in the postseason ranks second all-time behind Kenny Lofton (34). Also in game three, Canseco and Baines pulled off a double steal, Dave Henderson pilfered a sack, and Terry Steinbach was caught stealing home in the sixth inning but was safe on Pena's error. Manager Joe Morgan's slow-footed Boston Red Sox had the fewest steals in the majors (53) and the worst stolen base average (50.5 percent). Even Ellis Burks, who had stolen 73 bags in 93 attempts (78.5 percent) during his first three big league seasons, slumped to only 9 steals in 20 attempts (45 percent) in 1990. Burks did have the only Boston steal of the series.

While Oakland was destroying Boston in the ALCS, the Cincinnati Reds (91–71) needed six games to defeat Pittsburgh (95–67) in the closely fought NLCS. Both Pittsburgh (137 steals and 96 sacrifices) and Cincinnati (166 steals and 88 sacrifices) were good small ball teams and they combined for twelve steals in the series. Barry Larkin led the Reds by collecting three of their six steals, while Barry Bonds had two of Pittsburgh's six thefts. Larkin batted .295 lifetime with a .371 on-base percentage, a .444 slugging percentage, 59 sacrifices, 379 steals, and an impressive 83.1 percent basestealing average.

Lou Piniella's Reds upset the defending world champions with a shocking four-game sweep in the World Series. Mariano Duncan and Paul O'Neill stole the only bases for the Reds, while Oakland stole seven and were led by Rickey Henderson, who swiped three. Oakland improved upon its 75 percent basestealing average in the ALCS by swiping bags at a perfect 100 percent rate in the fall classic. But they didn't have a lot of opportunities to steal as the Reds pitchers held them to a .207 batting average and Jose Rijo dominated with a 2–0 record and a 0.59 ERA. There were three sacrifice bunts in the series, laid down by Carney Lansford and Bob Welch of Oakland, and Paul O'Neill of Cincinnati.

The National League pilfered more bags than the American League in 1990, 1,787 to 1,503. The senior circuit teams also laid down 193 more sacrifices, 876 to 683. Buck Rodgers's third-place Montreal Expos (85–77, NL East) were a small ball juggernaut, stealing 235 bags to lead the majors and laying down 87 sacrifices (3rd, NL). The last-place Atlanta Braves in the NL West laid down the fewest sacrifices in the NL (49) and only 18 of them (36.7 percent) were by position players. However, this was not as bad as the 1984 Philadelphia Phillies, who had only 39 sacrifice bunts and 31 of them were by the pitchers (79.5 percent). No Philadelphia position player had more than one sacrifice that season and 41-year-old Jerry Koosman led the team with fourteen. Jim Leyland's first-place Pittsburgh Pirates led the senior league with 96 sacrifices in 1990, while the AL West second-place Chicago White Sox led the AL with 75. The White Sox led the American League in sacrifices for four consecutive seasons from 1988 to 1991. Milwaukee led the junior circuit in steals from 1987 to 1990. They swiped 164 bags in 1990, but their .320 on-base percentage was tied for twelfth in the AL and they limped home with a 74–88 record (6th, AL East). St. Louis was burdened by a low on-base percentage and slugging percentage, the inability to score runs, and weak pitching. Their 221 steals were helpful, but not enough to overcome major deficiencies, as they occupied the cellar of the NL East with a 70–92 record. Jay Bell of Pittsburgh led the majors with 39 sacrifice bunts. Bell compiled an impressive 159 sacrifices during his career and laid down 111 from 1989 to 1993. He also led the majors in 1991 (30). Mike Gallego of Oakland and Billy Ripken of Baltimore led the AL with 17 sacrifices in 1990. Billy laid down 72 during his career, which was 62 more than his brother Cal.

Vince Coleman had one of his better seasons in 1990, which was his final season with the Cardinals. He batted .292 with a .340 on-base percentage, a .400 slugging percentage, and 77 steals in 94 attempts (81.9 percent), while winning his sixth and final NL stolen base title. Eric Yelding of Houston finished second with 64 steals, followed by Barry Bonds (52), Brett Butler (51), and Otis Nixon (50). Yelding's 64 steals represented 71.9 percent of his career total (89) and he never stole more than 11 in any other season. Bonds captured the first of seven NL MVP Awards and joined the 30–30 club for the first of five times during his career with 33 homers and 52 steals (80 percent stolen base average). Rickey Henderson batted .325 and led the AL in on-base percentage (.439), runs scored (119), and stolen bases (65) with an 86.7 percent basestealing average. He also launched 28 homers, matching his career high with the 1986 Yankees. Steve Sax (43) and Roberto Kelly (42) finished second and third in steals and accounted for 71.4 percent of the Yankees' 119 steals.

On May 9, Rickey Henderson scored from second on a 6–3 groundout in the eighth inning and then in the eleventh, he drew a bases loaded walk, to propel the Athletics to a 2–1 win over the Yankees. The game on May 29 was another case of mistaken identity and the imprecise nature of early baseball statistics. As the Athletics were on their way to a 2–1 loss against the Blue Jays, Henderson stole his 893rd bag, which was believed to surpass Ty Cobb's AL record of 892 steals. *The 2006 ESPN Baseball Encyclopedia* credits Cobb with 897 steals. The groundbreaking work, *Total Baseball* by John Thorn and Pete Palmer, came out the previous year in 1989 and served as the foundation of the newer, more accurate encyclopedias. Furthermore, it forced Macmillan to raise its own standards and try to put out a more accurate encyclopedia. However, the 9th edition of Macmillan's baseball encyclopedia that came out in 1993 still had a myriad of discrepancies, including crediting Cobb with 892 steals.

In 1990, Willie Wilson batted .290 with a .354 on-base percentage and 24 steals in 30 attempts (80 percent) during his fifteenth and final season in Kansas City. On June 13 he stole his 600th bag in an 11–4 triumph over California. The American League prevailed, 2–0, over the Nationals in the All-Star Game at Wrigley Field on July 10. The junior circuit stole four bags: two by Kelly Gruber and one apiece by Steve Sax and Jose Canseco. Barry Larkin pilfered the only bag for the NL.

The Indians broke a four-game losing streak with a 4–1 triumph over Kansas City in front of the home fans in Cleveland on August 1. Alex Cole made his major league debut on July 27 and quickly made a great impression. Against Kansas City on the first day of August he went 2 for 2 with two runs scored, one RBI, and five stolen bases, including stealing second and third in the opening inning. It was the first time a Cleveland Indians player stole five bags in a game. In total, the Indians stole six as Mitch Webster pilfered one of his 22 bases on the season. Tom Candiotti of Cleveland was four outs away from a no-hitter at Yankee Stadium on August 3 when the roof caved in, as the Yankees scored four unearned runs in the eighth inning to win the game, 6–4. Former Indian, Mel Hall, hit a three-run homer off reliever Doug Jones in the inning. It was another good day for Cole as he went 2 for 4 with two runs scored and two stolen bases. Each time he stole second it proved fruitful as he came around to score on a double and single. The seven steals in two consecutive games for Cole tied a big league record. The speedy fly chaser batted .300 during the season and finished fourth in the American League with 40 steals, despite playing in only 63 games.

The NL East last-place Montreal Expos were the best basestealing team in the majors in 1991, swiping 221 bags with young speed merchants Marquis Grissom (76) and Delino DeShields (56) leading the team. Grissom (429) and DeShields (463) combined to steal 892 bases during their careers. Grissom batted .272 lifetime with a .318 on-base percentage, a .415 slugging percentage, 227 homers, 38 sacrifices, and 429 steals in 545 attempts (78.7 percent). He led the major leagues in steals in both 1991 (76) and 1992 (78) with stolen base averages of 81.7 percent and 85.7 percent. Grissom accumulated his fair share of strikeouts and so did DeShields, who batted .238 in 1991 with a .347 on-base percentage, a career high 151 strikeouts, and 56 steals in 79 attempts (70.9 percent). The .238 average was an aberration early in his career, as he batted .289 or better during three of his first four seasons from 1990 to 1993, which were also his only seasons in Montreal. DeShields was a 6'1", 175-pound, left-handed hitting but right-handed throwing second baseman, who batted .268 lifetime with a .352 on-base percentage, a .377 slugging percentage, 57 sacrifices, 463 steals, and a 75.9 percent basestealing average. He stole at least 42 bags during six seasons, including his first four, and had his most prolific campaigns in 1991 and in 1997 with St. Louis (55). Grissom played for six big league teams, while DeShields played for five.

The St. Louis Cardinals (202), Atlanta Braves (165), New York Mets (153), and Oakland Athletics (151) were the other big league teams with at least 151 steals in 1991. The Pirates (99) and White Sox (76) led their respective leagues in sacrifices. Joe Torre's second-place Cardinals (84–78, NL East) almost became the first team since the 1912 Washington Senators with ten players with ten or more steals. On October 6 in their 7–3 loss to Chicago, Tom Pagnozzi was inserted into the game in the ninth inning and was gunned down by Hector Villanueva, while trying to steal his tenth bag. Jay Bell of Pittsburgh led the majors with 30 sacrifices, while Luis Sojo of California led the AL with 19. Rickey Henderson won his eleventh AL stolen base title with 58 bags and was followed by Roberto Alomar of Toronto (53), Tim Raines of Chicago (51), Luis Polonia of California (48), and Milt Cuyler of Detroit (41). Grissom took the NL stolen base title with 76 thefts and was followed by

Otis Nixon of Atlanta (72), DeShields (56), Ray Lankford of St. Louis (44), and Barry Bonds of Pittsburgh (43).

Joe Carter batted .259 lifetime with 396 long balls and 231 steals in 297 attempts (77.8 percent). John Cerutti, a southpaw hurler with Toronto, tagged him out unassisted while he wandered off first base in 1986. And then on April 23, 1991, Roger Clemens tagged him out unassisted the same way at Fenway Park. There was more unusual activity in the big leagues on May 22 when Dennis Eckersley picked off Kenny Williams of Toronto in the ninth inning of a 2–1 Oakland victory. Eckersley's last pickoff before this game came on June 29, 1987, against the Chicago White Sox. Remarkably, Kenny Williams was the man who was picked off.

The headline by the Associated Press on May 2, 1991, declared, "Henderson 'greatest' thief at 939." Oakland won the game, 7–4, against the Yankees before a home crowd of 36,139. The new king of thieves pilfered third base in the fourth inning to surpass Lou Brock as the all-time stolen base leader at 939. He triumphantly raised the bag above his head and pumped his left fist. Play was halted for five minutes and Henderson celebrated the moment while the crowd gave him a standing ovation and his teammates applauded from the top step of the dugout. He said, "Lou Brock was a great base-stealer, but today I'm the greatest of all time." Brock was on hand and graciously said, "Today, you might be the greatest competitor that ever ran the bases and I congratulate you. You are a legend in your own time." Henderson needed only 1,154 attempts, breaking the record in his thirteenth season, while Brock had accumulated his career total during nineteen seasons and 1,245 attempts. Henderson tried to break the record in the opening inning, but he was thrown out by Matt Nokes trying to pilfer second base with Tim Leary on the hill. He said he desperately wanted to capture the record and he had felt the pressure of the moment. It was a "dream come true." The Athletics recognized Henderson's achievement by giving him a 1991 Porsche and by donating $75,000 to charities that were selected by Henderson. The concession stands at the Coliseum were buzzing as people crowded in to buy T-shirts of Henderson, commemorating his achievement. There was a total of five steals in the game, four by Oakland and one by New York. Furthermore, Henderson was caught stealing two times in the game and was only three for eight during the early season competition.[66]

Jim Sundberg won six Gold Gloves and was widely recognized as an outstanding defensive catcher. He was reportedly Henderson's favorite catcher to steal against and stole 55 bags against him. The precocious speed merchant challenged the catcher right from the outset, stealing his first major league bag against him on June 24, 1979, when Sundberg was playing for the Rangers. Sundberg didn't remember that steal while being interviewed in 1991, but said that right before the 1983 All-Star break, "My arm was really hurting and he stole 10 bases off me in three games. So, he got about 20 percent of his career steals off me in just three days."[67]

Montreal swept the Braves in their three-game series, winning the finale at Olympic Stadium by a 7–6 score on June 16. Otis Nixon of Atlanta became the first major leaguer to steal six bags in a game since Eddie Collins did it on September 22, 1912. In total, Atlanta stole eight to tie a franchise record, while Montreal stole five, including the 32nd and 33rd thefts by Marquis Grissom and the 28th steal by Delino DeShields. Nixon stole second and third in the first, third, and ninth innings. He victimized the battery of southpaw Chris Nabholz and catcher Mike Fitzgerald in the first and third, while right-hander Barry Jones was on the hilltop in the ninth. Atlanta had six steals in the opening three frames with their two and three hole hitters, Terry Pendleton and Lonnie Smith, also pilfering one apiece.

Nixon went 3 for 5 out of the leadoff spot and scored two runs. The only reason he was in the lineup was because David Justice became sick. Nixon was perplexed as to why a writer approached him and congratulated him for his feat, saying, "To be honest, I would trade all those stolen bases and hits for a win." When he was told that he tied Collins's record, he said that he thought the record was held by "somebody like" Rickey Henderson or Vince Coleman and he didn't know who Eddie Collins was. Part of the reason why Atlanta lost the game was because left fielder Lonnie Smith got a late jump on a smash by DeShields and it fell to the ground, scoring two runs in the sixth inning.[68]

The day after Nixon became the first modern-era National League player with six steals in a game, the Hall of Fame called him, asking for his shoes. Nixon commented, "At least a part of me will be in the Hall." He wore black shoes, size 11. Nixon said that when he is taking his lead off first base with a lefty on the hill, he looks for a key that gives away whether they are coming home with the pitch or to first. Right-handers are easier to read. Furthermore, he doesn't get as big a lead as some other basestealers, taking about three and a half steps, but instead relies on a good jump. He insisted that every pitcher has a movement that tells him when they are going home: they may throw from the chest "or at a count ... one, two, three." Nixon, who was once timed in the 40-yard dash at 4.4 seconds, said it took him about three steps to be running at full speed. He said, "I could close my eyes and know when to slide; it's about seven steps." Nixon preferred the headfirst slide and unlike some players who slowed up before sliding, he instead would accelerate. He used a "short, compact slide" and disliked the "long, leaping slide." When Nixon slid feet first it was because he felt he had the base stolen and it wouldn't be a close play.[69]

The American League won the All-Star Game at the SkyDome, 4–2, on July 9. Ivan Calderon of the NL stole third base in the top of the second inning and Ozzie Guillen of the AL had the only sacrifice bunt in the game.

Tom Kelly's Minnesota Twins went from worst to first in 1991, winning 21 more games than 1990 and capturing the AL West title with a 95–67 record. Their small ball numbers were unexceptional with 107 steals (7th, AL) and 44 sacrifices (11th, AL). But once they got into the postseason they had their running shoes on and they set the pace from the outset of the ALCS versus Toronto (91–71). Minnesota jumped out to a 5–0 lead in the first three innings of game one, thanks to four stolen bases and held on for a 5–4 win at the Metrodome. The Twins won in five games and they stole eight cushions in the series: three by Dan Gladden, two apiece by Chuck Knoblauch and Shane Mack, and one by Chili Davis. Cito Gaston's Blue Jays stole seven bags as Devon White pilfered three, Roberto Alomar had two, while Kelly Gruber and Mookie Wilson had one apiece. The Blue Jays 148 steals were ranked second in the AL during the 1991 campaign. Shane Mack had a unique but undesirable accomplishment in the 1991 postseason as he was caught stealing home on two occasions: in game one of the ALCS and in game four of the World Series.

Brian Hunter of Atlanta was caught stealing home in the bottom of the second inning in game five of the NLCS as pitcher Tom Glavine struck out on the play. With the bases loaded, one out, and a 2 and 2 count on Glavine, third base coach Jimy Williams flashed the suicide squeeze sign in his direction. Hunter sprinted towards home plate, but the left-handed hitting Glavine couldn't make contact with Zane Smith's low and outside sinker and Hunter was tagged out by the third baseman in a rundown. Glavine was bunting at the pitch, seeing Hunter running home out of the corner of his eye, but admitted that he had missed the sign. Jim Leyland, the Pirates skipper, acknowledged that they were caught off guard by the squeeze play and were fortunate that Smith delivered a difficult pitch to bunt. Bobby Cox insisted that it was the perfect count to try the suicide squeeze because if Glavine, who was a terrific bunter, got the ball down, then they scored a run and if he fouled it off and struck out, then Lonnie Smith would have a chance to hit with the bases loaded. The inability to execute the suicide squeeze was costly as the Pirates prevailed 1–0.[70]

Minnesota wasn't the only team to go from worst to first in 1991 as the Atlanta Braves (94–68) turned the trick during Bobby Cox's first full season as their skipper. Jim Leyland's Pittsburgh Pirates, the winners of the NL East with a 98–64 mark, led the senior league in sacrifices for the second straight season (99), but Atlanta had the third most steals in the NL (165) heading into the NLCS. The Braves got great pitching from Steve Avery and John Smoltz, who each won two games, and they defeated the Pirates, four games to three. Ron Gant stole seven of Atlanta's ten bases. Pittsburgh stole six hassocks in the series, three by Barry Bonds, two by Gary Redus, and one by Andy Van Slyke.

Gene Larkin's bases-loaded single in the last of the tenth gave the Twins a 1–0 game seven victory and their second world title in five years. Lonnie Smith's baserunning blunder may have cost the Braves the world championship. Terry Pendleton hit a double in the eighth inning and Smith looked uncertain, hesitating at second base, which cost him dearly as he couldn't score on the long two-bagger, pulling up at third, and later being cut down at the plate as Sid Bream grounded into a 3–2–3 double play. The 1991 World Series was one of the best ever with three games going extra innings, including the final two. Chuck Knoblauch stole four bags for Minnesota, while Dan Gladden had two and Kirby Puckett pilfered one. Knoblauch was a renowned thief, stealing 407 bases during a twelve-year career. Atlanta stole five cushions as David Justice led the team with two. The Braves had four of the six sacrifices in the series as Rafael Belliard, who batted .375 in sixteen at-bats, led both teams with two sacrifice bunts.

Not many people gave Phil Garner's Milwaukee Brewers much of a chance to compete for the AL East title in 1992. Knowing that his team was incapable of hitting a large number of homers, Garner decided to make things happen on the bases and take the opposition out of their "comfort zones." With their rookie skipper leading the way, the Brewers went old school on the American League, stealing 256 bases with a respectable 69 percent basestealing average (4th, AL). The 256 steals was the most in the AL since Chuck Tanner's 1976 Oakland Athletics stole 341 bags. Furthermore, the Brewers became the first team since the 1901 Philadelphia Phillies with eleven players stealing ten or more bases. While one Detroit Tigers coach told Garner that his team's running "bordered on lunacy," Garner insisted that there was a "method in our madness." Tim Foli, the first base coach, was allowed to tell the runners when they should steal.[71] While it was not surprising to see Pat Listach (54 steals) and Darryl Hamilton (41) steal bags, which they were skilled at doing so in the minors, it was perhaps surprising to see big 6'1", 222-pound, John Jaha, steal ten bases in ten attempts during his first season or to see Dante Bichette, another big person, steal 18 in 25 attempts. Bichette had decent wheels and stole 152 bags during his career, including a career high of 31 with the 1996 Colorado Rockies when he also hit 31 homers, scored 114 runs, and drove in 141.

Garner insisted that you can't be afraid of being thrown out or you won't be any good. His running philosophy worked wonderfully in 1992 and they gave Cito Gaston's Blue Jays all they could handle, finishing four games behind them in second place with a 92–70 record. The Brewers hit the second fewest homers in the American League (82) and the third fewest in the majors. However, they finished fifth in runs scored (740), despite failing to lead the league in any major offensive category except stolen bases. They batted .268

during the campaign (2nd, AL), had a .330 on-base percentage (7th, AL), and a .375 slugging percentage (11th, AL). Their 61 sacrifice bunts ranked second in the junior circuit. In addition to having a formidable small ball offense, the Brewers had the junior league's best pitching staff (3.43 ERA) and defense (.986 fielding average).

The American League stole more bases than the National League in 1992, 1,704 to 1,560. However, the senior league's 130 steals per team surpassed the junior league's 121.7 steals per team. There were five big league teams with at least 160 steals: Milwaukee (256), St. Louis (208), Montreal (196), the Chicago White Sox (160), and California (160). Pat Listach secured the AL Rookie of the Year Award by beating out Kenny Lofton. But Lofton won the AL stolen base title with 66 thefts as Listach finished second (54). Listach won the hardware in 1992, but it was Lofton who would have the more accomplished career. Brady Anderson of Baltimore (53) was ranked third in steals, followed by Luis Polonia of California (51) and Roberto Alomar of Toronto (49). Conspicuously absent was 33-year-old Rickey Henderson, who stole 48 bags in 117 games and failed to make the top five for the first time since 1979, his first big league season when he played only 89 games. In the National League, Marquis Grissom won his second straight stolen base title with 78 sacks and was followed by his teammate Delino DeShields (46), Bip Roberts of Cincinnati (44), Steve Finley of Houston (44), and Ozzie Smith of St. Louis (43).

There was nothing exceptional about Henry Cotto's 23 steals in 1992, except if you consider he was caught stealing only two times for a 92 percent basestealing average. This was not unusual for the Seattle outfielder, who swiped 27 in 30 attempts (90 percent) in 1988 and 21 in 24 attempts (87.5 percent) in 1990. Cotto was a .261 career hitter with a low .299 on-base percentage, a .370 slugging percentage, 21 sacrifices, and 130 steals in 156 attempts (83.3 percent).

The two worst teams in the NL West had the two best sacrifice bunt totals in 1992: San Francisco (101) and Los Angeles

As first-year skipper Phil Garner prepared for the 1992 season, he knew that the prospects for his Milwaukee team were poor if they were going to rely on long balls for success. Instead he molded his team into an aggressive, daring, and reckless group of burglars, who pilfered a whopping 256 bags, the most in the American League since Chuck Tanner's Oakland Athletics swiped 341 cushions in 1976. The 1992 Milwaukee Brewers almost stole the AL East title from Toronto, finishing four games back with an impressive 92–70 record, despite hitting a measly 82 homers. They had a well-balanced basestealing attack with eleven players stealing ten or more bases. Pat Listach (54), Darryl Hamilton (41), and Paul Molitor (31) were the best three burglars on the club and they accounted for 49.2 percent of Milwaukee's steals. (George Brace photograph).

(102). Tony LaRussa's Athletics led the AL with 72 sacrifices, while Toronto and New York had the fewest (26). Brett Butler of the Dodgers led the majors with 24 sacrifice bunts, while Jerry Browne of Oakland led the AL with 16.

On May 1, Rickey Henderson stole his 1,000th bag in the first inning as Oakland went on to defeat Detroit, 7–6. On May 3, Alex Cole of Cleveland stole five bases in a game for the second time in his career. California won the contest, 6–3, as Cole went 4 for 4. Cole was only batting .206 for Cleveland in 41 games when he was traded to Pittsburgh on July 4 and batted .278 for the Pirates in 64 games the rest of the way.

At Three Rivers Stadium on June 15, Jeff King of Pittsburgh was caught stealing twice in the same inning in a 4–1 win by the Phillies. In the last of the fourth, King took off for second prematurely, intending to steal the bag and he got hung up in a rundown and joined pitcher Terry Mulholland and catcher Darren Daulton who "all converged on an uncovered first base like flies to an unguarded pickle." While Daulton was applying the tag at first base, Mulholland bumped King as he was sliding and the Phillies southpaw hurler was called for interference. Umpire Jim Quick allowed King to advance to second, but he was credited with a caught stealing. Mulholland facetiously said, "That was a pulling-guard type situation. I was trying to find a hole and run interference for Dutch." And then with a serious disposition, he confessed, "Actually, it was boneheaded of me not getting over there to cover earlier." He said he "reacted slowly" when Daulton caught him off guard by throwing behind the runner at first, instead of throwing through to second. Later in the inning, King was thrown out trying to steal third and he became the fifth big leaguer to be caught stealing twice in the same inning. Donell Nixon of the Giants was the last player to do it on July 6, 1988. With Barry Bonds out of the lineup with an injury, Mulholland's job was made easier and he went the distance for the win, giving up his one run on five hits and three walks.[72] Jim Fregosi's Phillies finished the campaign in last place in the NL East. However, in 1993 they would win 27 more games and capture the NL pennant for the first time since 1983.

On June 26, Tony Fernandez of San Diego was also thrown out twice in the same inning as the Padres defeated the Giants, 6–2. Fernandez stole 20 bags in 1992, but was also caught stealing 20 times. It was the worst stolen base average for a player with 20 steals since Jack Fournier of the 1921 St. Louis Browns stole 20 in 42 attempts (47.6 percent). On July 4, Fernandez didn't even make it to first base in the opening frame on a one-hopper to right field as Larry Walker of Montreal threw him out at first. The 1992 All-Star Game was played at Jack Murphy Stadium in San Diego on July 14 as the AL prevailed, 13–6. Roberto Alomar of the AL stole second and third in the second inning and scored on Joe Carter's single. Vince Coleman didn't walk a lot during his career, but on August 10 he drew five walks, which was 18.5 percent of his season total of 27. The Pirates defeated the Mets, 4–2, in sixteen innings at Shea Stadium. The Phillies fell to Houston, 3–2, on September 2, but Terry Mulholland had his fourteenth pickoff of the season, a major league record. The portsider was extremely skilled at preventing larceny, allowing only his second theft of the campaign on a delayed steal by Andujar Cedeno.

The Cleveland Indians prevailed over the Chicago White Sox, 2–1, on September 13 as Kenny Lofton scored both of the Indians runs. Lofton pilfered his 53rd and 54th bags to break Donie Bush's 1909 AL rookie record of 53 steals. It could be argued convincingly that Lofton deserved the 1992 Rookie of the Year Award, batting .285 with a .362 on-base percentage, 96 runs scored, 66 steals, and an 84.6 percent basestealing average. Lofton began his big league career in 1991 with Houston (20 games) before being traded to Cleveland on December 10, 1991. It was a regrettable deal for Houston as they lost a first-rate leadoff man and received Eddie Taubensee and Willie Blair in return. Lofton was an excellent leadoff man with high on-base percentages; large numbers of steals with good bases-stealing averages; the ability to bunt for a hit and affect the psychology and positioning of the defense; and large numbers of runs scored. Furthermore, he could run balls down in center field with the best of them. During his first five complete seasons in the AL from 1992 to 1996, he won the stolen base crown each year with 66, 70, 60, 54, and 75 thefts, respectively. His stolen base averages were equally impressive: 84.6, 83.3, 83.3, 78.3, and 81.5. Lofton is ranked 15th all-time with 622 steals and he is one of thirty-six players in the 500 stolen base club. Entering the 2010 season, the 500 stolen base club was as follows:

Player	Stolen Bases	Player	Stolen Bases
1. Rickey Henderson	1406	19. Maury Wills	586
2. Lou Brock	938	20. George Van Haltren	583
3. Billy Hamilton	914	21. Ozzie Smith	580
4. Ty Cobb	897	22. Hugh Duffy	574
5. Tim Raines	808	23. Bid McPhee	568
6. Vince Coleman	752	24. Brett Butler	558
7. Arlie Latham	742	25. Davey Lopes	557
8. Eddie Collins	741	26. Cesar Cedeno	550
9. Max Carey	738	27. Bill Dahlen	548
10. Honus Wagner	723	28. John Ward	540
11. Joe Morgan	689	29. Herman Long	537
12. Willie Wilson	668	30. (tie) Patsy Donovan	518
13. Tom Brown	657	30. (tie) Jack Doyle	518
14. Bert Campaneris	649	32. Barry Bonds	514
15. Kenny Lofton	622	33. (tie) Fred Clarke	509
16. Otis Nixon	620	33. (tie) Harry Stovey	509
17. George Davis	619	35. Luis Aparicio	506
18. Dummy Hoy	596	36. Paul Molitor	504

It appeared as if the Pittsburgh Pirates (96–66) would avenge the Braves (98–64) for defeating them in seven games in the previous season's NLCS. In the seventh game they held a 2–0 lead going into the last of the ninth at Atlanta–Fulton County Stadium when the Braves broke their hearts once again, scoring three, including the final two runs thanks to Francisco Cabrera's pinch-hit, two-run single with two outs. Otis Nixon proved instrumental in Atlanta's 6–4, game four triumph, as he went 4 for 5 with two runs scored and two RBIs. He batted .286 in the series and stole three of Atlanta's five bases. The other three steals in the series were by Ron Gant and John Smoltz of Atlanta, while Barry Bonds stole the only bag for Pittsburgh.

Tony LaRussa's Oakland Athletics faced off against Cito Gaston's Toronto Blue Jays in the ALCS, as they both had identical 96–66 records during the regular season. The Blue Jays finished seventh in the AL with 129 steals, but their 76.8 percent basestealing average was the best in the junior circuit and second only to Philadelphia (80.4 percent) in the majors. Oakland's 143 steals were fifth in the junior league and they had the circuit's third best basestealing average (70.8 percent). In the ALCS both teams ran the bases aggressively as Toronto won the series, four games to two, and stole seven bags. Roberto Alomar batted .423 with two homers and five steals, while Joe Carter batted only .192 and stole two bags. Oakland stole an eye-opening sixteen bases: seven by Willie Wilson; two apiece by Eric Fox, Rickey Henderson, and Walt Weiss; while Lance Blankenship, Mike Bordick, and Ruben Sierra each stole one. LaRussa's daring burglars had a terrific 88.9 percent basestealing average in the series, while Toronto compiled an inadequate 58.3 percent average and were weighed down by Devon White, who was 0 for 4 in stolen base attempts after stealing 37 hassocks during the regular season with a magnificent 90.2 percent basestealing average.

Otis Nixon's unsuccessful bunt was the final out of the 1992 World Series as Toronto defeated Atlanta in six games. There were four sacrifices in the series, two by each team. Once again, Alomar led the team by collecting three of Toronto's six steals. Atlanta was the aggressor in the series, stealing fifteen, including five apiece by Otis Nixon and Deion Sanders. Nixon and Sanders carried their weight in the series, batting .296 and .533 respectively, but the rest of the team wasn't any good. Both teams ran the bases efficiently: Toronto was 6 for 6 in stolen base attempts, while Atlanta was 15 for 18 (83.3 percent). The Blue Jays emerged victorious in game three, 3–2, thanks to their successful execution of small ball strategies. The game was tied at two entering the home half of the ninth when Alomar led off with a single and stole second. Carter was passed intentionally and then cleanup hitter, Dave Winfield, laid down a sacrifice bunt to move the runners to second and third. Winfield laid down only nineteen sacrifices during his twenty-two-year big league career in regular season competition. After Winfield's selfless act, pinch-hitter Ed Sprague was given an intentional free pass to set up a force play at home and a potential inning ending double play. Instead of taking their chances with the 25-year-old second-year player who batted .234 during the regular season, the veteran Candy Maldonado stepped into the batter's box after batting .272 during the regular season with a .357 on-base percentage and 20 homers. However, the book insists that the best way to escape without harm in this situation is to load the bases and take your chances with the next hitter and the book is usually right. But Maldonado singled to score the winning run and Toronto won in the ninth inning for the second straight game. And it was Cito Gaston who went against the book as he chose not to go to his bench and have the left-handed hitting Rance Mulliniks pinch-hit for the right-handed hitting Maldonado against the right-hander Jeff Reardon.

Second-place Montreal (94–68, NL East) and first-place Toronto (95–67, AL East) led their respective leagues in steals and basestealing average in 1993. Felipe Alou's Expos stole 228 bags with a terrific 80.3 percent basestealing average, while Toronto pilfered 170 bags with a laudable 77.6 percent basestealing average. Perhaps it was not surprising that Cito Gaston's Blue Jays led their league in steals, considering they had four players on the team who stole a combined 2,730 bags during their careers: Rickey Henderson (1,406), Paul Molitor (504), Roberto Alomar (474), and Devon White (346). Henderson began the season with Oakland, batting .327 with 17 homers, but he batted only .215 for Toronto after being traded on July 31. He maintained high stolen base percentages with both teams and finished the campaign with 53 bags and an 86.9 percent basestealing average. Kenny Lofton led the junior league with 70 thefts, followed by Luis Polonia (55), Roberto Alomar (55), Henderson (53), and Chad Curtis of California (48). In the NL, Chuck Carr of the expansion Florida Marlins won the stolen base crown with 58 bags and was followed by Marquis Grissom (53), Otis Nixon (47), Darren Lewis of San Francisco (46), and Gregg Jefferies of the St. Louis Cardinals (46). Carr played only eight big league seasons with a low .254 batting average, a .316 on-base percentage, 30 sacrifices, 144 steals, and a 73.5 percent basestealing average.

Runs scored and home runs increased significantly in both leagues in 1993, even if you account for expansion in the NL. When the National League expanded by two teams with new franchises in Colorado and Florida, for the first time since 1976 both leagues had the same number of teams. The NL stole 1,714 bases, while the AL swiped 1,549. The only teams with more than 152 steals were Montreal (228), Toronto (170), California (169), Cleveland (159), and St. Louis (153). There were three NL teams with at least 100 sacrifices: Los Angeles (107), San Francisco (102), and Montreal (100). The AL East fifth-place Boston Red Sox led the AL with 80 sacrifice bunts. It was the first time since 1946 that Boston led the junior circuit in sacrifices. An even more amazing fact is that during the first 24 seasons of divisional play from 1969 to 1992, the American League's team sacrifice bunt leader came from the AL West. Jose Offerman of Los Angeles led the NL in sacrifices by laying down 25 of his 73 career total. He stole 172 bases during his fifteen-year career with a disturbingly low 63.2 percent basestealing average. Joey Cora of the White Sox laid down 19 of his career 84 sacrifices to lead the AL.

On May 24, the Seattle Mariners defeated the California Angels, 4–3, in fourteen frames as Luis Polonia of the Angels tied an American League record by being caught stealing three times, twice on pitchouts. Jack McDowell pitched a three-hit shutout for Chicago on June 16 at the Oakland-Alameda County Coliseum as the White Sox prevailed, 4–0. Rickey Henderson got two of the three hits and stole the 1,066th base of his illustrious career. He must have felt on top of the world, knowing that he surpassed Yutaka Fukumoto in steals to become the number one thief in the world. Fukumoto played in the Japanese League from 1970 to 1988 and stole 1,065 bases.

The American League won its sixth straight All-Star Game in 1993 by a 9–3 score on July 13 at Oriole Park at Camden Yards. Devon White played in his second All-Star Game and went 1 for 2 with a double, a run scored, an RBI, and the only steal of the contest. White batted .273 during the season with 116 runs scored and 34 steals in 38 attempts. George Brett wasn't known for his wheels, but when he stole a base on August 29 in Kansas City's 5–4 triumph over Boston, he became the third major leaguer with at least 3,000 hits, 300 homers, and 200 steals. Willie Mays and Hank Aaron were the other two players on this short list.

The Toronto Blue Jays needed six games to defeat Gene Lamont's Chicago White Sox (94–68) in the ALCS. Roberto Alomar batted .292 and stole four of Toronto's seven bases. Henderson stole two, while Pat Borders swiped one. Alomar played in the postseason during seven campaigns and his twenty postseason steals is ranked fourth all-time behind Omar Vizquel (23), Rickey Henderson (33), and Kenny Lofton (34). Ozzie Guillen, Lance Johnson, and Tim Raines, stole one bag apiece for Chicago. Tony Fernandez laid down the only sacrifice bunt for Cito Gaston's club, while the Pale Hose collected five sacrifices: two apiece by Joey Cora and Ron Karkovice, and one by Guillen.

The Braves (104–58) outlasted the Giants (103–59) to win the NL West in the final authentic pennant race before baseball added an extra round of playoffs with a wildcard team and went to a three divisional setup. When the Phillies (97–65) downed the Braves, four games to two in the NLCS, the only steals were by Philadelphia's Dave Hollins and Mickey Morandini. Three players had two sacrifices in a single game: Otis Nixon laid down two sacrifice bunts in game four, while opposing pitchers Greg Maddux and Tommy Greene each did it in game six when Philadelphia secured the flag with a 6–3 triumph. And then Toronto won its second consecutive World Series, four games to two, as they pilfered seven bags against the fighting Phils. Alomar batted .480 in the fall classic and stole four cushions, while Henderson, Paul Molitor, and Devon White had one apiece. Molitor was the series MVP, batting .500 with 10 runs scored, 8 RBIs, and 6 extra-base hits (2 doubles, 2 triples, 2 homers). Philadelphia's seven steals were pilfered by Lenny Dykstra (4) and Mariano Duncan (3). Phillies hard-throwing right hander Curt Schilling laid down the only sacrifice bunt of the series in game five. The series ended in dramatic style when Joe Carter hit a three-run blast off closer Mitch Williams in the last of the ninth in game six to give the Blue Jays a come-from-behind 8–6 triumph in the final contest.

The players went on strike on August 12, 1994, refusing to accept a salary cap, which the owners demanded, and on September 14 the season was declared over as the owners and players were still at an impasse. This was bad news for the Montreal Expos, who were leading the NL East with a 74–40 record and they were also leading the NL in steals (137) and basestealing average (79.2 percent). Kansas City of the AL Central led the junior circuit with 140 steals, while the Baltimore Orioles stole 69 and had the majors' best basestealing average (84.1 percent). The Houston Astros (73) and Chicago White Sox (51) led their respective leagues in sacrifices. Craig Biggio won the only NL stolen base crown of his career with 39 thefts in 43 attempts. Kenny Lofton won his third straight AL stolen base crown with 60 thefts in 112 games. Pitcher Ken Hill of Montreal (16) and second baseman Pat Kelly of the New York Yankees (14) led their respective leagues in sacrifice bunts.

The players' strike extended through the scheduled Opening Day of the 1995 baseball season; when they resumed play in late April, they only played a 144-game schedule. Bobby Cox's Braves lost the World Series in 1991 and 1992, but in 1995 they got over the hump and prevailed over Cleveland in six games. Davey Johnson's Cincinnati Reds were the only team to steal more than three bags in the divisional series as they pilfered nine in their three-game sweep of Los Angeles, while the Dodgers failed to steal a base. Barry Larkin batted .385 in the series with four steals. While the Reds led the NL with 190 steals, it was Mike Hargrove's Cleveland Indians who led the junior circuit with 132 thefts. Against Lou Piniella's Seattle Mariners in the ALCS, the Indians stole nine bags in their four games to two victory, as Kenny Lofton led the way with five steals, while batting .458. Omar Vizquel stole three, while Wayne Kirby stole one. The Mariners also pilfered nine bags, including four by Vince Coleman. In Atlanta's four-game sweep of Cincinnati in the NLCS, both teams combined for six steals. The Braves stole two, including one by pitcher John Smoltz. Kenny Lofton batted only .200 in the World Series with six of Cleveland's eight steals, but his batting average was better than his team's .179 mark. The Braves pilfered five sacks,

Kenny Lofton was a tremendous leadoff hitter and defensive center fielder, who played in the postseason during eleven campaigns. He led the American League in stolen bases for five straight seasons from 1992 to 1996 with Cleveland. Kenny stole at least 54 bags during six seasons, including a career high of 75 thefts in 1996. He used his sprinter's speed to chase down balls in center field and frustrated opposing batters, catching balls that would ordinarily fall to the earth, and by using his great leaping ability to rob hitters of home runs and extra-base hits. He won four consecutive Gold Gloves from 1993 to 1996. (George Brace photograph).

including three by Marquis Grissom, who batted .360 in the series. Atlanta laid down all five of the sacrifice bunts as Rafael Belliard led the way with two, including one on a successful suicide squeeze.

The Braves won the opening game of the 1995 World Series by a 3–2 score before 51,876 frigid fans at Atlanta–Fulton County Stadium. Greg Maddux held Cleveland to only two hits in the route going performance. Kenny Lofton went 1 for 4 with two runs scored and entered the record books by stealing two bases in one inning, the first time it had been done in the fall classic since 1921. The game started inauspiciously for Atlanta as Lofton reached first on an error and pilfered second and third before scoring on a groundout by the three-hole hitter, Carlos Baerga. Lofton pushed the envelope in the ninth inning when he singled with one out and then went in motion, running with the pitch, as Vizquel grounded to second. He took off for third while the out was being recorded at first and when Braves first sacker, Fred McGriff, tried to cut him down at third, the throw eluded Chipper Jones and Lofton scampered across the plate. Lofton used his great foot speed to change the course of many games, but in this contest Cleveland came up short. The Braves scored what would be the winning run in the seventh inning when Rafael Belliard executed the suicide squeeze, allowing David Justice to score their second run in the inning. Justice was not blessed with great foot speed and stole only 53 bases in 99 attempts (53.5 percent) during his fourteen-year career. But speed is not as important as timing when executing the suicide squeeze, as the baserunner is instructed to break for home just before the pitcher releases the ball. If the timing is perfect than even an average bunt will score the runner. Belliard's bunt was beyond average and executed perfectly as he pushed a Julian Tavarez fastball towards the second baseman. If Indians skipper Mike Hargrove was expecting Bobby Cox to call for a suicide squeeze, he would have instructed his hurler to fire a pitchout. But if the pitcher is in his motion and recognizes that the squeeze play is on, then he is obligated to throw at the batter's head because the beanball is widely regarded as the best defense against the squeeze bunt. Therefore it is imperative that the batter conceals his intention until the last possible moment.

The two best teams in the NL Central, Cincinnati (190 steals) and Houston (176 steals), were the only major league teams with over 138 thefts in 1995, as the NL West last-place San Francisco Giants finished third with 138 steals. Kenny Lofton won his fourth straight AL stolen base crown with 54 thefts. Quilvio Veras, the Marlins 5'9", 166-pound, switch-hitting and right-handed throwing second baseman from the Dominican Republic, led the NL with 56 steals.

Home runs increased by 578 in the AL in 1996, an increase of almost 27 percent, while long balls increased in the NL by 303, which was nearly 16 percent. Despite the fact that home runs were being hit at a record or near record pace, stolen bases remained at healthy levels with 1,785 in the NL and 1,454 in the AL. During the 1990s sacrifice bunt totals in the AL began to drop precipitously. In 1996 the NL had 404 more sacrifices than the AL, 974 to 570. Mike Hargrove's Cleveland Indians (99–62) had the best record in the majors for the second straight season but in the ALDS, wall ball would prevail over small ball, as Davey Johnson's Baltimore Orioles (88–74) had a major league record 257 homers during the regular season and then crushed nine in their four-game victory over Cleveland in the first round of the playoffs. Eddie Murray stole the only base for the wildcard entrant, while the Indians purloined eleven, including five by Kenny Lofton and four by Omar Vizquel. Cleveland's eleven steals in the postseason was the second most as the three additional divisional series losers compiled only three thefts: Texas (1), Los Angeles (0), and San Diego

(2). Baltimore (1) and St. Louis (4) lost in the League Championship Series and combined to steal five bases during the postseason. The Yankees scored only one run in the first two games of the World Series and then stormed back against Atlanta, winning the next four. They stole eight bases in their three postseason series, while the Braves stole twelve. Bobby Cox's team laid down four of the six sacrifice bunts in the fall classic, including two by second baseman Mark Lemke. The ALCS was representative of the direction the game was headed as the Yankees stole only three bags and crushed ten homers, while Baltimore stole none and hit nine long balls. Fans were returning back to the game after the bitter strike of 1994–1995. They were enticed to do so partially because of a surfeit of dizzying long ball hitting that turned major league baseball into a version of Home Run Derby.

Don Baylor's Colorado Rockies were a well-balanced offensive team that finished third in the NL West with an 83–79 record. The Rockies led the majors with 201 steals and their impressive 75.3 percent basestealing average was the third best in the National League. For a team to have a 75 percent basestealing average is very good and generally puts it at or near the top of their league in that category, while an 80 percent or above mark is phenomenal, especially considering the few number of teams that have accomplished this feat. Tony LaRussa's Cardinals led the NL in sacrifice bunts (88), while Bob Boone's Royals (66) led the AL. Both St. Louis (149 steals, 4th NL) and Kansas City (195 steals, 1st AL) were well-rounded small ball teams, but the Cardinals won the NL Central (88–74), while the running Royals resided in the AL Central's basement (75–86). Pitchers Pedro Martinez and Denny Neagle each had 16 sacrifices to lead the NL, while Tom Goodwin led the AL with 21.

Kenny Lofton batted .317, scored 132 runs, and won his fifth and final AL stolen base crown with 75 thefts. He stole two bags in the All-Star Game at Veterans Stadium on July 9 as the NL won, 6–0. Lance Johnson, who finished second in the senior circuit with 50 thefts, stole 51.5 percent of the Mets' 97 bases during the season, and also stole one in the midsummer classic. Eric Young won his only stolen base crown in 1996, capturing the NL title with 53 bags. In Colorado's 16–15 win over Los Angeles on June 30, Young became the third major leaguer in the modern era to steal six bags in a game. He swiped second, third, and home in the third inning. Eric Young's major league career spanned from 1992 to 2006 and he batted .283 with 84 sacrifices, 465 steals, and a 73.5 percent basestealing average.

Through the 2009 season there were fifty-four, 30 homer–30 stolen base seasons in major league history, and thirty-eight of them came after 1988. In 1996 there were four 30–30 men: Barry Larkin (33 homers, 36 steals), Barry Bonds (42 homers, 40 steals), Dante Bichette (31 homers, 31 steals), and Ellis Burks (40 homers, 32 steals). Bonds stole his 40th on September 27 in a 9–3 Giants win over the Rockies and became only the second member of the 40–40 club after Jose Canseco. Alex Rodriguez (1998) and Alfonso Soriano (2006) were the next two players to join that list. Barry was a five time 30–30 man, while his father, Bobby, also did it five times. Andre Dawson's Florida Marlins lost to the San Francisco Giants on April 27 by a 6–3 score as Barry Bonds became the fourth major leaguer with at least 300 homers and 300 steals as he smashed two long balls. Barry joined his father, Dawson, and Willie Mays as the only players to accomplish this feat. Dawson played his final season in 1996, batting .276 in 42 games.

Chris Stynes of Kansas City stole his first major league base on May 12 in Seattle's 8–5 win. Ordinarily, this would be an unremarkable event, except for the fact that his first three steals came in the first inning as he stole second, third, and home. He pilfered another bag later in the game, but had only five during the season and forty-nine during his career. Perhaps even more remarkable for the Royals was when Bob Hamelin (11 career steals) and David Howard (23 career steals) stole home in back-to-back games in late May.

Gerald Williams had only ten career steals entering the game at Oakland on June 2, but he pilfered four bags to tie a team record and the Yankees stole eight total as they crushed the Athletics, 11–4. It was a close game until the ninth inning when they pushed across six markers to blow it open. The Yankees didn't run much when Buck Showalter was their manager from 1992 to 1995 but Joe Torre, who had been a National League guy during his entire playing and managerial career up until 1996, was changing that with an aggressive mentality. The other Yankee bases were pilfered by Bernie Williams, Ruben Rivera, and rookie Derek Jeter, who had two. Much to the consternation of Oakland catcher Terry Steinbach, Gerald stole third without a throw in the second inning and scored on a sacrifice fly after initially reaching base because of left fielder Allen Battle's two-base error. In the fourth stanza with Gerald Williams on third and Jeter at first, they pulled off a double steal with Williams stealing home. The Yankees aggressiveness distracted the Oakland pitchers. Before Gerald stole home in the fourth, he singled, stole second, and advanced to third on a wild pitch on ball four to Jeter. Steinbach insisted that it was the worst game he ever played as the ninth inning added to his misery. Gerald led off with a single and advanced to second on Rivera's one-base hit. When he stole third base it was the sixteenth time that a Yankee had pilfered four hassocks in a single contest. Steinbach's throw was off target and Williams scored on the catcher's second throwing error of the game. Joe Torre said, "Whatever it takes. We're not going to go toe-to-toe with teams hitting homers. We have to do something else. We're getting more comfortable with the running game. Today was the best all year." The victory gave the Yankees their first sweep at the Oakland Coliseum since 1979.[73]

As the game of baseball neared the end of the twentieth century and entered the twenty-first century, the straight steal of home had become a rarity, a relic from baseball's past. When a player steals home it's generally because the defense did something wrong or there was a double steal and the runner at third took off after the catcher threw to second. However, catchers are often reluctant to throw to second in such situations and will fake a throw and check the runner at third or perhaps fire the ball to the pitcher, hoping to catch the runner off third. A fast runner at third could also steal home on a pickoff throw to first base. In Jan Larson's article "Stolen Victories: Daring Dashes That Send the Fans Home Happy," he attributes the decline of the steal of home to a number of reasons. Pitchers are removed from the game far sooner than in the old days when they worked late into the game, got tired, and lost their concentration with ducks on the pond. With a runner on third, pitchers work from the stretch unlike the old days when they would often spin out of the windup. Also because players make so much money, managers are reluctant to allow them to steal home because they may get injured sliding into home plate or perhaps even worse, the batter could miss the sign and swing away, hitting a liner into the man's head.[74]

Lee Jenkins's outstanding article in the *New York Times* in April of 2006 titled "The Thieves Turn Timid" also provides great insight into this subject. He lists several other reasons why players are reluctant to steal home, including a surfeit of RBI hitters, managers who want to go for the big inning, and a fear of failure and looking bad. The best time to steal home is with two outs and a bad hitter at the plate. While a right-handed pitcher could see the runner take off from third, a southpaw is more desirable because his back is to the runner. Furthermore, a runner with average speed is often more likely to accomplish this feat because he may induce the pitcher to work from the windup and the pitcher may not pay attention to him at third. When Grady Sizemore had a straight steal of home in August 2005, he was the envy of all the thieves in the big show.[75]

The first four teams in the NL Central amassed the most steals in the senior circuit in 1997: first-place Houston (171), second-place Pittsburgh (160), third-place Cincinnati (190), and fourth-place St. Louis (164). The Detroit Tigers led the junior league with 161 thefts, while Minnesota was second in steals (151), first in stolen base average (74.4 percent), but last in sacrifices (20). The Los Angeles Dodgers (105) and the Kansas City Royals (51) led their respective leagues in sacrifices.

Brian Hunter of Detroit led the AL with 74 steals, his first season in the junior league after three seasons in Houston. During his ten-year career with six major league teams, he batted .264 with a .313 on-base percentage, a .346 slugging percentage, 27 sacrifices, and 260 steals with an 81 percent basestealing average. He stole 160 bases from 1997 to 1999 with totals of 74, 42, and 44, and basestealing averages of 80.4 percent, 77.8 percent, and 84.6 percent. Tony Womack of Pittsburgh won the first of three consecutive NL stolen base crowns with 60 bags and a superb 89.6 percent basestealing average. Womack was also the senior circuit's best thief in 1998 (58), while pilfering bags at a rate of 87.9 percent. And then with the Arizona Diamondbacks in 1999, he won another stolen base crown with 72 thefts, while stealing bases at an impressive 84.7 percent clip. Womack batted .273 lifetime with a .316 on-base percentage, 57 sacrifices, and 362 steals with a terrific 83.2 percent basestealing average.

Womack's 1997 stolen base crown was a gift, courtesy of Deion Sanders. The two-sport star sat out the 1996 season and then came roaring back in 1997, having a phenomenal April. On April 14, the Braves downed Sanders's Reds, 15–5, as Kenny Lofton of Atlanta had five hits, five runs scored, and two steals. Sanders tied a team record with four steals, wearing the cut-off sleeves to honor Jackie Robinson. Lofton batted .333 during the season with a .409 on-base percentage, but he stole only 27 bases and perhaps because he was unaccustomed to the new league, he was caught stealing 20 times for a 57.4 percent basestealing average, which was an anomaly for Lofton. At the end of April, Deion Sanders had a .385 batting average and 19 steals. When he left to join the Dallas Cowboys on September 5, he was leading the league with 56 steals and would have most likely won the NL stolen base crown if he had remained with the Reds.

Edgar Renteria, the Marlins second-year shortstop, led the majors with 19 sacrifice bunts, while Omar Vizquel led the AL with 16. Vizquel is one of the greatest bunters in the history of the game, whether he was trying to leg out a hit or move a runner along. A great bunter like Vizquel could also lay one down with a runner on first and less than two outs, intending to bunt for a hit, but if he is unsuccessful than at least he advanced the runner to second and had a productive out. Entering the 2010 season, Vizquel had 244 sacrifices and 389 steals with a 71.4 percent basestealing average. After the 2009 season he was ranked 42nd all-time in sacrifices and every man in front of him on that list played at least part of their career when sacrifice flies counted as sacrifice hits. He led the AL in sacrifices in 1997 (16), 1999 (17), and 2004 (20) with Cleveland and led the NL in 2005 with San Francisco as he laid down 20 sacrifices for the second straight season. Vizquel is an amazingly consistent sacrifice bunter with fourteen seasons of ten or more sacrifices. From 1999 to 2001 he teamed with Roberto Alomar to form one of the greatest middle infield combinations ever and on offense they were both outstanding small ball players. Vizquel's best basestealing seasons were in 1997 (43) and 1999 (42) when his success rates were 78.2 percent and 82.4 percent.

Brian Hunter had four hits and three steals on April 5 in the Tigers 15–12 triumph over the White Sox. Minnesota had nineteen consecutive steals before Denny Hocking was caught stealing in a 6–4 loss to Toronto on May 10. At Fenway Park on June 26, the fleet-footed Tigers defeated the iron-footed Red Sox, 10–6, as Hunter went 3 for 5 with two runs scored, two RBIs, and four stolen bases. Hunter induced southpaw Vaughn Eshelman to make a mistake in the first inning. He singled to start the game and then stole second. Eshelman caught Hunter off the middle bag and it looked as if he was going to be picked off. But his throw to third sailed into left field and Hunter scampered across the plate with the first tally. Scott Hatteberg was also behind the plate for the Sox two days later when the Tigers won, 9–2, and Damion Easley, Detroit's second baseman, went 2 for 3 with a double, two runs scored, and four stolen bases. Detroit won the first three games of the four-game set against Jimy Williams's Sox, a team that was missing several players to injuries or personal issues. The 1997 Tigers won 26 more games than in 1996, going from 53–109 (87 steals) to 79–83 (161 steals). Easley split the 1996 season between California and Detroit and then had a career high of 28 steals in 1997. He insisted that the reason they were going in the right direction was "Aggressiveness. On the bases, on the mound, everything." Hunter gave the credit to skipper Buddy Bell saying, "I don't know how he managed before, but he's been letting us run this year. He's a very aggressive manager." After the game on June 28 they had a 35–41 record, compared to 21–55 at the same juncture in 1996.[76]

Rickey Henderson of the San Diego Padres stole his 1,200th bag on July 14 in a 5–3 win over the Giants. He played for both San Diego (88 games) and Anaheim (32 games) in 1997, stealing a combined 45 bags with an outstanding 84.9 percent basestealing average. Barry Bonds stole the only base in the All-Star Game at Jacobs Field on July 8, but the American League emerged triumphant, 3–1. Edgar Martinez, who stole only 49 bags during his eighteen-year career with a low 62 percent basestealing average, tried to swipe the only bag for the AL, but was caught stealing.

It took the Florida Marlins only five seasons to win a world title as veteran skipper Jim Leyland led the wildcard Marlins (92–70) to the promised land in 1997. They needed seven games to defeat Cleveland (86–75) as Edgar Renteria's RBI single in the bottom of the eleventh inning gave the Marlins the championship as they won the final game, 3–2. Cleveland was the only team that did a lot of running in the playoffs as they stole sixteen cushions. In their hard fought, three games to two victory over the Yankees in the ALDS, they stole six bags: Omar Vizquel batted .500 and stole four bases, while Bip Roberts hit for a .316 clip and stole two. Marquis Grissom had three of their five steals in the ALCS as they defeated Baltimore in six games. The third game of the series was knotted at one in the twelfth inning at Jacobs Field when Marquis Grissom had a game-ending steal of home to give the Indians a 2–1 win. However, the steal of home was not aesthetically pure: Randy Myers's pitch went in the dirt and catcher Lenny Webster couldn't handle it. Webster refused to chase after the ball believing that Vizquel had tipped it on a bunt attempt. Initially, the play was ruled a passed ball, but on the following day the official scorer changed it to a stolen base, relying on rule 10.08(a). In the World Series, Vizquel had all five of Cleveland's steals. The Division Series losers only stole nine bases total: Yankees (3), Mariners (2), Giants (2), and Astros (2). The League Championship Series losers only stole seven in both rounds of the playoffs: Orioles (5) and Braves (2). While Cleveland stole sixteen in the postseason and Florida had seven thefts. In the autumn classic, the Indians had five of the six sacrifice bunts, including two by Vizquel. Vizquel's exceptional small ball skills were displayed under the bright lights of the postseason as he stole nine bags and laid down five sacrifice bunts.

For those baseball fans that enjoyed the harmonious balance of the 1970s and 1980s when small ball strategies were prevalent and home runs were being hit at healthy levels, they were perhaps dismayed to see baseball deteriorate in the 1990s, as the game fundamentally changed. Hitters now stood on top of the plate, wearing protective gear, and without much fear of an inside pitch, knowing that if the pitcher had the audacity to throw inside and hit them, then they could be fined and suspended for their actions. Batters were using thin-handled bats and swinging from their heels as strikeouts increased. Games took forever to end as managers would incessantly go to their bullpen, instead of allowing their starters to work deep into games. Home runs were flying out of the park as many people insisted that the reasons for this phenomenon were a livelier ball, shorter pitching deliveries, stronger players, better bat design, weaker pitching because of expansion, and smaller ballparks or in the case of Coors Field, a large ballpark, where home runs were plentiful because of the atmospheric conditions. Stolen bases were declining during the 1990s, but the far greater decline came in the use of the various bunt plays and the hit-and-run. While a minority of baseball fans found the game during the mid-to-late 1990s to be revolting, the majority of the baseball public was captivated by the home run explosion. The mob salivated over the home run chase in 1998 between Mark McGwire (70) and Sammy Sosa (66) as Roger Maris's home run record of 61 long balls was shattered. However, there was a darker side to this paradise, as fans would later find out that in 1998 the game was in the midst of what would later become known as the Steroid Era.

The National League expanded to sixteen teams in 1998, but the fourteen-team junior circuit still managed to pilfer more sacks, 1,675 to 1,609. For the first time ever, the NL had at least twice as many sacrifices than the AL, 1,167 to 538. The junior circuit's average of 38.4 sacrifices per team was the lowest in the history of the league, excluding the strike-shortened 1994 campaign. Gene Lamont's last-place Pittsburgh Pirates stole the most bases in the senior circuit with 159, while Larry Dierker's first-place Houston Astros stole the second most with 155. The Toronto Blue Jays led the junior circuit with 184 steals. Colorado (98) and Oakland (58) led their respective leagues in sacrifices, while the Detroit Tigers had a major league low 16 sacrifices. Neifi Perez, the Rockies shortstop, had 22 sacrifice bunts to lead the NL, while Mike Bordick of Baltimore led the AL with 15. Rickey Henderson, the aging 39-year-old speed merchant, batted .236 for Oakland but thanks to his league leading 118 walks, he had a good .376 on-base percentage and scored 101 runs. Furthermore, he won his twelfth and final AL stolen base crown with 66 steals in 79 attempts. Henderson became the oldest player to win a stolen base crown. Tony Womack led the NL with 58 thefts.

Larry Dierker's Houston Astros stole 492 bases from 1997 to 1999 with totals of 171, 155, and 166. However, he only managed 135 of their 162 games in 1999. During those three seasons it can be argued that the Astros were one of the best small ball teams in major league baseball. In his thoughtful book *My Team: Choosing My Dream Team from My Forty Years in Baseball*, Dierker provides many of his insights about the game. He accepts the sabermetric theory that stolen bases don't add much value to an offense, writing, "Stolen bases seem to be very important when you are watching a game but, statistically, they aren't worth that much. Psychologically, the running game can be disruptive and even one steal can win a close game. Over time, when you judge the value of a player, it is a mistake to fall in love with larceny."[77] Dierker prefers teams that give up few runs with good pitching and defense instead of teams with great hitting that give up a surfeit of runs. Perhaps, this is not surprising since Dierker was a pitcher in the big leagues for fourteen seasons. He insists that slow-footed teams with great hitters will have trouble on the road in larger ball-parks, while "A fast team with good pitchers and fielders can win on grass or Astroturf, in a big park or a small one."[78] Dierker believed in using the stolen base as a weapon as long as basestealing averages were at acceptable levels. While managing in the big leagues he relied on the sabermetric statistic that says that for a runner to break "even in terms of the runs his team scores" they have to have a 66.7 percent basestealing average, which is to steal two bases for every three attempts.[79] Most studies show that for a stolen base to not be counterproductive the success rate needs to be between 67 and 75 percent. However, statistics often do not account for the psychological affect a fast runner has on the pitcher, the way it alters the positioning of the fielders, and the way it helps the hitter. The former Astros manager believed that if you stole bases you needed high success rates to make it productive. Dierker also wrote the following, which is more consistent with a man whose teams stole a large number of bases:

> The SABR guys may know what the math says, but they don't know how a pitcher *feels* when a base stealer is dancing off the bag. As a manager, I preferred a team that attempted to steal a lot of bases. We ran often when we had a break-even 67 percent success rate — or even a little lower — because I *know* how I felt when a fast runner was taking a big lead and juking around trying to get a good jump. As a manager, I figured that if we could put more pressure on the opposing pitcher he wouldn't perform as well. In my mind, stealing, or even the threat of stealing, is important because it creates opportunities for hitters. There is no way to quantify the effect of this pressure.[80]

Most players that garner a large number of steals in recent times are usually going to have a stolen base percentage above 70 percent. A manager that values high basestealing averages will probably consider taking away the green light if the basestealer can't maintain that minimum percentage or at least above the break-even point. A great basestealer should have a stolen base percentage that is significantly better than the league average. Some people, for example, may consider Steve Sax's 1983 basestealing average of 65.1 percent as being adequate because it was only slightly below the National League average of 67.2 percent, which is also at the break-even point for stolen bases. But a better assessment is to characterize his rate as being poor. Sax was 56 for 86 in basestealing attempts that season and garnered the third most thefts in the senior circuit. Among the ten players that represented the top five burglars in each league, seven of them pilfered sacks at a rate of 82.6 percent or better, while the remaining two players had rates of 77.1 percent and 70.5 percent. Also consider that when Rickey Henderson stole 108 cushions, he was caught stealing only 19 times. He stole nearly twice as many bases as Sax and was thrown out eleven fewer times. There is usually far too much attention paid to the number of stolen bases and not enough attention paid to stealing rates. What made players like Rickey Henderson (80.8 percent), Tim Raines (84.7 percent), Vince Coleman (80.9 percent), Joe Morgan (81 percent), Willie Wilson (83.3 percent), and Davey Lopes (83 percent) great basestealers is not only that they amassed prodigious stolen base totals, but they also posted phenomenal basestealing averages. The difference between a player who steals 500 bags with an 80 percent basestealing average and one that steals 500 bags with a 65 percent basestealing average is huge. The player with the 65 percent average would be caught stealing 144 more times, a total of 269 versus 125.

But should managers curtail the stolen base attempts of players with low basestealing averages? Not necessarily, and in at least one situation this would be counterproductive. If, for example, there is a young player with blazing speed who is learning the game at the big league level, but is having difficulty reading the pitchers and has a low stolen base percentage, then it would behoove the manager to encourage the player to work harder and keep trying to steal bases. The last thing you want to do is to discourage such a player to the point where he may lose his confidence. If speed is that player's biggest asset, then a manager must be patient and wait until the player improves his skills, so he could best utilize that asset or tool. When Ron LeFlore came up to the big leagues, he was still learning the game, and stole 28 bases in 48 attempts during his second season for a pitiful 58.3 percent basestealing average. He stole 58 bags the next season in 1976 and improved his average to 74.3 percent. And then from 1978 to 1980 the light went on with stolen base totals of 68, 78, and 97, with basestealing averages of 80.9 percent, 84.8 percent, and 83.6 percent.

Stolen base totals can be misleading and what is often more important is basestealing averages and the situations in which players or teams are pilfering sacks. For example, there are two teams, one with 150 steals, which is a large number, while the other team stole a modest 90 bags. Let's say that the team that pilfered 150 bags stole 100 bases with their team trailing or leading by several runs and the team that stole 90 sacks garnered 70 of them while the score was tied or their team was trailing or leading by two or fewer runs. The second team stole 60 fewer bases, but their steals were more meaningful. Furthermore, if they had a higher basestealing average then it can be argued convincingly that they were much more productive while stealing bases. While basestealing totals can be misleading, most of the time they are not, and teams with a large number of steals are generally going to steal a higher percentage of bags in important situations and have a higher basestealing average.

Basestealing statistics can also be very misleading. In *The 2006 ESPN Baseball Encyclopedia* there is a statistic called Basestealing Runs, which measures the number of runs that are produced because of basestealing activity. The formula is as follows: (.22 times the number of stolen bases) minus (.35 times the number of caught stealing). So if a team had ten stolen bases in a month and seven caught stealing, the Basestealing Runs statistic would produce a negative number (-0.25). But what if the seven caught stealing came at times when it did not impact the final score of the game, but five of the stolen bases were garnered when the score was tied late in a game or when they were trailing by a run. And what if after stealing those five bags the players scored and their team went on to win the game. Furthermore, they would probably not have scored unless they stole those bags. The Basestealing Runs statistic would produce a negative number as if the team's basestealing activity was counterproductive. However, in this situation that would be far from the truth.

In his fifth and final major league season in 1998, Lou Frazier of the White Sox played only seven games, failed to collect a hit, and stole four bags. Amazingly, all four of his steals came on April 19 at SkyDome as the Blue Jays downed the Sox, 5–4, in twelve innings. Frazier led off for Chicago and went 0 for 3 with two walks, four steals, and one sacrifice bunt. Lou also reached base in the fifth inning on pitcher Juan Guzman's error when he laid down a bunt. He tied the White Sox record of four steals by Jimmy "Nixey" Callahan and George Davis in 1905. In total, there were eight steals in the game and five of them were by the Sox. Manager Jerry Manuel commented about Frazier, saying, "He didn't get a hit, but he created a lot of stuff." Frazier said, "That's the leadoff guy's job to get on whatever way you can and get in scoring position so they can get you in." He also provided some observations about stealing bases, "You don't have to be really fast, you just have to be smart."[81]

The Yankees won their ninth in a row with a 6–2 triumph against Montreal at Olympic

Stadium on June 10, but they lost Bernie Williams, who injured his right knee sliding into third base in the sixth inning. He stole third on the play, and then scored, and played a half inning in the field before being removed. In the eighth inning, Tim Raines stole his 800th bag to join Billy Hamilton, Ty Cobb, Lou Brock, and Rickey Henderson as the only players to reach that level. The former Expo was given large standing ovations throughout the series. At the age of 38, he proved he could still play well, batting .290 during the season with a .395 on-base percentage in 321 at-bats, while stealing eight bags in eleven attempts. The American League won the All-Star Game, 13–8, on July 7 at Coors Field as it stole six bags in six attempts, one apiece by Kenny Lofton, Ray Durham, Scott Brosius, Roberto Alomar, Ken Griffey, Jr., and Ivan Rodriguez. Tom Glavine of the NL had the only sacrifice bunt in the game. Glavine entered the 2008 season with 213 sacrifices, which was tied for 74th all-time and 2nd on the active list behind Omar Vizquel. The third and fourth players on the active list were longtime members of the Braves pitching triumvirate, Greg Maddux (174) and John Smoltz (135). Jason Kendall of Pittsburgh batted .327 in 1998 with a .411 on-base percentage and on September 21 he stole his 26th and final base of the season in an 8–1 loss to the Giants. He broke John Stearns's NL record for stolen bases for a catcher. Stearns stole 25 bags in 1978 for the Mets.

Joe Torre's New York Yankees dominated major league baseball in 1998, putting together a 114–48 record and sweeping Texas in three games in the ALDS, winning the ALCS in six games, and then capturing the world title with a four-game sweep of the Padres. The Yankees had a well-balanced offensive attack, finishing the regular season with 207 homers (4th, AL) and 153 stolen bases (2nd, AL). There were only eleven stolen bases in the divisional series: Cleveland (3), Atlanta (3), New York Yankees (2), Boston (1), Chicago Cubs (1), Houston (1), Texas (0), and San Diego (0). Houston lost in the Division Series to San Diego, three games to one, as their only victory came in game two when they pushed across a run in the last of the ninth to win 5–4. Ricky Gutierrez led off with a single and was sacrificed to second by Brad Ausmus. He stole third and then Craig Biggio was given an intentional free pass right before Bill Spiers drove him in with a one-base knock. New York (9) and Cleveland (6) combined for fifteen steals in the ALCS as Omar Vizquel of the Indians batted .440 and led both teams with four steals. When San Diego (2) defeated Atlanta (3), four games to two in the NLCS, both teams combined for only five steals. The Yankees and Padres each stole one base in the World Series. New York laid down five sacrifice bunts in the postseason: three by Derek Jeter and one apiece by Scott Brosius and Andy Pettitte. Pettitte's sacrifice was the only one in the fall classic.

Ordinarily, when a team loses sixteen more games than the previous year it's usually not a good sign. But this wasn't the case with the 1999 New York Yankees (98–64) as they overcame a number of injuries and personal issues during the regular season to win the AL East. They hit their stride once the postseason began, losing only one game in the playoffs and winning the World Series in four straight for the second season in a row to win their 25th world title. There were only seven steals in the two ALDS series as Cleveland led the way with five thefts. Boston and Texas each stole one, while the Yankees failed to pilfer a bag. In the NL, Atlanta (103–59) defeated Houston (97–65) in four games and both teams combined for seven steals. Bobby Valentine's wildcard Mets (97–66) upset Arizona (100–62) in the other NLDS series as they stole eight, while the Snakes from the Desert failed to steal a bag. Rickey Henderson of the Mets batted .315 with a .423 on-base percentage during the regular season and also scored 89 runs and stole 37 bags with a 72.5 percent basestealing average. Then Henderson batted .400 in the NLDS and stole a divisional series record, six bags.

The Red Sox stole four cushions in the ALCS, while the Yankees stole three as Joe Torre's club won in five games. Boston's ten errors led to their downfall. In the NLCS, Bobby Cox's Braves batted only .223 with five homers, but they stole a whopping fourteen bags and won the series over the Mets in six games. Valentine's team pilfered seven sacks. The Braves punched their ticket to the fall classic by putting together one of the greatest small ball exhibitions in postseason history during the sixth and final game of the series, a 10–9 triumph in eleven frames. They laid down three sacrifices and were 6 for 6 in stolen base attempts, including a double steal by Gerald Williams and Bret Boone in the first inning as both men advanced two bases on Mike Piazza's throwing error. Piazza was known as a poor throwing catcher and made two critical throwing errors in the final game. Atlanta garnered seven sacrifice bunts in the series and had a good 77.8 percent basestealing average. And then in the World Series the Braves running game was shut down as they stole only one bag and hit only one homer in the series. The Yankees stole five bags. Torre's team also laid down all three of the sacrifice bunts and one of them helped turn the tide in game one. The Yankees entered the top of the eighth inning, trailing by a 1–0 score. After the first two men reached base, Chuck Knoblauch was willing to give the Braves an out and advance two runners into scoring position. However, first baseman Brian Hunter made an error on the play to load the bases and the Yankees went on to score four runs in the stanza and win the game, 4–1.

Stolen bases increased in the NL from 1,609 in 1998 to 1,959 in 1999. The AL teams stole 213 fewer bases, a decline of about 12.7 percent. There were 31 fewer sacrifices in the AL than the previous year, while the NL had 70 fewer sacrifices. Technically, the Yankees had the fewest sacrifice bunts in the majors with 22. However, consider that Bruce Bochy's NL West fourth-place San Diego Padres laid down only 36 sacrifices and only eight of them were by position players (22.2 percent). Bochy's Padres were known to lay down a low number of sacrifice bunts, including four straight seasons from 1999 to 2002 when they had the fewest in the NL with totals of 36, 39, 29, and 45. San Diego finished no higher than fourth place during those seasons. The Padres did, however, lead the majors with 174 thefts in 1999. Mike Hargrove's first-place Cleveland Indians (97–65, AL Central) led the AL in both steals (147) and sacrifices (54).

Otis Nixon was in the twilight of his career in 1999, batting .205 for Atlanta during his final big league season and stealing 26 bags at a 78.8 percent rate. On April 23 against Florida, he stole his 600th bag. Rickey Henderson's Mets lost to San Diego on April 27 by a 6–2 margin as he stole his 1,300th bag. Damian Jackson batted .224 with a .320 on-base percentage for San Diego in 1999 and stole a career high 34 bags in 44 attempts. On June 28 he stole five bases, including one of home in an 8–7 win over Colorado at Qualcomm Stadium.

John Boles's Florida Marlins laid down the second fewest sacrifice bunts in the senior league in 2000 with 42, but they led the circuit with 168 steals. Luis Castillo, an exceptionally talented defensive second baseman with the Marlins, batted .334 in 136 games with a .418 on-base percentage, 101 runs scored, only 17 RBIs, and a major league leading 62 steals with a 73.8 percent basestealing average. Johnny Damon of Kansas City led the AL with 46 steals.

The Marlins were in crisis mode after an astonishing 6–2 defeat to San Diego at Pro Player Stadium on May 18. San Diego won two of the three games in the series as the Marlins three-day attendance of 21,888 was the worst in their history. The best crowd of the series showed up for the finale on the 18th, only 7,832 fans. Mike Phillips of the *Miami Her-*

ald pondered the question, "How can you steal 10 bases and not win?" While San Diego stole two bases in the game, the Marlins swiped ten: three apiece by Luis Castillo and Cliff Floyd; while Mark Kotsay and Preston Wilson had two apiece. Wilson joined the 30–30 club in 2000 with 31 homers and 36 steals, but he also struck out a disturbing 187 times. Florida established a team record with seven steals in the first three innings. Stan Spencer, a 6'4", 205-pound, right hander was on the mound when Florida pilfered their ten bags, while Wiki Gonzalez was behind the dish. The ten steals was one short of the St. Louis Cardinals NL record of eleven thefts, which was accomplished in a five-inning affair against Pittsburgh in the second game of a twin bill on August 13, 1916. Castillo had stolen fourteen in a row and seven in his last two games, which was one short of a 106-year-old senior league record by Walt Wilmot, who stole eight bags on August 6 and 7 of 1894, for the Chicago White Stockings, a franchise which later changed its name to the Cubs. Florida left eight men on base and were 3 for 11 with runners in scoring position. John Boles said, "It's not the worst loss of the year. It's one of the worst losses ever. I'm totally frustrated. I feel like my head is going to explode. I feel like my skin is on fire, like I'm going to have an anxiety attack." He insisted that the loss was the worst ever because they had plenty of opportunities to score and received "gifts" and "freebies," which they failed to take advantage of. Adding, "If you told me we would steal 10 bases in five innings, then how many runs do you think we would score? I would have said a lot. But it's the same old thing. It's the offense." Furthermore, the running game couldn't be blamed for the loss because they were not caught stealing in the contest.[82]

The Mets and Cubs opened the 2000 season at the Tokyo Dome in Japan, playing two games, which were the first major league regular season games played outside of North America. When the Mets won the second game, 5–1, in eleven frames, Rickey Henderson stole second and became the second player after Ted Williams with a stolen base in four decades. Eric Young of the Cubs stole five bags on May 14, but the Expos emerged victorious, 16–15. On September 3 in Cleveland's 12–11, thirteen-inning triumph over Baltimore, Kenny Lofton became the sixteenth player (8th American Leaguer) in the modern era to steal five or more bases in a game. He also became the second Cleveland Indians player to swipe five hassocks in a contest and it was the third time an Indians player had done so, as Alex Cole did it twice.

Joe Torre's club was spinning their wheels entering the 2000 postseason, losing 15 of their last 18 regular season games, and then facing stiff competition in the playoffs, unlike the previous two years. The ALDS against Oakland went the distance as they won in five games, and then they defeated the Mariners in six in the ALCS, before winning the World Series against the crosstown Mets in five games. During a season in which stolen bases plummeted in both leagues, by 332 in the NL and 165 in the AL, it was perhaps not surprising that there wasn't much running in the postseason. In 1999 there were 56 thefts in the postseason and in 2000 there were only 34. However, the postseason stolen base rate far exceeded the regular season rate despite the sharp decline. The four Division Series losers stole a total of nine bases: Oakland (2), Chicago White Sox (4), Atlanta (1), and San Francisco (2). The two LCS losers stole fourteen cushions in both rounds of the playoffs: Seattle (5) and St. Louis (9). Meanwhile, the Yankees (6) and Mets (5) combined to steal only eleven bases during the postseason. Torre's triumphant aggregation had the only steal in the fall classic. Bobby Valentine's Mets laid down three of the four sacrifices.

The Pale Hose got swept in the ALDS by Seattle, but Jose Valentin batted .300 with a .417 on-base percentage and pilfered three bags for the Sox. The Mariners won the finale,

2–1, thanks to Carlos Guillen's game-winning squeeze bunt which scored Rickey Henderson in the bottom of the ninth inning. Edgar Renteria of St. Louis batted .300 in their five-game loss to the New York Mets in the NLCS. He stole three bases in game two and laid down two sacrifice bunts during the series. The Yankees won the ALCS, four games to two over Seattle. They exploded for seven runs in the eighth inning to win game two, 7–1. The Bronx Bombers slaughtered the Mariners in that frame, despite the fact that Jorge Posada was caught stealing home on a botched squeeze bunt by Jose Vizcaino.

With Philadelphia's new skipper, the energetic Larry Bowa, steering the ship in 2001, the Phillies won 21 more games than in 2000 and finished second in the NL East with a 86–76 record. Bowa brought an aggressive mentality to the club as they stole 51 more bags than in the previous year. They led the senior circuit with 153 steals and a 76.5 percent bases-stealing average. Jimmy Rollins, their rookie shortstop, batted .274 with 97 runs scored and led the league in triples (12) and stolen bases (46). Rollins got a cup of coffee with Philadelphia in 2000 (3 steals), making his major league debut on September 17, and was not caught stealing by a catcher's throw until August 26, 2001, when Arizona's Damian Miller cut him down. He finished the season with only eight caught stealing and an 85.2 percent bases-stealing average. Jimmy shared the stolen base title with Colorado's second-year center fielder, Juan Pierre, who batted .327 with a .378 on-base percentage, 202 hits, and 108 runs scored. The mesmerizing Ichiro Suzuki brought his remarkable talent to the United States in 2001 and led the majors in batting average (.350), hits (242), and stolen bases (56).

Don Baylor's Chicago Cubs became the first team since the 1997 Dodgers with over 100 sacrifice bunts. Furthermore, their 117 sacrifices was the highest total in the big leagues since Gene Mauch's 1979 Minnesota Twins laid down 142 sacrifices. The South Siders of Comiskey Park paced the junior league with 63 sacrifices. Tom Glavine, Ricky Gutierrez, and Jack Wilson each had 17 sacrifices to lead the NL, while David Eckstein of Anaheim led the AL with 16 sacrifice bunts.

Rickey Henderson stole at least 22 bags for the twenty-third straight season. He batted .227 for San Diego, but thanks to his 81 walks, he compiled a .366 on-base percentage and stole 25 bags in 32 attempts. If people didn't realize that this man was one of the greatest players to ever step between the white lines, perhaps they came to their senses in 2001. Henderson became the all-time walks leader and the all-time runs scored leader during the season and also collected his 3,000th hit on the final day of the season. Tony LaRussa once said, "He was a great teammate and for a couple of years I thought he was the most dangerous hitter in the league. He could beat you in so many ways. I think he got a bad reputation because he didn't always express himself well. He came off as being more selfish than he really was. Believe it or not, he was a lot of fun—a great guy to have on the team."[83]

After shutting out Milwaukee and fanning fourteen, Greg Maddux was hammered for twelve hits in a 7–1 loss to San Diego at Qualcomm Stadium on May 8. San Diego had sixteen hits in the contest and eight steals. Henderson, Mark Kotsay, and Ryan Klesko each had two steals, while Damian Jackson and the 41-year-old Tony Gwynn stole one base. For Gwynn it was the 319th and final steal of his illustrious career as he would hang up his cleats at the end of the season. San Diego's pitcher Kevin Jarvis was the only player caught stealing, as he also wanted a piece of the action. The eight steals were garnered with Paul Bako behind the dish for Atlanta and there were three steals of third. Henderson stole second base on a pitchout in the fifth frame for the 1,375th bag of his career.

The Dodgers prevailed by an 8–4 score over the Rangers at Dodger Stadium on June 12. Darren Dreifort, the Dodgers 6'2", 211-pound right hander, stole home on the front end of a double steal to become the first pitcher to steal home since Rick Sutcliffe did it on July 29, 1988. Tim Raines stole his 808th and final base of his career on September 25 in Montreal's 2–0 loss to the Mets. He became the third player after Ted Williams and Rickey Henderson with a steal in four different decades.

Lou Piniella's 2001 Seattle Mariners were a small ball juggernaut and led the majors with 174 steals and a terrific 80.6 percent basestealing average, which was the first time since 1995 that a team finished above 80 percent. Their 116–46 record was even more astonishing, but they fell to the Yankees in five games in the ALCS. However, it was rookie manager Bob Brenly's Arizona Diamondbacks (92–70) that surprised the baseball world and won the World Series over the Yankees in seven games.

There wasn't much running in the postseason as the burglars pilfered 28 cushions, which was a decline of six from the previous year and it was a 50 percent decline from the 1999 total. The Division Series losers stole a total of seven bags: Oakland (3), St. Louis (3), Cleveland (1), and Houston (0). The League Championship losers, Seattle (6) and Atlanta (1), stole only seven in the postseason. The Diamondbacks (6) and Yankees (8) stole fourteen cushions in the postseason and combined for only three steals in the World Series. Arizona laid down five of the six sacrifices in the fall classic, four by Craig Counsell and one by Matt Williams. Scott Brosius had the only sacrifice bunt for the vanquished. Counsell collected six sacrifices in the postseason, including three in game four of the World Series. He wasn't the only player to be credited with three sacrifice bunts in a postseason game. Arizona conquered St. Louis in the NLDS in five games as both teams combined for fourteen sacrifices, eight by the Cardinals and six by the Diamondbacks. Placido Polanco of St. Louis had three sacrifices in game four.

In 2002 the Oakland Athletics' small ball deficient (46 steals, 20 sacrifices), sabermetrically oriented ballclub won over 100 games for the second straight season with a 103–59 record. But it was manager Mike Scioscia's small ball oriented Anaheim Angels who first secured the wild card and then won the World Series. The Angels had a .282 batting average (1st, AL), a .341 on-base percentage (4th, AL), a .433 slugging percentage (6th, AL), 851 runs scored (4th, AL), 1,603 hits (1st, AL), 152 homers (tied 10th, AL), 462 walks (11th, AL), 805 strikeouts (fewest, AL), 117 steals (3rd, AL), and 49 sacrifices (1st, AL). The Angels played excellent defense and were well schooled in the fundamentals: they ran the bases well, hit the cutoff man, threw to the right base, made productive outs with skilled place hitting, bunted runners along, and skillfully executed the hit-and-run play. Furthermore, they were the mirror opposite of the Athletics. While the Athletics preached patience at the plate, the Angels saw only 3.57 pitches per at-bat, the fewest in the AL. While sabermetricians often say that high strikeout totals are not alarming, the Angels were the best contact hitting team in the majors. While the Athletics eschewed small ball strategies, the Angels embraced them. During the eight seasons from 2002 to 2009, the Angels made the playoffs six times and won five AL West titles. Also during this time period the Angels were the best small ball team in the AL: they finished first in steals three times, second three times, and third twice. They were ranked at or near the top of the junior circuit in sacrifice bunts during most of these seasons and they were highly skilled at executing the squeeze play.

The Oakland Athletics also enjoyed great regular season success with their immensely talented general manager, Billy Beane. But the postseason had been a nightmare, losing games because of poor defense, the inability to execute the fundamentals, and poor baserunning — a runner who refused to slide at home plate on a close play, a runner who failed to touch home plate and instead of going back to correct his mistake, he shoved the catcher, while the on-deck hitter looked on apathetically, and a player who stopped running to argue with the umpire, insisting that the third baseman interfered with him. From 2000 to 2003 the Athletics were 0 and 9 in games that could advance them to the second round. During those nine games they made twelve errors, failed to hit in the clutch, averaged 2.67 runs per game, and hit only four homers in 390 at-bats. Billy Beane insisted after losing their series to Boston in the 2003 ALDS: "Anyone who wants to diminish what these guys have done with some historic item is either foolish or ignorant."[84] In Michael Lewis's book *Moneyball: The Art of Winning an Unfair Game*, Beane said that what happens in the playoffs is "fucking luck."[85] But what happens if your slow-footed, power-laden team, suddenly goes cold in the postseason? Well if your team does not execute the fundamentals, play good defense, and manufacture runs, then you're in big trouble. Runs are harder to come by in the postseason because playoff teams generally have the best pitching staffs; they go to a four man rotation; the best pitchers often come back and pitch on two or three days rest; and the weather turns cold. If your offense goes cold in the postseason, a capable small ball team could find a way to steal a few runs by laying down a safety squeeze, suicide squeeze, sacrifice bunt, bunting for a hit, stealing a base, being aggressive on the basepaths, executing a hit-and-run or by making productive outs and hitting behind the runner. If you could steal one game in a short series because of small ball tactics that may be enough to propel your team to victory or keep your team alive. Even the sabermetrically inclined Boston Red Sox had a new found appreciation of the stolen base when pinch-runner Dave Roberts stole second in the ninth inning of game four in the 2004 ALCS versus the Yankees. This is widely recognized as the most important play in that series, with skipper Terry Francona saying, "It was so important. If he doesn't steal that base, we're going home."[86]

Anytime you limit your options, like the Oakland Athletics did, it is more difficult to be successful. However, by 2006 things were beginning to change in the Bay Area. Beane appeared less ideological and more willing to allow his manager to use small ball strategies. The 2006 Athletics played excellent defense, had great team chemistry, and they even stole 61 bags, which was 30 more than the previous season. In the ALDS it was the Twins who exploded with critical mental and physical errors as they were swept in three games as the Athletics played good fundamental baseball. Eric Chavez, the Athletics third baseman, insisted that the 2006 version of the Athletics were not as talented as previous seasons, but they played as a team and coalesced as a unit. Chavez said, "Of all the other years, I can honestly say this is team baseball." He continued, "Every team is different. The addition of (Mark) Kotsay and (Jason) Kendall and Milton (Bradley), hard-nosed baseball players, is really the difference from teams of the past. Not to say those weren't good baseball players, but these are grittier, grinder baseball players. Frank (Thomas) is the only superstar. The rest of us just go out there and play real hard baseball."[87] This overachieving aggregation was swept by Detroit in the ALCS.

Over the years the legacy of the Athletics, consisting of great regular season success with a very low payroll, has been tarnished by postseason failure. While some general managers try to build a team that will be successful in both the regular season and postseason, Billy Beane appears to have built teams that are designed for regular season success. He even acknowledged this in *Moneyball*, saying, "My job is to get us to the play-offs. What happens after that is fucking luck."[88] Back in 2002, Billy Beane was heaped with lavish praise for his sabermetric approach to the game. Dan Le Batard wrote in the *Miami Herald* on September 30, 2002, "The Marlins are playing antiquated baseball. They steal bases and sacrifice bunt in a helium-inflated era of offense, risking too much for a mere one base, and the A's laugh at teams that still play this way." But it was the Marlins who had the final laugh as their authentically pure small ball team won the World Series in 2003.

The Angels success in the 2002 postseason had more to do with long balls than small ball, as they hit homers at a rate that far exceeded the regular season. They destroyed the Yankees pitching staff in the ALDS, winning in four games, while batting .376 with 31 runs scored, 9 homers, and 4 steals. They needed only five games to get by Ron Gardenhire's Twins in the ALCS. Anaheim batted .287 in the series with eight homers and three steals while Minnesota, a team that had a fairly low number of steals (79, 8th AL) and sacrifices (34, 9th AL) during the regular season, managed to pilfer only one base and failed to hit a homer in the series. The Angels won the World Series against San Francisco in seven games, batting .310 with 7 homers and 6 steals. Dusty Baker's Giants had four of the six sacrifice bunts in the autumn classic.

Stolen bases increased by 58 in the NL during the regular season and plummeted by 411 in the AL as the senior league outpaced the junior league, 1,514 to 1,236. The American League's stolen base total dropped by a whopping 25 percent from the previous year's 1,647 bags. In the postseason, Anaheim was the only team to do a lot of running. The four Division Series losers combined for only five steals: Atlanta (2), Arizona (1), Oakland (1), and the New York Yankees (1). Minnesota and St. Louis, the two Championship Series losers, stole three bases apiece in the postseason. Anaheim stole thirteen cushions in their three playoff series, while San Francisco stole seven.

Catcher Mike Matheny of St. Louis laid down two sacrifices in the NLDS as the Cardinals defeated the Diamondbacks in a three-game sweep. In their 12–2 opening game victory, Matheny had a sacrifice bunt that had a unique result during the six-run seventh inning. His sacrifice produced two runs and put two runners into scoring position, thanks to a disastrous throwing error by the southpaw reliever Greg Swindell. During San Francisco's four games to one NLCS victory over St. Louis, the Giants had some notable sacrifice bunt accomplishments. Rich Aurilia laid down three sacrifices in the series and Ramon Martinez had an RBI sacrifice bunt in the top of the ninth inning in game two, which was won by the Giants, 4–1.

The Florida Marlins and the Kansas City Royals led their respective leagues in steals with 177 and 140, respectively. The Montreal Expos (108) and the Anaheim Angels (49) led their league in sacrifice bunts. During the first two seasons of his career in 2001 and 2002, Jack Wilson, the Pirates shortstop, laid down 17 sacrifices to lead the NL. David Eckstein, the Angels overachieving shortstop, laid down 14 sacrifices and led the AL for the second straight season. Luis Castillo stole one more base (48) than Colorado's Juan Pierre to secure the senior circuit stolen base title. Alfonso Soriano led the AL with 41 steals.

Atlanta opened a three-game set against Los Angeles at Turner Field on May 7 as Brian Jordan of the Dodgers and Gary Sheffield of the Braves each hit two-out ninth inning homers as the game went into extra innings tied at five. Marquis Grissom was an aging 35-year-old outfielder for the Dodgers, whose best basestealing days were in the past. He singled to center field with one out in the top of the sixteenth and then stole second. Catcher Javy Lopez's throw was late and off target and rolled into center field after second baseman Marcus Giles couldn't handle it. Grissom advanced to third on the wild throw. Shawn Green was passed intentionally to put runners on the corners and then Paul Lo Duca grounded to Vinny Castilla at third as it appeared the Braves would escape the inning with a 5–4–3 double play. But first baseman Julio Franco couldn't handle Giles's relay throw that bounced off the dirt and Lo Duca was safe, while Grissom scored the go-ahead run and they held on for a 6–5 win. Manager Jim Tracy said, "We get a run because Shawn Green went hard into second base to disrupt a double play." Grissom and Sheffield stole bags in the game, while Rafael Furcal and Franco were thrown out stealing. There were four sacrifice bunts in the contest, including two by the Dodgers leadoff man, Cesar Izturis.[89]

The Marlins finished their season on September 29 with a 4–3 win in ten innings over Philadelphia at Pro Player Stadium. Florida's leadoff hitter, Luis Castillo, went 3 for 5 with one run scored and secured the stolen base title with three steals to beat out Juan Pierre by one. In the home half of the tenth inning, he singled to right field, stole second, advanced to third on a wild pitch, and scored on a sacrifice fly to the first baseman to win the game. The Phillies pilfered four sacks in the game, three by Jimmy Rollins and one by Doug Glanville.

In 2003, Lou Piniella's AL East last-place Tampa Bay Devil Rays led the AL in steals (142) and finished second in basestealing average (77.2 percent). Oakland stole only 48 bags and was fractionally better with a major league leading 77.4 percent stolen base rate. Florida (150) and Montreal (100) were the only NL teams with at least 100 steals, while the AL had four: Tampa Bay (142), Anaheim (129), Kansas City (120), and Seattle (108). It wasn't that long ago that teams with at least 100 steals were a dime a dozen. In fact in 1987 every NL team stole at least 109 bases and all but two AL teams stole at least 105. Florida's Juan Pierre stole 65 bases to lead the NL in 2003, while Carl Crawford of Tampa Bay led the AL with 55 steals.

Crawford batted .281 during his second season and had an 84.6 percent basestealing average. He had natural power and preferred to drive the ball, instead of guiding the ball around the field, and developed into a Rickey Henderson type of player during the next few years, who could hit home runs in the double digits, while also putting pressure on the defense with his blazing speed. However, unlike Rickey, he didn't walk a lot, wasn't very patient, and liked to attack the first pitch. Crawford's on-base percentages have been unexceptional at best and sometimes quite abysmal, including a low .309 mark in 2003, when he walked only 26 times in 151 games. Because he had speed to burn some people thought he was a prototypical leadoff hitter and after being drafted he was frustrated by the fact that his minor league coaches were telling him to hit down on the ball, grounders to the infield, so he could utilize his speed while hitting out of the left-hand side of the batter's box. He prefers hitting down in the order, in the number two or three holes and said, "Just because you can run fast, that doesn't make you a good leadoff hitter. That's one of the dumbest things that goes on in baseball. I was always frustrated leading off. I became passive and not the player I can be." Crawford was quoted in Paul White's exceptional article, "In the fast lane: Speed thrills but other skills important, too" in the April 16–22, 2008, issue of *USA Today Sports Weekly*. Crawford is a thoughtful person and had an interesting theory as to why Jose Reyes of the Mets slumped down the stretch in 2007, batting .205 in September. He insisted that basestealing takes a toll on a player's body and said that the reason why Reyes slumped was because his body got beaten up because of so many stolen base attempts. This is an interesting theory, but if this was true than players like Rickey Henderson, Lou Brock, Bert Campaneris, Joe Morgan, and Vince Coleman wouldn't have had excellent postseason performances.

The St. Louis Cardinals (87) and the Detroit Tigers (65) led their respective leagues in sacrifice bunts during the 2003 campaign. The sabermetrically oriented Toronto Blue Jays laid down only eleven sacrifices during the season and also finished last in the majors with 37 steals. Florida's Luis Castillo and Juan Pierre shared the NL sacrifice hit title with

San Francisco's ace pitcher Jason Schmidt as they each had fifteen. Ramon Santiago, a middle infielder with Detroit, batted only .225 in 444 at-bats, but led the majors with eighteen sacrifices.

The Florida Marlins played in the spacious Pro Player Stadium and in 2003 they prospered in this salubrious small ball environment with players who possessed an abundance of speed and the ability to play little ball. Their formula for success included good pitching, excellent defense, and great wheels. They excelled with a 53–28 home record, but struggled on the road (38–43), perhaps because of their lack of power. Their 157 homers were ranked eleventh in the National League and they failed to finish higher than fifth in batting average (.266, 5th), on-base percentage (.333, tied, 8th), and slugging percentage (.421, 6th). They led the senior league in only one major offensive category, stolen bases (150). Juan Pierre and Luis Castillo were excellent table setters and they helped the Marlins finish second in the NL with 82 sacrifice bunts. A late season surge allowed them to capture the wild card.

In the postseason Florida had more circuit clouts (14) than steals (8). However, ten of their homers came in the NLCS versus Chicago as they only had two apiece in the NLDS and the World Series. The Division Series losers combined for six steals as Oakland led the way with three, while Minnesota, San Francisco, and Atlanta each had one. The League Championship Series losers, Boston (5) and Chicago (6), stole eleven in the postseason. Kenny Lofton of the Cubs batted .286 with three steals in their five-game triumph over Atlanta in the NLDS and then batted .323 with Chicago's only steal in the seven-game NLCS. Florida (8) and their World Series opponent, the New York Yankees (11), stole nineteen bases in the playoffs but only two apiece in the fall classic.

Excluding the strike-shortened seasons of 1981 and 1994, 2004 was the first season since 1973 that no major league team stole at least 150 bags. The last-place Milwaukee Brewers and the first-place Anaheim Angels led their respective leagues in steals with 138 and 143. The Montreal Expos (100) and the Chicago White Sox (58) had the most sacrifices in each league. Royce Clayton of Colorado (24) and Omar Vizquel of Cleveland (20) won the sacrifice bunt titles. It was the first time since 1982 that the leaders in each league had at least twenty sacrifices each. Speedster Scott Podsednik of Milwaukee led the majors with 70 steals, while swiping bases at a terrific 84.3 percent clip. In the American League, Carl Crawford won his second straight stolen base title with 59 thefts.

Kris Benson of Pittsburgh won his second game of the campaign on April 18 in an 8–1 triumph over the Mets at Shea Stadium. He became the seventh major leaguer to lay down four sacrifices in a game and tied a major league record. On June 13, Pat Borders of Seattle stole his first base since June 5, 1994, in an 8–1 win over Montreal. The Dodgers lost to the Giants, 9–3, on June 24 but Paul Lo Duca stole home on the front end of a double steal with Juan Encarnacion on the back end.

It took the self proclaimed "Idiots" to kill the Curse of the Bambino and after 2004 the Red Sox no longer had to go into enemy territory with the chant of "1918, 1918" reigning down upon them. Terry Francona's Red Sox (98–64) were the American League's wild card entrant and for the third consecutive season a wild card team won the World Series. The Sox did not actually embrace small ball tactics, stealing 68 bags (11th, AL) and laying down an extremely low 12 sacrifices, which was the fewest in the majors. Even general manager Billy Beane's second-place Athletics had more than twice as many sacrifices than Boston with twenty-five. The 2004 Red Sox eschewed subtlety and instead relied on brute force. For much of the season they lacked defense and speed. However, their young general manager, Theo Epstein, helped rectify this problem with a couple of fine trading-deadline deals. Doug Mientkiewicz and Orlando Cabrera, a pair of excellent defensive infielders, were brought in to strengthen the defense. Cabrera also had good wheels. Dave Roberts began the season with Los Angeles, batting .253 with a .340 on-base percentage in 68 games, while stealing 33 bags in 34 attempts for a phenomenal 97.1 percent basestealing average. After he was traded to the Red Sox at the trading deadline, he batted .256 for Boston with five steals in seven attempts. And then in the American League Championship Series he made his presence felt with perhaps the most important steal in postseason history.

The Division Series losers combined to swipe fourteen bags: Atlanta (7), Minnesota (4), Los Angeles (2), and Anaheim (1). The New York Yankees (7) and the Houston Astros (9) stole sixteen in the postseason and lost in the Championship Series. The World Series participants, Boston and St. Louis, each stole seven bags in the playoffs. In the fall classic, Tony Womack and Larry Walker laid down sacrifice bunts for the Cardinals, while Derek Lowe had one for the Red Sox. After stealing 14 bags in 17 attempts (82.4 percent) for Kansas City, Carlos Beltran was traded to Houston and stole 28 bases in 28 attempts. Beltran's 93.3 percent success rate in 2004 was not an anomaly as he consistently posted sensational basestealing averages during his career. He was on fire in the playoffs, batting .455 with 2 steals in the NLDS and .417 with 4 steals in the NLCS. In Houston's three games to two win over Atlanta in the NLDS, Rafael Furcal of the Braves batted .381 with 3 steals. Boston's Johnny Damon batted .467 with 3 steals in the ALDS in their three-game sweep of Anaheim.

The Red Sox were bruised and bloodied, staggering up against the ropes, staring down the vicious right-hand of their opponent, when they suddenly collected themselves and mounted an unbelievable comeback in the ALCS. The Yankees held a three games to none lead and were up 4–3 heading into the last of the ninth in game four with their terrific closer Mariano Rivera standing on the small hill in the middle of the diamond. Kevin Millar had an impressive .383 on-base percentage during the regular season and he drew a walk to lead off the inning. Dave Roberts pinch-ran and stole second on a bang-bang play. Bill Mueller's single scored Roberts to tie the game. The Red Sox won in twelve innings, 6–4, and then won the next three games to secure the greatest comeback in postseason history.

Jose Reyes, the electrifying shortstop for the New York Mets, led the NL with 60 stolen bases in 2005 and compiled an 80 percent basestealing average. He pilfered 39.2 percent of the Mets league-leading 153 steals and was a prodigious thief despite compiling an abysmal .300 on-base percentage. Chone Figgins batted .290 with a .352 on-base percentage, 113 runs scored, and a major league leading 62 steals with a 78.5 percent basestealing average. He swiped 38.5 percent of the AL West first-place Angels' major-league-leading 161 steals. For the first time in major league history the two team league leaders in stolen base percentage finished above 80 percent: Philadelphia (81.1 percent) and Texas (81.7 percent). Jason Bay of Pittsburgh (21 steals, 95.5 percent) and Alfonso Soriano of Texas (30 steals, 93.8 percent) posted near perfect success rates. Both Scott Podsednik of the White Sox and Tony Womack of the Yankees had two, four-stolen-base games. On July 27, Ryan Freel purloined five sacks for the Reds as they defeated the Dodgers, 7–6. The San Francisco Giants and Washington Nationals led the NL with 91 sacrifice bunts. Omar Vizquel of the Giants (20) and Coco Crisp of the Indians (13) led their respective leagues in sacrifices. Crisp's thirteen sacs was the lowest total for a league leader since Paul Blair and Denny McLain each laid down thirteen to lead the AL in 1969.

The threat of the steal gave the Marlins a 2–0 win over Cincinnati on August 7 at the

Great American Ball Park. Ramon Ortiz, the Reds starter, had three errors on pickoff throws trying to catch Juan Pierre. It led to two unearned runs that were tallied by Pierre. He went 2 for 4 out of the leadoff spot and said, "I haven't been getting on base as much as I'd like to be. This shows that speed can play a part. You don't expect three bad pickoff throws. You see something new in baseball every day." Luis Castillo and Mike Lowell stole bases for the fast moving Fish. Matt Treanor, the Marlins catcher, and Ortiz laid down sacrifices.[90]

When Ozzie Guillen became the Chicago White Sox manager, he brought an aggressive mentality to his team and wanted them to push the envelope. However, during his first season as the skipper in 2004 (83–79, 2nd AL Central), his team stole only 78 bags, but led the AL with 58 sacrifices. Scott Podsednik, a skilled small ball practitioner, was brought into the fold to be the catalyst for the 2005 campaign and everything clicked. The Sox stole bases and took extra bases with an aggressive approach. They executed the various bunt plays and used the hit-and-run ubiquitously. Podsednik batted .290 with a .351 on-base percentage, 80 runs scored, and 59 steals with a 72 percent basestealing average. He played 129 games and perhaps not coincidentally, when he went on the disabled list the team struggled without their spark plug at the top of the lineup. Ozzie did not refer to his tactics as "small ball," but instead called it "smart ball." The Pale Hose collected 59 more stolen bases in 2005 than during the previous season, finishing third in the junior circuit with 137 thefts. And for the second straight season they led their league in sacrifices (53). Ozzie's club also had 37 bunt hits to lead the AL. They held off the upstart Cleveland Indians to win the AL Central with a 99–63 record, and then went on to win the World Series.

Scott Podsednik had a terrific postseason, batting .273 with one homer and one steal in their three-game sweep of Boston in the ALDS. In their five-game victory over the newly named Los Angeles Angels of Anaheim in the ALCS, he batted .294 with a .478 on-base percentage and three steals. And then in their four-game sweep of Houston in the fall classic, he compiled a .286 batting average with two triples, one homer, and two steals. He hit two homers during the postseason, but none during the regular season. The Division Series losers stole nine bases: Atlanta (4), New York Yankees (3), San Diego (2), and Boston (0). The Angels (3) and Cardinals (4) lost in the League Championship Series and stole a total of seven cushions in the playoffs, while Chicago (13) and Houston (8) combined for 21 steals in the postseason. Both teams stole five bags in the World Series. Phil Garner's Astros had five of the seven sacrifice bunts as Willy Taveras led the way with two. David Eckstein of St. Louis (game 2, NLDS), Steve Finley of the Los Angeles Angels of Anaheim (game 3, ALDS), and Juan Uribe of the Chicago White Sox (game 3, ALDS) each had an RBI sacrifice bunt in the postseason, executing the squeeze play. Finley teamed with Adam Kennedy for back-to-back sacrifice bunts in game two of the ALDS versus New York, while Joe Crede and Uribe had back-to-back sacrifices in game three of the ALDS versus Boston. Finley had four sacrifices in the Angels three games to two victory over the Yankees in the ALDS. The Houston Astros defeated the Atlanta Braves, 10–5, in game one of the NLDS and they laid down four sacrifices in the game.

Ichiro Suzuki stole his 39th straight base on September 30, 2006. His consecutive successful steals streak extended into the 2007 season, ending with 45 straight steals and breaking Tim Raines's 1995 AL record of 40. Moises Alou of San Francisco stole home on the front end of a double steal on September 27 with Ray Durham on the back end to join Paul Molitor, Minnie Minoso, and Dave Concepcion as the only players since 1957 to steal home after turning age forty. In the Rockies 14–8 victory over the Nationals on June 14, Cory Sullivan of Colorado became the eighth major leaguer to lay down four sacrifices in a game.

The Rockies (119) and Royals (52) led their respective leagues in sacrifice bunts, while Roy Oswalt of Houston (20) and Jose Lopez of Seattle (12) won the individual crowns. The Mets (146) and Angels (148) stole the most bases, as Jose Reyes (64) and Carl Crawford (58) were the most prodigious basestealers. Ichiro Suzuki of the Mariners (45 steals, 95.7 percent), Chris Duffy of the Pirates (26 steals, 96.3 percent), and Brandon Phillips of the Reds (25 steals, 92.6 percent) distinguished themselves because of their outstanding success rates.

Jim Leyland's wild card Detroit Tigers (95–67) won the AL pennant in 2006 on the back of their great pitching staff (3.84 ERA, 1st AL). They hit 203 homers (3rd, AL), stole 60 bases (11th, AL) and finished second in the junior circuit with 45 sacrifice bunts. However, they lost the World Series in five games to a team that won twelve fewer games than they did during the regular season. Tony LaRussa's Cardinals (83–78) secured the world title despite entering the playoffs with a pitching staff that compiled the ninth best ERA in the NL (4.54). Similar to Detroit they weren't much of a small ball team with 59 steals (14th, NL) and 71 sacrifices (9th, NL). There wasn't a lot of stealing in the postseason as well. The Division Series losers stole a total of six bags: Los Angeles Dodgers (2), San Diego Padres (2), New York Yankees (1), and the Minnesota Twins (1). The Mets stole seven in their two playoff series, while Oakland didn't steal a bag in their two rounds. The Cardinals (7) and Tigers (4) stole eleven bases in the postseason. St. Louis garnered four of the seven sacrifice bunts in the autumn classic and they were led by So Taguchi, who had two. In game four of the World Series, won by the Cardinals 5–4, Taguchi produced a run with his sacrifice bunt in the seventh inning, but he wasn't credited with an RBI because of pitcher Fernando Rodney's error. LaRussa is extremely fond of the squeeze play and there were two RBI sacrifice bunts for St. Louis in the postseason. David Eckstein, the supremely skilled bunter, executed the squeeze play with the bases loaded in the last of the sixth inning in game four of the NLDS, while Ron Belliard had a successful squeeze bunt in the top of the second inning in game seven of the NLCS.

The 2007 Phillies stole 138 bags and established a new major league record with a remarkable 87.9 percent basestealing average. Jose Reyes led the NL with 78 steals, while Carl Crawford and Brian Roberts shared the AL stolen base title with 50 bags. The New York Mets led the majors with 200 steals, becoming the first team since the 1996 Colorado Rockies (201) to steal at least 200 bags in a season. Baltimore paced the AL with 144 thefts. Colorado (83) and Texas (57) led their respective leagues in sacrifices. Juan Pierre of the Dodgers (20) and Corey Patterson of Baltimore (13) won the individual sacrifice bunt crown in the two leagues. Pierre was known to lay down 100 bunts a day during spring training and roll balls down the baseline to see which direction they would go. He once said, "The guys with speed should utilize it more. The bunt puts pressure on the defense. The threat of it puts pressure on the defense."[91]

Terry Francona's 2007 Boston Red Sox (96–66) captured the World Series title, their second championship in four seasons. Their pitching staff led the AL with a 3.87 ERA, while their feared hitters had the third best slugging percentage (.444) in the junior league. Boston stole a respectable 96 bases (7th, AL), led the circuit in basestealing average (80 percent), but laid down only 30 sacrifices (13th, AL). They still finished with twelve more sacrifice bunts than Oakland (18). The Athletics' total was extremely low, but that was still twice as many than the 2005 Texas Rangers, who laid down only nine sacrifices. It was an unusual 2007 postseason with five of the seven series ending in sweeps. None of the National League teams were involved in a series that didn't end in a sweep: Arizona swept Chicago in one NLDS series, while Colorado swept Philadelphia in the other NLDS series. Colorado swept Arizona in the NLCS and then Boston swept Colorado in the World Series. The Division Series losers stole a total of ten bags: Angels (5), Phillies (3), Yankees (1), and the Cubs (1). The League Championship Series losers, Cleveland (6) and Arizona (4), stole ten bags in the postseason. Boston (6) and Colorado (3) stole a total of nine. Julio Lugo and Alex Cora each had a sacrifice bunt for the Sox in the fall classic, while Yorvit Torrealba had one for the Rockies. Some of the notable small ball achievements in the postseason included the Angels stealing five bags in game two of the ALDS versus Boston, but losing by a 6–3 score. The Indians prevailed over the Yankees, 2–1, in game two of their Division Series clash and they laid down four sacrifices, including two by Asdrubal Cabrera, who had three in the series.

In 2008, Jacoby Ellsbury became the first Boston Red Sox player since Tommy Harper in 1973 to lead the junior circuit in steals, pilfering 50 of the Sox's 120 bags. Willy Taveras of the Colorado Rockies led the National League with 68 steals and he sported an exceptional 90.7 percent basestealing average. Clint Hurdle's Rockies led the NL with 90 sacrifices, while Ron Gardenhire's Twins led the AL with 52. Perhaps the most surprising small ball statistic in 2008 was that the sabermetrically oriented Toronto Blue Jays finished second in the American League with 48 sacrifice bunts. Chicago Cubs pitcher Ryan Dempster had the most sacrifice bunts in the NL with nineteen, while Minnesota Twins second baseman, Alexi Casilla, led the AL with thirteen.

The Tampa Bay Devil Rays were the worst team in baseball since their first season in 1998, but in 2008 they dropped the word "Devil" from their name and shockingly captured the AL East title (97–65) and then the American League pennant. Joe Maddon's running Rays led the majors with 142 steals, but they also laid down the fewest sacrifice bunts (23). They continued to push the envelope in the postseason, stealing a record twenty-four bags, including seven by Carl Crawford. However, Charlie Manuel's Phillies won the World Series title in five games. The Phillies were ranked third in the National League with 136 thefts and their outstanding 84.5 percent basestealing average was significantly better than Tampa Bay's 74 percent rate.

Philadelphia won the NL pennant once again in 2009, but was vanquished in the World Series by the New York Yankees. Both teams had superb lumber companies that excelled at long ball hitting and were skilled in larceny. The Phillies launched 224 homers (1st, NL) and stole 119 bags (2nd, NL), while the Bronx Bombers hit 244 bombs (1st, AL) and pilfered 111 sacks (7th, AL). Davey Lopes, the Phillies first base coach, orchestrated their running attack as they led the major leagues in basestealing average for the third consecutive season at 81 percent. Perhaps it wasn't surprising that the fate of Philadelphia's National League aggregation drastically improved when Lopes joined their coaching staff in 2007. From 2007 to 2009 the Phillies averaged 131 stolen bases per season and a remarkable 84.5 percent basestealing average. Lopes's thieves were highly efficient which was especially important because they played in the cozy confines of Citizens Bank Park, a home run haven where it is deleterious to give up outs because of reckless baserunning. Furthermore, the 2009 Phillies did not utilize the sacrifice bunt extensively, finishing fifteenth in the senior circuit with 55 and only 16 of them were by position players (29.1 percent).

The American League stole 224 more bases in 2009 than in 2008, an increase of 17 percent. They pilfered 1,541 cushions (110.1 per team), while the National League swiped 1,429 bags (89.3 per team). There were plenty of basestealing heroics early in the season as Dexter Fowler, the Colorado Rockies rookie center fielder, stole five bases on April 27. He was surpassed by Carl Crawford on May 3, when he became the fourth player in the modern era to steal six bases in a game. It appeared that Crawford would run away with the stolen base title, but when the curtain was lowered on the season, Jacoby Ellsbury had successfully defended his crown (70 steals, 85.4 percent), while Crawford finished second with sixty bags. Seven of the junior circuit teams stole at least 111 bases and they collectively finished a whopping 106 games *over* .500: Tampa Bay (194), Texas (149), Los Angeles (148), Oakland (133), Boston (126), Chicago (113), and New York (111). The 133 bags garnered by the Athletics was their highest total since 1992 (143). In the National League, the New York Mets' 122 steals was good enough to lead the circuit and Houston's Michael Bourn ran away with the stolen base crown with 61 thefts and an 83.6 percent stolen base percentage. The Cincinnati Reds (100) and the Seattle Mariners (56) led their respective leagues in sacrifice bunts, while Atlanta's pitcher Javier Vazquez (20) and Detroit's shortstop Adam Everett (15) secured the individual crowns.

As major league baseball entered the 2010 season the future of small ball looked strong having weathered the home run explosion of the 1990s and the early twenty-first century. Stolen bases were on the rise, apparently because baseball was now testing for performance-enhancing drugs and the Steroid Era appeared to have ended, therefore making small ball strategies like the stolen base more desirable as home run totals declined. There were other opinions as to why steals were increasing, such as poor defensive catchers, pitchers who are not concerned about controlling the running game, and pickoff moves that were ineffective. The four worst teams at throwing out basestealers in the fifty seasons before the 2008 campaign accomplished their ignominious feat in 2006 and 2007, including the 2007 Padres, who were the worst (9.6 percent). The thieves abused San Diego pitcher Chris Young in 2007, stealing 44 bags in 44 attempts against him. The 2009 Boston Red Sox were also dreadful at preventing larceny, gunning down only 13.2 percent of would-be basestealers.

The most important criteria when determining if a ballclub should be characterized as a "small ball team" is whether they steal a large number of bases. Teams that steal a large number of bases generally have fast players, and speed is the most important tool of a small ball player. Speed helps a player in the field. It helps them get infield hits, beat out bunts, stay out of the double play, take extra bases, and steal bases. The hit-and-run and the bunt-and-run are more effective with a fast baserunner. If a fast runner on first goes in motion with the pitch and the hitter grounds to short, they could take third on the throw to first. Or if they're on second and they go in motion with the pitch while the batter hits a ground ball, they could score a run while the out is being recorded at first. They could score from second on long drives to the outfield that are caught. And they could score from first on a double and take extra bases in a number of other situations. Speed allows a player to outrun his mistakes and psychologically demoralize the opposition. Furthermore, it often forces the defense to make mental and physical errors.

The future of the hit-and-run play is more uncertain. While the hit-and-run was ubiquitously employed during the 1980s, it has become more rare with the passage of time. There is also a statistical problem with the hit-and-run, considering there is no statistic. In the early twenty-first century some people who are ideologically inclined have suggested getting rid of the batting average statistic and replacing it with on-base percentage. If, for example, there are two players with a .350 on-base percentage, but one player has a .220 batting average and the other player has a .300 batting average, which player is more desirable or are they equal? Of course, the player with the .300 batting average is more desirable because he is more likely to get more extra-base hits and more RBIs. Alfonso Soriano is a player who doesn't walk a lot and has low on-base percentages. You could find a plethora of players with lower batting averages than Soriano but higher on-base percentages, but most of them aren't half as good as Soriano. Ultimately, there should be more statistics not fewer. If there were a large percentage of the baseball public that argued convincingly against using the sacrifice bunt, that doesn't mean we should stop tabulating the sacrifice bunt statistic. Because the sacrifice bunt statistic exists for a large part of major league baseball history, we could see patterns that help us learn about the evolution of the game. Unfortunately, this cannot be said of the hit-and-run. There is no statistic that measures the quantity and effectiveness of the hit-and-run. We know that Whitey Herzog and John McGraw both loved to use the hit-and-run. But which team used the hit-and-run more often, the 1911 New York Giants or the 1985 St. Louis Cardinals? Which team had a better success rate? These are questions that are apparently unable to be answered because there is no hit-and-run statistic. What is a good success rate for the hit-and-run? Is the hit-and-run play a good strategy? Do hitters have a substantially higher batting average when runners go in motion with the pitch? These are questions that are more easily answered with statistics, than without them. There should be more statistics in the game, not fewer. Statistics that measure the hit-and-run and productive outs. These statistics may be flawed, but many other statistics that are widely used are also flawed or at least provide an incomplete representation of how good or bad that player or team is. However, statistics that measure the hit-and-run and productive outs would provide a greater understanding of the game.

Since the 1980s there has been a small decline in the number of sacrifice bunts in the NL and a precipitous decline in the AL. As home runs skyrocketed during the 1990s and runs scored increased, the sacrifice bunt became less desirable as managers were unwilling to give up outs. Furthermore, there have been rigorous statistical evaluations conducted that prove that the sacrifice bunt is ineffective in most circumstances. *Baseball Prospectus'* study showed that with no outs and a runner on first base, teams scored an average of 0.896 runs an inning. However, if the batter sacrificed the runner to the keystone bag, to put the runner on second with one out, then they would score an average of 0.682 runs. The results are similar with a runner on second with no outs, compared to a runner on third with one out. However, some people have suggested that this study is flawed because the options are limited. These results are similar to those that were found by George Lindsey whose article "An Investigation of Strategies in Baseball" was published by *Operations Research* in the summer of 1963. Lindsey's research did show that it is beneficial to utilize the sacrifice bunt with runners on first and second and no outs. If they advanced to second and third with one out then their chances of scoring increased by a miniscule 0.09. However, the *Baseball Prospectus* study shows that the sacrifice bunt is an ineffective strategy in this situation. If a team has an abundance of speed then they could manufacture runs without relying heavily on the sacrifice bunt and improving their effectiveness. Lindsey's study puts the break-even point for a steal of second base with one out at 59 percent.

While the sacrifice bunt, in general, is not an effective strategy based on the statistics, there are a few situations where it should be employed. National League pitchers could help themselves immensely by having the ability to bunt runners over. American League starters have less time to perfect their bunting skills because they will only get a few at-bats each season during interleague play. The sacrifice bunt is an effective weapon in a close game during the late innings with a runner at first and no outs with an average hitter at the plate, or perhaps one that strikes out a lot or is inclined to hit into a double play because of his bad wheels. The same is true with a runner on second and no outs, who is sacrificed to third. And with runners on first and second with no outs, who advance to second and third on a sacrifice. If a team needs a run to tie or win the game or perhaps wants an insurance run, than the sacrifice bunt is important in these situations. And finally the sacrifice bunt could be used as an incidental weapon. Let's say there is a runner on first with no outs and a speed merchant at the plate who is also a terrific bunter. Juan Pierre fits this description perfectly. Pierre will often bunt for a hit in these situations and if he doesn't get a hit and is out at first, then at least he had a productive at-bat and is credited with a sacrifice. Every situation is different and one should not completely disregard subjective observations. There is a reason why managers continue to use the sacrifice bunt and even sabermetric organizations like Boston, Oakland, and Toronto lay down their fair share of sacrifices. If, for example, there is a runner on second in the early innings and no outs with a good bunter at the plate and the on-deck hitter is known to hit a lot of fly balls and has low strike-out totals, then the sacrifice bunt would be very desirable in this situation. But if the on-deck hitter strikes out a lot, then it may not be a good option to sacrifice the runner to third. The manager must also consider whether he thinks the opposing skipper would bring the infield in with a runner on third and one out and how this would affect the situation. Furthermore, there is a big difference between not bunting and not knowing how to bunt. If the manager is leading a team that knows how to bunt, then he could use the various bunt plays when it becomes desirable, but if they don't know how to bunt, then that limits their options.

Charts 1 and 3 in this book showed that the teams who finished at or near the top of their league in winning percentage stole significantly more bases than second division teams during the Deadball Era and for the period from 1920 to 1961. There was a correlation between successful teams and high stolen base totals. Conversely, second-division occupants had low stolen base totals, while the last-place teams were the worst thieves, stealing the fewest bases. Chart 5 determines if this is also true for the 1960s, 1970s, 1980s, and 1990s. On the far left side, cascading vertically, the decade and league are listed. The final three entries represents the total or aggregate number for the National League, American League, and combined major leagues. The seven categories listed horizontally are where teams will be positioned if they stole between 0–50 bases, 51–100 bases, 101–150 bases, 151–200 bases, 201–250 bases, 251–300 bases and 301 or more bases. The 1960s National League is the first "Decade/League" listed. The first number in parenthesis represents the number of teams who qualified for that category. During the 1960s in the senior league there were 24 teams who stole fewer than 51 bases. These 24 teams had a 1,826–2,009 record, which is 183 games *under* .500. The number -183 represents the number of games they finished under .500. Next, there are 65 teams who stole between 51 and 100 bases, finishing with a 5,224–5,221 record, which is 3 games *over* .500. There are seven teams that stole between 101 and 150 bases, finishing 109 games *over* .500. The two teams that stole between 151 and 200 bases finished an impressive 71 games *over* .500. So by examining this chart we know that the 89 teams that stole less than 101 bases during the 1960s in the NL, finished 180 games *under* .500, while the 9 teams that garnered 101 or more steals, finished 180 games *over* .500. There are no teams that stole at least 201 bases so the final three categories are left blank with a dash.

The strike-shortened seasons of 1981 and 1994 are not included in the results. This is because they would distort the results. For example, the 1981 Montreal Expos stole 138 bases in 108 games. If they played a 162-game schedule they would have surely stolen at least 151 bases and perhaps finished between 201 and 250 steals. However, the strike-shortened seasons of 1972 (156-game schedule) and 1995 (144-game schedule) are included. Chart 5 is listed below:

Decade/League	0–50	51–100	101–150	151–200	201–250	251–300	301+
1960s (NL)	(24) -183	(65) 3	(7) 109	(2) 71	—	—	—
1960s (AL)	(38) 5	(48) 62	(12) -37	(2) -30	—	—	—
1970s (NL)	(11) 11	(53) -606	(44) 369	(9) 139	(2) 57	(1) 30	—
1970s (AL)	(10) 3	(69) -58	(32) -136	(10) 147	(4) 31	—	(1) 13
1980s (NL)	—	(15) -237	(46) 8	(37) 153	(8) 39	(1) -3	(1) 40
1980s (AL)	(9) -11	(46) -234	(56) 90	(13) 195	(2) -40	—	—
1990s (NL)	—	(36) -255	(60) 171	(21) 112	(7) 7	—	—
1990s (AL)	(4) -16	(47) -66	(61) -33	(13) 58	—	(1) 22	—
total (NL)	(35) -172	(169) -1,095	(157) 657	(69) 475	(17) 103	(2) 27	(1) 40
total (AL)	(61) -19	(210) -296	(161) -116	(38) 370	(6) -9	(1) 22	(1) 13
total (ML)	(96) -191	(379) -1,391	(318) 541	(107) 845	(23) 94	(3) 49	(2) 53

The results are truly eye-opening and show that teams that stole 101 or more bases did substantially better than teams that stole fewer than 101 bases. The 475 major league teams that stole fewer than 101 bases from 1960 to 1999 performed poorly, finishing 1,582 games *under* .500. Conversely, the 453 teams that stole 101 or more bases were an outstanding 1,582 games *over* .500. Furthermore, the best category in the majors from 1960 to 1999 was the one where teams stole between 151 and 200 bases, finishing 845 games *over* .500. The 28 teams that stole 201 or more bases also performed extremely well, with teams that purloined 251 or more sacks posting superb records. However, the sample size is very small for the final two categories with only three teams stealing between 251 and 300 bases, finishing 49 games *over* .500. And only two teams with 301 or more steals, finishing an impressive 53 games *over* .500.

The 207 teams that stole 101 or more bases in the American League from 1960 to 1999, finished 280 games *over* .500, while the 271 AL teams that stole below 101 bases, finished 315 games *under* .500. While the AL teams that stole at least 101 bases did significantly better than the junior circuit teams that stole under 101 bases, they were not as severe as the NL results, which were truly astonishing. The 204 NL teams that stole fewer than 101 bases, finished a staggering 1,267 games *under* .500, while the 246 NL teams that stole 101 or more bases, finished an outstanding 1,302 games *over* .500. The National League during the 1970s had the most impressive results: the 11 teams that stole under 51 bags held their own, finishing 11 games *over* .500. However, the 53 teams that stole between 51 and 100 bases, which is a low or moderate total, finished a whopping 606 games *under* .500. The 44 teams that stole between 101 and 150 bases were 369 games *over* .500. And the 12 teams that stole at least 151 bags, representing three categories, were a combined 226 games *over* .500. Interestingly, there were no National League teams during the 1980s and 1990s that stole fewer than 51 bags. This is true during the 1980s even if you count the 1981 strike-shortened season, but it is not true during the 1990s if you count the 1994 strike-shortened season. In the American League during the 1990s, but excluding the 1994 campaign, there were only four teams with fewer than 51 steals: the 1991 Baltimore Orioles, 1992 Boston Red Sox, 1993 New York Yankees, and the 1995 New York Yankees.

Teams that stole at least 101 bases performed well during the first decade of the twenty-first century. From 2000 to 2009 there were 108 major league teams with 101 or more thefts and they finished 212 games *over* .500. The 51 National League teams collectively finished

2 games *under* .500 with a 4,128–4,130 record, while the 57 American League teams were 214 games *over* .500 with a 4,722–4,508 record. The eleven major league teams that pilfered 151 or more bags finished 125 games *over* .500: the five NL teams were 21 games *over* .500, while the six AL teams were 104 games *over* .500.

The results in Chart 5 are consistent with Charts 1 and 3 examined earlier in this book and show that teams that steal a large number of bases do better than teams that steal a low or moderate number of bases. Furthermore, from 1960 to 1999 these teams did substantially better. Again, this is not to suggest that stolen bases are the only reason why these teams are successful. Pitching is the most important component of a baseball team, while power hitting, run producing, and fielding are also extremely important. However, these results are quite revealing, not only because of the large discrepancy in winning percentage between teams that steal a large number of bases versus teams that steal a small number of bases, but also in the consistency of the results throughout the modern era. Teams that steal a large number of bases are generally the best small ball teams because they usually have fast runners and speed is the most important tool that a small ball player could possess. However, just because a player possesses good wheels doesn't mean he can execute the various small ball plays: bunts, steals, and the hit-and-run. But if he is fundamentally sound and could execute these plays by knowing how to bunt; how to steal a bag successfully; how to read a pitcher; how to take an extra base by studying the fielders and the various situations; and how to swing in a way that enhances his productivity; then small ball strategies are going to be more successful.

Why do teams that steal a large number of bases do better than teams that steal a low or moderate number of bases? There are probably several reasons for this, including the fact that speed helps a player at the bat, in the field, and on the bases. Slow-footed aggregations have to play station-to-station baseball, advancing one base at a time, waiting for the three-run homer, and are unable to manufacture runs because of their flat tires. They may have some great hitters on their club, but if they slump, then they're going to have difficulty scoring runs. Furthermore, if they have difficulty bunting or hitting behind the runner to make productive outs, they hurt their chances even more. Another important baseball fundamental is running the bases the right away, which is something that all players should learn regardless of how fast they are. In the early twenty-first century the Angels have had great baserunning teams, while their division rival, the Athletics, have had some horrible baserunning teams. Anytime a team like the Athletics limits their options by eschewing small ball strategies even if they have the players to execute these plays, then they hurt their chances. A team that possesses good power and speed and the ability to execute small ball strategies is going to have a great advantage over powerful, slow-footed aggregations that can't manufacture runs. Another reason why teams that steal a large number of bases are successful is psychological and unable to be quantified in statistics. These teams are generally much more aggressive than teams that steal a low or moderate number of bases: pushing the envelope, taking more chances, challenging the outfielders arm, laying down the suicide squeeze, and taking two bases on a groundout. Generally when a ballplayer is more aggressive they are going to be less uptight and showcase their talents to the best of their ability. But if you're constantly being told to play the game conservatively and take no risks, then you're going to be more uptight, perhaps unable to play the game to the best of your ability because you're afraid of making a mistake.

In the twenty-first century as major league baseball tries to clean up the game, reducing the use of performance-enhancing drugs, which were allegedly ubiquitously employed during the so-called Steroid Era, baseball teams may begin to value speed players once again like they did during the 1980s and early 1990s. The stolen base continued to be used as a weapon during the Steroid Era, remaining at healthy levels, despite the fact that many of the newer ballparks were home run havens and were lacking a quick, artificial turf surface, which put speed players in great demand during the previous decades. Was the decline in stolen bases during the 1990s and into the early twenty-first century the beginning of a lengthy downward trend, reminiscent of the four decade decline after the Deadball Era? This appears to be unlikely, considering that stolen bases increased in both leagues during 2006 and 2007, while there still remains a healthy respect for the speed game. Furthermore, stolen bases in the National League increased for four consecutive seasons from 2004 to 2007, and the American League's 1,541 thefts in 2009 was the circuit's highest total since 2001.

Appendix A

Stolen Base and Sacrifice Hit Totals
(Per League, Per Season, 1886–2009)

This chart lists the total number of stolen bases and sacrifice hits or bunts accumulated by the National League and American League teams for each season through 2009. It also lists the average number of stolen bases and the average number of sacrifice hits or bunts for each team in each league during each season. From 1908 through 1930 and also in 1939, sacrifice flies were counted as sacrifice hits. For the remaining seasons the sacrifice hits number represents the number of sacrifice bunts for that league.

National League

Year	Total Stolen Bases	Average	Total Sacrifice Hits	Average
1886	1339	167.4		
1887	2681	335.1		
1888	2301	287.6		
1889	2087	260.9		
1890	2259	282.4		
1891	2011	251.4		
1892	3201	266.8		
1893	2752	229.3		
1894	3148	262.3	1156	96.3
1895	2895	241.3	997	83.1
1896	3059	254.9	1163	96.9
1897	2705	225.4	1130	94.2
1898	2069	172.4	1346	112.2
1899	2668	222.3	1323	110.3
1900	1686	210.8	806	100.8
1901	1402	175.3	833	104.1
1902	1369	171.1	958	119.8
1903	1569	196.1	977	122.1
1904	1574	196.8	1044	130.5
1905	1601	200.1	1168	146
1906	1462	182.8	1304	163
1907	1382	172.8	1349	168.6
1908	1372	171.5	1655	206.9
1909	1516	189.5	1542	192.8
1910	1594	199.3	1529	191.1
1911	1691	211.4	1416	177
1912	1576	197	1362	170.3
1913	1576	197	1239	154.9
1914	1435	179.4	1394	174.3
1915	1194	149.3	1383	172.9
1916	1328	166	1293	161.6
1917	1145	143.1	1348	168.5

Year	Total Stolen Bases	Average	Total Sacrifice Hits	Average
1918	1029	128.6	1182	147.8
1919	1165	145.6	1213	151.6
1920	969	121.1	1418	177.3
1921	803	100.4	1441	180.1
1922	755	94.4	1381	172.6
1923	824	103	1113	139.1
1924	754	94.3	1123	140.4
1925	672	84	1079	134.9
1926	608	76	1489	186.1
1927	649	81.1	1531	191.4
1928	568	71	1494	186.8
1929	692	86.5	1309	163.6
1930	481	60.1	1317	164.6
1931	462	57.8	789	98.6
1932	445	55.6	761	95.1
1933	408	51	906	113.3
1934	362	45.3	651	81.4
1935	403	50.4	754	94.3
1936	401	50.1	761	95.1
1937	459	57.4	756	94.5
1938	354	44.3	673	84.1
1939	368	46	1137	142.1
1940	475	59.4	658	82.3
1941	411	51.4	784	98
1942	423	52.9	800	100
1943	384	48	878	109.8
1944	381	47.6	863	107.9
1945	527	65.9	844	105.5
1946	478	59.8	901	112.6
1947	361	45.1	687	85.9
1948	449	56.1	668	83.5
1949	364	45.5	679	84.9
1950	372	46.5	556	69.5
1951	453	56.6	621	77.6
1952	396	49.5	642	80.3
1953	342	42.8	574	71.8
1954	337	42.1	657	82.1
1955	377	47.1	563	70.4
1956	371	46.4	652	81.5
1957	399	49.9	510	63.8
1958	388	48.5	515	64.4
1959	439	54.9	548	68.5
1960	501	62.6	532	66.5
1961	468	58.5	572	71.5
1962	788	78.8	656	65.6
1963	684	68.4	732	73.2
1964	636	63.6	789	78.9
1965	745	74.5	709	70.9
1966	737	73.7	745	74.5
1967	694	69.4	729	72.9
1968	704	70.4	794	79.4
1969	817	68.1	891	74.3
1970	1045	87.1	819	68.3
1971	900	75	918	76.5
1972	954	79.5	865	72.1
1973	976	81.3	958	79.8
1974	1254	104.5	983	81.9

Year	Total Stolen Bases	Average	Total Sacrifice Hits	Average
1975	1176	98	1082	90.2
1976	1364	113.7	975	81.3
1977	1555	129.6	847	70.6
1978	1533	127.8	970	80.8
1979	1486	123.8	949	79.1
1980	1839	153.3	967	80.6
1981	1108	92.3	688	57.3
1982	1782	148.5	978	81.5
1983	1786	148.8	921	76.8
1984	1728	144	809	67.4
1985	1636	136.3	901	75.1
1986	1842	153.5	869	72.4
1987	1851	154.3	823	68.6
1988	1789	149.1	938	78.2
1989	1529	127.4	899	74.9
1990	1787	148.9	876	73
1991	1651	137.6	891	74.3
1992	1560	130	983	81.9
1993	1714	122.4	1110	79.3
1994	1141	81.5	758	54.1
1995	1602	114.4	947	67.6
1996	1785	127.5	974	69.6
1997	1817	129.8	1030	73.6
1998	1609	100.6	1167	72.9
1999	1959	122.4	1097	68.6
2000	1627	101.7	1062	66.4
2001	1456	91	1074	67.1
2002	1514	94.6	1134	70.9
2003	1294	80.9	1093	68.3
2004	1336	83.5	1190	74.4
2005	1349	84.3	1151	71.9
2006	1515	94.7	1190	74.4
2007	1564	97.8	1045	65.3
2008	1482	92.6	1049	65.6
2009	1429	89.3	1138	71.1

American League

Year	Total Stolen Bases	Average	Total Sacrifice Hits	Average
1901	1449	181.1	839	104.9
1902	1315	164.4	877	109.6
1903	1173	146.6	1035	129.4
1904	1207	150.9	1195	149.4
1905	1345	168.1	1335	166.9
1906	1535	191.9	1401	175.1
1907	1399	174.9	1254	156.8
1908	1350	168.8	1575	196.9
1909	1539	192.4	1583	197.9
1910	1671	208.9	1496	187
1911	1711	213.9	1465	183.1
1912	1823	227.9	1396	174.5
1913	1674	209.3	1295	161.9
1914	1657	207.1	1414	176.8
1915	1443	180.4	1580	197.5

Year	Total Stolen Bases	Average	Total Sacrifice Hits	Average
1916	1425	178.1	1537	192.1
1917	1268	158.5	1731	216.4
1918	974	121.8	1281	160.1
1919	916	114.5	1498	187.3
1920	751	93.9	1639	204.9
1921	684	85.5	1551	193.9
1922	696	87	1582	197.8
1923	743	92.9	1621	202.6
1924	747	93.4	1582	197.8
1925	716	89.5	1479	184.9
1926	667	83.4	1709	213.6
1927	788	98.5	1649	206.1
1928	700	87.5	1500	187.5
1929	639	79.9	1389	173.6
1930	598	74.8	1283	160.4
1931	624	78	650	81.3
1932	544	68	719	89.9
1933	452	56.5	791	98.9
1934	547	68.4	804	100.5
1935	480	60	794	99.3
1936	562	70.3	654	81.8
1937	562	70.3	663	82.9
1938	542	67.8	681	85.1
1939	589	73.6	1056	132
1940	478	59.8	608	76
1941	471	58.9	648	81
1942	538	67.3	684	85.5
1943	626	78.3	811	101.4
1944	539	67.4	834	104.3
1945	453	56.6	837	104.6
1946	406	50.8	722	90.3
1947	399	49.9	719	89.9
1948	363	45.4	749	93.6
1949	366	45.8	729	91.1
1950	278	34.8	693	86.6
1951	413	51.6	619	77.4
1952	375	46.9	712	89
1953	326	40.8	671	83.9
1954	358	44.8	675	84.4
1955	317	39.6	624	78
1956	348	43.5	601	75.1
1957	368	46	605	75.6
1958	353	44.1	531	66.4
1959	414	51.8	579	72.4
1960	422	52.8	661	82.6
1961	578	57.8	733	73.3
1962	560	56	705	70.5
1963	552	55.2	716	71.6
1964	540	54	673	67.3
1965	704	70.4	779	77.9
1966	718	71.8	710	71
1967	679	67.9	751	75.1
1968	811	81.1	713	71.3
1969	1033	86.1	778	64.8
1970	863	71.9	811	67.6
1971	865	72.1	884	73.7
1972	853	71.1	893	74.4

Year	Total Stolen Bases	Average	Total Sacrifice Hits	Average
1973	1058	88.2	592	49.3
1974	1234	102.8	751	62.6
1975	1348	112.3	791	65.9
1976	1690	140.8	818	68.2
1977	1462	104.4	917	65.5
1978	1471	105.1	1016	72.6
1979	1497	106.9	947	67.6
1980	1455	103.9	916	65.4
1981	913	65.2	564	40.3
1982	1394	99.6	762	54.4
1983	1539	109.9	640	45.7
1984	1304	93.1	626	44.7
1985	1461	104.4	648	46.3
1986	1470	105	646	46.1
1987	1734	123.9	632	45.1
1988	1512	108	692	49.4
1989	1587	113.4	727	51.9
1990	1503	107.4	683	48.8
1991	1469	104.9	733	52.4
1992	1704	121.7	682	48.7
1993	1549	110.6	701	50.1
1994	1117	79.8	449	32.1
1995	1331	95.1	541	38.6
1996	1454	103.9	570	40.7
1997	1491	106.5	547	39.1
1998	1675	119.6	538	38.4
1999	1462	104.4	507	36.2
2000	1297	92.6	566	40.4
2001	1647	117.6	533	38.1
2002	1236	88.3	499	35.6
2003	1279	91.4	533	38.1
2004	1253	89.5	541	38.6
2005	1216	86.9	469	33.5
2006	1252	89.4	461	32.9
2007	1354	96.7	495	35.4
2008	1317	94.1	477	34.1
2009	1541	110.1	497	35.5

Appendix B

Teams That Have Led Their League
(Stolen Bases and Sacrifice Hits in a Season)

This chart is a list, in reverse chronological order, of those National League and American League teams that have led their league in both stolen bases and sacrifice hits or bunts during a season. Teams that met this condition are included through the 2010 season. For teams listed after 1968 when divisional play began, their position represents where they finished in their division.

Year	Team	Position (Record)	Stolen Bases	Sacrifice Hits/Bunts
2008	Colorado Rockies	3rd (74–88)	141	90
1999	Cleveland Indians	1st (97–65)	147	54
1996	Kansas City Royals	5th, Last (75–86)	195	66
1986	St. Louis Cardinals	3rd (79–82)	262	108
1975	California Angels	6th, Last (72–89)	220	97
1966	Chicago White Sox	4th (83–79)	153	109
1965	Los Angeles Dodgers	1st (97–65)	172	103
1964	Los Angeles Dodgers	6th, tie (80–82)	141	120
1962	Los Angeles Dodgers	2nd (102–63)	198	83, tie
1960	Los Angeles Dodgers	4th (82–72)	95	102
1959	Los Angeles Dodgers	1st (88–68)	84	100
1956	Chicago White Sox	3rd (85–69)	70	86
1955	Chicago White Sox	3rd (91–63)	69	111
1953	Chicago White Sox	3rd (89–65)	73	120
1952	Chicago White Sox	3rd (81–73)	61	121
1951	Chicago White Sox	4th (81–73)	99	103
1950	Brooklyn Dodgers	2nd (89–65)	77	88
1949	Brooklyn Dodgers	1st (97–57)	117	102
1946	Brooklyn Dodgers	2nd (96–60)	100	141
1939	Chicago White Sox	4th (85–69)	113	154
1935	Boston Red Sox	4th (78–75)	91	137
1930	Pittsburgh Pirates	5th (80–74)	76	196
1928	Cincinnati Reds	5th (78–74)	83, tie	212
1924	Chicago White Sox	8th, Last (66–87)	137	232, tie
1919	Chicago White Sox	1st (88–52)	150	223
1908	Chicago Cubs	1st (99–55)	212	270
1904	Chicago White Sox	3rd (89–65)	216	197
1904	New York Giants	1st (106–47)	283	166
1902	Chicago White Sox	4th (74–60)	265	154
1902	Chicago Cubs	5th (68–69)	229	156
1901	Chicago White Sox	1st (83–53)	280	135, tie

Chapter Notes

Chapter 1

1. Dickson, *The New Dickson Baseball Dictionary*, 315.
2. Palmer and Gillette, *The 2006 ESPN Baseball Encyclopedia*, xii.
3. For discrepancies in baseball statistics, see Schwarz, *The Numbers Game*, 17, 155–72; Palmer and Gillette, *The 2006 ESPN Baseball Encyclopedia*, xi–xvi.
4. Dickson, *The New Dickson Baseball Dictionary*, 92.
5. Morris, *A Game of Inches*, 78.
6. Ibid., 79.
7. Ibid., 80.
8. Ibid., 80.
9. Schwarz, *The Numbers Game*, 18–19.
10. Morris, *A Game of Inches*, 81.
11. Frommer, *Old-Time Baseball*, 164.
12. Ibid., 165.
13. Scheinin, *Field of Screams*, 38.
14. Ibid., 49.
15. Frommer, *Old-Time Baseball*, 169.
16. Scheinin, *Field of Screams*, 63.
17. Gutman, *It Ain't Cheatin' If You Don't Get Caught*, 5.
18. Kavanagh and Macht, *Uncle Robbie*, 22–23; Scheinin, *Field of Screams*, 66.
19. Alexander, *John McGraw*, 40.
20. *New York Times*, 9 September 1898.
21. Alexander, *John McGraw*, 40.
22. Kavanagh and Macht, *Uncle Robbie*, 25.
23. *The Baseball Encyclopedia*, 5.

Chapter 2

1. *Washington Post*, 19 April 1901.
2. *New York Times*, 20 April 1901.
3. Jones, *Deadball Stars of the American League*, 481.
4. Anderson, *More than Merkle*, 23.
5. *Washington Post*, 25 April 1901.
6. Jones, *Deadball Stars of the American League*, 641.
7. *Washington Post*, 26 April 1901.
8. *New York Times*, 21 June 1901.
9. Simon, *Deadball Stars of the National League*, 147.
10. Steinberg, "The Spitball and the End of the Deadball Era," 7–8.
11. Robinson, *Matty*, 41.
12. Keetz, "Johnny Evers: The Find of the 1902 Season," 17.
13. *New York Times*, 13 July 1902.
14. *New York Times*, 3 August 1902.
15. Ibid.
16. *New York Times*, 24 April 1903.
17. Hynd, *The Giants of the Polo Grounds*, 127.
18. Robinson, *Matty*, 60.
19. Jones, *Deadball Stars of the American League*, 651.
20. *New York Times*, 23 April 1904.
21. Ibid.
22. Robinson, *Matty*, 61.
23. Jones, *Deadball Stars of the American League*, 707.
24. Ritter, *The Glory of Their Times*, 82.
25. Karst and Jones, *Who's Who In Professional Baseball*, 510.
26. Anderson, *More than Merkle*, 1.
27. Hynd, *The Giants of the Polo Grounds*, 139–40.
28. Ibid., 140.
29. Jones, *Deadball Stars of the American League*, 739–40.
30. Ribet, "The Chicago Baseball Wars: Competition in a hotbed of the game," 29.
31. Simon, *Deadball Stars of the National League*, 339–40.
32. Honig, *Baseball America*, 66.
33. Ritter, *The Glory of Their Times*, 60.
34. Scheinin, *Field of Screams*, 15.
35. Lane, *Batting*, 77.
36. Schwarz, *The Numbers Game*, 76.
37. Allen, *The World Series*, 62.
38. Ritter, *The Glory of Their Times*, 14–15.
39. Ibid., 189.
40. Anderson, *Pennant Races*, 18.
41. *Chicago Daily Tribune*, 3 July 1909.
42. Ibid.
43. *Chicago Daily Tribune*, 23 July 1909.
44. *New York Times*, 9 October 1909.
45. *New York Times*, 13 October 1909.
46. Simon, *Deadball Stars of the National League*, 251.
47. *Brooklyn Daily Eagle*, 26 August 1910.
48. *Washington Post*, 3 September 1910.
49. *Washington Post*, 4 September 1910.
50. Evers and Fullerton, *Touching Second*, 170.
51. Ibid., 171.
52. Ibid., 173.
53. Ibid., 176.
54. Ibid., 173.
55. *New York Times*, 29 September 1911.
56. Jones, *Deadball Stars of the American League*, 704.
57. Graham, *The New York Giants*, 67.
58. Ritter, *The Glory of Their Times*, 101.
59. Alexander, *John McGraw*, 4.
60. Ritter, *The Glory of Their Times*, 100.
61. Robinson, *Matty*, 45, 59, 162.
62. Lane, *Batting*, 57.
63. Ibid., 81.
64. Ibid., 151.
65. Ibid., 158.
66. Ibid., 180.

67. Hynd, *The Giants of the Polo Grounds*, 164.

68. *New York Times*, 30 April 1911.

69. Ibid.

70. Jones, *Deadball Stars of the American League*, 622.

71. James, *The New Bill James Historical Baseball Abstract*, 484.

72. *New York Times*, 4 May 1912.

73. *New York Times*, 28 May 1912.

74. Zingg, *Harry Hooper*, 103.

75. Ibid., 104.

76. Alexander, *John McGraw*, 170–71; Kavanagh and Macht, *Uncle Robbie*, 53–54.

77. Alexander, *John McGraw*, 169.

78. *Brooklyn Daily Eagle*, 22 May 1913.

79. *Philadelphia Inquirer*, 7 September 1913.

80. Ritter, *The Glory of Their Times*, 236.

81. Graham, *The Brooklyn Dodgers*, 49.

82. James, *The New Bill James Historical Baseball Abstract*, 777.

83. Jones, *Deadball Stars of the American League*, 510.

84. *New York Times*, 10 June 1915.

85. Graham, *The Brooklyn Dodgers*, 58.

86. *New York Herald*, 23 June 1916.

87. Fleitz, *Shoeless*, 127.

88. Jones, *Deadball Stars of the American League*, 625.

89. Zingg, *Harry Hooper*, 150.

90. Jones, *Deadball Stars of the American League*, 689.

91. Hynd, *The Giants of the Polo Grounds*, 208.

92. Fleitz, *Shoeless*, 146.

93. Goldstein, *Spartan Seasons*, 15.

94. Simon, *Deadball Stars of the National League*, 264.

95. Ritter, *The Glory of Their Times*, 227.

96. Barra, *Clearing the Bases*, 7.

97. Honig, *Baseball America*, 135.

98. Barra, *Clearing the Bases*, 2.

99. Simon, *Deadball Stars of the National League*, 294.

100. James, *The New Bill James Historical Baseball Abstract*, 454.

101. *New York Herald*, 15 August 1919.

102. *New York Herald*, 16 August 1919.

103. Macht, "The Cincinnati Base Hit," 154.

Chapter 3

1. Schwarz, *The Numbers Game*, 48–49.

2. Ibid., 48.

3. Ibid., 45.

4. Alexander, *John McGraw*, 231.

5. Lane, *Batting*, 64.

6. Jones, *Deadball Stars of the American League*, unnumbered page.

7. Simon, *Deadball Stars of the National League*, unnumbered page.

8. Jones, *Deadball Stars of the American League*, 496.

9. Ibid., unnumbered page.

10. Oakley, *Baseball's Last Golden Age*, 152–53.

11. Lane, *Batting*, 80.

12. Goldstein, *Spartan Seasons*, 132.

13. Goldstein, *Superstars and Screwballs*, 133–34.

14. Macht, "The 26-Inning Duel," 106.

15. *Chicago Daily Tribune*, 30 May 1920.

16. Puff, "Silent George Burns: A Star in the Sunfield," 113.

17. James, *The New Bill James Historical Baseball Abstract*, 709.

18. *New York Times*, 8 October 1922.

19. Ibid.

20. Allen, *The World Series*, 106.

21. *Washington Post*, 8 August 1923.

22. *New York Times*, 14 August 1923.

23. Browning, *Baseball's Greatest Season*, 89.

24. Ibid., 90.

25. Ibid., 11.

26. Carmichael, *My Greatest Day in Baseball*, 241.

27. Allen, *The World Series*, 118.

28. *Philadelphia Inquirer*, 7 May 1926.

29. *Washington Post*, 2 September 1926.

30. *New York Times*, 10 July 1927.

31. *New York Herald Tribune*, 11 July 1927.

32. *New York Herald Tribune*, 12 July 1927.

33. James, *The New Bill James Historical Baseball Abstract*, 813.

34. *Washington Post*, 5 June 1929.

35. *New York Times*, 23 July 1930.

36. Durocher with Linn, *Nice Guys Finish Last*, 82.

37. Ibid., 89–90.

38. Honig, *Baseball America*, 196.

39. Alexander, *Breaking the Slump*, 45.

40. Allen, *The World Series*, 127.

41. Carmichael, *My Greatest Day in Baseball*, 154.

42. *Philadelphia Inquirer*, 14 May 1931.

43. *New York Times*, 14 September 1931.

44. Simon, *Deadball Stars of the National League*, 166.

45. Obojski, *All-Star Baseball Since 1933*, 10.

46. Ibid., 7.

47. *New York Herald Tribune*, 3 July 1933.

48. *New York Herald Tribune*, 7 October 1933.

49. Stein and Peters, *Giants Diary*, 69.

50. Werber and Rogers, *Memories of a Ballplayer*, 115–16.

51. Ibid., 117–18.

52. Allen, *The World Series*, 138.

53. *Brooklyn Daily Eagle*, 16 May 1934.

54. Karst and Jones, *Who's Who In Professional Baseball*, 86.

55. *New York Times*, 27 August 1935.

56. Karst and Jones, *Who's Who In Professional Baseball*, 86.

57. Werber and Rogers, *Memories of a Ballplayer*, 58–59.

58. *Washington Post*, 5 May 1937.

59. Obojski, *All-Star Baseball Since 1933*, 31.

60. *Philadelphia Inquirer*, 30 April 1938.

61. *The Sporting News*, 12 July 1945.

62. Westcott, *Diamond Greats*, 354.

63. Ibid., 356.

64. Werber and Rogers, *Memories of a Ballplayer*, 179.

65. Creamer, *Baseball and Other Matters In 1941*, 295–96.

66. *Washington Post*, 26 June 1941.

67. Goldstein, *Spartan Seasons*, 133.

68. Spatz, "Snuffy Stirnweiss: Not Just a Wartime Player," 48.

69. *Washington Post*, 9 June 1944.

70. *New York Herald Tribune*, 14 May 1945.

71. *New York Herald Tribune*, 29 August 1945.

72. Durocher with Linn, *Nice Guys Finish Last*, 144.

73. Ibid., 431–32.

74. Turner, *When the Boys Came Back*, 238.

75. Seidel, *Ted Williams*, 165.

76. Kahn, *The Era*, 50.

77. Golenbock, *Bums*, 165.

78. Oakley, *Baseball's Last Golden Age*, 57.

79. Honig, *Baseball America*, 258.

80. Roberts and Rogers, *The Whiz Kids and the 1950 Pennant*, 52–53.

81. Robinson and Duckett, *I Never Had It Made*, 57.

82. Golenbock, *Bums*, 166.

83. *New York Herald Tribune*, 25 June 1947.

84. Oakley, *Baseball's Last Golden Age*, 52.

85. Goldstein, *Superstars and Screwballs*, 275.

86. *New York Herald Tribune*, 23 August 1948.

87. Oakley, *Baseball's Last Golden Age*, 85.

88. James, *The New Bill James Historical Baseball Abstract*, 117.

89. Golenbock, *Dynasty*, 3.

90. Turner, *When the Boys Came Back*, 48.

91. Lindberg, "Minoso By Any Other Name: From Cuban Comet to Chisox Goodwill Ambassador," 56.

92. *New York Times*, 1 September 1953.

93. Peary, *We Played the Game*, 215.

94. Hano, *Willie Mays*, 93.

95. Ibid., 92.

96. Durocher with Linn, *Nice Guys Finish Last*, 431.

97. Bjarkman, *Baseball with a Latin Beat*, 110.

98. Karst and Jones, *Who's Who In Professional Baseball*, 322.

99. Gough, "Nellie Fox: The long road to Cooperstown," 113.

100. Hano, *Willie Mays*, 123–24.

101. Oakley, *Baseball's Last Golden Age*, 254.

102. Bjarkman, *Baseball with a Latin Beat*, 230.

103. *New York Times*, 24 May 1957.

104. *New York Herald Tribune*, 14 June 1957.

105. *New York Herald Tribune*, 8 July 1957.

106. *New York Herald Tribune*, 12 July 1957.

107. Peary, *We Played the Game*, 409.

108. Oakley, *Baseball's Last Golden Age*, 287.

109. Voigt, *American Baseball: Vol. 3*, 21.

110. Peary, *We Played the Game*, 535–36.

111. Ibid., 436.

Chapter 4

1. Peary, *We Played the Game*, 506.

2. Durocher with Linn, *Nice Guys Finish Last*, 16–18.

3. *New York Times*, 27 August 1962.

4. *New York Times*, 8 September 1962.

5. *New York Times*, 24 September 1962.

6. Ibid.

7. Allen, *The World Series*, 214.

8. James, *The New Bill James Historical Baseball Abstract*, 250.

9. Gibson with Wheeler, *Stranger to the Game*, 85–86.

10. Westcott, *Diamond Greats*, 10.

11. Ibid., 10–11.

12. Ibid., 13.

13. Anderson, *Pennant Races*, 271.

14. Ibid., 263.

15. Ibid., 261.

16. Ibid., 321.

17. Dickey, *The History of the World Series Since 1903*, 217.

18. Gibson with Wheeler, *Stranger to the Game*, 132–33.

19. Ibid., 133–34.

20. *New York Times*, 25 September 1968.

21. Karst and Jones, *Who's Who In Professional Baseball*, 682.

22. Kuenster, *The Best of Baseball Digest*, 205.

23. Ibid., 205–06.

24. Ibid., 205.

25. *Washington Post*, 20 April 1969.

26. *New York Times*, 25 July 1970.

27. James, *The New Bill James Historical Baseball Abstract*, 738.

28. Neyer, *Rob Neyer's Big Book Of Baseball Lineups*, 112.

29. Durocher with Linn, *Nice Guys Finish Last*, 431–33.

30. James, *The New Bill James Historical Baseball Abstract*, 778.

31. *Boston Evening Globe*, 20 April 1973.

32. *Boston Globe*, 2 July 1973.

33. James, *The New Bill James Historical Baseball Abstract*, 498.

34. *Chicago Tribune*, 11 September 1974.

35. *Chicago Tribune*, 30 September 1974.

36. Dickson, *The New Dickson Baseball Dictionary*, 154.

37. Voigt, *American Baseball: Vol. 3*, 326.

38. Ibid., 197.

39. Dickson, *The New Dickson Baseball Dictionary*, 79.

40. James, *The New Bill James Historical Baseball Abstract*, 759.

41. *Chicago Tribune*, 16 August 1979.

42. Dickson, *The New Dickson Baseball Dictionary*, 65.

43. *Los Angeles Times*, 4 May 1980.

44. *Los Angeles Times*, 29 May 1980.

45. *Los Angeles Times*, 4 May 1980.

46. *Los Angeles Times*, 10 May 1981.

47. "Neyer On Sabermetrics and Race."

48. *Los Angeles Times*, 2 June 1982.

49. Okrent, *Nine Innings*, 242.

50. *New York Times*, 17 August 2003.

51. *Los Angeles Times*, 25 September 1983.

52. Ibid.

53. Dickson, *The New Dickson Baseball Dictionary*, 153.

54. *Chicago Tribune*, 11 June 1984.

55. *New York Times*, 30 September 1985.

56. *Chicago Tribune*, 2 August 1985.

57. Ibid.

58. Ibid.

59. *Chicago Tribune*, 3 August 1985.

60. Okrent, *Nine Innings*, 45.

61. *Chicago Tribune*, 27 June 1987.

62. *Los Angeles Times*, 25 June 1989.

63. James, *The New Bill James Historical Baseball Abstract*, 299.

64. *Los Angeles Times*, 25 June 1989.

65. *New York Times*, 10 October 1990.

66. *Atlanta Constitution*, 2 May 1991.

67. Ibid.

68. *Atlanta Constitution*, 17 June 1991.

69. *Atlanta Constitution*, 18 June 1991.

70. *Atlanta Constitution*, 15 October 1991.

71. *New York Times*, 8 March 1993.

72. *Philadelphia Inquirer*, 16 June 1992.

73. *New York Times*, 3 June 1996.

74. Larson, "Stolen Victories: Daring Dashes That Send the Fans Home Happy," 116–19.

75. *New York Times*, 2 April 2006.

76. *Boston Globe*, 29 June 1997.

77. Dierker, *My Team*, 108.

78. Ibid., 17.

79. Ibid., 18.

80. Ibid.

81. *Chicago Tribune*, 20 April 1998.

82. *Miami Herald*, 19 May 2000.

83. Dierker, *My Team*, 111.

84. Caple, "To err is human, but this is ridiculous."

85. Lewis, *Moneyball*, 275.

86. Bodley, "Forgotten plays led to famous ones."

87. *USA Today Sports Weekly*, 11–17 October 2006.

88. Lewis, *Moneyball*, 275.

89. *Los Angeles Times*, 8 May 2002.

90. *Washington Post*, 8 August 2005.

91. *New York Times*, 17 August 2003.

Bibliography

Books

Alexander, Charles C. *Breaking the Slump: Baseball in the Depression Era*. New York: Columbia University Press, 2002.

_____. *John McGraw*. 1988. Lincoln: University of Nebraska Press, 1995.

Allen, Lee. *The World Series: The Story of Baseball's Annual Championship*. New York: G.P. Putnam's, 1969.

Anderson, Dave. *Pennant Races: Baseball at Its Best*. New York: Doubleday, 1994.

Anderson, David W. *More Than Merkle: A History of the Best and Most Exciting Baseball Season in Human History*. Lincoln: University of Nebraska Press, 2000.

Barra, Allen. *Clearing the Bases: The Greatest Baseball Debates of the Last Century*. New York: St. Martin's, 2002.

The Baseball Chronicle: Year-by-Year History of Major League Baseball. Lincolnwood, IL: Publications International, 2003.

The Baseball Encyclopedia: The Complete and Definitive Record of Major League Baseball. 9th edition. New York: Macmillan, 1993.

Bingham, Dennis. "A Fan's-Eye View of the 1906 World Series." *Road Trips: A Trunkload of Great Articles from Two Decades of Convention Journals*. Cleveland, OH: Society for American Baseball Research, 2004.

Bjarkman, Peter C. *Baseball with a Latin Beat: A History of the Latin American Game*. Jefferson, NC: McFarland, 1994.

Browning, Reed. *Baseball's Greatest Season, 1924*. Amherst: University of Massachusetts Press, 2003.

Carmichael, John P. *My Greatest Day in Baseball: Forty-Seven Dramatic Stories by Forty-Seven Stars*. 1945. Lincoln: University of Nebraska Press, 1996.

Charlton, James, ed. *The Baseball Chronology: The Complete History of the Most Important Events in the Game of Baseball*. New York: Macmillan, 1991.

Creamer, Robert W. *Baseball and Other Matters in 1941: A Celebration of the Best Baseball Season Ever — in the Year America Went to War*. 1991. Lincoln: University of Nebraska Press, 2000.

Dickey, Glenn. *The History of the World Series Since 1903*. New York: Stein & Day, 1984.

Dickson, Paul. *The New Dickson Baseball Dictionary*. San Diego: Harcourt Brace, 1999.

Dierker, Larry. *My Team: Choosing My Dream Team from My Forty Years in Baseball*. New York: Simon & Schuster, 2006.

Durocher, Leo, with Ed Linn. *Nice Guys Finish Last*. New York: Simon & Schuster, 1975.

Evers, John J., and Hugh S. Fullerton. *Touching Second: The Science of Baseball*. Mattituck, NY: Amereon House, 1910.

Fleitz, David L. *Shoeless: The Life and Times of Joe Jackson*. Jefferson, NC: McFarland, 2001.

Frommer, Harvey. *Old-Time Baseball: America's Pastime in the Gilded Age*. Lanham, MD: Taylor, 2006.

Gershman, Michael. *Diamonds: The Evolution of the Ballpark*. Boston: Houghton Mifflin, 1993.

Gibson, Bob, with Lonnie Wheeler. *Stranger to the Game*. New York: Penguin, 1994.

Goldstein, Richard. *Spartan Seasons: How Baseball Survived the Second World War*. New York: Macmillan, 1980.

_____. *Superstars and Screwballs: 100 Years of Brooklyn Baseball*. New York: Dutton, 1991.

Golenbock, Peter. *Bums: An Oral History of the Brooklyn Dodgers*. New York: G.P. Putnam's, 1984.

_____. *Dynasty: The New York Yankees, 1949–1964*. 1975. Lincolnwood, IL: Contemporary, 2000.

Graham, Frank. *The Brooklyn Dodgers: An Informal History*. 1945. Carbondale: Southern Illinois University Press, 2002.

_____. *The New York Giants: An Informal History of a Great Baseball Club*. 1952. Carbondale: Southern Illinois University Press, 2002.

Gutman, Dan. *It Ain't Cheatin' If You Don't Get Caught: Scuffing, Corking, Spitting, Gunking, Razzing, and Other Fundamentals of Our National Pastime*. New York: Penguin, 1990.

Ham, Eldon. *Larceny and Old Leather: The Mischievous Legacy of Major League Baseball*. Chicago: Academy Chicago Publishers, 2005.

Hano, Arnold. *Willie Mays.* New York: Grosset & Dunlap, 1966.

Honig, Donald. *Baseball America: The Heroes of the Game and the Times of Their Glory.* 1985. New York: Barnes & Noble, 1997.

Hynd, Noel. *The Giants of the Polo Grounds: The Glorious Times of Baseball's New York Giants.* 1988. Dallas: Taylor, 1995.

James, Bill. *The New Bill James Historical Baseball Abstract.* New York: Free Press, 2001.

Jones, David, ed. *Deadball Stars of the American League.* Dulles, VA: Potomac, 2006.

Kahn, Roger. *The Era: 1947–1957, When the Yankees, the Giants, and the Dodgers Ruled the World.* New York: Ticknor & Fields, 1993.

Karst, Gene, and Martin J. Jones, Jr. *Who's Who in Professional Baseball.* New Rochelle, NY: Arlington House, 1973.

Kavanagh, Jack, and Norman Macht. *Uncle Robbie.* Lincoln, NE: Society for American Baseball Research, 1999.

Keetz, Frank. "Johnny Evers: The Find of the 1902 Season." *Road Trips: A Trunkload of Great Articles from Two Decades of Convention Journals.* Cleveland, OH: Society for American Baseball Research, 2004.

Kuenster, John, ed. *The Best of Baseball Digest.* Chicago: Ivan R. Dee, 2006.

Lane, F.C. *Batting: One Thousand Expert Opinions on Every Conceivable Angle of Batting Science.* 1925. Lincoln, NE: Society for American Baseball Research, 2001.

Lewis, Michael. *Moneyball: The Art of Winning an Unfair Game.* New York: W.W. Norton, 2003.

Macht, Norman L. "The Cincinnati Base Hit." *Road Trips: A Trunkload of Great Articles from Two Decades of Convention Journals.* Cleveland, OH: Society for American Baseball Research, 2004.

_____. "The 26-Inning Duel." *Road Trips: A Trunkload of Great Articles from Two Decades of Convention Journals.* Cleveland, OH: Society for American Baseball Research, 2004.

Morris, Peter. *A Game of Inches: The Stories Behind the Innovations That Shaped Baseball: The Game on the Field.* Chicago: Ivan R. Dee, 2006.

Nemec, David. *The Rules of Baseball: An Anecdotal Look at the Rules of Baseball and How They Came to Be.* New York: Lyons & Burford, 1994.

Neyer, Rob. *Rob Neyer's Big Book of Baseball Lineups: A Complete Guide to the Best, Worst, and Most Memorable Players to Ever Grace the Major Leagues.* New York: Simon & Schuster, 2003.

Oakley, J. Ronald. *Baseball's Last Golden Age, 1946–1960: The National Pastime in a Time of Glory and Change.* Jefferson, NC: McFarland, 1994.

Obojski, Robert. *All-Star Baseball Since 1933.* New York: Stein & Day, 1980.

Okrent, Daniel. *Nine Innings: The Anatomy of a Baseball Game.* Boston: Houghton Mifflin, 1985.

Palmer, Pete, and Gary Gillette, eds. *The 2006 ESPN Baseball Encyclopedia.* New York: Sterling, 2006.

_____. *The ESPN Baseball Encyclopedia.* 5th edition. New York: Sterling, 2008.

Peary, Danny, ed. *We Played the Game: 65 Players Remember Baseball's Greatest Era, 1947–1964.* New York: Hyperion, 1994.

Puff, Richard. "Silent George Burns: A Star in the Sunfield." *Road Trips: A Trunkload of Great Articles from Two Decades of Convention Journals.* Cleveland, OH: Society for American Baseball Research, 2004.

Quigley, Martin. *The Crooked Pitch: The Curveball in American Baseball History.* Chapel Hill, NC: Algonquin, 1984.

Ritter, Lawrence S. *The Glory of Their Times: The Story of the Early Days of Baseball Told by the Men Who Played It.* 1966. New York: William Morrow, 1984.

_____. *Lost Ballparks: A Celebration of Baseball's Legendary Fields.* New York: Penguin Studio, 1992.

Roberts, Robin, and C. Paul Rogers III. *The Whiz Kids and the 1950 Pennant.* Philadelphia: Temple University Press, 1996.

Robinson, Jackie, as told to Alfred Duckett. *I Never Had It Made.* 1972. Hopewell, NJ: Ecco Press, 1995.

Robinson, Ray. *Matty: An American Hero: Christy Mathewson of the New York Giants.* New York: Oxford University Press, 1993.

Scheinin, Richard. *Field of Screams: The Dark Underside of America's National Pastime.* New York: W.W. Norton, 1994.

Schwarz, Alan. *The Numbers Game: Baseball's Lifelong Fascination with Statistics.* New York: St. Martin's, 2004.

Seidel, Michael. *Ted Williams: A Baseball Life.* 1991. Lincoln: University of Nebraska Press, 2000.

Simon, Tom, ed. *Deadball Stars of the National League.* Washington: Brassey's, 2004.

Spatz, Lyle, ed. *The SABR Baseball List and Record Book: Baseball's Most Fascinating Records and Unusual Statistics.* New York: Scribner, 2007.

Stein, Fred, and Nick Peters. *Giants Diary: A Century of Giants Baseball in New York and San Francisco.* Berkeley: North Atlantic, 1987.

Szalontai, James D. *Close Shave: The Life and Times of Baseball's Sal Maglie.* Jefferson, NC: McFarland, 2002.

Turner, Frederick. *When the Boys Came Back: Baseball and 1946.* New York: Henry Holt, 1996.

Voigt, David Quentin. *American Baseball: Vol. 3, From Postwar Expansion to the Electronic Age.* University Park: Pennsylvania State University Press, 1983.

Werber, William M., and C. Paul Rogers III. *Memories of a Ballplayer: Bill Werber and Baseball in the 1930s.* Lincoln, NE: Society for American Baseball Research, 2001.

Westcott, Rich. *Diamond Greats: Profiles and Interviews with 65 of Baseball's History Makers.* Westport, CT: Meckler, 1988.

Zingg, Paul J. *Harry Hooper: An American Baseball Life.* Urbana: University of Illinois Press, 1993.

Magazine, Journal, and Internet Articles

Bodley, Hal. "Forgotten Plays Led to Famous Ones." *USAToday.com,* April 2, 2006.

Caple, Jim. "To Err Is Human, but This Is Ridiculous." *ESPN.com,* October 7, 2003.

Casway, Jerrold. "The Best Outfield Ever? The Phillies of the Gay Nineties." *Baseball Research Journal* 27, 1998.

Dittmar, Joe. "Baseball's Most Unbreakable Records: Polled from SABR's Records Committee." *Baseball Research Journal* 31, 2003.

Gough, David. "Nellie Fox: The Long Road to Cooperstown." *Baseball Research Journal* 26, 1997.

Larson, Jan. "Stolen Victories: Daring Dashes That Send the Fans Home Happy." *Baseball Research Journal* 36, 2007.

Lindberg, Richard C. "Minoso by Any Other Name: From Cuban Comet to Chisox Goodwill Ambassador." *The National Pastime: A Review of Baseball History* 12, 1992.

"Neyer on Sabermetrics and Race." *Baseball Musings,* July 21, 2003.

Peurzer, Richard J. "The Kansas City Royals' Baseball Academy." *The National Pastime: A Review of Baseball History* 24, 2004.

Ribet, Barrie. "The Chicago Baseball Wars: Competition in a hotbed of the game." *Baseball Research Journal* 28, 1999.

Smith, David W. "Sunny Jim Bottomley's Big Day: St. Louis Cardinals at Brooklyn Robins, September 16, 1924." *The National Pastime: A Review of Baseball History* 27, 2007.

Snyder, David L., and Michael K. Zitelli. "The Case for Curt Flood: Why He Should Be in Baseball's Hall of Fame." *Mound City Memories,* 2007.

Spatz, Lyle. "Snuffy Stirnweiss: Not Just a Wartime Player." *The National Pastime: A Review of Baseball History* 19, 1999.

Steinberg, Steve L. "The Spitball and the End of the Deadball Era." *The National Pastime: A Review of Baseball History* 23, 2003.

Verducci, Tom. "F's for the A's: Everyone in Oakland's Organization Gets Blamed for Team's Playoff Futility." *SI.com,* October 7, 2003.

Warburton, Paul. "The 1921 AL Race: Ruth's Greatest Season and the Yankees' First Pennant." *The National Pastime: A Review of Baseball History* 18, 1998.

Wiley, Ralph. "Squeeze play: Baseball's troubling issue." *ESPN.com.*

Williams, Pete. "Stealing First and Fielding with Your Head: Germany Schaefer and Babe Herman as Fools." *Baseball Research Journal* 19, 1990.

Wilson, Walt. "Chicago Scores 36 Runs: A Stampede by Anson's Colts." *Baseball Research Journal* 28, 1999.

Newspapers

Atlanta Constitution
Atlanta Journal-Constitution
Boston Globe (*Boston Evening Globe* and *Boston Sunday Globe*)
Brooklyn Eagle (*Brooklyn Daily Eagle*)
Chicago Tribune (*Chicago Daily Tribune*)
Los Angeles Times
Miami Herald
New York Herald
New York Herald Tribune
New York Times
Philadelphia Inquirer
The Sporting News
USA Today
USA Today Sports Weekly
Washington Post

Internet Sources

www.baseball-almanac.com
www.baseballlibrary.com
www.baseball-reference.com
www.retrosheet.org

Index